D0081026

Fraud Examination

W. STEVE ALBRECHT

Brigham Young University

CHAD O. ALBRECHT

Contributing Editor

Australia · Canada · Mexico · Singapore · Spain · United Kingdom · United States

Fraud Examination
W. Steve Albrecht

Editor-in-Chief:
Jack W. Calhoun

Team Leader:
Melissa S. Acuña

Acquisitions Editor:
Sharon Oblinger

Developmental Editor:
Ken Martin

Marketing Manager:
Keith Chasse

Production Editor:
Amy A. Brooks

Manufacturing Coordinator:
Doug Wilke

Compositor:
Lachina Publishing Services, Inc.

Printer:
Phoenix Color–Book Technology
Hagerstown, MD

Design Project Manager:
Casey Gilbertson

Internal Designer:
Casey Gilbertson

Cover Designer:
Casey Gilbertson

Printed in the United States of America
1 2 3 4 5 05 04 03 02

For more information contact South-Western, 5191 Natorp Boulevard, Mason, Ohio 45040. Or you can visit our Internet site at: http://www.swcollege.com

Library of Congress Cataloging-in-Publication Data
Albrecht, W. Steve.
Fraud examination / W. Steve Albrecht
p. cm.
Includes bibliographical references and index.
ISBN 0-324-16296-0
1. Fraud. 2. Fraud—Prevention. 3. Forensic accounting. 4. Fraud investigation. I. Albrecht, Chad O. II. Title.
HV6691 .A43 2002
364.16'3—dc21 2002071955

To
LeAnn and Jenny

ABOUT THE AUTHOR

W. Steve Albrecht is the Associate Dean of the Marriott School of Management and Arthur Andersen LLP Alumni Professor at Brigham Young University. His interest in fraud examination began about 25 years ago, when he was part of a research team that studied ways to better detect fraud. Since that time, he has written over 50 academic articles on fraud as well as several books and training courses for the AICPA and others.

Earlier in his career, Dr. Albrecht decided that he needed to get some "hands-on" investigative experience, rather than just approach the topic from an academic perspective. For a period of approximately six years, he worked closely with a Fortune 500 corporation, helping them coordinate fraud investigations and participating in those investigations. Since then, he has consulted with many other corporations in the areas of fraud prevention, fraud detection, and fraud investigation. Some of his work in the fraud area has involved interviewing actual fraud perpetrators.

Dr. Albrecht has been an expert witness in some of the largest fraud cases ever, including two current cases involving frauds of $2.6 billion and $400 million. Dr. Albrecht teaches frequently for the FBI and other governmental organizations, and he is a highly requested speaker on fraud-related topics all over the world. Steve was the first president of the Association of Certified Fraud Examiners (ACFE), was a member of COSO for four years, was on the AICPA task force that wrote SAS 82, and has served in several other fraud-related capacities with numerous organizations. In August 1998, he received the ACFE's Cressey Award the highest award given for achievement in fraud detection and deterrence.

Dr. Albrecht received his undergraduate degree in accounting from Brigham Young University, and his MBA and Ph.D. degrees from the University of Wisconsin at Madison. His writing also includes a financial accounting text and a principles of accounting text, both of which are in their eighth editions. With Robert Sack, he recently completed a major study (*Accounting Education: Charting the Course through a Perilous Future*) on the future of accounting education in the United States.

BRIEF CONTENTS

CONTENTS

PART ONE

Introduction to Fraud

PART TWO

Fraud Prevention

PART THREE

Fraud Detection

PART FOUR

Fraud Investigation

PART FIVE

Management Fraud

FOREWORD

According to the Association of Certified Fraud Examiners' 2002 Report to the Nation on Occupational Fraud and Abuse, organizations lose, on average, about 6 percent of their revenues to dishonesty from within.

If multiplied by the U.S. Gross Domestic Product, the cost of occupational fraud and abuse may run a staggering $600 billion annually. By the breadth of the definition, it covers all corporate dishonesty—from the mailroom to the boardroom. While executives are "cooking" the company's earnings to show better profits, purchasing agents are getting kickbacks from suppliers, and employees are embezzling money to improve their lifestyles.

Knowing how much fraud actually costs is a difficult—if not impossible—task. The cases we know about only represent the tip of the iceberg; those discovered tend to be greedy or careless. Executives and employees who are neither may well commit fraud throughout their entire careers and get away with it.

The huge cost of occupational fraud begs an obvious question: Why does it occur? The answers aren't easy. Although the simple answer is greed, it's a natural human trait, and even greedy people don't always lie, cheat, and steal. A more complete answer for corporate dishonesty involves three factors: the individual, the workplace, and society.

Individuals likely to commit occupational fraud are often on the financial ropes. This can occur when people spend more money than they make or when there is a personal financial crisis demanding immediate resolution. Although many of us have had such difficult situations, dishonest employees are more likely to salve their consciences with rationalizations that justify fraud. In short, they lack the convictions of their own ethics.

Workplace environments also contribute to occupational fraud. Organizations that are viewed by employees as uncaring, stingy, or dishonest run a much higher risk of being victimized from within. Many workers—in an attempt to right what they consider to be corporate wrongs—address these perceived injustices in a variety of ways: goldbricking, excessive absences, pilferage, and dishonesty.

Moreover, some organizations unwittingly contribute to the problem. By failing to establish reasonable safeguards and controls, companies make fraud too easy, and thus too tempting. Organizations have a duty to help keep the workforce honest. Societal conditions also influence the rate of occupational fraud. If dishonesty is easily accepted and goes largely unpunished, we can only expect it to thrive.

It was my own search for answers to occupational fraud over a decade ago that led me to W. Steve Albrecht. In the mid-1980s, after ten years with the FBI, I practiced as a fraud examiner. Increasingly, my corporate clients were referring me cases of embezzlement, corruption, and other misdeeds.

One client, certainly on the cutting-edge at the time, wanted help in developing an anti-fraud program. That request led me to the vast libraries of the University of Texas, where I discovered one of Dr. Albrecht's first published works on the subject, Deterring Fraud: The Internal Auditor's Perspective.

After reading this seminal research by Steve and his colleagues, I sought him out personally. Even though Steve had never heard my name, he graciously answered my questions and volunteered his valuable time to aid in further research on the topic of occupational fraud. After that, we stayed in touch.

Neither of us at that time could have imagined the paths our lives would take together. In 1988, Steve was a major influence in encouraging me to start the Association of Certified Fraud Examiners, and he served with distinction as its first president.

Since that time, the ACFE has grown to almost 30,000 members in over 120 countries. Steve's lifetime of contributions to the field of fraud detection and deterrence simply cannot be overstated. The ACFE recognized the enormity of Dr. Albrecht's body of work in 1998 when it honored him with its most valued prize: the Cressey Award.

However, the many awards Steve has received may not capture the kind of man he is. A devoted father and husband, Steve lives his life by high example. Regardless of his many accomplishments, you won't hear about them from him; humility is one of his most endearing traits. I am proud to call Steve Albrecht my friend.

Steve and I are of a common mind when it comes to fraud. First, the accounting community, which has the lion's share of responsibility to control occupational fraud, is ill-equipped for the job. Second, education is the cornerstone to preventing fraud. The more we know, the less likely we are to become victims.

The terms "fraud examination" and "forensic accounting" are often used interchangeably. However, they refer to different but overlapping concepts. The latter phrase, although highly popular as a euphemism for fraud investigation, actually refers to any kind of accounting work done for litigation purposes.

According to the Fraud Examiners Manual, fraud examination is a methodology for resolving allegations of fraud from inception to disposition. The process involves gathering evidence, taking statements, writing reports, and assisting in the detection and deterrence of fraud. Although many organizations employ fraud examiners, audit professionals and others also conduct fraud examinations on a limited, as-needed basis. The fraud examination field draws its common body of knowledge from four areas: accounting and auditing, fraud investigation techniques, the legal elements of fraud, and criminology and ethics.

For accountants, anti-fraud education has been practically non-existent for decades. One of the main reasons has been the lack of authoritative texts on the subject. Educators and students alike will find Fraud Examination to be a solution. Packed full of real examples, thought-provoking discussion issues and questions, this book is ideal for both undergraduate and graduate students.

Moreover, practitioners will find a great deal of guidance in resolving current cases. Managers and executives will benefit from understanding the myriad of issues that can assist them in deterring occupational fraud. And for all of us, Fraud Examination is a wonderfully engaging read.

Joseph T. Wells, CFE, CPA
Chairman of the Board of Directors
The Association of Certified Fraud Examiners
Austin, Texas
http://www.cfenet.com/home.asp

PREFACE

Fraud examination (sometimes called forensic accounting) is one of the most exciting careers for students studying accounting and business today. The AICPA has called forensic accounting one of the seven hot new "sizzling" career areas in accounting. It is estimated that there will be a shortage of between 25,000 and 50,000 security professionals in the next few years in the United States. Exciting opportunities for accounting and business students who become knowledgeable in fraud prevention, detection, and investigation abound in various federal agencies, such as the FBI and Postal Inspectors, major corporations, and professional service and consulting firms. Both the size and the number of frauds is increasing, which will result in an even greater demand for fraud-fighting professionals in the future.

Fraud is an extremely costly business problem. For example, not long ago a Fortune 500 automaker experienced a $436 million fraud. Because the fraud reduced the company's net income by $436 million from what it would have been and because the company had a profit margin (net income divided by net sales) of approximately 10 percent, the company would have to generate an additional $4.36 billion (10 times the amount lost in the fraud) in revenues to restore net income to its pre-fraud level. And, if you assume that an average car sells for $20,000, this company would have to make and sell an additional 218,000 cars ($4.36 billion divided by $20,000 sales price) to recover the effect on net income. In other words, this company faced a major business problem: it could either make and sell 218,000 more cars, or it could work hard to prevent these types of frauds from occurring in the future. When faced with the choice of generating that much additional revenue, which would have been difficult if not impossible, the company decided that reducing and eliminating future frauds was the more effective way to spend its money. As a result, it hired additional fraud and control experts and implemented extensive fraud prevention procedures. Eliminating fraud is a problem that every organization faces, and you can help them deal with this growing problem.

Even if you decide not to become a fraud expert, the topics you will study in this course will help you be a better professional in whatever career path you choose. The technology, interviewing, document examination, public records, and other tools you will study will make you a better consultant, auditor, tax professional, or manager, as well as a better and more astute investor.

As you will discover in this book, there is also a very active professional organization that deals with fighting fraud called the Association of Certified Fraud Examiners (ACFE), which currently has about 30,000 members and is based in Austin, Texas. This organization, as well as others, can provide future fraud training. In addition, the ACFE will provides its educational materials free of charge to institutions of higher learning that agree to offer a three-hour course entitled "Fraud Examination." These materials include 12 original videos of interviews with actual white-collar criminals. Most of the videos are in two 25-minute segments, for a total of 50 minutes in length. A complete listing of the ACFE's materials and other information can be found at the Association's Web site at http://www.cfenet.com/home.asp.

In this book, we cover seven different topics. Part 1, comprising Chapters 1, 2, and 3, provides an introduction to fraud and an overview of the fraud problem. Chapter 1 discusses the nature of fraud, Chapter 2 describes fraud perpetrators and their motivations for being dishonest, and Chapter 3 provides an overview of the different ways to fight and, hopefully, reduce fraud.

The second and third parts of the book focus on fraud prevention (Chapter 4) and fraud detection (Chapters 5 and 6.) Chapter 5 provides an overview of and discusses traditional fraud detection methods, while Chapter 6 introduces you to the use of technology to proactively detect fraud.

Part 4 covers the various elements of fraud investigation. In Chapter 7, we cover theft and concealment investigation methods; in Chapter 8, we discuss conversion investigative methods; and in Chapter 9, we cover various types of interviewing and other query approaches to investigating fraud. The interview techniques you learn in Chapter 9 will make you a more discerning husband or wife, parent, manager, employee, or friend.

Parts 5 and 6 discuss the various types of fraud. In Part 5, we include three chapters on management, or financial statement, fraud. In Chapter 10, we provide an overview of financial statement fraud and introduce a proactive model for detecting fraud and errors in the financial statements. In Chapter 11 we discuss both revenue- and inventory-related frauds, the two most common ways to manipulate financial statements. In Chapter 12, we discuss three other types of financial statement frauds: understating liabilities and expenses, overstating assets, and inadequate disclosures. These chapters will help you better understand and critique the financial statements of any organization. In Part 6, we discuss three other types of fraud. Chapter 13 covers fraud committed against organizations by employees, vendors, and customers. Chapter 14 introduces divorce and bankruptcy fraud, both of which are very common because people often try to hide assets that might be taken away in such proceedings. Chapter 15 discusses e-Business frauds, a new and growing type of fraud problem because of the increasing use of the Internet to conduct business.

The final part in the book includes only Chapter 16 and discusses options that victims have when deciding how to follow-up on frauds they experience. This chapter provides an overview of the criminal and civil statutes governing fraud legal proceedings and helps you understand the various ways organizations have to resolve dishonest acts.

We realize that there are many other fraud-related topics that we could have included. We have tried to strike a balance between brevity and topics of general interest and detailed investigation and specific knowledge that experienced professional fraud examiners would need. We also realize that, for most of you, this will be the only fraud-related course you will take in your college studies. We are certain, however, that it will be one of your most exciting and will spark an interest that will stimulate career-changing plans for some of you. At a minimum, after taking this course, you should be a much more careful investor and business decision maker. You will never view business transactions or reports the same way, and you will be a much more careful and skeptical observer and participant in future endeavors.

We are excited to share this exciting topic with you. We wish you success and enthusiasm as you study the pages of this book, and we welcome suggestions for improvement.

W. Steve Albrecht, Ph.D., CFE, CPA, CIA

ACKNOWLEDGMENTS

When South-Western approached me about writing this text, I determined that there was no way, given my other commitments, that I would have time to write a book on fraud. However, my son, Chad, who is an undergraduate business student at BYU and who is planning to pursue a Ph.D., stepped up and said, “Dad, we can write this together.” More than for any other reason, I wrote this book because of Chad’s motivation and help. While I take total responsibility for the contents of this book, especially any errors it might contain, Chad has helped with both the end-of-chapter materials and the chapters themselves. He has provided editing, drafting, and research help. On many occasions, he has told me that what I was writing didn’t make sense from a student perspective. In many ways, he is more than a contributing editor. When he completes his Ph.D., I will be honored to work with him as a co-author on the text.

For many years, Chad has had an intense interest in fraud detection and prevention. He has been my research assistant, has worked with me on fraud consulting engagements, and has traveled with me when I have been an expert witness. He has written several research papers on different aspects of fraud. One of the great joys in my life has been to write this book with Chad, whose help has made publishing this book possible.

Several reviewers provided valuable comments on the manuscript for this book. They were:

Michael Blue
Bloomsburg University

Thomas Buckoff
Buckoff, O-Halloran, and Eide Bailly, LLP

Gregory Claypool
Youngstown State University

Todd DeZoort
University of Alabama

Ross Fuerman
Suffolk University

George Gardner
Bemidji State University

Lawrence Gramling
University of Connecticut

William Haslinger
Hilbert College

Mark Morgan
Mississippi College and Mississippi State Tax Commission

Deborah Pavelka
Roosevelt University

Bonita Peterson
Montana State University

Barbara Reider
University of Montana

Mark Taylor
University of South Carolina

We are very grateful for the help of many other individuals who made this book possible. We appreciate the talented word processing help of Heather Hall, our secretary. We appreciate the able and talented editing of Ken Martin of South-Western. We also appreciate Brigham Young University for its support and for providing an environment of stimulation and challenge. Joseph T. Wells, Chairman of the Association of Certified Fraud Examiners (ACFE), has been inspiring and helpful in many ways. In this area of fraud examination, he has been our closest and most supportive friend. He and the ACFE have made their materials available to us in writing this book and, through their generous offer to support fraud education, will make their videos and other materials available to professors. Chairman Wells, through his work with the ACFE, has done more to fight fraud in the United States and the world than any other person we know. We also appreciate the help of valuable colleagues with whom we have collaborated previously. Gerald W. Wernz and Timothy L. Williams were co-authors on a previous book and several academic articles from which many ideas for this book were taken. Gregory J. Dunn and Conan C. Albrecht, my son, have been co-authors on journal articles from which ideas have been taken as well. We are also grateful to the many law firms, professional service firms, corporations, and government organizations that have provided us with consulting and expert witnessing opportunities to enrich our fraud experience and background. Finally, we are grateful to the students in our Winter 2002 fraud examination class at BYU, who made suggestions and helped develop ideas for end-of-chapter materials. Those students were:

Tegshee Bayarsaikhan
John Brown
Michael Drake
Thomas Farr
Jacob Given
David Harlow
Jeff Knowlton
Steven Leatherwood
Xuebei Luan
David Meilstrup
Justin Miller
Samuel Mulliner
Jonathan Muterra
Brent Nickel
Devin Osterhout
Samuel Picklesimer
Ned Prusse
Kathleen Skarda
Bernie Spears
Teodora Stantcheva
Brent Straton
Kevin Thompson
Juan Velasco
Tifani Walker
Josh Wardle
Rick Warne

PART ONE

INTRODUCTION TO FRAUD

The Nature of Fraud

After studying this chapter, you should be able to:

1. Understand the seriousness of the fraud problem and how it affects individuals, consumers, and organizations.
2. Define fraud.
3. Classify frauds into various types.
4. Understand the differences between criminal and civil fraud laws and how they relate to fraud.
5. Understand the types of fraud-fighting careers available today.

Enron is a multinational company that specializes in markets, in electricity, natural gas, energy, and other physical commodities. Enron initiated the wholesale natural gas and electricity markets in the United States. It was officially formed in 1985 as a result of the merger of Houston Natural Gas and InterNorth of Omaha, Nebraska. In 2000, Enron reported revenues of $101 billion, making it the seventh largest U.S. company in terms of revenue. In 2000, Enron employed 21,000 employees and operated in over 40 countries.

In October 2001, Enron was suspected of a large financial statement fraud. Its stock price, which reached a high of $90 earlier in the year, dropped to less than $1 in a matter of days. Unfortunately, in 2002, Enron is fighting to avoid collapse in one of the biggest corporate failures in U.S. history. At the time this book was published, Enron was being sued for some $25 billion, with new lawsuits being added almost daily.

Enron, citing accounting errors, had to restate its financial statements, cutting profits for the past three years by about 20%, or around $586 million. Many of the lawsuits against Enron allege that executives reaped personal gains from "off-the-book" partnerships, while the energy giant violated basic rules of accounting and ethics. As the accounting discrepancies became public knowledge, Enron investors lost billions of dollars, shattering their retirement plans. New York–based Amalgamated Bank, which lost millions in the fraud, is currently suing 29 top Enron executives. Enron has filed for Chapter 11 bankruptcy, making it the largest corporation to ever file for bankruptcy. In addition to Enron's internal accounting problems, its auditor, a "Big 5" CPA firm, allegedly instructed employees to destroy documents related to its work on Enron. The accounting firm is now under close scrutiny from regulators and others. While the discovery phase of this case has not yet occurred, the magnitude of this alleged fraud has shattered public confidence in America's financial reporting system.[1]

In reacting to the Enron scandal, The American Institute of Certified Public Accountants (AICPA) released the following statement to all AICPA members:

"Our profession enjoys a sacred public trust and for more than one hundred years has served the public interest. Yet, in a short period of time, the stain from Enron's collapse has eroded our most important asset: Public Confidence."[2]

Seriousness of the Fraud Problem

Enron is an example of a company whose management misrepresented the company and allegedly committed fraud. This is just one of the many types of frauds that are a major problem for businesses throughout the world.

Although most people and even researchers believe that fraud is increasing both in size and frequency, it is very difficult to know for sure. First, it is impossible to know what percentage of fraud *perpetrators* are caught. Are there perfect frauds that are never discovered, or are all frauds eventually discovered? In addition, many frauds that are discovered are handled quietly within the victim organization and never made public. In many cases, companies merely hide the frauds and quietly terminate or transfer perpetrators rather than make them public.

Statistics on how much fraud is occurring, whether it is increasing or decreasing, and how much the average fraud costs come from four basic sources:

1. Government agencies—Agencies such as the FBI or various health agencies publish fraud statistics from time to time, but only those statistics related to their *jurisdiction*. Generally, their statistics are not complete, are not collected randomly, and do not provide a total picture even of all the fraud in the areas for which they have responsibility.
2. Researchers—Researchers often conduct studies about particular types of fraud in particular industrial sectors. Unfortunately, data on actual frauds is difficult to get and, as a result, most research studies only provide small insights into the magnitude of the problem, even in the specific area being studied. Comprehensive research on the occurrence of fraud is rare and is not always based on sound scientific approaches.
3. Insurance companies—Insurance companies often provide fidelity bonding or other types of coverage against employee and other fraud. When fraud occurs, they undertake investigations and, as a result, have collected some fraud statistics. Generally, however, their statistics relate only to actual cases where they provided employee bonding or other insurance. At best, their look at the problem is incomplete.
4. Victims of fraud—Sometimes we learn about fraud from those who have been *victims*. In almost all industries, there is no organized way for victims to report fraud and, even if there were, many companies would choose not to make their fraud losses public.

The *Association of Certified Fraud Examiners (ACFE)* conducted one of the most comprehensive fraud studies ever undertaken in the mid-1990s. Based on voluntary reports of over 2,600 frauds, the ACFE estimated that fraud costs U.S. organizations more than $400 billion annually. It is estimated that the average organization's fraud losses are more than $9 per day per employee, and that about 6% of a company's total annual revenue is lost to fraud of various types.[3]

Even with the difficulties in measuring fraud, most people believe that fraud is a growing problem. Both the numbers of frauds committed and the total dollar amounts lost from fraud seem to be increasing. Because fraud affects how much we pay for goods and services, each of us pays not only a portion of the fraud bill but also for the detection and investigation of fraud. It is almost impossible to read a newspaper or business magazine without coming across multiple incidents of fraud. A recent issue of a national newspaper, for example, contains three fraud-related articles. The first discusses one of the nation's fastest growing grocery store chains; it is alleged that the company made sausage with spoiled green pork, coated slimy chicken with barbecue sauce before putting it in meat cases, and soaked aged, stinking fish in bleach before putting it out for sale. In addition, the grocery store chain is being hit with the largest child-labor complaint ever—more than 1,400 violations, including allowing teens to work around meat slicers and other dangerous equipment. The second article describes the attempt of voters in one state to recall the governor "because he is a crook." Recall backers cited five federal and state probes for corruption and tax evasion. The third article reports an investigation of a Little League team that won the Little League World Series. Allegedly, all 14 players on the team were ineligible and were allowed to play because of faked names and identification on official documents. The team won the World Series, but was stripped of the title after officials discovered that the players were ineligible.

The FBI has labeled fraud the fastest growing crime. The problem is so great that the FBI has committed approximately 24% of its resources to fighting fraud. At any given time, the FBI is investigating several hundred cases of fraud and embezzlement, most involving sums of more than $100,000.

Even more alarming than the increased number of fraud cases is the size of discovered frauds. In earlier times, if a thief wanted to steal from his or her employer, the perpetrator had to physically remove the assets from the business premises. Because of fear of being caught with the goods, frauds tended to be small. With the advent of computers, the Internet, and complex accounting systems, employees now need only make a telephone call, misdirect purchase invoices, bribe a supplier, manipulate a computer program, or simply push a key on the keyboard to misplace company assets. Because physical possession of stolen property is no longer required and because it is just as easy to program a computer to misdirect $100,000 as it is $1,000, the size and number of frauds have increased tremendously.

To understand how costly fraud is to organizations, consider what happens when fraud is committed against a company. Losses incurred from fraud reduce a firm's income on a dollar-for-dollar basis. This means that for every $1 of fraud, *net income* is reduced by $1. Since fraud reduces net income, it takes significantly more *revenue* to recover the effect of the fraud on net income. To illustrate, consider the $436 million fraud loss that a U.S. automobile manufacturer experienced a few years ago.[4] If the automobile manufacturer's *profit margin* (net income divided by revenues) at the time was 10%, the company would have to generate up to $4.36 billion in additional revenue (or 10 times the amount of the fraud) to recover the effect on net income. If we assume an average selling price of $20,000 per car, the company must make and sell an additional 218,000 cars. Considered this way, fighting fraud is a serious business. The automobile company can spend its efforts manufacturing and marketing additional new cars, or trying to reduce fraud, or a combination of both.

As another example, a large bank was the victim of a fraud that totaled $100 million in one year. With a profit margin of 5%, and assuming that the bank made $100 per year per checking account, how many new checking accounts must the bank generate to compensate for the fraud losses? The answer, of course, is up to 20 million new checking accounts ($100 million fraud loss ÷ 0.05 = $2 billion in additional revenues; $2 billion ÷ $100 per account = 20 million new accounts).

Because of different cost/revenue structures, the amount of additional revenues a firm must generate to recover fraud losses varies from firm to firm. It is easy to see that in order to maximize profits eliminating fraud should be a key goal of every business. The best way to minimize fraud is to prevent it from occurring. In this book, we will cover fraud prevention, as well as fraud detection and investigation.

What Is Fraud?

There are two principal methods of getting something from others illegally. Either you physically force someone to give you what you want, or you trick them out of their assets. The first type of theft we call robbery, and the second type we call *fraud*. Robbery is generally more violent and more traumatic than fraud and attracts much more media attention, but losses from fraud far exceed losses from robbery. Fraud always involves deception, confidence, and trickery.

Although there are many definitions of fraud, probably the most common is the following:

> *Fraud is a generic term, and embraces all the multifarious means which human ingenuity can devise, which are resorted to by one individual, to get an advantage over another by false representations. No definite and invariable rule can be laid down as a general proposition in defining fraud, as it includes surprise, trickery, cunning and unfair ways by which another is cheated. The only boundaries defining it are those which limit human knavery.*[5]

Fraud is deception that includes the following elements:

1. A *representation*
2. About a *material* point,
3. Which is *false*,
4. And *intentionally or recklessly* so,
5. Which is *believed*
6. And *acted upon* by the victim
7. To the victim's *damage*

Fraud is different from unintentional errors. If, for example, someone mistakenly enters incorrect numbers on a *financial statement,* is this fraud? No, it is not fraud because it was not done with intent or for the purpose of gaining advantage over another through false pretense. But, if in the same situation, someone purposely enters incorrect numbers on a financial statement to trick investors, then it *is* fraud!

One of the most famous frauds of all time was Charles Ponzi's investment scam.[6] Ponzi perpetrated a stamp fraud by promising to pay investors unusually high returns. Two interesting things about Ponzi's scheme were that (1) he never made any of the promised investments, but (2) he actually paid the promised returns—at least initially. To make the "investment" look legitimate, Ponzi duped investors into believing he was providing "returns," at least for a while. Thus, early on in the scam if someone invested $1,000 in his scheme, for example, he paid the promised return of $300 at the end of the year. In reality, the $300 was a refund of part of the original $1,000 investment, which left only $700 in the investment, but it appeared as though the investor was earning a 30% return. Thrilled with the high "returns," investors poured more money into the investment and spread the word about this hot investment. As a result, the scam grew quickly, and Ponzi pocketed nearly $20 million before he skipped the country and left investors to realize their losses.

Ponzi's scam is extremely helpful in understanding fraud. Certainly, the scheme involved deception. It also involved greed—greed by the *perpetrator and*—this is important—even greed by the *investors,* who wanted higher-than-sensible returns. Finally, Ponzi's scheme involved the element of *confidence.* If he had not paid the original $300 "returns," investors wouldn't have invested additional money. By paying early "returns," Ponzi gained investors' confidence and convinced them that he had a legitimate business. In fact, confidence is the single most critical element for a fraud to be successful. (The word "con," which means to deceive, comes from "confidence.") It is difficult to con anyone out of anything unless the deceived has confidence in the deceiver. We cannot be conned unless we trust the person trying to deceive us. Similarly, employers cannot con employees if they do not have their employees' trust and confidence. And, without investor confidence, fraudulent companies cannot con unsuspecting investors.

The following example illustrates the role that confidence plays in committing fraud: Two men enter a bank. One is dressed in a business suit and is well groomed. The second has scraggly hair, tattoos up and down both arms, is wearing tattered jeans, and is carrying a motorcycle helmet. Which one do you think is in the best position to successfully con a teller?

Most of us would agree that the man in the business suit is in a better position to defraud the bank. He is, simply put, much more likely to be trusted, stereotypes being what they are. Most people would argue that the scraggly fellow is unlikely to pull off a successful fraud because the bank employees are less likely to trust him initially.

One common response of fraud victims is disbelief: "I can't believe she would do this. She was my most trusted employee. . . . Or my best customer. . . . Or my best friend." Someone who understands fraud will sadly tell you, "What else could they be? They wouldn't have succeeded *without* your trust!" Indeed, fraud perpetrators are often the least suspected and the most trusted of all the people with whom victims associate.

One company's research revealed that its largest group of fraud perpetrators are people between the ages of 36 and 45.[7] The statistics don't tell us *why* this is the case, but one reason may be that this age group includes managers who have worked themselves into positions of trust. In addition, they are probably the group with the highest financial pressures. When young people graduate from college, they look ahead and think, "By the time I'm 40, I'll have my house and cars paid off and have savings to pay for my children's college." But, when many people reach 40, their houses and cars are mortgaged to the hilt and they have no savings to pay for their children's college. During this same time frame (36–45) people are also better positioned in their careers to commit fraud. Alas, any time opportunity and life pressures are present together, the number of cases of fraud climbs steeply, and the result for companies can be financial implosion.

Types of Fraud

The most common way to classify fraud is to divide frauds into those committed *against* an organization and those committed *on behalf* of an organization.

In occupational fraud—fraud committed against an organization—the victim of the fraud is the employee's organization. The Association of Certified Fraud Examiners defines this type of fraud as, *"The use of one's occupation for personal enrichment through the deliberate misuse or misapplication of the employing organization's resources or assets."*[8] Occupational fraud results from the misconduct of employees, managers, or executives. Occupational fraud can be anything from lunch break abuses to high-tech schemes. *The Report to the Nation on Occupation Fraud and Abuse* by the Association of Certified Fraud Examiners states that, "The key to occupational fraud is that the activity (1) is clandestine, (2) violates the employee's fiduciary duties to the organization, (3) is committed for the purpose of direct or indirect financial benefit to the employee, and (4) costs the employing organization assets, revenues, or reserves."[9]

The most common fraud committed on behalf of an organization—usually through actions of the top management—is fraudulent financial reporting. These frauds are committed to make reported earnings look better or to increase a company's stock price. Sometimes, executives misstate earnings in order to ensure a larger year-end bonus. Financial statement fraud often occurs in companies that are experiencing net losses or have profits much less than expectations.

In June, 2001, a "Big 5" CPA firm and three of its partners were fined by the Securities and Exchange Commission for allowing a client to engage in a series of improper accounting practices that inflated its earnings for several years. The fine against the CPA firm and its partners totaled $7 million. The firm agreed to pay the fine and settle the case, although it would not admit to or deny the allegations. The fines against specific partners were the first since the mid-1980s and were imposed by the SEC because it is trying to curb what it sees as a growing problem of accounting fraud.[10]

A more inclusive classification scheme divides fraud into the following six types:

1. Employee embezzlement
2. Management fraud
3. Investment scams
4. Vendor fraud
5. Customer fraud
6. Miscellaneous fraud

Fraud that doesn't fall into one of the first five types and may have been committed for reasons other than financial gain is simply labeled *miscellaneous fraud*. The other five types of fraud are summarized in the table below and are discussed in the paragraphs that follow.

Type of Fraud	Victim	Perpetrator	Explanation
1. Employee embezzlement or occupational fraud	Employers	Employees	Employees directly or indirectly steal from their employers.
2. Management fraud	Stockholders, lenders, and others who rely on financial statements	Top management	Top management provides misrepresentation, usually in financial information.
3. Investment scams	Investors	Individuals	Individuals trick investors into putting money into fraudulent investments.
4. Vendor fraud	Organizations that buy goods or services	Organizations or individuals that sell goods or services	Organizations overcharge for goods or services or nonshipment of goods, even though payment is made.
5. Customer fraud	Organizations that sell goods or services	Customers	Customers deceive sellers into giving customers something they should not have or charging them less than they should.

Employee Embezzlement

Employee embezzlement is another name for occupational fraud. As stated previously, in this type of fraud, employees deceive their employers by taking company assets. Embezzlement can be either direct or indirect. Direct fraud occurs when an employee steals company cash, inventory, tools, supplies, or other assets. It also occurs when employees establish dummy companies and have their employers pay for goods that are not actually delivered. With direct fraud, company assets go directly into the perpetrator's pockets without the involvement of third parties. Indirect employee fraud, on the other hand, occurs when employees take bribes or kickbacks from vendors, customers, or others outside the company to allow for lower sales prices, higher purchase prices, nondelivery of goods, or the delivery of inferior goods. In these cases, payment to employees is usually made by organizations that deal with the perpetrator's employer, not by the employer itself.

One example of direct employee fraud is the fraud perpetrated against Liahona Construction, which was in the home repair business. What management didn't know was, so was one of their employees. The employee used $25,000 of the company's supplies and equipment to do his own remodeling jobs, pocketing the profits himself.

Here is an example of indirect employee fraud: Mark, who worked for "Big D" Advertising. In his role as purchase agent, Mark paid a company in New York City nearly $100,000 for contracted work that should have cost about $50,000. The contractor then paid Mark a kickback of nearly $30,000. Only after someone noticed that the quality of work performed by the New York contractor decreased substantially was the fraud suspected and detected.

Management Fraud

As stated previously, *management fraud* is distinguished from other types of fraud both by the nature of the perpetrators and by the method of deception. In its most common form, management fraud involves top management's deceptive manipulation of financial statements. Well-known examples of alleged management fraud in recent years include Phar-Mor and Crazy Eddie, Inc., both of which supposedly overstated inventories on financial statements; and ZZZZ Best, ESM Government Securities, Regina Vacuum Company, and MiniScribe Corporation, all of which supposedly overstated revenues and/or receivables. In all these cases, management wanted stockholders to believe that the companies' financial positions were better than they really were.

To illustrate management fraud, consider John Blue, the CEO for a fast-growing music store chain. The company was opening new stores almost monthly. The fast-growing music chain had lots of business and was famous for its low prices. When the company went public, shares of the stock soared. Here is what the shareholders didn't know: The chain was selling the music below cost—it was *losing* money on each item sold. John and his CFO hid the losses by inflating inventories and recording fictitious revenues. The scam eventually unraveled when a top accountant reported the fraud. When word leaked out, shares of the company's stock became worthless overnight.

Investment Scams

Closely related to management fraud are *investment scams.* In these scams, fraudulent and usually worthless investments are sold to unsuspecting investors. Telemarketing fraud usually falls into this category, as does the selling of worthless partnership interests and other investment opportunities. Charles Ponzi is regarded as the father of investment scams. Unfortunately, he has not lacked for imitators. His form of deception is extremely common today, with one estimate being that one of every three Americans will fall prey to this type of fraud sometime during his or her lifetime.

The National Fraud Information Center states that in 2000 alone over $5 billion was lost from telemarketing fraud. What follows is a list of the top 10 types of telemarketing frauds in 1999 and 2000.[11]

1999 Top 10 Investment Scams		2000 Top 10 Investment Scams	
Work-at-home schemes	16%	Prizes/sweepstakes	18%
Prizes/sweepstakes	15%	Magazine sales	14%
Telephone slamming	15%	Credit-card offers	13%
Advance-fee loans	11%	Work-at-home schemes	10%
Magazine sales	10%	Advance-fee loans	7%
Telephone cramming	9%	Telephone slamming	7%
Credit-card offers	5%	Credit-card loss protection	4%
Travel/vacations	3%	Buyers' clubs	3%
Credit-card loss protection	2%	Telephone cramming	2%
Investments	2%	Travel/vacations	2%

Consider Brian, a hard-working college student, who was victimized by an investment scam. During the day, Brian attended school, and at night, to support himself, he was a waiter at a downtown diner. On a good night, Brian brought home about $90 in tips. During a period of three years, Brian saved almost $1,200. One day at lunch, Brian's friend, Lance, told him about a startup company in Canada. "If you get in now," Lance said, "you'll be in on the bottom floor. You'll make *at least* three times your money in only a couple of weeks." That same night, Brian accompanied Lance to a meeting describing the investment opportunity. The following day they each invested $1,000. Lance and Brian had never been so excited. They thought the opportunity was almost too good to be true—and unfortunately, they were right! The investment *was* too good to be true. The whole venture was a scam, and Brian and Lance never saw their $1,000 again, let alone any of the exorbitant earnings they were promised.

Vendor Fraud

Vendor fraud has been in the news time and again over the years because of significant overcharges by major vendors on defense and other government contracts. Vendor fraud, which is extremely common in the United States, comes in two main varieties: (1) fraud perpetrated by vendors acting alone, and (2) fraud perpetrated through collusion between buyers and vendors. Vendor fraud usually results in either an overcharge for purchased goods, the shipment of inferior goods, or the nonshipment of goods even though payment was made.

A recent Department of Defense case is a typical vendor fraud. As a result of a joint FBI/Department of Defense investigation, an Illinois-based corporation pleaded guilty to false claims and conspiracy charges pertaining to cost overruns and executive personnel expenses charged to the Department of Defense. The corporation agreed to make restitution of $115 million to the government. The corporation later agreed to an additional payment of $71.3 million to resolve pending administrative and noncriminal issues and to dismiss certain officers proven criminally culpable through investigation.[12]

Customer Fraud

In *customer fraud,* customers either do not pay for goods purchased, or they get something for nothing, or they deceive organizations into giving them something they should not have. For example, consider the bank customer who walked into a branch of a large bank one Saturday morning and convinced the branch manager to give her a $525,000 cashier's check, even though she had only $13,000 in her bank account. The manager believed she was a very wealthy customer and didn't want to lose her business. Unfortunately for the bank, she was a white-collar thief, and she proceeded to defraud the bank of over $500,000. In another customer fraud, six individuals sitting in a downtown Chicago hotel room pretended to be representatives of large corporate customers, made three calls to a Chicago bank, and had the bank transfer nearly $70 million to their accounts in another financial institution in New Jersey. Once the money was transferred to New Jersey, it was quickly transferred to Switzerland, withdrawn, and used to purchase Russian diamonds.

Criminal and Civil Prosecution of Fraud

When people commit fraud, they can be prosecuted criminally and/or civilly. To succeed in a criminal or civil prosecution, it is usually necessary to show that the perpetrator acted with *intent* to defraud the victim. This is best accomplished by gathering evidential matter. *Evidential matter* consists of the underlying data and all corroborating information available. In a later chapter, we will discuss types of evidence and the role evidence plays in successful prosecution and/or litigation.

Criminal Law

Criminal law is that branch of law that deals with offenses of a public nature. Criminal laws generally deal with offenses against society as a whole. They are prosecuted either federally or by a state for violating a *statute* that prohibits some type of activity. Every state and the federal government have statutes prohibiting a wide variety of fraudulent and corrupt practices. Some of the principal federal statutes are as follows:

Statute	Title and Code	Description
Bribery of Public Officials and Witnesses	Title 18, U.S. Code § 201	Bribery is punishable by up to 15 years in prison, a fine of up to three times the thing of value given or received, and disqualification of officer.
Anti-Kickback Act of 1986	Title 41, U.S. Code § 51 to 58	This act outlaws the giving or receiving of any thing of value by a subcontractor to a prime contractor in United States Government contracts. Willful violations are punished by a fine and up to 10 years in prison.
Mail Fraud	Title 18, U.S. Code § 1341	"Whoever, having devised or intending to devise any scheme or artifice to defraud, or for obtaining money or property by means of false or fraudulent pretenses, representations, or promises, . . . for the purpose of executing such scheme or artifice or attempting so to do, places in any post office or authorized deposits or causes to be deposited any matter or thing whatever to be sent or delivered by an private or commercial interstate carrier, . . . shall be fined under this title . . . or imprisoned."
Bank Fraud	Title 18, U.S. Code § 1344	Any scheme to defraud federally insured financial institutions by customers, officers, employees, and owners. Covers banks, savings and loans, credit unions, and other financial institutions insured by government agencies.

continues

Statute	Title and Code	Description
Racketeer Influenced and Corrupt Organizations (RICO) Statute	Title 18, U.S. Code § 1961	This statute makes it an offense for any person associated with an "enterprise" engaged in interstate commerce to conduct the affairs of the enterprise through a "pattern of racketeering activity." A pattern is defined as two or more enumerated criminal violations.
Computer Frauds	Title 18, U.S. Code § 1030	Section 1030 punishes any intentional, unauthorized access to a "protected computer" for the purpose of obtaining restricted data regarding national security, obtaining confidential financial information, using a computer which is intended for use by the U.S. government, committing a fraud, or damaging or destroying information contained in the computer.
Securities Fraud	Rule10(b)5 Securities Act of 1934, § 17(a)	It is unlawful for an insider who has material inside information to purchase or sell the company's securities, irrespective of whether the insider deals directly or through an exchange. The anti-fraud provisions impose civil liability on those who perpetrate or who aid and abet any fraud in connection with any offer and sale of securities.
Foreign Corrupt Practices Act (FCPA)	Title 15, U.S. Code § 78m, 78a(b), 78dd-1, 78dd-2, 78ff	This law outlaws bribery of foreign officials by U.S. companies for business purposes. The FCPA also requires that SEC-regulated companies keep accurate books and records, and have sufficient internal controls to assure that "access to assets is permitted only in accordance with management's . . . authorization," to prevent slush funds and bribe payments.
Tax Evasion	Title 26, U.S. Code § 7201	Failure to report income from fraud or bribes may be prosecuted as tax evasion, or for filing a false return. Also, bribes may not lawfully be deducted as business expenses.

A variety of statutes cover fraudulent activity. Usually, when perpetrators are convicted, they serve jail sentences and/or pay fines. Before perpetrators are convicted, they must be proven guilty "beyond a reasonable doubt." Juries must rule unanimously on guilt for the perpetrator to be convicted. Recent cases of people who were convicted criminally include: the CEO of Financial News Network, who was sentenced to five years in prison for spinning companies he controlled into a plot that inflated FNN's sales; the CEO of Towers Financial, who was sentenced to 20 years for a Ponzi-like scheme that defrauded investors of $450 million; and Donald Ferrarini, who was convicted in February of 1999 and sentenced to 12 years and one month in prison for reporting nonexistent revenues that made his income-losing company look like a profit maker.[13]

Civil Law

Civil law is the body of law that provides remedies for violations of private rights. Civil law deals with rights and duties between individuals. Civil claims begin when one party files a complaint against another, usually for the purpose of gaining financial restitution. The purpose of a civil lawsuit is to compensate for harm done to another individual. Unlike criminal cases, juries in civil cases need not consist of twelve jurors but may have as few as six jurors. The verdict of the jury need not be unanimous. Civil cases are often heard by judges instead of juries. To be successful, plaintiffs in civil cases must only prove their case by the "preponderance of the evidence." In other words, there need only be slightly more evidence supporting the plaintiff than supporting the defendant. In both civil and criminal proceedings, the parties often call expert witnesses to give their opinion on matters thought to be too technical for the jurors or judge to understand. Fraud examiners and accountants are often used as experts in fraud cases to compute and testify to the amount of damages. When fraud is committed, criminal prosecution usually proceeds first.

The following table identifies the major differences between a civil and criminal case.

	Criminal Case	Civil Case
Purpose	To right a wrong	To obtain a remedy
Consequences	Jail and/or fines	Restitution and damage payments
Burden of Proof	"Beyond a reasonable doubt"	"Preponderance of evidence"
Jury	Jury must have 12 people	May consist of fewer than 12 persons
Organization	Determination by a grand jury that sufficient evidence exists to indict	Filing of a claim by a plaintiff
Verdict	Unanimous verdict	Parties may stipulate to a less than unanimous verdict
Claims	Only one claim at a time	Various claims may be joined in one action

Fraud-Related Careers

As the number of frauds and the amounts of fraud losses increase, so do the opportunities for successful careers in fraud-fighting. In fact, just recently, *U.S. News and World Report* identified fraud examination as one of the fastest growing and most financially rewarding careers.[14] The American Institute of Certified Public Accountants recently touted fraud examination/fraud auditing as one of the six fastest growing and most profitable opportunities for accountants.[15] Although there are numerous opportunities for fraud-fighting professionals, careers in forensic work can be broadly classified according to employer, as shown in the table below.

Employer	Types of Work
Government	FBI, Postal Inspectors, Criminal Investigation Division of the IRS, U.S. Marshals, inspector generals of various governmental agencies, state investigators, and law enforcement officials.

continues

Employer	Types of Work
CPA firms, forensic accounting firms, litigations support firms, and law firms	Conduct investigations, support firms in litigations, do bankruptcy-related fraud work, serve as expert witnesses, consult in fraud prevention and detection, and provide other fee-based work.
Corporations	Prevent, detect, and investigate fraud within a company. Includes internal auditors, corporate security officers, and in-house legal counsels.
Organizations that are being sued, or organizations suing in civil cases	Lawyers to defend and/or prosecute cases.
Universities, hospitals, technology corporations, etc.	Consult, serve as expert witnesses, extract evidence from computers and servers, investigate public records, and serve on grand or trial juries.

Taken together, the cost of fighting fraud is very high. In high-profile civil cases, it is not uncommon for defendants and plaintiffs to spend tens of millions of dollars defending and prosecuting alleged frauds. Many large fraud cases involve multiple law firms, multiple lawyers from each firm, multiple investigators, and expert witnesses and large support staffs. Often, after spending large sums of money defending or prosecuting a fraud case, a pre-trial settlement is reached, with no public announcement of the terms of the settlement.

You will find your study of fraud examination to be very helpful—whether or not you become a professional fraud-fighter. As a businessperson, understanding the tremendous costs of fraud losses and learning to recognize fraud warning signs may someday mean the difference between your business surviving or failing. If you become a financial consultant, you will be better equipped to help your clients avoid high-risk and fraudulent investments. As an investor, you will learn skills that help you distinguish between fraudulent and profitable investments. If you become an auditor, you will find the document examination and evidence-gathering skills you learn here invaluable. If you work with taxes, you will be alert to when information from clients is questionable. And, the interviewing skills you will learn will stand you in good stead in numerous endeavors.

You may find, to your surprise, that fraud examination and forensic accounting are not only rewarding and challenging, they are also intriguing (what good mystery isn't?) and endlessly interesting. We hope you enjoy the adventure.

New Terms

Association of Certified Fraud Examiners (ACFE): An international organization, based in Austin, Texas, dedicated to fighting fraud and white-collar crime.

Civil law: The body of law that provides remedies for violations of private rights.

Criminal law: The branch of law that deals with offenses of a public nature.

Customer fraud: Customers not paying for goods purchased, getting something for nothing, or deceiving organizations into giving them something they should not have.

Employee embezzlement: Employees deceiving their employers by taking company assets.

Evidential matter: The underlying data and all corroborating information available about a fraud.

Financial statements: Reports such as the balance sheet, income statement, and statement of cash flows, that summarize the financial status and results of operations of a business entity.

Fraud: "A generic term that embraces all the multifarious means which human ingenuity can devise, which are resorted to by one individual, to get an advantage over another by false representations. No definite and invariable rule can be laid down as a general proposition in defining fraud, as it includes surprise, trickery, cunning and unfair ways by which another is cheated. The only boundaries defining it are those which limit human knavery."

Investment scams: The selling of fraudulent and worthless investments to unsuspecting investors.

Jurisdiction: The limit or territory over which an organization has authority.

Management fraud: Deception perpetrated by an organization's top management through the manipulation of financial statement amounts or disclosures.

Miscellaneous fraud: Deception that doesn't fall into any of the other five categories of fraud.

Net income: An overall measure of the performance of a company; equal to revenues minus expenses for the period.

Perpetrator: A person who has committed a fraud.

Profit margin: Net income divided by total revenues. Also known as return on sales, profit margin percentage, profit margin ratio, operating performance ratio.

Revenue: Increases in a company's resources from the sale of goods or services.

Statute: A law or regulation; a law enacted by the legislative branch of a government.

Vendor fraud: An overcharge for purchased goods, the shipment of inferior goods, or the nonshipment of goods even though payment is made.

Victim: The person or organization deceived by the perpetrator.

Questions and Cases

Discussion Questions

1. What is fraud?
2. How does fraud affect individuals, consumers, and organizations?
3. List and describe the five different types of frauds.
4. What is the difference between civil and criminal laws?
5. For each of the following, indicate whether it is a characteristic of a civil or a criminal case:
   a. Jury may consist of fewer than 12 jurors.
   b. Verdict must be unanimous.
   c. Multiple claims may be joined in one action.
   d. "Beyond a reasonable doubt."
   e. Purpose is to right a public wrong.
   f. Purpose is to obtain remedy.
   g. Consequences of jail and/or fines.
   h. Juries may have a less-than-unanimous verdict.
6. What are some of the different types of fraud-fighting careers?
7. How do employee fraud and management fraud differ?
8. Do you think the demand for careers in fraud prevention and detection is increasing or decreasing? Why?

9. Why are accurate fraud statistics hard to find?

True/False

1. All frauds that are detected are made public.
2. Perpetrators use trickery, confidence, and deception to commit fraud.
3. One of the most common responses to fraud is disbelief.
4. Manufacturing companies with a profit margin of 10% must usually generate about 10 times as much revenue as the dollar amount from the fraud in order to restore net income to its pre-fraud level.
5. Fraud involves using physical force to take something from someone.
6. Telemarketing fraud is an example of employee embezzlement.
7. When perpetrators are convicted of fraud, they often serve jail sentences and/or pay fines.
8. Management fraud is deception perpetrated by an organization's top management.
9. Most people agree that fraud-related careers will be in demand in the future.
10. In civil cases, fraud experts are rarely used as expert witnesses.
11. Many companies hide their losses from fraud rather than make them public.
12. The only group/business that must report employee embezzlement is the federal government.
13. Advances in technology have had no effect on the size or frequency of frauds committed.
14. Fraud losses generally reduce a firm's income on a dollar-for-dollar basis.
15. The single most critical element for a fraud to be successful is opportunity.
16. Fraud perpetrators are often those who are least suspected and most trusted.
17. Unintentional errors in financial statements are a form of fraud.
18. Occupational fraud is fraud committed on behalf of an organization.
19. Companies that commit financial statement fraud are often experiencing net losses or have profits less than expectations.
20. Indirect fraud occurs when a company's assets go directly into the perpetrator's pockets without the involvement of third parties.
21. In vendor fraud, customers don't pay for goods purchased.
22. A negative outcome in a civil lawsuit usually results in jail time for the perpetrator.
23. When fraud is committed, criminal prosecution usually proceeds first.

Multiple Choice

1. Why does fraud seem to be increasing at such an alarming rate?
   a. Computers, the Internet, and technology make fraud easier to commit and cover up.
   b. Most frauds today are detected, whereas in the past many were not.
   c. A new law requires that fraud be reported within 24 hours.
   d. People don't understand the consequences of fraud to organizations and businesses.

2. Which of the following is *not* an important element of fraud?
   a. Confidence
   b. Deception
   c. Trickery
   d. Intelligence
3. Fraud is considered to be:
   a. A serious problem that continues to grow
   b. A problem felt by a few individuals, but not by most people
   c. A mild problem that most businesses need not worry about
   d. A problem under control
4. People who commit fraud are usually:
   a. New employees
   b. Not well-groomed, and have long hair and tattoos
   c. People with strong personalities
   d. Trusted individuals
5. "The use of one's occupation for personal enrichment through the deliberate misuse or misapplication of the employing organization's resources or assets" is the definition of which of the following types of fraud?
   a. Employee embezzlement or occupational fraud
   b. Investment scams
   c. Management fraud
   d. Vendor fraud
6. Corporate employee fraud-fighters:
   a. Work as postal inspectors and law enforcement officials
   b. Prevent, detect, and investigate fraud within a company
   c. Are lawyers that defend and/or prosecute fraud cases
   d. None of the above
7. Investment scams most often include:
   a. An action by top management against employees
   b. Worthless investments or assets sold to unsuspecting investors
   c. An overcharge for purchased goods
   d. Nonpayment of invoices for goods purchased by customers
8. Which of the following is *not* true of civil fraud?
   a. Usually begins when one party files a complaint
   b. The purpose is to compensate for harm done to another
   c. Must be heard by 12 jurors
   d. Only "the preponderance of the evidence" is needed for plaintiff to be successful
9. Future careers in fraud will most likely be:
   a. In low demand
   b. In about the same demand as now
   c. Low paying
   d. In higher demand and financially rewarding

10. Studying fraud will help you to:
    a. Learn evidence-gathering skills
    b. Avoid high-risk and fraudulent activities
    c. Learn valuable interviewing skills
    d. All of the above
11. Which of the following is *not* a reliable resource for fraud statistics?
    a. FBI agencies
    b. Health agencies
    c. Insurance organizations
    d. Fraud perpetrators
12. Which of the following statements is true?
    a. Bank robberies are more costly than frauds.
    b. Fraud is often labeled the fastest growing crime.
    c. FBI agencies are spending approximately 35% of their time on fraudulent activities.
13. Which of the following is *not* an element of fraud?
    a. False representation
    b. Accidental behavior
    c. Damage to a victim
    d. Intentional or reckless behavior
14. What is the best way to minimize fraud within an organization?
    a. Detection of fraud
    b. Investigation of fraudulent behavior
    c. Prevention activities
    d. Research company activities
15. What is the most important element in successful fraud schemes?
    a. Promised benefits
    b. Confidence in the perpetrator
    c. Profitable activities
    d. Complexity
16. Which of the following characters is least likely to be involved in a fraud?
    a. Middle-aged person who has a middle management position
    b. A long-haired teenager wearing leather pants
    c. Recent college graduate
    d. Senior executives who have obtained stock options
17. Which of the following is *not* a fraud type?
    a. Direct employee embezzlement
    b. Indirect employee embezzlement
    c. Supervisor fraud
    d. Investment scams
18. Which of the following is *not* a form of vendor fraud?
    a. Overcharge for purchased goods
    b. Shipment of inferior goods
    c. Nonshipment of goods even though payment is made
    d. Not paying for goods purchased

19. Civil law performs which of the following functions?
    a. Remedy for violation of private rights
    b. Remedy for violations against society as a whole
    c. Punishment for guilt "beyond reasonable doubt"
    d. Monetary reimbursement for federal damages
20. Fraud-fighting includes what type of careers?
    a. Professors
    b. Lawyers
    c. CPA firms
    d. All of the above

Short Cases

Case 1. Clever, Inc., is a car manufacturer. Its 2002 income statement is as follows:

Clever, Inc.
Income Statement
For the year ended Dec. 31, 2002

Sales revenue	$20,000
Less cost of goods sold	10,000
Gross margin	$10,000
Expenses	8,000
Net income	$ 2,000

Alexander, Inc., is a car rental agency based in Florida. Its 2002 income statement is as follows:

Alexander Inc.
Income Statement
For the year ended Dec. 31, 2002

Sales revenue	$20,000
Expenses	15,000
Net income	$ 5,000

During 2002, both Clever, Inc., and Alexander, Inc., incurred a $1,000 fraud loss. How much additional revenue must each company generate to recover the losses from the fraud? Why are these amounts different? Which company will probably have to generate less revenue to recover the losses?

Case 2. You are having lunch with another business student. During the course of your conversation, you tell your friend about your exciting fraud examination class. After you explain the seriousness of fraud in the business world, she asks you two questions:

1. What is the difference between fraud and an unintentional error?
2. With all the advances in technology, why is fraud a growing problem? With advanced technology, shouldn't companies, police, the FBI, and others be able to prevent and detect fraud much more easily?

Case 3. For each of the following examples, identify whether it is an employee embezzlement, management fraud, investment scam, vendor fraud, customer fraud, or miscellaneous fraud.

1. Marcus bought a $70 basketball for only $30, simply by exchanging the price tags before purchasing the ball.
2. Craig lost $500 by investing in a multilevel marketing scam.
3. The Bank of San Felipe lost over $20,000 in 2002. One of its employees took money from a wealthy customer's account and put it into his own account. By the time the fraud was detected, the employee had spent the money and the bank was held responsible.
4. The CEO of Los Andes Real Estate was fined and sentenced to six months in prison for deceiving investors into believing it made a profit in 2002, when it actually lost over $150 million.
5. The government lost over $50 million in 2002 because many of its contractors and subcontractors charged for fictitious hours and equipment on a project in the Middle East.
6. A student broke into the school's computer system and changed his grades in order to be accepted into college.

Case 4. Some students in your fraud examination class are having a hard time understanding why statistics on fraud are so difficult to obtain. What would you say to enlighten them?

Case 5. You're telling your husband about your classes for the new semester. He's intrigued by the idea of your becoming a fraud detective, but he wants to know whether you will have job security and what kinds of jobs you might get. How would you respond to his questions?

Case 6. A newspaper from June 2001 contains the following story:[16]

Sweepstakes Company Agrees to Pay Up

Publishers Clearing House agreed to pay $34 million in a deal with 26 states to settle allegations the sweepstakes company employed deceptive marketing practices. The $34 million will cover customer refunds, legal expenses, and administrative cost to the states. Each state's share has yet to be determined. In the lawsuits, state attorneys general accused Publishers Clearing House of deceptive marketing for its sweepstakes promotions. The suit alleged that the company was misleading consumers by making them believe they had won prizes or would win if they bought magazines from Publishers Clearing House.

As part of the settlement, the company will no longer use phrases like "guaranteed winner." "This will in fact revolutionize the sweepstakes industry," Michigan Attorney General Jennifer Granholm stated. "We listened to the states' concerns and have agreed to responsive and significant changes that will make our promotions the clearest, most reliable and trustworthy in the industry," said Robin Smith, chairman and CEO of the Port Washington, N.Y.–based company.

Publishers Clearing House reached an $18 million settlement last August with 24 other states and the District of Columbia, though the other states opted not to join. The states involved in the latest settlement are: Arizona, Arkansas, Colorado, Connecticut, Delaware, Florida, Indiana, Iowa, Kansas, Kentucky, Maine, Maryland, Massachusetts, Michigan, Minnesota,

> *Missouri, New Jersey, North Carolina, Oregon, Pennsylvania, Rhode Island, Tennessee, Texas, Vermont, West Virginia, and Wisconsin.*

Based on this information do you believe Publishers Clearing House has committed fraud? Why or why not?

Case 7. A bookkeeper in a $3,000,000 retail company had earned the trust of her supervisor, so various functions normally reserved for management were assigned to her, including the authority to issue and authorize customer refunds. She proceeded to issue refunds to nonexistent customers and created documents with false names and addresses. She adjusted the accounting records and stole about $15,000 cash. She was caught when internal audit sent routine confirmations to customers on a mailing list and received excessive "return-to-sender" replies. The investigation disclosed a telling pattern. The bookkeeper initially denied accusations but admitted the crime upon presentation of the evidence.

You are a lawyer for the retail company. Now that the fraud has been detected, would you prosecute her criminally or civilly, or both? What process would you use to try to recover the $15,000?

Case 8. You are a new summer intern working for a major professional services firm. During your lunch break each day, you and a fellow intern, Bob, eat at a local sandwich shop. One day, Bob's girlfriend joins you for lunch. When the bill arrives, Bob pays with a company credit card and writes the meal off as a business expense. Bob and his girlfriend continue to be "treated" to lunch for a number of days. You know Bob is well aware of a recent memo that came down from management stating casual lunches are not valid business expenses. When you ask Bob about the charges, he replies, "Hey, we're interns. Those memos don't apply to us. We can expense anything we want."

1. Is fraud being committed against the firm?
2. What responsibility, if any, do you have to report the activity?

Case 9. After receiving an anonymous note indicating fraudulent activities in the company, XYZ Company officials discover that an employee has embezzled a total of $50,000 over the past year. Unfortunately, this employee used an assumed identity and has vanished without a trace. The CFO at XYZ wants to know how badly this fraud has hurt the company. If XYZ has a profit margin of 7%, how much additional revenue will XYZ most likely have to generate to cover the loss?

Case 10. Your friend John works for an insurance company. John holds a business degree and has been involved in the insurance business for many years. John shares some recent company gossip with you. He has heard that the internal auditors estimate the company has lost about $2,500,000 because of fraud in the last few years. Because you are a Certified Fraud Examiner, John asks you how this will affect the company's profitability. John doesn't have access to the company's financial information.

Compute the additional revenues needed to make up for the lost money, assuming that the company has a profit margin of 5%, 10%, and 15%. Give examples of three types of fraud that could affect the insurance company. Who are the victims and who are the perpetrators?

Extensive Case

Case 11. The credit-card industry is all too familiar with the high cost and pervasive problem of fraud. In fact, it is estimated that between 9% and 12% of all U.S. credit-card transactions are fraudulent. A large percentage of the costs to issue and service credit cards involves the detection and prevention of fraud. VISA, MasterCard, American Express, and institutions that facilitate the use of debit and credit cards have gone to great lengths to learn the behavior of fraudsters so they can recognize patterns and predict behavior. These organizations keep databases of all fraudulent transactions in order to analyze data and devise new strategies to combat this persistent problem. Many banks use expensive fraud-detection software to try to stop fraudsters before their scams become too big. For instance, patterns suggest that people using stolen credit cards often go to gas stations to see if the credit card will authorize an unattended gas pump. If the gas purchase is authorized, the thieves then go directly to jewelry stores, electronics stores, or footwear stores and spend as much money as they can as fast as they can. Computer software can detect this pattern and then decline subsequent transactions.

Another problem that credit-card institutions face is the protection of their Bank Identification Number (BIN). This number identifies the member bank that issues credit cards and is used in the account number of cardholders. Fraudsters have become very sophisticated at either creating their own credit cards with valid BINs or stealing cards and changing the numbers of an active account. They can spend a lot of money before anyone notices a problem. Also, if certain protections are not put in place when a new credit-card institution is starting up and its BIN number first becomes valid in the network of bankcard authorizing systems, fraudsters can steal large amounts of money. At this point, the institution may not even have any valid credit cards yet, but since its BIN is active, valid credit-card numbers that include the BIN could potentially be authorized. When a mistake is made in putting these protections in place, it is not uncommon for an issuing bank to lose $1 million in a weekend before the error is noticed.

On a more personal level, "identity theft" is on the increase. This theft occurs when someone uses your name and personal information to do such things as open up credit-card accounts. Identity thieves find information in garbage dumps or anywhere they can gather information about you. One common scheme is for a fraudster to call people on the phone, posing as an employee of their bank. They manage to learn all kinds of information about people, such as social security numbers, place of birth, and PIN numbers without much effort. Another scheme occurs in restaurants with dishonest waiters. Dishonest waiters often have a device on their belt that looks like a pager. In reality it is a reader that can store information from the magnetic stripe on the back of your credit card. They swipe your card just before they charge you for the meal, and they have enough information to make a fake credit card. Credit-card schemes are as numerous as there are fraudsters.

1. Is this problem just a concern for the institutions that issue credit cards? How are you affected?
2. How can you protect yourself from "identity fraud"?

Internet Assignment

Your best friend wants to know why "on earth" you are taking a fraud examination class. He is curious about what careers this class prepares you for. Go to the Internet and find information about two different careers that you could pursue in the field of fraud examination. Write two or three brief paragraphs about what you found. Remember to include the web sites where your information came from, so that your friend can do some investigating of his own.

Debate

For the past year, you've been working as a secretary/processor for a local construction company, XYZ Homes, which specializes in the building of low-cost, limited-option homes. You left a comfortable, good-paying job to work for XYZ because it was family-owned and operated by some long-time friends.

Soon after you began working for XYZ, you noticed questionable behavior on the part of Mr. and Mrs. XYZ's two sons, who are company salesmen. In fact, you are positive that they are falsifying documents to increase their commissions and to trick local banks into approving mortgages to customers who don't meet credit standards.

You are trying to decide how to handle the situation when one of the sons approaches you and asks you to produce and sign a memo to a bank, falsely stating that a certain potential home buyer is credit-worthy. You refuse to do so and, after much consideration, approach Mr. XYZ about the situation. To your surprise, he simply brushes off your comments as unimportant and laughingly states that "boys will be boys."

What would you do in this situation? Is the fact that you correctly refused to produce and sign a false memo enough, or are you obligated to report these crimes to the banks and proper authorities? Discuss the options, responsibilities, and implications you are facing.

End Notes

1. Laura Goldberg and Ralph Bivins, "Enron's Former Chief Financial Officer Surfaces," *Wall Street City,* Dec. 13, 2001.
2. "Letter to Members," transcript of Barry Melancon, January 24, 2002. http://www.aicpa.org/infor/letter_02_01.htm
3. The Association of Certified Fraud Examiners. 1996. *The Report to the Nation on Occupation Fraud and Abuse.* Austin, TX: ACFE, p. 4.
4. "McNamara's Money Game," *Newsday: The Long Island Newspaper,* April 16, 1992, pp. 4–5.
5. *Webster's New World Dictionary, College Edition.* 1964. Cleveland and New York: World, p. 380.
6. Charles K. Ponzi Web site, http://www.mark-knutson.com.
7. This statistic is the proprietary information of a major financial institution for which the author was a consultant.
8. The Association of Certified Fraud Examiners. 1996. *The Report to the Nation on Occupation Fraud and Abuse,* Austin, TX: ACFE, p. 4.
9. Ibid., p. 9.
10. U.S. Securities and Exchange Commission, Litigation Release No. 17039, June 19, 2001 (http://www.sec.gov).
11. http://www.fraud.org/telemarketing/teleset.htm. June 19, 2001, The National Fraud Information Center.
12. Federal Bureau of Investigation. 1989. *White Collar Crime: A Report to the Nation,* p. 6, Department of Justice, Washington, D.C.
13. Securities and Exchange Commission, Litigation Release No. 16489, March 29, 2000, Release No. 38765, June 24, 1997 (http://codesign.scu.edu/505/set02/005/webproject/page6.htm).
14. "Careers to Count On," *U.S. News and World Report,* Cover Story, February 18, 2002.
15. http://aicpa.org/nolimits/job/paths/ndex.htm
16. News Release, Iowa Department of Justice, Attorney General Tom Miller, June 26, 2001. http://www.state.ia.us/government/ag/PCH_settlement_release_IA.htm

CHAPTER TWO

Who Commits Fraud and Why

After studying this chapter, you should be able to:

1. Understand who commits fraud.
2. Understand why people commit fraud.
3. Understand the fraud triangle.
4. Understand how life pressures contribute to fraud.
5. Understand why opportunities must be present in order for fraud to be committed.
6. Identify controls that prevent and/or detect fraudulent behavior.
7. Identify noncontrol factors that provide opportunities for fraud.
8. Understand why people rationalize.

I, Dennis Greer, am making this statement on my own, without threat or promises, as to my activities in regard to the activity of kiting between Bank A and Bank B. As of May 19XX, I was having extreme emotional and financial difficulties. For religious reasons, I was required without notice to move out of where I was living, and I had no place to go. Also, my grandmother—the only family member I was close to—was dying. I had to live out of my car for 3½ weeks. At the end of this time, my grandmother died. She lived in Ohio. I went to the funeral and I returned with a $1,000 inheritance. I used this money to secure an apartment. The entire sum was used up for the first month's rent, deposit, and the application fee. From that time, mid-June, until the first part of August, I was supporting myself on my minimum-wage job at the nursery. I had no furniture or a bed. I was barely making it. I was feeling very distraught over the loss of my grandmother and problems my parents and brother were having. I felt all alone. The first part of August arrived and my rent was due. I did not have the full amount to pay it. This same week, I opened a checking account at Bank B. I intended to close my Bank A account because of a lack of ATMs, branches, and misunderstanding. As I said, my rent was due and I did not know how to meet it. On an impulse, I wrote the apartment manager a check for the amount due. I did not have the funds to cover it. I thought I could borrow it, but I could not. During the time I was trying to come up with the money, I wrote a check from my Bank B account to cover the rent check and put it into Bank A. I did not know it was illegal. I knew it was unethical, but I thought since the checks were made out to me that it wasn't illegal. This went on for about a week—back and forth between banks. I thought I could get the money to cover this debt but I never did. My grandmother's estate had been quite large, and I expected more money, but it was not to happen. After a week of nothing being said to me by the banks, I began to make other purchases via this method. I needed something to sleep on and a blanket and other items for the apartment. I bought a sleeper sofa, a desk, a modular shelf/bookcase, dishes, and also paid off my other outstanding debts—college loans, dentist bill, and credit. I was acting foolishly. No one had questioned me at the banks about any of this. I usually made deposits at different branches to try to avoid suspicion, but when I was in my own branches, no *one said a thing. I thought maybe what I was doing wasn't wrong after all. So I decided to purchase a new car, stereo, and a new computer to use at home for work. Still, I did not have a problem making deposits at the banks. But, I was feeling very guilty. I knew I needed to start downsizing the "debt" and clear it up. I began to look for a better-paying job. Finally, last week I got a call from Bank B while I was at work: They had discovered a problem with my account. I realized then that the banks had found out. Later that day, I got another call from Bank A. They told me that what I had been doing was illegal and a felony. I was in shock. I didn't know it was that bad. I realize now how wrong what I did was. From the start, I knew it was unethical, but I didn't know it was indeed a crime until now. I have had to do a lot of thinking, praying, and talking to those close to me about this. I am truly sorry for what I have done, and I don't EVER plan to do it again. All I want now is to make amends with the banks. I do not have the money to pay back either bank right now. I realize this hurts them. I want to try to set this right, whether I go to prison or not. I am prepared to work however long it takes to pay the banks back in full with reasonable interest from a garnishment of my wages from now until the full amount is paid and settled. I committed this act because I was feeling desperate. I was emotionally a wreck and physically tired. I felt I didn't have a choice but to do what I did or return to living in my car. I know now that what I did was wrong, and I am very sorry for it. I am attempting to seek psychological counseling to help me deal with and resolve why I did this. I feel I have a lot to offer society, once I am able to clean up my own life and get it straightened out. I pray the bank employees and officers will forgive me on a personal level for the hardship my actions have caused them, and I want to make full restitution. I have done wrong, and I must now face the consequences. This statement has been made in my own words, by myself, without threat or promise, and written by my own hand.*

Dennis Greer

The names of the perpetrator and the banks have been changed in this case. However, this is a true confession written by a person who committed the fraud of kiting—using the "float time" between banks to give the impression that he had money in his accounts. This is a fraud perpetrated by a customer.

In Chapter 1, we talked about what fraud is; the seriousness of the problem; different types of frauds, including customer frauds like Greer's; how much fraud costs organizations; and the difference between civil and criminal law. In this chapter, we discuss who commits frauds and why they commit fraud. To prevent, detect, and investigate fraud, you must understand what motivates fraudulent behavior and why otherwise honest people behave unethically.

Who Commits Fraud

Past research has shown that anyone can commit fraud.[1] Fraud perpetrators usually cannot be distinguished from other people by demographic or psychological characteristics. Most fraud perpetrators have profiles that look like those of other honest people.

Several years ago, the author was involved in a study of the characteristics of fraud perpetrators. In this study, fraud perpetrators were compared with (1) prisoners incarcerated for property offenses and (2) a noncriminal sample of college students. The personal backgrounds and psychological profiles of the three groups were compared, and the results indicated that incarcerated fraud perpetrators are very different from other incarcerated prisoners. When compared to other criminals, they are less likely to be caught, turned in, arrested, convicted, and incarcerated. They are also less likely to serve long sentences. In addition, fraud perpetrators are considerably older. Although only 2% of the property offenders are female, 30% of fraud perpetrators are women. Fraud perpetrators are better educated, more religious, less likely to have criminal records, less likely to have abused alcohol, and considerably less likely to have used drugs. They are also in better psychological health. They enjoy more optimism, self-esteem, self-sufficiency, achievement, motivation, and family harmony than other property offenders. Fraud perpetrators also demonstrate more social conformity, self-control, kindness, and empathy than other property offenders.[2]

When fraud perpetrators were compared with college students, they differed only slightly. Fraud perpetrators suffer more psychic pain and are more dishonest, more independent, more sexually mature, more socially deviant, and more empathetic than college students. However, fraud perpetrators are much more similar to college students than they are to property offenders. The following diagram illustrates the differences among the three groups:

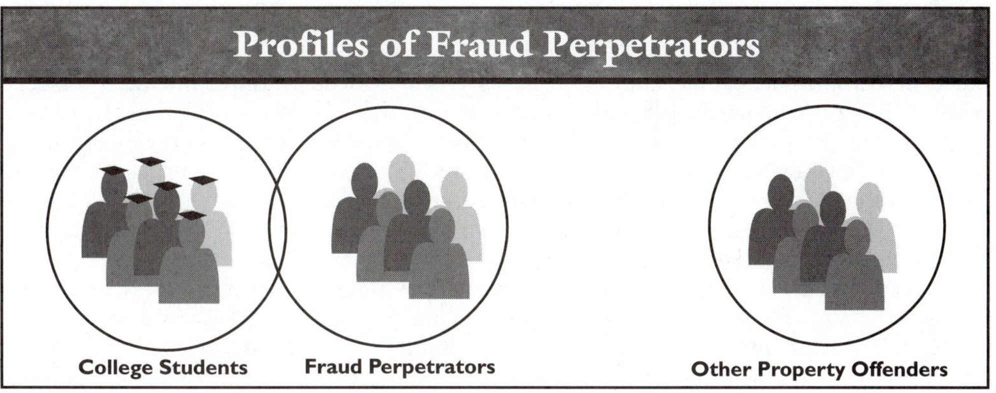

It is important to understand the characteristics of fraud perpetrators because they appear to be very much like people who have traits that organizations look for in hiring employees, seeking out customers and clients, and selecting vendors. This knowledge helps us to understand that (1) most employees, customers, vendors, and business associates and partners fit the profile of fraud perpetrators and are probably capable of committing fraud, and (2) it is impossible to predict in advance which employees, vendors, clients, and customers will become dishonest. In fact, when fraud does occur, the most common reaction by those around the fraud is denial. Victims can't believe that individuals who look and behave much like them and who are usually well trusted can behave dishonestly.

Why People Commit Fraud

Although there are thousands of ways to perpetrate fraud, Dennis Greer's fraud in the chapter opening vignette illustrates three key elements common to all of them. His fraud includes: (1) a perceived pressure, (2) a perceived opportunity, and (3) some way to rationalize the fraud as acceptable. These three elements make up what we call the fraud triangle.

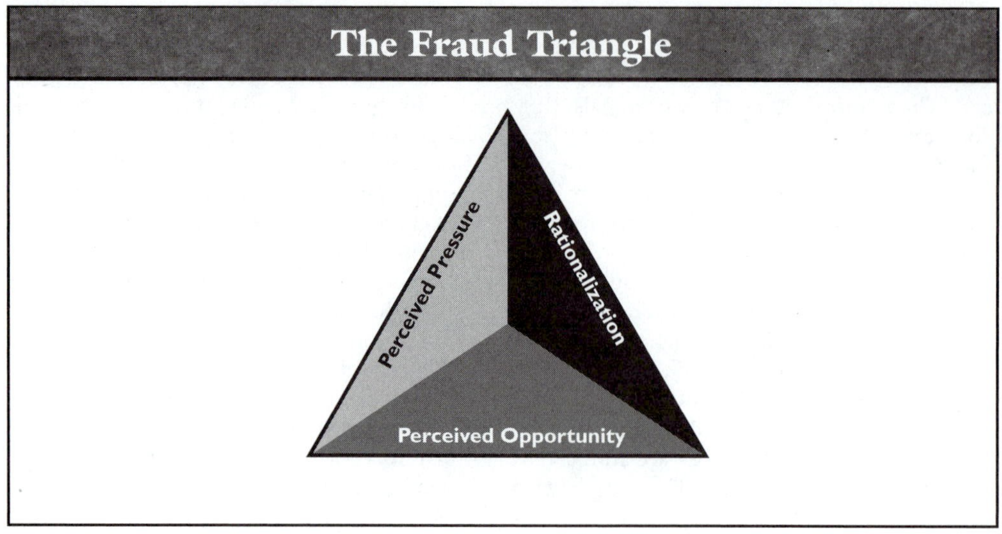

After moving into an apartment, Greer could not pay the second month's rent. Faced with having to choose between dishonesty or living in his car, he chose to be dishonest. Every fraud perpetrator faces some kind of *perceived pressure.* Most pressures involve a financial need, although nonfinancial pressures (such as the need to report results better than actual performance, frustration with work, or even a challenge to beat the system) can also motivate fraud. In Greer's case, he had a real pressure, not a perceived one. We may look at fraud perpetrators and say "they didn't have a real pressure." But it doesn't matter what we think—it is only what is in the fraud perpetrator's mind that matters. Later in this chapter we will discuss the different kinds of pressures that trigger fraudsters.

Greer found a way to commit fraud by repeatedly writing bad checks to give the impression that he was depositing real money in his accounts. He didn't need access to cash, to use force, or even to confront his victims physically. Rather, he simply wrote checks to himself in the privacy of his own apartment and deposited them in two different banks. His weapons of crime were a pen and checks from the financial institutions. Whether or not Greer could actually get away with the crime didn't matter. What mattered was that Greer believed he could conceal the fraud—in other words, he had a *perceived opportunity.*

Fraud perpetrators need a way to *rationalize* their actions as acceptable. Greer's rationalizations are twofold: (1) He didn't believe what he was doing was illegal, although he recognized it might be unethical, and (2) he believed he would get an inheritance and be able to pay the money back. In his mind, he was only *borrowing,* and, although his method of borrowing was *perhaps* unethical, he would repay the debt. After all, almost everyone borrows money.

Perceived pressure, perceived opportunity, and rationalization are common to every fraud. Whether the fraud is one that benefits the perpetrators directly, such as employee fraud, or one that benefits the perpetrator's organization, such as management fraud, the three elements are always present. In the case of management fraud, for example, the pressure may be the need to make earnings look better to meet debt covenants, the opportunity may be a weak audit committee, and the rationalization may be that "we'll only cook the books until we can get over this temporary hump."

Fraud resembles fire in many ways. For a fire to occur, three elements are necessary: (1) oxygen, (2) fuel, and (3) heat. These three elements make up the "fire triangle," as shown on the next page. When all three elements come together, there is fire.

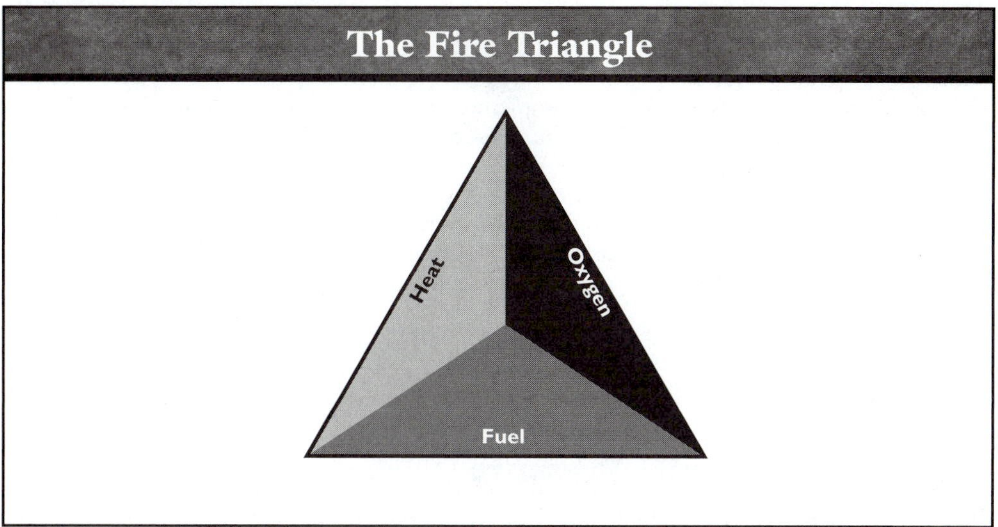

Firefighters know that a fire can be extinguished by eliminating any one of the three elements. Oxygen is often eliminated by smothering, by using chemicals, or by causing explosions, as is the case in oil well fires. Heat is most commonly eliminated by pouring water on fires. Fuel is removed by building fire lines or fire breaks or by shutting off the source of the fuel.

As with the elements in the fire triangle, the three elements in the fraud triangle are also interactive. With fire, the more flammable the fuel, the less oxygen and heat it takes to ignite. Similarly, the purer the oxygen, the less flammable the fuel needs to be to ignite. With fraud, the greater the perceived opportunity or the more intense the pressure, the less rationalization it takes to motivate someone to commit fraud. Likewise, the more dishonest a perpetrator is, the less opportunity and/or pressure it takes to motivate fraud. The following scale illustrates the relationship between the three elements:

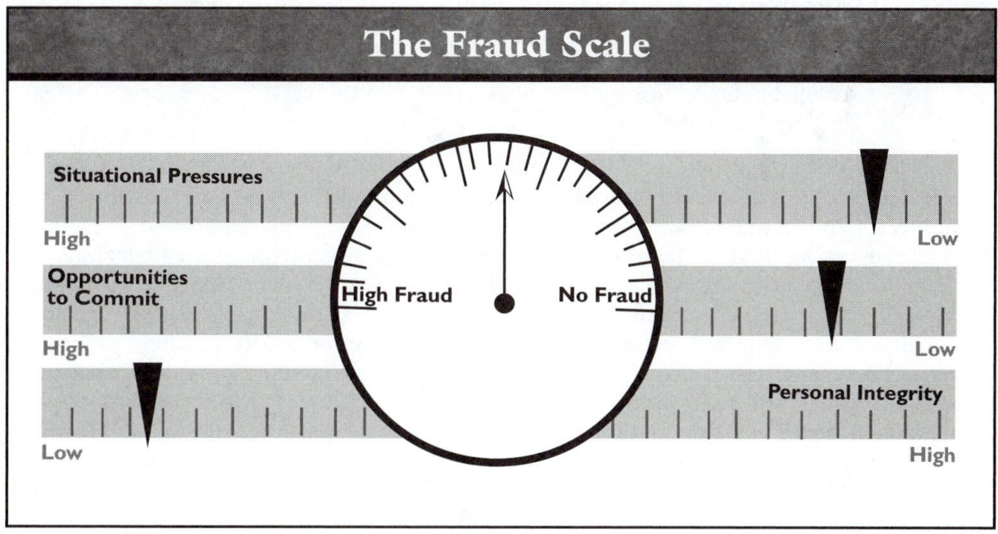

As we show in later chapters, people who try to prevent fraud usually work on only one of the three elements of the fraud triangle: opportunity. Because fraud-fighters generally believe that opportunities can be eliminated by having good internal controls, they focus all or most of their preventive efforts on implementing controls and ensuring adherence to them. Rarely do they focus on the pressures motivating fraud or on the rationalizations of perpetrators.

It is interesting to note that almost every study of honesty reveals that levels of honesty are decreasing.[3] Given the interactive nature of the elements in the fraud triangle, society's retreat from this value presents a scary future for companies combatting fraud. Less honesty makes it easier to rationalize, thus requiring less perceived opportunity and/or pressure for fraud to occur.

Rationalizations and varying levels of honesty, as well as fraud opportunities, are discussed later in this chapter. We now turn our attention to the pressures that motivate individuals to commit fraud.

The First Element: Pressure

Fraud is perpetrated to benefit oneself or to benefit an organization, or both. Employee fraud, in which individuals embezzle from their employers, usually benefits the perpetrator. Management fraud, in which an organization's officers deceive investors and creditors (usually by manipulating financial statements), is most often perpetrated to benefit an organization and its officers. In this section we will discuss the different pressures that motivate individuals to perpetrate fraud on their own behalf. Most experts on fraud believe these pressures can be divided into four types: (1) financial pressures, (2) vices, (3) work-related pressures, and (4) other pressures.

Financial Pressures

Studies conducted by the author show that approximately 95% of all frauds involve either financial or vice-related pressures.[4] What were Greer's financial pressures? He was living in his car, he didn't have furniture or other necessities, and he was broke. Here are the common financial pressures associated with fraud that benefits perpetrators directly:

1. Greed
2. Living beyond one's means
3. High bills or personal debt
4. Poor credit
5. Personal financial losses
6. Unexpected financial needs

This list is not exhaustive, and these pressures are not mutually exclusive. However, each pressure in this list has been associated with numerous frauds. We know of individuals who committed fraud because they were destitute. We know of perpetrators who were living lifestyles far beyond that of their peers. When one perpetrator was caught embezzling over $1.3 million from his employer, investigators discovered that he spent the money on monogrammed shirts and gold cuff links, two Mercedes Benz cars, an expensive suburban home, a beachfront condominium, furs, rings, and other jewelry for his wife, a new car for his father-in-law, and a country club membership. Most people would say he didn't have real financial pressures. But to him, the pressures from his desire to acquire these luxuries were enough to motivate him to commit fraud.

Financial pressures can occur suddenly or can be long-term. Unfortunately, very few fraud perpetrators inform others when they are having financial problems. As an example, consider Susan Jones. Susan had worked at the same company for over 32 years. Her integrity had never been questioned. At age 63, she became a grandmother—and immediately thereafter, a spendaholic. She bought everything she could get her hands on for her two grandchildren. She even became addicted to the Home Shopping Network, a cable TV channel. During the three years prior to her retirement, Susan stole over $650,000 from her employer. When caught, she was sentenced and served one year in prison. She also deeded everything she and her husband owned to her former employer in an attempt to pay the employer back. By giving her employer her home, her retirement account, and her cars, she repaid approximately $400,000 of the $650,000 she stole. She also entered into a restitution agreement to pay back the remaining $250,000 she still owed. And, because she hadn't paid income taxes on the $250,000 of fraudulent "income," the IRS required her to make monthly tax payments after she got out of prison.

The fact that someone has been an "honest" employee for a long time (32 years in Susan's example) appears to make no difference when severe financial pressures occur or an individual perceives that such pressures exist. One study found that whereas approximately 30% of frauds are perpetrated by employees during their first three years of employment, 70% are committed by employees with 4–35 years of experience, and the age group with the highest rate of fraud are individuals between 35 and 44 years old.[5]

Financial pressure is the most common pressure that drives people to commit fraud. Usually when management fraud occurs, companies overstate assets on the balance sheet and net income on the income statement. They usually feel pressured to do so because of a poor cash position, receivables that aren't collectible, a loss of customers, obsolete inventory, a declining market, or restrictive loan covenants that the company is violating. Regina Vacuum's management committed massive financial statement fraud. The main pressure that drove them to fraud was that their vacuum cleaners were defective—parts melted—and thousands were being returned. The large number of returns reduced revenues significantly and created such income pressures that management intentionally understated sales returns and overstated sales.[6]

Vice

Closely related to financial pressures are "vices"—addictions such as gambling, drugs, and alcohol—and expensive extramarital relationships. As an example of how these vice problems motivate a person to commit fraud, consider one individual's confession of how gambling led to his dishonest acts:

> *As I sat on the stool in front of the blackjack table I knew I was in trouble. I had just gambled away my children's college fund. I stumbled to my hotel room, hoping to wake up and realize this evening was nothing more than a nightmare. While driving back to San Jose from Reno Sunday morning, I could not face the embarrassment of telling my wife. I had to come up with the money. I was sure that if I had only $500, I could win the money back. But how could I get $500? A short time later at work, an accounts payable clerk came to my office seeking assistance with a problem. The clerk was matching invoices with purchase orders. He had found an invoice for $3,200 that did not match the purchase order. Immediately, I realized how I could get the $500 "loan." My company was a fast-growing microchip producer whose internal controls were quite good on paper but were often not followed. The company had a policy of paying, without secondary approval, any invoice of $500 or less. I decided to set up a dummy company that would issue invoices to my employer for amounts up to $500. I was confident my winnings from these "borrowings" would not only allow me to replace the college fund, but would also allow repayment of the "loan." I couldn't*

> *believe how easy it was to "borrow" the money. The first check showed up in a P.O. box I had opened a few days earlier. I called my wife with the bad news. Together with the controller, I would have to fly to Los Angeles over the weekend to meet with lawyers over a company matter. Within minutes, I was on my way to Reno. Upon arrival, I went straight to the craps tables. By 4:00* A.M.*, I was not only out of money but was in the hole over $600. I was concerned about the losses, but not as worried as before. I would just submit more fictitious bills to the company. Over the next few months, my fraud progressed to the point where I had set up two more dummy companies and insisted that accounts payable clerks not verify any invoice of less than $750. No one questioned my changing the policy because I had worked for the company for over 14 years and was a "trusted" employee. After one year, I had replaced the college fund and purchased a new automobile; I had stolen over $75,000. I was caught when the internal auditors matched addresses of vendors and found that my three dummy vendors all had the same P.O. box.*

Vices are the worst kind of pressure—out-of-control lifestyles are frequently cited as the trigger that drives previously honest people to commit fraud. We know of female employees who embezzled because their children were on drugs and they couldn't stand to see them go through withdrawal pains. We also know of "successful" managers who, in addition to embezzling from their companies, burglarized homes and engaged in other types of theft to support their drug habits. To understand the addictive nature of these vices, consider the following confessions from reformed gamblers.

- "Gambling was the ultimate experience for me—better than sex, better than any drug. I had withdrawal tortures just like a heroin junkie."
- "I degraded myself in every way possible. I embezzled from my own company; I conned my six-year-old out of his allowance."
- "Once I was hooked, any wager would do. I would take odds on how many cars would pass over a bridge in the space of 10 minutes."
- "I stole vacation money from the family sugar jar. I spent every waking hour thinking about getting to the track."
- "After I woke up from an appendectomy, I sneaked out of the hospital, cashed a bogus check, and headed for my bookie. I was still bleeding from the operation."
- "I'll never forget coming home from work at night, looking through the window at my family waiting for me, and then leaving to place a couple more bets. I was crying the whole time, but I had simply lost all control."

If someone will steal from his six-year-old child or sneak out of a hospital still bleeding from an operation to feed his addiction, he will certainly steal from his employer or commit other types of fraud. The number of embezzlers who trace their motivation for embezzlement to alcohol, gambling, and expensive extramarital relationships is high. However, the number who steal for drugs may even be higher. Consider these confessions of former addicted drug users.

- "I began living with a man who was a heavy drug user. We had a child, but the relationship didn't last. By the time it ended, I was high on drugs and alcohol so much of the time I could barely manage to make it to work every day."
- "I was the branch manager of a large bank. But secretly I was shooting up in my office all day and stealing money from my employer to finance it."
- "One day my daughter stretched out her little arms in front of me. She had made dots with a red pen on each of the creases in her arms. 'I want to be just like my Daddy,' she said proudly."

- "My wife and I literally whooped for joy at the sight of our newborn son: a 7-pound baby with big eyes and rosy cheeks—normal and healthy looking. But we both knew the moment we had been dreading was now just hours away. The baby would be going through withdrawal. We didn't want him to suffer because of our awful habit. And we had to keep the doctors from finding out he had drugs in his system, or he would be taken from us and placed in foster care. We felt we had no choice. When the nurses left the room, I cradled our baby in my arms and clipped a thin piece of heroin under his tongue."
- "I lost my job. I was robbing and stealing every day to support my habit, which cost $500 per day."

Someone who will clip a piece of heroin under a newborn baby's tongue or burglarize homes to support her habit will surely look for ways to embezzle from employers or commit other types of fraud.

Work-Related Pressures

Whereas financial pressures and vices motivate most frauds, some people commit fraud to get even with their employer. Factors such as not enough recognition for job performance, dissatisfaction with the job, fear of losing one's job, being overlooked for a promotion, and feeling underpaid motivate many frauds. Here is an example.

> *I began my career at the XYZ Company as a staff accountant. I am a religious person. In fact, I spent a year volunteering with a nonprofit agency that provided relief to people in need of food and shelter. Because of this experience and because of my six years with the company, I was considered a person of impeccable character and a very trusted employee. The president of XYZ is a workaholic and considers an eight-hour day to be something a part-time employee works. As a result, I spent six years working in my finance position, putting in between 12 and 14 hours per day. During this period, I was paid a salary, with no overtime compensation. Early in my career, the extra hours didn't bother me; I considered them an investment in my future. Soon, I was named manager of the purchasing department. After two years in that position, I realized that the 12- to 14-hour days were still an expected way of life at the company. I was becoming bitter about the expectation of overtimes and felt that the company "owed me" for the time I had worked for "nothing." I decided to get my "pay" from the company. Working with a favored vendor, I accepted kickbacks to allow over $1.5 million in overcharges to the company. I figured the $80,000 I received in kickbacks was compensation that I deserved.*

Other Pressures

Once in a while, fraud is motivated by other pressures, such as a spouse who insists on an improved lifestyle or a desire to beat the system. One perpetrator, for example, embezzled over $450,000 so that her husband could drive a new car, enjoy a higher lifestyle, and eat steak instead of hamburger. One famous computer consultant who is now retained by major companies to help them deter and detect computer fraud once felt personally challenged to "commit the perfect crime." After purchasing and taking delivery of over $1.5 million in inventory that was paid for by accessing a large company's computer records, he was caught when one of his inventory managers figured out what was going on.

All of us face pressures in our lives. We have legitimate financial needs, we make foolish or speculative investments, we are possessed by addictive vices, we feel overworked and/or underpaid, or we simply want more than we have. We sometimes have a difficult time distinguishing between wants and needs. Indeed, the objective of most people in capitalistic societies is to obtain wealth. We often measure success by how much money or wealth a person has. If you say you have a very successful relative, you probably mean that he or she lives in a big house, has a cabin or a condominium, drives expensive automobiles, and has money to do whatever he wants. But most of us don't put our success ahead of our honesty and integrity.

To some people, however, being successful is more important than being honest. If they were to rank the personal characteristics they value most in their lives, success would rank higher than integrity. Psychologists tell us that most people have a price at which they will be dishonest. Individuals with high integrity and low opportunity need high pressure to be dishonest.

Most of us can think of scenarios in which we, too, might commit fraud. If for example, we were starving, and we worked in an environment where cash was abundant and not accounted for, and we really believed that we would repay the money taken to feed ourselves, we might commit fraud. The U.S. president most famous for his honesty, Abraham Lincoln, once threw a man out of his office, angrily turning down a substantial bribe. When someone asked why he was so angry, he said, "Every man has his price, and he was getting close to mine."[7] One thing is for certain—eliminating pressures in the fraud triangle has an effect similar to removing heat from the fire triangle. Without some kind of pressure, fraud rarely occurs.

The Second Element: Opportunity

A perceived opportunity to commit fraud, to conceal it, or to avoid being punished is the second element in the fraud triangle. In this section we discuss opportunity. First, we examine controls that increase opportunities for individuals to commit fraud in organizations. Then, we provide a number of scenarios to illustrate noncontrol issues that should be considered when deciding whether a fraud opportunity is present.

At least six major factors increase opportunities for individuals to commit fraud in organizations. The following list is not exhaustive, but it does show system weaknesses that create opportunity.

1. Lack of or circumvention of controls that prevent and/or detect fraudulent behavior.
2. Inability to judge quality of performance.
3. Failure to discipline fraud perpetrators.
4. Lack of access to information.
5. Ignorance, apathy, and incapacity.
6. Lack of an audit trail.

Control Factors: Controls That Prevent and Detect Fraud

Having an effective control structure is probably the single most important step organizations can take to prevent and detect employee fraud. There are three components in a company's control structure: (1) the control environment, (2) the accounting system, and (3) control procedures or activities. The accounting profession and the Committee of Sponsoring Organizations (COSO) have defined these components; here we discuss only those components that are most effective in deterring fraud.

The Control Environment

The *control environment* is the work atmosphere that an organization establishes for its employees. The most important element in an appropriate control environment is *management's role and example.* There are numerous instances in which management's dishonest or inappropriate behavior was learned and then modeled by employees. In the famous Equity Funding case, management wrote insurance policies on individuals who didn't exist and sold them to other insurance companies. Seeing this dishonest behavior, one employee said to himself, "It doesn't make sense to have all these fictitious people live forever. I'll knock a few of them off and collect death proceeds. My actions won't be any different from those of the management of this company." In another case, employees realized top management was overstating revenues. In response, the employees began overstating expenses on their travel reimbursement forms, billing for hours not worked, and perpetrating other types of fraud.

Proper *modeling* (being an example) and proper *labeling* (communication) are some of the most important elements in effective control environments. When management models unacceptable behavior, the control environment is contaminated. Similarly, if management models a behavior that is inconsistent with good control procedures, the effectiveness of the control system is eroded. When a manager says, "Don't loan keys or share passwords with others," and then shares her password or keys, she sends mixed signals and her inappropriate behavior may eventually be copied by other employees. In other words, "actions speak louder than words." Management's example is the most critical element of the control environment when it comes to preventing fraud. Inappropriate behavior by management encourages others to justify overriding and ignoring control procedures.

The second critical element in the control environment is *management's communication.* Communicating what is and is not appropriate is crucial. Just as parents who are trying to teach their children to be honest must communicate often and openly with them, so must organizations clearly label what is and is not acceptable. Codes of conduct, orientation meetings, training, supervisor/employee discussions, and other types of communication that distinguish between acceptable and unacceptable behavior should be routine activities.

To be an effective deterrent to fraud, communication must be consistent. Messages that change based on circumstances and situations serve not only to confuse employees but also to encourage rationalizations. One reason so many frauds occur in "crash" projects is that the regular control procedures are not followed. Inconsistent messages relating to procedures and controls abound. Strikes, mergers, bankruptcies, and other dramatic events often result in inconsistent communication and increase fraud.

The third critical element in creating the proper control structure is *appropriate hiring.* Research shows that nearly 30% of all people in the United States are dishonest, another 30% are situationally honest (honest where it pays to be honest and dishonest where it pays to be dishonest), and 40% are honest all the time.[8] Although most organizations are convinced that their employees, customers, and vendors are among the 40% who are honest, this usually isn't the case.

When dishonest individuals are hired, even the best controls will not prevent fraud. For example, a bank has tellers, managers, loan officers, and others who have daily access to cash and can steal. Because it is impossible to deter all bank fraud, banks hope that personal integrity, together with preventive and detective controls and the fear of punishment, will deter theft.

As an example of the consequences of poor hiring, consider the case of a famous country singer who was raped a few years ago. The singer checked into a well-known hotel. A few hours after her arrival, there was a knock on her door, accompanied by the words "Room Service." She hadn't ordered anything but thought that maybe, because she was famous, the hotel was bringing her a basket of fruit or some complimentary wine. When she opened the door, a hotel custodian burst into her room and raped her. She later sued the hotel for $2.5 million and won. The basis of her lawsuit was that locks on the door were inadequate, and the hotel had inadequate hiring procedures because the custodian had previous arrest records and had been fired from previous jobs because of rape.[9]

If an organization does not screen job applicants carefully and hires dishonest individuals, it will be victimized by fraud, regardless of how good its other controls are. To understand how sound hiring practices help prevent fraud and other problems, consider a company that decided to take extra precautions in its hiring practices. They first trained all persons associated with hiring decisions to be expert interviewers and secondly required them to thoroughly check three background references for each prospective employee. Because of these extra precautions, over 800 applicants (13% of the applicant pool) who would have been hired were disqualified. These applicants had undisclosed problems, such as falsified employment information, previous arrest records, uncontrollable tempers, alcoholism, drug addiction, and a pattern of being fired from previous jobs.

The effects of poor hiring practices are illustrated in the following excerpt from an article in *Business Week Online:*

> *These days, it's tempting to hire the first person who seems capable of doing a job. But do you know what lurks behind that spiffy resume? The Association of Certified Fraud Examiners estimates that employee fraud costs small companies an average of $120,000 per incident. It's a good idea to check the backgrounds of all applicants. At the very least, you'll be certain the person has the credentials they claim. . . . Three years ago managers hired a security expert to conduct background checks on employees and potential hires, examining credit and criminal backgrounds and verifying education and experience. Good thing they did—the company was on the verge of hiring a director of finance who turned out to have neither the MBA nor any of the experience he said he had.*[10]

The fourth fraud-deterring element of the control environment is a *clear organizational structure.* When everyone in the organization knows exactly who has responsibility for each business activity, fraud is less likely to be committed. Such structures make it easier to track missing assets and harder to embezzle without being caught. Strict accountability for job performance is critical for a good control environment.

As an example of how failure to assign proper custody resulted in a fraud, consider the case of "Jane Doe":

> *I was one of eight tellers in a medium-sized bank. Because we all had access to money orders and bank checks, I stole 16 money orders. I didn't use them for two weeks to see if anyone would notice them missing. Then, I used one for $300. After nothing being said during the next two weeks, I used seven more.*

In this case, someone independent from the teller should have had responsibility for reconciling money orders on a daily basis.

The fifth element of the control environment is *an effective internal audit department, combined with security or loss prevention programs.* Although most studies have found that internal auditors detect only about 20% of all employee frauds (others are detected through tips, by alert employees, or accidentally), the mere presence of internal auditors provides a significant deterrent effect.[11] Internal auditors provide independent checks and cause potential perpetrators to question whether they can act and not be caught. A visible and effective security function, in conjunction with an appropriate loss prevention program, helps ensure that fraud is properly investigated and that control weaknesses and violations are appropriately punished.

Taken together, the five elements—(1) proper management modeling, (2) good communication or labeling, (3) effective hiring procedures, (4) clear organizational structure and assigned responsibilities, and (5) an effective internal audit department and security function—create an atmosphere in which fraud opportunities are decreased because employees see that fraud is neither acceptable nor tolerated. Relaxing any one of these elements increases opportunities for committing fraud.

The Accounting System

The second component of the control structure is a good *accounting system*. Every fraud is comprised of three elements: (1) the theft, in which assets are taken; (2) concealment, which is the attempt to hide the fraud from others; and (3) conversion, in which the perpetrator spends the money or converts the stolen assets to cash and then spends the money. An effective accounting system provides an *audit trail* that allows frauds to be discovered and makes concealment difficult. Unlike bank robbery, in which there is usually no effort to conceal the theft, concealment is a distinguishing element of fraud.

Frauds are often concealed in the accounting records. Accounting records are based on transaction documents, either paper or electronic. To cover up a fraud, paper or electronic documentation must be altered or misplaced. Frauds can be discovered in the accounting records by examining transaction entries that have no support or by probing financial statement amounts that are not reasonable. Without a good accounting system, distinguishing between actual fraud and unintentional errors is often difficult. A good accounting system ensures that recorded transactions are (1) valid, (2) properly authorized, (3) complete, (4) properly classified, (5) reported in the proper period, (6) properly valued, and (7) summarized correctly.

Control Activities (Procedures)

The third component of the control structure is good *control activities (or procedures)*. Individuals who own their own businesses and are the sole "employee" probably do not need many control procedures. Although these people may have ample opportunity to defraud their own business, they have no incentive to do so. They wouldn't steal from themselves, and they would never want to treat customers poorly. However, organizations that involve many employees must have control procedures so that the actions of employees are congruent with the goals of management or the owners. In addition, with control procedures, opportunities to commit and/or conceal frauds are eliminated or minimized. No matter what the business is, whether it is the business of operating a financial institution, a grocery store, or a Fortune 500 company, or the business of investing personal assets, there are five primary control procedures or activities:

1. Segregation of duties or dual custody
2. System of authorizations
3. Independent checks
4. Physical safeguards
5. Documents and records

Although there are thousands of control activities used by businesses, they are basically all variations of these five basic procedures. Good fraud detection and prevention efforts involve matching the most effective control procedures with the various risks of fraud. As an illustration of how control procedures can be used to achieve goal congruence and prevent fraud, consider the following situation:

> *Mark was a seventh grader. At the annual parent-teacher conferences, Mark's parents discovered that he was getting straight As in all of his classes except one—a German class in which he was getting an F. When Mark's parents later asked him about the class, he said, "I hate the teacher. She is*

a jerk and I refuse to work for her." After discussions with the teacher and Mark, Mark's parents decided to implement three controls, so that his actions would be consistent with the desires of his parents. First, Mark's parents printed up some simple forms (documents) for the teacher to check off each day. These pieces of paper contained two simple statements: (1) Mark (was) (was not) prepared for class today, and (2) Mark (was) (was not) responsible in class today. The teacher would circle the appropriate response to each phrase, initial the paper, and send it home with Mark. By insisting on reading the note each night, Mark's parents were performing an independent check on his performance. In addition, his rollerblades were taken away until his grade improved. Taking away his right to play street hockey on his rollerblades was a variation of an authorization control. (He lost his authorized use.) When Mark's parents invoked the three controls of (1) documents, (2) independent checks, and (3) taking away an authorized activity, his behavior performance in German changed to become more in line with the goals of his parents. By the end of the term, his grade in German changed from an F to a B.

Segregation of Duties and Dual Custody. Activities can usually be better controlled by invoking either *segregation of duties* or dual-custody control. Segregation of duties involves dividing a task into two parts, so that one person does not have complete control of the task. Dual custody requires two individuals to work together at the same task. Either way, it takes two people to do one job. This control, like most preventive controls, is most often used when cash is involved. For example, the opening of incoming cash in a business is usually done by two people or by segregating duties. The accounting for, and the handling of, cash are separated so that one person does not have access to both. Fred R.'s example shows the ease with which fraud can be perpetrated when accounting for and custody of assets are not separated.

Fred R. worked for a medium-size homebuilder. He was in charge of writing checks as well as reconciling bank statements. Over a period of time, Fred stole over $400,000 by manipulating the check register and forcing the bank reconciliation to balance. If, for example, his employer owed a subcontractor $15,000, Fred would write the check for $15,000 and write $20,000 on the check stub. Then, using the next check, he would write himself a check for $5,000 and mark the check stub "voided." When the bank statement was returned, he would destroy the checks written to himself and force the reconciliation.

Fred's fraud could easily have been caught, if not prevented, if someone besides Fred was either reconciling the bank statements *or* writing the checks. There are at least three critical functions that even small business owners should either set up as segregated duties or always do themselves: (1) writing checks, (2) making bank deposits, and (3) reconciling bank statements.

Because two individuals are involved, dual custody or segregation of duties is usually the most expensive of all controls. Labor costs are high, and hiring two people to complete one job is a luxury that most businesses don't believe they can afford. This control always involves a trade-off between higher labor cost and less opportunity for error and fraud. Besides being expensive, good dual custody is often difficult to enforce. When two individuals are working on the same task, they shouldn't take their eyes or their minds off the task to answer telephones, use the restroom, respond to a question, or even sneeze. A fraud that was perpetrated in a supposed "dual-custody environment" is the case of Roger M., who made the following confession:

> *In January 20XX, I took the amount of $3,062 in cash, which was contained in a disposable night drop bag. I concealed my actions by putting it inside a night drop envelope that I processed on the same day. I have no real excuse for taking money. I saw an easy way of taking the money, and I took advantage of it. Circumstances that made it seem easy to take the money without being caught or observed were that I was situated on the customer side of the merchant vault, which obscured the view of my dual-custody partner. I have reimbursed the bank today (January 27, 20XX) the amount of $3,062.*

System of Authorizations. The second internal control procedure is a proper system of authorizations. Authorization control procedures take many forms. Passwords authorize individuals to use computers and to access certain databases. Signature cards authorize individuals to enter safe deposit boxes, to cash checks, and to perform other functions at financial institutions. Spending limits authorize individuals to spend only what is in their budget or approved level.

When people are not authorized to perform an activity, the opportunity to commit fraud is reduced. For example, when individuals are not authorized to enter safe deposit boxes, they cannot enter and steal the contents of someone else's box. When individuals are not authorized to approve purchases, they cannot order items for personal use and have their companies pay for the goods. As the following case shows, the failure to enforce authorization controls makes the perpetration of fraud quite simple.

> *Mary and Ron had been customers of a certain bank for many years. Because Ron owned a jewelry store, they maintained a safe deposit box at the bank to store certain inventory. Most employees of the bank knew them well because of their frequent visits to make deposits and conduct other business. What was unknown to the bank employees was that Mary and Ron were having marital difficulties, which ended in a bitter divorce. After the divorce, they canceled their joint safe deposit box. Ron came in to the bank a short time later and opened a new safe deposit box, with his daughter as cosigner. Because Mary was bitter about the divorce settlement, she entered the bank one day and told the safe deposit custodian (who had been away on vacation when she and Ron closed their box) that she had lost her key and needed to have the box drilled. Because the custodian knew Mary and didn't know the old box had been closed and a new one opened, Mary arranged to force open the box. Without any problems, the box was drilled and Mary emptied the contents. When Ron tried to open the box a few days later, he discovered what had happened. Because Mary was not a signer on the account at the time the box was forced open, the bank was completely liable and settled out of court with the jeweler for $200,000. This fraud was allowed to be perpetrated because the authorization control of matching signatures to a signature card was not performed.*

Independent Checks. The theory behind *independent checks* is that if people know their work or activities are monitored by others, the opportunity to commit and conceal a fraud is reduced. There are many varieties of independent checks. The Office of the Controller of the Currency (OCC) requires that every bank employee in the United States take one week's vacation (five consecutive days) each year. While employees are gone, others are supposed to perform their work. If an employee's work piles up while he or she is out for the week, this "mandatory vacation" control is not working as it should and the opportunity to commit fraud is not eliminated.

Periodic job rotations, cash counts or certifications, supervisor reviews, employee hotlines, and the use of auditors are other forms of independent checks. One large department store in Europe has a complete extra staff of employees for its chain of department stores. This staff goes to a store and works while everyone who is employed there goes on vacation for a month. While they are gone, the transient staff operates the store. One purpose of this program is to provide complete, independent checks on the activities of store employees. If someone who is committing fraud is forced to leave for a month, the illegal activity is often discovered.

To illustrate the creative use of independent checks, consider the case of a Baskin-Robbins ice cream store in Washington, D.C.

> *Upon entering this 31-flavors establishment, the customer is greeted by a smiling cashier. Two large signs hang on the wall behind the cashier. One sign reads, "If you have problems with service, please call the manager at this telephone number." The other reads, "If you get a star on your sales receipt, you receive a free sundae."*

In an ice cream store or any other retail establishment, one of the easiest ways to perpetrate fraud is to accept cash from customers and either not ring it into the cash register or ring it in as a lesser amount. If the store happens to sell ice cream, cones can be made a little smaller during the day to cover for the extra ice cream used in sales that are not entered into the cash register. The purpose of the Baskin-Robbins signs is to encourage customers to receive and examine their sales receipts. In order for customers to be able to look for a star, sales receipts must be issued. If the cashier charges $2 for an ice cream cone and rings only $1 into the cash register, sooner or later a customer will report the embezzlement.

Physical Safeguards. Physical safeguards protect assets from theft by fraud or other means. *Physical safeguards,* such as vaults, safes, fences, locks, and keys, take away opportunities to commit fraud by making it difficult for people to access assets. Money locked in a vault, for example, cannot be stolen unless someone gains unauthorized access or unless someone who has access violates the trust. Physical controls also protect inventory by storing it in locked cages or warehouses; small assets such as tools or supplies by locking them in cabinets; and cash by locking it in vaults or safes.

Documents and Records. The fifth control procedure involves using *documents or records* to create a record of transactions and an audit trail. Documents rarely serve as preventive controls, but they do provide excellent detective tools. Banks, for example, prepare kiting-suspect reports as well as reports of employee bank account activity to detect abuse by employees or customers. Most companies require a customer order to initiate a sales transaction. In a sense, the entire accounting system serves as a documentary control. Without documents, no accountability exists. Without accountability, it is much easier to perpetrate fraud and not get caught.

Summary of the Controls That Prevent or Detect Fraud

The control environment, the accounting system, and the many variations of the five control procedures work together to eliminate or reduce the opportunity for employees and others to commit fraud. A good control environment establishes an atmosphere in which proper behavior is modeled and labeled, honest employees are hired, and all employees understand their job responsibilities. The accounting system provides records that make it difficult for perpetrators to gain access to assets, to conceal frauds, and to convert stolen assets without being discovered. Together, these three components make up the control structure of an organization. The following table summarizes these components and their elements:

Internal Control Structure		
Control Environment	**Accounting System**	**Control Activities or Procedures**
1. Management philosophy and operating style, modeling 2. Effective hiring procedures 3. Clear organizational structure of proper modeling and labeling 4. Effective internal audit department	1. Valid transactions 2. Properly authorized 3. Completeness 4. Proper classification 5. Proper timing 6. Proper valuation 7. Correct summarization	1. Segregation of duties 2. Proper procedures for authorization 3. Adequate documents and records 4. Physical control over assets and records 5. Independent checks on performance

Unfortunately, many frauds are perpetrated in environments in which controls that are supposed to be in place are not being followed. Indeed, it is the overriding and ignoring of existing controls, not the lack of controls, that allow most frauds to be perpetrated.

Noncontrol Factor: Inability to Judge the Quality of Performance

If you pay someone to construct a fence, you can examine the completed job and determine whether or not the quality of work meets your specifications and is consistent with the agreed contract. If, however, you hire a lawyer, a doctor, a dentist, an accountant, an engineer, or an auto mechanic, it is often difficult to know whether you are paying an excessive amount or receiving inferior service or products. With these kinds of contracts, it is easy to overcharge, perform work not needed, provide inferior service, or charge for work not performed. As an example of fraud perpetrated by a professional whose work quality could not be assessed, consider the following excerpt from a *Los Angeles Times* article.

> *A dermatologist who was struck and killed after walking into freeway traffic last week had been under investigation by the state medical board for allegedly faking diagnoses of skin cancer to collect higher fees. Dr. Orville Stone, who once headed the dermatology department at UC Irvine Medical Center, was accused by five former employees of using cancerous patients' skin tissue to fake diagnoses for hundreds of other patients. . . . Last Friday, the day after the board served a search warrant at his Huntington Beach practice, . . . Stone, 61, walked in front of traffic on the San Bernardino Freeway near Indio, the California Highway Patrol said. "He basically parked his car, walked down to the embankment and walked in front of the path of a truck and was struck by four other cars." The Highway Patrol listed the death as suicide. Former employees accused Stone of hoarding cancerous moles or skin tissue he removed from at least 3 patients. He then would take healthy tissue from patients, diagnose them as having cancer and switch tissues, sending the diseased tissue to a laboratory for analysis. Stone normally charged about $50 to remove non-cancerous skin tissue and about $150 to remove cancerous ones.*[12]

Another example of this noncontrol factor is the case of Sears Automotive in California:

> *Prompted by an increasing number of consumer complaints, the California Department of Consumer Affairs completed a one-year investigation into allegations that Sears Tire and Auto Centers overcharged their customers for auto repair services. The undercover investigation was conducted in two phases. In the first phase, agents took 38 cars known to have defects in the brakes and no other mechanical faults to 27 different Sears Automotive Centers in California during 1991. In 34 of the 38 cases, or 89% of the time, agents were told that additional work was necessary, involving additional costs. Their average amount of the overcharge was $223, but in the worst case, which occurred in San Francisco, agents were overcharged $585 to have the front brake pads, front and rear springs, and control-arm bushings replaced. Although a spokesman for Sears denies the allegations and says that Sears will fight any attempt to deprive them of their license to do auto repair work in California, the evidence of fraud is substantial. In one case, Ruth Hernandez, a citizen of Stockton, California, went to Sears to have new tires put on her car. While she was there, the mechanic informed her that she also needed new struts, which would cost an additional $419.95. When Mrs. Hernandez sought a second opinion, she was told her struts were fine. The Sears mechanic later admitted to having made an incorrect diagnosis.*[13]

To understand why a well-established, reputable company such as Sears might commit such a fraud, it is important to know that Sears had quotas for parts, services, and repair sales for each eight-hour shift. Allegedly, mechanics who consistently did not meet their quotas either had their hours reduced or were transferred out of the parts and service department. Apparently, faced with the pressure to cheat or fail, and believing that customers would not know whether the parts and services were actually needed, many service center employees decided to commit fraud.

Noncontrol Factor: Failure to Discipline Fraud Perpetrators

Criminologists generally agree that rapists have the highest rate of repeat offenses (recidivism) of all criminals. The next highest category of repeat offenders is no doubt fraudsters who are neither prosecuted nor disciplined. An individual who commits fraud and is not punished or is merely terminated suffers no significant penalty and often resumes the fraudulent behavior.

Fraud perpetrators often command respect in their jobs, communities, churches, and families. If they are marginally sanctioned or terminated, they rarely inform their families and others of the real reason for their termination or punishment. On the other hand, if they are prosecuted, they usually suffer significant embarrassment when family, friends, and business associates find out about their offenses. Indeed, humiliation is often the strongest factor in deterring future fraud activity.

Because of the expense and time involved in prosecuting, many organizations simply dismiss dishonest employees, hoping to rid themselves of the problem. What these organizations fail to realize is that such action is shortsighted. They may rid themselves of one fraudster, but they have also sent a message to others in the organization that perpetrators will not suffer significant consequences for their actions. Indeed, lack of prosecution gives others "perceived opportunity" that, when combined with pressure and rationalization, can result in additional frauds in the organization. Perceived opportunity is removed when employees understand that perpetrators will be punished according to the law, not merely terminated.

In a society in which workers are mobile and often move from job to job, termination often helps perpetrators build an attractive resume, but it does not deter future fraud. A man we'll call John Doe is a classic example of someone whose termination (he was not otherwise punished) allowed him to get increasingly attractive jobs at increased salary levels. His employment and fraud history for 14 years is shown below.

Occupation	Job Length	Amount Embezzled
Insurance sales	10 months	$ 200
Office manager	2 years	1,000
Bookkeeper	1 year	30,000
Accountant	2 years	20,000
Accountant	2 years	30,000
Controller & CFO	6 years	1,363,700
Manager	Still employed	?

According to one reference who described John Doe's fraud, he was never prosecuted. His victim organizations either felt sorry for him, thought prosecution would be too time-consuming and too expensive, or merely chose to pass the problem on to others. As a result, every succeeding job Doe obtained was better than his previous one until he eventually became a controller and CFO making $130,000 a year. By only terminating him, his victims helped him build a resume and secure increasingly attractive jobs.

Noncontrol Factor: Lack of Access to Information

Many frauds occur because victims don't have access to information possessed by the perpetrators. This is especially prevalent in large management frauds that are perpetrated against stockholders, investors, and debt holders. In the famous ESM fraud case, for example, the same securities were sold to investors several times. Yet, because only ESM possessed those investment records, victims didn't know of the fraudulent sales.[14]

A classic example in which lack of information played a major role in the fraud is the Lincoln Savings and Loan case. On January 6, 1992, Charles Keating and his son, Charles Keating III, were convicted on 73 and 64 counts, respectively, of racketeering and fraud. Charles Keating created sham transactions to make Lincoln Savings look more profitable than it really was in order to please auditors and regulators. He was able to perpetrate the schemes because auditors and regulators were not given complete access to transactions. One transaction, known as the *RA Homes sale,* was structured as follows:

> *On September 30, 1986, defendants Keating and others caused a subsidiary of Lincoln Savings to engage in a fraudulent sale of approximately 1,300 acres of undeveloped land northwest of Tucson, Arizona, to RA Homes, Inc., at a price of approximately $25 million, consisting of a $5 million cash down payment and a $20 million promissory note, secured only by the undeveloped land. Defendants Keating and others caused Lincoln to record a sham profit of approximately $8.4 million on the sale. RA Homes agreed to purchase the land only after Keating orally (1) promised that Lincoln would reimburse RA Homes for the down payment on the purchase, (2) agreed that the Lincoln subsidiary would retain responsibility for developing and marketing the property, and (3) guaranteed that RA Homes would be able to sell the land at a profit within a year following the purchase.*[15]

Auditors didn't know about the oral commitments, all of which violated accounting standards for recording real estate sales. Subsequent to these oral agreements, in supposedly separate transactions, Keating loaned RA Homes $5 million (to cover the down payment) and then continued to manage, market, and develop the "sold" property. When the real estate agent, who thought he had an exclusive selling arrangement, discovered that the 1,300 acres had supposedly been sold by Charles Keating himself, he contacted Charles Keating for commissions on the sale and was told that no real estate commission was due because the land had just been "parked" with RA Homes. With the higher reported profits of his company, Lincoln Savings and Loan was able to appear profitable and further perpetrate its fraud on investors and others.[16]

Most investment scams and management frauds depend on their ability to withhold information from victims. Individuals can attempt to protect themselves against such scams by insisting on full disclosure, including audited financial statements, a business history, and other information that could reveal the fraudulent nature of such organizations.

Noncontrol Factor: Ignorance, Apathy, and Incapacity

Older people, individuals with language difficulties, and other vulnerable citizens are often victims of fraud because perpetrators know that such individuals may not have the capacity or the knowledge to detect their illegal acts. Vulnerable people are, unfortunately, easier to deceive. For example, consider the following:

> *A nurse with purple hands was charged with embezzling money from patients' rooms at a local hospital. The nurse's hands were purple because invisible dye had been put on money planted in a purse used to trap the embezzler. The nurse was on loan from a temporary-help agency. Two sisters reported to hospital security that money was taken from their purses, which were left unattended in their father's room. A check of the staff roster showed that the nurse was alone in the room just before the money was discovered missing. Hospital security put a purse containing dye-covered bills in a room. Later that day, a supervisor reported that the nurse had dye on her hands. When confronted, the nurse first said she accidentally knocked the purse to the floor and her hands were stained while she was replacing the items. After further questioning, however, the nurse admitted to taking the money from the women's purses.*

The nurse realized that elderly patients were an easy target for theft. In hospital rooms, where patients are often under the influence of sedating drugs, victims don't always recognize that they have been robbed.

Frauds called *pigeon drops* take specific advantage of elderly victims. In such thefts, perpetrators often pose as bank examiners trying to catch dishonest bankers, or they use some other scheme to get elderly or non-English-speaking customers to withdraw money from banks. When these customers leave the bank with their money, the perpetrators grab the money and flee instead of examining it as promised, knowing the elderly person has no chance to catch them.

Investment scams also take advantage of elderly people. In the AFCO fraud case, a real estate investment scam, elderly victims were persuaded to take out mortgages on their homes. Sales pitches like the following convinced them that it was a good idea:

- Do you know you have a sleeping giant in your home that you are not using?
- Your home is worth $100,000, is completely paid off, and you could get $80,000 out of it with no debt to you.
- If you are willing to borrow and invest $80,000, we'll make the mortgage payments, pay you interest of 10% on the money you're making nothing on now, and buy you a new luxury car to drive.

A financially prudent person would recognize that the perpetrators could not possibly pay the 10% interest they were promising on the loan, plus the new car, but many of the victims found the offer too good to refuse. As a result, several hundred elderly, retired citizens invested a total of over $39 million in the AFCO scam.

Noncontrol Factor: Lack of an Audit Trail

Organizations go to great lengths to create documents that provide an audit trail so that transactions can be reconstructed and understood at a later time. Many frauds, however, involve cash payments or manipulation of records that cannot be followed. Smart perpetrators understand that their frauds must be concealed. They also know that such concealment usually involves manipulation of financial records. When faced with a decision about which financial record to manipulate, perpetrators almost always manipulate the income statement, because they understand that the audit trail will quickly be erased. Here is an example:

> *Joan Rivera was the controller for a small bank. Over a period of four years, she stole more than $100,000 by having a larger bank pay her credit card bills. She covered her fraud by creating accounting entries like the following:*
>
> Advertising Expense 1,000
> Cash 1,000
>
> *Joan used this approach because she knew that at year-end all expense accounts, including advertising expense, would be closed and brought to zero balances. If bank auditors and officials didn't catch the fraud before year-end, the audit trail would be erased and the fraud would be difficult to detect. On the other hand, she knew that if she covered the cash shortage by overstating outstanding checks on the bank reconciliation, the cash shortage would be carried from month to month, creating a "permanent" concealment problem. She also knew, for example, that if she manipulated the inventory, an asset, that inventory shortage would carry over into the next period.*

Joan was not caught until she got greedy and started using other fraud methods that were not as easily concealed.

The Third Element: Rationalization

So far, we have discussed the first two elements of the fraud triangle: perceived pressure and perceived opportunity. The third element is rationalization. To see how rationalization contributes to fraud, let's look at the infamous case of Jim Bakker and Richard Dortch. These men were convicted on 23 counts of wire and mail fraud and one count of conspiracy to commit wire and mail fraud. As a result of their conviction, the perpetrators of one of the largest and most bizarre frauds in U.S. history were sent to jail. In his remarks to the court prior to Jim Bakker's sentencing, prosecutor Jerry Miller summarized this PTL (Praise-the-Lord) fraud with the following comments:

> *The biggest con man to come through this courtroom, a man corrupted by power and money and the man who would be God at PTL, is a common criminal. The only thing uncommon about him was the method he chose and the vehicle he used to perpetrate his fraud. He was motivated by greed, selfishness, and a lust for power. He is going to be right back at it as soon as he gets the chance. Mr. Bakker was a con man who in the beginning loved people and used things, but he evolved into a man, a ruthless man, who loved things and used people.*[17]

How did Jim Bakker, the beloved TV minister of the PTL network, rationalize the committing of such a massive fraud? Here is his story.

> *PTL had a modest beginning in 1973 when it began operating out of a furniture showroom in Charlotte, North Carolina. By October 1975, it had purchased a 25-acre estate in Charlotte, North Carolina, and had constructed Heritage Village, a broadcast network of approximately 70 television stations in the United States, Canada, and Mexico on which the PTL ministry's show was aired. PTL's corporate charter stated that the religious purposes of the organization were: (1) establishing and maintaining a church and engaging in all types of religious activity, including evangelism, religious instruction, and publishing and distributing Bibles; (2) engaging in other religious publication; (3) missionary work, both domestic and foreign; and (4) establishing and operating Bible schools and Bible training centers. Over the following 11 years, PTL built a multimillion-dollar empire that consisted of PTL and a 2,300 acre Heritage USA tourist center valued at $172 million. Specific activities of the organization included Heritage Church with a weekly attendance of over 3,000; Upper Room prayer services where counselors ministered to people; Prison Ministry, with a volunteer staff of over 4,000; Fort Hope, a missionary outreach house for homeless men; Passion Play, a portrayal of the life of Christ in an outdoor amphitheater; a dinner theater; a day care center; Heritage Academy; a summer day camp; the Billy Graham Home; workshops; and a Christmas nativity scene that had been visited by over 500,000 people.*
>
> *PTL also had a wide range of activities that were ultimately deemed by the IRS to be commercial. In one such venture, PTL viewers were given an opportunity to become lifetime partners in a hotel for $1,000 each. Bakker promised that only 25,000 lifetime partnership interests would be sold and that partners could use the hotel free each year for 4 days and 3 nights. In the end, however, 68,412 such partnerships were sold. Through this and simi-*

> *lar solicitations, Jim Bakker's PTL had amassed gross receipts of over $600 million, much of which had been used to support the extravagant lifestyle of Bakker and other officers of PTL. Time and time again, Bakker misled worshippers, investors, and his faithful followers by misusing contributions, overselling investments, evading taxes, and living an extravagant lifestyle.*[18]

How could a minister perpetrate such a large and vicious fraud in the name of religion? Most people believe that Jim Bakker's ministry was initially sincere, inspired by a real desire to help others and to teach the word of God. He believed that what he was doing was for a good purpose and rationalized that any money he received would directly or indirectly help others. He even recognized at one time that money might be corrupting him and his empire. In 1985, he said, "I was going to say to listeners, 'Please stop giving.' But, I just couldn't say that."[19] What started out as a sincere ministry was corrupted by money. Jim Bakker stated on a television program, "I have never asked for a penny for myself. . . . God has always taken care of me." His rationalizations increased to the point that one trial attorney, in her closing argument, stated, "You can't lie to people to send you money—it's that simple. What unfolded before you over the past month was a tale of corruption—immense corruption. . . . What was revealed here was that Mr. Bakker was a world-class master of lies and half-truths."[20]

Jim Bakker rationalized his dishonest acts by convincing himself that the PTL network had a good purpose and that he was helping others. In a similar way, folklore has it that Robin Hood defended his dishonest acts by arguing that he "stole from the rich and gave to the poor."

Nearly every fraud involves rationalization. Most perpetrators are first-time offenders who would not commit other crimes. Rationalizing helps them hide from the dishonesty of their acts. Here are some common rationalizations used by fraudsters:

- The organization owes it to me.
- I am only borrowing the money—I will pay it back.
- Nobody will get hurt.
- I deserve more.
- It's for a good purpose.
- We'll fix the books as soon as we get over this financial difficulty.
- Something has to be sacrificed—my integrity or my reputation. (If I don't embezzle to cover my inability to pay, people will know I can't meet my obligations and that will be embarrassing because I'm a professional.)

Certainly, there are countless other rationalizations. These, however, are representative and serve as an adequate basis to discuss the role rationalization plays in fraud.

It is important to recognize that there are very few, if any, people who do not rationalize. We rationalize being overweight. We rationalize not exercising enough. We rationalize spending more than we should. Most of us rationalize being dishonest. Here are two examples:

> *A wife works hard, saves her money, and buys a new dress. When she puts it on for the first time, she asks her husband, "How do you like my new dress?" Realizing that the wife worked hard for the money and that she must really like the dress or she wouldn't have purchased it, the husband says, "Oh, it's beautiful," even though he really doesn't like it. Why did the husband lie? He probably rationalized in his mind that the consequence of telling the truth was more severe than the consequence of lying. "After all, if she likes it, I'd better like it, too," he reasons. Unfortunately, not wanting to hurt his wife's feelings resulted in lying, which is dishonest. In fact, the husband will pay for his dishonesty. His wife will continue to wear the dress because she believes her*

husband likes it. What the husband could have said is, "Honey, you are a beautiful woman and that is one reason I married you. I like most of the clothes you buy and wear, but this dress is not my favorite."

You go to your mother-in-law's for dinner. For dessert, she bakes a cherry pie. Even though you don't like pie, you lie and say, "This pie is delicious." Why did you lie? Because you rationalized that you didn't want to hurt your mother-in-law's feelings and that, in fact, it would make her feel good if you complimented her cooking. As in the dress example, you will pay for your dishonesty because your mother-in-law, believing you like her cherry pie, will serve it again the next time you visit. Dishonesty could have been avoided by remaining silent or by saying, "Mom, you are an excellent cook, and I really like most of the food you cook. However, cherry pie is not my favorite."

We rationalize dishonesty by our desire to make other people feel good. The same sort of rationalization often enables fraud to be perpetrated. Sometimes it's lying to oneself. Sometimes it's lying to others. For example, the following rationalization allows us to break the law: You get in your car and start down the freeway. You see a sign that says, "65 miles per hour." What do you do? Most likely you will go faster than 65, justifying your speeding by using one or more of the following rationalizations.

- Nobody drives 65. Everyone else speeds.
- My car was made to go faster.
- Sixty-five miles per hour is a stupid law. Going faster is still safe.
- I must keep up with the traffic or I'll cause an accident.
- It's all right to get one or two speeding tickets.
- I'm late.
- The speed limit is really 72 or 73.

Is it OK to break the law and speed just because "everyone else is doing it"? What if everyone else were committing fraud? If so, would that make it right for you to commit fraud?

Take income tax evasion. Many people underpay taxes with the following rationalizations:

- I pay more than my fair share of taxes.
- The rich don't pay enough taxes.
- The government wastes money.
- I "work" for my money.

To understand the extent of income tax fraud, consider that, in 1988, for the first time, the IRS required taxpayers who claimed dependents to list social security numbers for their dependents. In 1987, 77 million dependents were claimed on federal tax returns. In 1988, the number of dependents claimed dropped to 70 million. Fully one-tenth of the dependents claimed—7 million dependents—"disappeared." The IRS determined that in 1987 and probably in previous years, over 60,000 households had claimed four or more dependents who didn't exist, and several million had claimed one or more who didn't exist.[21]

Claiming dependents who don't exist is one of the easiest-to-catch income tax frauds. Yet, rationalizations were strong enough to drive millions of citizens to blatantly cheat on their tax returns.

When interviewed, most fraud perpetrators say things like, "I intended to pay the money back. I really did." They are sincere. In their minds, they rationalize that they will repay the money, and since they judge themselves by their intentions, and not their actions, they do not see themselves as criminals. Their victims, on the other hand, tend to take an entirely different view!

Summary

In concluding this chapter, we examine a famous fraud case. Jerry Schneider, at age 21, was the model West Coast business executive, bright and well educated. Schneider differed from this image in only one respect: Starting in 1971, he embezzled over $1 million from Pacific Telephone Company. Here is the story of his fraud.

Jerry Schneider's fraud had its genesis at a warm, open-air evening party where he and some friends had gathered for drinks, socializing, and small talk. Schneider was the young president of his own electronics corporation. This night, the talk was of organized crime and whether or not it could be profitable. "All these press stories of the big-time killings, and the crooks who build palaces down in Florida and out here on the coast, aagh. . . ," said a cynical male voice, "they're cooked up for the movies."

Schneider recognized the speaker as a young scriptwriter whose last outline—a crime story set among the Jewish mafia—had been turned down. "Not so," he said. "Some of them clean up. Some of them walk away clean, with a huge pot. You only hear of the ones that don't. The others become respectable millionaires."

A lawyer asked, "You believe in the perfect crime, do you?"

"Yes, if what you mean is the crime that doesn't get detected. I don't say nobody knows it has been done—though there must be some of those, too. But I'm sure there are crooks clever enough to figure ways to beat the system."

Long after everyone had left the party, Jerry Schneider was still thinking about whether or not there was a perfect crime. He had a great knowledge of computers and he thought maybe he could use his knowledge to perpetrate the perfect crime. Finally, about 2:00 A.M. he felt sick about the whole idea.

No one knows why Schneider later changed his mind. An investigator with the district attorney's office in Los Angeles believes it was because Jerry got possession of a stolen computer code book from Pacific Telephone Company. Schneider accessed the company's computer from the outside. Exactly how he did it was not fully revealed at his trial. He used a touch-tone telephone to place large orders with Pacific's supply division, inserting the orders into the company's computer. He then programmed Pacific Telephone's computers to pay for the merchandise. After he received the merchandise, he sold it on the open market.

Schneider was caught when an embittered employee noticed that much of the stuff Schneider was selling was Pacific's. The employee leaked to the police a hint about how Schneider had acquired the material. An investigation revealed that huge amounts of equipment were missing from Pacific's dispatch warehouse. Invoices showed that the equipment had been ordered and authorized for dispatch. The goods had then been packaged and put out on the loading bays ready for collection. Schneider had collected the goods himself, always early in the morning. To avoid the scrutiny of a gate guard and a tally clerk, who would have required bills of lading, Schneider left home at two and three in the morning night after night, in a pickup truck painted to look like a company transport.

Schneider merely drove in among the assorted wagons and freight piles. He had somehow acquired keys, and documents issued by the computer gave him access to the yard. The inexperienced night security guards not only let him through but even offered him cups of coffee and cigarettes as he and his men loaded the equipment.

Schneider started to have fears about what he was doing—the morality of it and the cheating it involved. He had intended the theft to be just a brilliant near-scientific feat. Jerry began to realize that the effort of the crime was greater than the reward. In Schneider's words, "It got so that I was afraid of my ex-employees, men I knew were aware of what I was up to because they'd seen the stuff come in, day after day, and go out again as our stuff. I began to feel hunted. Scared." The crime left him short of sleep, exhausted, and feeling guilty. In addition, the value of the stolen material passing into his possession was rising dramatically.[22]

Schneider robbed Pacific Telephone of nearly $1 million worth of equipment. His crime is interesting because his rationalization was "to see if the perfect crime could be committed." In fact, he probably couldn't have rationalized committing the crime for any other reason. When he was asked whether he considered himself an honest man, Schneider responded with a firm "yes." When he was asked whether, if he saw a wallet on the sidewalk, he would pocket it or try to return it to the owner, his answer was that he was like everyone else—he'd try to return it if it was at all possible. However, when he was asked whether, if he saw $10,000 lying in an open cash box in a supermarket and nobody was watching him, if he would take the money, he answered, "Sure, I would. If the company was careless enough to leave the money there, it deserved to have the money taken."[23]

Schneider's pressures were greed, retaliation (it was revealed at his trial that he hated Pacific Telephone Company), and a compulsion to prove his superiority. Schneider is a man with strong self-discipline. He is a strict vegetarian who does a lot of physical exercise. He works hard, and is brilliant and successful at whatever he undertakes. There is little doubt that he could be a valued and even trusted executive at most corporations. His tremendous knowledge of computers allowed him opportunities to get keys and passwords.

Schneider's "perfect crime" failed. It would have never happened, however, had he *not* acted on a personal challenge and rationalized that he was only playing a game—a game of intellectual chess with a faceless company. For several years after he was caught, Jerry Schneider worked as a security fraud consultant.

New Terms

Accounting system: Policies and procedures for recording economic transactions in an organized manner.

Audit trail: Documents and records that can be used to trace transactions.

Control environment: A set of characteristics that defines good management control features other than accounting policies and control activities.

Control activities or procedures: Specific error-checking routines performed by company personnel.

Documents and records: Documentation of all transactions in order to create an audit trail.

Independent checks: Periodical monitoring of the work or activities of others.

Labeling: Teaching and training.

Modeling: Setting an example.

Perceived opportunity: A situation where people believe they have a favorable or promising combination of circumstances to commit fraud and not be detected.

Perceived pressure: A situation where people perceive they have a need to commit fraud; a constraining influence on the will or mind, as a moral force.

Physical safeguards: Vaults, fences, locks, and so on that protect assets from theft.

Rationalization: Self-satisfying but incorrect reasons for one's behavior.

Segregation of duties: Division of tasks into two parts, so one person does not have complete control of the task.

System of authorizations: A system of limits on who can and cannot perform certain functions.

Questions and Cases

Discussion Questions

1. What types of people commit fraud?
2. What motivates people to commit fraud?
3. What is the fraud triangle, and why is it important?
4. What is the fraud scale, and how does it relate to pressure, opportunity, and integrity?
5. What are some different types of pressures?
6. What are some of the controls that prevent and/or detect fraudulent behavior?
7. What are some common noncontrol factors that provide opportunities for fraud?
8. How does rationalization contribute to fraud?

True/False

1. When hiring, it is usually difficult to know which employees are capable of committing fraud, especially without performing background checks.
2. The three elements of the fraud triangle are a perceived pressure, a perceived opportunity, and rationalization.
3. Management's example or model is of little importance to the control environment.
4. Good controls will often increase opportunities for individuals to commit fraud within an organization.
5. Effective fraud-fighters usually put most of their time and effort into minimizing the pressures on perpetrators to commit fraud.
6. The greater the perceived opportunity or the more intense the pressure, the less rationalization it takes for someone to commit fraud.
7. Fraud can be perpetrated to benefit oneself or to benefit one's organization.
8. Fraud perpetrators who are prosecuted, incarcerated, or severely punished usually commit fraud again.
9. Many organizations merely dismiss dishonest employees because of the expense and time involved in prosecuting them.
10. Appropriate hiring will not decrease an organization's risk of fraud.
11. An individual who owns his or her own business and is the sole employee needs many control procedures.

12. A proper system of authorization helps ensure good internal controls.
13. Good documents and records are some of the best preventive controls.
14. Many frauds occur because victims don't have access to information possessed by the perpetrators.

Multiple Choice

1. Fraud perpetrators:
   a. Look like other criminals.
   b. Have profiles that look like most honest people.
   c. Are usually very young.
   d. None of the above.
2. Which of the following is *not* one of the three elements of fraud?
   a. Perceived pressure
   b. Perceived opportunity
   c. Rationalization
   d. Intelligence
3. Which of the following is a common perceived pressure?
   a. The ability to outsmart others
   b. Opportunity to cheat others
   c. A financial need
   d. The ability to "borrow" money by committing fraud
4. If pressures and opportunities are high and personal integrity is low, the chance of fraud is:
   a. High
   b. Medium
   c. Low
   d. Very low
5. Which of the following is *not* a common type of fraud pressure?
   a. Vice
   b. Work-related pressures
   c. Financial pressures
   d. Pressure to outsmart peers
6. Opportunity involves:
   a. Opportunity to conceal fraud
   b. Opportunity to avoid being punished for fraud
   c. Opportunity to commit fraud
   d. All of the above
   e. None of the above
7. Which of the following is *not* one of the three elements of the control system of an organization?
   a. The control environment
   b. The accounting system
   c. Management
   d. Control activities or procedures

8. Which of the following noncontrol factors provide opportunities for fraud?
   a. Inability to judge the quality of performance
   b. Lack of access to information
   c. Failure to discipline fraud perpetrators
   d. Lack of an audit trail
   e. All of the above
9. Who generally has the highest risk of becoming a fraud victim?
   a. Businessperson
   b. Older, less educated people
   c. College students
   d. None of the above
10. How frequently do most people rationalize?
   a. Often
   b. Sometimes
   c. Rarely
   d. Never
11. Which of the following kinds of pressures is most often associated with fraud?
   a. Work-related pressures
   b. Financial pressures
   c. Vice pressures
   d. All of the above
12. Which of the following is *not* a control procedure?
   a. Use of documents and records to create an audit trail
   b. Independent checks
   c. Decreasing work-related pressure
   d. Physical safeguards
13. It is the _______ and _______ of existing controls, not the _______ of controls, that allow most frauds to be perpetrated.
   a. existence, use, lack
   b. lack, ignoring, existence
   c. overriding, ignoring, lack
   d. overriding, lack, use
14. On what element of the fraud triangle do most fraud-fighters usually focus all or most of their preventive efforts?
   a. Perceived pressure
   b. Perceived opportunity
   c. Perceived weak internal controls
   d. Rationalization
15. Which of the following is *not* a control activity (procedure)?
   a. System of authorizations
   b. Appropriate hiring procedures
   c. Independent checks
   d. Documents and records
   e. All of the above are control activities.

16. Which of the following is *not* a common vice that motivates people to commit fraud?
    a. Gambling
    b. Drugs
    c. Expensive extramarital relationships
    d. Alcohol
    e. All of the above are vices that motivate people to commit fraud.
17. Which of the following is *not* a way that management can establish a good control environment?
    a. Having a clear organizational structure
    b. Proper training
    c. Communicating openly
    d. Appropriate hiring procedures
    e. All of the above are ways that management can establish a good control environment.
18. Which of the following is *not* an element of most frauds?
    a. Taking assets
    b. Concealment
    c. Breaking and entering
    d. Conversion

Short Cases

Case 1. You are an auditor for Jefferson Retailers and have discovered the following problems with their accounting system. For each problem, tell which of the five internal control procedures is lacking. Also, recommend how the company should change its procedures to avoid the problem in the future.

1. Jefferson Retailers' losses due to bad debts have increased dramatically over the past year. In an effort to increase sales, the managers of certain stores have allowed large credit sales to occur without review or approval of the customers.
2. An accountant hid his theft of $200 from the company's bank account by overstating outstanding checks on monthly reconciliation. He believed the manipulation would not be discovered.
3. Michael Meyer works in a storeroom. He maintains the inventory records, counts the inventory, and has unlimited access to the storeroom. He occasionally steals items of inventory and hides his thefts by overstating the physical inventory accounts.
4. Receiving reports are sometimes filled out days after shipments have arrived.

Case 2. In the early 1990s, the top executive of a large oil refining company based in New York was convicted of financial statement fraud.[24] One issue in the case involved the way the company accounted for its oil inventories. In particular, the company purchased crude oil from exploration companies and then processed the oil into finished oil products, such as jet fuel, diesel fuel, and so forth. Because there was a ready market for these finished products, as soon as the company purchased the crude oil, it recorded its oil inventory at the selling prices of the finished products less the cost to refine the oil (instead of at cost). Besides the fraud in the case, this type of accounting was questioned because it allowed the company to recognize profit before the actual sale and refining of the oil. This method was even accepted by one of the large CPA firms. If you were the judge in this case, would you be critical of this accounting practice? Is "aggressive" accounting a warning signal that fraud might be occurring?

Case 3. Helen Weeks has worked for Bonne Consulting Group (BCG) as the executive secretary in the administrative department for nearly 10 years. Her apparent integrity and dedication to her work quickly earned her a reputation as an outstanding employee and resulted in increased responsibilities. Her present responsibilities include arranging for outside feasibility studies, maintaining client files, working with outside marketing consultants, initiating the payment process, and notifying the accounting department of all openings or closings of vendor accounts.

During Helen's first five years of employment, BCG subcontracted all of its feasibility and marketing studies through Jackson & Co. This relationship was subsequently terminated because Jackson & Co. merged with a larger, more expensive consulting group. At the time of termination, Helen and her supervisor selected a new firm to conduct BCG's market research. However, Helen never informed the accounting department that the Jackson & Co. account had been closed.

Her supervisor allowed Helen to sign the payment voucher for services rendered, and Helen continued to process checks made payable to Jackson's account. Because her supervisor trusted her completely, he also allowed her to sign for all voucher payments less than $10,000. The accounting department processed the payments, and Helen distributed the payments. She opened a bank account in a nearby city under the name of Jackson & Co., where she made deposits. She paid all of her personal expenses out of this account.

You have recently been hired by BCG to detect and prevent fraud.

1. What internal controls are missing at BCG?
2. What gaps in control gave Helen the opportunity to perpetrate the fraud?
3. How could this fraud have been detected?

Case 4. The following describes an actual fraud in a communications company:

What Jane Doe did in her spare time didn't concern the New York public relations firm where she worked. "We thought she was just playing cards with the girls," says John Brown, the president of the Public Group, the firm that employed her for nine years.

She was such a trusted employee that her bosses put her in charge of paying bills, balancing bank accounts, and handling other cash-management chores. They didn't realize their mistake until Doe took a sick leave and they discovered she had been pocketing company funds for years. The money stoked a gambling habit that took the 60-year-old widow on weekend junkets to casinos in the Bahamas, Monte Carlo, and Las Vegas. In all, the company claims she stole about $320,000.

Doe pleaded guilty to one count of grand theft and four counts of check forgery. She was placed on 10 years' probation and ordered to attend meetings of a chapter of Gamblers Anonymous, the national self-help group.

1. What were Doe's perceived opportunities?
2. What pressure did she have to commit fraud?
3. How did the fact that Doe was a trusted employee give her more opportunity to commit fraud?
4. How do addictions such as gambling motivate people to commit fraud?

Case 5. The following describes an actual investment fraud.[25]

Mr. Armstrong allegedly committed one of the most common frauds in finance: making big promises to investors that he couldn't deliver. Mr. Armstrong stands accused of securities fraud after trying to cover up millions of dollars in bets on the yen and other markets that went horribly wrong.

A criminal indictment is probably not the ending that the 49-year-old Armstrong envisioned when he fell in love with business as a boy. His love affair with trading made him an active stamp dealer at just 13, but by 1972 he was kicked out of the stamp world's most elite trading fraternity, amid accusations of selling rare stamps that he didn't own and thus could not deliver.

Undaunted, he fought his way back to respectability and became a stamp expert—and eventually an authority on the far-more-sophisticated financial markets on which he was widely quoted. His self-confident forecasting style made him a hit in Japan, where Armstrong is now accused of bilking investors out of $950 million.

Documents that he used to sell his investments show that he promised potential buyers a guaranteed yield of 4% on the fixed-rate instrument, a strong selling point in a country where interest rates on government bonds are less than half that. Moreover, the securities offered further returns as high as 25%, depending on market conditions.

Armstrong's bets on the markets eventually began to turn against him. The Securities and Exchange Commission says that from late 1997, Armstrong racked up increasingly bigger losses on large investments he made in currencies and options. Between November 1997 and August 1999, SEC officials say he lost $295 million in trading the yen alone—all of it clients' money. "In the wake of the discovery of the fraud," the SEC said in its civil complaint that was filed, "Armstrong has transferred millions of dollars from Princeton Global accounts into foreign-bank accounts he controls." SEC officials declined to disclose how much money he may have transferred overseas, or to what countries.

On two previous instances, Armstrong did face commodities trading scrutiny. In 1985, the agency overseeing commodities trading in the United States lodged a complaint against him for failing to register and maintain proper investment records. Then in June 1987, the same agency fined him $10,000 and suspended his trading privileges for a year for improper risk disclosure and misrepresentation of his trading returns. Part of the complaint was related to advertising in a Princeton newsletter.

1. How did trust contribute to Armstrong's fraud?
2. Lack of access to information is one of the noncontrol factors that provides opportunities for fraud. How would investor knowledge about Armstrong's background have affected his ability to perpetrate the fraud?

Case 6. Alexia Jones is the sole worker on the night shift at a local 24-hour pharmacy. Because management is cost conscious and business is slow at night, Alexia is responsible for doing the accounting from the previous day. Alexia has two children, and her husband does not work. Alexia has strong pressure to provide well for her family.

1. Is the pharmacy at risk for fraud? Why or why not?
2. How does the fraud scale help us to determine if risk for fraud is high or low in this situation?
3. You have been retained by the pharmacy as a business consultant. What information should you provide to the owner of the pharmacy concerning fraud?

Case 7. Bob's Country Kitchen, a small family-owned restaurant in northern New York, has seen a drop in profitability over the past three years and the owners want to know why. Bob's has been a local favorite for 20 years. Two brothers, Tom and Bob, opened it in the early

1980s because they couldn't find a burger they liked. Bob's initially served only hamburgers, but rapidly expanded to a wider menu. Bob's was so popular in the late 1980s that the brothers hired several people to help manage the restaurant's day-to-day operation. Until that point, Tom and Bob managed the place themselves.

The brothers felt that their new management was doing a good job and so they gradually became less and less involved. In 2000, they gave up all management duties to Joel, a friend of the family employed by Bob's for 15 years. Bob's has no computer system in place for customer orders. Each order is written on a pad with a duplicate carbon, one copy is taken to the kitchen, and the other is given to the customer. All customers pay at the old cash register at the front of the restaurant, after which their receipts are pegged on a tack and are totaled at day's end to determine total sales. Bob and Tom have noticed a gradual decline in profits over the past three years and, until now, figured it was because of increased restaurant competition in the area.

However, it struck the brothers as odd that revenues have increased substantially but profits have not. When asked about this disturbing trend, Joel says it is because of the large increase in the cost of food and that he has to pay employees more with the increased competition. Bob and Tom have no reason to disbelieve Joel, since he is a trusted family friend. Joel's responsibilities at Bob's include preparing the nightly deposits, managing accounts payable, handling payroll, and performing the bank reconciliations. He also writes and signs all checks. No one checks his work.

1. What possible opportunities does Joel have to commit fraud?
2. What flags may be signaling a possible fraud here?
3. Which internal controls would you put in place to prevent future abuses?

Case 8. "But I intended to pay it all back, I really did," Joe Swankie said as he talked to his manager. "How did I ever get into this situation?" he thought.

Two years ago Joe received the promotion he had been working for. His new manager told him he had a promising future. Joe and his wife quickly purchased a new home. Not long after, Joe and his wife Janae had their fourth child, and life was great. After having their fourth child, Janae soon quit work to spend more time with the kids.

Then things started to turn upside down. The economy took a downturn, and negatively impacted Joe's company. His pay, which was based on commission, was reduced nearly 50%. Joe continued to work hard but thought he should be paid more. Unable to find another job, Joe grudgingly decided to stay with the company even with the lower pay.

Not long after he started receiving lower commissions, Joe noticed that controls over the petty cash fund were loose. Records weren't reviewed very often, and when small shortages occurred, they were usually written off. One week Joe took $50. When questioned by his wife, Joe said he had found a few odd jobs after work. Joe continued to take small amounts for a couple of weeks. After realizing that no one was noticing the shortage, he began to take up to $100 a week.

One day another employee saw Joe take some cash from the fund and put it in his wallet. When questioned, he stated that it was a reimbursement the company owed him for supplies. An investigation ensued and Joe's fraud was discovered.

1. Identify the opportunities, pressures, and rationalizations that led Joe to commit this fraud.
2. What simple procedures could the company have implemented to prevent the fraud from occurring?

Case 9. Johnson Manufacturing, a diversified manufacturer, has seven divisions that operate in the United States, Mexico, and Canada. Johnson Manufacturing has historically allowed its divisions to operate independently. Corporate intervention occurs only when goals are not met. Corporate management has high integrity, although the board of directors is not very active. Johnson screens every employee before hiring them. Johnson feels its employees are all well educated and honest.

The company has a code of conduct, but there is little monitoring of employees. Employee compensation is highly dependent on the performance of the company.

During the past year, a strong new competitor entered one of the Johnson's highly successful markets. The competitor is undercutting Johnson's prices. Johnson's manager of this unit, Sue Harris, has responded by matching price cuts in hopes of maintaining market share. Sue is very concerned because she cannot see any areas to reduce costs so that growth and profitability can be maintained. If profitability is not maintained, the division managers' salaries and bonuses will be reduced.

Sue has decided that one way to make the division more profitable is to overstate inventory, since it represents a large amount of the division's balance sheet. She also knows that controls over inventory are weak. She views this overstatement as a short-run solution to the profit decline due to the competitor's price cutting. Sue is certain that once the competitor stops cutting prices or goes bankrupt, the misstatements in inventory can be corrected with little impact on the bottom line.

1. What factors in Johnson's control environment have led to and facilitated Sue's manipulation of inventory?
2. What pressures did Sue have to overstate inventory?
3. What rationalization did she use to justify her fraud?

Case 10. In October of 2001, a former optometrist was sentenced to seven years in New Jersey State prison for conspiracy, theft by deception, falsifying records, and falsification of records relating to medical care, as part of a massive health insurance fraud. In addition to his prison sentence, the optometrist was ordered to pay a criminal insurance fraud fine of $100,000 and restitution of $97,975. The state is also in the process of seeking an additional $810,000 in civil insurance fraud penalties.[26]

The optometrist was found guilty of false insurance billing for providing eyeglasses and routine eye exams at no cost or at reduced cost, and making up the difference by billing insurance carriers for services not rendered to patients. The optometrist also had his office staff create approximately 997 false patient records and charts and falsely bill insurance carriers for prescribed optometric services that were not rendered to his patients. He billed insurance companies for optometric treatments and tests for ocular conditions that patients did not actually suffer. The optometrist was also charged for falsifying patient records and charts.

What noncontrol factors provided the optometrist with an opportunity to commit fraud?

Case 11. FCS Fund Management is an investment marketing business with sales of over $10 million and with offices in Norwich, Connecticut, Dubai, and Hong Kong. The firm sells high-yield investments offering returns of up to 20%. FCS has clients in the United Kingdom, Europe, and the Middle East, many of whom are U.S. expatriates. FCS sells its investment products through salesmen operating in these locations. The CEO, James Hammond, knows that many of the accounts are, or might be, misleading, false, or deceptive in that they purported to confirm the existence of genuine investments. Yet, because the investments and even many of the investors are in other countries, he knows he can't be sued, even if the investments are fraudulent. Therefore, he isn't as concerned about due diligence as he would be if the investments were in the United States.

Describe how the rationalization element of the fraud triangle is operative here.

Case 12. Len Haxton owns a local CPA firm with four separate offices in a medium-size town. He and his wife started the firm 20 years ago, and they now have over 50 full-time employees. Recently, Len discovered that one of his employees has stolen more than $20,000 from the business over the past six months because of lax internal controls. He is furious about the situation, but is uncertain about whether he should initiate a criminal investigation or just fire the employee.

1. List four reasons why Len should have the employee prosecuted.
2. List three reasons why Len might not want to seek prosecution of his employee.
3. If you were Len, what would you do?

Case 13. As a new employee in a large, national company, you are excited about your career opportunities. You hope that senior staff will eventually perceive you as a "rising star." During your first week of training, you are assigned a mentor. The mentor will help you learn your way around the company and answer any questions you may have about your work. As it turns out, your mentor is a rising star. One day, she takes you out to lunch. While you are eating, you and she discuss company policies. She explains expense reimbursement. Company policy dictates that expenses such as lunch are the responsibility of the employee and are not reimbursable. The exception to this policy is for lunches with clients and potential recruits, or for other work-related circumstances. She tells you "off the record" that nobody really follows this policy, and that you can always find a "business purpose" to justify your lunch expenses with fellow employees, as long as you don't do it every day. "Besides, our supervisors don't really scrutinize expense reimbursement requests below $25, so why worry about it?"

1. Is it a fraud to charge the company for personal lunches that you submit as business expenses?
2. What elements of fraud, if any, are present in this situation?
3. How would you respond to your mentor, or to other employees that may encourage you to pick up the tab for lunch with the understanding that you will charge the company for the lunch?

Case 14. You own a local department store in a small town. Many of your employees have worked for you for years, and you know them and their families very well. Because your business is relatively small, and because you know your employees so well, you haven't worried about establishing many internal controls. You do set a good example for how you expect your employees to work, you are actively involved in the business, and you provide adequate training to new employees. One day you become suspicious about an employee at a checkout desk. You fear that he may be stealing from the company by altering the day's totals at his register. He has worked for you for 15 years, and he has always been honest and reliable. After several weeks of investigation, you discover that your fears are correct—he *is* stealing from the company. You confront him, and he admits to stealing $25,000 over several years. He explains that, at first, he stole mainly to pay for small gifts for his wife and young children. But then last year his wife lost her job, they had another child, and he wasn't sure how to pay all of the bills.

1. What elements of fraud are present in this case?
2. How might you have detected this fraud earlier, or prevented it from happening?
3. How will you approach your interactions with employees and your relationships with them in the future?

4. Do you feel a better system of internal controls, such as surveillance cameras and an improved computer system, are necessary or justified to prevent future frauds?

Case 15. In 2001, a prominent New York fertility doctor was sentenced to more than 7 years in prison for his insurance fraud conviction. Dr. Niels Lauersen received a 7-year, 3-month sentence and was ordered to pay $3.2 million in restitution and an additional $17,500 in fines.[27]

Lauersen was convicted of pocketing $2.5 million during a 10-year period. Prosecutors say he stole from insurance companies by falsely billing fertility surgeries that were not covered by insurance as gynecological surgeries. Tearful former patients called out to Lauersen and wished him well as he was led away. He is now in prison.

At his sentencing, the judge said, "You were a medical doctor at the top of your profession and a public figure at the apex of New York society. Your fall from prestige has been Faustian in its dimensions." The probation report recommended that Lauersen be sentenced to 14 years' imprisonment. Lauersen, 64, has lived in the United States since 1967, when he left Denmark. His lawyer, Gerald Shargel, argued for leniency, saying Lauersen had an honorable purpose: to make it affordable for women with fertility problems to have children.

"This is a very tough sentence. This is a very unusual case," Shargel said. Shargel said his client treated 14,000 women, delivering 3,000 children in a single year.

1. What pressure might have motivated Lauersen to commit fraud?
2. What opportunity enabled him to commit fraud?
3. How did Lauersen rationalize his fraudulent activities?
4. How could Lauersen have both helped his patients and not lied or stolen from the insurance company?

Case 16. Full-of-Nature is a vitamin supplement company in New York that makes different herbal pills for gaining muscular strength, losing weight, and living a healthier life. You have been hired to audit Full-of-Nature, and you soon realize that company practices are deceptive and misleading. You notice the following frauds being committed and are writing a report to the Board of Directors about what should be done to fix the problems. For each fraud, list one control procedure that was not followed and suggest how the company should eliminate the fraud and deal with the perpetrator.

1. Journal entries for consulting expenses, when traced back, show five companies using the same post office box for receiving consulting fees from Full-of-Nature. You discover that the accountant has been embezzling money and listing it as consulting expenses.
2. The warehouse manager has been stealing pills to help his son get stronger (he wants his son to play football). To cover the losses, he issued credit memos to customers, showing that they returned bad goods that were replaced with new pills.
3. The CEO decided he didn't want to pay payroll taxes anymore, so he fired all of his employees and re-hired them as contractors. However, he still withholds payroll taxes and keeps the money for himself.
4. The accounts payable clerk likes to go shopping with the company checkbook and always buys herself a little something when she orders office supplies. However, since she is the one who handles office supplies, no one knows what was purchased for the company and what was ordered for her living room.

Extensive Cases

Case 17. GreenGrass is a small, family-operated company whose core service is in horticultural care and lawn care for local customers. GreenGrass's owner has used company revenues over the years to cover the costs of his children's college education. At the same time, he has given his children some work experience at the company and opportunities to earn spending money. The company has grown steadily over the last few years, and the manager has hired many employees outside the family to keep up with the demand of the increasing number of customers. GreenGrass is housed in a small office building, and only one employee runs operations in the company office. The owner was originally in charge of this aspect of GreenGrass, but now leaves it to his trusted friend, Sam Hudsen, who has experience in accounting and information systems. Sam schedules the routes of all employees and is also responsible for payments, receipts, and balancing the books.

GreenGrass performs two major services. First, it provides lawn care using insecticides, fertilizer, and weed killers. Eight employees are responsible for this activity. They each drive a truck and collect money from the customers they serve. They also load and mix chemicals in the tanks they use during the day. The second service is lawn mowing care. Usually, a four-man crew is responsible for all the machines they use, and they are assigned certain lawns on their daily schedule. It is in the lawn mowing service that Sam employs his own children. The lawn mowing team is thus made up of younger workers than the lawn care team.

Profits increased steadily as the company picked up new clients. However, the owner noticed that last year's accounts were different. Revenues increased only marginally, and expenses increased more than they should have. The owner has noticed that his interactions with his friend in the office have been fewer. Also, employees finish their routes later in the day than in previous years.

1. What are some of the fraud opportunities in GreenGrass?
2. What symptoms of fraud exist, and what should the owner look for if he believes fraud may be occurring?
3. What steps should be taken to make sure fraud does not occur, and what are the costs associated with these steps?

Case 18. James Watkins, an ambitious 22-year-old, started an entertainment business called Best Club after he graduated from California State University. Best Club initially failed because James ignored day-to-day operations and cost controls. One year later, James was heavily in debt. Despite his debt, he decided to open another location of Best Club because he was confident that Best Club would eventually bring him financial success.

However, as expenses increased, James could not meet his debts, and he turned to insurance fraud to save his business. He staged a break-in at a Best Club location, then claimed a loss. In addition, James reported fictitious equipment to secure loans, falsified work order contracts to secure loans, stole money orders for cash, and added zeros to customers' bills who paid with credit cards. James lived the "good life," with an expensive house and a new sports car.

Two years later, James decided to take Best Club public. He falsified financial statements to greatly improve the company's reported financial position. In order to avoid the SEC's scrutiny of his financial statements, James merged Best Club with Red House, an inactive New York computer firm, and acquired Red House's publicly owned shares in exchange for stock in the newly formed corporation. James personally received 79% of the shares, making him worth $24 million on paper, and he continually raised money from new investors to pay off debts. A few months after going public, Best Club's stock sold for $21 a share, and the company's book value was $310 million. James was now worth $190 million on paper. A short time later, James met John Gagne, president of AM Company, an advertising service. John agreed to raise $100 million, via junk bonds, for Best Club to buy out Sun Society, a travel service.

These efforts, together with television appearances, made James "hot," and his reputation as an entrepreneurial genius grew. However, all this changed after an investigative report by a major newspaper that chronicled some of James's early credit-card frauds. Within two weeks, Best Club's stock plummeted from $21 to $5.

After a criminal investigation, James was charged with insurance, bank, stock, and mail fraud, money laundering, and tax evasion, and Best Club's shares were selling for just pennies. A company once supposedly worth hundreds of millions of dollars dropped in value to only $48,000.

From this case, identify:

1. The pressures, opportunities, and rationalizations that led James to commit his fraud.
2. The flags that could have signaled the fraud.
3. Controls or actions that could have detected James's behavior.

Internet Assignments

1. Visit the Association of Certified Fraud Examiners web site, http://www.cfenet.com/home.asp, and answer the following questions:
   a. How many professionals make up the Association of Certified Fraud Examiners?
   b. What are the requirements for becoming a Certified Fraud Examiner?
   c. What is the overall mission of the Association of Certified Fraud Examiners?
   d. What does a Certified Fraud Examiner (CFE) do? What are some of the professions from which they originate?
   e. Take the CFE Practice Quiz. Do you have what it takes to be a Certified Fraud Examiner?
   f. List a few of the products offered on the web site for training people interested in fraud examination. Which materials would be most beneficial to you in your profession? Why?
   g. What service does the Association provide so that individuals can anonymously report allegations of ethical violations, fraud, waste, and abuse? How does this service work?
   h. Visit the Media Center. Click on Fraud Statistics and list a couple of fraud statistics that you find surprising. Click on Fraud Follies and read a humorous story about fraud.
2. The Serious Fraud Office (SFO) is a government agency in the United Kingdom that investigates and prosecutes serious frauds. Its web site contains press releases of recently settled cases. These cases provide excellent examples of the fraud triangle at work.

   Visit the web site of the SFO at http://www.sfo.gov.uk, and click on press releases. Choose a case that interests you and describe the fraud in terms of the fraud triangle. Clearly identify the elements of perceived pressure, rationalization, and perceived opportunity.

End Notes

1. See, for example, W. S. Albrecht, D. Cherrington, R. Payne, A. Roe, and M. Romney, *How to Detect and Prevent Business Fraud,* Prentice-Hall, 1981.
2. See "Red-Flagging the White-Collar Criminal," *Management Accounting,* by Marshall B. Romney, W. Steve Albrecht, and David J. Cherrington, March 1980, pp. 51–57.
3. For example, several studies on retail theft over time by Richard C. Hollinger (University of Florida) and others have shown that a higher percentage of employees were dishonest in later years than in earlier years. Other studies have found similar results.
4. See *How to Detect and Prevent Business Fraud,* op. cit.
5. This was a proprietary study performed for one of the author's fraud clients.
6. http://www.better-investing.org
7. From speech by Lynn Turner, former chief accountant of U.S. Securities and Exchange Commission, given at the 39th Annual Corporate Counsel Institute, Northwestern University School of Law, October 12, 2000.
8. Richard C. Hollinger. 1989. *Dishonesty in the Workplace: A Manager's Guide to Preventing Employee Theft.* Park Ridge, Ill.: London House Press, pp. 1–5.
9. http://www.biography.com/features/sweethearts/cframes.html
10. Alison Stein Wellner, "Background Checks," *Business Week Online,* Aug. 14, 2000.
11. For example, see *2002 Report to the Nations: Occupational Fraud and Abuse,* Association of Certified Fraud Examiners, Austin, Texas, pp. 11.
12. "Doctor Listed as Suicide Was Target of Fraud Investigation," *Los Angeles Times,* Dec. 10, 1992, p. A3.
13. Kevin Kelly, "How Did Sears Blow the Gasket? Some Say the Retailer's Push for Profits Sparked Its Auto-Repair Woes," *Business Week,* June 29, 1992, p. 38; and Tung Yin, "Sears Is Accused of Billing Fraud at Auto Centers," *Wall Street Journal,* June 12, 1992, Western Ed., p. B1.
14. From the video, "Cooking the Books," Association of Certified Fraud Examiners, Austin, Texas.
15. From the personal notes of the author, who testified as an expert witness before a June 1990 grand jury, U.S. District Court for the Central District of California.
16. From the personal notes of the author, who testified as an expert witness before a June 1990 grand jury, U.S. District Court for the Central District of California.
17. *Anatomy of a Fraud: Inside the Finances of the PTL Ministries,* by G. Tidwell and J. McKee, John Wiley & Sons, March 1993.
18. Facts about the PTL case were taken from "PTL: Where Were the Auditors?" a working paper by Gary L. Tidwell, Associate Professor of Business Administration, School of Business and Economics, College of Charleston, Charleston, South Carolina.
19. Ibid.

20. Ibid.
21. http://www.house.gov/ways_means/socsec/106Cong/5-11-00/5-llhost.htm
22. From an unpublished interview with Jerry Schneider by Donn Parker of the Stanford Research Institute. Author Steve Albrecht was privileged to read Donn's files in his office. To read about the case, go to http://www.arts/uwaterloo/ca/acct/ccag/chapter 2/chpt2sect1topic6.htm.
23. Ibid.
24. This fraud occurred at Arochem Corporation. The author was an expert witness in this case.
25. Securities and Exchange Commission, Litigation Release No. 16279, September 13, 1999; http://www.sec.gov/litigation/litrelease.htm.
26. Office of Attorney General, Jack J. Farmer, Jr., Attorney General, January 11, 2002, New Jersey Department of Law and Public Safety, "Former Monmouth County Optometrist Sentenced to Seven Years in State Prison for Insurance Fraud."
27. State of New York, Department of Health, 8'11'01-101, "State Health Department Suspends License of Niels Lauersen, M.D."

CHAPTER THREE

Fighting Fraud: An Overview

After studying this chapter, you should be able to:

1. Understand the importance of fraud prevention.
2. Understand the importance of early fraud detection.
3. Distinguish between different approaches to fraud investigation.
4. Choose between different legal actions that can be taken once fraud has occurred.

During the past two years, Mark-X Corporation has uncovered three major frauds. The first fraud involved a division manager overstating division profits by reporting fictitious revenues. Faced with declining sales and fearful of not receiving his annual bonus and possible termination, the manager inflated service contract amounts to overstate revenues by $22 million. The second fraud was committed by the purchasing department manager. In his responsibility to secure uniforms for company employees, he gave favored treatment to a certain vendor. In return for allowing the vendor to charge higher prices and provide inferior service, the vendor hired the purchasing manager's daughter as an "employee" and paid her over $400,000 for essentially rendering no service. In fact, when investigated, the daughter didn't even know the location of the vendor's offices or telephone number (for whom she supposedly worked). The daughter then funneled the bribes to her father, the purchasing agent. As a result of this kickback scheme, Mark-X purchased $11 million of uniforms at inflated prices. The third fraud involved two warehouse managers who stole approximately $300,000 in inventory. They perpetrated the fraud by issuing credit memos to customers who supposedly returned defective merchandise and were given product replacements. In fact, the merchandise was never returned. Instead, the credit memos concealed the theft of "high value" merchandise from the warehouse.

All three of these frauds were reported in newspapers and brought significant embarrassment to the company's management and board of directors. The investigation of the frauds also cost the company a tremendous amount of money. And, in a meeting of the board of directors, the chairman made the following comment to the CEO: "I am sick and tired of our dirty laundry hitting the newspapers. If there is one more high-profile fraud in this company, three of us will resign from the board and we will also recommend that you be replaced."

Following the board meeting, the CEO called a meeting with the CFO, the internal audit director, in-house legal counsel, and the director of corporate security. In the meeting, he told them that unless the company successfully developed a proactive fraud program, they would all lose their jobs. The CEO then reviewed the three frauds with the group. His final words were, "I don't care how much you spend, but I want the best proactive fraud-mitigating program possible. Hire whatever consultants you need, but get me a proactive fraud program that I can report to the board."

What advice would a consultant give this company? Probably to embark on four key activities. The four activities are (1) fraud prevention, (2) early fraud detection, (3) fraud investigation, and (4) follow-up legal action and/or resolution. Comprehensive fraud programs focus on all four. Mark-X focused its fraud efforts on the last two: investigation and legal action. These are the least effective and most expensive fraud-fighting efforts.

In this book, we cover all the activities that companies have found useful in minimizing this growing problem. Chapter 4 discusses prevention. Chapters 5 and 6 cover detection. Chapters 7–10 cover investigation. Chapters 11–15 discuss various kinds of fraud and e-business frauds. Chapter 16 discusses important follow-up activities. In this chapter, we provide an overview of a comprehensive fraud-fighting program. You will then have a structure to help you understand the kinds of fraud-fighting efforts that are available.

Fraud Prevention

Preventing fraud is the most cost-effective way to reduce losses from fraud. Once a fraud has been committed, there are no winners. Perpetrators lose—they suffer humiliation and legal consequences. They must make tax and restitution payments, and they also face financial penalties and other consequences. Victims lose—assets have been stolen and they must now incur legal fees, lost time, negative publicity, and other adverse consequences. Organizations and individuals that install proactive fraud prevention measures find that the measures pay big dividends. Because investigating fraud can be very expensive, *preventing* it is crucial.

As we noted in Chapter 2, people commit fraud because of three factors: (1) perceived pressure, (2) perceived opportunity, and (3) some way to rationalize the fraud as acceptable. We then introduced a scale showing that these factors differ in intensity from instance to instance. When perceived pressures and opportunities are high, a person needs less rationalization to commit fraud. When perceived pressures and opportunities are low, a person needs more rationalization. Unfortunately, sometimes pressures and/or the ability to rationalize are so high that, no matter how hard an organization tries to prevent fraud, theft still occurs. Indeed, fraud is often impossible to prevent, especially in a cost-effective way. The best an organization can hope for is to minimize the costs of fraud.

Certain organizations have significantly higher levels of employee fraud and are more susceptible to fraudulent financial reporting. Research consistently shows that almost all organizations have fraud of one type or another.[1] Only those organizations that carefully examine their risk for fraud and take proactive steps to create the right kind of environment succeed in preventing fraud.

Fraud prevention involves two fundamental activities: (1) creating and maintaining a culture of honesty and integrity, and (2) assessing the risk of fraud and developing concrete responses to minimize risk and eliminate opportunity.

Creating a Culture of Honesty and Integrity

There are several ways to create such a culture: (1) Insist that top management model appropriate behavior. (2) Hire the right kind of employees. (3) Communicate expectations throughout the organization and require periodic written confirmation of acceptance of those expectations. (4) Create a positive work environment. And (5) develop and maintain effective policies for punishing perpetrators once fraud occurs.

Research in moral development strongly suggests that honesty is reinforced when proper examples are set—sometimes referred to as "the tone at the top."[2] Management cannot act one way and expect others in the organization to behave differently. Management must reinforce through its own actions that dishonest, questionable, or unethical behavior will not be tolerated.

The second element is hiring the right employees. People are not equally honest, nor do they embrace equally well-developed personal codes of ethics. In fact, research indicates that many people, when faced with significant pressure and opportunity, will behave dishonestly rather than face the "negative consequences" of honest behavior (for example, loss of reputation or esteem, failure to meet quotas or expectations, exposure of inadequate performance, inability to pay debts, etc.). If an organization is to be successful in preventing fraud, it must have effective hiring policies that distinguish between marginal and highly ethical individuals, especially when they recruit for high-risk positions. Proactive hiring procedures include such things as conducting background investigations on prospective employees, thoroughly checking references and learning how to interpret responses to inquiries about candidates, and testing for honesty and other attributes.

The third critical element—communicating expectations—includes (1) identifying appropriate values and ethics, (2) fraud awareness training that helps employees understand potential problems they may encounter and how to resolve or report them, and (3) communicating consistent punishment of violators. For codes of conduct to be effective, they must be written and communicated to employees, vendors, and customers. They must also be developed in such a manner that management and employees "own" them. Requiring employees to confirm in writing that they understand the organization's expectations goes a long way toward creating a culture of honesty. In fact, many organizations have found that annual written confirmations are very effective in both preventing frauds and detecting them before they become large. The punishment for fraud must be clearly communicated by top management throughout the organization. For example, a strong statement from management that dishonest actions will not be tolerated and that violators will be terminated and prosecuted to the fullest extent of the law do help prevent fraud.

The fourth element in creating an honesty-driven culture involves developing a positive work environment. Research indicates that fraud occurs less frequently when employees have feelings of ownership toward their organization than when they feel abused, threatened, or ignored by it.[3] Factors associated with high levels of fraud that detract from a positive work environment include the following:

1. Top management that does not care about or pay attention to appropriate behavior.
2. Negative feedback and lack of recognition of job performance.
3. Perceived inequities in the organization.
4. Autocratic rather than participative management.
5. Low organizational loyalty.
6. Unreasonable budget expectations.
7. Unrealistically low pay.
8. Poor training and promotion opportunities.
9. High turnover and/or absenteeism.
10. Lack of clear organizational responsibilities.
11. Poor communication practices within the organization.

The last critical element is the organization's policy for handling fraud once it occurs. No matter how well developed the culture of honesty and integrity in an organization, it is still likely to experience some fraud. How the organization reacts to incidents of fraud sends a strong signal that affects the rate at which future incidents occur. An effective policy for handling fraud assures that the facts are investigated thoroughly, firm and consistent actions are taken against perpetrators, risks and controls are assessed and improved, and communication and training are ongoing.

Assessing and Mitigating the Risk of Fraud

Neither fraud committed by top management on behalf of an organization nor fraud committed against an organization can occur without opportunity, as we noted in Chapter 2. Organizations can eliminate opportunity by (1) accurately identifying sources and measuring risks; (2) implementing appropriate preventative and detective controls; (3) creating widespread monitoring by employees; and (4) installing independent checks, including an effective audit function.

Identifying sources and measuring risk means that an organization needs a process in place that both defines areas of greatest risk and evaluates and tests controls that minimize those risks. In identifying risk, organizations should consider organizational, industry, and country-specific characteristics that encourage and discourage fraud.

Risks that are inherent in the environment of an organization can be addressed with an appropriate system of control. Once risks have been assessed, the organization can identify processes, controls, and other procedures that can minimize risks. Appropriate internal systems include well-developed control environments, effective accounting systems, and appropriate control procedures.

Research has shown that employees and managers—not auditors—detect most frauds.[4] Therefore, employees and managers must be taught how to watch for and recognize fraud. To involve employees in the all-important monitoring process, provide a protocol for communication. Such protocol details to whom employees should report suspected fraud and what form their communication should take. The protocol should assure confidentiality and stress that retribution will not be tolerated. Organizations that are serious about fraud prevention must make it easy for employees and managers to come forward and must reward (not punish) them for doing so.

Fraud Detection

Suppose that in a fraud perpetrated by a bank teller, the following amounts were taken on the noted dates:

4-1	$10	5-8	$20	6-5	$50	7-16	$600
4-4	$20	5-9	$30	6-9	$30	7-23	$600
4-7	$20	5-12	$30	6-10	$40	8-4	$20
4-9	$20	5-13	$30	6-11	$30	8-8	$20
4-10	$20	5-14	$30	6-12	$50	8-11	$30
4-14	$40	5-15	$30	6-13	$50	8-14	$30
4-16	$30	5-16	$40	6-16	$50	8-19	$20
4-22	$30	5-19	$40	6-17	$50	8-22	$40
4-23	$30	5-20	$40	6-18	$30	8-26	$400
4-24	$30	5-21	$40	6-20	$70	8-27	$600
4-25	$30	5-22	$20	6-23	$100	8-28	$400
4-28	$30	5-27	$30	6-24	$200	9-2	$400
4-29	$30	5-28	$40	6-25	$400	9-5	$100
4-30	$30	5-29	$40	6-26	$600	9-12	$100
5-1	$20	5-30	$50	7-8	$400	9-15	$200
5-5	$30	6-2	$40	7-9	$700	9-16	$400
5-6	$30	6-3	$50	7-14	$400		
5-7	$20	6-4	$50	7-15	$600		

When caught, the teller made the following statement: "I can't believe I was able to do this for so long without anyone ever suspecting a thing, especially when I began taking larger and larger amounts."

As you can see, this fraud started very small, with the teller stealing larger and larger amounts as it continued. When he wasn't caught, the perpetrator's confidence in his scheme increased, and he became greedy. In fact, you will note that, after July 23, there is a two-week period where the theft stopped. The reason why this pause occurred? Auditors came to the branch where he worked. You will also notice that once the auditors left, the teller resumed embezzling but only stole small amounts. That is, for a short time, he tested the system to make sure the auditors hadn't detected him or put processes in place that would reveal his theft. Once he again had confidence that he wouldn't be caught, the amounts stolen escalated into hundreds of dollars per day.

Although the amounts involved in our example are small, the pattern is all too typical. Most frauds start small and, if not detected, continue to get larger and larger. Events that scare or threaten the perpetrator result in discontinuance of the theft, which is then resumed when the threats pass. Because those that commit fraud increase the amounts they steal, in most cases, amounts taken just before discovery far exceed those taken earlier. In one case, the amounts taken *quadrupled* every month during the period of the fraud! Indeed, small frauds are just large frauds that got caught early. And, in cases where top management or owners are perpetrating the fraud, prevention is difficult, so early detection is critical. Consider the following fraud:

> *The president of a New Hampshire temporary service company intentionally misclassified employees as independent contractors rather than as employees of his company. The misclassification enabled him to avoid paying $211,201 in payroll taxes over a three-year period. In addition, he provided an insurance company with false information on the number of people he actually employed, thereby avoiding $426,463 in workers' compensation premiums.*[5]

When fraud is committed by owners of small organizations, who perform the accounting tasks themselves, as in this case, fraud is not preventable. If owners commit fraud, there is nothing anyone can do to stop them. Rather, the emphasis in these situations must be on detecting the fraud.

Because most frauds increase dramatically over time, it is extremely important that frauds, when they occur, be detected early. Detection, of course, involves steps and actions taken to uncover a fraud. It does not include investigations taken to determine motives, extent, method of embezzlement, or other elements of the theft. As you will discover in the next chapter, fraud is unlike other crimes in which the occurrence of the crime is easily recognized. Because fraud is rarely obvious, one of the most difficult tasks is determining whether one has actually occurred.

Detection usually begins when employees, managers, or victims notice "red flags," symptoms such as disturbing trends in numbers, or missing assets that indicate something is awry. Unfortunately, red flags don't always mean that fraud is occurring. There are two primary ways to detect fraud: (1) by chance and (2) by proactively searching for and encouraging early recognition of symptoms. In the past, most frauds were detected by accident. Unfortunately, by the time detection occurred, the frauds had been going on for some time and the losses were large. In most cases, individuals in the victim organizations suspected that fraud was occurring but did not come forward because they weren't sure, didn't want to wrongly accuse someone, didn't know how to report the fraud, or were fearful of being branded a whistle-blower.

In recent years, organizations have implemented a number of initiatives to better detect fraud. Probably the most common detection initiative has been hotlines whereby employees, co-workers, and others can phone in anonymous tips. Some hotlines are maintained within the company, and others are outsourced to independent organizations. (The Association of

Certified Fraud Examiners, for example, provides a fee-based hotline service.) Organizations that have installed hotlines now detect many frauds that would previously have gone undetected, but they also pay a price for doing so. Not surprisingly, many calls do not involve fraud at all. Some are hoaxes; some are motivated by grudges, anger, or a desire to do harm to an organization or individual; and some are about reasonable red flags that are caused by factors other than fraud.

Except for hotlines, organizations have only recently undertaken other serious proactive detection efforts. Advances in technology now allow organizations to analyze and mine databases to search for red flags. Banks, for example, use software that identifies suspected kiting. These programs draw the bank's attention to customers who have high volumes of bank transactions in short periods of time. Insurance companies use programs that examine claims within a short time after purchasing insurance. Some programs systematically identify the kinds of frauds that may be occurring by cataloging the various symptoms those frauds generate, and then building real-time queries into their computer systems to search for these symptoms. Fraud-detection research, mostly using computer search techniques, is now being conducted by academics and other investigators. Anyone who is seriously interested in understanding and fighting fraud should follow this research.[6]

Fraud Investigation

Mark is the CEO of McDonald's Incorporated, and his wife Jane is a partner in the CPA firm of Watkiss and McCloy. After a hard day at work, they met at a local restaurant for dinner. Mark told Jane about a curious incident that happened at work and showed her the anonymous note he got: "You had better look into the relationship between John Beasley (the manager of the purchasing department) and the Brigadeer Company (a supplier) because something fishy is going on." He had no idea who sent him the note and wasn't sure what to do about it. He told Jane that he was concerned about possible collusion and thought he ought to pursue the "lead." Jane couldn't believe what she was hearing. "What a coincidence," she mused. "Something very similar happened to me today." She described how a junior auditor approached her, confiding in her that he was concerned that a client's sales were overstated. The auditor explained that he had found some sales contracts without support (normally, significant documentation supported the contracts), all signed at the end of the accounting period. He was concerned that the client was artificially inflating revenues to improve the company's financial performance.

Both situations need to be investigated. If Mark doesn't investigate the anonymous tip, he may never uncover a possible kickback fraud and inflated purchasing costs for the company. Likewise, Jane needs to follow up on the client's potential revenue problem.

There are at least three reasons why auditors must determine whether clients are overstating revenues. First, the company's shareholders could face significant losses. Second, the auditors' failure to discover the overstatement can expose them to legal action (and consequent losses). Finally, and perhaps most important of all, an overstatement of revenues exposes management's integrity to such serious doubt that the firm can become "unauditable."

Both of these situations create a "predication of fraud." *Predication* refers to circumstances that, taken as a whole, would lead a reasonable, prudent professional to believe a fraud has occurred, is occurring, or will occur. Fraud investigations should not be conducted without predication. A specific allegation of fraud against another party is not necessary, but there must be some reasonable basis for concern that fraud may be occurring. Once predication is present, as in these cases, an investigation is usually undertaken to determine whether or not fraud is occurring, as well as the who, why, how, when, and where elements of the fraud. The purpose of an investigation is to find the truth—to determine whether the symptoms actually represent fraud or whether they represent unintentional errors or other factors. Fraud investigation is a complex and sensitive matter. If investigations are not properly conducted, the reputations of innocent individuals can be irreparably injured, guilty parties can go undetected and be free to repeat the act, and the offended entity may not have information to use in preventing and detecting similar incidents or in recovering damages.

Approaches to Fraud Investigation

Investigations must have management's approval. Because they can be quite expensive, investigations should be pursued only when there is reason to believe that fraud has occurred (when "predication" is present). Investigative approaches vary, although most investigators rely heavily on interviews.

Fraud investigations can be classified by the types of evidence produced or by the elements of fraud. Using the first approach, the *evidence square* below shows the four classifications of evidence:

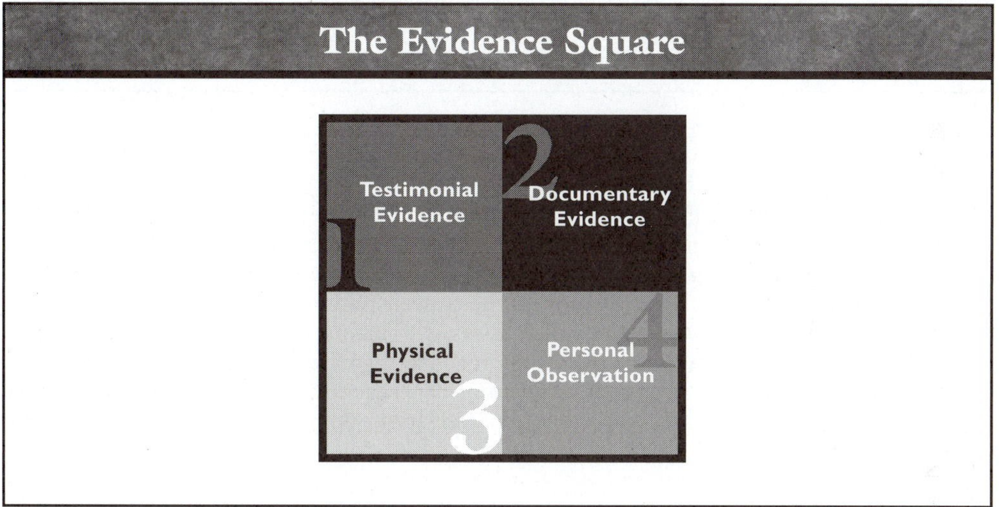

The four types of evidence that can be collected in fraud investigations are as follows:

1. *Testimonial evidence,* which is gathered from individuals. Specific investigative techniques used to gather testimonial evidence include interviewing, interrogation, and honesty tests.
2. *Documentary evidence,* which is gathered from paper, computers, and other written or printed sources. Some of the most common techniques for gathering this evidence include document examination, public records searches, audits, computer searches, net worth calculations, and financial statement analysis.
3. *Physical evidence* includes fingerprints, tire marks, weapons, stolen property, identification numbers or marks on stolen objects, and other tangible evidence that can be associated with the act. The gathering of physical evidence often involves forensic analysis by experts.
4. *Personal observation* involves evidence that is collected by the investigators themselves, including *invigilation,* surveillance, and covert operations, among others.

Many professionals prefer to classify investigative approaches according to the three elements of fraud, as shown in the triangle on the next page.

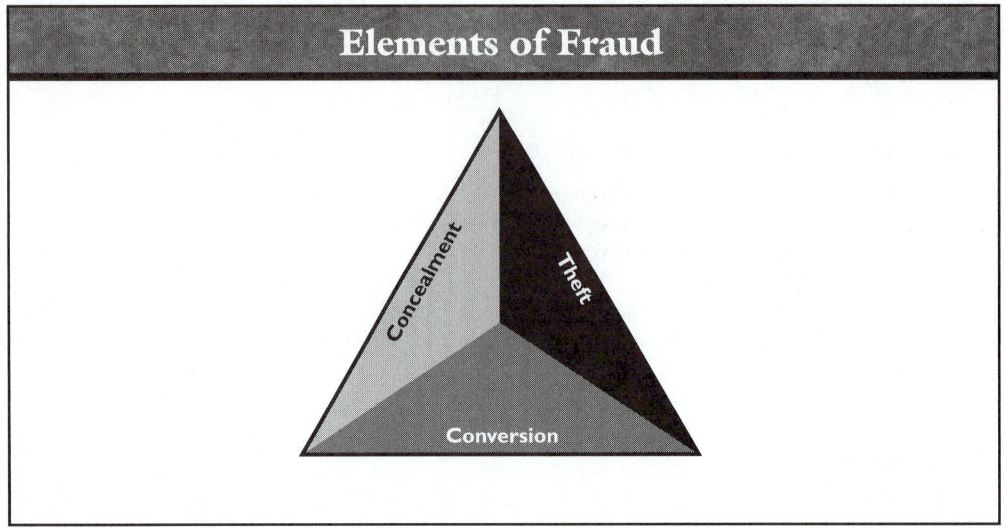

Investigation of the theft involves efforts to catch the perpetrator(s) in the act itself and information-gathering efforts. Investigation of the concealment focuses on records, documents, computer programs and servers, and other places where perpetrators might try to conceal or hide their deceit. Investigation of the conversion involves searching out the ways in which perpetrators have spent the stolen assets. A fourth set of investigative techniques, *inquiry methods,* has to do with the overall approach as it applies to all these elements. Thus, this approach to classifying investigative techniques is called the fraud triangle plus inquiry approach. In Chapter 7, we will discuss the investigation methods that fall in each of these four categories.

Conducting a Fraud Investigation

For now, it is important to know that fraud investigators need some way to coordinate the investigation. Some investigations are very large and conducting investigative steps in the wrong order or doing them inappropriately can lead to a failed investigation and other problems. In fact, it is extremely important that you understand the significant risks that investigators face.

You must also remember that investigating a fraud is a traumatic experience for everyone involved, including the perpetrators. As we stated previously, most fraud perpetrators are first-time offenders who have pristine reputations at work, and in their community, family, and church. Sometimes, admitting that they are being investigated for fraud or have committed fraud is more than they can take. Consider the following obituary:

> *Memorial services for John Jones will be held Thursday, May 5, 19XX, at the Springer-Wilson funeral home. John was 35 at the time of his death. He was preceded in death by his mother, Jane Jones, and a younger brother, Tom Jones. John is survived by his wife, Rebecca, and four children ages 9, 7, 6, and 4. He is also survived by three brothers, a sister, and his father. In lieu of flowers, please make contributions to the Improvement Memorial Fund for Children.*

This is the obituary of a person who embezzled $650,000 from his employer. Over a seven-year period, he embezzled nearly half of all cash received from customers. When the company finally determined that he was stealing, they called and asked him to meet with the company's lawyers the next morning. John did two things that night after receiving the telephone call. He called his attorney and told her that he had been stealing from his employer for seven years and asked her to represent him at the meeting with the company's attorneys the next morning. Then, a couple of hours later, he drove into some nearby mountains and committed suicide, a tragic demonstration of why investigations *must* be conducted carefully.

Maintaining high ethics in conducting investigations is also important. As a minimum, investigations of fraud must proceed as follows:

1. They must be undertaken only to "establish the truth of a matter under question."
2. The individuals who conduct the investigation must be experienced and objective. If such individuals do not exercise care in choosing words to describe the incident or do not maintain a neutral perspective, their objectivity immediately becomes suspect in the eyes of management and employees. Investigators should never jump to conclusions.
3. Any hypothesis investigators have about whether or not someone committed fraud should be closely guarded when discussing the progress of an investigation with others. Even though good investigators often form preliminary opinions or impressions, they must objectively weigh every bit of information against known facts and evidence and must always protect the confidentiality of the investigation.
4. Investigators must ensure that those who have a need to know (for example, management) are kept apprised of investigation activities and agree to the investigation and techniques employed.
5. Good investigators must ensure that all information collected during an inquiry is independently corroborated and determined to be factually correct. Failure to corroborate evidence is a common mistake of inexperienced investigators.
6. Investigators must exercise care to avoid questionable investigative techniques. Experienced investigators make sure that the techniques used are scientifically and legally sound and fair. Thoroughness and dogged tenacity, not questionable techniques, lead to successful conclusions.
7. Investigators must report all facts fairly and objectively. Communications throughout the term of an investigation, from preliminary stage to final report, should be carefully controlled to avoid obscuring facts and opinions. Communications, including investigative reports, must not only include information obtained that points to guilt, but must also include facts and information that may exonerate. Ignoring and failing to document information is a serious investigative flaw, with potential for serious consequences.

Legal Action

One of the major decisions a company, stockholders, and others must make when fraud is committed is what kind of follow-up action should be taken. Why the fraud occurred should always be determined, and controls or other measures to prevent or deter its reoccurrence should be implemented. The bigger and often troubling question that must then be addressed is what legal action should be taken with respect to the perpetrators.

Most organizations and other victims of fraud usually make one of three choices: (1) take no legal action; (2) pursue civil remedies; and/or (3) pursue criminal action against the perpetrators, which is sometimes done for them by law enforcement agencies. Although we addressed civil and criminal law in Chapter 1 and will discuss legal action in future chapters, it is appropriate to briefly review some of the pros and cons of each alternative here.

Research shows that legal action is taken against perpetrators in less than half of all fraud cases.[7] Management often wants only to get the fraud behind it as quickly as possible. They understand that pursuing legal action is expensive, time-consuming, sometimes embarrassing, and is often *considered* an unproductive use of time. Thus, management most often terminates perpetrators, but sometimes it doesn't even go that far. Unfortunately, when organizations do not pursue legal action, the word spreads quickly that "nothing serious will happen if you steal from the company." Employees who receive this message are more likely to steal than are employees who understand that punishment "to the letter of the law" will follow for all dishonest acts. When one Fortune 500 company changed its stance on fraud from "the CEO is to be informed when someone is prosecuted for fraud" to "the CEO is to be informed when someone who commits fraud is not prosecuted," the number of frauds in the company decreased significantly.

Civil Action

As you learned in Chapter 1, the purpose of a civil action is to recover money or other assets from the perpetrators and others associated with the fraud. Civil actions are quite rare in cases of employee fraud (because perpetrators have usually spent the money), but are much more common when frauds involve other organizations. Vendors who pay kickbacks to company employees often find themselves the target of civil actions by victim companies, especially if losses are high. Likewise, stockholders and creditors who suffer losses from management fraud almost always sue not only the perpetrators, but usually the auditors and others associated with the company as well. The plaintiff's lawyers are usually more than willing to represent shareholders in a class-action, contingent fee lawsuit.[8]

Criminal Action

Criminal action can only be brought by law enforcement or statutory agencies. Organizations that decide to pursue criminal action against perpetrators must work with local, state, or federal agencies to get their employees or other perpetrators prosecuted. As we noted in Chapter 1, criminal penalties involve fines, prison terms, or both. Perpetrators may be required to enter into restitution agreements to pay back stolen funds over a period of time. Pursuing criminal penalties for fraud is becoming more and more common. Corporate executives who commit fraud are often given 10-year jail sentences and are ordered to pay fines equal to the amounts they embezzled. However, it is much more difficult to get a criminal conviction than it is to get a judgment in a civil case. Whereas only a preponderance of the evidence (more than 50%) is necessary to win a civil case, convictions are only successful if there is proof "beyond a reasonable doubt" that the perpetrator "intentionally" stole money or other assets.

Summary

Most organizations spend most of their fraud-fighting dollars investigating frauds once predication is present. Investigation is only one of four major activities related to fraud. Organizations that do not work proactively at fraud prevention and detection can find themselves frequently targets of fraud schemes, and the scams come at a greater cost. In addition, even when organizations successfully investigate fraud, they often merely terminate perpetrators rather than seek legal action because termination is "the easy way out." Unfortunately, organizations that only terminate or do not sanction perpetrators also experience more fraud than organizations who enforce strict prosecution policies. Perpetrators are often first-time offenders and may be respected employees, clients, vendors, or customers. If they are terminated, they usually do not tell even their families the reason for their termination.

Because they do not suffer the humiliation that ensues when friends, family members, and other loved ones become aware of their crime, perpetrators often undertake fraudulent activities again when opportunities present themselves.

Organizations must decide how much fraud they are willing to tolerate. Although it is difficult to get accurate statistics, research indicates that money spent on proactive prevention and detection and rigorous, legal follow-up tends to reduce future occurrences of fraud.[9] One Fortune 500 company with approximately $25 million of known fraud annually decided to take proactive steps to reduce fraud. The company worked hard on prevention, including making a video that was shown periodically to train employees in fraud awareness (as well as awareness training in other undesirable activities, such as substance abuse, safety violations, and discrimination). The company also provided employees with cards that specified who they should contact if they saw any of these problems. A proactive code of conduct was developed, and every employee signed it each year. It also focused on detection methods, including computer search techniques and a fraud hotline. Finally, it developed a comprehensive fraud policy specifying who and how potential frauds would be investigated and what actions would be taken against fraud perpetrators. Its efforts paid large dividends, especially given the multiplier effect we discussed in Chapter 1. In only a couple of years, known frauds in the organization totaled less than $1 million annually.

New Terms

Autocratic management: Management conducted by a few key people who do not accept advice or participation from other employees.

Collusion: Fraud perpetrated by two or more employees or others, each of whose job responsibilities is necessary to complete the fraud.

Control environment: The actions, policies, and procedures that reflect the overall attitudes of top management, the directors, and the owners about control and its importance to the entity.

Documentary evidence: Evidence gathered from paper, documents, computer records, and other written, printed, or electronic sources.

Embezzlement: Theft or fraudulent appropriation of money through deception; often used interchangeably with the term fraud.

Evidence square: A categorization of fraud investigative procedures that includes testimonial evidence, documentary evidence, physical evidence, and personal observation.

Independent checks: Procedures for verifying and monitoring other controls.

Inherent risks: A business's susceptibility to fraud, assuming that appropriate controls are not in place.

Internal control structure: Specific policies and procedures designed to provide management with reasonable assurance that the goals and objectives it believes important to the entity will be met.

Invigilation: Imposing strict temporary controls on an activity so that, during the observation period, fraud is virtually impossible. Involves keeping detailed records before, during, and after the invigilation period and comparing suspicious activity during the three periods to obtain evidence about whether fraud is occurring.

Kickback fraud: Fraud perpetrated by an employee and the employee's vendor or customer. Usually involves the employee buying goods or services from the vendor at an overstated price or giving the customer a lower-than-normal price, and in return the vendor or customer pays the employee a "kickback."

Kiting: Fraud that conceals cash shortages by (1) transferring funds from one bank to another and (2) recording the receipt on or before the balance sheet date and the disbursement after the balance sheet date.

Participative management: Management style that expects everyone in the organization to take ownership and responsibility for their conduct and responsibilities and that allows input into decisions.

Personal observation evidence: Evidence that is sensed (seen, heard, felt, etc.) by investigators.

Physical evidence: Evidence of a tangible nature—includes fingerprints, tire marks, weapons, stolen property, identification numbers or marks on stolen objects, and so on.

Predication: Circumstances that, taken as a whole, would lead a reasonable, prudent professional to believe that a fraud has occurred, is occurring, or will occur.

Testimonial evidence: Evidence based on querying techniques, such as interviewing, interrogation, and honesty testing.

Questions and Cases

Discussion Questions

1. Why is fraud prevention so important?
2. Preventing fraud is the most cost-effective way to reduce losses from fraud. Why is fraud prevention more cost-effective than fraud detection or investigation?
3. How does building a culture of honesty and integrity help to reduce the possibility of fraud?
4. How does a company assess and minimize its risk of fraud?
5. Why is early detection of fraud important?
6. Why is early recognition of fraud symptoms important?
7. Why is it important to conduct a thorough investigation when fraud is suspected?
8. Predication refers to circumstances that would lead a reasonable professional to believe that fraud has occurred. Why should you not conduct a fraud investigation without predication?
9. Describe the evidence square.
10. How is the evidence square useful in thinking about fraud investigation?
11. For each of the following, identify whether the evidence would be classified as testimonial evidence, documentary evidence, physical evidence, or personal observation.
    a. Surveillance
    b. Tire marks
    c. Honesty test
    d. Interview
    e. A computer hard drive
    f. A financial statement analysis
    g. Invigilation
    h. A paper report
    i. Identification numbers on vehicles
    j. Audit of financial statements
    k. Check stubs
    l. Fingerprints
    m. Background checks
    n. Interview
12. What are some of the legal actions that can be pursued after a fraud has been discovered?

True/False

1. Once fraud has been committed, there are no winners.
2. Fraud prevention involves two fundamental activities: (1) a hotline for tips and (2) assessing the risk of fraud and developing concrete responses to minimize risk and to eliminate opportunities for fraud.
3. Developing a positive work environment is of little importance in creating a culture of honesty.
4. No matter how well developed an organization's culture of honesty and integrity, most organizations will still have some fraud.

5. Research has shown that employees and managers, not auditors, detect most frauds.
6. Organizations that want to prevent fraud must make it easy for employees and others to report suspicious activities.
7. If a perpetrator is not caught, his confidence in the scheme will decrease and he will become less and less greedy.
8. Once predication is present, an investigation is usually undertaken to determine whether or not fraud is actually occurring.
9. Most investigators rely heavily on interviews to obtain the truth.
10. Physical evidence includes evidence gathered from paper, computers, and other written documents.
11. The fraud triangle plus inquiry approach is an effective way to categorize investigative techniques.
12. Legal action taken by an organization can affect the probability of whether fraud will reoccur.
13. Investigating fraud is the most cost-effective way to reduce fraud losses.
14. Fraud prevention includes taking steps to create and maintain a culture of honesty and integrity.
15. Effective hiring policies that discriminate between marginal and highly ethical individuals contribute to an organization's success in preventing fraud.
16. Expectations about punishment must be communicated randomly among work groups if fraud is to be prevented.
17. Frauds typically start large and get smaller as perpetrators try to conceal their theft.
18. Fraud is difficult to detect because some fraud symptoms often cannot be differentiated from factors such as unintentional errors.
19. The three elements of the fraud triangle by which the investigative techniques are often classified are (1) the theft, (2) concealment efforts, and (3) conversion methods.
20. Organizations often want to avoid embarrassment and expense, so they terminate perpetrators without having them prosecuted further.
21. Criminal conviction is much more difficult to achieve than a civil judgment because there must be proof "beyond a reasonable doubt" that the perpetrator intentionally stole assets.

Multiple Choice

1. The most effective way to reduce losses from fraud is by:
   a. Detecting fraud early
   b. Implementing proactive fraud detection programs
   c. Preventing fraud from occurring
   d. Severely punishing perpetrators
2. To successfully prevent fraud, an organization must:
   a. Identify internal control weaknesses
   b. Explicitly consider fraud risks
   c. Take proactive steps to create the right kind of environment
   d. All of the above

3. The best way for management to model appropriate behavior is to:
    a. Enforce a strict code of ethics
    b. Set an example of appropriate behavior
    c. Train employees about appropriate behavior
    d. Make employees read and sign a code of conduct
4. Which of the following is *not* a proactive way for a company to eliminate fraud opportunities?
    a. Severely punishing fraud perpetrators
    b. Assessing risks
    c. Implementing appropriate preventive and detective controls
    d. Creating widespread monitoring of employees
5. Most frauds start small and:
    a. If not detected, continue to get larger
    b. Usually decrease in amount
    c. Remain steady and consistent
    d. None of the above
6. Which type of fraud is usually most difficult to prevent?
    a. Investment scams
    b. Fraud committed by a small business owner
    c. Employee fraud
    d. Customer fraud
7. ___________ refers to the circumstances, taken as a whole, that would lead a reasonable, prudent professional to believe fraud has occurred, is occurring, or will occur.
    a. Circumstantial evidence
    b. Investigation
    c. Service of process
    d. Predication
8. An evidence classification scheme that includes testimonial evidence, documentary evidence, physical evidence, and personal observation is referred to as the:
    a. Investigative square of evidence
    b. Investigation square
    c. Evidence square
    d. Fraud triangle plus inquiry approach
9. An evidence classification scheme that includes the theft, concealment, conversion, and inquiry methods is referred to as the:
    a. Investigative square
    b. Evidence square
    c. Fraud triangle plus inquiry approach
    d. Investigative square of evidence
10. Usually, for everyone involved—especially victims—the investigation of fraud is very:
    a. Pleasant and relaxing
    b. Educational
    c. Exciting
    d. Traumatic and difficult

11. To prevent fraud from reoccurring, most organizations and other fraud victims should:
    a. Take no legal action
    b. Pursue civil remedies
    c. Pursue criminal remedies
    d. Pursue either civil or criminal action
12. All of the following are ways to create a culture of honesty and integrity *except*:
    a. Creating a positive work environment
    b. Hiring the right kind of employees
    c. Having top management model appropriate behavior
    d. Eliminating opportunities for fraud
13. The "tone at the top" when related to fraud refers to management's attitude about:
    a. Office parties
    b. Fraud prosecution
    c. Employee absenteeism
    d. How it models and labels appropriate behavior
14. Research shows that fraud occurs less frequently when employees feel:
    a. Abused by management
    b. Threatened
    c. Challenged with unreasonable performance goals
    d. Ownership in the organization
15. Opportunities to commit fraud can be eliminated by identifying sources of fraud, implementing controls, and through independent checks. One other effective way of eliminating opportunities is
    a. Teaching employees to monitor and report fraud
    b. Terminating and punishing employees who commit fraud
    c. Failing to terminate or punish employees who commit fraud
    d. Identifying red flags—symptoms of fraud.
16. Drawbacks to establishing a hotline for employees to report fraud include all of the following *except:*
    a. Expense
    b. Many incidents reported are hoaxes motivated by grudges
    c. Fraud symptoms reported are caused by non-fraud factors
    d. This method for finding fraud is outdated
17. "Predication of fraud" is defined as:
    a. Reasonable belief that fraud has occurred
    b. Irrefutable evidence that fraud has been committed
    c. Motivation for committing fraud
    d. Punishment of fraud perpetrators
18. Which of the four types of evidence includes interrogation and honesty testing?
    a. Testimonial
    b. Documentary
    c. Physical
    d. Personal observation

19. The three elements of fraud are:
    a. Theft, rationalization, and opportunity
    b. Pressure, opportunity, and conversion
    c. Theft, concealment, and conversion
    d. Theft, pressure, and opportunity
20. Most often victims of fraud do not take legal action against perpetrators. This is because legal action can be:
    a. Unproductive
    b. Embarrassing
    c. Expensive
    d. All of the above
21. Arguments for taking legal action against perpetrators of fraud include:
    a. Huge cash settlements from prosecuting fraud are an excellent source of revenue
    b. Legal action usually results in positive publicity for the company
    c. Prosecution keeps lawyers busy
    d. Prosecution discourages reoccurrence of fraud

Short Cases

Case 1. You are a consultant for Long Range Builders, a company that specializes in the mass production of wood trusses. Their trusses are used in the building of houses throughout the United States, Canada, and Mexico. As you implement a fraud prevention program, you intend to stress the importance of creating a company culture of honesty and integrity.

1. What critical elements are key factors in creating an ethical culture?
2. How would you implement these elements in your company?

Case 2. You are the fraud expert for a large Fortune 500 company located in Miami, Florida. In a recent meeting with the executive committee, one officer explains that the fraud prevention program, which teaches managers and employees how to detect and report fraud, costs the company $150,000 a year. He then argues that it is a waste of time and money for the company to educate employees and managers about fraud. "Is it not the responsibility of the auditors to detect fraud?" he questions. The president asks you to explain why managers and employees should be educated in the detection of fraud.

1. What would you tell the committee about the importance of training managers and employees in fraud detection?
2. The president next asks you about effective ways to involve employees and managers in the prevention and detection of fraud. What would you tell her?

Case 3. You recently got an MBA, and you now work for Roosevelt Power Plant. Your boss, Mr. Jones, recently described to you a large fraud that has recently taken place in the company. He wants to know what actions you think should be taken to ensure that fraud of this magnitude does not occur again. After analyzing company procedures, you present your recommendations to Mr. Jones. He is puzzled by one item: "Create a culture of honesty and create a positive work environment for employees." He wants to know how a positive work environment could possibly prevent or detect fraud.

1. How would you answer Mr. Jones?
2. What would you tell him about negative work environments and fraud?

Case 4. It is important to hire employees who are honest and who have a well-developed personal code of ethics. Derek Bok, former law professor and president of Harvard University, has suggested that colleges and universities have a special obligation to train students to be more thoughtful and perceptive about moral and ethical issues.[10] Others have concluded that it is not possible to "teach" ethics. What do you think? Can ethics be taught? If you agree that colleges and universities can teach ethics, how might the ethical dimensions of business be taught to students?

Case 5. In 2001, the country of Peru was thrown into political turmoil as its president, Alberto Fujimori, was accused of conspiring with the head of the national army to accept bribes and steal money from the government. As a result, Fujimori fled the country to avoid impeachment and prosecution. Fujimori had been elected 10 years earlier based on his promises to lower inflation and combat terrorism. He was not, however, elected for his honesty. Indeed, many people expressed the thought, "All of our presidents steal from us, but he steals the least." What could the Peruvian people have done to avoid the frauds committed by President Fujimori?

Extensive Case

Case 6. Peter Jones, a senior accountant, and Mary Miller, a junior accountant, are the only accountants for XYZ Company, a medium-size business. Peter has been with the company for over four years and is responsible for the purchasing department. Mary has worked for the company for a little over five years, and has neither applied for a vacation nor taken any days off in the last three years. She is responsible for cash receipts and disbursements. She also collects the cash from the register, counts it and matches it with receipts, records daily receipts, and then puts the money in the safe. Once a week she takes the paperwork to her supervisor, Susan Lowe, who checks it. Mary recently resigned from the company. At the time of her resignation, Peter was asked to take over Mary's responsibilities while the company looked for a replacement. Peter soon realized that accounting records had been manipulated and funds have been embezzled. Investigations reveal that approximately $30,000 has been stolen.

1. What factors do you think allowed this fraud?
2. How could this fraud have been avoided?

Internet Assignments

1. Visit the web site of the National White Collar Crime Center—http://www.nw3c.com. This site is funded through a grant from the Department of Justice. Its purpose is to assist federal law enforcement agencies in the investigation and prevention of white-collar crime. The Center also has a college internship program. Find the research topics on their web page, read the study on health care fraud, and answer the following questions:
    1. What group is the largest perpetrator of health care fraud?
    2. What is health care fraud?
    3. What are the current losses and why are they expected to double?
    4. Why is Medicare the largest target of fraudulent acts?

2. Go to http://www.fraud.org/ and learn about the National Fraud Information Center (NFIC). What do they do, and specifically, how do they make it easy for people to report fraud?

Debate

Fred is a friend of yours and works with you at the same company. He is a well-respected and trusted employee. He has five young children and is a leader in his community. You have discovered that Fred has embezzled $3,000 over a period of several years. Although this is not much money for your company, you suspect that if you don't report him, the problem may worsen. On the other hand, he has young children, and he has done so much good in the company and the community. If you report him, he may go to prison because your company has an aggressive fraud-prosecution policy. Should you report him for such a small amount of money?

End Notes

1. Almost every year, KPMG Forensic and Investigative Services conducts a fraud survey. These surveys show that almost all companies surveyed have major frauds. For information about the surveys, contact Michael D. Carey, NY (212-872-6825).
2. For example, read the research of the Social and Moral Research Group, University of Maryland (http://www.education.umd.edu/Depts/EDHD/faculty/killen/SMDRG).
3. See, for example, *Theory O: Creating an Ownership Style of Management,* discussed at http://www.nceo.org/pubs/theoryo.html.
4. See, for example, *2002 Report to the Nation: Occupational Fraud and Abuse,* Association of Certified Fraud Examiners, Austin, Texas, 2002.
5. "Scheme to Save Over $637,000 Ends in Conviction," http://www.ifb.org/FFDOCS/ff1096.htm#scheme.
6. See, for example, "Conducting a Pro-Active Fraud Audit," W. Steve Albrecht, C. C. Albrecht, and J. G. Dunn, *Journal of Forensic Accounting,* Volume II, No. 2, Dec. 2001, pp. 203–218.
7. See, for example, *Deterring Fraud: The Internal Auditor's Perspective,* W. Steve Albrecht, K. Howe, and M. Romney, The Institute of Internal Auditors, Altamonte Spring, Florida, 1984.
8. Class-action lawsuits are permitted under federal law and some state rules of court procedure in the United States. In a class-action suit, a relatively small number of aggrieved plaintiffs with small individual claims can bring suit for large damages in the name of an extended class. After a fraud, for example, 40 bondholders who lost $40,000 might decide to sue, and they can sue on behalf of the entire class of bondholders for all their alleged losses (say $50 million). Lawyers are more than happy to take such suits on a contingency fee basis (a percentage of the judgment, if any).
9. See, for Example, "The Three Factors of Fraud," W. Steve Albrecht and G. Wernz, *Security Management,* July 1993, pp. 95–97.
10. Bok, Derek, *Beyond the Ivory Tower: Social Responsibility of the Modern University,* Harvard University Press, Cambridge, Mass., p. 123, 1982.

PART TWO

FRAUD PREVENTION

CHAPTER FOUR

Preventing Fraud

After studying this chapter, you should be able to:

1. Help create a culture of honesty, openness, and assistance.
2. Eliminate opportunities for fraud.
3. Understand the importance of good internal controls.
4. Discourage collusion between employees and outside parties.
5. Inform outside vendors of company policies.
6. Understand how to monitor employees.
7. Provide a response line for anonymous tips.
8. Conduct proactive fraud auditing.
9. Create an effective organization to minimize fraud.

Margaret worked for First National Bank, and for 34 years, she was an honest and trusted employee, but in the three years prior to her retirement, she embezzled over $600,000. Discovered after she retired, once the fraud was known, Margaret suffered severe consequences. The bank took possession of her home and her retirement account. Her husband, who supposedly knew nothing of her fraud, contributed the proceeds of his retirement account to the bank. The bank took possession of virtually every asset the couple owned. Margaret still owes the bank over $200,000 and must make regular payments toward meeting the agreement. She was prosecuted and incarcerated for one year. Her friends, her children, and her grandchildren all know that their grandmother is a convicted felon. When Margaret was released from prison, she was ordered to seek active employment so she could start making restitution payments. Failure to make regular payments is a violation of her parole, and would return her to prison. Margaret and her husband endured the humiliation of seeing her crime covered extensively in the local newspaper. As they were required to do, the bank submitted a criminal referral form to the Office of the Controller of the Currency (OCC), and the OCC turned over a copy of it to the IRS. The IRS levied fines, penalties, interest, and back taxes on Margaret because of the over $600,000 in income that she failed to report on her tax returns. (In subsequent negotiations, the portion she paid back by turning over her assets was determined to be a nontaxable loan.) Margaret will never be able to get a job, buy life or car insurance, or do many things we take for granted without informing people that she is a convicted felon. Her life and reputation, and the life and reputation of her family, will never be the same.

There are no winners in fraud. At best, a person committing fraud enjoys a higher lifestyle for a while. In the end, however, their crime costs them dearly in anguish and hardship. The victims of fraud, the companies and people from whom funds are stolen, also lose. Margaret's bank saw its name splashed across the front pages of the local newspapers. Customers terminated business relationships with the bank for fear that "if the bank can't safeguard funds, then my money is not safe there." And the bank stands to lose the money that Margaret still owes them (over $200,000), plus all the interest, because it is unlikely that Margaret will be able to pay back the remaining amount. Jobs that are available to convicted felons don't pay much. And this doesn't include the costs incurred by the bank for the hundreds of hours spent investigating, preparing for the trial, and then testifying.

Clearly, fraud prevention is where the big savings are. When there is no fraud, there are no detection or investigation costs. The organization's reputation doesn't take a hit, and employee morale doesn't suffer. Management doesn't have to make tough termination and prosecution decisions. Valuable work time can be put to productive uses—like *making* money.

Not Everyone Is Honest

Remember this statement. It is a sad fact, but a true one. Would that most people were so honest that fraud simply wasn't an issue and that organizations would not have to be vigilant in closing opportunities for fraud or have to give so much thought to their culture. Unfortunately, that is not the case. More people than we like to admit are capable of committing fraud. And when placed in an environment of low integrity, poor controls, loose accountability, or high pressure, such people become increasingly dishonest. Examples abound where workers adopted the dishonest practices of top management. In the famous Equity Funding case, management created fictitious policyholders and wrote insurance policies on them.[1] The fraudulent policies were then sold to other insurance companies or reinsurers. Not surprisingly, an employee of the company then thought to himself, "I might as well get in on the action. It doesn't make sense that all these fake insurance policies are written and no one ever dies." So he caused a few of the fictitious people to "die" and collected the death proceeds.

Organizations have a choice. They can create either a low-fraud environment or a high-fraud one. In this chapter, we identify factors in low-fraud environments that prevent fraud. We look at ways to create a culture of honesty, openness, and assistance—key attributes in low-fraud environments. We then see how organizations can eliminate opportunities to commit fraud and create expectations that fraud will be punished. And lastly, we show how to combine fraud prevention, detection, and investigation efforts to provide comprehensive fraud-fighting programs to organizations.

Creating a Culture of Honesty, Openness, and Assistance

Four factors in fraud prevention are crucial in creating a culture of honesty, openness, and assistance. These factors are: (1) hiring honest people and training them in fraud awareness; (2) creating a positive work environment; (3) disseminating a well-understood and respected code of conduct or ethics; and (4) providing employee assistance programs (EAPs).

Hiring Honest People and Training Them in Fraud Awareness

Effectively screening applicants so that only honest employees are hired is, of course, very important. As stated earlier in this book, studies indicate that nearly 31% of Americans are dishonest, 30% are situationally honest, and only 40% are honest all the time.[2] Studies also show that 25% of all frauds are committed by employees who have worked for the company three years or less. Individuals with gambling, financial, drug, or past criminal problems should not be hired, or, at least, if hired, the adverse information about their backgrounds should be known.

With today's stringent privacy laws, it is essential that companies develop and use good employee screening policies. Even in highly controlled environments, dishonest employees with severe pressures do commit fraud.

Because of privacy laws, organizations must be creative in their hiring processes. Many banks, for example, now use credit report companies or other methods to determine whether prospective employees and customers have had credit problems in their past. Banks now routinely fingerprint new employees and customers and compare the fingerprints with law enforcement records. Other organizations hire private investigators or use publicly available databases to investigate people's backgrounds. Pen-and-pencil honesty tests are more widely used now as screening tools. Some companies train interviewers to conduct more thorough interviews as well as to check multiple background references.

One such company, for example, extensively trains interviewers so that they know which questions are legal to ask (and which are not), and so that they can recognize deception and lying, and legally probe applicants' backgrounds. Their standard policy now requires that three previous references be called instead of one. And it is considered a negative outcome if no gratuitously positive information is received in any of the three background checks. Over a three-year period, this company found that 851 prospective employees, or 14% of all applicants, had undisclosed problems, such as previous unsatisfactory employment, false education or military information, criminal records, poor credit ratings, physical or mental illness, alcoholism, or uncontrolled tempers. People with these types of problems generally find it easier to rationalize dishonest acts, and simply not hiring such people can reduce fraud.

As an example of poor screening, consider the following fraud:

> *A controller defrauded his company out of several million dollars. During the investigation, the company found that he had been fired from three of his previous five jobs, all in the last eight years. He was discovered when the CEO came to the office one night and found a stranger working in the accounting area. The nighttime "visitor" had been hired by the controller/swindler to do his work for him—because the swindler had no training in accounting!*

Once people are hired, it is important that they participate in employee awareness programs that educate them about what is acceptable and unacceptable, how they are hurt when someone is dishonest, and what actions they should take if they see someone being dishonest. Comprehensive awareness programs educate employees about how costly fraud and other business abuses are. Employees need to know that fraud takes a direct bite out of their benefits, and that no dishonest acts of any kind will be tolerated. Most companies with successful fraud awareness programs package fraud training with other sensitive issues that are also important to employees, such as employee safety, discrimination, substance abuse, and the availability of employee assistance programs.

One company, for example, educates all employees about business abuses and gives them small cards to carry in their wallets. The cards list four possible actions employees can take if they suspect that abuses are taking place. They can (1) talk to management, or call (2) corporate security, (3) internal audit, or (4) an 800 hotline number. Employees can either provide the information anonymously or disclose their identities. This company also developed its own video about company abuses, including fraud, which is shown to all new employees. New posters relating to the awareness program are posted conspicuously throughout the organization on a regular basis. Because of these awareness programs, fraud and other abuses in the company have decreased substantially.

Creating a Positive Work Environment

A culture of honesty, openness, and assistance cannot be created without a positive work environment. Positive work environments do not happen automatically; rather, they must be cultivated. It is a simple fact that employee fraud and other dishonest acts are more prevalent in some organizations. Why, you might ask? Actually, would that more organizations asked this question because the answer is worth millions to them. Fortunately, two elements—open-door policies and positive personnel and operating procedures—go far in "inoculating" organizations against fraud.

Open-door policies prevent fraud in two ways. First, many people commit fraud because they have no one to talk to. When people keep their problems to themselves, they lose perspective about the appropriateness of their actions and about the consequences of wrongdoing. This loss of perspective can lead to making decisions to be dishonest. Second, open-door policies help managers and others to be aware of employees' pressures, problems, and rationalizations. This awareness enables managers to take proactive steps to prevent fraud. Studies show that most frauds (71% in one study) are committed by someone acting alone.[3] Having people to talk to can prevent this type of fraud. One embezzler said, in retrospect, "Talk to someone. Tell someone what you are thinking and what your pressures are. It's definitely not worth it . . . It's not worth the consequences."[4]

Consider Micky: As the controller for a small fruit-packing company, Micky embezzled over $212,000. When asked why, he said, "Nobody at the company, especially the owners, ever talked to me. They treated me unfairly. They talked down to me. They were rude to me. They deserve everything they got."

Research shows that personnel and operating policies are key factors in high- and low-fraud environments.[5] Uncertainty about job security, for example, is associated with high-fraud environments. Other personnel and operating conditions and procedures that appear to contribute to high-fraud environments include the following:

- Managers who don't care about or pay attention to honesty (who model apathetic or inappropriate behavior)
- Inadequate pay
- Lack of recognition for job performance
- Imposition of unreasonable budget expectations
- Expectations that employees live a certain lifestyle (like belong to a country club)
- Perceived inequalities in the organization
- Inadequate expense accounts
- Autocratic or dictatorial management
- Low company loyalty
- Short-term business focus
- Management by crisis
- Rigid rules
- Negative feedback and reinforcement
- Repression of differences
- Poor promotion opportunities
- Hostile work environments
- High turnover and absenteeism
- Cash flow problems or other financial problems
- Reactive rather than proactive management
- Managers with wheeler-dealer, impulsive, insensitive, emotional, or dominant personalities
- Rivalrous rather than supportive relationships
- Poor training
- Lack of clear organizational responsibilities
- Poor communication practices

These conditions and procedures create high-fraud environments. For example, crisis and rush jobs open up additional opportunities for committing fraud. When special projects are hurried toward completion, normal controls are often set aside or ignored. Corners are cut; signatures are obtained to authorize uncertain purchases; reimbursements are made rapidly, with little documentation. Record keeping falls behind and cannot be reconstructed. Inventory and supplies come and go rapidly and can easily be manipulated or misplaced. Job lines and responsibilities are not as well defined. In a recent interview, the controller of a Fortune 500 company indicated that his company experienced three large frauds in one year. Two of them, both in the millions of dollars, occurred while the company was completing crash projects.

Examples of frauds that succeeded (at least for a while) because of the operating conditions noted above are indeed numerous; we describe two here for your edification. Inadequate pay motivated the first one, and unreasonable expectations motivated the second one.

One long-time employee felt unfairly passed over for a raise. He earned $30,000 a year and decided that he was entitled to a 10% raise. He therefore proceeded to steal $250 a month—*exactly* 10% of his salary. His morals "permitted" him to steal that much because he felt that much was "owed to him," but he could not, and did not, embezzle one cent more—that would have been "dishonest"![6]

A division manager of a large conglomerate was directed to increase his division's segment margin by 20% during the coming year. When he realized he would not meet budget, he fabricated his reports and overstated assets rather than fail. He concluded that it was better to be dishonest than not meet his assigned budget.[7]

Developing a Company Code of Ethics

A culture of honesty, openness, and assistance cannot be created without a well-defined and respected company code of ethics or conduct. Literature on moral development suggests that if you want people to behave honestly, you must label honest behavior and you must model it.[8] Companies that succeed in preventing fraud have effective labeling programs; these usually involve instituting a "code of ethics" or "code of conduct." Clearly defined codes of ethics delineate what is acceptable and what is unacceptable. Having employees periodically read and sign the company's code of ethics not only reinforces their understanding of what constitutes appropriate and inappropriate behavior, it also underscores the fact that this is important to the company. Expectations are clarified, and clear expectations reduce fraud. Clearly specified codes also inhibit rationalizations. Statements like "It's really not that serious," "You would understand if you knew how badly I needed it," "I'm really not hurting anyone," "Everyone is a little dishonest," or "I'm only temporarily borrowing it," don't seem so justifiable when they are held up for everyone to discuss and discredit. When employees are required to acknowledge that they understand the organization's expectations, they buy into the idea that fraud hurts everyone, that not everyone is a little dishonest, that the organization won't tolerate dishonest acts, that dishonest behavior is serious, and that unauthorized borrowing is not acceptable.

Implementing Employee Assistance Programs

One of the three elements of the fraud triangle is perceived pressure. Pressures that push people to commit fraud are often ones that perpetrators consider to be unsharable or that they believe have no possible legal solutions. This is where *employee assistance programs* (EAPs) come in. Employees with effective avenues for dealing with personal pressures are much less likely to commit fraud. Formal EAPs help employees deal with substance abuse (alcohol and drugs), gambling, money management, and health, family, and personal problems.

One study of Fortune 500 companies found that 67% of companies surveyed had formal EAPs.[9] Most respondents felt that fewer than 10% of their company's employees ever used their EAPs, and only 50% of respondents felt that their EAPs returned less than $1 for every $1 spent. Other research has shown, however, that when used effectively, EAPs can return between $3 and $6 for every $1 spent.[10] When asked what type of problems their EAPs addressed, 67% of respondents in the previously cited study[11] stated alcohol and drug problems, 63% identified emotional problems, 57% identified family and marital problems, 38% covered gambling problems, 37% covered personal financial problems, and 32% provided legal assistance. In addition, 11% provided investment counseling, and 92% of all respondents felt that assisting employees with personal financial pressures helped prevent employee fraud. These two perpetrators might have benefited from EAP assistance, for example:

> *An unmarried woman became pregnant. She didn't want anyone to know, and needing money desperately, she stole $300 from her company. Then, realizing how easy it was, she stole another $16,000 before being detected.*

> *An employee of a large bank embezzled over $35,000. When she was caught and asked why, she stated that her son was "hooked on heroin at a cost of nearly $500 per day." She couldn't stand to see him go through withdrawal pains, so she embezzled to support his habit.*

Eliminating Opportunities for Fraud

In Chapter 2, we introduced the fraud triangle—perceived pressure, perceived opportunity, and rationalization. As you now know, when these three elements come together, the likelihood of fraud being perpetrated increases dramatically. If even one element is missing, fraud is unlikely. In this section, we look at ways to eliminate opportunity. The seven methods we cover reduce either actual or perceived opportunity, and all of them together combine with the environmental factors we described earlier to create comprehensive fraud prevention programs.

Installing Good Internal Controls

The most widely recognized way to deter fraud is with a good system of controls. The Institute of Internal Auditors' standard on fraud, for example, states the following:[12]

> *Deterrence consists of those actions taken to discourage the perpetration of fraud and limit the exposure if fraud does occur. The principal mechanism for deterring fraud is control. Primary responsibility for establishing and maintaining control rests with management.*

> *Internal auditing is responsible for assisting in the deterrence of fraud by examining and evaluating the adequacy and the effectiveness of control, commensurate with the extent of the potential exposure/risk in the various segments of the entity's operations. In carrying out this responsibility, internal auditing should, for example, determine whether:*

> *a. The organizational environment fosters control consciousness.*
> *b. Realistic organizational goals and objectives are set.*
> *c. Written corporate policies (e.g., codes of conduct) exist that describe prohibited activities and the action required whenever violations are discovered.*
> *d. Appropriate authorization policies for transactions are established and maintained.*
> *e. Policies, practices, procedures, reports, and other mechanisms are developed to monitor activities and safeguard assets, particularly in high-risk areas.*
> *f. Communication channels provide management with adequate and reliable information.*
> *g. Recommendations need to be made for the establishment or enhancement of cost-effective controls to help deter fraud. (See SIAS No. 1,* Control: Concepts and Responsibilities.*)*

As stated in Chapter 3, an organization's *internal control structure* should include (1) a good control environment, (2) a good accounting system, and (3) good control procedures (activities) as well as good communication and monitoring. As stated in a Committee of Sponsoring Organizations (COSO) report, the *control environment* sets the tone of an organization, and is largely responsible for employees being conscious (and therefore vigilant) about controls.[13] It is the foundation for all other components of internal control; it provides discipline and structure. Key factors in the control environment include the integrity, ethical values, and competence of the entity's people, management's philosophy and operating style, the way management assigns authority and responsibility and organizes and develops its people, and the attention and direction provided by the board of directors. The control environment also includes well-defined hiring practices, clear organization, and a good internal audit department.

A good accounting system is, of course, key. Information must be valid, complete, and timely. The system should also provide information that is properly valued, classified, authorized, and summarized.

Good control procedures (activities) are the policies and practices that provide physical control of assets, proper authorizations, segregation of duties, independent checks, and proper documentation. (Physical control, proper authorization, and segregation of duties are controls for preventing fraud, whereas independent checks and documents and records facilitate early detection.) A control system that meets these requirements provides reasonable assurance that the organization's goals and objectives will be met and that fraud will be reduced, prevented, and deterred.

Obviously, people who own their own company and are the company's sole employee do not need many internal controls. They are unlikely to steal from their own company or to serve their own customers poorly. However, in organizations with hundreds or thousands of employees and even with only two or three employees, controls are absolutely necessary to ensure that employees behave the way they should.

No internal control structure can ever be completely "fraud-proof," no matter how much care is taken in its design and implementation. Even with the best possible control system in place, its effectiveness still depends on the competency and dependability of the people enforcing it. Consider, for example, a policy that requires dual counting of all incoming cash receipts. If either of the two employees involved in the task fails to understand the instructions, or is careless in opening and counting incoming cash, money can easily be stolen or miscounted. One of the employees might understate the count intentionally to cover up a theft of cash. Dual custody works only if both people pay full attention to the task and completely understand how it is to be performed.

Because of the inherent limitations of controls, a control system by itself never provides absolute assurance that fraud will be prevented. Trying to prevent fraud using only a good control system is analogous to fighting a fire in a skyscraper with a garden hose. When combined with other methods, however, controls are an extremely important part of every fraud prevention program.

To determine what kind of control procedures (activities) an organization should have in place, it is important to identify the nature of the risks involved and the types of abuses that could result from these risks. Based on this assessment, controls can be installed that eliminate or mitigate the risks identified. And the controls, of course, need to be monitored and tested to ensure that they work and are being followed.

Another factor in determining which controls to implement is their cost/benefit analysis. For example, the most appropriate control from a risk perspective involves segregation of duties, but this control is also quite expensive. In small businesses with only a few employees, segregation of duties may be too costly or even impossible. There are always "compensating" alternatives that are less expensive. For example, in a small service business with eight employees, the owner might personally sign all checks and reconcile all bank statements to control cash.

Often the problem is not a lack of controls, but the overriding of existing controls by management or others. Consider the role of controls in the theft of $3.2 million from a small bank. Marjorie, head of accounting and bookkeeping in a small bank, was responsible for all proof reconciliations and activities. Over a seven-year period, she embezzled $3.2 million, about 10% of the bank's assets. Auditors and management knew about the lack of segregation of duties in her department, but believed they had compensating controls in place that would provide "reasonable assurance" that fraud was not possible. Here are some of the compensating controls and the ways in which they were overridden:

1. All deposits and transfers of funds were supposed to be made through tellers. Yet, proof employees made transfers for bank officers and for themselves directly through proof. Most employees were aware of this practice, but because it was done at the president's request, they didn't think about its weaknesses.
2. All documents were supposed to be accessible to external auditors. Yet, Marjorie kept a locked cabinet next to her desk, and only she had the key. A customer whose statement was altered by Marjorie complained, but was told that he would have to wait until Marjorie returned from vacation, because the documentation on his account was in her locked cabinet.
3. Auditors were supposed to have access to all employees, but Marjorie told her employees not to talk to auditors. Thus, all questions were referred to her during audits.
4. Every employee and every officer of the bank was required to take a consecutive two-week vacation. At Marjorie's request, management allowed this control to be overridden. Based on her memos, that "proof would get behind if she took a two-week vacation," Marjorie took her vacation one day at a time. In addition, no one was allowed to perform her most sensitive duties while she was away.
5. General ledger tickets were supposed to be approved by someone other than the person who completed the ticket. To override this control, Marjorie had her employees pre-sign 10 or 12 general ledger tickets, so she wouldn't have to "bother" them when they were busy.
6. There were supposed to be opening and closing procedures in place, but many employees had all the necessary keys and could enter the bank at will.
7. An effective internal audit function was supposed to be in place. For a period of two years, however, no internal audit reports were issued. Even when the reports were issued, internal audit did not check employee accounts or perform critical control tests, such as surprise openings of the bank's incoming and outgoing cash letters to and from the Federal Reserve.
8. Incoming and outgoing cash letters were supposed to be microfilmed immediately. This compensating control was violated in three ways. First, letters were not usually filmed immediately. Second, for a time, letters were not filmed at all. Third, Marjorie regularly removed items from the cash letters before they were filmed.
9. Employees' accounts were not regularly reviewed by internal audit or by management. On the rare occasions when accounts were reviewed, numerous deposits to and checks drawn on Marjorie's account that exceeded her annual salary were not questioned.
10. Loans were supposed to be made only to employees who met all lending requirements, as if they were normal customers. At one point, the bank made a $170,000 mortgage loan to Marjorie, without asking her to explain how she would repay the loan or how she could afford such a house.
11. Employees in proof and bookkeeping were not supposed to handle their own bank statements. Yet, employees regularly pulled out their own checks and deposit slips before statements were mailed.

12. Managers were supposed to review key daily documents, such as the daily statement of condition, the significant items and major fluctuation report, and the overdraft report. Either managers didn't review these reports, or they didn't pay close attention when they did review them. The daily statement of conditions fluctuated by as much as $3 million. The significant items and major fluctuation report revealed huge deposits to, and checks drawn on, Marjorie's account. In addition, Marjorie appeared on the overdraft report 97 times during the first four years she was employed by the bank.

If these controls had been in place and effective, Marjorie's fraud would have been detected in its early stages and possibly prevented altogether. Because management and internal auditors continually overrode controls, the bank's "reasonable assurance" deteriorated to no assurance at all.

Having a good system of internal control is the single most effective tool in preventing and detecting fraud. This cannot be stated strongly enough. It is simple: Control procedures prevent fraud. Control procedures also assist in early detection. Unfortunately, in practice, control procedures are rarely followed the way they were designed to be followed. Why does this happen? Sometimes employees emulate management's lackadaisical attitude toward controls. Other times, managers properly model and label good control procedures, but employees don't comply because of disinterest, lack of rewards or punishments for complying, lack of focus, and many other reasons. As you can see, control procedures provide only reasonable assurance at best; they are therefore only one element of a comprehensive fraud prevention plan.

Discouraging Collusion

As stated previously, approximately 71% of all frauds are committed by individuals acting alone. The remaining 29% involve collusion and are not only difficult to detect, they often involve the largest thefts. Because collusive fraud develops slowly (it takes time to get to know others well enough to trust that they will cooperate and not blow the whistle), many collusions can be prevented by simply requiring mandatory vacations or job transfers. When organizations leave one employee in close contact with the same vendors or customers for long periods of time, the risk of individuals deciding to profit personally increases dramatically. An example is the case where an accounts receivable employee "managed" a customer's receivables to benefit both himself and the customer at the expense of the company.

Unfortunately, two business trends are likely to increase collusion fraud. The first trend is the increasingly complex nature of business today. In complex environments, trusted employees often operate in isolated or specialized surroundings. The second trend is the increasing prominence of supplier alliances, where oral agreements replace paper trails and closer relationships exist between buyers and suppliers. Certainly, increased cost savings and productivity can be had from supplier alliances, but this does not diminish their increased risk for fraud. How much these trends will affect fraud is unknown, but fraud does appear to be on the rise. All too frequently, it is people whom we "trust" and "have confidence in" who commit most frauds. In reaction to a fraud perpetrated by a trusted vendor, one manager noted, "I just couldn't believe he would do it. It's like realizing your brother is an ax murderer."

The problem with trusting people too much is that opportunity and temptation increase. A helpful analogy is that of a company that nearly a century ago was looking for someone to drive its wagons over a rugged mountain.

> *The interviewer asked the first prospective driver, "How close to the edge of the cliff can you get without going over? "Why, I can maneuver within six inches without any problems," was his response. Asked the same question, the second interviewee responded, "I can drive within three inches of the*

edge without going over the cliff." The third and final applicant responded, "I will drive as far away from the edge as I possibly can, because it is foolish to place yourself in a risky position." Guess which one got the job!

Fraud is just like the "how close should we get to the cliff" situation. When risk is higher, more problems occur. Therefore, in environments where preventive and detective controls are minimal or absent, employees should be regularly reviewed, periodically transferred or rotated, or required to take prolonged periods of vacation. Had any of these procedures been in place, Robert might not have committed his fraud:

Robert was the chief teller in a large New York bank. Over a period of three years, he embezzled more than $1.5 million. Only after the fraud was discovered was it learned that Robert had a compulsive gambling habit. He took the money by manipulating dormant accounts. When customers complained about their accounts, Robert was always the one who explained the discrepancies. His excuse? "It's a computer error." He later said that the bank placed far too much trust and supervisory authority in him, and admitted that had there been one other supervisor sharing responsibility, or had a one-week mandatory vacation requirement been combined with periodic rotations, Robert wouldn't have succeeded in defrauding the bank.

When employees are solely responsible for large contracts, bribes and kickbacks are a possibility. In some cases, employees double or triple their salaries by allowing increases in costs of purchased goods of less than 1%. Purchase and sales frauds are the most common kickback frauds. When opportunity is too high, even individuals who otherwise live by professional codes of conduct will sometimes commit fraud. Take the ESM fraud case that we mentioned in Chapter 2.

A partner in the firm accepted under-the-table payments from his client, in return for staying quiet about fraudulent financial transactions. The fraud exceeded $300 million. The CPA was the partner-in-charge of this contract for over eight years. For not disclosing the fraud, he received a paltry $150,000. Had ESM not allowed him to manage this contract job for such a long time, his participation in the scheme would have been impossible.

Alerting Vendors and Contractors to Company Policies

Sometimes otherwise innocent vendors and customers are drawn into fraud by the central perpetrators because they fear that if they don't participate, they will lose the business relationship. In most cases, such customers or vendors have only one or two contacts with the firm. They are often intimidated by the person who requests illegal gratuities or suggests other types of illegal behavior. A periodic letter to vendors that explains the organization's policy of no gifts or gratuities helps vendors understand whether company buyers and sellers are acting in accordance with the rules. Such letters clarify expectations, which is very important in preventing fraud. Many frauds are uncovered when, after receiving such a letter, vendors express concern about their buying or selling relationships.

A large chicken fast-food restaurant discovered a $200,000 fraud involving kickbacks from suppliers. After investigating the fraud, the restaurant management decided to write letters to all vendors, explaining that it was against company policy for buyers to accept any form of gratuities from suppliers. The letters promptly uncovered two additional buyer-related frauds.

A precaution that discourages kickback-type frauds is including a "right-to-audit" clause on the back of all purchase invoices. These clauses alert vendors that the company reserves the right to audit their books at any time. This makes vendors much more reluctant to make bribery payments. A right-to-audit clause is also a valuable tool in fraud investigations.

Monitoring Employees

People who commit fraud and then hoard their proceeds are virtually nonexistent. Perpetrators almost always use their stolen money to support expensive habits. When fellow employees pay close attention to the enhanced lifestyle that results from these expenditures, fraud is often detected early. Fraudsters spend their stolen funds conspicuously—like Marjorie, whose case we visited earlier in this chapter.

Marjorie started working for the bank in 1980. During her first four years of employment, she took out a debt consolidation loan of approximately $12,000 and had 97 personal overdrafts. During the next seven years, the period of her fraud, her salary never exceeded $22,000 per year. Yet, fellow employees and officers of the bank knew that she:

- Took several expensive cruises
- Built a home on a golf course, costing $600,000
- Purchased a Rolls-Royce, a Jeep Cherokee, an Audi, and a Maserati
- Was a heavy consumer of expensive jewelry (including 16 diamonds and sapphires), designer clothes, electronic gear, and snowmobiles, to name a few of her habits
- Routinely hired limousines
- Held extravagant parties
- Bought a condominium for her mother-in-law
- Purchased an art glass collection costing over $1.5 million
- Took many domestic trips to buy art glass
- Had a beautifully furnished home

Anyone paying attention would have realized that her lifestyle was flagrantly out of line with her income. When someone did finally ask how she afforded it all, she said that her husband received one-third of an inheritance of $250,000. The story, of course, wasn't true, but even if it had been, $83,333 wouldn't have paid for the Maserati, let alone all the other luxuries she was continually purchasing.

Close monitoring facilitates early detection. It also deters frauds because potential perpetrators realize that "others are watching."

Tip Hotlines

Even with advances in technology, fraud is most commonly detected through tips. One company noted that 33% of its frauds were detected through tips, whereas only 18% were detected by auditors. In another company that experienced over 1,000 frauds in one year, 42% were discovered through tips and complaints from employees and customers. A good whistle-blowing program is an extremely effective prevention tool. When employees know that colleagues have an easy, anonymous way to report suspected fraud, they are more reluctant to commit it.

Unfortunately, too few organizations have effective tip programs. In a study of Fortune 500 companies, only 52% of the respondents indicated that their companies had formal whistle-blowing systems. Of the companies that did provide ways for employees to report suspicious acts, 16% had toll-free hotlines, 17% directed employees to discuss the matter with their managers, and 29% told them to contact corporate security directly.[14]

Creating an Expectation of Punishment

Fear of punishment really does deter dishonesty. Swift and consistent punishment makes employees stop and think before they embark on a path of crime. But note that merely being terminated is not meaningful punishment. Real punishment involves having to tell family members and friends about one's dishonest behavior. Because they are usually first-time offenders, fraud perpetrators loathe the humiliation of having to tell their loved ones that they are thieves. Termination can be shrugged off with excuses like "The company laid me off."

A strong prosecution policy that lets employees know that dishonest acts will be harshly punished, that not everyone is dishonest, and that unauthorized borrowing from the company will not be tolerated, is essential in reducing fraud. Although prosecution is often expensive and time-consuming, and it certainly raises concerns about unfavorable press coverage, not prosecuting is only cost effective in the short run. In the long run, failure to prosecute sends a message to other employees that fraud is tolerated and that the worst thing that can happen is termination. Because of today's privacy laws and high job turnover rates, termination alone does not deter fraud. Like a good code of ethics, a strong policy of punishment prevents potential fraudsters from hiding behind their rationalizations.

Proactive Fraud Auditing

Very few organizations audit for fraud. Rather, their auditors conduct financial, operational, and other audits, and investigate fraud only if it is suspected. Organizations that proactively audit for fraud create an awareness among employees that their actions are subject to review at any time. By increasing the fear of getting caught, proactive auditing reduces fraudulent behavior.

Good fraud auditing involves four steps: (1) identifying risk exposures, (2) identifying the fraud symptoms for each exposure, (3) building audit programs that proactively look for symptoms and exposures, and (4) investigating identified symptoms. One company used computerized auditing techniques to compare employees' telephone numbers with vendors' telephone numbers. The search revealed 1,117 instances in which telephone numbers matched, indicating that the company was purchasing goods and services from employees—a direct conflict of interest.

Preventing Fraud—A Summary

To summarize the points made thus far, fraud is reduced and often prevented (1) by creating a culture of honesty, openness, and assistance and (2) by eliminating opportunities to commit fraud. The components of these two activities are shown in the following diagram:

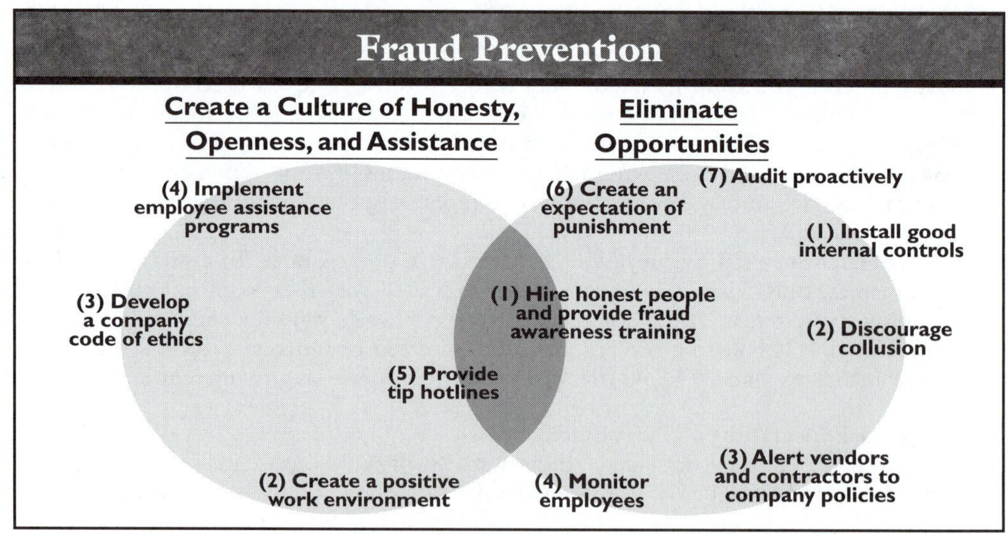
Fraud Prevention
Create a Culture of Honesty, Openness, and Assistance
Eliminate Opportunities
(4) Implement employee assistance programs
(3) Develop a company code of ethics
(5) Provide tip hotlines
(2) Create a positive work environment
(1) Hire honest people and provide fraud awareness training
(6) Create an expectation of punishment
(7) Audit proactively
(1) Install good internal controls
(2) Discourage collusion
(4) Monitor employees
(3) Alert vendors and contractors to company policies

Organizations that follow these recommendations have significantly fewer fraud problems. One company that worked hard at implementing these steps reduced known fraud from an average of more than $20 million per year to less than $1 million per year.

A Comprehensive Approach to Fighting Fraud

Now it is time to combine prevention with detection, investigation, and follow-up to create a comprehensive approach to fighting fraud. As mentioned earlier, the author conducted a survey of fraud-fighting strategies of Fortune 500 companies. Questionnaires were sent to each company, asking those most responsible for fraud prevention to respond. Of the 242 responses, 62% (150 responses) came from directors of internal audit, 28% (67 responses) from directors of corporate security, and 10% (25 responses) from personnel or human resource directors. Many respondents wrote that no one person was "most responsible" for fraud prevention.[15]

The diversity in the job titles of the respondents, combined with comments that rarely was anyone primarily responsible for preventing fraud, is a discouraging commentary on the status of fraud prevention in the United States. Fraud is a costly problem for organizations. Yet, responsibility for preventing it is often seen as belonging to "someone else." Independent auditors maintain they can't detect fraud because it isn't their responsibility and because their materiality levels are too high.[16] Internal auditors argue that their function is to evaluate controls and to improve operational efficiency. If they happen to find fraud, they'll pursue it and report it, but fraud isn't their primary responsibility. Corporate security officers, in most organizations, believe that theirs is an investigative role and that they are responsible for pursuing reported frauds, not deterring them. They don't focus on prevention or detection. Managers view "running the business" as their primary responsibility and seldom acknowledge the possibility that fraud can occur in their organization. Fraud is something that "happens elsewhere." Further, they don't know how to handle fraud when it does occur. Employees, who are often in the best position to prevent and detect fraud, don't know what to do or whom to talk to when they have suspicions, and they frequently feel that it is unethical or unwise to blow the whistle or report fellow employees.

Because "nonownership" of the problem prevails in most businesses, frauds like the Ackroyd Airlines one will continue to occur.

> *Jerry Watkins worked for Ackroyd Airlines for 17 years. During this time, he held positions in accounting, finance, and purchasing. Jerry had three children, two boys and one girl, and he and his family were active in the community and in their church. Jerry coached both Little League baseball and football. Both he and his wife, Jill, had college degrees, worked full-time, and shared a long-term goal of sending their children to college. Yet, each year the Watkins spent most of what they made and saved very little for college tuition and other expenses.*
>
> *Jerry had been working at Ackroyd for 15 years when Jerry's son Steve entered a well-known Ivy League college. A year later, Jerry, who handled the family finances, realized they could no longer cover Steve's college expenses, let alone save for their other two children's college. Jerry, a proud man, could not bring himself to admit this shortfall to his family. He already had a large mortgage and crushing credit-card debt, and he knew he couldn't borrow more money.*
>
> *Feeling desperate, Jerry began to embezzle money from Ackroyd Airlines. He knew of several other thefts in the company, and the perpetrators had not*

been prosecuted. In fact, the company merely transferred the employees. Jerry also rationalized that he would pay the money back sometime. His position as purchasing manager made it easy to take kickbacks from a vendor who had previously approached him with favors to get business. At first, Jerry took only small amounts. As time passed, however, he increasingly relied on the money to meet all kinds of extra "needs." He felt guilty about the kickbacks but knew that company auditors didn't consider fraud a serious threat. Anyway, he felt the company would understand if they knew how badly he needed the money. Significant good was coming from his "borrowing": His children were getting an education they could not otherwise afford, and Ackroyd didn't really miss the money. Eventually this "honest" employee stole several hundred thousand dollars.

What is alarming here is that Jerry's case is not unusual. Jerry never signed a code of conduct. Ackroyd's auditors never proactively searched for fraud. The company didn't have an EAP to help employees with their finances and other needs. Furthermore, as Jerry was well aware, the company never took actions harsher than terminating fraud offenders.

Organizations and Fraud—The Current Model

Like Ackroyd Airlines, many organizations do not have a proactive approach to fraud. Because fraud prevention is not emphasized in many companies, there is significant confusion about who has responsibility for detecting, preventing, and investigating it. The model that organizations typically use for dealing with fraud, often by default, is shown below.[17]

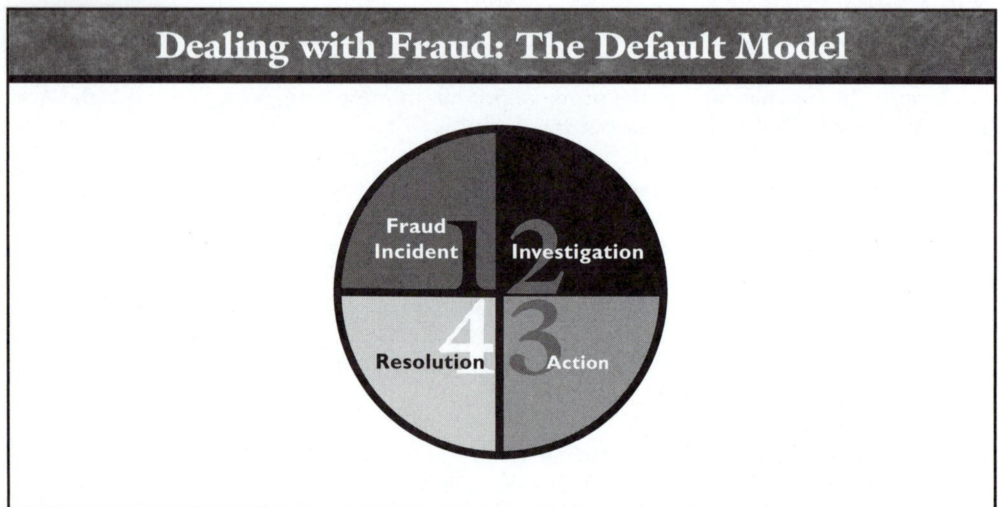

This model is characterized by four stages. In stage 1, a fraud incident occurs in an environment where formal awareness training and other prevention measures do not exist. The firm then shifts into a crisis mode, because it wants to (1) identify the perpetrator, (2) avoid publicity, (3) recover the losses, and (4) minimize the fraud's impact on the organization. The firm, caught unawares, is caught up in the emotions of crisis.

Stage 2 is the investigation. Here both security and internal audit become involved, and most of the investigative work centers around interviewing and document examination. The investigation may or may not lead to resolution, takes extensive time, and is often costly.

In stage 3, the investigation now complete, the company decides what actions to take regarding the perpetrator(s). Their choices are take no action, terminate or transfer only, or terminate and seek prosecution.

In stage 4 the file is closed, loose ends are tied together, the employee is replaced (thereby incurring additional costs), new controls may (or may not) be implemented, and the problem is otherwise resolved. At this point in the default model *no further action is taken*—until another fraud occurs. Unfortunately, fraud does not decrease; it instead becomes a recurring problem. Now let's look at a much better approach to fighting fraud—the fraud-savvy model below.

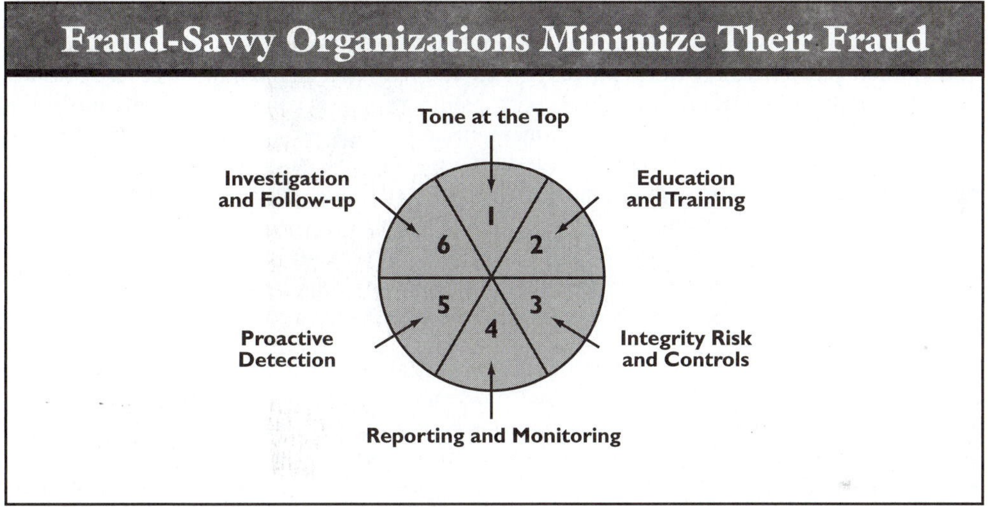

As you can see, there are six elements in the fraud-savvy model. First, and probably most important, is management, the board of directors, and key others setting a positive "tone at the top." This involves two steps: (1) developing and promoting a company code of conduct that everyone "owns," and (2) modeling appropriate behavior (otherwise known as "walking the talk").

When the management of one company changed its attitude from "we want to know when someone who commits fraud is prosecuted" to "we want to know when someone who commits fraud *isn't* prosecuted" and made fraud against the company, along with safety, discrimination, and substance abuse, significant issues in the organization, the number and size of their frauds decreased substantially. Likewise, top management cannot accept expensive perks and gifts from vendors and others and be surprised when employees do the same.

The second element in the fraud-savvy model is educating employees and others about the seriousness of the problem and showing them what they can do if they suspect fraud. As we have repeatedly said, it is fraud prevention—*not* detection and *not* investigation—that results in big savings. Therefore, significant attention should be given to proactive fraud education initiatives, rather than to dealing with losses already incurred.

Fraud awareness training helps prevent fraud and ensures that frauds that do occur are detected in their early stages, thus limiting the organization's financial exposure and minimizing fraud's impact on the work environment. Education must include instructing vendors and other outsiders, not just employees, about company expectations.

The third fraud-fighting element involves risk assessment and a good internal control system. We discussed internal controls earlier in this chapter. It is important to note that having a good system of controls in place means that every fraud will be studied to determine why it occurred, with an emphasis on implementing controls that will prevent future occurrences.

Fraud analysis involves determinations by people in management, audit, security, human resources, control, and finance on why and how the fraud occurred. The focus is on the individuals involved, the controls that were either compromised or absent, the environment that facilitated the fraud, and related factors. This step is crucial in developing effective preventive measures. Developing appropriate solutions does not take long once the appropriate parties come together. Obviously, new controls that do not meet the cost-effectiveness test may not be implemented. The decision not to implement, however, should be based on a cost/benefit analysis, and not be made by default because the proper analysis was not conducted.

The fourth element has to do with installing reporting and monitoring systems. Fraud reporting must be facilitated. With murder, bank robbery, or assault, there is no question about whether a crime has been committed. Fraud, on the other hand, is a crime that can go on for years if co-workers are not alert to the red flags that signal fraud. Because hotlines and other reporting systems often don't exist, employees rarely volunteer information about potential fraud symptoms. This is unfortunate, because employees are in the best position to recognize dishonest behavior and to question red flags. Monitoring means that internal auditors, external auditors, and management all watch the performance of audits and reviews. Employees and vendors who know that a stringent monitoring and reporting system is in place are much less likely to commit fraud. Effective prevention involves concerted efforts to create in the minds of potential perpetrators that their activities will be uncovered. Note that whether perpetrators will actually be caught doesn't matter as much as that they *think* they will.

Reporting also involves disseminating information about the fraud to those who can benefit from it. This is not about giving local newspapers all the tawdry details. In fact, until there is a conviction, that sort of publication is ill-advised, because it can lead to libel suits for slander. Rather, dissemination in this context means depersonalizing the case (that is, disguising the identities of the perpetrators and other people involved) and publishing it internally in a security newsletter or in memos that are distributed to auditors, security personnel, and appropriate management and employees. Such generic publications of fraud have a tremendous impact, because they help employees understand that fraud happens in their own organization and that it is *their* problem, one that they can work to prevent.

The fifth element in a fraud-savvy system is about having proactive detection methods in place. No matter how good prevention efforts are, fraud will still be committed. And, because the damage from fraud grows geometrically over time, it is important to detect it early. Proactive detection methods, such as those that we discuss in Chapter 6, are not only effective in detecting fraud, but knowledge that they are actively used is a good deterrent.

Conducting effective investigations and follow-up is the final element in our fraud-savvy model. Investigations are much more likely to be effective when formal fraud policies are in place that specify who will carry out the investigation, how they will do it, and when they will do it. Investigation procedures should carefully lay out (1) who will conduct the investigation, (2) how the matter will be communicated to management, (3) whether and when law enforcement officials will be contacted, (4) who will determine the scope of investigation, (5) who will determine the investigation methods, (6) who will follow up on tips of suspected fraud, (7) who will conduct interviews, review documents, and perform other investigation steps, and (8) who will ultimately determine the corporate response to fraud, disciplines, control, and so on. Policies regarding follow-up actions against perpetrators should also be in place.

Taking no action should not be a possibility and, whenever possible, perpetrators should be prosecuted. A strong prosecution policy needs the support of top management, and they must be informed if someone commits fraud and is not prosecuted. Gone are the days when prosecution resulted in bad publicity. Today people realize that fraud is every organization's problem. And more and more people also understand that organizations that take a tough stance on prosecution stand to significantly reduce future frauds *and* to be more profitable as a result.

As we stated previously, fear of punishment is the single greatest factor in deterring dishonest acts. Companies with successful prosecution policies also install their own internal investigation experts. They recognize that in order to obtain cooperation from law enforcement officers and the justice system, it is almost always necessary to conduct their own very thorough and very complete investigation (including obtaining a signed confession) *before* overworked law enforcement agencies and criminal justice systems can prosecute.

New Term

Employee Assistance Programs (EAPs): Programs that help employees deal with problems such as substance abuse, gambling, money management and debt, health, family, and other pressures.

Questions and Cases

Discussion Questions

1. How do organizations create a culture of honesty, openness, and assistance?
2. What are different ways that companies can eliminate opportunities for fraud?
3. Why should companies adopt a code of ethics?
4. Why are good internal controls important?
5. How can organizations discourage collusion?
6. Why is it important to inform outside vendors of company policies concerning payments to buyers?
7. How can organizations monitor their employees?
8. How is proactive fraud auditing conducted?
9. How do anonymous tip hotlines help prevent fraud?
10. Why is it important for companies to create effective organizational structures?

True/False

1. Even with the right opportunity or significant pressure, most people would probably not steal or embezzle.
2. Studies show that a positive and honest work culture in a company does little to prevent fraud.
3. An important factor in creating a culture of honesty, openness, and assistance in the workplace is maintaining an employee assistance program.
4. A good internal control system can ensure the absence of fraud.
5. When fraud is committed, the problem is often not a lack of controls, but the overriding of existing controls by management and others.
6. The two elements in creating a positive work environment are (1) having an open-door policy and (2) having positive personnel and operating procedures.

7. Not prosecuting fraud perpetrators is cost-effective both in the short run and the long run.
8. Even a good system of internal controls will often not be completely effective because of fallibilities of the people applying and enforcing the controls.
9. The increasingly complex nature of business helps to decrease the number of collusive frauds.
10. Tips and complaints are the most common way fraud is detected.

Multiple Choice

1. People will often be dishonest if they are placed in an environment of:
   a. Poor controls
   b. High pressure
   c. Low integrity
   d. Loose accountability
   e. All of the above
2. ______________________ is/are factor(s) in creating a corporate culture of honesty and openness.
   a. Hiring honest people
   b. Performing criminal background checks
   c. Not having an open-door policy
   d. Having a well-understood and respected code of ethics
   e. a and d
   f. All of the above
3. The following personnel and operating policy(ies) contribute to high-fraud environments:
   a. Management by crisis
   b. Rigid rules
   c. High employee lifestyle expectations
   d. Poor promotion opportunities
   e. All of the above
4. ______________________ is usually the single most effective tool in preventing and detecting fraud.
   a. Monitoring employees
   b. Having a good system of internal controls
   c. Developing a well-written company code of ethics
   d. Strict hiring procedures
5. A company's control environment includes:
   a. The tone that management establishes toward what is honest and acceptable behavior
   b. Corporate hiring practices
   c. Having an internal audit department
   d. All of the above
6. Which of the following factors generally results in a high-fraud environment?
   a. Hiring honest people
   b. Providing an EAP
   c. Autocratic management
   d. a and b

7. Which of the following aspects of fraud usually results in the largest savings?
   a. Fraud prevention
   b. Fraud detection
   c. Fraud investigation
   d. It is impossible to tell.
8. Which of the following is usually the most effective tool in preventing and detecting fraud?
   a. Discouraging collusion between employees and customers or vendors
   b. Effective investigations of fraud symptoms
   c. Having a good system of internal controls
   d. Creating an expectation of punishment in the company
9. Which of the following is the default fraud model that describes most firms?
   a. Fraud incident, assessing risk, investigation, reporting
   b. Fraud incident, investigation, action, resolution
   c. Assessing risk, fraud incident, investigation, resolution
   d. Assessing risk, investigation, implementing a fraud program, reporting
10. The "tone at the top" is an important element in fighting fraud and involves:
   a. Doing a good job of integrity risk assessment
   b. Having a positive organization where effective fraud teaching and training are conducted
   c. Setting a proper example or modeling appropriate management behavior
   d. b and c

Short Cases

Case 1. Karen, a friend of yours, recently started her own business, the Bike and Boulder Company (B&B). B&B specializes in the sale of mountain bikes and rock climbing equipment. Karen is putting the finishing touches on her company policies and procedures. She knows you are taking a fraud examination class and asks you to review what she has completed thus far. You quickly notice that Karen has neglected to address fraud and fraud prevention in her policies and procedures.

What policies and procedures would you suggest Karen implement to prevent and detect fraud at B&B?

Case 2. Because ABC Company suffered large losses from fraud last year, senior management has decided to be more proactive in implementing a fraud prevention environment. In interviewing employees, they find that many employees are unclear about which behaviors are ethical and which are not.

What could management do to better educate employees about ethical behavior?

Case 3. Jason works at a new software development company. The company has been in existence for only two years, so everybody works extra hours and spends all of their time developing new products. Because everybody is busy, there is very little time for manager-employee interviews. The culture of the company is trusting and fun. When Jason started with the company, the only agreement he had to sign was an agreement to not give company software secrets to other organizations. Earlier in the year, Jason learned of an instance where another employee in accounting was fired. The reason was rumored to be fraudulent behavior, but nobody really knew the reason.

What about this organization's operating procedures encourage fraudulent behavior?

Case 4. Nellie works for a large Fortune 500 company. She heads the information systems department and works closely with the accounting department. The company works with many associates and handles numerous buyer and supplier companies. Nellie knows a lot about the database systems and accounting practices in the company. She also works closely with buyers and suppliers to create data communication lines. Recently, Nellie has become concerned about the integrity and reliability of the accounting and information systems. The company has grown to a point where she cannot manage or supervise all the activities performed in these areas.

What proactive steps can Nellie take to ensure systems and accounting integrity and prevent fraudulent behavior?

Case 5. While performing an audit of TCC Corporation, the audit team noticed something that didn't "look right." The company's receivables aging report showed that bank loan eligible receivables were approximately \$91 million. The audit team calculated the bank loan eligible receivables to be approximately \$50 million. The client didn't identify specific accounts in writing off bad debts, there was extremely slow credit memo processing, and items that management had not focused on remained uncollectible and ineligible for financing. In addition, over the last two years, the company's credit department has had unusually high turnover—four different people have held the credit manager position under an intimidating CFO. The current credit manager is a friend of the CFO, having worked with him at a previous company. After looking at some invoices and asking about customer information to confirm, the credit manager admitted to creating false documents and arranging fictitious sales with clients—all with the CFO's full knowledge.

1. What red flags point to the possibility of fraud here?
2. What is the main problem in this case that allowed the fraud to occur?

Case 6. Joseph Gonzales recently bought a new business that includes a small 20-room motel and coffee shop. He hired a young couple to run the business and plans to pay them a monthly salary. The couple will live for free in a small apartment behind the motel office and will be in charge of the daily operations of the motel and coffee shop. They will also be responsible for hiring and supervising the four or five part-time employees who clean the rooms, cook, and wait on customers in the restaurant. The couple will also maintain records of rooms rented, meals served, and payments received (which can be in the form of cash, checks, or credit cards). They will make weekly deposits of the business's proceeds at the local bank. Joseph lives about six hours away and will only be able to visit periodically.

What are your two biggest concerns concerning possible fraud on the part of the couple? For each concern, identify a possible control that could reduce the risk of fraud.

Case 7. Danny has worked at Gant Chevrolet for two years. He feels fortunate to have held his job for so long, considering his past, because he was fired for fraudulent activities in two different companies. His boss, Mr. Gant, is a pretty cold person and only says hello to Danny upon arriving and leaving work each day. All of the guys at work tend to slack a little here and there. They don't mind eating lunch at the company's expense, and there is a general lack of order about the place. Danny has been feeling low on cash lately, having just moved into a home that is perhaps a little too expensive. With this internal pressure and no one on whom to unload his troubles or with whom to talk, Danny decides to steal parts from the parts garage and sell them on the street for cash.

What could Gant Chevrolet have done to prevent Danny's fraud?

Case 8. Mary S. owns a small flower shop. With only 12 employees, the environment is one of trust. Mary personally knows each employee, and most have worked at the shop since its opening. Although few controls exist, Mary is the only person allowed to sign checks. Mary's good friend, Steve, is very important to the business. Not only is he the head accountant, but he also helps maintain relationships with vendors. Steve is the proud father of two sons, one of whom started college just last year. Although immensely proud, Steve was worried about making tuition payments and maintaining the family's lifestyle, and he was right, because after his son's freshman year, things got really tight. Not wanting his son to know that the family was hurting financially, he reluctantly agreed to take "just one" payment from a vendor who wanted special preference with the company. The first kickback was hard to accept, but the second one was easier. Soon Steve was easily covering his son's tuition and more. He bought expensive jewelry for his wife and took extravagant trips. Because Mary knew the family's circumstances, she wondered where the money was coming from. Steve told Mary that his wife inherited some stocks from an aunt. Mary trusted him, so she believed his story. She didn't become suspicious until one day she tried to contact a vendor directly. Steve did not allow her to do so and insisted that she talk to the vendor through him. Mary soon discovered that Steve was "on the take."

How could this fraud have been prevented?

Case 9. Jim was the chief teller in a large bank. Over a period of three years, he embezzled $4.5 million by manipulating dormant accounts. When a customer complained about his account, Jim was always the one to explain the discrepancy. He usually used the excuse that "it's a computer error."

What internal control weaknesses allowed this fraud to occur?

Case 10. A controller of a small fruit-packing company in California stole $212,000 from the company. When asked why, he said "Nobody at the company (especially the owners) ever talked to me. They treated me unfairly, they talked down to me, and they were rude to me. They deserve everything they got."

What could the company have done to prevent this fraud?

Case 11. May 13, 1988, a Friday incidentally, will long be remembered by a major Chicago bank. Embezzlers nearly escaped with $69 million! Arnand Moore, who was released after serving four years of his eleven-year sentence for a $180,000 fraud, decided it was time to get in on something bigger and better. Naming himself "Chairman," he assembled Herschel Bailey, Otis Wilson, Neal Jackson, Leonard Strickland, and Ronald Carson to form his "Board." The "Board" convinced an employee of the Chicago bank to provide their "in." The caper required one month of planning in a small hotel in Chicago, and took all of 64 minutes to complete.

The bank employee had worked for the bank for eight years in the wire-transfer section, which dispatches multimillion-dollar sums around the world via computers and phone lines. Some of the bank's largest customers send funds from their accounts directly to creditors and suppliers. For electronic transfers, most banks require that a bank employee call back another executive at the customer's offices to reconfirm the order, using various code numbers. All such calls are automatically taped. The crooked employee participated in these deposits and confirmations and had access to all the code numbers and names of the appropriate executives.

The "Board's" targets were Merrill Lynch, United Airlines, and Brown-Forman Corporation (distillers). The gang set up phony bank accounts in Vienna under the false names of "Lord Investments," "Walter Newman," and "GTL Industries." At 8:30 A.M., a gang member posing as a Merrill Lynch executive called the bank to arrange a transfer of $24 million to the account of "Lord Investments," and was assisted by one of the crooked employee's unsuspecting co-workers. In accordance with the bank's practice of confirming transfers with a second executive, the employee stepped in and called another supposed executive who was actually Bailey, his partner in crime. Bailey's unfaltering, convincing voice

was recorded automatically on the tape machine, and the crooked employee then wired the funds to Vienna via the New York City bank. The same procedure followed at 9:02 and 9:34 A.M. with phony calls on behalf of United Airlines and Brown-Forman. The funds were initially sent to Citibank and Chase Manhattan Bank, respectively.

On Monday, May 16, the plot was uncovered. The "Chairman" and his "Board" were discovered due to no effort on the part of the Chicago bank or any investigative authority. Although bank leaders do not like to admit just how close the culprits came to getting away, investigators were amazed at how far the scheme proceeded before being exposed. Had the men been a little less greedy; had they stolen, say, "only" $40 million; or had they chosen accounts that were a little less active, they might have been touring the world to this day! The plot was discovered because the transfers overdrew the balances in two of the accounts, and when the companies were contacted to explain the NSF transactions, they knew nothing about the transfers.

How could this fraud have been prevented? Why is this a difficult fraud to prevent?

Extensive Case

Case 12. You own a moderate-sized company. You started your business over 20 years ago, and it has experienced impressive growth and profitability. The only frustrating thing is that you know the company's profits would be significantly higher if you could rid it of fraud. Your accountants estimate that the company has lost approximately 7% of its earnings to fraud over the past five years.

The company has adequate controls in place, and you try to ensure that people don't override them. However, since you are the owner, you often bypass certain controls. You aren't out to rob the company, so the controls don't apply to you, you tell yourself.

You try to keep a close eye on most aspects of the business, but with 500 employees, it's difficult to know everything that is going on. Employees have been caught in fraudulent activities in the past, but you have never bothered to prosecute them. You don't want the negative publicity, and you see no reason to publicly humiliate former employees—their shame won't bring back the money they've stolen.

What aspects of the company can you change in order to reduce the amount of fraud you are experiencing? Use the five factors described in the chapter that create a culture of honesty, openness, and assistance to explain your answer.

Internet Assignments

1. As mentioned in the chapter, the Committee of Sponsoring Organizations (COSO) produced a report on internal control. They also have published a report on fraudulent financial reporting.

   Visit their web site at http://www.coso.org. Click on "Publications." Then read Chapter Two, Recommendations for the Public Company. Report on any similarities/differences.
2. Perform an Internet search for the phrase "insurance fraud statistics." You will find several references to the insurance fraud-fighting efforts of different states (e.g., Massachusetts, Pennsylvania, and Utah). Study a couple of these web sites to see how serious the states consider insurance fraud to be. Which state do you believe has done the best work in fighting insurance fraud?

Debate

1. You work for a small manufacturing firm, where it is clearly too expensive to have proper segregation of duties. Because of this lack of control, management

knows that opportunities to perpetrate fraud exist within the company. Management is particularly concerned with possible collusion between purchasing agents and vendors because of the relatively small size of the company and the fact that a single purchasing agent is often solely responsible for a vendor's account. Management knows now that a lot of money can be saved by proactive prevention and not merely acting on a crisis basis. They are establishing an open-door policy where all employees are encouraged to talk about pressures and opportunities they face on the job. Management also wants to establish a hotline where employees can report suspicious activity.

1. Is an employee hotline necessary?
2. Is this sort of "whistle-blowing" ethical?
3. What can management do as they establish this hotline to encourage employees to actually use it?

2. During the past year, your company discovered three major frauds. The first was a $3.9 million theft of inventory that had been going on for six years. The second was a $2.8 million kickback scheme involving the most senior purchasing agent. She allowed certain customers to overcharge for products in return for personal payments and other favors. The third was an overstatement of receivables and inventories by a subsidiary manager to enhance reported earnings. Without the overstatement, his unit's profit would have fallen far short of budget. The amount of overstatement has yet to be determined. All three of these frauds have been reported in the financial newspapers and have embarrassed the company.

   In response to these incidents, the Board of Directors has demanded that management take "positive steps to eliminate future fraud occurrences." In their words, they are "sick and tired of significant hits to the bottom line and negative exposure in the press." The responsibility to develop a program to eradicate fraud has fallen on your shoulders. You are to present a comprehensive plan to prevent future frauds at the Board's next meeting. In devising your strategy, outline the roles the following groups will play in preventing fraud:

   1. Top management
   2. Middle management
   3. Internal audit
   4. Corporate security
   5. Audit committee
   6. Legal counsel

   Have six groups (or six students) assume the six positions above and discuss each group's responsibility in preventing fraud. Debate the issues.

End Notes

1. http://home.nycap.rr.com/dhancox/articles/equity.htm
2. See, for example, John Kula, Director of Fraud and Security Consulting for Arthur Andersen, as quoted in Jerry Thomas, "Prosecution of White-Collar Crime Rising," *Chicago Tribune,* June 10, 1991, p. B1.
3. See, for example, "Report to the Nation: Occupational Fraud and Abuse," Association of Certified Fraud Examiners, Austin, Texas, 1995.

4. From the video "Red Flags of Fraud," which profiles three perpetrators. This video was produced by the Association of Certified Fraud Examiners, Austin, Texas.
5. See *Fraud: Bringing Light to the Dark Side of Business,* W. Steve Albrecht, G. W. Wernz, and T. L. Williams, Irwin Professional Publishing, 1995, New York, p. 258.
6. From an unpublished interview with the fraud perpetrator by Donn Parker of the Stanford Research Institute. Author Steve Albrecht was privileged to read Donn's files in his office.
7. This fraud occurred at the AMI Company and was related in a speech by Bob Sack, former Enforcement Director at the SEC, at a conference on Corporate Ethics at Brigham Young University.
8. For example, read the research of the Social and Moral Research Group, University of Maryland (http://www.education.umd.edu/depts/EDAD/faculty/killen/SMDRG).
9. W. Steve Albrecht and J. Wernz, "The Three Factors of Fraud," *Security Management,* July 1993, pp. 95–97.
10. "Organizational Structures to Deal with Employee Fraud," with Ed McDermott and Timothy L. Williams, *Security Journal,* Vol. 1, Number 5, 1990, pp. 258–270.
11. Albrecht and Wernz, op. cit.
12. *Deterrence, Detection, Investigation, and Reporting of Fraud* (Maitland, Fla.: Institute of Internal Auditors), pp. 3–4.
13. Committee of Sponsoring Organizations, *Internal Control—Integrated Framework,* Treadway Commission, 1992. Their web site is http://www.coso.org.
14. "Organizational Structures to Deal with Employee Fraud," op. cit.
15. Ibid.
16. Independent auditors examine the consolidated financial statements of an organization. In that role, they are primarily concerned only with amounts significantly large enough to affect the financial statements. In some cases, amounts of several million dollars are considered "immaterial."
17. Part of the material that follows was previously published in "How Companies Can Reduce the Cost of Fraud," W. Steve Albrecht, E. A. McDermott, and T. L. Williams, *The Internal Auditor,* February, 1994, pp. 28–35.

PART THREE

FRAUD DETECTION

Recognizing the Symptoms of Fraud

After studying this chapter, you should be able to:

1. Understand how symptoms help in the detection of fraud.
2. Identify and understand accounting fraud.
3. Identify internal controls that help detect fraud.
4. Identify and understand analytical anomalies that can indicate fraud.
5. Understand how changes in lifestyle help detect fraud.
6. Understand how behavioral symptoms help detect fraud.
7. Evaluate tips and complaints as fraud symptoms.

Elgin Aircraft has claims processing and claims payment departments to administer its health care plans. The company is self-insured for claims under $50,000. Claims above this amount are forwarded to an independent insurance company. The claims processing department verifies the necessary documentation for payment and then forwards the documentation to the claims payment department. The claims payment department approves and signs the payment.

Elgin employees can choose between two different insurance plans. The first is a health maintenance organization (HMO) plan in which employees go to approved doctors. Elgin has a contract with a group of medical doctors who treat the employees for a set fee. The second plan allows employees to go to doctors of their own choice, but only 80% of their medical bills are paid by Elgin.

Management thus believed that the company had an excellent internal control system. In addition, the company continually had various auditors on their premises: government contract auditors, defense auditors, outside auditors, and internal auditors. Health claims were processed via an extensive form filled out by attending physicians and a statement from their offices confirming the dollar amount of the treatment. This form was given to the claims processing department, which verified the following:

- *That the patient is an employee of Elgin Aircraft.*
- *That treatments are covered by the plan.*
- *That amounts charged are within approved guidelines.*
- *That the amount of the claims per individual for the year are not over $50,000; if they are, a claim is submitted to the insurance company.*
- *Which plan the employee is on, and that the calculation for payment is correct.*

After these items are verified, claims are forwarded to the claims payment department, which pays the doctors directly. No payments ever go to employees.

One day, a defense auditor observed the claims payment manager taking her employees to lunch in a chauffeured limousine. The auditor was curious about how the manager could afford such an extravagant gesture and was concerned that the lunch and limousine were being paid for by the federal government. In speaking with the vice president of finance, he learned that the manager was "one of the company's best employees." He also learned that she had never missed a day of work in the last 10 years. Her department had one of the best efficiency ratings in the entire company.

Concerned about the limousine and other factors, the auditor began an investigation that revealed that the claims payment department manager had embezzled $12 million from Elgin Aircraft over four years. Her scheme involved setting up 22 dummy doctors who submitted medical bills for employees who did not have many medical claims during the year. She also created fake claims forms and submitted them to the claims processing department. The claims processing department sent the approved forms to the claims payment department, which then paid the dummy doctors.

Fraud is a crime that is seldom observed. When a body is discovered and the person has obviously been murdered, there is no question that a crime has been committed. The dead body is proof enough. Likewise, when a bank is robbed, there is no question that a crime has been committed. Everyone in the bank, including customers and employees, witnessed the robbery. In most cases, the entire episode is captured on video and can be replayed for doubters. But with fraud, it is not always apparent that a crime has been committed. That is why careful observers watch for red flags, the symptoms of fraud.

Symptoms of Fraud

A person's lifestyle changes, a document goes missing, a general ledger is out of balance, someone acts suspiciously, an accounting relationship doesn't make sense, or an anonymous tip is phoned in. As much as these situations may arouse our suspicions, they are only symptoms; they are not conclusive proof of fraud. There may be other explanations for these flags. Maybe the person has recently come into an inheritance, the documents really are lost, or the general ledger is out of balance because of an error. The suspicious actions may be caused by family dissension or personal problems. Accounting anomalies may be the result of unrecognized changes in underlying economic factors. A tip may be motivated by a grudge or by someone settling a score.

To detect fraud, managers, auditors, employees, and examiners must learn to recognize symptoms and pursue them until they are satisfied that fraud has or has not been committed. Unfortunately, many symptoms of fraud go unnoticed, or the symptoms are recognized but not vigorously pursued. Many frauds would be detected earlier if symptoms were routinely investigated.

Symptoms of fraud divide into six types: (1) accounting anomalies, (2) internal control weaknesses, (3) analytical anomalies, (4) extravagant lifestyles, (5) unusual behaviors, and (6) tips and complaints. In this chapter we discuss all six types in detail. But first, we will show how each type of symptom could have alerted management, auditors, and others that fraud was occurring at Elgin Aircraft.

Several *accounting anomalies* at Elgin Aircraft could have alerted auditors to the fraud. The claim forms from the 22 phony doctors all originated from two addresses: a post office box and a business located in a nearby city and owned by the manager's husband. The checks paid to the phony doctors were sent to the same two addresses. Checks were deposited in the same two bank accounts and contained handwritten rather than stamped endorsements.

Why were none of these accounting anomalies recognized? Because management trusted the perpetrator and auditors merely matched claim forms with canceled checks. The auditors did not ask the following key questions:

- Are these payments reasonable? (There were claims for hysterectomies for men.)
- Do the endorsements make sense?
- Why are all these checks going to, and the bills coming from, the same two addresses?

A major difference between auditors and fraud examiners is that most auditors merely match documents to see whether support exists and is adequate. Auditors and examiners who detect fraud go beyond ascertaining the mere existence of documents. They determine whether the documents are real or fraudulent, whether the expenditures make sense, and whether all aspects of the documentation are in order.

Significant *internal control weaknesses* were ignored by Elgin's auditors. First, the manager of the claims payment department had not taken a vacation in 10 years. Second, employees never received confirmation of medical payments so they could determine whether medical claims paid on their behalf were in fact incurred by them. Third, payments to new doctors were neither investigated nor cleared by the company.

Allowing employees to forgo vacations is a serious control weakness that should always be questioned. One of the most effective ways to deter fraud is to implement a system of independent checks. Employee transfers, audits, and mandatory vacations all provide independent checks on employees. As noted in Chapter 2, the Office of the Controller of the Currency requires all bank employees in the United States to take at least one week of consecutive vacation days each year. Many frauds come to light when employees go on vacation and thus cannot cover their tracks. In Elgin's case, had another employee made payments during the manager's absence, the common addresses or the fraudulent payments might have been recognized.

The lack of payment confirmation to employees is another serious control weakness. In Elgin's case, doctors were paid for hysterectomies, tonsillectomies, gall bladder surgeries, and other procedures that were never performed. Had employees been aware of payments made on their behalf for services they were not receiving, they might have complained, and the scheme would have been discovered much sooner.

Another problem is that even if the auditors and managers had noticed the internal control weaknesses, they still might not have uncovered the fraud. Most likely, they would have recommended that the control weaknesses be fixed without giving thought to the possibility that the weaknesses were already being exploited. A major difference between an auditor who uncovers fraud and one who does not is that the first auditor, upon discovering the weakness, immediately endeavors to determine whether the weakness has been exploited and takes measures to correct it. The second auditor ignores or minimizes the possibility of exploitation.

Before doctors are cleared for payment, some type of background check should be conducted to determine whether they are legitimate doctors. Just as Dun & Bradstreet checks should be performed on companies with which business is conducted, the legitimacy of doctors should be verified by checking with state licensing boards, medical groups, or even telephone books.

Analytical anomalies are relationships, procedures, and events that do not make sense, such as a change in a volume, mix, or price that is not reasonable. In the case of Elgin Aircraft, several analytical anomalies should have alerted others to the fraud. The sheer volume of insurance work performed by the fictitious doctors was very high—$12 million worth over a period of four years. Another analytical anomaly was that no outside insurance companies made payments to any of these doctors. That is, these doctors treated *only* employees who incurred less than $50,000 in medical expenses in any given year, for which only Elgin would be paying. Finally, medical costs for the company increased significantly (29%) during the four years of the fraud.

Several lifestyle symptoms at Elgin Aircraft should have been recognized. How common is it for managers to take employees to lunch in a limousine? An inquiry by the Defense Department auditor revealed that the manager paid for the limousine from personal funds and that she was independently wealthy. She told employees that she had recently inherited money from her husband's parents. All her employees knew that she lived in a very expensive house, drove luxury cars, and wore expensive clothes and jewelry. With such wealth, someone should have wondered why she worked and especially why she never took vacations. Although wealthy people often work because they love their job, rarely do they forgo vacations.

Several behavioral symptoms should have alerted others that something was wrong. Employees in the department regularly joked that their manager had a "Dr. Jekyll and Mrs. Hyde" personality. Sometimes she was the nicest person around, and other times she went through periods of unexplained anger. Interviews with employees revealed that her highs and lows had become more intense and more frequent in recent months.

With the Elgin Aircraft fraud, there were no tips or complaints. No employees came forward, and legitimate doctors were still getting business, so they had no reason to complain. Indeed, the only party being hurt was Elgin Aircraft.

The Elgin Aircraft scam was discovered because an observant auditor noticed a common symptom of fraud. In this chapter we discuss how understanding common symptoms helps us detect fraud much more effectively.

Accounting Anomalies

Common accounting anomalies involve problems with source documents, faulty journal entries, and inaccuracies in ledgers.

Irregularities in Source Documents

Source documents can be either electronic or paper and include checks, sales invoices, purchase orders, purchase requisitions, and receiving reports. Here are the red flags to watch for in source documents:

- Missing documents
- "Stale items" (old items that continue month to month) on bank reconciliations
- Excessive voids or credits
- Common names or addresses of payees or customers
- Increases in past due accounts receivable
- Increased reconciling of items
- Alterations on documents
- Duplicate payments
- Second endorsements on checks
- Document sequences that do not make sense
- Questionable handwriting on documents
- Photocopied documents

To illustrate how these flags can signal that embezzlement is taking place, we will describe three actual frauds. The first case involved suspicious photocopied documents; the second case involved an increase in past due accounts receivable; and the third one involved excessive voids or credits. Examine these three cases carefully—*many* frauds have been detected through suspicious source documents.

The first case was detected by an alert internal auditor who was examining authorizations for new equipment purchases. Further investigation revealed a large, collusive fraud. So what got the auditor's attention? A thin line running through a photocopied letter! The auditor came across the letter in a vendor invoice file. In it the manufacturer *appeared* to suggest that the vendor should replace some very expensive equipment. But here was this line that looked like a cut-and-paste job—was something missing? Yes, as it turned out. The manufacturer had also laid out in the letter the case for repairing the machine parts, but the vendor cut out that paragraph. Why? Because they got commissions on the *sale* of new equipment, *not* on the repair of existing equipment.

In the second case, a fraud was detected by recognizing an increase in past due accounts receivable. This employee fraud was committed against a Fortune 500 company that we will call "XYZ Foods."

> *"Mark Rogers" was the accounts receivable department manager at XYZ Foods. In this position, he developed a close relationship with one of the company's largest customers and used the relationship to defraud his employer. In return for a kickback, he offered to "manage" his company's receivable from the customer. By "managing" the large receivable, Rogers permitted the customer to pay later than was normally required, and the customer's bills were not recognized as delinquent or past due. Because the receivable involved millions of dollars, paying 30–60 days later than required cost XYZ $3 million in lost interest. Mark's kickbacks totaled $350,000.*

Mark's fraud was discovered when an alert co-worker realized that XYZ's accounts receivable turnover ratio was decreasing substantially. The co-worker prepared an aging schedule of individual accounts receivable balances, which identified Mark's customer as the source of the problem. A subsequent investigation revealed the kickback scheme.

Excessive credit memos were the tipoff in the third fraud. This case involved a supervisor in the shipping department of a wholesale-retail distribution center warehouse facility.

> *The supervisor was responsible for the warehouse's overall operations and was also accountable for a cash fund that was used to give change to customers who picked up their cash-on-delivery (COD) orders at the warehouse. Established procedures called for the supervisor to issue the customer a cash receipt, which was recorded in a will-call-delivery log book. The file on the customer order was eventually matched with cash receipts by accounting personnel, and the transaction would then be closed.*
>
> *Over approximately one year, the supervisor stole small amounts of money. He concealed the theft by submitting credit memos (with statements such as "billed to the wrong account," "to correct billing adjustment," or "miscellaneous") to clear the accounts receivable file. The accounts were matched with the credit memo, and the transaction then closed. A second signature wasn't needed on the credit memos, and accounting personnel did not question the credit memos originated by the supervisor of the warehouse.*

At first, the supervisor submitted only two or three fraudulent credit memos a week, totaling approximately $100. After a few months, however, he increased the amounts to about $300 per week. To give the appearance of randomness, so as to keep accounting personnel from becoming suspicious, the supervisor intermixed small amounts with large ones.

The fraud surfaced when the supervisor accidentally credited the wrong customer's account for a cash transaction. By coincidence, the supervisor was on vacation when the error surfaced and was thus not able to cover his tracks when accounting personnel queried the transaction. The accounts receivable clerk then questioned the manager of the warehouse, who investigated the problem. The manager scrutinized cash receipts and discovered the fraud.

Faulty Journal Entries

Accounting is a language, just as English and Japanese are languages. For example, consider the following journal entry:

Legal expense	5,000	
Cash		5,000

In plain English, this entry says "An attorney was paid $5,000 in cash." In the language of accounting, this entry says "Debit Legal Expense; credit Cash." People who speak both "accounting" and English know that these statements mean exactly the same thing.

The problem with the language of accounting is that it can easily be manipulated to lie. For example, how do we know that the attorney was actually paid $5,000? Maybe an employee embezzled $5,000 in cash and attempted to conceal the fraud by labeling the theft as a legal expense. Smart embezzlers often conceal their actions in exactly this way, realizing that fraudulent Legal Expense is closed to Retained Earnings at the end of the accounting period, making the audit trail difficult to follow. To recognize when journal entries are fact and when they are fiction, investigators learn to be alert to the symptoms that indicate "cooked" journal entries.

Embezzlers usually steal assets, such as cash or inventory. (No one steals liabilities!) To conceal their theft, embezzlers must find a way to decrease either the liabilities or the equities. Otherwise, the records won't balance and embezzlers will be quickly detected. Smart embezzlers understand that decreasing liabilities is not a good concealment method. In reducing payables, amounts owed to others have to be eliminated from the books. This manipulation will be recognized when vendors do not receive the payments they are owed. When the liability becomes delinquent, they will notify the company, and subsequent investigation will reveal the fraud.

Smart embezzlers thus realize that most equity accounts should not be altered. The owners' equity balance is decreased by paying dividends and expenses and is increased by selling stock and earning revenues. Embezzlers rarely conceal their frauds by manipulating either dividends or stock accounts, because these accounts have relatively few transactions and alterations are quickly noticed. In addition, transactions involving stock or dividends usually require the board of directors' approval and are monitored closely.

So what is left? Revenues and expenses. These two areas decrease the right side of the accounting equation and make the accounting records balance. Balancing the equation by manipulating revenues requires that individual revenue accounts be reduced. However, since revenues increase or are zero, but rarely decrease, a decrease in a revenue account would quickly draw attention. Therefore, embezzlers who manipulate accounting records to conceal their fraud often "balance" the accounting equation by increasing expenses. Increasing expenses decreases net income, which decreases retained earnings and owners' equity, thus leaving the accounting equation in balance, as shown here.

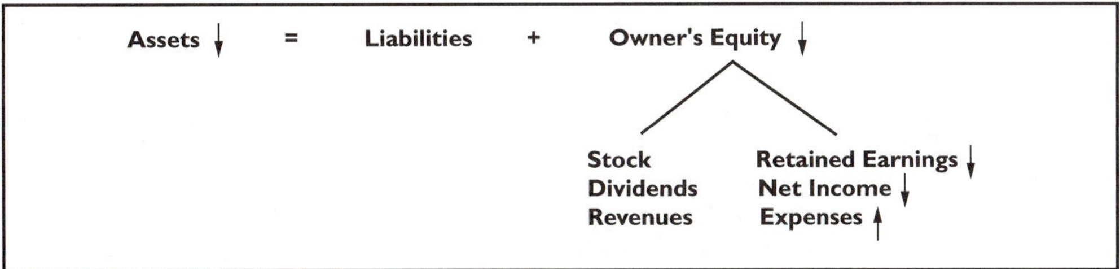

Recording an expense to conceal fraud involves a fictitious journal entry. Fraud detectors must be able to recognize signs that a journal entry may not be legitimate and may be concealing a fraud. Manipulating expense accounts also has the advantage that expenses are closed or brought to zero balances at year-end, thus obscuring the audit trail. The following entries are common symptoms of fraud:

- Journal entries without documentary support
- Unexplained adjustments to receivables, payables, revenues, or expenses
- Journal entries that do not balance
- Journal entries made by individuals who don't normally make such entries
- Journal entries made near the end of an accounting period

To see how you can ferret out suspicious journal entries, we describe two actual embezzlements. The symptom in the first case, a $150,000 embezzlement by the controller of a bank, was uncovered because of undocumented journal entries.

> *"John Doe" was the controller of a small bank we'll call "ABC Bank." Over a period of several years, he embezzled approximately $150,000 from ABC by telephoning correspondent banks and having them pay his personal credit-card bills. He concealed his fraud by creating fictitious journal entries that recognized the shortages as advertising expense. The total amount of advertising expense was large and the resulting increase in expense was relatively small, so no one questioned the legitimacy of his journal entries. Because he was the bank's controller and in charge of all accounting, he did not even need to forge documentation to support the entries. He was caught when he got greedy and deposited in his own personal bank account a duplicate $10,000 payment from a bank customer. When the customer realized he had paid twice, he asked for a refund, and the deposit was traced to Doe's account.*

Had anyone questioned the undocumented journal entries, Doe's fraud would have been quickly discovered. And had Doe not gotten greedy, his fraud might have continued indefinitely.

In the second case, journal entries were used to manipulate income at Lincoln Savings and Loan. In this fraud, journal entries were made at the end of accounting periods to artificially inflate reported net income. For many successive quarters, large journal entries recorded fictitious revenues that took Lincoln Savings and Loan from a loss to a profit position.

The accounting firm that reviewed Lincoln's transactions concluded that 13 transactions overstated income by more than $100 million. The auditors called the transactions the most egregious misapplication of accounting they had ever seen. If Lincoln's auditors and regulators had noted the pattern of last-minute entries earlier, Lincoln's investors would have been spared millions of dollars in losses.

Inaccuracies in Ledgers

Recall from your accounting courses that a ledger is defined as "a book of accounts." In other words, all transactions related to specific accounts, such as Cash or Inventory, are summarized in the ledger. The accuracy of account balances in the ledger is often proved by checking that the total of all asset accounts equals the total of all liability and equity accounts. Many frauds manipulate receivables from customers or payables to vendors. Most companies have master (control) receivable and payable accounts, the total of which should equal the sum of all the individual customer and vendor account balances. Two common fraud symptoms relating to ledgers then are

1. A ledger that does not balance
2. Master (control) account balances that do not equal the sum of the individual customer or vendor balances

The first symptom is found in frauds in which the cover-up in the accounting records is not complete. For example, a perpetrator embezzles inventory (an asset) but neglects to record expenses or effect a decrease to the right-hand side of the accounting equation. That is, the actual inventory balance, as determined by a physical count, is lower than the recorded amount of inventory, and the ledger doesn't balance. Another example is the theft of cash accompanied by failure to record an expense so that total assets are less than total liabilities plus owners' equity.

The second symptom indicates manipulation of an individual customer or vendor's balance without a balancing alteration in the ledger's master receivable or payable account. That is, the sum of the individual customer or vendor balances does not agree with the master account balance.

A fraud characterized by this second ledger symptom was perpetrated by the bookkeeper for a small bank, the First National Bank. Using the following schemes, she embezzled over $3 million from the bank, which had only $30 million in total assets.

> *Using two different schemes, "Marjorie" defrauded First National Bank of over $3 million. In the first scheme she wrote personal checks on her bank account at First National to pay for expensive art, jewelry, automobiles, home furnishings, and other expensive acquisitions. Then, when her cleared check was sent from the Federal Reserve to the bank (in the incoming cash letter), she allowed the overall demand deposit account balance to be reduced but pulled her checks before they could be processed and deducted from her personal account. The result was that the master demand deposit account balance was lower than the sum of the bank's individual customers' demand deposits.*
>
> *In the second scheme she made deposits into her account using checks drawn on other banks and then pulled the checks before they were sent in the outgoing cash letter to the Federal Reserve. Thus, her checks were never deducted from her accounts at the other banks. In fact, her accounts at the banks did not contain sufficient funds to cover the checks if they had been processed. The result was that the individual demand deposit balances increased, but the master demand deposit account balance did not.*

Both schemes had the effect of making the master demand deposit account balances lower than the sum of the individual account balances. Over time, as Marjorie wrote checks and made fictitious deposits, the discrepancy in the ledger balances grew larger and larger.

At the end of each accounting period, to cover her tracks and prevent auditors from discovering the fraud, Marjorie pulled previously used bank checks (cashier's checks) and sent them in the outgoing cash letter to the Federal Reserve. Because the Federal Reserve procedures are automated, no one there ever personally examined the checks or noticed that they had been processed several times. (In fact, some of the checks were totally black.) Her fraud was assisted by the Federal Reserve's policy of giving immediate credit to First National for the total amount supposedly contained in the outgoing cash letter. The next day, as the checks were processed using bank routing numbers, the Federal Reserve would realize that the official checks were not drawn on other banks but were really First National's own checks and would reverse the credit previously given to First National. The reduction would again throw First National's ledger accounts out of balance. But, for one day—the day the auditors examined the records—the bank's books would be balanced and the shortage would be "parked" at the Federal Reserve. Because the financial statements were prepared for that one day, the bank records balanced for the auditors.

This fraud could easily have been discovered if someone had noticed that, although the books balanced at month-end, they were out of balance the rest of the month. Bank managers received daily statements of condition and other reports that showed demand deposit balances significantly different from the balances on the financial statements. They never questioned these unusual balances.

This fraud could also have been uncovered if someone had recognized many other symptoms. For example, Marjorie had significant personality conflicts with other employees, and she lived far beyond what her income could have supported. In addition, individual accounting records were altered, and a previous fraud at the same bank indicated the need for better reporting procedures that, if implemented, would have made Marjorie's fraud impossible. Surprisingly, the fraud was not discovered until a check that Marjorie had reused several times was kicked out of a Federal Reserve sorter because it could not be read.

Internal Control Weaknesses

As discussed in previous chapters, fraud occurs when pressure, opportunity, and rationalization come together. Many individuals and organizations have pressures. Everyone rationalizes. When internal controls are absent or overridden, the fraud triangle is completed, and the risk for fraud increases greatly.

As we discussed in Chapter 2, internal control is composed of the control environment, the accounting system, and control procedures. Common internal control weaknesses that make fraud easier to perpetrate include the following:

- Lack of segregation of duties
- Lack of physical safeguards
- Lack of independent checks
- Lack of proper authorization
- Lack of proper documents and records
- Overriding of existing controls
- Inadequate accounting system

Many studies have found that frauds are most commonly committed by overriding existing internal controls.[1] We give two examples that show how control weaknesses facilitate fraud. In the first example, a customer defrauded a bank of over $500,000. The second is a famous fraud that continued over several years.

> *"Lorraine" was a customer of Second National Bank. She had opened her account 16 months earlier, and she often made deposits and withdrawals in the hundreds of thousands of dollars. She claimed to be a member of a well-known, wealthy family. She drove a Porsche, dressed very nicely, and had earned the trust and confidence of the bank's branch manager. One day, she approached the manager and said that she needed a cashier's check in the amount of $525,000. The manager, realizing that she had only $13,000 in her account, first denied the request. Then, deciding that she was a valued customer, and based on her promise to cover the shortage the next day, gave her the cashier's check. Lorraine, of course, was not who she claimed to be. In fact, she had embezzled over $5 million from her employer; all the funds going through her bank account were stolen. Her employer had already apprehended her but had promised not to prosecute if she repaid the company. She was therefore stealing from Second National in order to repay the money.*

As it turned out, Second National did have a control requiring two signatures on all cashier's checks exceeding $500,000. However, the bank manager, who was an imposing figure, ordered his assistant to sign the cashier's check. And, the assistant merely followed orders. As a result, the independent-signature control was compromised. There were two signatures, but they were not independent. The assistant and the manager joined the ranks of the unemployed soon thereafter.

The famous Hochfelder case also shows how internal control weakness can open the door to fraud. This case went all the way to the U.S. Supreme Court before it was decided that Ernst & Ernst (now Ernst & Young), a large public accounting firm, was not negligent in performing their audit.

> *Lester B. Nay, the president of First Securities Co. of Chicago, convinced certain customers to invest funds in high-yielding escrow accounts. Problem was, there were no such accounts. Nay then dipped into customer funds for his own personal use.*
>
> *The transactions did not follow the usual protocol used for dealings between First Securities and its customers. First, customer correspondence was done solely by Nay. Because of a "mail rule" that Nay imposed, such mail was opened only by him. Second, their checks were made payable directly to Nay. Third, the escrow accounts were not reflected on the books of First Securities, nor in filings with the SEC, nor in connection with the customers' other investment accounts. The fraud was uncovered only after Nay's suicide.*
>
> *Respondent customers sued in district court for damages against Ernst & Ernst as aiders and abetters under Section 10b-5 of the 1933 SEC Act. They alleged that Ernst & Ernst failed to conduct a proper audit, which would have led them to discover the mail rule and the fraud. The court reasoned that Ernst & Ernst had a common-law and statutory duty of inquiry into the adequacy of First Securities' internal control system, because the firm had contracted to audit First Securities and to review the annual report filings with the SEC.*

The U.S. Supreme Court reversed the decision of the Court of Appeals and concluded that the interpretation of Section 10b-5 requires an "intent to deceive, manipulate or defraud." Justice Powell wrote, in the Supreme Court's opinion: "When a statute speaks so specifically in terms of manipulation and deception, and of implementing devices and contrivances—the commonly understood terminology of intentional wrongdoing—and when its history reflects no more expansive intent, we are quite unwilling to extend the scope of the statute to negligent conduct."

The Supreme Court pointed out that in certain areas of the law, recklessness is a form of intentional conduct for purposes of imposing liability.[2]

In this case, the mail rule that required that no one except Lester B. Nay open the mail was an internal control weakness. Had it not been allowed, Nay's fraud would have been revealed much earlier and investors would not have lost nearly so much money.

Analytical Anomalies

Analytical anomalies are procedures or relationships that are unusual or too unrealistic to be believable. They include transactions or events that happen at odd times or places; that are performed by or involve people who would not normally participate; or that include odd procedures, policies, or practices. They also include transactions and amounts that are too large or too small, that occur too often or too rarely, that are too high or too low, or that result in too much or too little of something. Basically, analytical anomalies are anything out of the ordinary.

Common examples of analytical anomalies include the following:

- Unexplained inventory shortages or adjustments
- Deviations from specifications
- Increased scrap
- Excess purchases
- Too many debit or credit memos
- Significant increases or decreases in account balances
- Physical abnormalities
- Cash shortages or overages
- Excessive late charges
- Unreasonable expenses or reimbursements
- Strange financial statement relationships, such as
  - increased revenues with decreased inventory
  - increased revenues with decreased receivables
  - increased revenues with decreased cash flows
  - increased inventory with decreased payables
  - increased volume with increased cost per unit
  - increased volume with decreased scrap
  - increased inventory with decreased warehousing costs

The Mayberry fraud was detected by investigating analytical anomalies.

The internal auditors for the Mayberry Corporation, a conglomerate with about $1 billion in annual sales, were going over the company's sheet metal division. Past audits showed favorable outcomes with few audit findings. This year, however, something did not seem right. Their observation of inventory revealed no serious shortages, and yet inventory seemed dramatically overstated. Why would inventory increase fivefold in one year?

> *Suspecting something was wrong, the auditors performed some "midnight auditing." Their investigation revealed that sheet metal inventory was grossly overstated. The auditors were almost deceived. Local management falsified the inventory by preparing fictitious records. The auditors verified the amount of inventory shown on the tags and deposited their verifications in a box in the conference room they used during the audit. A manager added spurious tags to the box at night. However, since there wasn't enough time to fabricate a large number of reasonable tags, some fabrications showed very large rolls of sheet metal. The manager also substituted new inventory reconciliation lists to conform with the total of the valid and spurious tags.*

The fraud was discovered when the auditors analyzed the numbers. First, they converted the purported $30 million of sheet metal inventory into cubic feet. Second, they determined the capacity of the warehouse used to store the inventory. At most, it could store only one-half the reported amounts; it was far too small to house the total. Third, they examined the inventory tags and found that some rolls of sheet metal had to weigh 50,000 pounds. However, none of the forklifts used to move the rolls lifted over 3,000 pounds. Finally, the auditors verified the reported inventory purchases. Purchase orders supported an inventory of about 30 million pounds, yet the reported amount was 60 million pounds.

Faced with this evidence, managers admitted that they grossly overstated the value of the inventory to show increased profits. The budget for the sheet metal division called for increased earnings, and without the overstatement, earnings fell far short of target.

In this case, the relationship between amounts recorded and the weight and volume that the recorded amounts represented did not make sense. Unfortunately, few managers or auditors ever think to examine physical characteristics of inventory.

Sometimes, it is not unusual relationships that signal fraud but transactions or events that don't make sense. Such was the case in the Regal Industries fraud.

> *"Don" was the business manager for Regal Industries. In this position, he often arranged and paid for services performed by various vendors. An alert accountant caught Don committing fraud. The accountant first noted that payments were made to an Oldsmobile dealership, even though the company had only a few company cars and all were Cadillacs. The accountant also thought it strange that the company cars were serviced at an Oldsmobile dealership rather than the Cadillac dealership. Maybe, he reasoned, the Oldsmobile dealership was closer, but upon checking, he discovered that it was not. Further investigation revealed that although payments were also made to the Oldsmobile dealership for body damage to company cars, no claims were filed with insurance companies. And the monthly payments to the Oldsmobile dealer were always the same amount. The combination of factors—wrong dealer, body damage expense with no insurance claims, monthly expenditures of the same amount—did not make sense. The accountant concluded that the only legitimate explanation for these anomalies would be a fixed-fee maintenance contract with the Oldsmobile dealer to service the company's Cadillacs. An investigation revealed that no such maintenance contract existed. Further investigation confirmed that Don's girlfriend worked at the Oldsmobile dealership, and that Regal Industries (unbeknownst to them) was buying her a car.*

In this case, an alert accountant saved Regal approximately $15,000. Unfortunately, many accountants and auditors would miss this fraud. They would note the check paid to the Oldsmobile dealer, would match it with the invoice that Don's girlfriend supplied each month, and have been satisfied. They wouldn't have asked themselves whether the expenditure made sense or why a company would service Cadillacs at an Oldsmobile dealership.

Recognizing analytical anomalies is an excellent way to detect fraud. This is how one longtime fraud investigator uncovered his first fraud. This discovery, which determined his lifelong career, still is an excellent example of the use of analytical anomalies. Here is his career-changing experience.

> *It was the summer of 1956. That's what I remember, at least, though it was a long time ago and things get distorted when you look back. And, I have looked back quite a bit since then, for the entire episode was quite an eye-opener for an 18-year-old kid. I was a "numbers man" then and still am. Mathematics is an art to me. I find a beauty in pure numbers that I never see in the vulgar excesses that most of society chases after. You might wonder, then, what I was doing working in a movie theater that summer—the summer that Grace Kelly became a princess and the whole country seemed to worship the cardboard stars on the silver screens. Well, the truth is, I spent the summer in a movie theater because I needed employment. I'd just graduated from South High and was waiting to begin college. To earn money, I took a job as a ticket taker at the Classic Theater. As movie theaters go, the Classic was one of the best. Not in terms of elegance: it wasn't one of those gild and velvet-lined monstrosities with fat plaster babies and faux chandeliers. No! What the Classic had was a certain charm in the same way that drive-in hamburger joints of the decade did. I think the style was called deco-modern and it made me feel a bit like I was rushing toward the 21st century. So the place wasn't all bad, though it was not the kind of job that a dedicated numbers man usually sought. But as it turned out, my numbers did come in useful. For that's how I caught on to him, you see; it was because of the numbers.*
>
> *Ticket taking is not the most exciting job there is, and I didn't find it a real intellectual challenge. My mind was free to wander, and I got in the habit of noting the number of each ticket that I tore: 57, 58, 59, 60. The numbers would march to me in a more or less consecutive order as they came off the roll that the ticket seller sold from: 61, 62, 63, 64. But sometimes, I noticed, the sequence would be off. A whole chunk of numbers would appear that should have come through earlier: 65, 66, 40, 41, 42. It would happen almost every time I worked. I thought it was odd and was curious about what could be disturbing the symmetry of my numbers. The world of numbers is orderly and logical; for every apparent irrationality, there is an explanation. I began to use the puzzle as a mental game to occupy my working hours. Noting each time the sequence was off, I came to realize that it always happened after my daily break. The manager, "Mr. Smith," would relieve me while I was on break. I watched closer and noticed another fact: the numbers would always be off while the ticket seller, who had the break after mine, was being relieved. Mr. Smith filled in for the ticket seller too.*
>
> *Until this point, the amateur detective work had been merely a way to pass the time. I began to suspect that something wrong was going on, and it made me uncomfortable. After more observation and thought, I solved Mr. Smith's scheme. When he relieved me as ticket taker during my break, he would pocket the tickets instead of tearing them in two. Then, when he*

> *relieved the ticket seller, he would resell the tickets he had just pocketed and keep the cash. Thus, the ticket numbers that I saw coming through out of sequence were really coming through for the second time.*

Although this was a small fraud, it demonstrates the "rule" that when things don't look right, they probably aren't right. If the ticket taker had not been fascinated with numbers, the manager probably wouldn't have been detected. The manager was trusted more than other workers. The number of tickets he pocketed was small in relation to the total number of tickets sold in a day, and so the owner did not see a large drop in profits. Every night, the bookkeeper computed the total number of tickets sold, using the beginning and ending ticket numbers, and compared the total to the cash taken in. Unfortunately, the balance was not wrong. The theater hired separate people to sell and take tickets specifically to avoid this type of fraud. But because Smith was the manager, no one perceived a problem with letting him do both jobs while others were on break. There is probably no way Smith's fraud would have been caught if it had not been for a "numbers man" who saw relationships that did not make sense.

The story that numbers tell also shows up in financial statements. To people who understand accounting, financial statements tell a very particular kind of story, and the elements of the story must be internally consistent. Many large financial statement frauds would be discovered much sooner if statement preparers, auditors, analysts, and others understood numbers in the financial statements the way the ticket taker understood his numbers.

MiniScribe Corporation's fraud is one of the best examples of numbers not making sense.[3] MiniScribe, based in Denver, manufactured computer disk drives. Here is a description of MiniScribe's financial statement fraud and an analysis of the numbers that did not make sense.

> *On May 18, 1989, MiniScribe Corporation announced that the financial statements issued for 1986, 1987, and the first three quarters of 1988 could not be relied upon because they grossly overstated sales and net income.*
>
> *Only the year before, MiniScribe had been voted the most "well-managed" personal computer disk drive company. Company sales increased from $113.9 million in 1985 (the year it lost IBM, its largest customer) to a reported $603 million in 1988. In April 1985, Quentin Thomas Wiles was appointed CEO and director of the company, and hopes were high that he would lead the company out of financial trouble. Under his management, the company's sales and profits steadily increased, even amid downturns in the market and severe price cutting in the industry. Unfortunately for investors, the financial statement numbers were fraudulent.*
>
> *Wiles used his strict, overbearing management style to turn failing companies into successes. At MiniScribe, he set stringent goals: Each manager would increase sales and income, and failure would not be tolerated. In an effort to please Wiles, reports were forged and manipulated throughout the company. One marketing manager revealed that division managers were told to "force the numbers" if they needed to. Thus, the fraud began with managers simply touching up internal documents as they moved up the line. Wiles continued, however, to push for increases in sales, even during recession and periods of industrywide price cutting. This pressure led managers to invent various schemes to make the company look better than it really was:*
>
> - *Packaging bricks, shipping them, and recording them as sales of hard drives.*

- *Dramatically increasing shipments to warehouses and booking them as sales.*
- *Shipping defective merchandise repeatedly and booking the shipments as sales.*
- *Shipping excess merchandise that was not returned until after financial statements were released.*
- *Understating bad debts expense and the allowance for doubtful accounts.*
- *Changing shipping dates on shipments to overseas customers so that revenues were recognized before sales were made.*
- *Changing auditors' working papers.*

The result was a significant overstatement of net income and sales. Inventory records as of the end of 1987 revealed $12 million on hand; in reality, it was more like $4 million. In 1989, the company booked a $40 million charge to income to offset these overstatements. On January 1, 1990, the company filed for bankruptcy, listing liabilities of $257.7 million and only $86.1 million in assets.

Several analytical anomalies indicated that things were not right at MiniScribe. First, the company's results were not consistent with industry performance. During the period of the fraud, severe price cutting was going on, sales were declining, and competition was stiff. MiniScribe Corporation reported increases in sales and profits, while other companies reported losses. MiniScribe had very few large customers and had lost several major customers, including Apple Computer, IBM, and Digital Equipment Corporation (DEC). MiniScribe also fell behind on its payments to suppliers. Returns to suppliers forced MiniScribe's major supplier of aluminum disks, Domain Technologies, into bankruptcy.

In addition, the numbers reported at the end of each quarter were amazingly close to the projections made by Wiles. Financial results were the sole basis for management bonuses. Receivables increased significantly, and yet the allowance for doubtful accounts was far less than the industry average. An aging of receivables revealed that many accounts were old and probably not collectable. A simple correlation of inventory with sales would have revealed that although reported sales were increasing, inventory was not increasing proportionately. Indeed, the financial statement numbers did not make sense. Relationships in the statements, relationships with industry standards, and an examination of MiniScribe's customers revealed analytical anomalies that suggested something was seriously wrong. Unfortunately, by the time these anomalies were recognized, many people had a lot of lost money.

Extravagant Lifestyles

Most people who commit fraud do so under financial pressure. Sometimes the pressures are real; sometimes they represent simple greed. Once perpetrators meet their financial needs, however, they often continue to steal, using the embezzled funds to improve their lifestyles. They buy new cars. They buy other expensive toys, take vacations, remodel their homes or move into more expensive houses, buy expensive jewelry or clothes—the money goes many places. Few perpetrators save what they steal. Indeed, most immediately spend everything they steal. As they grow confident, they steal more and spend more. Soon they live far beyond what they can reasonably afford. Here are two examples.

> *"Kay" embezzled nearly $3 million from her employer. She and her husband worked together to perfect the scheme over a period of seven years. Because they knew they might someday get caught, they decided not to have children. With their stolen funds, they purchased a new, expensive home (worth $500,000) and five luxury cars—a Maserati, a Rolls-Royce, a Jeep Cherokee, and two Audis. They filled their home with expensive artwork and glass collections. They bought a boat and several expensive computers, and they paid cash to have their yard extensively landscaped. They frequently invited*

Kay's co-workers to parties at their home and served expensive foods, including lobster flown in from the East Coast. Yet none of the employees noticed the change in lifestyle. They did not note, for example, that Kay drove a different car to work every day of the week, and that they were all extremely expensive. (This is hard to believe—but it happened!)

Randy stole over $600,000 from his friend's (and employer's) small company. The business constantly had cash flow problems, but Randy drove a Porsche, bought a cabin in the mountains, and took expensive vacations. At one point, he even loaned his friend $16,000 to keep the business going. Never once did his friend (the owner) question where the money was coming from, even though Randy was paid less than $25,000 a year.

Embezzlers are people who take shortcuts to appear successful. Very few crooks, at least those who are caught, save the embezzled money. The same motivation that compels them to steal compels them to seek immediate gratification. People who can delay gratification rarely embezzle.

Lifestyle changes are the easiest of all symptoms to detect. If managers, co-workers, and others pay attention, they will notice that embezzlers live lifestyles that their incomes do not support. Although lifestyle changes only provide circumstantial evidence of fraud, such evidence is easy to corroborate. Bank records, investment records, and tax return information are difficult to access, but property records, Uniform Commercial Code (UCC) filings, and other records are easy to check to determine whether assets have been purchased or liens have been removed.

Unusual Behaviors

Research in psychology indicates that when people (especially first-time offenders, as many fraud perpetrators are) commit a crime, they are overwhelmed by fear and guilt.[4] These emotions express themselves in an extremely unpleasant physical response called stress. Individuals then exhibit unusual and recognizable coping mechanisms, as shown below.

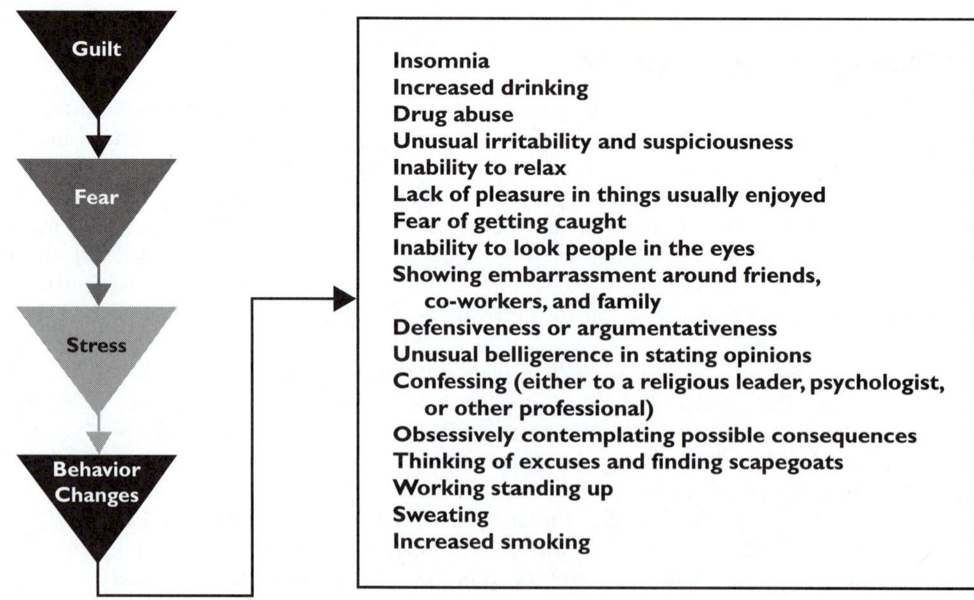

No particular behavior signals fraud; rather, changes in behavior (in conjunction with the other symptoms we've been discussing) are signals. People who are normally nice become intimidating and belligerent. People who are normally belligerent suddenly become nice.

Even perpetrators recognize their behavioral changes. A woman who stole over $400,000 said, "I had to be giving off signals. I couldn't look anyone in the eye." A man who embezzled over $150,000 said, "Sometimes I would be so wound up I would work 12 or 14 hours a day, often standing up. Other times I would be so despondent I couldn't get off the couch for over a week at a time." Eddie Antar, mastermind of the Crazy Eddie fraud described here, became very intimidating and finally vanished.[5]

> *From 1971 to 1987, Crazy Eddie, Inc., a 42-store retail company located in New York, New Jersey, Connecticut, and Pennsylvania, sold entertainment and consumer electronic products. Eddie installed his father, brother, uncle, cousin, and his father's cousin as officers of the company. He also allegedly overstated inventory by over $65 million. As the fraud progressed, he became increasingly overbearing. Finally, overwhelmed by fears that he would be caught and prosecuted, he skipped the country and ended up in Israel. He has since been extradited to the United States and is now facing charges for his fraud.*

Donald Sheelen, CEO of Regina Vacuum Company, and Lester B. Nay, CEO of First Securities of Chicago, are two perpetrators for whom the stress caused by committing fraud caused behavioral changes. Neither was able to cope with the stress of the fraud. Sheelen went to his priest *before* his fraud was discovered and confessed his entire scheme. Nay, after penning a suicide note detailing how he defrauded investors of millions of dollars, committed suicide.[6]

The following case illustrates how stress changes behavior.

> *"Johnson Marine" is an industrial diving company that services marine-related problems all over the eastern United States. The firm salvages downed aircraft in oceans, lays submarine pipelines, inspects dams, conducts insurance recoveries, and performs search-and-rescue missions. Johnson's part-time accountant, "Rick Smith," uncovered a serious fraud that was perpetrated by "Joseph Simons," vice president of the company. After Rick was hired by the office manager, Joseph told Rick to report only to him, to pay bills only when he directed Rick, and to take all his questions only to Joseph. It was obvious to Rick that Joseph intimidated the office manager. Joseph treated the office manager like a slave and continually reminded him that if he didn't mind his own business, he would find himself without a job.*
>
> *Rick's first task was to update all the balances in accounts payable. Upon close inspection, he found very few of the 120 balances to be correct. He spent a week fixing them, only to be criticized by Joseph, who told Rick to find more productive work and not worry about trivial things. When Rick tried to identify the petty cash system, he found that petty cash had not been reconciled in over five months, and that a negative difference of $13,600 existed between checks written to replenish the cash box and total receipts in the cash box. Rick immediately told Joseph—who directed him to make an adjusting entry on the computer to fix the problem.*
>
> *Rick's next discovery came when he reviewed the company's life insurance policies, two of which were for over $1 million. Joseph was listed as beneficiary.*

Next, Rick noticed that large balances were accruing on the company's American Express card. Although overdue notices were piling up, Joseph forbade Rick to pay the bill. Rick asked the president about it, who said that the company didn't have an American Express card. The "nonexistent" credit card showed a balance of over $5,500! A similar problem occurred with the Phillips 66 bill. Again, Joseph told Rick not to pay the bill, even though they were receiving final notices. Rick later learned that the company used only Chevron cards.

Looking back over the accounts payable balances, Rick noticed that an account with TMC Consulting had an outstanding balance over 90 days old. He tried to find out more about the account, but there was nothing on file. By coincidence, while he was looking at the account information, Rick saw that the address was 10 Windsor Circle—a diving catalog addressed to Joseph had been sent to the same place two weeks earlier. Upon printing out a history of the company's transactions with TMC Consulting, Rick found five $2,000 payments on the account spread over a period of several months. He presented this information to the president, who confronted Joseph. Joseph stalled the president until the next day but never came back. Investigation revealed that he had moved to California, leaving no forwarding address.

In this case, Joseph's intimidating personality kept the office manager and others at bay. Although the office manager sensed something was wrong, he was never given the chance to find out. The office manager was continually blamed when petty cash was out of balance, yet never allowed to balance it. In fact, Joseph constantly blamed others for problems. In retrospect, employees understood that Joseph's intimidating behavior was his way of keeping the fraud from being discovered and of dealing with the stress he felt for committing the crime.

Once in a while, someone commits a fraud or other crime and does not feel stress. Such people are called sociopaths or psychopaths. They feel no guilt because they have no conscience. The following case exemplifies this.[7]

Confessed killer Mark Hoffman's ability to pass a lie detector test left two nationally known polygraph experts baffled and anxious to question the dealer in bogus documents on how he passed the test.

Hoffman pleaded guilty to the bombing deaths of two people, which he carried out to avoid exposure of his fraudulent documents dealings. He was judged truthful in an earlier polygraph test during which he denied his involvement with the slayings.

What puzzled the polygraph experts the most? That Hoffman did not merely squeak by on the tests—in fact, he passed with flying colors! On the plus-minus scale used to gauge truthfulness, a score of plus 6 is considered a clear indication that the subject is not lying; but Hoffman scored twice that—plus 12. The point here? Sociopaths can and do pass polygraph tests, and with ease. Apparently, one must first have a conscience in order for polygraphs to be reliable. And we don't yet have a test for that!

Tips and Complaints

Auditors are often criticized for not detecting more frauds. Yet, because of the nature of fraud, auditors are often in the worst position to detect it. Recall that the elements of fraud form a triangle:

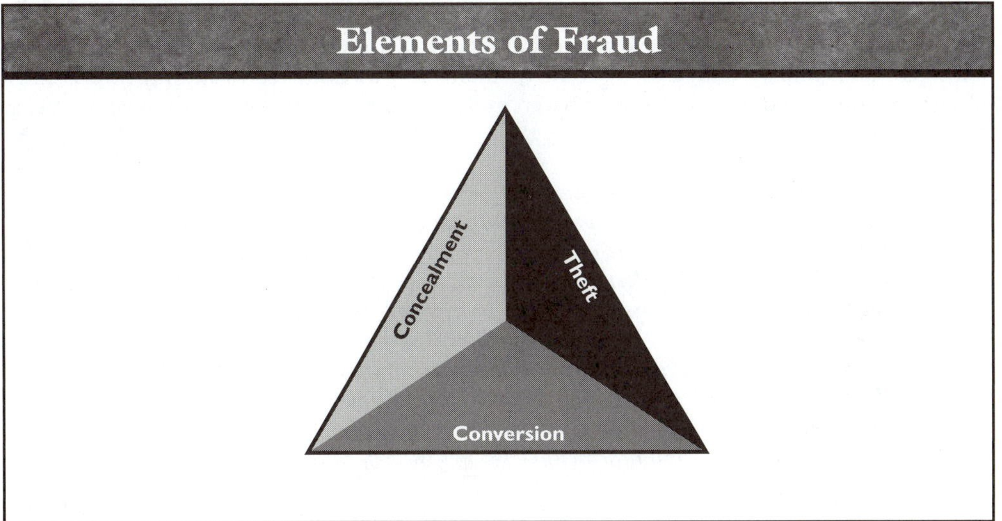

Theft is the actual taking of cash, inventory, information, or other assets. Theft can occur manually, by computer, or by telephone. *Concealment* involves the steps taken by the perpetrator to hide the fraud. In concealment, financial records are altered, cash or inventory is miscounted, or evidence is destroyed. *Conversion* has to do with selling stolen assets or converting them into cash and then spending the cash. If the asset taken is cash, the conversion is the spending of the stolen funds. As we noted previously, virtually all perpetrators spend their stolen funds.

A fraud can be detected during any of these elements of the crime. Someone may witness the theft—the perpetrator taking cash or other assets. Someone may notice that records have been altered or cash or inventory miscounted. And the lifestyle changes that perpetrators almost inevitably make when they convert their embezzled funds are often highly visible.

Who in an organization is in the best position to recognize each of these elements? Certainly, for the theft, it is not the auditors. Auditors are rarely present when funds are stolen. Rather, they spend one or two weeks conducting periodic audits, and the thefts often stop during this period. Instead, co-workers, managers, and other employees are the ones who usually detect fraud during the theft. That said, auditors are frequently key in detecting fraud through its concealment. If audit samples include altered documents, miscounts, or other concealment efforts, auditors may suspect fraud. Even so, company accountants and even co-workers are still in the better position to detect fraud through the concealment. Auditors rarely detect fraud during its conversion: They won't know that the employee rolling into the parking lot in a BMW recently drove a used Ford Focus. This is where co-workers, friends, and managers come in; only they are in a position to notice the changes that come about when the conversion of stolen assets begins.

Co-workers and managers are in the best position to detect fraud, but they are often the least trained to recognize it. Even so, many frauds are found out by employees, friends, managers, customers, and other untrained people providing tips or complaining that something is wrong. One large company, for example, which uncovered over 1,500 individual frauds, uncovered 43% of them through customer complaints and employee tips.

Complaints and tips are categorized as fraud symptoms rather than actual evidence of fraud because many tips and complaints turn out to be bogus. It is often difficult to know what motivates a person to complain or provide a tip. Customers, for example, may complain because they think they're being taken advantage of. Employees may phone in tips for reasons of malice, personal problems, or jealousy. Tips from spouses and friends may be motivated by anger, divorce, or blackmail. Therefore, tips and complaints must be treated with care and initially only as symptoms of fraud, not as evidence of it. Individuals must always be considered innocent until proven guilty. Remember, tips can also be spurious, as the following example shows.

> *Joan worked in a bank. One day, Joan approached the bank branch's operations manager and informed him that two weeks ago she saw Jean, a co-worker, place a bundle of bills (currency) in her blouse. She stated that she hadn't been able to sleep for two weeks, so she finally decided to inform the bank. For several days, auditors and security people scoured the bank's records and cash vault. Employees cried, and suspicion and distrust abounded. Finally, the fraud investigators discovered that Jean had been sleeping with Joan's boyfriend, and that Joan's tip was false and motivated by jealousy. Joan resigned, but because of the nature of the triggering circumstances, branch management could not inform all employees about what happened.*

In most organizations, co-workers and others suspect and may even know that fraud is occurring, but they do not come forward with their information. Why? They hesitate for several reasons. First, knowing for certain that fraud is taking place is almost impossible. There are no dead bodies or videotapes of the crime, so all that potential informants see are symptoms. They may note changes in lifestyle, strange behavior, or company inventory stashed in a garage. But no one wants to accuse wrongly. Even when their suspicions are strong, there is always the possibility that a legitimate reason exists.

Second, informants may hesitate to come forward because they have heard the horror stories about what happens to whistle-blowers. Even though such reports are often exaggerated, people fear that they will suffer similar reprisals if they become informants.

Third, employees and others are frequently intimidated by the perpetrators. Subordinates are especially afraid to come forward with their suspicions when the perpetrator is their superior. One fraud continued for six years, even though seven co-workers knew about it. The perpetrator was so dominant that others feared him, and he routinely fired people who questioned his integrity.

Fourth, many of us have been conditioned from grade school on to believe that squealing, tattling—and therefore, whistle-blowing—is not acceptable. This is a societal code that needs to be looked at differently. Technically, one who does not tell on another is an ethnological liar. Not squealing is the creed of the Mafia. To illustrate the general reluctance to become informants, consider the following actual event.

> *Scott was a junior in high school, enrolled in a word processing class. He was informed that students' grades for the class would be mostly determined by how many processed projects they completed. The teacher informed the students that they must work alone, and, in fact, that working together constituted cheating and would result in an F for the course. One night, Scott informed his dad that the best grade he could get in word processing was a B unless he cheated, and then he could probably get an A.*
>
> *"What do you mean?" Scott's dad asked.*
>
> *"Well," said Scott, "our grades are mostly based on the number of jobs we complete. And while we have been told we must work alone, a number of student groups have formed in the class. Each member of the group completes a*

> *certain number of projects and then they all copy each other's disks as though they had completed the projects themselves. There is no way I can complete as many projects alone as a group of three or four students can. I have been invited to work in a group, but I don't know whether I should. What do you think I should do, Dad? Should I cheat and get an A or settle for a B?"*
>
> *Needless to say, Scott's dad was very frustrated. Although he didn't want Scott to cheat, he didn't want him to be disadvantaged and earn a B either. His counsel to Scott was to do neither but to go to the teacher and inform her what was happening. Scott's quick reply was "I can't." When asked why, Scott said, "These are my friends," he said, "and it wouldn't be right to squeal on them."*

There is another reason most employees and others do not come forward with their suspicions or knowledge of fraud: Organizations don't make it easy. In most organizations, employees do not know whom they should contact if they suspect fraud, how the information should be conveyed, or what consequences will ensue if they do come forward. In addition, they don't know whether their tips will remain anonymous.

Organizations that are effective in identifying tips and complaints as fraud symptoms have found that they need to encourage employees to submit tips. Employees must be given easy avenues for whistle-blowing. Domino's Pizza, for example, allegedly has a hotline for drivers to call if managers send them out with so little time that they have to speed in order to deliver a pizza within the allotted 30 minutes. Complete anonymity is guaranteed. Another company includes fraud in its list of undesirable actions along with drug use, safety violations, discrimination, and harassment. It trains all employees so that they know what to do if they see any of these activities. The company provides seminars for new hires, posters and other periodic reminders, a billfold card that lists alternative actions employees can take if they witness violations, and videos that are shown periodically. Employees are told, and the information is reinforced on the billfold card, that they have five options if they suspect problems in any of these areas: (1) They can talk to their manager or to their manager's manager. (2) They can call corporate security at a specified number. (3) They can call internal audit at a specified number. (4) They can call a companywide ombudsman, who will forward the complaint or tip. Or (5) they can call an 800-number hotline, which connects them to an independent monitoring service that screens the calls, guarantees anonymity, and forwards the information to relevant company individuals who can deal with the problem.

Hotlines are not substitutes for maintaining an open environment in which employees feel comfortable about reporting known or suspected fraudulent activities. Hopefully, employees will feel comfortable enough to report such activities to someone in their management chain, to an internal auditor, to corporate security, or to legal counsel. They should, however, be kept aware of the hotline option and encouraged to use it if they feel this is the most appropriate option.

Companies that provide hotlines detect numerous frauds that would otherwise go undetected. These companies also report that hotline use is somewhat erratic, with periods of considerable use and periods of very little use. What is important is to create a reporting option for employees who would not otherwise reveal suspected activities.

Many organizations use hotlines managed by third parties. Some organizations have even gone so far as to reward employees for legitimate tips. Although research suggests that hotlines are an excellent fraud detection tool, the evidence about rewarding employees for tips is mixed at best.[8]

The GE fraud and the Revere Armored Car Company fraud were both detected by tips and complaints. Here is what happened at GE:[9]

A few years ago, John Michael Gravitt, a machine foreman at GE, stood up at an assertiveness training session and told the class that GE was ripping off the government. He told approximately 30 colleagues that the time cards going into supervisors' offices were not the same ones coming out. Within a few minutes several other foremen confirmed Gravitt's story. Even after his outburst in class, Gravitt's superiors still pressured him to coax his subordinates to cheat on their time cards. Gravitt was told that if his subordinates would not alter their own time cards, he was to do so. When Gravitt refused, his supervisors altered the cards for him. According to Gravitt, the process was hardly subtle. "With black or blue felt-tipped pens, they (the supervisors) altered the billing vouchers. Usually they scrawled the number of a project safely within cost constraints over the number of a job that was already running over budget." Foremen who refused to falsify vouchers had their vouchers sent to the unit manager, Robert Kelly. Kelly then completed the blank vouchers himself. When Kelly died, his successor, Bill Wiggins, continued the falsification of time cards and billing vouchers. At one time, Wiggins told Gravitt that GE was a great big pie and that everyone who participated (in cheating) got a piece; those who did not participate did not get a slice.

Falsifying time cards became a way of life at GE. One foreman confessed to personally altering 50–60% of his subordinates' time cards during an eight-month period. Once, when Gravitt told his foreman that he could go to jail for altering cards, the foreman replied that he was only carrying out orders and that there was no chance of getting caught. Finally, Gravitt decided to alert someone who could do something about the problem. One weekend he slipped into a secretary's office and photocopied about 150 altered time cards and billing vouchers. He wrote an eight-page letter explaining what had been going on. The next week, he delivered the letter and the photocopies to Brian H. Rowe, the senior vice president in charge of the engine plant. Gravitt was dismissed from GE that same day. A subsequent investigation by the FBI and the Defense Contract Audit Agency revealed that $7.2 million of idle time had been falsely billed to the U.S. government. They also found that 27% of the time-sheet vouchers in the shop where Gravitt worked had been falsified during the three years Gravitt worked at GE.

John Gravitt's tips were the sole reason GE's fraud was detected. GE did everything in its power to prevent Gravitt from coming forward.

In the Revere Armored Car case, the informants were competitors.[10]

The revelation of fraud at Revere Armored Car began when some competitors, tired of losing customers to Revere's cutthroat prices, installed a video camera. In December 1992, the competitors taped a Revere delivery of $100 million to the New York Federal Reserve Bank's Buffalo branch. They were hoping for evidence of shoddy security, and they got it. The tape showed the driver and a guard leaving the truck in the parking lot of a highway restaurant, locked but unguarded, its engine running, while they went inside to eat. The competitors presented their tape to Lloyds of London, the underwriting group that insured Revere for $100 million. The tape demonstrated to Lloyds the "ease with which someone could whack 'em" and prompted Lloyds to hire an investigator to check out Revere. Among other things, the investigation also turned up evidence of more sinister wrongdoings. Based on the evidence, federal authorities launched a pre-dawn raid

> *on Revere headquarters and found what may be the biggest scandal ever in the armor-truck industry: millions of dollars missing, allegedly pilfered by Revere owners Robert and Susanna Scaretta. Of the $84.6 million that banks say they had in storage at Revere, only $45 million was retrieved. Apparently the Scarettas had run up significant gambling debts. They may also have used Revere as a money-laundering operation for illegal gambling proceeds. Among the banks that lost considerable amounts in this fraud were Citibank, which lost more than $11 million, and Marine Midland Bank, which lost nearly $34.8 million.*

This fraud was perpetuated because the banks and Lloyds of London did not perform adequate due diligence. Neither the banks nor Lloyds regularly monitored Revere's operations. Had it not been for the competitor's tip, this fraud might be going on today. Revere also commingled funds of different banks rather than keeping them separate. Even though large amounts were stolen, Revere always had enough money on hand to satisfy auditors of any one bank at a given time.

Summary

Fraud is a crime that is seldom visible. Instead we only observe symptoms or "red flags" that indicate that fraud may be occurring. These symptoms often relate to the motivations behind fraud (pressure, opportunity, or rationalization) or to the elements of fraud (theft, concealment, or conversion). Just because someone observes symptoms of fraud doesn't necessarily mean that fraud has been committed. Symptoms can be caused by other factors. Sudden extravagant expenditures, for example, could truly be because of an inheritance. A dramatic increase in an accounts receivable balance might mean that one or two large customers are going bankrupt. Changes in behavior usually do indicate something besides fraud—perhaps a traumatic event, like a divorce or a death in the family. But the point is, *not always*. Fraud is *always* a possibility.

To detect fraud, managers, auditors, employees, and examiners must learn to recognize symptoms and pursue them until they obtain evidence that proves fraud is *or* is not occurring. Unfortunately, many symptoms of fraud go unnoticed, or recognized symptoms are not vigorously pursued. If symptoms were vigorously pursued, many frauds could be detected earlier.

Symptoms of fraud can be separated into six groups:

1. *Accounting anomalies:* Because accounting records are often manipulated to conceal fraud, anomalies and problems with accounting documents—either electronic or paper journals, ledgers, or financial statements—are excellent symptoms of fraud.
2. *Internal control weaknesses:* One of the main purposes of internal control procedures is to safeguard assets. When controls are absent or weak (or overridden), they facilitate fraud being perpetrated.
3. *Analytical anomalies:* These are relationships, records, or actions that are too unusual or unrealistic to be believed. They include transactions or events that happen at odd times or places, activities that are performed by, or involve, people who would not normally participate in them, as well as peculiar procedures and policies. Other anomalies that should be scrutinized carefully include amounts that are too large or too small, that occur too often or too rarely, or that result in excesses or shortages.
4. *Lifestyle symptoms:* Once perpetrators meet the financial needs that motivated them to commit fraud, they usually continue to steal and then use the money to

enhance their lifestyles. They may buy expensive cars or other personal items, take extravagant trips, remodel their homes or purchase more expensive ones, or buy expensive jewelry or clothes.

5. *Unusual behaviors:* When people commit crimes (especially first-time offenders, as many perpetrators are), they are engulfed by feelings of fear and guilt. These emotions express themselves in unusual behavior. It is not one particular behavior that often signals fraud; rather, it is a pattern of changes in behavior. People who are accommodating become intimidating and belligerent, people who are belligerent become easy to work with, and so forth.
6. *Tips and complaints:* People who are in the best position to detect fraud are usually those closest to the perpetrator—family members, friends, co-workers, managers, and others, not the auditors or fraud examiners. These individuals often provide tips or complaints that suggest that fraud is being committed. Although such complaints and tips are often legitimate, they can also be motivated by a desire to get even, or by frustration or personal vendettas, or by numerous other reasons.

New Terms

Accounting anomalies: Inaccuracies in source documents, journal entries, ledgers, or financial statements.

Analytical anomalies: Relationships, procedures, or events that do not make sense.

Elements of fraud: The theft act, concealment, and conversion that are present in every fraud.

Internal control weakness: Weakness in the control environment, accounting system, or the control activities or procedures.

Psychopath: A person with a personality disorder, especially one manifested in aggressively antisocial behavior.

Questions and Cases

Discussion Questions

1. How do fraud symptoms help in detecting fraud?
2. Why do internal control weaknesses help detect fraud?
3. What are accounting symptoms?
4. What are analytical symptoms?
5. How can lifestyle changes help in detecting fraud?
6. How can behavioral symptoms help in detecting fraud?
7. The text points out that tips and complaints are not evidence of fraud but instead are fraud symptoms. Do you agree with this statement and why?
8. How can tips and complaints help in detecting fraud?
9. What circumstances make it difficult for auditors to detect fraud? Who is more likely to be in a better position to detect fraud?
10. According to the chapter, which groups (auditors, managers, co-workers, company accountants, or friends) are in the best position to observe fraud symptoms in each of the three elements of fraud? Which group is surprisingly absent in each element?
11. What is the act of theft as it applies to fraud?

12. What is conversion?
13. What is concealment?

True/False

1. Analytical anomalies are present in every fraud.
2. Recording an expense is one way to conceal the theft of cash.
3. A check is an example of a source document.
4. Internal control weaknesses give employees opportunities to commit fraud.
5. Internal control is composed of the control environment, the accounting system, and control procedures (activities).
6. Analytical fraud symptoms are the least effective way to detect fraud.
7. Most people who commit fraud use the embezzled funds to save for retirement.
8. As fraud perpetrators become more confident in their fraud schemes, they steal and spend increasingly larger amounts.
9. First-time offenders usually exhibit no psychological changes.
10. Psychopaths feel no guilt because they have no conscience.
11. Fraud can be detected in all three elements of fraud.
12. The fraud elements consist of concealment, conversion, and completion.
13. Auditors can best help detect fraud in conversion.
14. Some complaints and tips turn out to be unjustified.
15. Fraud is a crime that is seldom observed.
16. Because of the nature of fraud, auditors are often in the best position to detect its occurrence.
17. Most people who commit fraud are under financial pressure.
18. Studies have found that the most common internal control problem when frauds occur is having a lack of proper authorizations.
19. Fraud perpetrators who manipulate accounting records to conceal embezzlements often attempt to balance the accounting equation by recording expenses.
20. Employee transfers, audits, and mandatory vacations are all ways to provide independent checks on employees.

Multiple Choice

1. Which of the following is true regarding fraud?
   a. It is easily identified.
   b. It is seldom observed.
   c. When a fraud occurs, there is no question whether or not a crime has been committed.
   d. Many witnesses are usually available when fraud occurs.
2. Which of the following is *not* a fraud symptom related to source documents?
   a. Duplicate payments
   b. Missing documents
   c. A tip from an employee
   d. Photocopied documents

3. Which of the following is a fraud symptom related to an internal control weakness?
    a. Lack of proper authorization
    b. Lack of independent checks
    c. Inadequate accounting system
    d. Lack of physical safeguards
    e. All of the above
4. In the three elements of fraud (theft act, concealment, conversion), who is usually in the best position to detect the fraud?
    a. Co-workers and managers
    b. Customers
    c. Owners
    d. Vendors
5. When people commit a crime, they usually:
    a. Become engulfed by emotions of fear and guilt
    b. Experience no changes in behavior
    c. Become friendly and nice
    d. Experience a lower stress level
6. Most people who commit fraud:
    a. Use the embezzled funds to build a savings account
    b. Give the embezzled funds to charity
    c. Experience no change in their lifestyle
    d. Use the embezzled funds to improve their lifestyle
7. Which of the following is *not* a reason why co-workers and others hesitate to come forward with their suspicions?
    a. It is usually impossible to know for sure that fraud is taking place.
    b. They have read or heard horror stories about what happens to whistle-blowers.
    c. Employees and others are sometimes intimidated by perpetrators.
    d. Many people believe that it is not good to squeal on others, even when it appears that they are doing something wrong.
    e. People hesitate for all of the above reasons.
8. Which of the following is *not* a category of employee fraud symptoms?
    a. Accounting anomalies
    b. Analytical anomalies
    c. Tips and complaints
    d. Firm structure
9. Embezzlement of assets reduces the left side of the accounting equation. To conceal the theft, the embezzler must find a way to reduce the right side of the accounting equation. A perpetrator would most likely reduce the right side of the equation by:
    a. Reducing accounts payable
    b. Paying dividends
    c. Increasing expenses
    d. Altering stock accounts

10. Which of the following is *not* a fraud symptom related to journal entries?
    a. Unexplained adjustments to receivables, payables, revenues, or expenses
    b. Journal entries that do not balance
    c. Journal entries without documentary support
    d. Journal entries made near the beginning of accounting periods
11. Which of the following is *not* a common internal control fraud symptom or problem?
    a. Lack of segregation of duties
    b. Unexplained adjustments to receivables, payables, revenues, or expenses
    c. Lack of independent checks
    d. Overriding of existing controls
12. Once in a while, someone commits fraud or another crime and does not feel stress. Such people are referred to as:
    a. Psychopathic
    b. Altruistic
    c. Philanthropic
    d. Magnanimous
13. Fraud is usually detected by recognizing and pursuing:
    a. Synonyms
    b. Symptoms
    c. Equity
    d. Legends
14. A letter is most likely to be fraudulent if:
    a. It is signed only by one person
    b. It is addressed to an individual, rather than a department
    c. It is a photocopy of an original letter
    d. It is written on outdated company letterhead
15. If a perpetrator has stolen assets, which of the following is the easiest way to conceal the theft?
    a. Reduce liabilities (such as payables)
    b. Manipulate dividend or stock accounts
    c. Increase other assets (such as receivables)
    d. Increase expenses
16. Which of the following are common fraud symptoms relating to ledgers?
    a. A ledger that does not balance
    b. A ledger that balances too perfectly
    c. Master account balances that do not equal the sum of the individual customer or vendor balances
    d. Both (a) and (c)

Short Cases

Case 1. The balance sheet and income statement for ABC Company for the years 2002 and 2003 are as follows:

Balance Sheet

	2002	2003
Cash	$ 460	$ 300
Accounts receivable	620	480
Inventory	1,000	730
Total assets	$2,080	$1,510
Accounts payable	$ 580	$ 310
Notes payable	500	100
Common stock	400	500
Retained earnings	600	700
Total liabilities and stockholders' equity	$2,080	$1,510

Income Statement

	2002	2003
Net sales	$ 550	$ 840
Cost of goods sold	120	160
Gross margin	$ 430	$ 680
Expenses:		
Salaries	$ 100	$ 150
Warehousing costs	80	120
Advertising	60	90
Taxes	45	75
Total expenses	$ 285	$ 435
Net income	$ 145	$ 245

Perform vertical and/or horizontal analysis of the statements and identify two things that appear to be unusual and could be possible symptoms of fraud.

Case 2. Cal Jr. is the night manager at a local doughnut shop that is doing very well. The shop sells doughnuts 7 days a week, 24 hours a day. Cal runs the graveyard shift by himself, because none of the other employees want to work at night. Since the shop opened six months ago, Cal hasn't been able to find anyone to work for him and therefore has not missed one day of work. Cal makes his deposit every morning before going home.

Cal feels overworked and underpaid. Cal maintains a clean work environment and is considered a valuable employee. The franchise owner, Kenny Count, has praised Cal for his hard work and dedication to the company. Kenny's only concern is that, once or twice a week, an entire batch of traditional glazed doughnuts are thrown away because of overbaking.

Recently, Cal has yelled at people on shifts before and after him for seemingly insignificant reasons. He was originally hired because he got along with everyone and was easygoing. His recent irritability may stem from the fact that business is slowing down and he doesn't have much interaction with anyone at night. He also complains that he isn't getting very much sleep. One day Cal comes to work in a new BMW M3, the car of his dreams, saying that his dad helped him buy the car.

1. What areas of the business are most at risk for fraud?
2. Identify any symptoms of fraud that appear to exist at the doughnut shop.
3. What steps could be taken to reduce opportunities for fraud?

Case 3. James owns a small Internet service provider business. Recently, customers have been complaining that they are overcharged and are not receiving timely customer service. Billing rates seem to increase without notice.

Five years ago, James used funding from several different investors in order to start his service. Currently, he has 17 outstanding bills to be paid, all with late charges. Five of the bills include notices stating that lawsuits are pending. Also, he hasn't paid dividends to investors in two years.

Every day James drives either his Mercedes Benz or his new Lexus to work. Before starting the business, James drove only one car, a Suzuki Samurai. James now lives in a palatial home and owns very expensive furniture. Employees constantly ask James for new equipment, but the "boss" refuses to update the old equipment. Two weeks ago, James was irate and fired one of his accounting clerks for not depositing some checks on time. James is known for losing his temper.

1. Discuss any fraud symptoms that are present in this case.
2. Why would complaints from customers be a fraud symptom?

Case 4. Joan, along with three of her best friends, started her own ranching operation in Hawaii. The business began with 2 bulls and 20 heifers. After their first year, the business was turning profits, and everything seemed to be going well. The heifers were bred each year by using a new patented technique, and the steer population grew to 100 in two years. Most of their heifers produced twins, and 90% were male. This allowed for future breeding of the remaining 10%.

New investment is needed, so limited partners are invited to join the partnership with an initial investment of $20,000 each. The partnership interests are advertised as "hot in the hands" and "very exclusive." In interviews, Joan describes the investments as a "double-your-money, sure thing." She states that the best way to get in is to act within 10 days of the initial offering of the investment. The annual report of the company shows enormous growth, with the pro forma statements predicting phenomenal success. Because of the exorbitant food prices in Hawaii, Joan says she can demand a premium for all cattle sold.

Based on this scenario, what symptoms of fraud exist?

Case 5. ABC Corp., a retailer, had the following comparative balance sheets at December 31, 2003:

	Year Ended	
	12/31/02	**12/31/03**
Cash	$ 800,000	$ 900,000
Accounts receivable	4,000,000	4,250,000
Inventory	9,000,000	8,500,000
Warehouse (net)	10,000,000	10,500,000
	$23,800,000	$24,150,000
Accounts payable	$ 1,490,000	$ 1,400,000
Notes payable	12,000,000	13,200,000
Stockholders' equity	10,310,000	9,500,000
	$23,800,000	$24,150,000

Interest expense was $1.7 million in 2002 and $1.5 million in 2003. Other companies with credit ratings comparable to ABC's can borrow at 9%.

Based on this information, do you have reason to believe that ABC is underreporting its liabilities? Discuss what symptoms you looked for and the results of your analysis. Estimate the extent to which liabilities may be underreported.

Case 6. You are a staff auditor on a very important audit. Your assignment is the audit of two parts of your client's purchasing department. After several days of studying purchase orders and sales invoices, you notice that three vendors have identical addresses. After further examination, you notice that the documents have only one of the two required signatures for purchases of those accounts. You decide to interview the purchasing manager in charge of those accounts, but discover that he is "out to lunch." While you wait for him, you notice through his office window a very nice Bose™ stereo system. It's the same system you've been wanting, but will only be able to afford after you make partner.

What symptoms of fraud exist?

Case 7. You have been hired by a small firm to analyze its accounts receivable department and to assess its susceptibility to fraud. The company operates a table manufacturing facility. The only employee in accounts receivable is Joanne, an employee of 10 years. Joanne opens all cash receipts, credits the clients' accounts, and deposits the money at the bank. What fraud-related risks does this company face, and what changes, if any, should be made?

Case 8. Sally was aware of a fraud being committed by one of her co-workers, but she never reported it. What are some possible reasons for her failure to come forward?

Case 9. John Parker, Jr., is the manager at a local store. The store opened four years ago and has been doing very well. With current business growing, Parker decides to hire James Peter as an accountant. When Peter starts work, he finds several things that, on the surface, appear to be unusual. For example, six receiving documents are lost, the general ledger is out of balance, one e-customer has complained that he is continually overcharged, and another customer complains that he doesn't receive timely service. Parker lives in an expensive house and has several beautiful sports cars.

As a class, discuss whether fraud could be occurring. Does fraud actually exist, or are only fraud symptoms present?

Extensive Case

Case 10. In June of a recent year, allegations of fraud regarding repair contracts for work onboard United States Naval Ships (USNS) were reported to law enforcement agents. The allegations indicated that fraud was rampant and could possibly impact the seaworthiness of these vessels. A task force of agents from the FBI, Defense Criminal Investigative Service, and the Naval Criminal Investigative Service was quickly formed to investigate. The task force agreed that the most effective approach to investigating possible fraud was the use of an undercover operation utilizing a covert contracting business. Management at Bay Ship Management (BSM), the entity in charge of getting contracts for USNS, were demanding that their employees process a high volume of contracts in faster times. When employees began to quit because of the pressure, BSM made sure it did not garner attention from government supervisors. BSM had close relationships with some of the subcontractors, but always maintained an appearance of independence from these subcontractors.

1. What are some of the symptoms of fraud in this case?
2. What questions would you ask yourself about fraud symptoms that might help you investigate this fraud?
3. Why would an undercover operation be the most effective approach to investigate?

Internet Assignments

1. How many different web sites can you find that deal with fraud auditing and detection? Try a few different search strings in a search engine and see what sites are available. Also, locate the Association of Certified Fraud Examiners web site at http://www.cfenet.com. What services do they offer?
2. Locate the web site of the American Society of Questioned Document Examiners (ASQDE) at http://www.asqde.org. What is the ASQDE? What is its purpose?

End Notes

1. See, for example, *Deterring Fraud: The Internal Auditor's Perspective,* The Institute of Internal Auditors, W. Steve Albrecht, K. Howe, and M. Romney, 1984.
2. *Auditing and Assurance Services: An Integrated Approach,* 9th Edition, A. Arens, R. Elder, and M. Beasley, Prentice-Hall, Upper Saddle River, New Jersey, 2003, p. 119.
3. See http://www.sec.gov/litigation/admin/34-39589.txt, Auditing and Accounting Enforcement Release No. 1007, January 28, 1998.
4. *Fraud: Bringing Light to the Dark Side of Business,* W. Steve Albrecht, G. Wernz, and T. Williams, Irwin Professional Publishing, New York, 1995, p. 126.
5. http://www.sec.gov/litigation/litreleases/lr15814.txt, Litigation Release No. 15814, July 16, 1998.
6. From the video "Cooking the Books," produced by the Association of Certified Fraud Examiners, Austin, Texas.
7. http://www.connect-a.net/users/drshades/hofmann.htm
8. A number of years ago, several companies, mostly large department stores (e.g., Macy's, Bloomingdale's, Marshall Field) offered rewards for hotline tips. In recent years, these companies have stopped paying rewards because they received too many false alerts. Most organizations that manage hotlines now do not recommend that rewards be given.
9. "Bounty Hunter: Ex-Foreman May Win Millions for His Tale about Cheating at GE," Gregory Stricharchuk, *Wall Street Journal,* June 23, 1998, A1.
10. Fred R. Bleakley, "Suspicions of Rivals Open Up a Scandal at Armored-Car Firm," *Wall Street Journal,* February 17, 1993, p. A1.

Proactive Approaches to Detecting Fraud

After studying this chapter, you should be able to:

1. Understand the importance of proactive fraud detection.
2. Understand the role commercial data-mining software plays in detection.
3. Understand the advantages and disadvantages of data mining and digital analysis.
4. Understand Benford's law.
5. Understand inductive fraud detection.
6. Understand how fraud is detected by analyzing financial statements.

In 1996, Yasuo Hamanaka, a trader for Sumitomo Trading Company of Japan, was convicted of committing fraud totaling approximately $2.6 billion. Mr. Hamanaka, widely thought to be a trading genius, supposedly controlled 5% of the world's copper market and 50% of the copper futures traded on the London Metals Exchange. Unfortunately, Mr. Hamanaka was not a genius at all but a rogue trader, and many of his trades were fictitious, causing tremendous losses for his company. His fictitious trading had been going on for several years, starting quite small in the late 1980s and eventually increasing to several hundred million dollars a year before he was caught in 1996.

Mr. Hamanaka was first employed in the copper trading division of Sumitomo Corporation in the mid-1980s. Copper trading had not been profitable, and another employee began creating some fictitious off-the-books transactions to make the division look profitable. Before retiring, this employee brought Mr. Hamanaka into the fraud. Hamanaka was much more successful in "managing" the fraud so it wouldn't be detected by his colleagues. Most of his dishonest transactions were conducted through Sumitomo's Hong Kong affiliate that didn't follow the controls established by the Tokyo headquarters. Through a series of complicated swap, hedge, and other types of derivatives and futures transactions, he was able to fool his superiors at Sumitomo into believing he was making huge profits for the company. In fact, in the early 1990s, Sumitomo featured Mr. Hamanaka in its annual report as its "star" trader. Before he was caught through an investigation of the Commodity Futures Trading Corporation (CFTC) in the United States, Hamanaka was widely known as "Mr. 5%." In subsequent civil litigation, a number of U.S. and international firms were sued by Sumitomo for complicity with Hamanaka. Most of these cases were settled out of court, so we will never know whether Mr. Hamanaka acted alone or whether he had accomplices.

Hamanaka's fraud is typical in that it started small and grew geometrically over time. Had it been detected early on, Sumitomo Corporation would have saved itself billions of dollars. Proactive fraud detection is one of the most effective ways to minimize a company's losses due to fraud.

In Chapter 5, we discussed the symptoms of fraud and how to recognize them. Most frauds are detected by management and fellow employees—by accident, through a tip or complaint of wrongdoing—rather than by proactive efforts of auditors and fraud examiners. Historically, the primary detection methods used were whistle-blower hotlines and statistical sampling. Because of developments in technology, however, new methods are now used to detect fraud and identify fraud perpetrators. In this chapter, we spend most of our time discussing ways to use technology to detect fraudulent transactions on the resulting financial statements. The high cost of fraud to business and its high growth rate make the use of these new methods critical to minimizing the occurrence of fraud.

Proactive Fraud Detection

As we discussed in Chapter 5, detecting fraud is different from investigating it. Fraud detection involves identifying symptoms that often indicate fraud is being, or has been, committed. Fraud investigation, on the other hand, is about examining and studying the symptoms or red flags once they have been identified. Fraud investigation involves determining who committed the fraud, the scheme(s) used, when it was committed, what motivated it, and how much money or other assets were taken. Obviously, an investigation cannot proceed until a fraud has been detected. Because symptoms can be caused by factors other than fraud, investigators must remain objective and neutral, assuming neither guilt nor innocence.

In this chapter, we address proactive ways that help us suspect fraud early on. We then examine two technology-based inductive detection methods and one inductive detection method. In the second section we demonstrate how financial statements can be analyzed to detect fraud. Finally, we will discuss how technology is used to detect or identify fraud perpetrators. This innovative technology that is being created by some forward-looking firms is an exciting new development in fraud detection.

Inductive Method Number 1: Commercial Data-Mining Software

One of the most popular detection approaches uses commercial data-mining software, such as Audit Command Language (ACL), to look for anomalies in databases. To illustrate the application of such software, let's consider the case of "XYZ Corporation." Believing that a high-risk area for fraud indicated kickbacks from vendors to buyers, XYZ used a data-mining package to examine purchasing trends of various products. Sorting their records by vendor and by volume (an enormous task before the advent of this software), the company observed that total purchases from one vendor were increasing, even though total purchases from all other vendors were decreasing. Upon further analysis, the company also found that the favored vendor's prices were increasing at a faster rate. These patterns were suspect, especially considering the number of complaints about this vendor's products. XYZ investigated further and discovered that their buyer was accepting kickbacks. The bribery caused XYZ to purchase more than $11 million of unneeded inventory and supplies.

Purchasing patterns frequently signal kickback fraud because, once a buyer starts accepting kickbacks, the control of transactions switches from buyer to vendor. Once the vendor takes control of the relationship, prices often increase, the volume for the favored vendor increases, purchases from other vendors decrease, and, sometimes, even the quality of the goods purchased decreases.

In this and other such database searches for fraud, suspicious patterns are symptoms of fraud, not evidence of it. The reasons why buyers are purchasing more from one vendor and less from others may, in fact, be legitimate, even if the favored vendor's prices are higher. Perhaps the favored vendor's quality is superior or their deliveries more timely.

The major advantage of commercial data-mining software is that it is easy to use. On small databases, it does an excellent job of identifying trends, anomalies, and other unusual activity. Because it is so easy to use, it is very popular.

Although commercial data-mining software can be extremely helpful in detecting fraud, it does have disadvantages. The most obvious one is that the databases kept by large corporations are, by definition, very large. Therefore, querying information onto several zip disks or CDs limits the amount of data that can be transferred. Once the information is queried (and summarized), it is static and cannot be recombined in different ways with the original corporate data. Transferring all corporate data in its original form involves the transfer of *terabytes* of information, a scope of data that is both costly and time-consuming. Further, applications such as ACL generally have spreadsheet-like interfaces and can only analyze small data sets. This size limitation also drives the requests for zip disks and CDs rather than for the entire corporate data set. Often, inherent limitations in analyzing such large data sets with limited software and data storage adversely affect results. Without further manipulating the data and modeling various combinations of red flags, generic data-mining programs end up identifying thousands of "fraud symptoms." Further, these general-purpose programs often cannot be refined enough to focus on actual frauds. Because of their general-purpose use, there is often no way to eliminate false signals.

Inductive Method Number 2: Digital Analysis of Company Databases

Data-mining software packages are one kind of inductive analysis. Another type searches company databases in a manner similar to analytical review procedures already familiar to most accountants. The idea behind these analyses is to use the company's own databases to search for accounting anomalies or unusual or unexpected relationships between numbers.

One common analysis applies Benford's law to various types of data sets. To understand Benford's law, suppose someone hands you a stack of 10,000 random invoices and asks you to estimate how many of the dollar amounts on them begin with the digit 1. You might guess that the answer is about 1 in 9, but the truth is that some integers show up as first digits in data sets much more often than others.

In 1881, the American astronomer Simon Newcomb noticed that the first pages of books of logarithms were much more soiled than the remaining pages. In 1938, Frank Benford applied Newcomb's observation to various types of data sets. According to Benford's law, the first digit of random data sets will begin with a 1 more often than with a 2, a 2 more often than with a 3, and so on. In fact, Benford's law accurately predicts for many kinds of financial data that the first digits of each group of numbers in a set of random numbers will conform to the distribution pattern shown in the chart below. Note that Benford's law applies only to numbers that describe similar items; it does not apply to assigned numbers, such as personal ID numbers or lists where the numbers have built-in minimums or maximums or have pre-assigned patterns.

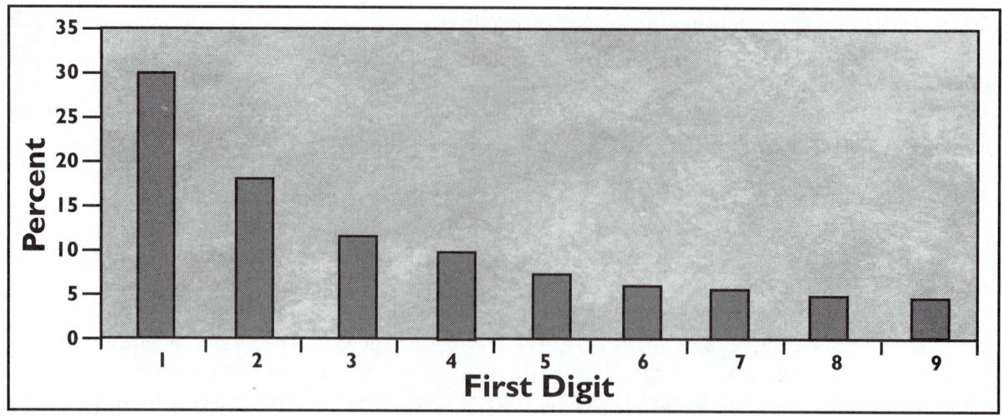

As the chart indicates, the first digit is expected to be a 1 about 30% of the time, whereas a 9 is expected as the first digit only about 4.6% of the time. This means that if you compare the distribution of the first numbers in a small set from your 10,000 invoices to Benford's distribution and find that for 70% of your invoice numbers the first digit is an 8 or a 9, you probably have a fraud.

One company, a multibillion dollar organization we will call "Company X," decided to test its data from supplier invoices against Benford's law. First, Company X analyzed the first digits of dollar amounts on its total population of 820,651 supplier invoices and plotted the results against the expectations of Benford's law and an upper and lower bound. The following chart shows the results:

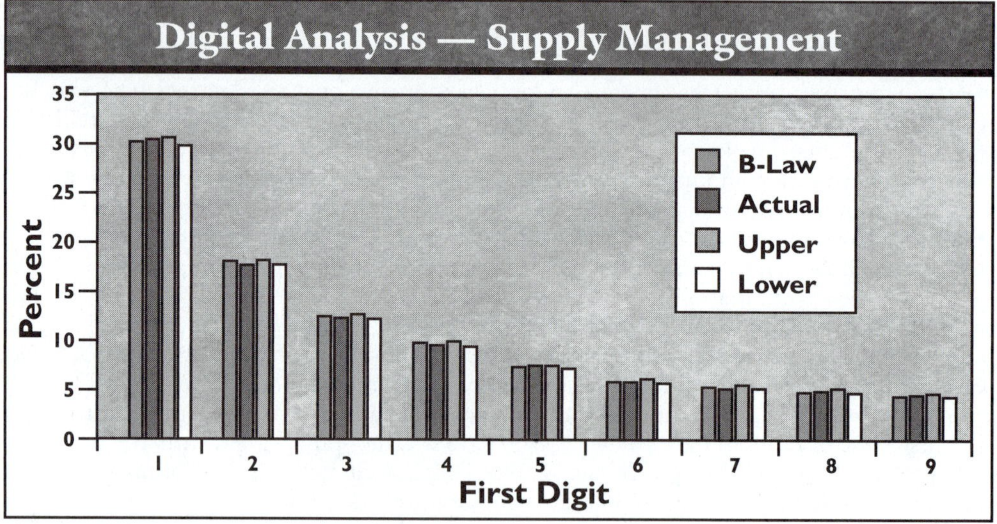

The company's results for its entire population of supplier invoices tracked Benford's predicted results closely. In fact, for all digits except 2, their actual results fell within Benford's upper and lower bounds. Such close tracking might cause many managers to decide that all is well in supply management and move on to other business. Fortunately, those in charge of this analysis knew that just because the entire population looked good did not rule out the possibility that specific populations would still deviate and thereby indicate fraud. So Company X compared the first digits of dollar amounts on invoices from *each* supplier against Benford's distribution. The following four charts show the results for four suppliers.

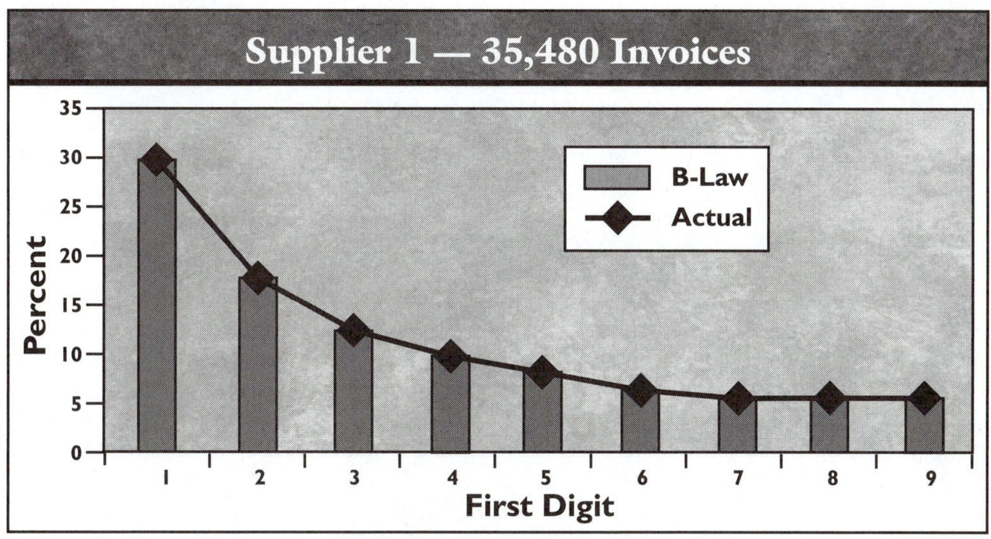

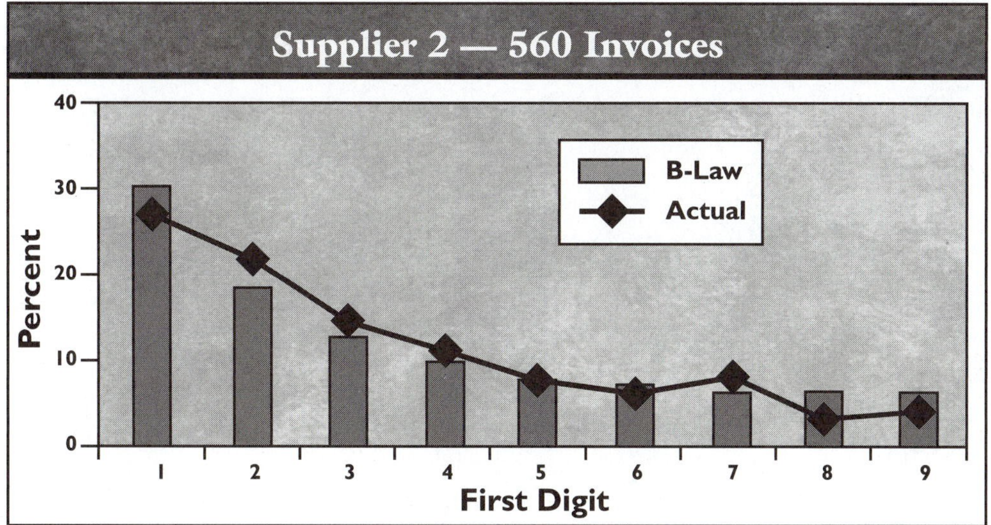

Supplier 1 appears to be in good shape. Their actuals conform closely to Benford's predictions. Although no upper and lower bounds are shown, the actual distribution is obviously within bounds at all points.

Supplier 2 also follows the general slope, but the results are not so precise. Even though the results conform to the general shape of the distribution, the variances are still enough to convince most fraud examiners that a follow-up is in order.

Suppliers 3 and 4 (below) have some major problems. Random distributions of first digits simply do not follow the predicted patterns. Fraud examiners should be highly suspicious of these results. Supplier 4 particularly looks rigged; someone has attempted to use numbers that would look random. In other words, someone tried to use every digit approximately the same number of times as every other digit.

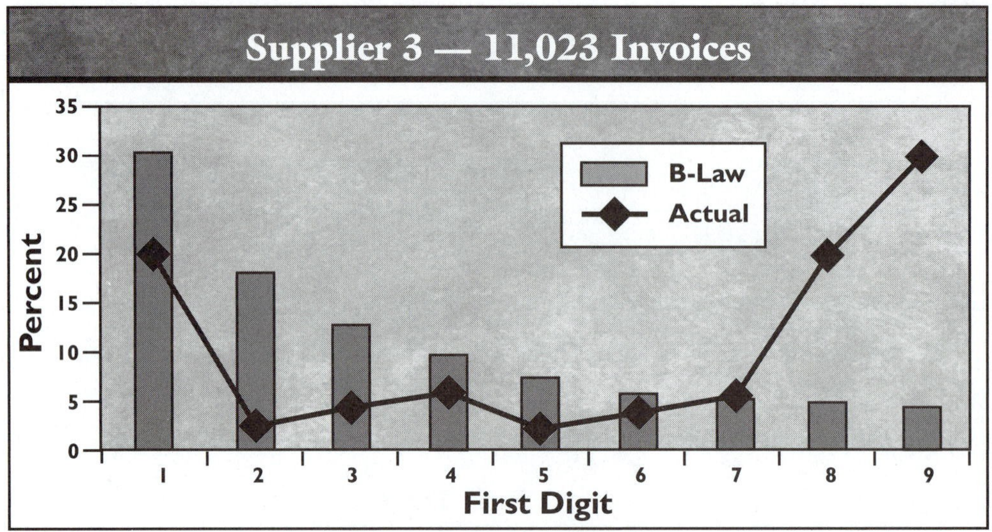

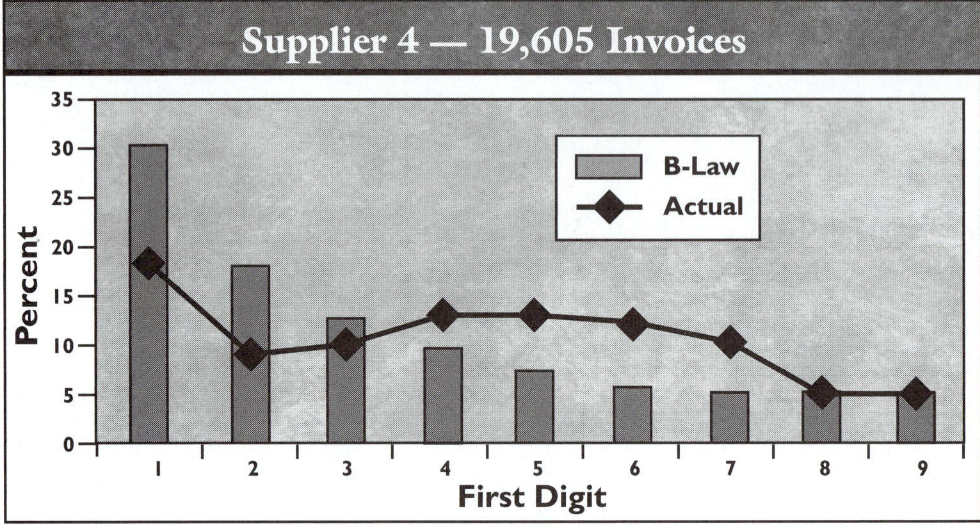

One major advantage in using Benford's law to detect fraud is that it is the least expensive method to implement and use. And, since you apply it to the company's own databases (that is, you don't query data that is then analyzed by consultants or others), potential suspects are less likely to know you are trying to detect fraud. Fraud perpetrators are certainly easier to catch if they have not ceased their activities because they believe someone suspects them.

A major disadvantage of Benford's law is that using it is tantamount to hunting fraud with a shotgun—you pull the trigger and hope that a few pellets hit something important. To understand what this means, consider Company X again. What would have happened if the analysts had stopped after seeing that all vendor invoices taken together tracked Benford's predictions so closely? They might very well have concluded that their organization was free from fraud.

Another shortfall of relying solely on Benford's law is that it only broadly identifies the possible existence of fraud; it fails to narrow possibilities to a manageable field of promising leads. Once anomalies are identified by Benford's law, the fraud examiner must still determine the nature of the fraud being perpetrated and the identity of the perpetrator.

Deductive Fraud Detection

The two detection methods we've just discussed are quite similar. They examine large databases (or infer from a sample to a larger population) in an effort to find anomalies that suggest the existence of fraud. Both methods are, in many ways, a "shotgun" approach. No particular type of fraud is suspected; rather, various types of analysis are performed on databases in the hope that something will show up. In contrast, the final detection method we discuss in this chapter uses a deductive approach. It determines what kinds of frauds can occur in a particular situation and then uses technology and other methods to determine if those frauds exist. It follows a five-step process:

1. Understanding the business or operations to be studied.
2. Understanding what kinds of frauds could occur (fraud exposures) in the operation.
3. Determining the symptoms that the most likely frauds would generate.
4. Using databases and information systems to search for those symptoms.
5. Following up on symptoms to determine if actual fraud or other factors are causing them.

Bank Fraud Case

One example of this detection approach involves a small bank with five branches. Realizing that controls were quite loose, especially those involving top management, the board of directors decided that a risk analysis would be cost effective. The risk assessment would determine major management fraud exposures, identify symptoms those frauds would generate, and then search 16 years of bank data for the symptoms. The tests revealed the following symptoms:

- Exception reports, reflecting fraudulent transactions, which exhibited unusual, atypical, and otherwise questionable patterns of supervisory overrides, transactions with no apparent business purpose, and transactions involving unusually large amounts. This symptom occurred at least 211 times.
- Journal vouchers containing only one signature, containing incorrect information, and/or reflecting transfers between different customers' accounts. This symptom occurred at least 20 times on exception reports.
- Deposit slips with missing information, incomplete names, or where the name of the depositor did not match the name on the passbook and/or the account name in the bank's records. This symptom occurred in at least 41 of 56 exception reports.
- Deposits and withdrawals exceeding $1,000 in one executive's passbook account. This symptom occurred in 39 of 85 exception reports.
- Deposits and withdrawals from the same account made on the same day or within a short period of time and appearing on the exception reports. This symptom occurred on every exception report.
- Bank checks reflecting transfers between different customers' accounts or checks with altered dates. All 11 exception reports contained this symptom.

- Withdrawal vouchers and checks containing purported customer signatures readily distinguishable upon comparison with the customers' signatures. This symptom occurred at least 73 times.
- Large negative available balances in slush accounts and other customer accounts. This symptom appeared 15 times.
- Deposit slips of customer funds between accounts of different customers and/or deposits of customer checks where cash was received back. This symptom occurred in 8 of 9 exception reports.
- CDs closed prematurely, with proceeds placed in lower interest-bearing passbook accounts, sometimes with large penalties. This symptom occurred in 36 of 42 exception reports.
- Customers not present when accounts were opened and closed or when transactions were effected in the account. This symptom occurred numerous times.
- Large withdrawals of cash by executives from customers' accounts. Out of 234 exception reports, withdrawals happened in 129 of them.
- The mailing of customer account statements to executives instead of to the customer, without written authorization. This happened with at least 40 accounts.

Follow-up investigation of the "symptoms" found that one executive vice president had embezzled several million dollars through various schemes over several years.

Oil Company Case

A second case involves a search for fraud in one of the world's largest oil refineries. The refinery's situation provided an excellent search laboratory because it involved tens of thousands of vendor and employee transactions. Its two databases gave the investigators a data-rich environment to explore. The databases contained detailed information on material acquisitions, project status, and vendor labor billings showing hours worked by individuals. During the period investigated, 41 vendors had transactions with the refinery totaling over $1 million each, 242 vendors had transactions totaling over $100,000 each, 497 vendors had transactions totaling over $25,000 each, for a total of 1,983 vendors. The period studied produced over 47,000 vendor invoices, and at least that many expense reimbursement, payroll, and other employee-driven transactions. In addition, because the refinery was heavily unionized and employed many second- and third-generation employees, the company believed that there might be employees who knew about frauds but were reticent to come forward with information.

As part of the database search, the investigators developed customized queries that combined data in new and different ways. In addition, a "time engine" was developed that analyzed fraud symptoms by time period as well as by individual, invoice, product, purchase order, and other factors under consideration. Using this approach, a number of possible fraud symptoms were observed. Because of management's interest and the availability of the data, detection efforts focused primarily on various types of vendor and contractor fraud. The following table identifies the types of possible fraud identified, the symptoms associated with the various frauds, and some of the searches that were performed.

Type of Fraud	Red Flags Identified	Red-Flag Searches
Vendor(s) committing fraud	Overcharging for goods purchased	Price increases greater than 30% for four consecutive years

continues

Type of Fraud	Red Flags Identified	Red-Flag Searches
Vendor(s) committing fraud (continued)	Providing poor quality goods	Work orders with cost overruns exceeding 50% Dollar amount, number, and percentage of goods returned to vendor
	Billing more than once for the same purchase	Duplicate invoice numbers Vendors with invoices for the same amount on the same day Multiple invoices for the same item description by vendor
	Short shipping	Quantity paid for exceeds quantity received, ranked by dollar differences
	Billing for goods not ordered or shipped	Vendors with sequential invoices
Employee(s) committing purchasing fraud	Establishing dummy vendors	Two or more suppliers with same telephone number and/or address Matching of vendors paid with company's master vendor list and with Dun & Bradstreet listings Contractors with common names, first two letters match exactly, and 90% of the name is the same Employee and vendor telephone numbers are the same Contractors with only one buyer for all contracts
	Purchasing goods for personal use	Purchase orders with zero dollar amounts by buyer Invoices exceeding purchase order dollar amount ranked by dollar difference Invoices without valid purchase order
Vendor and company employee(s) committing fraud in collusion	Kickbacks or other favors	Price increases greater than 30% for four consecutive years Dollar amount, number, and percentage of items returned by vendor and buyer Payments without receiving reports Increased volume of purchases by vendor and buyer Combination of increased prices and increased purchases from specific vendors

continues

Type of Fraud	Red Flags Identified	Red-Flag Searches
Contractor(s) committing fraud	Charging more hours than actually worked	Ranking of hours worked by contractor employee
	Working excessive overtime for higher per-hour rates	Ranking of overtime hours worked per two-week pay periods by contractor and contractor employee Ranking of contractors with rising overtime charges
	Overbilling for equipment used	Trends in equipment rental rates by type of equipment by contractor Differences between standard (allowed) rates and actual rates by contractor over time
	Billing for equipment not used	Equipment charges when no labor is charged
	Billing at the wrong rates	Licenses of workers for various crafts vs. licenses issued by states Changes in craft designation for employees by contractor
	Charging higher labor rates than allowed	Contractor employees with significant jumps in labor rates Ranking of labor rates by craft by contractor Contractors with outrageous rates per hour
	Charging for fake employees	Contractor employee social security numbers arranged by ascending numbers
Company employee(s) committing contractor-related fraud	Charging for more hours than contractor actually worked and paying fictitious employees	Employees ranked by hours worked per pay period
	Working excessive overtime for higher rates	Employees with rising overtime charges Employees with high overtime per time card
Contractor and company employee(s) committing fraud in collusion	Kickbacks for favors	Increased volume of work by vendor by buyer Higher than normal rates for services

continues

Type of Fraud	Red Flags Identified	Red-Flag Searches
Contractor and company employee(s) committing fraud in collusion (continued)	Kickbacks for favors (continued)	Excessive charges for equipment use Contractors with rapidly rising invoic amounts Increasing trend of equipment rental rates by contracting employee Amounts contracted by contractor by buyer Invoices with outrageous costs per hour
All types of fraud	Nonrandomness in invoice numbers and amounts	Benford's digits tests

Although the actual instances of fraud at the oil refinery are still being investigated (or litigated), the detection effort led to both discoveries of fraud and data errors. In addition, several of the findings that did not involve fraud resulted in valuable information for management. Here are some of the red flags identified:

- The search for the dollar amount, number, and percentage of returned items by vendor uncovered three suspicious vendors. The refinery was rejecting over 50% of goods received from these vendors, due to poor quality. Two of these were small suppliers, but one represented a relationship with one of the refinery's largest vendors.
- The search for multiple invoices for the same item description by vendor uncovered six invoices for the same amounts from the same vendor on the same day, all for $1,044,000. Three invoices from the same vendor, on the same day, for the same items, each for $900,000, were also found.
- Using various combinations of red flags, four companies that appeared to be committing large-scale contractor fraud were identified. The refinery no longer conducts business with two of these vendors and is pursuing recovery.
- The search for price increases greater than 30% per year for four consecutive years uncovered one company that had increased prices 581,700% and another that had increased prices by 331,879%. In total, 35 companies had raised prices over 1,000%, and 202 companies had raised prices over 100%.
- No incidences were found where employee and vendor telephone numbers were the same, but six employees had the same addresses as vendors.
- Of the 319 vendors with common names and addresses, all but two of these had reasonable explanations for the coincidence.
- The search for vendors not listed in the master file uncovered one unapproved vendor from whom the company had purchased $791,268 of services. Purchases from all other unapproved vendors totaled less than $10,000.
- In 20 purchases over $100,000, the quantity paid for was greater than the quantity received.
- The search for high-volume purchases by vendor uncovered only one vendor with unusually high transactions. The company paid $56,201 for items with unit prices of 19 cents and 12 cents each. The volume on these items far exceeded the refinery's needs.
- The search for contractor employees with excessive overtime was one of the most useful analyses. Four companies had employees who reported working 150+ hours over 20 consecutive two-week pay periods. Employees of one company

submitted time cards from different locations for the same periods. Another company's employees averaged 2,046 hours of overtime for the year. In one year, ten companies had averages of over 200 overtime hours per two-week period, 388 had some overtime, and hundreds had no overtime.

- Per-hour charges by craft and by company and employee ranged from $56.11 per hour to $15.43 for the same craft. Also, 40 companies had standard deviations for rates billed that were over 40% of the average rates billed for the same craft.
- Invoices from seven companies exceeded purchase order amounts by over $100,000. The largest difference was $713,791 on an original invoice of $21,621.
- The search for vendors with sequential invoices revealed 19 vendors that submitted sequentially numbered invoices in over 50% of all invoices. With one vendor, over 83% of the invoices submitted were sequential.
- The search uncovered three companies with over 100 zero-amount purchase orders.
- Nine contractors had cost overruns exceeding 50% and $100,000. The highest percentage overrun was 2,431%.
- Finally, only 65 companies could not be matched with Dun & Bradstreet listings. Except in a few instances, purchases from nonlisted companies were small.

Which Transaction-Based Approach Is Best?

Each of the transaction-based approaches we've described has advantages and disadvantages. Using commercial data-mining software is usually the most inexpensive approach. However, its usefulness is limited when databases are large. In addition, the generic searches that such software performs often lead to excessive listings of possible fraud symptoms. In one case, for example, applications using Microsoft's FoxPro led to over 26,000 possible symptoms. The major advantage of commercial data-mining software is that it is easy to use and can be quickly modified and applied.

Statistical analyses, such as using Benford's law, can be performed on databases of any size. They are most useful when a particular type of fraud, such as vendor kickbacks, is suspected. However, statistical analyses also tend to identify large numbers of symptoms.

The major disadvantage of the deductive approach is that it is more expensive. However, the data and output can be continuously modified and refined until most alternative explanations are eliminated.

In deciding which approach to use, consider the size of the databases to be analyzed and whether or not the search is a one-time or multiple-application activity. If the refined analyses of the deductive approach can be used repeatedly or be automated as a real-time fraud detection activity, it is both preferable and cost-effective. On the other hand, if the databases are small and the search a one-time-only application, commercial data-mining software is preferable.

All of these methods are proactive approaches in that they can detect fraud early and can pay large dividends. Early detection of fraud not only results in significant cost savings, but the idea that fraud detection activities are in place and used routinely can be a strong deterrent.

Analyzing Financial Statements Reports That Result from Transactions to Detect Fraud

Financial statements are the end product of the accounting cycle. They can be viewed as summaries of all the transactions that occurred during a specific period of time. Fraud can be detected anywhere along the way—through transaction source documents, journal entries of the transactions based on those documents, ledger balances (which are summaries of journal entries)—and finally in the resulting financial statements (which summarize the ledger totals in prescribed formats). Unless a fraud is large, however, it may not affect summarized financial statements significantly enough to be detected. Large frauds, however, are a different "animal," and can often be detected through financial statements. Small frauds are usually detected by focusing on source documents or other symptoms.

To detect fraud through financial statements, investigators focus on unexplained changes. For example, in most companies, very few customers pay cash at the time of purchase. Rather, their payments are made by check, based on monthly bills. As a result, revenues normally do not increase without a corresponding increase in accounts receivable. Similarly, an increase in revenues should be accompanied by an increase in cost of goods sold and in inventory purchased and accounts payable balances. Also, inventory levels don't usually increase while purchases and accounts payable remain constant. In all cases, unexplained changes must be the focus of attention.

To understand how financial statement changes can signal fraud, one must be familiar with the nature of the three primary financial statements. Most organizations publish periodic balance sheets, income statements, and statements of cash flow. The balance sheet is a position statement. It shows what an organization's asset, liability, and equity balances are at a *specific* point in time (like a snapshot). A balance sheet prepared as of December 31, 2002, for example, reveals what the organization owns and owes on that date only. A balance sheet prepared on January 3, 2003 (three days later), may show drastically different numbers. Because a balance sheet is a position statement as of a specific date, it must be converted to a change statement before it can be used to detect fraud. The changes can then be analyzed to determine whether they make sense or represent symptoms that should be investigated.

An income statement shows what an organization's revenues, expenses, and income were for a period of time. An income statement prepared for the year ending December 31, 2002, for example, would reveal revenues, expenses, and income for the 12 months January through December, 2002. Although an income statement is for a period, rather than as of a specific date, it is not a change statement. Like a balance sheet, it must also be converted to a change statement before it can be used effectively as a fraud detection tool.

Balance sheets and income statements are converted from position and period statements to change statements in four ways: (1) comparing account balances in the statements from one period to the next, (2) calculating key ratios and comparing them from period to period, (3) performing horizontal analysis, and (4) performing vertical analysis. The first approach compares numbers in the statement from one period to the next. For example, the accounts receivable balance of one period is compared to the balance in a subsequent period to see whether the change is in the expected direction and whether the magnitude of change is reasonable, given changes in other numbers. Unfortunately, because financial statement numbers are often large and difficult to compare, assessing levels of change can be difficult.

In the second approach—converting balance sheets and income statements to change statements—key financial statement ratios are calculated and changes in these ratios from period to period are compared. The quick ratio (also called the acid-test ratio) and the current ratio assess a company's liquidity. Accounts receivable turnover and inventory turnover ratios assess a company's operational efficiency. Debt-to-equity and times-interest-earned ratios assess a company's solvency. Profit margin, return on assets, return on equity, and earnings per share ratios assess profitability. By examining ratios, it is possible to see whether resulting changes in liquidity, efficiency, solvency, and profitability are as expected. Changes in ratios that do not make sense are often the result of fraudulent activity by managers.

Detecting fraud through financial statement ratios is much easier than assessing changes in the financial statement numbers themselves. Ratios usually involve small, easily understood numbers that are sensitive to changes in key variables. In addition, benchmarks for most ratios are well known. Common ratios that can be used to detect fraud are shown in the following table.

Common Ratios		
1. Current ratio	=	$\frac{\text{Current Assets}}{\text{Current Liabilities}}$
2. Quick ratio (acid-test)	=	$\frac{\text{Current Assets (minus Inventory)}}{\text{Current Liabilities}}$
3. Accounts receivable turnover	=	$\frac{\text{Sales}}{\text{Average Accounts Receivable}}$
4. Days in receivable	=	$\frac{365}{\text{Receivable Turnover}}$
5. Receivable percentage	=	$\frac{\text{Accounts Receivable}}{\text{Total Assets}}$
6. Bad debt percentage	=	$\frac{\text{Bad Debt Expense}}{\text{Average Accounts Receivable}}$
	=	$\frac{\text{Bad Debt Expense}}{\text{Total Sales}}$
7. Inventory turnover	=	$\frac{\text{Cost of Goods Sold}}{\text{Average Inventory}}$
8. Days in inventory	=	$\frac{365}{\text{Inventory Turnover}}$
9. Cost of goods sold percentage	=	$\frac{\text{Cost of Goods Sold}}{\text{Sales}}$
10. Inventory percentage	=	$\frac{\text{Inventory}}{\text{Total Assets}}$
11. Property, plant, and equipment (PPE) turnover	=	$\frac{\text{Sales}}{\text{Average PPE}}$
12. PPE percentage	=	$\frac{\text{PPE}}{\text{Total Assets}}$

continues

Common Ratios		
13. Sales return percentage	=	$\frac{\text{Sales Returns}}{\text{Total Sales}}$
14. Debt to equity (leverage)	=	$\frac{\text{Total Liabilities}}{\text{Stockholders' Equity}}$
15. Debt percentage	=	$\frac{\text{Total Liabilities}}{\text{Total Assets}}$
16. Profit margin	=	$\frac{\text{Net Income}}{\text{Net Sales}}$
17. Earnings per share	=	$\frac{\text{Net Income}}{\text{Number of Shares of Stock}}$

The third approach—converting balance sheets and income statements to change statements—uses vertical analysis, which converts financial statement numbers to percentages. For a balance sheet, total assets are set at 100% and all other balances are a percentage of total assets. A simple example of vertical analysis of a balance sheet is shown below.

JOHN DOE COMPANY
Vertical Analysis of Balance Sheet
December 31, 2003 and 2002

	2003		2002	
Cash	$ 64,000	8%	$ 50,000	5%
Accounts receivable	96,000	12	100,000	10
Inventory	160,000	20	200,000	20
Fixed assets	480,000	60	650,000	65
Total assets	$800,000	100%	$1,000,000	100%
Accounts payable	$ 16,000	2%	$ 70,000	7%
Mortgage payable	80,000	10	120,000	12
Bonds payable	160,000	20	200,000	20
Common stock	400,000	50	400,000	40
Retained earnings	144,000	18	210,000	21
Total liabilities and equity	$800,000	100%	$1,000,000	100%

Vertical analysis is a very useful fraud detection technique, because percentages are easily understood. When we spend $1 or part of $1, we know what it means. If we spend it all, we know we have spent 100%. Similarly, all through school, we scored 70 or 80 or 90% on examinations. Everyone understands which of these scores is good, which is bad, and what the percentage represents. Changes in cumbersome financial statement balances can be readily assessed by converting the numbers to percentages. Understanding that sales increased 20%, for example, is much easier than understanding that sales increased from $862,000 to $1,034,400.

When vertical analysis is used to analyze changes in income statement balances, gross sales are set at 100% and all other amounts are converted to a percentage of sales. A simple example of an income statement converted to percentages by using vertical analysis is shown below.

JOHN DOE COMPANY
Vertical Analysis of Income Statement
For the Period Ending December 31, 2003 and 2002

	2003		2002	
Sales	$1,000,000	100%	$800,000	100%
Cost of goods sold	600,000	60	400,000	50
Gross margin	$ 400,000	40%	$400,000	50
Expenses:				
Selling expenses	$ 150,000	15%	$120,000	15%
Administrative expenses	100,000	10	88,000	11
	$ 250,000	25%	$208,000	26
Income before taxes	$ 150,000	15%	$192,000	24%
Income taxes	60,000	6	80,000	10
Net income	$ 90,000	9%	$112,000	14%

In this example, the cost of goods sold increased from 50% of sales in year 1 to 60% of sales in year 2. Does this change make sense? Why would the cost of sales increase twice as much as sales? Possible explanations include (1) inventory costs rose faster than sales prices, (2) inventory is being stolen, and (3) the accounting records are not accurate. An analyst can easily determine which of these (or other) factors caused the unusual changes.

The fourth approach—converting balance sheets and income statements to change statements—uses horizontal analysis. Horizontal analysis resembles vertical analysis in that it converts financial statement balances to percentages. However, instead of computing financial statement amounts as percentages of total assets or gross sales, it converts the percentage change in balance sheet and income statement numbers from one period to the next. Simple examples of horizontal analysis of a balance sheet and horizontal analysis of an income statement are shown below.

JOHN DOE COMPANY
Horizontal Analysis of Balance Sheet
December 31, 2003 and 2002

	2003	2002	Change	% Change
Cash	$ 50,000	$ 64,000	$(14,000)	(22)%
Accounts receivable	100,000	96,000	4,000	4
Inventory	200,000	160,000	40,000	25
Fixed assets	650,000	480,000	170,000	35
Total assets	$1,000,000	$800,000	$200,000	25
Accounts payable	$ 70,000	$ 16,000	$ 54,000	338
Mortgage payable	120,000	80,000	40,000	50
Bonds payable	200,000	160,000	40,000	25
Common stock	400,000	400,000	-0-	-0-
Retained earnings	210,000	144,000	66,000	46
Total liabilities and equity	$1,000,000	$800,000	$200,000	25

JOHN DOE COMPANY
Horizontal Analysis of Income Statements
For the Period Ending December 31, 2003 and 2002

	2003	2002	Change	% Change
Net sales	$1,000,000	$800,000	$200,000	25%
Cost of goods sold	600,000	400,000	200,000	50
Gross margin	$ 400,000	$400,000	0	0
Expenses:				
Selling expenses	$ 150,000	$120,000	$ 30,000	25
Administrative expenses	100,000	88,000	12,000	14
	$ 250,000	$208,000	$ 42,000	20
Income before taxes	$ 150,000	$192,000	$ (42,000)	22
Income taxes	60,000	80,000	(20,000)	25
Net income	$ 90,000	$112,000	$ 22,000	(20)

Horizontal analysis is the most direct method of focusing on changes. With ratios and vertical analysis, statements are converted to numbers that are easier to understand, and then the numbers are compared from period to period. With horizontal analysis, the changes in amounts from period to period are converted to percentages (change ÷ Year 1 amount = % change).

As an example of the usefulness of vertical and horizontal analysis, consider the ESM fraud described below by an expert witness in the case.

> *I received a call from an attorney asking me to be an expert witness in a major fraud case. The case was ESM Government, a securities dealer that had been in the news recently. The attorney indicated that the large accounting firm he was defending was being sued for some $300 million by the insurance commission for negligent auditing. The suit related to the firm's audit of a savings and loan that had invested in ESM. To defend the firm, the attorney was trying to understand the nature and extent of the fraud as well as to obtain an independent opinion on whether his client was negligent in performing the audit.*
>
> *The attorney requested that I analyze the financial statements to determine whether fraud existed and, if so, in which accounts. In my analysis, I used both horizontal and vertical analyses. My converted financial statements are shown below and on page 160.*

ESM GOVERNMENT
Horizontal Analysis*

	Year 1 to Year 2	*Year 2 to Year 3*	*Year 3 to Year 4*
Assets			
Cash	1,684%	(40%)	(67%)
Deposits	0	0	0
Receivables from brokers and dealers	(91)	1,706	102
Receivables from customers	19.5	(48)	(23)

continues

ESM GOVERNMENT
Horizontal Analysis*

	Year 1 to Year 2	Year 2 to Year 3	Year 3 to Year 4
Securities purchased under agreement to resell	(3)	(44)	205
Accrued interest	0	190	487
Securities purchased not sold at market	829	13	120
Total assets	7.5	(38)	183
Liabilities and S.E. Equity			
Short-term bank loans	898	40	14
Payable to brokers and dealers	(72)	658	33
Payable to customer	50	(64)	158
Securities sold under agreement to repurchase	(3)	(44)	232
Accounts payable and accrued expenses	192	(100)	55
Accounts payable—parent and affiliates	279	(25)	(4)
Common stock	0	0	0
Additional contributed capital	0	0	0
Retained earnings	127	113	21

*Dollar amounts are omitted to simplify the presentation.
Note: This horizontal analysis, based on ESM's actual financial statements, was prepared by Steve Albrecht.

ESM Government
Vertical Analysis

	$ (Year 1)	%	$ (Year 2)	%	$ (Year 3)	%	$ (Year 4)	%
Assets								
Cash	$ 99,000	0.000	$ 1,767,000	0.001	$ 1,046,000	0.001	$ 339,000	0.000
Deposits	25,000	0.000	25,000	0.000	25,000	0.000	25,000	0.000
Receivables from brokers and dealers	725,000	0.000	60,000	0.000	1,084,000	0.001	2,192,000	0.001
Receivables from customers	33,883,000	0.024	40,523,000	0.027	21,073,000	0.022	16,163,000	0.006
Securities purchased under agreement to resell	1,367,986,000	0.963	1,323,340,000	0.867	738,924,000	0.781	2,252,555,000	0.840
Accrued interest	433,000	0.000	433,000	0.000	1,257,000	0.001	7,375,000	0.003
Securities purchased not sold at market	17,380,000	0.010	161,484,000	0.106	182,674,000	0.193	402,004,000	0.150
Total assets	$1,420,531,000		$1,527,632,000		$946,083,000		$2,680,653,000	
Liabilities and equity								
Short-term bank loans	$ 5,734,000	0.005	$ 57,282,000	0.037	$ 80,350,000	0.085	$ 91,382,000	0.034
Payable to brokers and dealers	1,721,000	0.001	478,000	0.000	3,624,000	0.004	5,815,000	0.000
Payable to customers	2,703,000	0.002	4,047,000	0.003	1,426,000	0.002	3,683,000	0.000
Securities sold under agreement to repurchase	1,367,986,000	0.963	1,323,340,000	0.867	738,924,000	0.781	2,457,555,000	0.917
Accounts payable and accrued expenses	272,000	0.000	796,000	0.000	591,000	0.001	1,377,000	0.000
Accounts payable—parent and affiliates	33,588,000	0.020	127,604,000	0.084	95,861,000	0.101	92,183,000	0.014
Common stock	1,000	0.000	1,000	0.000	1,000	0.000	1,000	0.000
Additional contributed capital	4,160,000	0.040	4,160,000	0.003	4,160,000	0.004	4,160,000	0.000
Retained earnings	4,366,000	0.040	9,924,000	0.006	21,146,000	0.022	24,497,000	0.010
Total liabilities and equity	$1,420,531,000		$1,527,632,000		$946,083,000		$2,680,653,000	

Note: This vertical analysis, based on ESM's actual journal, was prepared by Steve Albrecht.

> *Based on my analysis, I drew three conclusions. First, if there were fraud, it had to be in either the "securities sold under agreement to repurchase (repo) account" or in the "securities purchased under agreement to resale (reverse repo)" account. I was not familiar with either of these accounts, but recognized them as being the only accounts large enough to hide massive fraud. Second, I wondered why these two accounts would have identical balances in three of the four years. After I realized that these accounts were really only payables and receivables for the company, my concern heightened. It did not make sense that a company's receivable balance should exactly equal its payable balance in even one year, let alone three in a row. Third, the numbers in the financial statements jumped around randomly. There were large changes from year to year, and often these changes were in opposite directions. In a stable company, only small, consistent changes from year to year are the norm.*
>
> *I called the attorney with my conclusions, and stated that I wasn't sure whether the financial statements were fraudulent but that there were three very significant red flags. I also stated that if fraud were present, it would have to be in the repo and reverse repo accounts.*
>
> *Based on this analysis, I was retained as an expert witness in the case. I did not testify, however, because the case was settled out of court for less than $5 million.*

Examples of financial statement fraud abound. Some of these frauds are missed by auditors, but they could be easily detected using horizontal or vertical analysis. In many cases, the unexplained changes are obvious; in other cases, they are subtle. Unfortunately, however, managers and even auditors generally use ratios, horizontal analysis, and vertical analysis only as tools for assessing an organization's performance. Rarely do they use these measures to detect fraud.

The third financial statement—the statement of cash flows—is already a change statement and doesn't need to be converted. The statement of cash flows shows the cash inflows and cash outflows during a period. A graphic description of this statement is shown below.

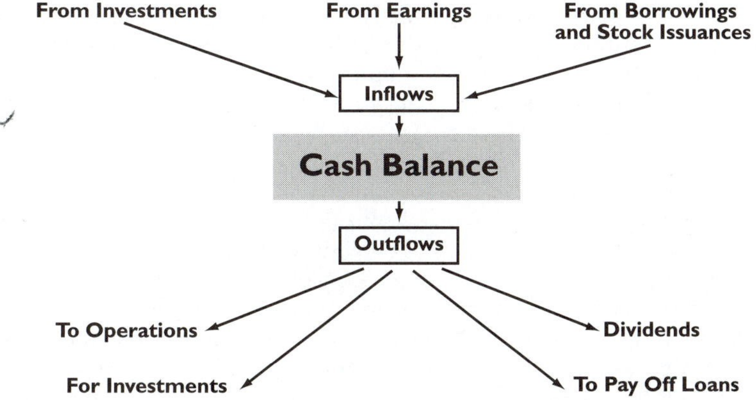

Increases or decreases that do not make sense serve as red flags and should be investigated. Because the statement of cash flows focuses on changes, it can be used to answer such questions as:

- Is the increase in cash flow as expected?
- Why did receivables go up (down)?
- Why did inventory increase (decrease)?
- Why did payables increase (decrease)?
- Why was there an increase in payables when inventory decreased?
- Why were assets sold (bought)?
- Where did the cash come from to pay dividends?

Detecting or Identifying Fraud Perpetrators

Thus far our discussion in this chapter has focused on identifying fraudulent transactions. In this last section of the chapter, we discuss the exciting developments in using technology to identify fraud perpetrators and other high-risk individuals. Every time an individual moves, applies for a job or loan, is married, applies for a driver's or other license, takes a certifying examination, is arrested, logs onto the Internet, or conducts any kind of business transaction, identifying data are captured. Like walking in the sand on the beach, we leave financial and other footprints almost anytime we do anything. Relevant information from these records, such as telephone number, address, name, affiliations, and criminal activity, are cross-referenced across databases to search for predictive matches and evaluations.

While cross-correlations such as these might seem simple, they are actually complicated. The major problem is that personal data contains so many inconsistencies. For example, assume that your address is 925 South, 700 East, Jackson, New Jersey, 00035-4658. The following are ways in which you might write your address:

925 S. 700 East, Jackson, New Jersey, 00035-4658
925 So. 700 East, Jackson, New Jersey, 00035-4658
925 So. 700 E., Jackson, New Jersey, 00035-4658
925 S. 700 E. Jackson, New Jersey, 00035-4658
925 South 700 E. Jackson, New Jersey, 00035-4658
All of these combinations with N.J. instead of New Jersey
All of these combinations with NJ instead of New Jersey
All of these combinations with 00035 instead of 00035-4658
Other variations

Finding ways to combine these "non-obvious" relationships is the problem. One company, Systems Research & Development Corporation (SRD) of Las Vegas, for example, has used "fuzzy logic" algorithms to make associations that are normally difficult for humans to detect. Their technology identifies alarming non-obvious relationships between individuals and companies. For example, employee data provide information on residence, banking, phone number, and affiliations. These records can be cross-referenced for criminal activity or to highlight questionable relationships, such as supervisors and their direct subordinates having the same addresses.

Approaches like SRD's can quickly search through vast sources of data to identify relationships within an organization to (1) detect potential collusion between employees and vendors, (2) identify suspect relationships between employees and customers, (3) locate repeat risk management claims across a corporation, and (4) find employees or clients who are "in cahoots" with lists of known criminals. What's even more impressive is that these kinds of technologies are very fast and can be used in almost any setting. For example, in approximately eight seconds, someone at an airline counter checking in for a flight or purchasing a ticket can be identified as someone appearing on a terrorist list, someone shopping at a store can be identified as a person who passes bad checks, someone betting at a blackjack table at a casino can be identified as a person who has previously been caught cheating, someone applying for a driver's license can be recognized as a person owing back child support, or someone proposing to your daughter could be identified as one having a criminal record.

Three case studies recently conducted by SRD, for example, found the following:

> *Case 1.* The data from a large consumer product distributor with more than 800,000 employees was analyzed. The analysis revealed 564 employees who had vendor or criminal relationships and 26 employees who were in fact vendors.
>
> *Case 2.* In collusion testing at a major Las Vegas resort, an analysis of more than 20,000 employees (current and terminated), all vendors, customers, in-house arrests and incidents, and their known list of problem people, they found 24 active players who were known criminals, 192 employees who had possible vendor relationships, and seven employees who were in fact vendors.
>
> *Case 3.* A government organization's 10,000 employees, 75,000 vendors, and more than 50,000 known problem people were analyzed. The analysis found 140 employee relationships with vendors, 1,451 vendor relationships to security concerns, 253 employee relationships to security concerns, two vendors who constituted a security concern, and some employees who were either a security concern or vendor.

As these types of technology-based programs become more refined, other non-obvious relationships will become capable of being examined. For example, individuals who have one or two pieces of identification in common but some elements that are different will be able to be analyzed to see if they have relationships.

While these types of programs are useful in identifying fraud perpetrators or other troublemakers, there is some concern that they could be used by individuals who want to cause harm, injury, or loss to others. Unfortunately, those are risks of our new information economy. As one person recently observed, with developments such as those described here, "there is just no place to hide anymore."

Summary

Proactive fraud detection methods, especially the high-tech ones, are in their infancy. For years, the only detection method possible, other than hotlines, was discovery sampling, which we will cover in Chapter 7.

With respect to fraud, developments in technology have been both good news and bad news. Computers have given creative perpetrators many new opportunities to commit fraud. Some of these frauds have been much larger than we thought possible. Perpetrators understand that exploiting vulnerabilities in technology means they don't need to physically move the stolen assets. Rather, they merely make a telephone call, key in a transaction, or speak into voice recording instruments. "So if I'm going to steal," the reasoning goes, "I might as well add a few zeros and make life interesting." However, just as technology has made some frauds easier to commit, it has also made detection much easier.

In this chapter, we discussed three transaction-based technology fraud detection approaches. We also discussed how financial statement analysis can detect fraud. We have also discussed new developments that focus on perpetrators, rather than on transactions, to detect fraud. These are currently the most effective methods, but new approaches continue to be developed. Current applications of technology are one of the most exciting areas in fraud research.

When proactive approaches are used, remember that symptoms you observe are just that—only symptoms. Although they may indicate actual fraud, factors other than fraud can also create symptoms. Therefore, symptoms should be thoroughly investigated before you conclude that fraud exists.

New Terms

Accounting cycle: Procedures for analyzing, recording, classifying, summarizing, and reporting the transactions of a business.

Accounts receivable turnover ratio: The rate at which a company collects its receivables; computed by dividing sales by average accounts receivable.

Audit command language (ACL): Popular commercial data-mining software; helps investigators detect fraud.

Balance sheet: Financial statement that reports a company's assets, liabilities, and owners' equity as of a particular date.

Benford's law: Mathematical algorithm that accurately predicts that, for many data sets, the first digit of each group of numbers in a random sample will begin with a 1 more than a 2, a 2 more than a 3, a 3 more than a 4, and so on; predicts the percentage of time each digit will appear in a sequence of numbers.

Commercial data-mining software: Commercial software packages that use query techniques to detect patterns and anomalies in data that may suggest fraud.

Current ratio: Measure of the liquidity of a business; equal to current assets divided by current liabilities.

Database: Set of interrelated, centrally controlled data files that are stored with as little redundancy as possible. A database consolidates many records previously stored in separate files into a common pool of data and serves a variety of users and data processing applications.

Debt-to-equity ratio: The number of dollars of borrowed funds for every dollar invested by owners; computed as total liabilities divided by total equity.

Deductive fraud detection: Determining the types of frauds that can occur and then using query techniques and other methods to determine if those frauds may actually exist.

Horizontal analysis: Tool that determines the percentage *change* in balance sheet and income statement numbers from one period to the next.

Income statement: Financial statement that reports the amount of net income earned by a company during a specified period.

Inductive fraud detection: Proactively searching for fraud by identifying anomalies or unusual or unexpected patterns and/or relationships, without determining in advance the kinds of fraud you are looking for.

Inventory turnover ratio: A measure of the efficiency with which inventory is managed; computed by dividing cost of goods sold by average inventory for a period.

Profit margin: Measure of the profit generated from each dollar of revenue; calculated by dividing net income by revenue.

Quick (acid-test) ratio: Measure of a firm's ability to meet current liabilities, computed by dividing net quick assets (all current assets, except inventories and prepaid expenses) by current liabilities.

Return on equity: Measure of the profit earned per dollar of investment; computed by dividing net income by equity.

Risk assessment: The identification, analysis, and management of risk, such as the risk associated with the possibility of fraud.

Statement of cash flows: Financial statement that reports an entity's cash inflows (receipts) and outflows (payments) during an accounting period.

Statistical analysis: The use of statistics and number patterns to discover relationships in certain data, such as Benford's law.

Vertical analysis: Tool that converts financial statement numbers to percentages so that they are easy to understand and analyze.

Questions and Cases

Discussion Questions

1. Why is it important to proactively detect fraud?
2. What is the purpose of commercial data-mining software?
3. What are the advantages of using commercial data-mining software to detect fraud?
4. What are the disadvantages of using commercial data-mining software?
5. What are the advantages of statistical analysis to detect fraud?
6. What are the disadvantages of statistical analysis?
7. What is Benford's law?
8. What is deductive fraud detection?
9. How can fraud be detected by analyzing financial statements?
10. What is the significance of unexplained changes in financial statements in detecting fraud?
11. What are some of the difficulties in trying to correlate customers, vendors, or employees with known problem people?

True/False

1. Unusual patterns always indicate the existence of fraud.
2. Transferring all corporate data in its original form can involve the transfer of terabytes of information.
3. Statistical analysis uses the company's database to search for normal relationships between numbers.
4. According to Benford's law, the first digit of random sets of numbers will begin with a 9 more often than with an 8.
5. When using Benford's law, potential suspects are less likely to know you are trying to detect fraud than if you use more direct detection techniques.
6. Understanding the kinds of frauds that can occur is not important when using a deductive detection method.
7. Statistical analysis, such as Benford's law, can be performed on databases of any size.
8. Proactive fraud detection can pay large dividends and is an effective way to reduce the cost of fraud in any organization.
9. Unexplained changes are common in financial statements.
10. Balance sheets must be converted to change statements before they can be used in detecting fraud.
11. Vertical analysis is a more direct method than horizontal analysis in focusing on changes in financial statements from one period to another.
12. Vertical analysis is a useful detection technique because percentages are easily understood.
13. It is impossible to identify an employee who has a previous arrest record, but who changes his name and lives at the same address.

Multiple Choice

1. When detecting fraud, it is important that fraud investigators:
   a. Remain objective and neutral
   b. Assume guilt
   c. Assume innocence
   d. None of the above
2. Data mining:
   a. Determines the cost of fraud
   b. Identifies possible fraud suspects
   c. Looks for anomalies in databases
   d. All of the above
3. Once a buyer starts accepting kickbacks from a supplier:
   a. Prices often increase
   b. Purchases from other vendors often decrease
   c. The supplier usually takes control of the purchasing relationship
   d. All of the above
4. The most obvious disadvantage of data mining is:
   a. Databases are very large and often cannot be analyzed using off-the-shelf products
   b. High cost
   c. The decrease in employee morale
   d. None of the above
5. Benford's law:
   a. Is usually unsuccessful as a fraud detection tool
   b. Predicts that the first digit of random number sets will begin with a 1 more often than a 2, a 2 more often than a 3, and so on
   c. Applies to personal ID numbers
   d. All of the above
6. A detection method that focuses on the kinds of frauds that can occur and then uses technology to determine whether those frauds actually exist is called:
   a. Fishing fraud detection
   b. Data mining
   c. Deductive fraud detection
   d. Benford's law
7. When deciding which detection method to use, it is important to:
   a. Determine the advantages and disadvantages of each approach
   b. Identify the costs involved
   c. Determine which method will meet the client's objectives
   d. All of the above
8. Fraud is best detected through financial statements by focusing on:
   a. Unexplained changes in financial statement balances
   b. Consistencies
   c. Intuition
   d. Management's behavior when financial statements are released

9. The most effective way to convert balance sheets and income statements from position and period statements to change statements is to:
   a. Compare balances in the statements from one period to the next
   b. Calculate key ratios and compare them from period to period
   c. Perform horizontal and vertical analysis
   d. All of the above
10. Profit margin, return on assets, and return on equity are all examples of:
    a. Vertical analysis
    b. Key financial statement ratios
    c. Horizontal analysis
    d. None of the above
11. When vertical analysis is performed:
    a. Ratios are used to detect fraud.
    b. Changes in significant balance totals are examined.
    c. Financial statement balances are converted to percentages.
    d. Total revenues are compared to total expenses.
12. Horizontal analysis is different from vertical analysis in that:
    a. There is no difference between horizontal and vertical analysis.
    b. Horizontal analysis calculates the percentage change in balance sheet and income statement numbers from one period to the next, while vertical analysis converts balances in a single period to percentages.
    c. Horizontal analysis converts balances in a single period to percentages, while vertical analysis calculates the percentage change in balance sheet and income statement numbers from one period to the next.
    d. Key ratios are compared from one period to the next.
13. Which of the following is *not* a disadvantage of using commercial data-mining software to detect fraud?
    a. It is a static approach, and results cannot be recombined in different ways.
    b. Data-mining software can only be used to analyze small data sets.
    c. Commercial data-mining software often identifies thousands of possible fraud symptoms.
    d. All of the above are possible disadvantages of using commercial data-mining software to detect fraud.
14. Benford's law is:
    a. The most expensive of all the digital analysis methods to implement and use
    b. The most effective way to identify actual frauds
    c. A method that uses vertical financial statement analysis
    d. An effective way to identify anomalies in data sets
15. If a search reveals that an employee and a vendor have the same telephone number, this result may indicate:
    a. Vendors are overcharging for goods purchased.
    b. Employees may be establishing dummy vendors.
    c. Contractors are billing at the wrong rates.
    d. A vendor is receiving kickbacks or other favors.

16. When conducting financial statement analysis, which ratio will be the most useful in determining whether a company has erroneously inflated accounts receivable?
    a. Current ratio
    b. Profit margin
    c. Accounts receivable turnover
    d. Debt percentage

Short Cases

Case 1. Boxer Incorporated has hired you as a consultant to implement a proactive fraud detection program in the company. One of the owners, Priscilla Boxer, asks you to give a presentation to several executives about the different approaches you are considering. After evaluating the company, you narrow the possibilities down to two choices: (a) commercial data-mining software and (b) statistical analysis, such as Benford's law.

1. List the advantages and disadvantages of each approach.
2. What factors will you need to know to make your decision?

Case 2. A large manufacturing business has hired you as a fraud detection specialist. The first day on the job, your boss asks you the following questions:

1. What is Benford's law?
2. In what situations is it appropriate to use Benford's law, and in what situations is Benford's law inappropriate?

Case 3. Dennis Jones, an old college friend, contacted you last week. Dennis owns several car washes, and he believes that financial statement fraud may be occurring. (He pays each car wash manager a bonus if a certain level of profits is earned and is worried that some managers are overstating profits to earn a higher bonus.) Dennis is coming over today to see whether you can help him determine if his suspicions are valid. He is bringing along the financial statements for each car wash (income statements, balance sheets, and cash flow statements) for the last five years.

What kind of financial statement analysis could you perform to help Dennis detect possible fraud?

Case 4. Your boss knows you are taking a fraud examination course at a local university. He is interested in learning more about proactive fraud detection and asks you to prepare a short memo briefly explaining proactive fraud detection methods and approaches. List three proactive fraud detection approaches and briefly explain them.

Case 5.

There once was a corporation from Nantucket,
Its controls leaked like holes in a bucket.
Smelling trouble with the buyer,
And with the supplier,
They determined to fix it or chuck it.

This limerick accurately depicts Bucket Corp., which manufactures wood furniture. Bucket has enjoyed several years of good profits, but now recently sees some alarming trends in its bottom line. Although not drastic, Bucket's profits first stagnated, and are now beginning to decline. After some cost analysis and investigation of financial records, the company has determined that the problem may be coming from the procurement division of operations.

The following is a small random sample of invoices from various vendors:

Supplier	Product	Price/Ton	Qty.	Total
Woods 'R' Us	Oak	$157.00	2	$314.00
	Cherry	75.00	3	225.00
	Cedar	125.00	1.5	187.50
	Spruce	42.00	3	126.00
Harris Lumber	Oak	215.00	4	860.00
	Cherry	115.00	8	920.00
	Cedar	140.00	6	840.00
	Spruce	80.00	9	720.00
Lumber Jack's	Oak	158.00	1	158.00
	Cherry	74.00	2	148.00
	Cedar	124.00	2	248.00
	Spruce	43.00	3	129.00
Small's Lumber	Oak	156.00	3	468.00
	Cherry	76.00	3	228.00
	Cedar	127.00	1	127.00
	Spruce	41.00	4	164.00

What could the CFO do to investigate the potential problems in the procurement department of Bucket Corp.? Do you think it is possible there is fraud involved? Why?

Case 6. By ordering unnecessary products at inflated prices, the purchasing manager of XYZ Company defrauded his employer of over $40,000 over a two-year period.

How could you have detected this fraud?

Case 7. As CEO of your company, you've been going over your financial statements and have noticed something disturbing. You perform a horizontal analysis and find that sales have been increasing at a rate of 3% per year, while inventory has risen at a rate of 29% per year.

1. Could fraud be occurring? Why or why not?
2. Assuming that fraud is being committed, how would you investigate?

Case 8.

Amount	Description	Check No.
$ 235.65	Payment to US West for phone bill	2001
$ 654.36	John's Heating and Cooling for fixing A/C in December	2002
$4,987.36	Sharky's Used Car Dealership for Yugo Truck	2003
$ 339.13	Salt River Project for power in December	2004
$ 475.98	Arizona Department of Internal Revenue for taxes	2005
$ 254.14	Grainger Corp. for power tools	2006
$ 504.17	Home Depot for outdoor carport	2007
$ 171.54	Steelin's consulting for help with computer network	2008
$ 326.45	Payment to US West for phone bill in January	2009
$ 477.67	Bank of America for loan payment	2010

1. Compare the first-digit frequency in the above transactions with Benford's law. What are the results?
2. Could fraud be occurring in this organization?

Case 9. As an internal auditor for CRA, Inc., you are assigned to a team working on an ongoing project to identify possible fraud. The project started as a data-mining exercise to analyze the company's databases and identify possible problems. The project was started last year, but because of budget problems, it was delayed until this year. Most of the data mining is complete, but the team is having problems sorting through all the information. Your manager is certain that this data-mining approach is the best method in a large company such as CRA.

1. Discuss the strengths and possible weaknesses of the data-mining approach for CRA.
2. What other approaches should be considered?

Case 10. Large frauds can often be detected by performing financial statement analysis. Although such analysis can raise areas of concern, not all red flags are the result of fraudulent activities. Reasonable explanations often exist for anomalies in financial statements.

The statement of cash flows is one financial statement that is analyzed in order to identify possible fraud. This statement for Kelly Enterprises, Inc., for a three-year period is shown below.

Kelly Enterprises, Inc.
Statement of Cash Flows
For the Period Ended December 31, 2002

In millions	**2002**	**2001**	**2000**
Cash from Operations			
Net income	$900	$800	$ 450
Change in accounts receivable	(706)	(230)	25
Change in accounts payable	150	45	90
Change in inventory	50	(15)	25
Depreciation	105	90	65
Net cash from operations	499	690	655
Cash from Investing			
Additions to property, plant, and equipment	(950)	(690)	(790)
Proceeds from sale of securities	25	56	15
Net cash from investing	(925)	(634)	(775)
Cash from Financing			
Borrowings of long-term debt	250	150	34
Cash dividends	(140)	(85)	(45)
Net cash from financing	110	65	(11)
Increase (decrease) in cash	**$(316)**	**$121**	**$(131)**

1. Identify possible red flags.
2. Indicate if reasonable explanations exist for the areas of concern.

Case 11. By examining first digits, Company XXX suspects fraud. You are asked to review the following sample of invoices to make sure they make sense. You are familiar with several fraud detection methods and are eager to try out Benford's law.

INVOICE AMOUNTS

$149,200.00	$ 19,489.00	$1,134.00
1,444.00	12,485.00	446.00
1,756.00	26,995.00	678.00
91.59	235,535.00	456.00
2,250.00	59,155.00	341.00
38,005.00	109,995.00	890.00
45,465.00	212,536.00	402.00
112,495.00	685.00	467.00
137,500.00	765.00	465.00
37,300.00	234.00	1,516.00
36,231.00	435.00	375.00
26,695.00	1,045.00	679.00

Do you suspect possible fraud? Why?

Extensive Cases

Case 12. You are in your first month as an internal auditor in the corporate offices of Cover-Up Fraud-Mart, a large regional variety store chain based in Los Angeles. Your manager has just given you a general overview of the company's problems with fraud. In fact, losses from fraud exceed losses from shoplifting by tenfold, and management wants your perspective on what it can do to proactively detect fraud. From your fraud auditing class, you know that the deductive approach is one of the most effective detection methods.

1. What is the difference between the two inductive fraud detection methods discussed in this chapter and this deductive method?
2. List the five steps involved in the deductive fraud detection method.

Case 13. Using the financial information provided below and on the following pages, compute the required ratios list on the ratio analysis sheet, and then complete the horizontal and vertical analysis worksheets.

ABC Company
Balance Sheet
As of December 31, 2002

ASSETS	**2002**	**2001**	**2000**
Current assets			
Cash	$ 501,992	$ 434,215	$ 375,141
Accounts receivable	335,272	302,514	241,764
Inventory	515,174	505,321	310,885
Prepaid expenses	251,874	231,100	136,388
Total current assets	$1,604,312	$1,473,150	$1,064,178
Property, plant, and equipment	765,215	735,531	705,132
Accumulated depreciation	(218,284	(196,842	(175,400
TOTAL ASSETS	$2,151,243	$2,011,839	$1,593,910

LIABILITIES			
Current liabilities			
Accounts payable	$ 248,494	$ 366,864	$ 322,156
Accrued liabilities	122,192	216,533	215,474
Income taxes payable	10,645	25,698	22,349
Current portion of long-term debt	42,200	42,200	42,200
Total current liabilities	$ 423,531	$ 651,295	$ 602,179
Long-term liabilities			
Long-term debt	425,311	400,311	375,100
TOTAL LIABILITIES	$ 848,842	$1,051,606	$ 977,279
STOCKHOLDERS' EQUITY			
Common stock	$ 370,124	$ 356,758	$ 320,841
Additional paid-in capital	29,546	24,881	21,910
Retained earnings	578,594	273,880	75,315
Total stockholders' equity	$ 978,264	$ 655,519	$ 418,066
TOTAL LIABILITIES AND STOCKHOLDERS' EQUITY	$1,827,106	$1,707,125	$1,395,345

ABC Company
Income Statement
For the Period Ended December 31, 2002

	2002	**2001**	**2000**
Sales	$1,572,134	$1,413,581	$1,158,417
Cost of goods sold	601,215	556,721	500,702
Gross profit	$ 970,919	$ 856,860	$ 657,715
EXPENSES			
Advertising	$ 55,153	$ 50,531	$ 42,150
Depreciation	21,442	21,442	21,442
Bad debts	20,151	18,934	17,943
Legal	17,261	10,207	9,701
Miscellaneous	91,014	31,214	29,104
Rent	148,321	142,078	141,143
Repairs and maintenance	14,315	13,642	11,932
Salaries and wages	47,121	45,312	39,142
Utilities	15,912	15,643	14,217
Total expenses	$ 430,690	$ 349,003	$ 326,774
Net income before income tax	$ 540,229	$ 507,857	$ 330,941
Income tax expense	216,092	203,143	132,376
NET INCOME	$ 324,137	$ 304,714	$ 198,565
Number of shares of stock outstanding	35,913	26,786	23,712

ABC Company
Ratio Analysis
December 31, 2002

LIQUIDITY RATIOS:	**12/31/02**	**12/31/01**	**Change**	**% Change**
Current ratio				
Current assets ÷ Current liabilities				
Quick ratio				
(Current assets − Inventory) ÷ Current liabilities				
Accounts receivable turnover				
Sales ÷ Average accounts receivable				
Days sales in accounts receivable				
365 ÷ Accounts receivable turnover				
Inventory turnover				
Cost of goods sold ÷ Average inventory				
PROFITABILITY/PERFORMANCE RATIOS:				
Profit margin				
Net income ÷ Net sales				
Gross profit margin (%)				
Gross profit ÷ Sales				
Earnings per share				
Net income ÷ Number of shares of stock				
Sales ÷ Total assets				
Sales ÷ Total assets				
Sales ÷ Working capital				
Sales ÷ (Current assets − Current liabilities)				
EQUITY POSITION RATIOS:				
Owners' equity ÷ Total assets				
Total stockholders' equity ÷ Total assets				
Current liabilities ÷ Owners' equity				
Current liabilities ÷ Total stockholders' equity				
Total liabilities ÷ Owners' equity				
Total liabilities ÷ Total stockholders' equity				

ABC Company
Income Statement
For the Period Ended December 31, 2002

	2002	2001	$ Change	% Change
Sales	$1,572,134	$1,413,581		
Cost of goods sold	601,215	556,721		
Gross profit	$ 970,919	$ 856,860		
EXPENSES				
Advertising	$ 55,153	$ 50,531		
Depreciation	21,442	21,442		
Bad debts	20,151	18,934		
Legal	17,261	10,207		
Miscellaneous	91,014	31,214		
Rent	148,321	142,078		
Repairs and maintenance	14,315	13,642		
Salaries and wages	47,121	45,312		
Utilities	15,912	15,643		
Total expenses	$ 430,690	$ 349,003		
Net income before income ta	$ 540,229	$ 507,857		
Income tax expense	216,092	203,143		
NET INCOME	$ 324,137	$ 304,714		

ABC Company
Balance Sheet
As of December 31, 2002

ASSETS	**2002**	**% Total Assets**	**2001**	**% Total Assets**	**2000**	**% Total Assets**
Current assets						
Cash	$ 501,992	_______	$ 434,215	_______	$ 375,141	_______
Accounts receivable	335,272	_______	302,514	_______	241,764	_______
Inventory	515,174	_______	505,321	_______	310,885	_______
Prepaid expenses	251,874	_______	231,100	_______	136,388	_______
Total current assets	$1,604,312		$1,473,150		$1,064,178	
Property, plant, and equipment	765,215	_______	735,531	_______	705,132	_______
Accumulated depreciation	(218,284)	_______	(196,842)	_______	(175,400)	_______
TOTAL ASSETS	$2,151,243		$2,011,839		$1,593,910	
LIABILITIES						
Current liabilities						
Accounts payable	$ 248,494	_______	$ 366,864	_______	$ 322,156	_______
Accrued liabilities	122,192	_______	216,533	_______	215,474	_______
Income taxes payable	10,645	_______	25,698	_______	22,349	_______
Current portion of long-term debt	42,200	_______	42,200	_______	42,200	_______
Total current liabilities	$ 423,531		$ 651,295		$ 602,179	
Long-term liabilities						
Long-term debt	425,311	_______	400,311	_______	375,100	_______
TOTAL LIABILITIES	$ 848,842		$1,051,606		$ 977,279	
STOCKHOLDERS' EQUITY						
Common stock	$ 370,124	_______	$ 356,758		$ 320,841	
Additional paid-in capital	29,546	_______	24,881	_______	21,910	_______
Retained earnings	578,594	_______	273,880	_______	75,315	_______
Total stockholders' equity	$ 978,264		$ 655,519		$ 418,066	
TOTAL LIABILITIES AND STOCKHOLDERS' EQUITY	$1,827,106		$1,707,125		$1,395,345	

Internet Assignments

1. Read the article entitled "Following Benford's Law, or Looking Out for No. 1" found at http://256.com/gray/info/benfords.html. The article mentions that a statistics professor can easily discern if students flipped a coin 200 times or if they merely faked it. Of this exercise, the professor stated, "Most people do not know the real odds of such an exercise, so they cannot fake data convincingly." How does that exercise relate to Benford's law and detecting fraud?
2. Go to http://idagroup.com/v1n1701.htm and answer the following questions.
   1. What is a neural network?
   2. How can neural networks be used to detect fraud?
   3. Which industries will benefit most from neural network technology?
   4. Who is developing this technology?
3. Credit-card companies are very concerned with the growing problem of credit-card fraud. They spend enormous amounts of money each year on detection. Go to the web site of a large credit-card company, such as Visa, MasterCard, or American Express. What are some of the proactive measures these institutions are taking to control fraud and to persuade the public that it is safe to use credit cards?

Debate

You are the new controller of a major U.S. manufacturing firm. In your previous employment, you detected multiple varieties of fraud. The CFO of your new company informs you that top management is concerned about possible fraud in the organization and is interested in taking a proactive approach both to detecting fraud and deterring fraud. After noting that he has recommended you for the fraud detection assignment, the CFO tells you that he is a little nervous about how much these investigative approaches will cost and asks you to keep your choices simple and inexpensive. You and the CFO are good friends, and you've never had a problem suggesting ideas about upcoming projects in the past. You know that to be most effective in completing your new assignment, you should do some extensive data analysis because of the large size of the company and its databases.

Have one person take the position of the CFO who wants to keep analyses simple and another the position of the controller who believes more extreme approaches are necessary. Debate the appropriateness of the various detection approaches, including the deductive approach, for your company. Explain why data-mining using commercial software may not be sufficient.

PART FOUR

FRAUD INVESTIGATION

Investigating Theft and Concealment

After studying this chapter, you should be able to understand:

1. Methods for investigating theft.
2. How to coordinate investigations using vulnerability charts.
3. The nature of surveillance and covert operations.
4. The effectiveness of invigilation in investigating fraud.
5. How physical evidence can be used in fraud investigations.
6. Methods for investigating concealment.
7. The value of documents in fraud investigations.
8. The importance of obtaining documentary evidence.
9. How to perform discovery sampling to obtain documentary evidence.
10. How to obtain hard-to-get documentary evidence.

No single promotion lured more people to McDonald's than its popular monopoly game—until August of 2001—when it was discovered that the monopoly game was a fraud. An employee at Simon Marketing, which ran the monopoly game on behalf of McDonald's, was responsible for the fraud. Simon Marketing allegedly bilked McDonald's out of $13 million worth of game prizes.

In a quiet, upper-class subdivision of brick and stucco mansions in Lawrenceville, Georgia, Jerome Jacobson spent six years promoting one of the largest promotional (and fake) contests ever held. As Simon's longtime manager of game security, Jacobson, 58, traveled the country and randomly placed winning peel-off contest stickers on things like soft-drink cups and french fry boxes at McDonald's restaurants and inserted instant-winner tickets in magazines and Sunday newspaper circulars. However, the FBI says that Jacobson devised his own cash-in scheme, embezzling winning game pieces and instant tickets. In turn, he sold them to prearranged winners for kickbacks of $50,000 or more.

Jacobson pocketed at least $50,000 each from up to 13 separate $1 million prizewinners. The government's lengthy complaint described Jacobson as a savvy manipulator and the fraud's ringleader, willing to double-cross those who dared hold back payments. Jacobson recruited at least two accomplices who acted as recruiters themselves.

In exchange for negotiated payments, the "winners" received winning game pieces and instant prize tickets. They were also instructed at length on how to disguise their actual residences and what to tell McDonald's about where and how they had picked up game pieces and instant-winner tickets.

According to federal prosecutors, at least 17 recruits won ill-gotten prizes. Besides the 13 winners of the $1 million game, one recipient won a 1996 Dodge Viper valued at about $60,000. Others won cash prizes of $100,000 and $200,000.

Had an informant not contacted the Jacksonville FBI office last year, the contest scam allegedly orchestrated by Jacobson might have continued indefinitely. FBI agents obtained court permission for several telephone wiretaps and tailed Jacobson and others. McDonald's also agreed to delay issuing checks to winners, which helped the FBI secure evidence from wiretaps.[1]

In Chapter 3, we provided an overview of fraud investigation. The two approaches to fraud investigation are (1) the evidence square approach and (2) the fraud triangle plus inquiry approach. The fraud triangle plus inquiry approach, together with the various investigative techniques, is shown below.

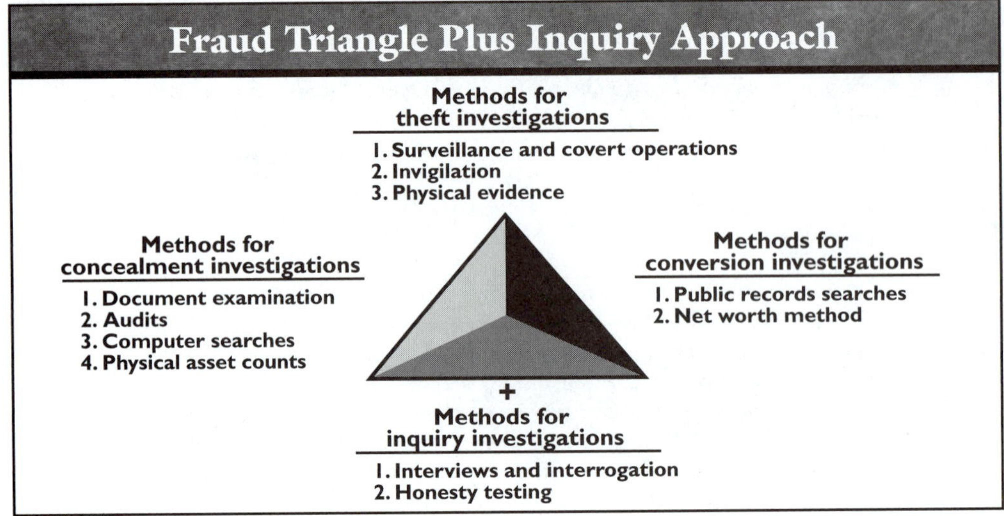

In this chapter, we discuss different methods for investigating theft and concealment, as well as various techniques for gathering the documents and evidence. Methods for investigating conversion are examined in Chapter 8.

In deciding which methods to use, effective investigators focus on gathering the strongest type of evidence for the fraud at hand. For example, because inventory frauds involve the transporting of stolen goods, investigators focus on the theft. In payroll frauds, such as excess overtime charges or "ghost" employees on payrolls, focusing on concealment efforts is often the best strategy. Payroll frauds involve tampered records (the concealment) and documentary evidence is usually easy to find.

In collusion and kickback frauds, however, documentary evidence doesn't always exist, although purchasing records occasionally show increased prices or increased work by a particular vendor. As a result, investigation techniques that work on concealment often don't work well on kickback scams. With these frauds, investigators frequently investigate the theft, using tailing or wiretaps (as in the McDonald's case), or they gather circumstantial public-record evidence in order to show that the perpetrator is living beyond his or her income. Inquiry methods are helpful in all types of fraud investigations.

Theft Investigation Methods

Seasoned fraud investigators are careful to begin their investigations in a manner that does not arouse suspicion and, more important, does not incriminate innocent people. Therefore, they initially involve very few people, and they avoid words like "investigation" ("audit" and "inquiry" usually suffice). They choose techniques that are not likely to be recognized as an investigation—at least in the beginning. As the inquiry proceeds, they work inward toward the prime suspect, until finally he or she is confronted in an interview. The following diagram illustrates this pattern.

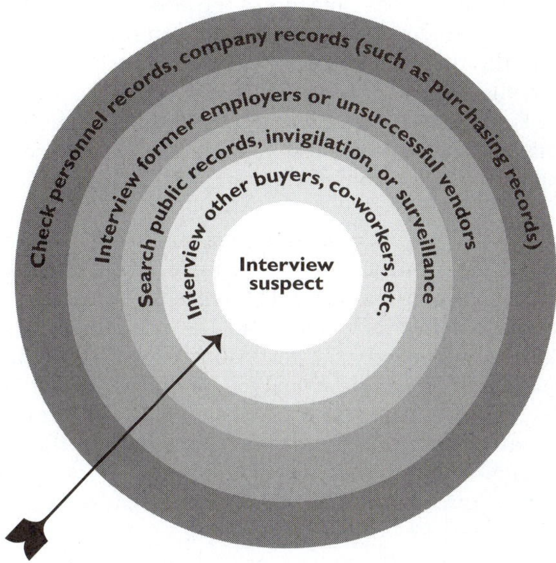

Suppose you are investigating a purchasing employee who is suspected of taking kickbacks. You might proceed through these seven steps:

1. Check employee's personnel records for evidence of liens or other financial difficulties, or for previous problems.
2. Perform a "special audit" of the purchasing function to examine trends and changes in prices and purchasing volume from various vendors.
3. Search public records and other sources to gather evidence about the suspect's lifestyle.
4. Perform surveillance or other covert operations.
5. Interview former buyers and unsuccessful vendors.
6. Interview current buyers, including the suspect's manager (only if collusion with management is not suspected).
7. Simultaneously interview the suspected buyer and the suspected vendor.

Several of these steps can be undertaken without arousing suspicion. For example, security personnel, auditors, and fraud examiners commonly examine personnel records during normal audits. Similarly, searching purchasing records and public records does not create suspicion, because this is a normal audit procedure and it can be performed offsite.

Properly performed surveillance is done without the perpetrator's knowledge. Only when interviews begin is the suspect likely to become aware of the investigation. Even then, interviews are normally conducted first with individuals who are objective and who are not currently associated with the suspect, and then work inward until the suspect is finally interviewed. Starting tangentially and working inward avoids alerting suspects too early that they are being investigated and also avoids undue stress or suspicion among other employees. In addition, this process protects the subject of the investigation, in case evidence reveals that the individual is innocent.

Coordinating an Investigation

When beginning a fraud investigation, constructing a vulnerability chart is often useful. Vulnerability charts coordinate the various elements of the possible fraud, including (1) assets that were taken or are missing, (2) individuals who have opportunities to commit fraud, (3) promising methods to use in the theft investigation, (4) concealment possibilities, (5) conversion possibilities, (6) symptoms observed, (7) pressures on possible perpetrators, (8) potential rationalizations for the fraud, and (9) key internal controls that had to be compromised for the theft to occur. The vulnerability chart shown here identifies factors that need to be examined in a fraud investigation for a bank customer who complained that her deposit was not credited to her account.

Investigations begin with questions, and the vulnerability chart is a good place to organize your initial answers. What was taken? In our example, assets taken could include the customer's deposit. Who had opportunity(ies)? The teller who processed the transaction, the operations officer who supervised the teller, and the proof operator who processed the deposit. How were the assets moved? List the possibilities, for this and for the remaining questions. As your investigation continues, you will no doubt add items and cross others off.

Vulnerability charts can be prepared for every potential fraud. For example, frauds involving stolen inventory and overcharged goods are also shown in the vulnerability chart on page 183. The advantage of such charts is that they force investigators to consider every aspect of a fraud. When symptoms are observed, a decision must be made whether or not to investigate.

Surveillance and Covert Operations

Surveillance and covert or undercover operations are investigation techniques that rely on the senses, especially hearing and seeing. Surveillance or observation means watching and recording (on paper, film, or magnetic tape) physical facts, activities, and movements that constitute the theft. Technically, the three types of surveillance are (1) stationary or fixed point, (2) moving or tailing, and (3) electronic surveillance.

Simple fixed-point or stationary observations can be conducted by anyone. In conducting these observations, the investigator locates the scene to be observed, anticipates the action that is most likely to occur at the scene, and either keeps detailed notes on all activities involving the suspect or records them on film or tape. The detailed records should include date and day of observation, name of the observer, names of corroborating witnesses, the position from which the observation was made, its distance from the scene, and the time the observation began and ended, along with a detailed time log of all movements and activities of the suspect. An example of a surveillance log is shown on pages 184–185. The person under surveillance was suspected of taking kickbacks from a vendor.

Vulnerability Chart

What was taken?	Who had opportunity?	How were assets moved?	How was theft concealed?	How are assets converted?	Red-flag symptoms?	Possible Motive(s)		Key Internal Controls
						Pressures	Rationalization	
Customer deposit	Teller Operations officer Proof operator	Entering verified credits Stealing check; endorsing it	Destroying deposit slip Forged signature Entering credit in own account	Unlimited	Changed behavior Changed lifestyle Customer complaint	Tax lien New home Divorce	Feels underpaid or poorly treated	Use processing jacket Certification Teller counts customer receipts
Goods delivered	Receiving trucker	Not received Truck	Night Included with trash	Fenced Used personally	Control not followed Goods not counted	New car Spouse laid off	Passed over for promotion	Receiving report
Overcharged for goods	Purchasing agent	N/A	Kickback	Cash Hire spouse	Extravagant lifestyle Asset sold inexpensively	Maintain lifestyle	Greed	Bids

Surveillance Log	
January 29, 2002 Date/Time	**Event**
6:30 pm	Instituted surveillance at Flatirons Country Club, 457 W. Arapahoe, Boulder, CO.
6:40 pm	Alex Tong and unidentified white male seen leaving racquetball courts and entering locker rooms.
7:00 pm	Both men seen leaving locker room.
7:05 pm	Tong and white male enter club restaurant and order drinks. White male orders beer; Tong orders orange liquid drink.
7:10 pm	Twosome order dinner.
7:25 pm	Dinner arrives. Tong has white, cream-based soup and club sandwich. White male has steak and potatoes.
7:30 pm	Break: Surveillance terminated.
7:36 pm	Surveillance re-instituted. Twosome still eating at table.
7:55 pm	Tong goes to restroom. White male remains at table.
8:00 pm	Tong returns to table.
8:15 pm	Twosome order two drinks.
8:25 pm	White male requests check.
8:30 pm	Check arrives and is presented to white male. White male hands credit card to waitress without examining check.
8:35 pm	Waitress returns, gives bill to white male, who signs bill. Waitress gives yellow slip to white male. No indication of Tong attempting to pay check.
8:40 pm	White male removes envelope from portfolio and gives it to Tong. Tong looks pleased and places envelope in his pocket. Twosome leave and are seen getting into a Mercedes Benz and a 2002 Lexus, respectively, and drive away.

continues

Surveillance Log	
January 29, 2002 Date/Time	**Event**
8:45 pm	Waitress is interviewed. She displays a copy of a Citibank Gold MasterCard charge slip in the name of Christopher D. Ballard, account number 5424-1803-1930–1493. Card expires 03/2006. The amount of the check is $78.65. Waitress is given $20 cash tip for information.
9:00 pm	Surveillance terminated.

Mobile observation, or tailing, which was used in the McDonald's fraud, is much more risky than stationary surveillance. In one case, an internal auditor was shot at while tailing a suspect. Although the potential rewards for this type of surveillance are high and can include identifying the receiver of stolen goods or the payer of bribes or kickbacks, the chances of failure are also high. Tailing is a job best left to professionals.

Electronic surveillance of employees, using video cameras, is frequently used. Wiretapping, another form of surveillance, can only be used by law enforcement officers. Electronic surveillance may also have limited value in investigations of employee frauds and many other white-collar crimes because of concerns regarding employees' privacy in the workplace. However, it is useful in kickback schemes, such as the McDonald's case, where law enforcement is involved. Several corporations have instituted strict controls over all forms of electronic surveillance, including video, electronic mail (e-mail) privacy, wiretapping, and access to PCs.

Surveillance and covert operations are legal as long as they do not invade a person's reasonable expectation of privacy under the Fourth Amendment to the Constitution, which protects people from unreasonable searches. Legal counsel and human resources should always be consulted before any form of surveillance takes place. In addition, organizations should implement strict protocols regarding the use of any form of surveillance to ensure that controls are in place and that the "reasonable person" test is given to every application. The net value of surveillance can be more than offset by problems caused by inappropriate or improper application of the techniques.

Undercover operations are both legal and valid, provided they are not "fishing expeditions." Undercover operations are costly and time-consuming and should be used with extreme care. Use them only when (1) large-scale collusion is likely, (2) other investigation methods fail, (3) the investigation can be closely monitored, (4) there is significant reason to believe the fraud is occurring or reoccurring, (5) the investigation is in strict compliance with the laws and ethics of the organization, (6) the investigation can remain secretive, and (7) law enforcement authorities are informed when appropriate evidence has been accumulated.

Three actual undercover operations will highlight some of the risks involved. In the first instance, which was successful, collusion was suspected. The undercover agent obtained valuable evidence that led to the conviction of several individuals. The other two (unsuccessful) undercover operations were concerned with suspected drug dealing at manufacturing facilities. (No organization can tolerate drug dealing. If the employee purchasing and using drugs on the job is involved in a car accident on the way home from work, for example, the organization can be liable.) In the second operation, the agent became fearful and quit. In the third operation, the agent became sympathetic to the suspects and was not helpful.

Invigilation

In invigilation, suspects are closely supervised during an examination period. Such strict temporary controls are imposed on an activity that, during the period of invigilation, fraud is virtually impossible. As noted in earlier chapters, opportunity is one of the three conditions that must exist for fraud to occur. When controls are so strict that opportunities to commit fraud are nonexistent, a fraud-free baseline can be established. If detailed records are kept before, during, and after the invigilation period, evidence about whether fraud is occurring can be obtained. The following diagram outlines an invigilation:

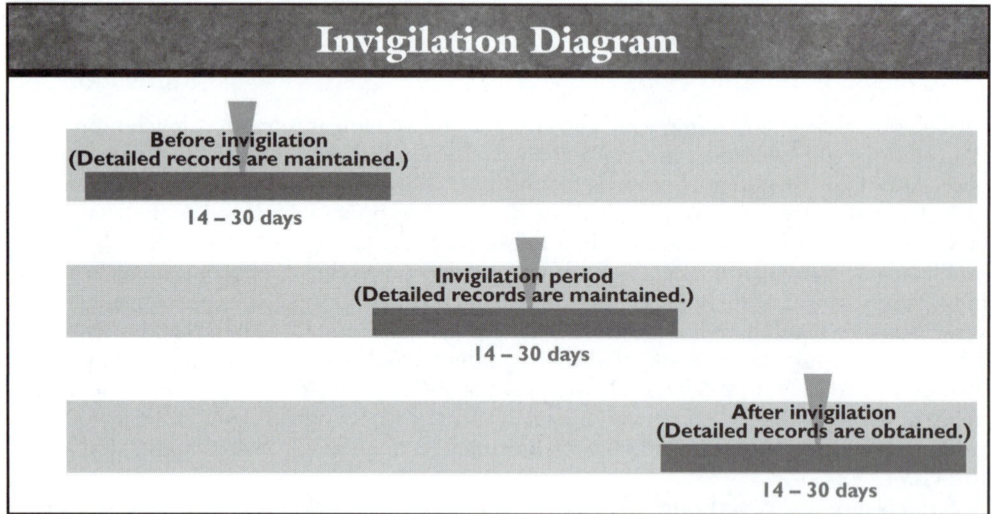

The following invigilation detected a fraud involving inventory losses:

> *An oil distributor was experiencing inventory losses of 0.23% of inventory. The manager suspected fraud but was not sure how or when it was occurring. Observation and other investigation methods failed to produce evidence. For a 30-day period, the installation was saturated with security guards and auditors. Every movement of goods both in and out was checked, all documents were verified, and inventory and equipment were regularly reviewed. During the invigilation period, losses ceased. Afterward, records kept at the plant were examined for absolute, proportional, and reasonableness changes during the invigilation period. Two service stations—which before the exercise bought an average of only 2,000 gallons of gasoline a week—suddenly doubled their orders. During the 30 days, in fact, each received more than 19,000 gallons. In addition, a shift foreman, who in 23 years of service had taken no sick leave, was away from work on 19 of the 30 days. Two or three months were allowed to elapse, and during this time, covert observation was maintained on the service stations, whose weekly orders had by this time reverted to the 2,000-gallon level. Using night vision equipment and cameras, unrecorded deliveries to the service stations were observed. The owners were interviewed, and their books examined. They were subsequently charged with fraud extending back two years and involving 62,000 gallons of gasoline.*

This invigilation took place in a large company, but this tool can also be used in smaller organizations, as the following example shows:

> *"Mark" owned an auto tune-up shop. The company had 12 bays, 12 mechanics, and one accountant, "John," whom Mark completely trusted, handled all accounting duties, including cash receipts, bank deposits, the writing of checks, payroll, and taxes. Each year, Mark's business serviced more cars, but cash flow decreased. Not knowing what to do, Mark consulted a friend, who was a CPA. The friend performed various cost, volume, and profit analyses and informed Mark that his business should be profitable. He suggested that someone might be embezzling. John was the only employee in a position to embezzle. Mark's friend suggested an experiment, and Mark agreed. Mark first made copies of all bank statements and other cash records for one month. He then told all employees, including John, that he was thinking about selling the shop and that the prospective buyer insisted on daily audited records for one month. During this month, an outside CPA came by daily to count cash receipts, make bank deposits, write all checks, and check on parts and inventory. After one month, Mark informed all employees that the sale had fallen through and that he had decided not to sell the shop. Following the invigilation period, Mark again copied bank statements and other cash records for one month. To Mark's surprise, cash paid by customers as a percentage of total receipts (customers either paid by check, credit card, or cash) was 7% before the investigation, 15% during the one-month invigilation period, and returned to the approximately 7% level in the following month. Faced with the evidence, John admitted that he had been embezzling cash from Mark's business. A subsequent analysis revealed that he stole more than $600,000.*

Invigilation can be expensive. Use it only with management's approval, and restrict it to a discrete and self-contained area of the business. Most commonly, it is used in such high-risk areas as expensive inventory, areas with poor controls over the receipt and loading of goods, and areas with poor controls over accounting records.

When using invigilation, management must decide on the precise nature of the increased temporary controls necessary to remove fraud opportunities. Past records should be analyzed to establish an operating baseline for the unit under review. This baseline must include such things as normal losses, the number and nature of transactions per day, the number and type of exceptional transactions, and vehicle movements in and out of the facility. To get an accurate reading, experts generally agree that invigilations must continue for at least 14 days. In individual cases, however, the optimal duration will depend on the frequency and nature of transactions.

Once in a while, invigilation backfires. One company, for example, was suffering significant small tool losses from its manufacturing plant. To determine who was taking the tools, the company checked all workers' lunch boxes as they exited the facility. The practice so upset employees that they caused a work slowdown that was more expensive than the fraud losses.

Physical Evidence

The final theft investigation technique is the analysis of physical evidence. This technique involves analyzing objects such as inventory, assets, and broken locks; substances such as grease and fluids; traces such as paints and stains; and impressions such as cutting marks, tire tracks, and fingerprints. Physical evidence was used to discover who was involved in the 1993 bombing of the World Trade Center in New York City. The vehicle identification number engraved on the axle of the rented van that contained the explosives made it possible to trace the van to a rental agency. When the perpetrator came back to the rental agency to recover his deposit and make a claim that the van had been stolen, the FBI arrested him.

Another use of physical evidence involved the famed detective William J. Burns, who once solved a counterfeit currency conspiracy by tracking down a single clue to its source.[2] Here is how he solved the case. Burns used a four-digit number preceded by "xx," which was imprinted on a burlap covering to a sofa shipped from the United States to Costa Rica. In the sofa were hidden nearly 1 million counterfeit pesos. By tracing the clue to its source, Burns gained a great deal of evidence, blew the case wide open, and was instrumental in sending the counterfeiters to Sing Sing State Prison. Burns proceeded as follows:

1. Located and called on burlap manufacturers.
2. Learned the significance of the imprinted number on the burlap covering, and how it might help him trace the specific piece of burlap to its purchaser.
3. Dug for the precise four-digit order number in a pile of old, discarded order forms.
4. Located the retail dry goods store that sold the particular piece of burlap.
5. Asked a retail clerk about the purchase of interest and obtained a description of the person who purchased the burlap: a little old lady dressed in black and wearing a shawl.
6. Located the purchaser. (Burns later learned that she bought the burlap for her son-in-law.)
7. Invented a pretense to take the young retail clerk with him to call on the lady, so that the clerk would later be able to identify her.
8. Checked out a number of furniture moving companies to locate the one that moved the old couch containing the pesos to the docks.
9. Questioned a succession of dockhands until he found one who remembered loading the sofa. The dockhand also remembered the undue concern of a dark, handsome man, who constantly urged the dock hands to handle the sofa with care. The dockhand said he was sure he could identify the man.
10. Located the man who was so concerned for the sofa's safe shipment.
11. Discovered that the man, whose name he now knew, traveled to Costa Rica shortly before the shipment of the peso-packed sofa. He was accompanied by a beautiful woman who traveled under her real name.
12. Learned who engraved the counterfeit plates used to print the pesos. The engraver turned out to be the son of a lithographer in a plant owned by the two people who had traveled to Costa Rica. The chief product of the plant was revolutionary literature that tied in with the plot to overthrow the Costa Rican government.

Concealment Investigation Methods

Surveillance and covert operations, invigilation, and physical evidence are all methods for investigating theft. These methods are used less frequently in fraud investigations because they are more expensive and require more expertise than other techniques. For certain frauds, however, especially those involving the theft of tangible assets, they often deliver the strongest evidence. Methods for investigating concealment, on the other hand, deal with manipulation of source documents, such as purchase invoices, sales invoices, credit memos, deposit slips, checks, receiving reports, bills of lading, leases, titles, sales receipts, money orders, cashier's checks, or insurance policies.

Aspects of Documentary Evidence

Most concealment-focused investigations involve ways to gather documents that have been manipulated. When faced with a choice between an eyewitness and a good document as evidence, most fraud experts will opt for the document. Unlike witnesses, documents do not forget, they cannot be cross-examined or confused by attorneys, they cannot commit perjury, and they never tell inconsistent stories on two different occasions. Documents often contain extremely valuable information for detecting and proving fraud. A canceled check is a good example of documentary evidence. Besides the potential for fingerprints, a canceled check gives a lot of other useful information. Take the check shown below, which provides the following information:

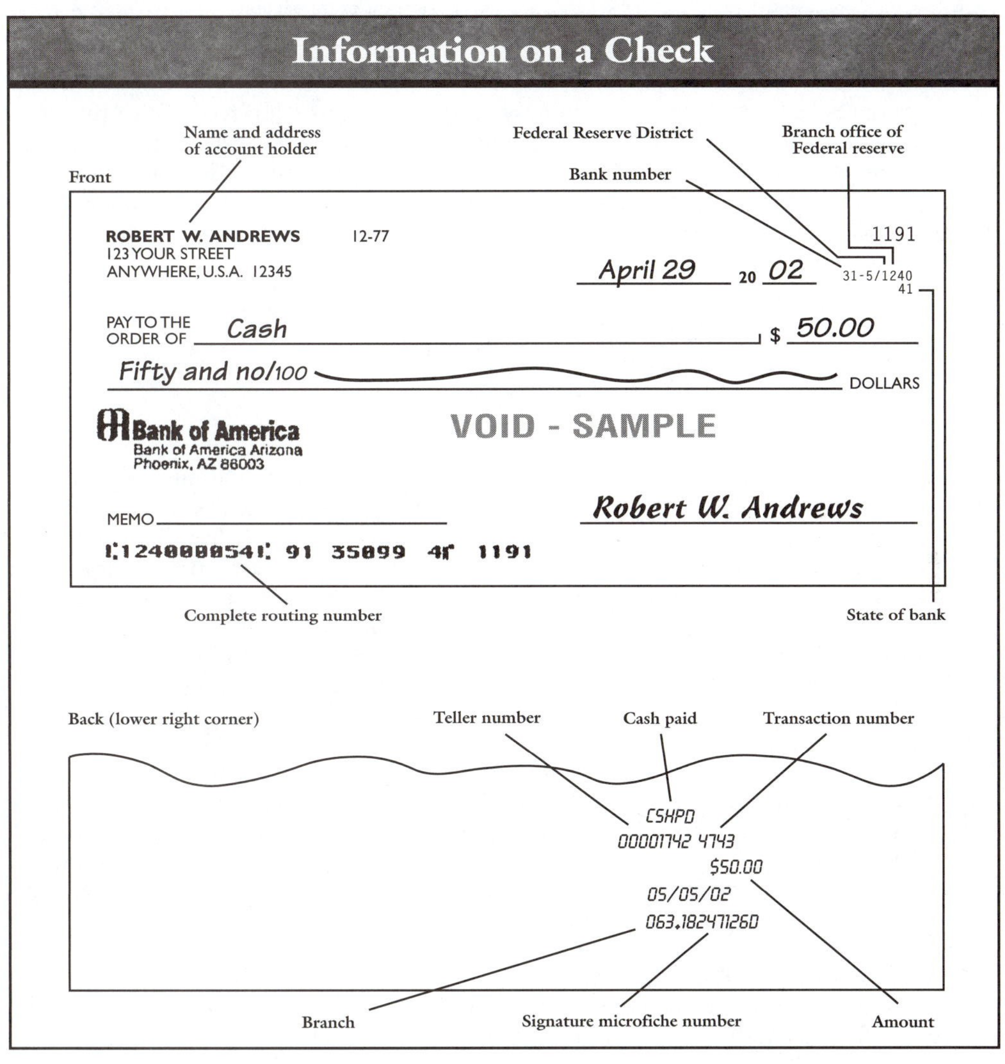

Information about the Maker and the Maker's Bank	Information about the Bank That Processes the Check
1. Name and address of the account holder 2. Bank number of the maker's bank, including: a. City and state of bank b. Bank name 3. Bank routing number of the maker's bank including: a. Federal Reserve District b. Branch office of Federal Reserve c. State of the maker's bank 4. Maker's account number 5. Check number 6. Amount processed	1. Branch number where processed 2. Teller who processed the transaction 3. Sequence number of the transaction 4. Information about the nature of the transaction, including: a. Whether the check was cashed b. Whether it was deposited c. Whether it represented a payment 5. Account number of the person who presented the check 6. Date of transaction 7. Amount of transaction

If you are investigating a kickback or forgery scheme, a check will direct you to the teller who processed the transaction and who may remember valuable information about the suspect. In addition, a check allows you to assemble a paper trail of the entire transaction.

Because documents make up a great deal of evidence in most fraud cases, investigators need to understand the legal and administrative aspects of handling them—specifically, the following aspects:

- Chain of custody of documents
- Marking of evidence
- Organization of documentary evidence
- Rules concerning original versus copies of documents

Chain of Custody

From the time documentary evidence is received, its chain of custody must be carefully maintained so that the evidence will be admitted in court. Basically, the chain of custody has to do with the records kept on when a document is received and what happened to it after its receipt. The records should note anytime the document left the care, custody, or control of the examiner. Contesting attorneys will make every attempt to suggest to the jury that the document has been altered or tampered with. A memorandum should be written that describes when the document came into the hands of the examiner, and subsequent memoranda should note whenever the status of the document changes.

Marking the Evidence

When documentary evidence is received, it should be uniquely marked so that it can be later identified. Use a transparent envelope to store it, with the date received noted and the initials of the examiner written on the outside. Make a copy of the document and store the original document in the envelope in a secure place. During the investigation, use copies of the document and keep them in the same file with the original. Such safeguards preserve the condition of the original for its use during trial.

Organization of the Evidence

Fraud cases often create enormous amounts of documentary evidence. In one case, 100 people worked full-time for over a year to input key words into a computer—just so that documents could be called up on demand during the trial. Literally millions of documents were involved. In the Lincoln Savings and Loan Association case, the judge created a "document depository," which contained *millions* of documents, that attorneys, FBI agents, and others were able to access as they prepared for trial.

Because the volume of documents can be large, a consistent organization scheme *from the start* is imperative. Fraud experts disagree about which scheme is most effective. Some prefer documents organized by witnesses, some prefer chronological organization, and still others prefer organization by transaction. Whichever method is used, a database should be maintained that includes (1) dates of documents, (2) sources of documents, (3) the dates on which documents were obtained, (4) brief descriptions of document contents, (5) subjects of documents, and (6) an identifying or bates number. ("Bates" numbers are used by attorneys involved in litigation to track all documents.)

Original Documents versus Photocopies

Original documents are always preferable to photocopies as evidence. In fact, depending upon the jurisdiction, usually only four situations permit the introduction of photocopies (which are considered secondary evidence) in a court of law. In these situations (listed below), the court must have proof that an original document existed and that the secondary evidence copy is a genuine copy of the original.

1. The original document has been lost or destroyed without the intent or fault of the party seeking to introduce the secondary evidence.
2. The original document is in the possession of an adverse party who fails to produce it after a written notice to do so, or when the party in possession is outside the jurisdiction of the subpoena power of the court.
3. The document or record is in the custody of a public office.
4. The original documents are too voluminous to permit careful examination, and a summary of their contents is acceptable.

Frauds sometimes go undetected because auditors and others are satisfied with photocopies rather than original documents. In the ZZZZ Best case, one of the principals was said to be a master of the copy machine. According to one source, "He could play the copy machine as well as Horowitz could play the piano."[3] Anytime photocopies are used, investigators should be suspicious.

Obtaining Documentary Evidence

Accessing and accumulating documentary evidence is a key part of the investigation of concealment. In the remainder of this chapter, we identify ways to obtain such evidence. Examiners with backgrounds in computers, statistics, and/or accounting usually have an advantage in investigating documentary evidence.

Documentary evidence is sometimes obtained by chance or through tips. Once in a great while, auditors and others come across documents that provide evidence of fraudulent activities. These documents may be recognized because of blatant alterations or forgeries, or because informants bring them to the organization's attention. These are lucky breaks, and luck is famously unreliable. Fortunately, there are more reliable ways to obtain documentary evidence.

Audits

Auditors conduct seven types of tests, and each type yields a form of evidence: (1) tests of mechanical accuracy (recalculations), (2) analytical tests (tests of reasonableness), (3) documentation, (4) confirmations, (5) observations, (6) physical examinations, and (7) inquiries. Because checking documentation is a central part of their work, auditors can often gather documentary evidence without arousing suspicion. Auditors use both manual and computer procedures to gather documentary evidence.

To illustrate the role auditors can play in fraud investigations, consider the fraud at Elgin Aircraft, which we described in Chapter 5. The defense auditor recognized several symptoms at Elgin, including (1) the limousine (a lifestyle symptom), (2) the suspect never missed a day's work (a behavioral symptom), and (3) claims with employees were not verified (a control weakness). He therefore decided to investigate, suspecting that the manager of the claims department was committing fraud. Reasoning that the easiest way for her to commit fraud was to set up phony doctors and bill the company for fictitious claims, the auditor gathered documentary evidence in the form of checks paid to various doctors to ascertain whether the doctors and claims were legitimate.

The auditor knew it would be impossible to determine conclusively whether fraud was being perpetrated without looking at every check. He also realized that, because he had no proof of fraud, his suspicions did not justify his personally examining the total population of all 6,000 checks (which were numbered 2000 through 8000). Balancing his need to examine the checks against time limits the auditor realized that he had three alternatives. He could audit the checks by looking at a few of them, he could draw a random sample and use statistical sampling techniques to examine the checks, or he could do a computer search and examine certain attributes of all checks.

If the auditor chose the first alternative and analyzed in detail, say, 40 checks, he could conclude that the manager was committing fraud only if one or more of the selected checks was made out to a fictitious doctor. However, if the 40 checks did *not* include payments to fictitious doctors, the only conclusion he could draw was that there was no fraud in his sample of 40. Without drawing a random sample and using proper sampling procedures, no conclusions could be made about the total population. This result would not be reliable.

Discovery Sampling

A better approach to assembling documentary evidence in many situations uses a form of statistical sampling called discovery sampling. Discovery sampling allows auditors to make generalized inferences about the population based on sample results, as shown in the following diagram.

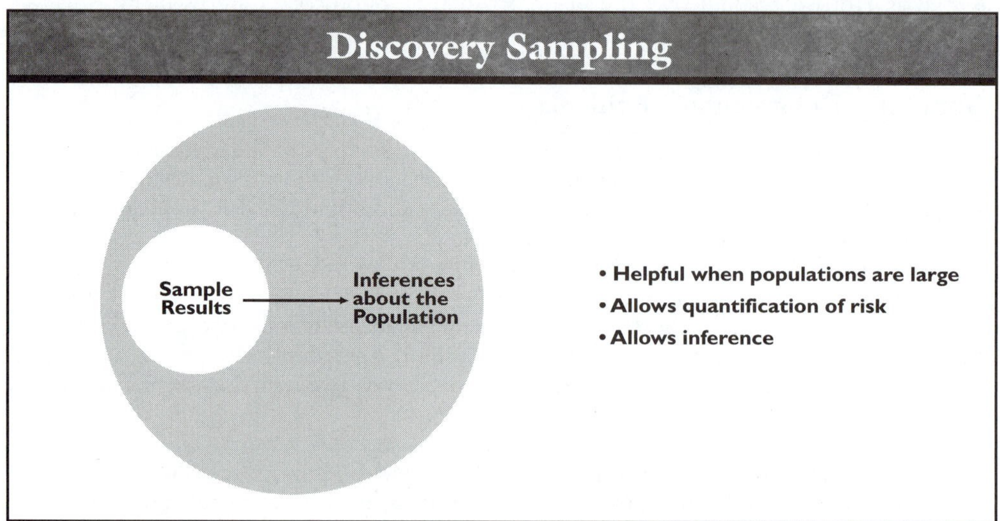

Discovery sampling is the easiest of all statistical sampling variations to understand. Basically, if auditors can read a table, they can conduct discovery sampling. Discovery sampling deals with the probability of discovering at least one error in a given sample size if the population error rate is a certain percentage. A type of attribute sampling, which is based on normal probability theory, discovery sampling is sometimes referred to as stop-and-go sampling. It involves two steps: (1) drawing a random sample and (2) constructing a table to make inferences about the population from the sample. To illustrate, let's assume that the defense auditor decided to use discovery sampling to examine checks payable to doctors. First, he used a random number generator or a random number table to select the checks to be examined. A sample list of random numbers is shown in the following table.

Partial Table of Random Numbers

Item	(1)	(2)	(3)	(4)	(5)	(6)	(7)	(8)
1000	37039	97547	64673	31546	99314	66854	97855	99965
1001	25145	84834	23009	51584	66754	77785	52357	25532
1002	98433	54725	18864	65866	76918	78825	58210	76835
1003	97965	68548	81545	82933	93545	85959	63282	61454
1004	78049	67830	14624	17563	25697	07734	48243	94318
1005	50203	25658	91478	08509	23308	48130	65047	77873
1006	40059	67825	18934	64998	49807	71126	77818	56893
1007	84350	67241	54031	34535	04093	35062	58163	14205
1008	30954	51637	91500	48722	60988	60029	60873	37423
1009	86723	36464	98305	08009	00666	29255	18514	49158
1010	50188	22554	86160	92250	14021	65859	16237	72296
1011	50014	00463	13906	35936	71761	95755	87002	71667
1012	66023	21428	14742	94874	23308	58533	26507	11208
1013	04458	61862	63119	09541	01715	87901	91260	03079
1014	57510	36314	30452	09712	37714	95482	30507	68475
1015	43373	58939	95848	28288	60341	52174	11879	18115
1016	61500	12763	64433	02268	57905	72347	49498	21871
1017	78938	71312	99705	71546	42274	23915	38405	18779
1018	64257	93218	35793	43671	64055	88729	11168	60260
1019	56864	21554	70445	24841	04779	56774	96129	73594
1020	35314	29631	06937	54545	04470	75463	77112	77126
1021	40704	48823	65963	39659	12717	56201	22811	24863
1022	07318	44623	02843	33299	59872	86774	06926	12672
1023	94550	23299	45557	07923	75126	00808	01312	46689
1024	34348	81191	21027	77087	10909	03676	97723	34469
1025	92277	57115	50789	68111	75305	53289	39751	45760
1026	56093	58302	52236	64756	50273	61566	61962	93280
1027	16623	17849	96701	94971	94758	08845	32260	59823
1028	50848	93982	66451	32143	05441	10399	17775	74169
1029	48006	58200	58367	66577	68583	21108	41361	20732
1030	56640	27890	28825	96509	21363	53657	60119	75385

To use a random number table, the auditor had to make four decisions:

1. Where to start in the table to select check numbers.
2. Which direction he would move through the table.
3. What to do with numbers outside the desired range (in this case, that didn't fall between 2000 and 8000).
4. Which four of the five digits to use (given that the checks were all four-digit numbers).

Let's assume that the auditor started with the top-left number (37039), moved through the table from left to right and from top to bottom, skipped numbers that fell outside the relevant range, and used the first four digits of each number. The checks selected for examination were thus checks 3703, 6467, 3154, 6685, 2514, 2300, and so forth. (How many he needed to select is discussed next.) Randomly choosing the checks to be examined allowed the auditor to make inferences about the population, not just about the sample.

Once the checks were selected, the next step involved using a discovery sampling table, such as the one below, to draw conclusions about the checks. If the auditor found a check in the sample made out to a fictitious doctor, he could then be 100% certain that fraud existed. If he did not find such a check, he still had to examine all 6,000 checks to be absolutely certain that there was no fraud. If he sampled anything less than 100% of the checks and did not find fraud, discovery sampling allowed him to decide how much risk he was willing to assume. In other words, discovery sampling allowed the auditor to quantify risk. Using the table below, if the auditor sampled 300 checks and found none made out to fictitious doctors, he would be 95% confident that the true population fraud rate did not exceed 1%, 78% confident that no more than 0.5% of the checks were fraudulent, and so forth. The entire table is based on the assumption that no fictitious checks are found. (Again, if the auditor found even one fictitious doctor, he would be 100% certain that fraud existed.)

Discovery Sampling Table								
	Probability (percentage) of including at least one error in the sample							
	Rate of Occurrence in the Population (%)							
Sample Size	0.01	0.05	0.1	0.2	0.3	0.5	1	2
50		2	5	9	14	22	39	64
60	1	3	6	11	16	26	45	70
70	1	3	7	13	19	30	51	76
80	1	4	8	15	21	33	55	80
90	1	4	9	16	24	36	60	84
100	1	5	10	18	26	39	63	87
120	1	6	11	21	30	45	70	91
140	1	7	13	24	34	50	76	94
160	2	8	15	27	38	55	80	96
200	2	10	18	33	45	63	87	98
240	2	11	21	38	51	70	91	99
300	3	14	26	45	59	78	95	99+
340	3	16	29	49	64	82	97	99+
400	4	18	33	55	70	87	98	99+
460	5	21	37	60	75	90	99	99+
500	5	22	39	63	78	92	99	99+
800	8	33	55	80	91	98	99+	99+
1,000	10	39	63	86	95	99	99+	99+
1,500	14	53	78	95	99	99+	99+	99+
2,500	22	71	92	99	99+	99+	99+	99+

The more confident the auditor wanted to be and the smaller the risk he wanted to assume, of *not* identifying fraudulent checks, the larger the sample that had to be examined. Population size appears to make little difference in sample size, unless the sample becomes a significant part of the population (usually greater than 10%), and then the confidence level is higher and the risk lower than indicated in the table.

Even with discovery sampling, auditors can never be certain that fraud does not exist in a population of checks. Although discovery sampling does allow inferences to be made about the problem, there are still two possibilities: that the sample is not representative of the population (sampling risk), and that the auditor examines a fraudulent check and does not recognize it (nonsampling risk). Discovery sampling allows auditors to quantify both risk and samples until they have sufficient evidence that fraud does not likely exist.

Documentation. Investigators need to document the method they use for determining sample size (that is, the specified population error rate and confidence level) and the method they use to select the sample. This means recording the name of the book or computer program from which the random number table was taken and also the rules used to determine the starting point and progress through the table. Such documentation may be important if the sample is later expanded, if another person reviews the sampling plan, or if the procedure becomes evidence in court.

Errors. If investigators find errors using discovery sampling, they must determine whether the errors were unintentional or indicate fraud. For example, in our preceding example, finding payments to fictitious vendors was predetermined to be indicative of fraud. However, errors in check amounts could be due to unintentional mathematical or typing errors or could be intentional overpayments in a fraud kickback scheme. Such evaluations are aided if what constitutes error and fraud is defined beforehand.

Sampling Risk. Investigators need to understand the sampling risks associated with discovery sampling. This is the risk that the sample is *not* representative of the population. To reduce sampling risk, investigators can increase sample size or use a random number table or generator to select the items to be examined.

Nonsampling Risk. Investigators must also consider nonsampling risk, which is the risk that a finding will be misinterpreted. For instance, investigators may not recognize that an examined item contains an error, they may misjudge an error as unintentional when it is actually intentional, or they may not recognize that a document is forged. Nonsampling risk cannot be quantified, but it can be minimized by careful planning, performance, and evaluation of the sampling procedure.

Computer Searches

As an alternative to discovery sampling, auditors may perform their search by computer (see Chapter 5). This allows all checks to be examined. Using this approach, auditors select a variable of interest, such as addresses of payees, checks mailed to post office boxes, or payments made to certain doctors. If the variables they identify are reliable signals of fraud, this approach can be very effective in determining whether fraud exists. For example, a fraud examiner who suspects procurement fraud might use computer searches to seek out and then possibly compare the following items:

- Timing of bids
- Pattern of bids
- Dates of disposal with reorders of goods
- Amount of work by a given vendor
- Pattern of hiring new vendors
- Vendors with post office boxes as addresses
- Number of sole-source contracts
- Price changes in purchased items
- Company employees with vendor officers
- Vendors with Dun & Bradstreet
- Vendor addresses with company use
- Number of rush orders

Similar computer searches can gather documentary evidence relating to any kind of fraud. Using computer searches to investigate fraud may well be the most promising of all investigative procedures for the future.

Comparison of Discovery Sampling and Computer Sampling

In the Elgin Aircraft case, the claims payment manager embezzled more than $12 million over a five-year period by making payments to 22 fictitious doctors. The payments were sent to two common addresses: a business in a nearby city that was owned by the manager's husband and a post office box that the manager rented. Both discovery sampling and a computer search could have detected this fraud.

Let's assume the Elgin Aircraft auditor used discovery sampling. He first selected checks and then confirmed whether the doctors being paid were legitimate. He had three choices with which to determine legitimacy: (1) examine the doctors' listings in telephone books, (2) confirm their medical licenses with the state licensing board, or (3) make inquiries through medical associations. The moment he found one fictitious doctor, he stopped sampling and examined the entire population to determine the extent of the fraud.

Now let's assume the auditor used a computer search. He matched addresses of doctors and found that payments to 22 doctors were being sent to two common addresses. Checking out the addresses, he found that one was the business owned by the manager's husband and the other was her post office box.

What is the risk that discovery sampling will not catch the fraud? The fraud will not be found (1) if the sample chosen is not representative of the population (sampling risk) and (2) if fraudulent checks are examined and not recognized as fraudulent (nonsampling risk). With the computer search, the risk lies in not selecting the correct variable to query.

Hard-to-Get Documentary Evidence

Some documentary evidence is extremely difficult to obtain, although recent laws have made such records more easily accessible. The three most common examples are private bank records, tax returns, and brokerage records. Usually, such evidence can only be obtained in three ways: (1) by subpoena, (2) by search warrant, or (3) by voluntary consent. *Subpoenas duces tecum* are orders issued by a court or a grand jury to produce documents. Failure to honor such a subpoena is punishable by law. Only agents of the grand jury or the court (usually law enforcement officers) can obtain documents by subpoena; this is one reason to coordinate fraud investigations with law enforcement officials.

The second way to obtain hard-to-get documentary evidence is with a search warrant. A judge issues a search warrant when there is probable cause to believe that documents have been used in committing a crime. Search warrants are executed only by law enforcement officials and are generally used only in criminal cases.

The third and most common way to obtain private documents is by voluntary consent, which can be either oral or written. An example of a consent that allows a fraud examiner to access private bank records is shown on page 197. Often initial interviews with fraud suspects are conducted in order to obtain permission to access bank or brokerage records, rather than to obtain a confession (see Chapter 9). The leverage of possible termination as an employee or a vendor is used to get such permission.

Document Experts

Sometimes it is necessary to determine whether a document is authentic. Documents of interest can be genuine, counterfeit, fraudulent, or forged. Document examination, the purview of experts in the field, applies forensic chemistry, microscopy, and photography to determine whether documents are genuine. Document experts can determine whether a document was written by the person whose signature it bears; whether it was forged; whether it was altered by additives, deletions, obliterations, erasures, or photocopying; whether the handwriting is genuine; whether the entire document was printed on the same machine; whether it was printed on the date it bears or before or after; whether two or more documents are significantly different or substantially the same; and whether pages have been substituted in a document.

XYZ Corporation

Customer consent and authorization for access to financial records

I, *Arnold Fox McCune*, having read the explanation of my rights which is attached to
(Name of Customer)

this form hereby authorize the *XYZ Corporation Credit Union* to disclose these financial records:
(Name and Address of Financial Ins.)

All Bank Account Records, including checking accounts, savings and loans from 1/1/2001 to present

to *Michael R. Blair and Robert W. Jacobs* for the following purpose(s): *Administrative Purposes*

I understand that this authorization may be revoked by me in writing at any time before my records, as described above, are disclosed, and this authorization is valid for no more than three months from the date of my signature.

August 16, 2001

Arnold F. McCune
(signature of customer)
318 E. Birch Street
Ann Arbor, MI 48159
(Address of Customer)
Michael R. Blair

The following table lists questions that investigators commonly encounter when they examine disputed documents or documents of unknown origin. Document experts can usually answer these questions.

Questions That Arise with Disputed Documents

Handwriting:

1. Is the signature genuine?
2. Is the continued writing genuine?
3. Was the writing disguised?
4. Who did any unknown writing?
5. Can the hand printing, if any, be identified?
6. Can the handwritten numerals, if any, be identified?
7. Which was written first, the signature or the writing above it?
8. Can the forger be identified?
9. Is the handwriting or signature consistent with the date of the document?

Printing:

1. What make and model of printer was used? During what years was the particular make and model used?
2. Can the individual printer that was used be identified?
3. Was the printing done before or after any handwriting and/or signatures?
4. Was the printing done on the date of the document or later?
5. Who did the actual printing?
6. Was the printing on the document all done at one time, or was some of it added at a later time? How much was added later?
7. Were copies made using the original document?
8. Are the copies genuine?
9. Can the printer or the document be identified from a carbon tape?

continues

Questions That Arise with Disputed Documents

Alterations and additions:

1. Was the document altered in any way or added to at a later time? Were pages added, parts torn or cut off, purposely wrinkled or stained, etc.?
2. What original date or matter was altered or added to?
3. When was the alteration or addition made?
4. Who made the alteration or addition?
5. Has the photograph on an ID card or other ID document been removed and replaced with another?

Age:

1. Is the age of the document in accordance with its date?
2. How old are the paper, the printing, the ink, the seal, etc.?
3. Is there evidence of the manner or location in which the document was kept?

Copies:

1. Are the photocopies or photostatic reproductions copies of other documents?
2. What type of copy machine was used? What brand?
3. Can the individual copier be identified?
4. In what year was the particular make and model used? Produced?
5. Was any portion of the copy not on the original document? Was it pasted up?
6. Is there any indication that pages are missing on the copies that were part of the original?
7. Can the copy be traced to and identified as the particular original document that was its source?

Other:

1. Can machine-printed matter be identified?
2. Can the check-writer, the adding machine, the addressograph machine, or other machine be identified?
3. Was the envelope resealed?
4. Can the stapler, glue, pin, clip, or other fastener be identified?
5. Is the printed document genuine or counterfeit? If counterfeit, can the original document used as a reproduction source be determined?
6. What processes were used to print the counterfeit document?
7. Could the printing source or counterfeiter be identified if located?

Characteristics of handwriting:

1. Basic movement of the handwriting—clockwise, counterclockwise, and straight-line—indicating direction, curvature, shapes, and slopes of the writing motions.
2. Slant—forward, backward, or in between.
3. Manner in which letters with loops are curved, and the size, shape, and proportion of the loops.
4. Peculiarities in the approach strokes and the upward strokes in the first letter of a word and in capital letters.
5. Characteristic initial and terminal strokes; their length and their angle in relation to letters and words.
6. Gaps between letters in specific letter combinations.
7. Manner in which the capital letters are formed, and the additional hooks or flourishes some writers place at the start or end of these letters.
8. Relative smoothness, tremor, or hesitation in the writing. Some writing flows smoothly and is free of hesitation. Other writing shows hesitation in the formation of some letters or defective line quality in the writing as a whole.
9. Manner in which the writer varies pressure in certain pen strokes, and variations in the weight and width of stroke lines.
10. Proportion and alignment of letters; the length or height and size of capital letters compared with lower case letters.
11. Manner in which the letter *t* is crossed, and the height and slant of the crossing—near the top of the *t* or lower down, straight or at an angle, with a flourish or plain; whether words ending in *t* are crossed.
12. Location of the dot over the letter *i* and its relationship to the location of the letter itself.

continues

Questions That Arise with Disputed Documents

13. Types of ending strokes in words ending in the letters *y*, *g*, and *s*.
14. Open or closed letter style, as seen in such letters as *a* and *o*, and in letters that combine upward or downward strokes with loops, such as *b*, *d*, *o*, and *g*. Are the circles in these letters open or closed, broad or narrow?
15. Separation of letters within a word (for example, separating a *t* from the remainder of the word, or separating a whole syllable from the rest of the word).
16. Characteristics of the portions that appear above and/or below the line is such letters as *f*, *g*, and *y*.
17. Relative alignment of all letters; the uniformity and spacing of letters, words, and lines.
18. Alignment of lines.
19. Use and positioning of punctuation.
20. Indications that the writing instrument was lifted off the writing material between words and sentences.

Becoming a skilled examiner of questioned documents requires extensive and specialized training. Although most fraud investigators are not trained document examiners, they do need to understand two important elements relating to document examination: (1) when to have a document examined by an expert and (2) the responsibility of the investigator with respect to questioned documents. If one or more of the following warning signs exist, a document should probably be submitted for examination:

1. Abrasions or chemical pen or pencil erasures
2. Alterations or substitutions
3. Disguised or unnatural writings
4. Use of two or more different colors of ink
5. Charred, mutilated, or torn pages
6. Pencil or carbon marks along the writing lines
7. Existence of lines made during photocopying
8. Signs of inconsistency or disruption in the continuity of the content
9. Any suspicious appearance or unusual form

In dealing with questioned documents, fraud investigators are responsible for taking the following steps:

- Collecting, protecting, identifying, and preserving the questioned document in as good a condition as possible
- Collecting and being able to prove to the document examiner the origins of adequate comparison specimens
- Submitting both the questioned and the comparison documents to the examiner

Two well-known organizations of document experts offer help in fraud investigations. The first is the FBI Laboratory Division, Document Section.

> *The Document Section, FBI Laboratory Division, provides expert forensic assistance and examinations of physical evidence. These services are available to all federal agencies, U.S. attorneys, and the U.S. military in connection with both criminal and civil matters. These services are available to all duly constituted state, county, municipal, and other nonfederal law enforcement agencies in the United States in connection with criminal matters. All expenses for these services, including provision of expert witnesses to testify to the results of their examinations in judicial proceedings and the travel expenses of these experts, are borne by the FBI.*

Examinations of questioned documents include the full range of traditional examinations and comparisons, including, but not limited to, the following: handwriting and signatures, hand printing, typewriting, altered and obliterated documents, charred or burned paper, writing materials, photocopies, and many others.

The second organization of document experts is a private group, the American Board of Forensic Document Examiners, Inc. (ABFDE).[4] The ABFDE's background, functions, and purpose are as follows:

The need to identify forensic scientists qualified to provide essential professional services for the nation's judicial and executive branches of government as well as the community in general has been long recognized. In response to this professional mandate, the American Board of Forensic Document Examiners, Inc., was organized in 1977 to provide, in the interest of the public and the advancement of the science, a program of certification in forensic document examination. In purpose, function, and organization, the ABFDE is thus analogous to the certifying board[s] in various other scientific fields.

The objective of the Board is to establish, enhance, and maintain, as necessary, standards of qualification for those who practice forensic document examination and to certify as qualified specialists those voluntary applicants who comply with the requirements of the Board. In this way, the Board aims to make available to the judicial system, and other public, a practical and equitable system for readily identifying those persons professing to be specialists in forensic document examination who possess the requisite qualifications and competence.

Certification is based upon the candidate's personal and professional record of education and training, experience, and achievement, as well as on the results of a formal examination.

The Board is a non-profit organization in the District of Columbia. Its initial sponsors are the American Academy of Forensic Sciences and the American Society of Questioned Document Examiners. The Board is composed of officers and other directors who serve staggered terms and are elected from among nominees of designated nominating organizations or serve at-large.

Summary

Investigation techniques for fraud can be divided into four groups: (1) theft investigation methods, (2) concealment investigation methods, (3) conversion investigation methods, and (4) inquiry investigation methods. Theft investigation methods include surveillance and covert operations, invigilation, and physical evidence. Concealment investigation methods include document examination, audits, computer searches, and physical asset counts.

Theft investigation methods are used less often than other methods. They tend to be more expensive and require more expertise than other methods. For certain frauds, however, especially those involving the theft of tangible assets, they often offer the best evidence available.

Concealment investigation techniques usually focus on obtaining documentary evidence. Documents usually make up a significant and reliable amount of the evidence used in fraud cases. Investigators should understand both the legal and the administrative aspects of documentary evidence and the various ways in which such evidence may be accumulated and examined.

New Terms

Chain of custody: Maintaining detailed records about documents from the time they are received in the investigation process until the trial is completed. Helps to substantiate that documents have not been altered or manipulated since coming into the investigator's hands.

Concealment investigative methods: Investigating a fraud by focusing on the cover-up efforts, such as the manipulation of source documents.

Covert operations: Placing an agent in an undercover role in order to observe the suspect.

Discovery sampling: Sampling used in fraud detection that assumes a zero expected error rate. The methodology allows an auditor to determine confidence levels and make inferences from the sample to the population.

Document examiner: Specialized investigator who applies forensic chemistry, microscopy, photography, and other scientific methods to determine whether documents or other evidence are genuine, forged, counterfeit, or fraudulent.

Electronic surveillance: Using video, e-mail, wiretapping, and so on to watch fraud suspects.

Fixed point surveillance: Watching a fraud suspect from a fixed point, such as a restaurant, office, or other set location.

Invigilation: Imposing strict temporary controls on an activity so that, during the observation period, fraud is virtually impossible. Involves keeping detailed records before, during, and after the invigilation period and comparing suspicious activity during the three periods to obtain evidence about whether fraud is occurring.

Lien: Claim on property for the satisfaction of just debt.

Marking the evidence: Placing unique identification tags or descriptions on documents when they are received, so that they can be identified during the investigation and trial process.

Mobile observation: Another term for tailing.

Moving surveillance: Another term for tailing; involves following suspects wherever they go (within limits) and observing or recording their activities.

Nonsampling risk: Risk that a sample will be examined and the characteristics of the sample will be misinterpreted.

Physical evidence: Objects such as inventory, assets, broken locks, fingerprints, tire tracks, and other tangible evidence that can be used in an investigation to provide information about a fraud or other crime.

Population: Collection of all units with similar characteristics from which samples are drawn.

Sample: Portion of the population that is examined in order to draw inferences about the population.

Sampling risk: Risk that a sample is not representative of the population.

Search warrant: Order issued by a judge that gives the investigator consent to search a suspect's personal information, such as bank records, tax returns, or their premises.

Static surveillance: Another term for fixed-point surveillance.

Stationary surveillance: Locating a scene to be observed, anticipating the actions that are most likely to occur at the scene, and keeping detailed notes on tape or film on all activities involving the suspect.

Subpoena (*subpoena duces tecum*): Order issued by a court or a grand jury to produce documents or to appear before a court.

Surveillance: Investigation technique that relies on the senses, especially hearing and seeing.

Tailing: Secretly following a fraud suspect in an attempt to gain additional information; another name for moving surveillance.

Theft investigation methods: Investigation methods that focus on the actual transfer of assets from the victim to the perpetrator; helps determine how the theft was committed and often includes methods such as surveillance and covert operations, invigilation, and the obtaining of physical evidence.

Vulnerability chart: Tool that coordinates the various elements of a fraud investigation to help identify possible suspects.

Questions and Cases

Discussion Questions

1. What methods are used to investigate theft in suspected frauds, and how are they used?
2. How do vulnerability charts help in the coordination of fraud investigations?
3. When is surveillance helpful in investigating fraud?
4. What is invigilation?
5. How is physical evidence used to investigate fraud?
6. What are the most commonly used techniques for investigating concealment?
7. How do documents help in fraud investigations?
8. Why is it important to obtain documentary evidence?
9. How is discovery sampling used to obtain documentary evidence?
10. What are the different ways investigators obtain hard-to-get documentary evidence?

True/False

1. The fraud triangle plus inquiry approach is an effective way to understand the various types of investigative methods.
2. One advantage of vulnerability charts is that they force investigators to consider all aspects of a fraud.
3. Electronic surveillance is often of limited value in the investigation of employee fraud because of concerns regarding employees' privacy rights.
4. Photocopies are always preferable to original documents as evidence.
5. There is no difference between forensic document experts and graphologists.
6. Surveillance is a technique for investigating theft that relies on the examination of documents.
7. Mobile observation is usually much more risky than stationary surveillance.
8. During invigilation, no controls are imposed on any activities.
9. Methods used to investigate concealment sometimes involve the study of documents that have been manipulated.
10. Discovery sampling is probably the most difficult of all statistical sampling variations to understand.
11. As long as a sample is selected randomly, it will always be representative of the population as a whole.
12. Even if photocopies of original documents are allowed to be introduced as evidence in a court of law, they are still considered secondary evidence.

13. A canceled check typically shows the account number of the person who presented the check, the teller who processed the check, and the sequence number of the transaction.
14. Random number tables are ineffective and should not be used when selecting random samples from a population.
15. Using a computer can be a very effective approach for determining whether fraud exists because auditors can look at entire populations.
16. "Bates" numbers are identifying numbers that attorneys use to track documents during litigation.

Multiple Choice

1. Which of the following is *not* a category used in the fraud triangle plus inquiry approach?
    a. Theft investigative techniques
    b. Concealment investigative techniques
    c. Action investigative techniques
    d. Conversion investigative techniques
2. When beginning an investigation, fraud examiners should use techniques that will:
    a. Not arouse suspicion
    b. Identify the perpetrator
    c. Determine the amount of the fraud
    d. Identify when the fraud occurred
3. When conducting an investigation, which of the following words should be avoided when conducting interviews?
    a. Audit
    b. Inquiry
    c. Investigation
    d. Record examination
4. When beginning a fraud investigation, which of the following methods is most useful in identifying possible suspects?
    a. Preparing an identification chart
    b. Preparing a vulnerability chart
    c. Preparing a surveillance log
    d. None of the above
5. Invigilation:
    a. Is most commonly associated with crimes such as robbery, murder, and property offenses
    b. Can create tremendous amounts of documentary evidence
    c. Provides evidence to help determine whether fraud is occurring
    d. All of the above
6. In a fraud investigation, documents usually:
    a. Contain extremely valuable information
    b. Are rarely used in court
    c. Are not reliable sources of information
    d. Are only valuable in obtaining a confession

7. Chain of custody refers to:
    a. Marking on a document so it can later be identified
    b. A record of when a document is received and what has happened to it since its receipt
    c. Databases used in trials to assist lawyers
    d. The way in which courts are organized
8. Marking documentary evidence is important to ensure that:
    a. Documents are legal
    b. Databases can be created with valuable information
    c. Documents can be identified later
    d. Marking documentary evidence is not important.
9. Discovery sampling:
    a. Is a type of variables sampling
    b. Is one of the more difficult statistical sampling methods to understand
    c. Is never used in conducting a fraud examination
    d. Deals with the probability of discovering at least one error in a given sample size if the population error is a certain percentage
10. Documentary evidence such as private tax returns can usually only be obtained by:
    a. Subpoena
    b. Search warrant
    c. Voluntary consent
    d. All of the above
11. Which of the following is true regarding document experts?
    a. They cannot usually determine whether a document was written by the person whose signature the document bears.
    b. They cannot usually determine whether a document has been forged.
    c. They cannot usually determine whether the date the document bears is the date the document was written.
    d. None of the above.
12. Which of the following is *not* a benefit of statistical sampling?
    a. It allows auditors to be certain that fraud does not exist in a population.
    b. It is helpful when populations are large.
    c. It allows quantification of risk.
    d. It allows inference about a population.
13. When is a photocopy *not* acceptable as evidence in a court of law?
    a. When the original document has been lost or destroyed without the intent or fault of the party seeking to introduce the copied document as secondary evidence
    b. When the original document has been lost by the fraud examiner
    c. When the document or record is in the custody of a public office
    d. When the original documents are too voluminous to permit careful examination

14. Which of the following methods of gathering documents is based primarily on luck?
    a. Documents discovered during audits
    b. Hard-to-get private documents that are subpoenaed
    c. Documents discovered through searching public sources
    d. Documents provided by tipsters
15. Which of the following is true of graphologists?
    a. They can only perform their work in laboratory settings.
    b. Their work is the same as that of forensic document experts.
    c. They study handwriting as a way to interpret and identify personalities.
    d. They are required to be members of the ABFDE organization.
16. What can fraud examiners conclude if one or more instances of fraud are found in a sample taken from a population?
    a. There is a slight risk that fraud exists in the population.
    b. The population contains fraud.
    c. The sample may not have been randomly selected, and thus no conclusions can be drawn.
    d. The sample is most likely not representative of the population as a whole.
17. What can fraud examiners conclude if their tests confirm that no instances of fraud are present in a sample taken from a population?
    a. There is virtually no risk that fraud exists in the population.
    b. The population contains no fraud.
    c. Only that no fraud is present in that particular sample.
    d. The sample is most likely not representative of the population as a whole.
18. How are most frauds concealed?
    a. By shredding source documents
    b. By converting to a paperless office without paper transactions
    c. By creating fictitious documents or altering source documents
    d. By firing employees who will not go along with the fraud

Short Cases

Case 1. The management of AAAA Company observes that the company's cash outflows have been increasing much more rapidly than its inflows. Management cannot understand the change; from their perspective it has been "business as usual." Management asks you, a fraud expert, to help them understand what is going on.

You decide that the best place to start your investigation is to take a sample of canceled checks and verify that both the controller and another manager signed them—a procedure required by company policy. Check numbers for the period range from 100 to 800.

Using the random number table on page 193, select a random sample of 15 checks to examine by following this procedure:

- Start from the bottom left of the table.
- Move through the table from left to right and from bottom to top.
- Skip numbers outside the relevant range.
- Use the middle three digits of each number.

Case 2. You have selected a random sample of 15 checks from a population of 800 checks; the checks have the following numbers: 664, 789, 650, 136, 365, 538, 800, 657, 110, 136, 398, 645, 214, 544, and 777. Based on this sample, what conclusions can you make in each of the following situations?

1. Check #365 is not properly signed and was paid to a fictitious vendor.
2. No suspicious checks were found in the sample of 15 checks you evaluated.

Case 3. As lead accountant for a small company, you notice that inventory purchases from a certain vendor have increased dramatically over the past few months, even though purchases from other vendors have decreased. You suspect that something may not be right.

Which method(s) would you use to investigate your suspicions?

Case 4. While auditing a client, the CEO asks you to look carefully at the cash flow. You notice that cash flows have decreased every year. Upon learning of your findings, the CEO remarks, "I seem to bring in more customers every year, but the cash is not there." You tell him that fraud may be occurring, and he asks you to investigate. You agree that the most likely place for a fraud to be occurring is cash collections.

Which investigative method(s) would be best for finding the fraud?

Case 5. ABC Company is a relatively small dry-cleaning operation with a very steady level of business. Since the company hired a new employee, however, cash inflows have decreased and the amount of promotional coupon redemptions have increased dramatically. The owner of the company was initially impressed with this new employee, but now has suspicions regarding her cashiering practices. When comparing cash sales to check and credit-card sales, the owner notes that the coupon redemption rate is dramatically higher for cash sales. The owner doesn't want to wrongly accuse the employee, but does want to find out whether fraud is occurring. The owner asks you to recommend a reliable way to gather evidence that could determine if fraud is occurring.

What are some possible investigation methods you could suggest?

Case 6. A bank manager's responsibility is making loans. Auditors discovered that several loans he made over a 5-year period have not been repaid. A fraud investigation reveals that the manager has been receiving kickbacks from risky clients in exchange for extending them loans. His loans have cost the bank millions of dollars in uncollectable loans. You are asked to determine the amount of kickbacks the manager has taken.

1. What types of records would you search to find information about the manager's assets?
2. Which of the records searches do you think would be the most helpful in this case? Why?

Case 7. Enron, the largest corporation ever to file for Chapter 11 bankruptcy protection, was number 7 on the Fortune 500 list of the largest companies in America as ranked by revenues at the time of its bankruptcy. It is alleged that Enron executives condoned questionable accounting and financial statement fraud, the disclosure of which caused the downward spiral in Enron's stock price and the financial ruin of thousands of employees and investors. In addition to Enron's internal accounting problems, it is alleged that its auditor, Arthur Andersen, instructed employees to destroy documents related to its work for Enron.

Based on your understanding of a fraud examiner's responsibilities regarding documents, what should the audit firm personnel have done with their documents if they suspected fraud?

Case 8. You are a fraud examiner who has been hired by Bellevue Company to carry out an investigation. Bellevue is a beverage company that has experienced increased shipments of beverages but no increase in revenue. Management suspects that inventory is being shipped to unknown places or is being stolen.

How can you use invigilation to determine whether inventory is being stolen or shipped to unknown locations? Briefly explain how you would carry out this investigative procedure.

Case 9. Marlin Company has suspected something "fishy" for several months. It knows that its profits have been slowly decreasing, but revenues have been rising. After consulting with you, a fraud expert, the company decides to investigate the purchasing patterns of its three purchasing agents—Curly, Larry, and Moe. You intend to examine a random sample of purchase invoices and verify their accuracy and validity. Curly's invoices are numbered 0000–0999, Larry's 1000–1999, and Moe's 2000–2999.

When you approach Curly, Larry, and Moe, they seem somewhat defensive. They begin to harass one another, blaming each other for the mess they find themselves in. Moe even twitches their noses and slaps their heads. Curly attempts to retaliate by poking Moe in the eye, but misses and hits Larry instead. The CFO, Mr. Rutin-Tutin, exclaims, "Would you three stooges quit fooling around and produce the invoices immediately?!"

The three shuffle off to their offices, grumbling all along the way. They return a couple of hours later with photocopies of their invoices. When Mr. Rutin-Tutin asks where the original invoices are, they explain that they always copy and destroy the originals for easier storage. Annoyed and fed up with the three morons, Mr. Rutin-Tutin hands you the stacks of photocopied invoices and tells you to do your thing.

What is wrong with this picture? Are you suspicious that there is fraud present? What is a possible first step in verifying the invoices?

Case 10. A man in Los Amigos County is discovered committing workers' compensation fraud. He is currently receiving disability benefits, and surveillance shows him working at an automobile auction. The investigator interviews the owner of the auction and finds that the claimant is being paid $200 per week in cash for washing vehicles and performing other shop tasks. Surveillance video shows the man carrying 25-pound bags of pet food, loading boxes, and rummaging through a trash dumpster. Obviously, he is not seriously injured.

1. Is surveillance the proper method to use in this case? Why?
2. What are some of the restrictions you have to be careful about in conducting surveillance?

Case 11. This chapter described the case of a manufacturing firm that had problems with employee theft of tools. The company decided to search every employee's lunch box at the end of each shift. The employees were enraged and caused a work slowdown.

Give three alternatives for how the company could have investigated this theft effectively without causing morale problems.

Case 12. Someone in your company is taking money from the petty cash fund. Complete a vulnerability chart similar to the one on page 183 to help you coordinate the various aspects of the fraud investigation.

Extensive Cases

Case 13. John Doe, a fraud examiner, has been hired by ABC Corporation to investigate a suspicious shortage of cash. John Doe could spend his time and money interviewing witnesses to the crime or collecting documents that would confirm fraud. As with most fraud examiners, he chooses to collect supporting documents instead of interviewing witnesses. Explain why John and most other fraud examiners prefer documents over witnesses, and then describe elements of good document care.

Case 14. Jim is the owner and president of ZZZ Company. When he and his close friend, Dan, graduated with their MBAs, they dreamed about being successful and making lots of money. They have been employed at the same company for years, working their way up to senior management; and Dan is now CEO and Jim is a senior executive. ZZZ Company has been highly successful the entire time that Jim and Dan have worked for the company. Stock prices have increased every year, and revenues have grown by a compounded rate of 20% per year. However, Jim is becoming a little suspicious of the company's results because the earnings per share are always equal to Wall Street's projections. In the past couple of years, Jim has noticed that his friend's personal life has unraveled. Dan is now divorced, and he seems to struggle financially, even though Jim knows that Dan makes plenty of money. One night Jim stops by Dan's office to respond to some e-mails he couldn't get to during the day. He notices that Dan is working late as well. Jim initially assumed that he was working late because it was close to the end of the quarter. However, after reviewing the quarter's results, Jim is again suspicious because the results exactly match Wall Street's forecasts. Jim concludes he needs to investigate the company's financial reporting practices.

What issues must Jim consider as he formulates his investigation strategy?

Internet Assignments

Today many data analysis tools are available to assist fraud examiners when they search for possible fraud. Visit the Association of Certified Fraud Examiners' web site and list some of the computer-aided data analysis tools and services available to fraud examiners (http://www.cfenet.com).

Debates

1. The Discount Plus Company has been concerned about its cash flows for some time. Since the company began five years ago, Discount's business has increased steadily, yet cash flows remain virtually the same every year. You have been hired by Discount Plus to detect possible fraud in the company. Discount's management is almost certain that one of its accountants is embezzling cash and informs you that they have already installed surveillance cameras in possible "problem areas." In addition, management is considering some form of covert operation to detect the fraud.

   What problems or dilemmas is Discount's management facing by installing cameras and implementing a covert (undercover) operation? Team up with another student (or group of students) and debate opposite sides of the question of whether surveillance cameras should be installed.

2. An excerpt from the Fourth Amendment reads: "The right of the people to be secure in their persons, houses, papers, and effects, against unreasonable searches and seizures, shall not be violated, and no Warrants shall issue, but upon probable cause, supported by Oath or affirmation, and particularly describing the place to be searched, and the persons or things to be seized."

   In 2002, suspecting a Mr. Dayley of running an illegal gambling and loan sharking operation, the FBI obtained a federal search warrant. They entered Mr. Dayley's residence and searched through various records. Suspecting most of the records were contained on a personal computer, the FBI attempted to access various files.

Unable to access the needed files because of password barriers, the FBI installed a system known as a "Key Logger System," or KLS. This system determines the keystrokes made on a computer and thus allowed the FBI to discover the password. The discovery led to evidence that links Mr. Dayley to the suspected illegal operation.[5]

Were Mr. Dayley's Fourth Amendment rights violated?

End Notes

1. Gary Strauss, "Informant Key to Unlocking Scam Behind Golden Arches," *USA Today*, (Aug. 24, 2001).
2. See *Fraud: Bringing Light to the Dark Side of Business*, W. Steve Albrecht, G. W. Wernz, and T. L. Williams, Irwin Professional Publishing, 1995, New York, p. 151.
3. From the video "Cooking the Books," produced by the Association of Certified Fraud Examiners, Austin, Texas.
4. The author wishes to point out the difference between forensic document experts and graphologists, as commonly practiced in North America. Forensic document experts typically practice in a laboratory setting. They examine documents for fingerprints, indented writing, handwriting or typewriting, similarities, and so on. They generally possess accredited degrees in various applied sciences. Graphology (a term used in conjunction with some forensic document experts in Europe) is practiced in North America by individuals (graphologists) who generally undertake home study courses in handwriting and its application to personalities. We strongly urge caution in differentiating between forensic document experts and graphologists when seeking the truth in investigations that require expert review of questioned documents.
5. Based on a true case from http://lawlibrary.rutgers.edu/fed/html/scarfo2.html-1.html.

Conversion Investigation Methods

After studying this chapter, you should be able to:

1. Explain why finding out how perpetrators convert and spend their stolen funds is important.
2. Understand how federal, state, and local public records can assist in following the financial "tracks" of suspected perpetrators.
3. Access information via the Internet to assist in the investigation of a suspected fraud perpetrator.
4. Perform net worth calculations on suspected fraud perpetrators and understand how net worth calculations are effective in court and in obtaining confessions.

Phar-Mor, a dry goods retailer based in Youngstown, Ohio, was founded in 1982 by Mickey Monus.[1] *Within 10 years, Phar-Mor was operating in nearly every state, with over 300 stores. The retailer's business strategy was to sell household products and prescription drugs at prices lower than other discount stores. Phar-Mor's prices were so low and its expansion so rapid that even Wal-Mart, the king of discount prices, was nervous.*

Unfortunately, what appeared to be one of the fastest growing companies in the United States was committing massive fraud. In reality, the company never made a legitimate profit. Investigators eventually determined that Phar-Mor overstated revenues and profits by over $500 million. Mickey Monus personally pocketed more than $500,000.

Monus loved the good life and being where the action was. He diverted $10 million from revenues to prop up the National Basketball Association (the defunct minor-league basketball venture), and personally assembled the All-American Girls (a professional cheerleading squad). His stolen money got spent at expensive bars, playing golf at expensive country clubs, paying off his credit-card balances, and adding rooms to his house. Monus bought an expensive engagement ring for his fiancée, and at their poolside wedding at the Ritz Carlton Hotel, his bride wore an 18-karat gold mesh dress worth $500,000. Monus's spend-a-holic personality exhibited itself in countless ways. Many were the times that he would walk into the office at 3 in the afternoon and say, "Let's go to Vegas"—and he meant right then! Once there, a limo would whisk him to Caesar's Palace, where a suite awaited him 7 days a week, 24 hours a day. Monus routinely gave employees $4,000 to gamble with. As one employee said, "He was at home in the 'world of big bets and make-believe.'" To Monus, life was truly a game.[2]

The Phar-Mor fraud is not the only one whose perpetrators enjoyed the good life. In another case, a perpetrator who confessed to embezzling $3.2 million was asked in her deposition the following question:

> *How would you describe your lifestyle during the period when the fraud was being perpetrated?*

Her response was:

> *Extravagant. I drove expensive, very nice cars. We had an Audi 5000 Quattro, a Maserati Spider convertible, a Jeep Cherokee, and a Rolls-Royce. We bought expensive paintings, art, and glasswork. We held expensive parties, serving steak and lobster. We bought a condominium for my parents. We took cruises and other expensive vacations. And I wore expensive clothes, fur coats, diamonds, and gold jewelry.*

The lifestyles of Mickey Monus and this embezzler were extreme, but they demonstrate a common theme: Rarely do perpetrators save what they steal. Although most perpetrators begin their thefts because of a perceived critical need (the $3.2 million perpetrator stole initially to repay a debt consolidation loan), they frequently continue to embezzle after their immediate need is met. And the money usually goes to improve their lifestyles. An important focus in investigations, therefore, involves determining how perpetrators "convert" or spend their stolen funds. As we discussed previously, conversion is the third element of the fraud triangle. Certain frauds, such as kickback schemes, do not generate fraudulent company records, and investigating the theft and concealment elements of some frauds is, for practical purposes, impossible. Accordingly, these frauds are most easily be detected and investigated by focusing on lifestyle changes and other conversion attempts.

Most investigations of conversion involve searching public records and other sources to trace purchases of assets, payments of liabilities, and changes in lifestyle and net worth. When people enter into financial transactions, such as buying assets, they leave tracks or "financial footprints." Trained investigators, who know how to follow, study, and interpret these tracks, often find valuable evidence that supports allegations of fraud.

Conversion searches are performed for two reasons: first, to determine the extent of the embezzlement and, second, to gather evidence that can be used in interrogations to obtain a confession. Effective interviewers, without tipping their hand, often get suspects to admit that his or her only income is earned income. Then by introducing evidence of a lifestyle and associated expenditures that cannot be supported by the earned income, interviewers make it difficult for the suspect to explain the source of the unknown income. Cornered suspects sometimes break down and confess.

To become proficient at conversion investigations, fraud examiners need to understand that (1) federal, state, and local agencies and other organizations maintain information that can be accessed in searches; (2) several types of information are available from each of those sources; and (3) the net worth method of analyzing spending information is especially helpful in determining probable amounts of embezzled funds.

Many federal, state, and local agencies maintain public records in accordance with various laws. Much of this information can be accessed by anyone who requests it, but some of it is protected under privacy laws that prevent disclosure to the public. Federal records are generally not as useful as state and local records in fraud investigations, but they are helpful in certain situations. Because of the bureaucracies involved, accessing federal records is time-consuming and costly. In addition, several private organizations, such as credit reporting agencies and companies that maintain computer databases, as well as Internet sources, also provide valuable information about a person's lifestyle and spending habits.

Federal Sources of Information

Most federal agencies maintain information that can be helpful in investigations of fraud.

Department of Defense

The Department of Defense maintains records on all military personnel, both active and inactive. Military information is maintained by branch of service. This department also contains information on individuals who may be a threat to national security. The department regularly shares information with other federal agencies, such as the Federal Bureau of Investigation (FBI) and Central Intelligence Agency (CIA).

Military records are not confidential and provide valuable information that can help you trace a person's whereabouts through changing addresses. Military records are also helpful in searching for hidden assets, because individuals often buy property and other assets using previous addresses. The web site of the Department of Defense is http://www.defenselink.mil.

Department of Justice

The Department of Justice is the federal agency charged with enforcing federal criminal and civil laws. It maintains records related to the detection, prosecution, and rehabilitation of offenders. The Department of Justice includes U.S. Attorneys, U.S. Marshals, and the FBI. The Drug Enforcement Administration (DEA) is the agency of the Department of Justice charged with enforcing laws against narcotics trafficking.

The FBI is the principal investigative agency of the Department of Justice. Criminal matters not assigned to other U.S. agencies are assigned to the FBI. The FBI thus investigates bank fraud, organized crime, and trade in illegal drugs. The FBI is also responsible for national security within U.S. borders.

The FBI maintains several databases and other records that can be accessed by state and local law enforcement agencies. The major database maintained by the FBI is the National Crime Information Center (NCIC). The NCIC contains information on stolen vehicles, license plates, securities, boats, and planes; stolen and missing firearms; missing persons; and individuals who are currently wanted on outstanding warrants. The FBI also maintains the Interstate Identification Index (III), which is an outgrowth of the NCIC and benefits state and local law enforcement agencies. The III contains arrest and criminal records on a nationwide basis.

Some states maintain databases for their states similar to the one maintained by the NCIC. To gain access to all such databases, you must present identifying information, such as your birth date or Social Security number. These databases are not generally available to private investigators. A need to obtain access to these databases is a good reason to involve local law enforcement in a fraud investigation. The web site of the U.S. Department of Justice is http://www.usdoj.gov.

Bureau of Prisons

This agency operates the nationwide system of federal prisons, correctional institutions, and community treatment facilities. It maintains detailed records on persons who have been incarcerated in the various federal facilities. The web site of the U.S. Bureau of Prisons is http://www.bop.gov.

Internal Revenue Service

The IRS enforces all internal revenue laws, except those dealing with alcohol, firearms, tobacco, and explosives, which are handled by the Bureau of Alcohol, Tobacco, and Firearms. IRS records are not available to the public. The web site of the Internal Revenue Service is http://www.irs.gov.

Secret Service

The Secret Service is responsible for protecting the President of the United States and other federal dignitaries. It also deals with counterfeiting, theft of government checks, interstate credit-card violations, and some computer crimes. The web site of the Secret Service is http://www.ustreas.gov/usss.

Postal Service

The Postal Service is a quasi-governmental organization that has responsibility for the U.S. mail and for protecting citizens from loss through theft that uses the mail system. Postal inspectors are some of the best and most helpful federal investigators. They handle major fraud cases involving the use of mails, and they work for the prosecution of offenders who violate postal laws. Postal inspectors share jurisdiction with other federal, state, and local agencies.

Postal inspectors can be very helpful in investigations of employee fraud, investment scams, or management frauds. Perpetrating a fraud in the United States is difficult without using the mail system. Thus, we find that bribes and kickbacks and false advertisements are often made through the mail, and stolen checks and funds are often deposited in banks by sending them through the mail. Because the use of mail is so common in frauds, the federal mail statutes are the workhorse statutes in federal crimes. It behooves you, as a fraud investigator, to be familiar with mail fraud statutes and to know your local postal inspectors. They can be very helpful in all kinds of fraud investigations. The web site of the Postal Service is http://www.usps.gov.

Central Intelligence Agency

The CIA is responsible to the President of the United States. It investigates security matters outside the United States, whereas the FBI has jurisdiction for security within the U.S. The web site of the Central Intelligence Agency is http://www.cia.gov.

Social Security Administration

The Social Security Administration (SSA) has information about individuals' Social Security numbers. This agency can be helpful in identifying the area where a perpetrator was residing when a Social Security number was issued. Because every Social Security number contains information about the area (first three digits), the group (middle two digits), and the person's serial number (last four digits), Social Security information is extremely useful in fraud investigations. Once an individual's unique Social Security number is known, numerous federal, state, local, and private records can be accessed. The web site of the Social Security Administration is http://www.ssa.gov.

Other Federal Sources of Information

Many other federal sources of information are available. The ones discussed above indicate the range and variety in the types of records available. For additional federal sources, see the United States Federal Government Agencies Directory at http://www.lib.lsu.edu/gov/fedgovall.html.

State Sources of Information

Some state agencies also maintain information that can be helpful in fraud investigations.

State Attorney General

The attorney general for each state enforces all state civil and criminal laws, in cooperation with local law enforcement agencies. Most state attorneys general have investigative arms (similar to the FBI for the Department of Justice), such as the State Bureau of Investigation. This agency contains records relating to individuals who have been convicted of a breach of state civil and criminal laws. The National Association of Attorney Generals has a web site at http://www.naag.org.

Bureau of Prisons

The Bureau of Prisons for each state maintains the network of state prisons and administers state corrections departments. It maintains records on all individuals who have been incarcerated in state prison systems, as well as on individuals who are on probation or parole.

Secretary of State

The Secretary of State maintains all types of records relating to businesses and Uniform Commercial Code (UCC) filings. Every corporation must file documents in the state in which it was chartered. These documents, which are usually maintained by the Secretary of State's office, reveal incorporators, bylaws, articles of incorporation, the registered agent, and the initial board of directors and officers. These records are public information and can be very helpful in gathering information about organizations that are perpetrating fraud. They can confirm whether the organization is legally conducting business and whether its taxes have been paid. They can also provide names of partners, principal shareholders, board members, and business affiliations. This information is valuable in tracing assets, establishing conflicts of interest, identifying dummy companies, and determining changes in financial status.

Secretary of State offices also usually maintain UCC filings. Such records contain information about chattel mortgages (non–real estate transactions) and about loans to individuals or businesses on equipment, furniture, automobiles, and other personal property. UCC records can identify collateral on purchased and leased assets, the nature of the lending company, where a person banks, and whether the person has a need for money. UCC records are sometimes available in a county clerk's office (depending on the state). Much of the information maintained by a Secretary of State's office concerning businesses and UCC filings is online at the National Association of Secretaries of State at http://nass.stateofthevote.org/busreg/busreg.html.

Department of Motor Vehicles

Driver's license records are maintained by the Department of Motor Vehicles and are publicly available in most states. These records enable you to access a person's driving history, address, convictions for traffic violations, name, date of birth, address of birth, and photograph.

Department of Vital Statistics

This department maintains birth records. These records, although quite difficult to obtain, contain information about a person's date and place of birth and parents.

Department of Business Regulation

Most states have a department of business regulation or a similar agency that maintains licensing information about various professionals. Licensing information is generally maintained on accountants, attorneys, bankers, doctors, electricians, plumbers, contractors, engineers, nurses, police officers, firefighters, insurance agents, bail bondsmen, real estate agents, security guards, stock brokers, investment bankers, teachers, servers (food handler's permit), and travel agents, among others.

Licensing information that helps you access industry guidelines also leads you to an individual's memberships, specializations, current business addresses, history of business complaints, grievances, and charges, investigations, and professional credentials.

As an example of how helpful this information can be, suppose you are investigating a fraud similar to the Elgin Aircraft example in Chapter 5, in which dummy doctors are set up. A quick check with the Department of Business Regulation in the relevant state will disclose whether the doctors being paid are legitimate.

County and Local Records

Counties and other local agencies maintain records that are especially useful in fraud investigations. The nature of these records varies from state to state and from county to county.

County Clerk

County clerks maintain numerous records on local citizens, including voter registration records and marriage licenses. Marriage and voting records are always useful in fraud investigations. Voter registration records, for example, state a person's name, current address, past addresses, age, date of birth, social security number, signature, and telephone number, whether listed or unlisted. Even if a person has not voted, his or her family members (such as son, daughter, and spouse) may have voted, and thus voter registration records still provide valuable information.

Marriage records are maintained in the county clerk's office in the county of residence at the time of marriage. They often list the full legal names of the couple, their dates of birth, their Social Security numbers, their addresses at the time of marriage (and usually their parents' addresses as well), driver's license numbers, passport numbers, prior marriages, and the witnesses to those marriages. Once this information has been obtained, numerous databases and other sources of information can be accessed.

County Land Office and Tax Assessor's Office

These offices contain real estate records for land located in the county. There are two common ways to trace real estate records. Land ownership is normally found in the County Land Office or in the office of the Recorder of Deeds. Property tax records, maintained by the County Assessor's Office, also contain property records. Property records are indexed by address or legal description or by the owner's name, or they may be indexed by the name of the seller or the buyer. County Land Office records identify owned assets, indebtedness, mortgage holders, trustees or straw buyers, and people who knew a person before and after a sale. Property tax records contain information about a property's legal description and current assessed value and the taxpayer's current status. These records are helpful in identifying assets purchased and liens removed by a perpetrator.

County Sheriff and Other Officers

Offices such as that of the city police, the county constable, probation officers, and bail bondsmen contain information about criminal charges, indictment statements, pre-trial information reports, conviction statements, incarceration information, and probation information.

Local Courts

Various local courts maintain records on past law violators, including such pre-trial information as personal history, employment history, personal and physical information, prior charges, divorces and property settlement agreements, personal injury lawsuits, financial claims and litigation, fraud claims and co-conspirators, bankruptcies, wills, and probates. Bankruptcy information, which can also be found at various sites online, includes the current status of bankruptcy cases, creditor lists, debts, assets, and information on character. These records can show how assets might be hidden. Information about wills and probates helps identify the assets (and sources of the assets) of perpetrators. Many perpetrators often justify their extravagant lifestyles by claiming to have inherited money. Such claims can be validated or dismissed from information contained in wills and probate.

Permit Departments

Permit departments supply information on fire permits (hazardous chemicals), health permits (pollutants), elevator permits, and building permits. Permit-issuing departments can be helpful in identifying the nature and location of businesses, new leases, and recent construction.

Private Sources of Information

Hundreds of sources of private information are available to those who understand where to find them. Utility records (gas, electric, water, garbage, and sewer), for example, supply the names of persons billed, show whether or not a person lives or owns property in the service area, and identify the types of utilities a business uses.

Another way to gain financial information is through the former spouse of a suspected fraud perpetrator. Many times, former spouses have documents, including bank documents, that turn out to be key in investigations.

A surprising source of valuable financial information is the "trash cover." Trash cover involves looking through a person's trash for possible evidence. Note that searching trash while it is in the possession of a person is against the law. However, once the trash leaves the suspect's home, sidewalk, or fenced area, investigators can usually freely and legally search the trash. In the months of January, February, and March these searches often uncover valuable tax information. During all times of the year, it is always possible to find credit-card information, bank statements, and other valuable information.

Various credit reporting companies maintain private credit records on both individuals and organizations. Reporting agencies are of two types: (1) file-based credit reporting agencies, which develop information from their credit files, and (2) public records and investigative agencies, which gather most of their information through interviews. Credit bureaus are used primarily by retail organizations.

Credit reporting companies typically maintain the following information:

- Consumer information, such as addresses, ages, family members, and incomes
- Account information, such as payment schedules, items purchased, and buying habits
- Marketing information, such as customer breakdowns by age, sex, and income levels
- Information on current and former employees

Information maintained by credit reporting agencies is governed by the Fair Credit Reporting Act of 1971. This act regulates activities of credit, insurance, and employment investigations. Under the law, a consumer-reporting agency must, on request, furnish information to an individual that is also furnished to a third party. If adverse action is to be taken against an employee as a result of third-party information, the employee must be given advance notice. The three major credit reporting agencies are as follows:

- Experian, http://www.experian.com
- Equifax, http://www.equifax.com
- TransUnion, http://www.tuc.com

Financial Institution Records

Financial institution records (including banks, brokerage, and insurance companies) are essential elements of investigations. Bank records can be obtained through a court subpoena, search warrants, a civil summons, or civil discovery. Financial institutions often sell the rights to search and retrieve records from their databases.

Until 1999, when the Gramm-Leach Bliley Act was passed, investigators could only gain information from a financial institution by using false pretenses. Using false pretenses is illegal under the new Act, but it does allow banks and other financial institutions to share customer information with anyone they want, including selling it to database companies. Before financial institutions can sell or disclose confidential customer information, they must provide customers the opportunity to "opt out" of information sharing; that keeps their information private. However, most people do not provide written notice to the bank denying the bank the right to sell their personal bank information (opting out), so bank information is more readily available than ever before. Many Internet sites, for a fee, provide information such as bank account number, bank name, bank address, approximate account balance, city and state of the bank, withdrawals, deposits, savings, wire transfers, full transactions of the bank accounts, credits, collateral records, debits, transactions of loans, bankruptcies, transaction details, and outstanding loans.

Publicly Available Databases

An increasing number of publicly available and/or commercial databases provide helpful information. Dialog, for example, contains 900 databases that provide information about individuals' and companies' backgrounds, employment histories, professional papers, and technical information. Many publicly available databases contain bankruptcy, court records, real estate, tax lien, UCC filing, and other important financial information. Valuable web sites of commercial and/or public databases, along with a brief description of the type of information available on each, are listed here.

Dun & Bradstreet: http://www.zapdata.com The Dun & Bradstreet databases contain information on over 12 million U.S. businesses and millions of contacts for each of those businesses. Dun & Bradstreet also publishes several directories that provide background and financial information on businesses.

Dialog: http://www.dialog.com/index.shtml Dialog's 900 databases contain over 12 terabytes of high-volume information. Content areas include business, science, technology, media, news, property, law, government, and more.

LexisNexis: http://www.lexis-nexis.com LexisNexis provides access to thousands of worldwide newspapers, magazines, trade journals, industry newsletters, tax and accounting information, financial data, public records, legislation records, and data on companies and executives.

Newsnet: http://www.newsnet.telebase.com/brainwave This specialty database gives in-depth information such as patent, bankruptcy, UCC filings, medical updates, and business profiles.

KnowX: http://www.knowx.com One of the most comprehensive databases available, KnowX can help you find out where a former tenant lives, what business name is being used, whether a potential employer is involved in any lawsuits, and what assets an employee has.

Data Quick: http://www.dataquick.com These databases contain property profiles, mortgage information, asset ownership information, and other valuable information.

CDB Infotek: http://www.cdb.com CDB Infotek provides government and businesses with access to critical county, state, and federal public records. Its 1,600 databases contain more than 4 billion public records including UCC filings and other corporate documents.

ProQuest: http://www.proquest.com ProQuest provides access to thousands of current periodicals, as well as out-of-print and rare books, dissertations, newspapers, and other valuable information.

EBSCO Information Systems: http://www.epnet.com This site contains many large databases that include full text periodicals, scholarly journals, U.S. and international newspapers, reference books, and even detailed pamphlets.

SEC's Edgar Database: http://www.sec.gov/edgar.shtml This database is useful for investigating companies. The web site offers free access to financial information on all public companies.

Harte-Hanks: http://www.hartehanksmi.com Harte-Hanks's databases track technology installations, business demographics, and key decision makers at more than 400,000 locations.

Online Sources of Information

With the Internet, investigations can be conducted much more easily and faster than ever before. Searches of both public and private databases can be conducted on the Internet. With the touch of a key, it is possible to access critical county, state, and federal records, including UCC filings. Using the Internet, you can identify bankruptcy, tax lien, civil judgment records, background checks, asset identifications, and criminal records. You can access locations and telephone numbers of every county department in the United States. You can even access specific information, such as how many traffic tickets a person has, or the amount of money in a person's bank account. There are literally thousands of web sites that are helpful in conducting fraud investigations, with new ones being added daily. Below is a sampling of valuable web sites for fraud investigators, along with a brief description of the type of information available on each. Some web sites offer investigation services for a fee. Others contain information that you can search yourself.

Internet sources are dynamic—they change often. The ones we list were current at the time this book was published.

US Search: http://www.ussearch.com US Search offers instant people searches, background checks, and instant civil and criminal court record searches. A free online credit report is available.

Discreet Research: http://www.date411.com Discreet Research offers an extensive line of public records, including business reports, telephone searches, pre-employment information, motor vehicle records, license verifications, county criminal records, metro criminal records, state criminal records, outstanding warrants, prison records, civil records, and other valuable information.

BRB Publications: http://www.brbpublications.com BRB Publications is a public records research library that offers access to records of over 26,000 government agencies. It also has links to over 650 state, county, city, and federal databases.

Confi-chek Online Public Records: http://www.confi-chek.com For a fee, Confi-chek conducts background checks, asset identifications, and searches for criminal records. Information on personal real property, bankruptcy, tax liens, civil judgments, and criminal records can be obtained here.

Verifacts Online: http://www.verifacts.com Verifacts Online offers instant online reports, including credit reports, social security checks, criminal investigations, and eviction and rental histories.

Hogan Information Service: http://www.hoganinfo.com Hogan Information Service collects bankruptcy, tax lien, civil judgment records and other types of public record information. This site also performs specific client requests, such as traffic ticket, eviction, and criminal record filings for a fee.

Social Security Death Index: http://www.ancestry.com/search/rectype/vital/ssdi/main.htm Go to this site to access information provided by the Social Security Administration.

National Driver Register: http://www.nhtsa.dot.gov/people/perform/driver The National Driver Register is a computerized database of information on drivers who have had their licenses revoked or suspended, or who have been convicted of serious traffic violations, such as driving while impaired by alcohol or drugs.

Free Public Records Sites: http://www.publicrecordfinder.com This web site lists over 6,000 links to government sites that offer free searches of public records.

State Motor Vehicle Records: http://www.webgator.org/gator78.htm The State Motor Vehicle Records web site gives locations and telephone numbers of every county motor vehicle department in the United States.

Search Systems: http://www.pac-info.com Search Systems gives access to over 4,740 different databases that include such information as license, birth certificate, driving records, and bankruptcies.

National Courts and Court Records: http://www.webgator.org/gator75.htm This web site includes information about bankruptcy courts for all 50 states.

Criminal Histories: http://www.webgator.org/gator206.htm The criminal histories web site gives links to state web sites where criminal information can be accessed.

Black Book Online: http://www.crimetime.com/online.htm Black Book Online provides searches on bankruptcies, mail drops, corporations, real estate, businesses, death records, state records, federal records, and other valuable information.

Public Records: http://www.docusearch.com/free-links.html Public Records is a detailed collection of 300 links to databases containing public information.

Cemeteries and Obituaries: http://www.webgator.org/gator210.htm This web site gives links to cemeteries, organized by state, as well as obituaries and other information.

NetrOnline: http://www.netronline.com/public_records.htm NetrOnline is an information portal to official state web sites, and Tax Assessors' and Recorders' offices that have developed web sites for retrieving public records. The public records includes copies of deeds, parcel maps, GIS maps, tax data, ownership information and indexes, and other information.

The preceding web sites provide information useful in conducting investigations. The following sites provide information about how to begin an investigation and questions you may have while you conduct it.

How to Investigate.com: http://www.howtoinvestigate.com/information.htm This site gives information on how to conduct an investigation.

Public Records Information Sources: http://www.ahhapeoplefinder.com/information.htm Public Records Information Sources gives information about credit bureaus, business reports, government agencies, state and federal records, and the directory industry.

Investigative Resource Center: http://www.factfind.com/public.htm The Investigative Resource Center gives information on public and open source records, and corporate records.

Legal Resource Center: http://www.crimelynx.com/investigation.html The Legal Resource Center gives numerous government links, criminal justice statistics, record searches, and other valuable information.

Private Investigator: http://www.geocities.com/Athens/7374/links.html This web site gives information on various databases, postal address references, investigative organizations, and credit reporting.

The Net Worth Method

Once investigators compile information about spending and lifestyle from public records and other sources, they usually want to determine the extent of the stolen funds. The most common way to make such determinations is through net worth calculations. Essentially, the net worth method uses the following formula, which is based on a person's assets (things owned), liabilities (debts), living expenses, and income.

The Net Worth Calculation

1. Assets − Liabilities = Net Worth
2. Net Worth − Prior Year's Net Worth = Net Worth Increase
3. Net Worth Increase + Living Expenses = Income
4. Income − Funds from Known Sources = Funds from Unknown Sources

From public records and other sources, investigators determine an individual's purchases of real estate, automobiles, and other assets. Such records also state whether liens have been removed, thus identifying whether loans have been paid. Combining public sources information with information collected from interviews of landscapers, furniture and automobile dealers, and other relevant parties, and with information gathered through subpoenas provides a reasonably accurate accounting of assets and liabilities.

When people have income, they either purchase additional assets, pay off liabilities, or improve their lifestyles, thus increasing living expenses. Known income subtracted from unknown income gives a reasonable estimate of unknown funds. Verifying or eliminating other sources of funds (such as inheritances, gambling winnings, and gifts) gives a good estimate of the amount of stolen funds.

The net worth method for determining amounts embezzled has gained favor among fraud investigators in recent years. The FBI regularly uses this method, as does the DEA, which uses it to determine whether suspected narcotics traffickers have income from illegal drug sales. The IRS uses it to estimate unreported income in tax fraud cases. Because only assets and reductions in liabilities that can be discovered enter into the calculation, net worth calculations tend to give a conservative estimate of stolen funds. The bad news is, embezzlers typically spend increasing amounts on food, jewelry, vacations, and other luxuries that are difficult to track and cannot be factored into net worth calculations. The good news is, because these calculations are conservative, the amounts determined to be stolen are usually readily accepted as evidence by courts. They also often facilitate obtaining confessions from suspects. An effective and often fruitful way to interrogate suspects is to present accurate information regarding their expenditures and lifestyle that they cannot justify from their income.

To illustrate the net worth method, reconsider the following example that was described in a case at the end of Chapter 2:

> *Helen Weeks worked for Bonne Consulting Group (BCG) as the executive secretary in the administrative department for nearly 10 years. Her apparent integrity and dedication to her work quickly earned her a reputation as an outstanding employee and resulted in increased responsibilities. She soon made arrangements for outside feasibility studies, maintained client files, worked with outside marketing consultants, initiated the payment process, and notified the accounting department of all openings or closings of vendor accounts. During Helen's first five years of employment, BCG subcontracted all its feasibility and marketing studies through Jackson & Co. This relationship was subsequently terminated because Jackson & Co. merged with a larger, more expensive consulting group. At the time of the termination, Helen and her supervisor selected a new firm to conduct BCG's market research. However, Helen never informed the accounting department that the Jackson & Co. account was closed. Her supervisor trusted her completely and allowed her to sign for all voucher payments less than $10,000. Helen continued to process checks made payable to Jackson's account. The accounting department continued to process the payments, and Helen distributed the payments. She opened a bank account under the name Jackson & Co. and deposited the checks in the account. She paid all her personal expenses out of this account.*

Let's say we are investigating Helen's fraud. As part of our investigation, we have searched public records and other sources and have accumulated the following financial information on Helen Weeks.

Financial Data for Helen Weeks			
	Year 1	Year 2	Year 3
Assets:			
Residence	$100,000	$100,000	$100,000
Stocks and bonds	30,000	30,000	42,000
Automobiles	20,000	20,000	40,000
CD	50,000	50,000	50,000
Cash	6,000	12,000	14,000

continues

Financial Data for Helen Weeks	Year 1	Year 2	Year 3
Liabilities:			
Mortgage balance	90,000	50,000	-0-
Auto loan	10,000	-0-	-0-
Income:			
Salary		34,000	36,000
Other		6,000	6,000
Expenses:			
Mortgage payments		6,000	6,000
Auto loan payments		4,800	4,800
Other living expenses		20,000	22,000

With this information, we can use the net worth method to estimate how much Helen may have embezzled. These calculations are shown below.

Comparative Net Worth–Asset Method	End Year 1	End Year 2	End Year 3
Assets:			
Residence	$100,000	$100,000	$100,000
Stocks and bonds	30,000	30,000	42,000
Auto	20,000	20,000	40,000
CD	50,000	50,000	50,000
Cash	6,000	12,000	14,000
Total assets	$206,000	$212,000	$246,000
Liabilities:			
Mortgage balance	$ 90,000	$ 50,000	$ —
Auto loan	10,000	—	—
Total liabilities	$100,000	$ 50,000	$ —
Net worth	$106,000	$162,000	$246,000
Change in net worth		$ 56,000	$ 84,000
Plus total expenses		30,800	32,800
Total		$ 86,800	$116,800
Less known income		40,000	42,000
Income from unknown sources		$ 46,800	$ 74,800

Based on this calculation, we determine that Helen had at least $46,800 of unknown income in year 2 and $74,800 of unknown income in year 3. This information can be used in court to obtain a criminal conviction, civil judgment, or even an order against Helen, and it can also be used to obtain a confession. A good investigator, armed with this data, may well get a confession from Helen. She would first be asked to state her income and other sources of funds. The investigator would then show that she cannot maintain her lifestyle and pay her debts without additional income. Seeing that her story and the reality conflict, Helen might confess.

Summary

In previous chapters, we covered ways to investigate theft and concealment. In this chapter, we discussed ways to investigate conversion. Essentially, conversion investigations involve two steps: (1) using publicly available sources and other sources to determine a person's spending habits and other information, and (2) calculating a person's net worth to estimate the amount of money stolen. We identified various sources of information, including (1) federal sources, (2) state sources, (3) local sources, (4) county and local records, (5) financial institution records, (6) commercial and publicly available databases, and (7) online or Internet sources.

New Terms

Gramm-Leach Bliley Act: Passed in 1999, this law prohibits the use of false pretenses to access the personal information of others. It does allow banks and other financial institutions to share or sell customer information, unless customers proactively "opt out" and ask that their information not be shared.

National Crime Information Center (NCIC): The major criminal database maintained by the FBI. This database contains information on stolen vehicles, securities, boats, missing persons, and other information helpful in fraud investigations.

Net worth method: Analytical method that estimates a suspect's unexplained income. Liabilities are subtracted from assets to give net worth, then the previous year's net worth is subtracted to find the increase in net worth. Living expenses are then added to the change in net worth to determine a person's total income, and finally known income is subtracted from total income to determine the unknown income.

Opting-out right: Right of customers to give written notice to financial institutions that prohibits the institution from sharing or selling customer's personal information.

Postal inspectors: Inspectors or investigators hired by the U.S. Postal Service to handle major fraud cases that are perpetrated through the U.S. mail system.

Trash investigation: Searching through a person's trash for possible evidence in an investigation.

Questions and Cases

Discussion Questions

1. What are common ways to investigate conversion of stolen assets?
2. What are "financial footprints"?
3. Why is it important to know how perpetrators convert and spend their stolen funds?
4. What are the differences between public and private sources of information?
5. How do state, federal, and local public records assist fraud investigations?
6. How does the Internet assist in determining the net worth of suspected perpetrators?
7. Why are net worth calculations so valuable?

True/False

1. Perpetrators usually save what they steal.
2. One common investigation procedure determines how perpetrators convert or spend their time.
3. Investigations of perpetrators' net worth and lifestyles help investigators know what class of society the perpetrators are from.
4. It is always necessary to involve a federal law enforcement agent in order to access federal databases.
5. The Secretary of State maintains many types of records relating to business and Uniform Commercial Code filings.
6. Counties and other local agencies that contain records are usually not very useful in fraud investigation.
7. Private credit records are maintained on both individuals and organizations by various credit reporting companies.
8. Several publicly available databases provide information that can be helpful in investigations.
9. The net worth method is rarely, if ever, helpful in actual fraud investigations.
10. For various reasons, the net worth method tends to be a conservative estimate of amounts stolen.
11. Conversion is the third element of the fraud triangle.
12. The Gramm-Leach Bliley Act of 1999 made it more difficult for officials and private citizens to access information from financial institutions.
13. Before financial institutions can sell or disclose confidential customer information, they must provide customers with the opportunity to "opt out" from information sharing.
14. Federal agencies provide better records than state or county agencies for conversion investigations.
15. When people convert stolen cash by entering into financial transactions, such as buying assets, they leave tracks that investigators can follow.
16. Private financial institutions can usually sell confidential customer information.
17. The net worth method cannot help in determining the extent of stolen funds.
18. An increase in a person's net worth plus living expenses equals the person's income.

Multiple Choice

1. Although most perpetrators begin their thefts because of a perceived critical need, they continue to embezzle in order to:
   a. Beat the system
   b. Fulfill an inner desire to commit fraud
   c. Improve their lifestyle
   d. Achieve a higher self-esteem
2. Evidence gathered from public records can be useful in
   a. Identifying with the suspect
   b. Obtaining a confession
   c. Making the suspect feel at ease
   d. None of the above

3. The net worth method of analyzing financial information can help to determine:
   a. The suspect's feelings about the organization
   b. Possible perpetrators of the fraud
   c. The suspect's personality characteristics
   d. The amount of embezzled funds
4. Which of the following organizations maintain public information that can be accessed in record searches?
   a. Local agencies
   b. State agencies
   c. Federal agencies
   d. All of the above
5. How useful are local and county records in fraud investigations?
   a. Very useful
   b. Not useful
   c. Somewhat useful
   d. Aren't allowed in the investigation of fraud
6. Which of the following laws regulates activities of credit, insurance, and employment investigations?
   a. Fair Investigation Act of 1980
   b. Fair Credit Reporting Act of 1971
   c. Credit, Insurance, and Employment Investigation Act
   d. There is no governing law.
7. The net worth method is effective:
   a. As evidence in court
   b. To help obtain a confession
   c. To conduct an interview of suspects
   d. All of the above
8. Conversion investigations focus on how suspects:
   a. Had opportunities to steal
   b. Had motives to commit fraud
   c. Spent stolen money
   d. Committed the actual theft
9. Which of the following are possible uses of conversion-based investigation techniques?
   a. Searching public records to trace purchases of assets and payments of liabilities
   b. Attempting to locate previous spouses' bank account records
   c. Locating significant amounts of money held by related parties
   d. All of the above
10. Most conversion investigations involve searching public records and other sources to trace:
    a. Purchases of assets
    b. Payments of liabilities
    c. Changes in lifestyle
    d. Net worth
    e. All of the above

11. A database of criminal records maintained by the FBI is the:
    a. CIA
    b. III
    c. NCIC
    d. a and c
    e. b and c
12. Which are usually some of the best and most helpful federal fraud investigators?
    a. Officers of the Secret Service
    b. Employees of the Bureau of Prisons
    c. Officers of the Department of Vital Statistics
    d. Postal inspectors
13. Which source could you use to access valuable financial information in a fraud investigation?
    a. Financial institutions
    b. Internet sites
    c. The former spouse of a suspected fraud perpetrator
    d. Trash
    e. All of the above
14. The net worth method is a calculation based on a person's:
    a. Assets, liabilities, equity, and living expenses
    b. Assets, liabilities, equity, and income
    c. Assets, liabilities, income, and living expenses
    d. Assets, income, and living expenses

Short Cases

Case 1. Given the following information, determine whether there is a likelihood of illegal income. If so, determine the amount of unknown income.

Financial Data

	Year 1	Year 2	Year 3
Assets:			
Residence	$100,000	$100,000	$100,000
Baseball cards	15,000	15,000	25,000
Automobiles	-0-	30,000	50,000
Paintings	50,000	150,000	250,000
Cash	6,000	12,000	14,000
Liabilities:			
Mortgage balance	100,000	50,000	-0-
Auto loan	-0-	30,000	-0-
Income:			
Salary		34,000	36,000
Other		6,000	6,000
Expenses:			
Mortgage payments		6,000	6,000
Auto loan payments		4,800	4,800
Other living expenses		20,000	20,000

Case 2. You are auditing a bank and someone provides you an anonymous tip that an employee is embezzling money from the bank. You decide to investigate the allegation.

Your interviews with other bank employees confirm that the suspected embezzler has been acting very strange lately. Some employees have seen the employee crying in the bathroom and acting strange in other ways. The bank recently downsized due to poor economic growth, yet the suspect recently bought a new Lexus.

From some "helpful" hints from bank employees and through your own investigation, you discover that the mortgage taken out by the suspect three years ago for his personal home has recently been paid in full.

After calculating the suspect's net worth, you determine that he has about $249,000 income from unknown sources this year alone.

1. What are possible explanations for why the suspect (1) is experiencing emotional changes, and (2) has had an increase in unknown income?
2. Can you conclude from these facts that the suspect has indeed been committing fraud?

Case 3. Bill James is being investigated for embezzling over $700,000 from ABC Capital Management, for whom Bill has worked for nearly 10 years. When co-workers noticed the new "toys" Bill was buying, they jokingly asked him to tell them his stock picks as they wanted in too! Bill told them that they better go adopt some rich relatives. "My Uncle Eddie didn't have any kids, so he left a chunk of his money to each of us nephews."

Explain how you might go about checking the validity of Bill's claim to a recent inheritance. Include in your discussion the relevant information you need about Uncle Eddie and where you could find that information.

Case 4. Homegrown Gardens, LLP, is a $10 million nursery and garden retailer in Colorado. Homegrown employs about 20 full-time and seasonal employees. The majority of the plants and nursery stock Homegrown sells comes from Monromio Nurseries, a wholesaler based in Oregon. Monromio is recognized throughout the West for the quality of the plants it grows and sells. Homegrown is generally happy to pay the premium prices that Monromio's plants command, because they pass the extra costs on to their customers, who value the high-quality plants they sell. However, Barry Greenstem, one of Homegrown's managing partners, is visibly upset after speaking with the owners of other nurseries at a recent trade show in Atlanta. Although Monromio has increased their prices across the board, Monromio's price hike to Homegrown is larger than the average. Barry suspects that Betty Stevenson, Homegrown's assistant manager in charge of purchasing nursery stock, may be accepting kickbacks from Monromio in return for allowing higher purchase prices. Betty and her husband, Mike, purchased a new SUV, a houseboat, and several ATVs last year and moved into a new, larger house this year. Barry knows Betty's salary isn't high enough to support the new lifestyle and he doubts that Mike's job as a city employee would provide large enough raises to justify the new "toys." Barry hires you to perform a net worth investigation of Betty and Mike to determine the amount of any unknown income. Your search of public and private records reveals the following information:

	Year Before Last	Last Year	This Year
Assets:			
Personal residence	$70,000	$70,000	$200,000
Automobiles	15,000	45,000	45,000
Houseboat		30,000	30,000
ATVs		12,000	12,000

	Year Before Last	Last Year	This Year
Liabilities:			
Mortgage balance	35,000	30,500	100,000
Auto loan	2,500		
Loan on houseboat		15,000	11,000
Income:			
Betty's salary	25,000	25,500	26,000
Mike's salary	35,000	36,000	37,000
Expenses:			
Mortgage payments	4,500	4,500	13,000
Auto payments	1,800	1,800	
Houseboat payments		2,400	2,400
Other living expenses	15,000	17,000	15,000

Using this information, calculate the amount of income from unknown sources, if any, using the net worth method.

Case 5. You manage a car dealership in a large city. Many of your sales employees are very successful, and have purchased their own vehicles from your dealership. Your dealership finances the sale of some of these vehicles. One employee recently paid off the balances on a couple of new vehicles purchased from your dealership. You discover this information after investigating complaints from customers about this particular employee's actions. His sales are down, and customer complaints about his attitude abound. He previously worked for two other car dealers, both of which were satisfied with his performance. This employee is in charge of having used cars reconditioned by various automobile repair shops.

1. What signs of unusual behavior and lifestyle symptoms are present in this case, and what are some possible causes for them?
2. How might this employee be defrauding the company?

Case 6. Janet Moody is one of XZY Company's most trusted employees. She never complains about her work and rarely misses work due to illness or vacation. The company has been successful over the years, but is now having cash flow problems. Because of the recent downturn in the company, you take a closer look at all the company's financial records. When you ask Janet about the recent cash flow problems, she responds, "I don't know what is going on. I only do the reporting. Ask those who manage the company." This behavior differs from Janet's normal pleasant deportment. As you continue your investigation, you discover that the reported financial results do not match what the company is doing, but you can't determine why. You decide to investigate Janet further.

1. What are some behavior and lifestyle changes that you should look for?
2. What resources can you use to conduct your research?

Case 7. Using the net worth method, analyze the following financial data for potential signs of fraud or embezzlement. Do your results indicate that this person could be committing some type of fraud? If so, why do you think so? What other factors might you consider to determine whether fraud has been committed, other than the final total income from other sources (if any)? Is this scenario realistic?

	Year 1	Year 2	Year 3	Year 4	Year 5
Assets					
Residence	200,000	200,000	275,000	275,000	275,000
Automobile	50,000	50,000	75,000	75,000	90,000
Stocks and bonds	75,000	75,000	100,000	100,000	125,000
Cash	15,000	16,500	18,150	19,965	21,962
Liabilities					
Mortgage balance	175,000	50,000	125,000	107,000	40,000
Auto loan balance	40,000	20,000	35,000	25,000	10,000
Income					
Salary		100,000	107,000	125,000	133,750
Other		10,000	10,000	10,000	10,000
Expenses					
Mortgage loan payments		12,000	18,000	18,000	18,000
Auto loan payments		7,000	10,000	10,000	13,000
Other living expenses		30,000	33,000	36,300	39,930

Case 8. The following financial data were collected during a fraud investigation:

	Year 1	Year 2	Year 3
Assets			
Residence	280,000	280,000	280,000
Automobile	18,000	45,000	45,000
CD	5,000	15,000	15,000
Cash	8,000	8,000	2,000
Stock portfolio	3,500	15,000	15,000
Boat		15,000	15,000
Liabilities			
Mortgage	200,000	180,000	100,000
Auto loan	12,000	30,000	
Other loan		18,000	
Income			
Salary	55,000	90,000	130,000
Investment	800	800	800
Expenses			
Mortgage expense	18,000	18,000	18,000
Auto expense	5,000	9,000	9,000
Living Expenses	20,000	20,000	20,000

1. Without calculating the amount of unknown income, indicate possible red flags or trends you notice in the numbers above.
2. Now calculate the amount of income and unknown income, using the numbers given. Does it appear that a possible fraud exists? Could there be other explanations for the unknown income?

Case 9. After searching public records and other sources, you accumulate the following financial information for John Dough:

	Year 1	Year 2	Year 3
Assets			
Residence	$150,000	$150,000	$150,000
Residence #2			85,000
Stocks and bonds	10,000	20,000	35,000
Automobiles	18,000	35,000	35,000
Boat		22,000	22,000
CD	8,000	27,000	50,000
Cash	3,500	7,500	18,000
Liabilities			
Mortgage balance #1	84,000	42,000	15,000
Mortgage balance #2			85,000
Auto loans	12,000	38,000	
Boat loan		22,000	5,000
Income			
Salary		49,000	55,000
Interest/other		5,000	7,000
Expenses			
Mortgage payments		15,000	26,000
Auto loan payments		6,000	6,000
Boat loan payments		3,500	5,000
Other living expenses		22,000	31,000

Given the above financial information, determine whether there is a likelihood of illegal income. If so, determine the amount.

Case 10. Mr. I. M. Bezzle works in the purchasing department for Big Time Inc. During the 12 years that he has worked there, he has been a trusted employee and has sole responsibility for the company's purchasing function. He started working for the company in 1990 for $30,000 a year and now makes $100,000 a year. Fellow employees and friends have noticed that his lifestyle has improved substantially recently since his promotion to purchasing manager. Based on an anonymous tip, the CEO asks you to look into the situation.

What steps would you take to investigate the possibility of fraud here?

Case 11. Tom works for XYZ Company and is suspected to have embezzled funds from the company. By searching databases on the Internet, talking with his ex-wife, and searching through his trash, you gather the following information:

Assets	$120,000
Liabilities	70,000
Living expenses	50,000
Known income	60,000
Prior year's net worth	10,000

1. Use these data to figure out Tom's income from unknown sources by performing a net worth calculation.
2. How can this information be used to motivate Tom to confess that he has stolen from XYZ Company?

Case 12. Sarah Welch was hired 15 years ago by Produce-R-Us, an importer of rare and exotic fruits. Produce-R-Us was started by an immigrant family 20 years ago and has grown to a national company with sales of $10 million annually. Although the business has grown, the family-owned business strives to maintain a "family atmosphere" and stress trust. Because of Sarah's honesty and hard work, the manager quickly promoted her, and she now signs checks for amounts under $5,000 and also has responsibilities for Accounts Payable. Now, however, the owners are suspicious of Sarah's recent lifestyle changes and have hired you to determine whether Sarah is embezzling from the company. Public records reveal the following:

	Year 1	Year 2	Year 3
Assets			
Personal residence	$100,000	$100,000	$100,000
Automobiles	20,000	40,000	90,000
Stocks and bonds	30,000	30,000	30,000
Boat		30,000	30,000
CDs	25,000	25,000	50,000
Liabilities			
Mortgage balance	90,000	40,000	
Auto loan	10,000	5,000	
Income			
Salary	37,000	40,000	42,000
Other	4,000	4,000	4,000
Expenses			
Mortgage payments	6,000	6,000	6,000
Auto loan payments	2,000	2,500	2,500
Other living expenses	15,000	15,000	20,000

Perform a net worth calculation, using the data above.

Extensive Cases

Case 13. Steve (Slick) Willy (age 45) just got out of jail. As a reformed citizen on parole, Slick decides to go into business for himself. He starts a collections company to help companies collect debts. The terms of his parole stipulate that he pay restitution payments to the federal government of $400 a month, or 10% of his income, whichever is greater. As his parole officer, you notice that after a year out of jail, Slick makes some interesting purchases. First, he buys a new Jaguar which he drives to parole meetings. Second, he moves into an expensive neighborhood on the north side of town and takes a cruise to Jamaica with his 17-year-old girlfriend. Yet, he has never been late making his $400 monthly payments to the federal government. After obtaining a subpoena for his bank records, you notice that he has only $1,000 in his account. About this time, you receive a call from a man who is making payments to Slick's collection company. He states that Slick is threatening to break his legs and hurt his family if he doesn't pay Slick's company. The man says Slick demands the checks be made out to a woman, not a company.

This complaint convinces you to investigate Mr. Willy and his girlfriend. A search of UCC filings in the county shows that Slick's girlfriend owns three cars costing $90,000, a $250,000 house, and a company called Tak'In It From You. You check her bank account and see that more than $50,000 is moving through the account each month. You decide to dig through Slick and his girlfriend's trash a few times each month. In these searches, you find evidence that support the following: three car payments totaling $1,000 per month; a $1,500 monthly mortgage payment; a credit-card balance of $6,000, with $100 monthly payments; a balance of $12,000 owed to Home Shopping Network, with $500 monthly payments; $400 food payments during the past two weeks; and a $3,500 payment to Jamaican cruise lines. After searching the girlfriend's trash, you talk to her neighbors, friends, and co-workers and determine that she and Slick spend between $1,500 and $2,000 a month on miscellaneous items and trips. One neighbor tells you that Slick just gave his girlfriend a two-carat diamond ring. Slick's girlfriend works as a waitress at a small restaurant and makes only $15,000 a year.

Use this information to prepare a net worth analysis of Slick's girlfriend. (Ignore interest in your calculations.)

Case 14. You receive an anonymous tip that your controller is embezzling assets from your company. You begin your investigation by interviewing several employees in the accounting department, who report no unusual behavior or sudden changes in the suspect's standard of living. One interviewee does report that the controller has gone on a number of extravagant vacations.

You perform a net worth analysis, based on a search of public records, and find the following information:

	Year 1	Year 2	Year 3
Total assets	80,000	82,000	85,000
Total liabilities	40,000	41,000	41,000
Net worth	40,000	41,000	44,000
Change in net worth		1,000	3,000
Living expenses		36,000	36,000
Total income		37,000	39,000
Less known income	35,000	35,000	36,000
Unknown income		2,000	3,000

1. Based on the evidence gathered in your search, what conclusions can you make about the controller?
2. Would you feel comfortable using the evidence above in an interview to obtain a confession? Why or why not?
3. What additional investigating could you pursue to obtain more evidence?

Case 15. Use the following financial data to prepare a comparative net worth assessment:

	Year 1	Year 2	Year 3
Assets			
Residence	$50,000	$50,000	$200,000
Stocks and bonds	10,000	10,000	10,000
Automobiles	15,000	15,000	40,000
Cash	5,000	8,000	20,000
Liabilities			
Mortgage balance	40,000	30,000	0
Auto loan	8,000	5,000	0
Student loans	10,000	8,000	0

	Year 1	Year 2	Year 3
Income			
Salary	30,000	35,000	40,000
Other	0	1,000	1,000
Expenses			
Mortgage payments	$ 5,000	$ 5,000	$ 0
Car payments	1,000	5,000	2,500
Student loan payments	1,000	1,000	500
Other living expenses	15,000	15,000	20,000
Total living expenses	$22,000	$26,000	$ 23,000

Internet Assignments

1. The Postal Service site contains lots of information on detecting mail fraud and the investigation efforts of the Postal Service.
   a. Access the United States Postal Service web site at http://www.usps.gov. Find the site entitled "US Postal Inspection Service." (*Hint:* Use the keyword search at http://www.usps.gov; search for "fraud" or other similar words.) Review and become familiar with the fraud services provided by the Postal Inspection Service.
   b. Give a brief overview of the Postal Inspection Service.
   c. What does the Postal Inspection Service recommend in order to protect you against phony "one-shot" credit-card offers?
   d. Name five characteristics of telemarketing fraud schemes.
2. An increasingly common way to commit fraud is to use the Internet. The Department of Justice now devotes an entire page on its web site to Internet fraud. Visit the site at http://www.usdoj.gov/criminal/fraud/Internet.htm and identify three types of Internet fraud.
3. Go to http://www.howtoinvestigate.com/information.htm. Read the section entitled *Information Record Sources: local records, county records, state records, federal records, and national records.*
   a. Records are collected and maintained at three levels by government and private organizations. Name these three levels.
   b. Credit bureaus gather credit data about individuals from a vast network of retailers, businesses, and financial institutions. In exchange for these data, they provide credit information to all their members. List three giant commercial credit bureaus.
   c. What are open records? What rights do you have to use them?
   d. What are semi-open records? Give examples.
   e. What are closed records?
4. Go to http://howtoinvestigate.com/busback.htm. Read the section entitled *Business Background Investigations.*
   a. What does a complete business investigation include?
   b. Suppose you hire someone to perform some work on your house. Who do you call to find out if the contractor is licensed to conduct business in your area?

Debate

1. You are performing an audit of a small Internet startup company that recently went public. During the audit, you frequently converse with the employees, with whom you have a comfortable relationship. In one conversation, an employee mentions the strange behavior of a co-worker.

   Apparently, this suspect employee comes to work very early and stays late. He is stressed at work and very irritable. Although many of the company's founders are enjoying the economic fruits of the IPO, this person did not own any stock in the company at the time of the IPO and thus did not earn much money when the company went public. Nevertheless, this person drives a new Porsche Boxter.

   Your debate topic: Is there sufficient evidence to determine whether this employee appears to be committing fraud?
2. This chapter discussed techniques for conversion investigations that involve searching public records to identify changes in lifestyle and the net worth of alleged fraud perpetrators. You recently became a Certified Fraud Examiner and have joined a local fraud examination firm. Your manager explains how he prefers to work with private sources of information and not involve local law enforcement agencies in the conversion investigation stage of his cases. You disagree and feel that local law enforcement can be an excellent resource.

   Pair up with someone in your class. One of you take the position of the manager and the other take the position of the new CFE. Discuss the advantages and disadvantages of involving law enforcement agencies in your fraud investigations.

End Notes

1. Most of the facts for the Phar-Mor vignette were taken from the video, "How to Steal 500 Million." *Frontline* by PBS Video. PBS 1992. Some facts were taken from an article in the *Wall Street Journal.* (See Gabriela Stern, "Chicanery at Phar-Mor Ran Deep, Close Look at Discounter Shows," *Wall Street Journal,* Jan. 20, 1994, p. 1.)

2. Mark F. Murray, "When a Client Is a Liability," *Journal of Accountancy,* Sept. 1992, pp. 54–58.

3. Jack Bologna, *Forensic Accounting Review* (Plymouth, Michigan), April 1993, p. 2.

CHAPTER NINE

Inquiry Methods and Fraud Reports[1]

After studying this chapter you should be able to:

1. Describe the different types of honesty testing.
2. Understand the interviewing process.
3. Plan and conduct an interview.
4. Understand the nature of admission-seeking interviews.
5. Describe the different deceptions and lies used by perpetrators.
6. Prepare a fraud report.

Don Restiman was purchasing manager for Emerald Enterprises. During a four-year period, he accepted over $400,000 in bribes from one of Emerald's suppliers by having the supplier hire and pay his daughter, Jane, as a supposed "salesperson." Jane deposited her "paycheck" into an account she shared with her father. They used the money to buy real estate, automobiles, and other valuables. Fraud was suspected in the purchasing department for several reasons, which included increased amounts of purchases from the vendor, unnecessary purchases, purchases of goods at increased prices, and prices significantly higher than those of competitors.

Two skilled investigators interrogated Jane. They asked her about the specifics of her "job." As the interview proceeded, it became obvious through both verbal and nonverbal cues that she was lying. She was unable to answer such simple questions as, "Where are the company's headquarters located?" "What is the address and telephone number of your office?" "What companies do you sell to?" and "Who are your closest co-workers?"

After several obvious lies, her attorney asked if he and his client could step outside the room for a few moments. Her attorney convinced Jane that she was perjuring herself. When they returned, Jane confessed that she was lying about being employed at Emerald. In the presence of her attorney, she signed a prepared written confession that made prosecution of her father easier.

In this chapter, we conclude our discussion of investigation methods by discussing how to query people (witnesses or suspects), through interviews and various types of honesty testing.

Honesty Testing

The most common inquiry method (and the most common of all investigation techniques) is the interview. However, at least three other methods can also solicit information about a person's honesty: (1) pencil-and-paper tests, (2) graphology, and (3) voice stress analysis and polygraphs.

Pencil-and-Paper Test

Pencil-and-paper honesty tests are objective tests that elicit information about a person's honesty and personal code of ethics. They are used more frequently as employee screening devices than as tools to determine whether someone has committed a crime. Pencil-and-paper tests are considered to be between 50% and 90% accurate. Some of the more common ones are the Reid Report, the Personnel Selection Inventory, and the Stanton Survey. They use questions such as:

True False 1. It is natural for most people to be a little dishonest.
True False 2. People who are dishonest should be sent to prison.

Answers to these and similar questions create a profile of a person's personal code of conduct, on which his or her risk to a business can be assessed. According to the developers of these tests, one of their advantages is that the results can be tabulated by a computer in a matter of minutes, making them ideal for applicant screening or initial identification of possible suspects. These kinds of tests are now used by a large number of retailers in the United States.

Graphology

Graphology is the study of handwriting for the purpose of character analysis. Its use has increased substantially in past years. Graphology is used in fields in which employee integrity is important, such as banking, manufacturing, and insurance. About 350 graphologists currently work as consultants to U.S. businesses. Note, however, that many fraud investigators are skeptical about the reliability of graphology.

Voice Stress Analysis and Polygraphs

Voice stress analysis determines whether a person is lying or telling the truth by using a mechanical device connected to the person. Polygraphs are more complicated than voice stress analyzers in that they attempt to assess stress, and hence lying, by measuring key physical responses. The theory is that people feel guilty when they lie or are dishonest. The guilt feelings produce stress, which results in changes in behavior. Polygraphs measure pulse rate, blood pressure, galvanic skin response, and respiration. Like voice stress analyzers, polygraphs sometimes lead to incorrect decisions because they frighten innocent people. In addition, they rarely detect psychopathic liars, who feel no stress when they lie because they do not have a conscience.

The Employee Polygraph Protection Act passed a number of years ago has made the use of polygraphs more difficult. Although polygraphs are still legal, investigators must meet 11 conditions in order to use them—one of which is that investigators must inform suspects that they don't have to take the test if they don't want to.

Polygraphs and voice stress analyzers are only as good as the experts who administer them. In the hands of inexperienced administrators, they can be dangerous. Most experts agree that individuals who pass polygraph examinations are probably innocent, but that failure does not necessarily imply certain guilt.

Interviewing—An Overview

Interviewing is by far the most common technique used to investigate and resolve fraud. An *interview* is a question-and-answer session designed to elicit information. It differs from ordinary conversation in that it is structured (not free-form) and has a purpose. It is the systematic questioning of individuals who have knowledge of events, people, and evidence of a case under investigation. Good interviewers quickly zero in on suspects and can usually get admissions from guilty parties. Interviews also help obtain (1) information that establishes the essential elements of the crime, (2) leads for developing cases and gathering other evidence, (3) the cooperation of victims and witnesses, and (4) information on the personal backgrounds and motives of witnesses. Interviews are conducted with victims, complainants, contacts, informants, clients or customers, suspects, expert witnesses, police officers, clerks, janitors, co-workers, supervisors, disgruntled spouses or friends, vendors and former vendors, and anyone who might be helpful in the investigation. There are three types of interviews: (1) friendly, (2) neutral, and (3) hostile. Each type is handled differently.

The friendly interviewee goes above and beyond what is normally expected in order to be (or at least appear to be) helpful. Although friendly witnesses can be helpful, experienced investigators take care to determine their motives. In some cases, the motive truly is a sincere desire to help. However, possible motives also include a desire to get even with the suspect or to direct attention away from the interviewee as a suspect.

Neutral interviewees have nothing to gain or lose from the interview. They have no hidden motives or agendas, and they are usually the most objective and helpful of all interviewees.

Hostile interviewees are the most difficult to interview. They are often associated in some way with the suspect or the crime. Friendly and neutral interviewees can be questioned at any time, and appointments can be made in advance, but hostile interviewees should generally be questioned without prior notice. Surprise interviews provide hostile interviewees with less time to prepare defenses.

Characteristics of a Good Interview

Good interviews share common characteristics. Interviews should be of sufficient length and depth to uncover relevant facts. Most interviewers tend to get too little, rather than too much, information. A good interview focuses on pertinent information and quickly steers talk away from irrelevant information. Extraneous or useless facts unnecessarily complicate the gathering and analysis of information. Interviews should end on a positive note.

Interviews should be conducted as closely as possible to the event in question. With the passage of time, memories of potential witnesses and respondents become faulty, and critical details can be lost or forgotten. Good interviews are objective. They endeavor to gather information in a fair and impartial manner.

Characteristics of a Good Interviewer

Good interviewers share certain characteristics. Above all, they are "people persons," and interact well with others. Successful interviewers are people with whom others are willing to share information. Good interviewers do not interrupt respondents unnecessarily. Volunteered information, as opposed to responses to specific questions, is often pertinent information. Good interviewers display interest in the subject and in what is being said.

The person being interviewed (also called the respondent, interviewee, witness, suspect, or target) must understand that interviewers are attempting to obtain only the relevant facts and are not "out to get" someone. This can best be done by phrasing questions in a nonaccusatory manner. Little is accomplished when interviewers are formal, ostentatious, or attempt to impress respondents with their authority. Information gathering is best accomplished by interviewing in an informal and low-key manner.

If respondents perceive that interviewers are biased, or are attempting to confirm foregone conclusions, respondents are less likely to cooperate. Accordingly, interviewers should make every effort to demonstrate a lack of bias.

Professionalism in the interview often involves a state of mind and a commitment to excellence. Interviewers should be on time, be professionally attired, and be fair in all dealings with respondents. It is vital that interviewers not appear to be a threat, but rather as people who put others at ease. If respondents perceive that they are the target of an inquiry, they will be less likely to cooperate.

Understanding Reaction to Crisis

Fraud, like death or serious injury, is a crisis. People in crisis have a predictable sequence of reactions. Interviewers who understand these reactions are much more effective than interviewers who do not. The sequence of reactions is as follows:

1. Denial
2. Anger
3. Rationalization or bargaining
4. Depression
5. Acceptance

Denial functions as a buffer after people receive unexpected or shocking news. It allows people who are affected by or connected with the fraud to collect themselves and to mobilize other, less radical defenses. Denial screens out the reality of the situation. Some studies show that carefully balanced psychological and physiological systems must be maintained for people to function normally.[2] To avoid sudden and severe disruption of this psychological equilibrium, which can destroy or incapacitate a person, the most immediate recourse is denial, which is a strategy to maintain the status quo. Because people in denial refuse to acknowledge the stress at either the cognitive or the emotional level, they do not initiate behavioral changes that help them adjust to the new reality.

Denial takes many forms: People appear temporarily stunned or dazed; they refuse to accept the information given; they insist that there is some mistake; or they do not comprehend what has been said. Denial acts as a "shock absorber" to reduce the impact of sudden trauma. Denial of fraud gives perpetrators time to alter, destroy, or conceal valuable documents and records. It also creates delays, which can mean that witnesses disappear or become confused, and that valuable documentary evidence is lost. When denial cannot be maintained any longer, feelings of anger, rage, and resentment follow.

The anger stage is difficult to cope with, because anger is usually directed in every direction and it is also projected onto the environment—at times, even randomly. Anger arises because attempts to return to the old psychological status quo fail and are met with frustration. Suspects direct their anger at friends, relatives, and co-workers. Sometimes suspects direct their anger inward; this can result in feelings of guilt, but not always. Suspects are not the only ones to feel anger, however. Managers and other employees become hostile to auditors and investigators—perceive them as cruel or unfeeling, a reaction not unlike that of the ancient Greeks who murdered messengers bearing evil tidings.

The anger stage is a dangerous time to resolve frauds. While angry, managers and others can insult, harm, slander, or libel suspects and may terminate them without due cause. The result can be lawsuits—for slander, libel, assault, battery, or wrongful termination. An angry manager of a fast-food restaurant who believed an employee was stealing had the police handcuff the employee and drag him out of the store in front of customers. The employee, who was later found innocent, sued and won $250,000 in damages. In other situations, victims' angry reactions allowed criminals to get legal settlements larger than the amounts they stole.

People in the rationalization stage attempt to justify the dishonest act and/or to minimize the crime. During this stage, managers believe they understand why the crime was committed and often feel that the perpetrator's motivation was almost justifiable. Managers may feel during this period that the perpetrator is not really a bad person, that a mistake was made, and that perhaps he or she should be given one more chance. Interviews during this stage are often not objective and can be detrimental to attempts to uncover the truth, or harmful to future prosecution efforts. Rationalization leads to failure to prosecute, easy penalties, and weak testimonies. Rationalization is the last attempt of the affected group to return to the former psychologically steady state.

As attempts to resolve the problem fail, hope diminishes. Managers are faced with the emotional burden of the truth. As trauma emerges, symptoms of depression appear: people are sad, and many withdraw or lose interest in the environment. Like the stages of denial, anger, and rationalization, depression is a normal part of the coping process necessary for eventual psychological readjustment. In this stage, managers no longer deny or rationalize the dishonest act. Their anger is replaced by a sense of loss and disappointment—or sometimes embarrassment that the fraud happened on "their watch." During this stage, managers and others often become withdrawn and uncooperative. They may be unwilling to volunteer information or to assist with the investigation. Interviews conducted during this stage are often less useful than those held later. Thus, it is crucial to take the state of mind of potential witnesses into consideration during interviews.

Individuals experience different behaviors as they attempt to adjust to "life after fraud." A small fraud with minimal impact may only have a small psychological impact on individuals, whereas larger frauds with significant ramifications (such as embarrassment, loss of client, public exposure, or job jeopardy) often have larger psychological impacts. Individuals can cycle through the emotions of denial, anger, rationalization, and depression a number of times. Some people fluctuate between two phases as they strive to reach a new psychological equilibrium.

Eventually, people reach a state in which they no longer experience depression or anger; rather, they have a realistic understanding of what happened. Acceptance is not a happy state; it is an acknowledgement of what happened and a desire to resolve the issue and move on. This phase is often precipitated by a knowledge of the facts surrounding the fraud, including a knowledge of the motivations of the perpetrator. It is during this phase that interviews are most useful and witnesses most cooperative.

To demonstrate how these reactions play out during fraud investigations, consider the following fraud, which we discussed in Chapter 5. The case involved a supervisor in the shipping department of a wholesale-retail distribution center warehouse facility stealing over $5,000. The supervisor was responsible for overall operations of the warehouse and was also accountable for a cash fund used to give change (usually amounts between $25 and $500) to customers who came to the warehouse to pick up COD orders. The established procedures called for the supervisor to issue the customer a cash receipt, which was recorded in a will-call delivery logbook. The file containing details on the customer order was eventually matched with cash receipts by accounting personnel, and the transaction closed.

Over approximately one year, the supervisor stole small amounts of money. He concealed the fraud by submitting credit memos (with statements such as "billed to the wrong account," "to correct billing adjustment," and "miscellaneous") to clear the accounts receivable file. Per the procedures, the accounts were matched with the credit memo, and the transactions closed. A second signature was not needed on credit memos, and accounting personnel asked no questions about the supervisor's credit memos. At first, the supervisor submitted only two or three fraudulent credit memos a week, totaling approximately $100. After a few months, however, the amount increased to approximately $300 per week. To give the appearance of randomness, and to keep the accounting personnel from becoming suspicious, the supervisor intermixed comparatively large credit memo amounts with smaller ones.

The fraud surfaced when the supervisor accidentally credited the wrong customer's account for a cash transaction. By coincidence, the supervisor was on vacation when the error surfaced and was thus unable to cover his tracks when accounting personnel queried the transaction. Because of his absence, the accounts receivable clerk questioned the manager of the warehouse, who investigated the problem. The manager scrutinized cash receipts and determined that the potential for fraud existed.

Stage 1. Denial

Because of the possibility of fraud, the general manager and the warehouse manager started their own investigation of the warehouse cash fund. Sensing a serious problem, they decided to wait until the supervisor returned from vacation before taking further action. Both managers were anxious and somewhat irritable as they waited for the supervisor to return. Each manager later said that his work performance was adversely affected by the shock and their preoccupation with the problem. Both managers rationalized that the supervisor could probably explain the error; after all, he had been with the firm for three years and they considered him a model employee.

Later, after the close of the investigation, both managers admitted that they tried to deny that the falsified credit memos represented intentional fraud. Because of their denial, they didn't take advantage of readily available evidence during the suspected employee's absence.

Company procedure required managers to contact either corporate security or the internal audit department if a fraud was suspected. However, because they trusted the supervisor, both managers convinced themselves that there was no possibility of fraud—that the whole thing was a mistake. When the supervisor returned from vacation, the managers asked him to discuss the situation. Still in the denial stage, the managers simply asked the supervisor to explain his handling of the cash fund. The supervisor—now thrown into his own first stage of crisis, denial—told them that he didn't know what they were talking about. Had he offered some explanation, the managers, who were still denying fraud, probably would have been satisfied and terminated their investigation.

But the supervisor denied the existence of the credit memos, and the managers knew this to be untrue, so they sent the supervisor back to work and also decided to investigate further. From an investigative standpoint, sending the supervisor back to his job was a risky action. He was again in control of the original credit memos and cash transaction logs and could have easily destroyed evidence. Simply "losing" the records would have concealed the fraud and jeopardized the investigation. At this point, the warehouse managers requested the assistance of internal audit to review the matter further. A full week passed before assistance was made available.

Stage 2. Anger

During this week's waiting period, both managers decided that fraud had indeed been committed. They discussed their feelings and decided to confront the employee. This time they vowed they would get answers. Clearly, both managers had progressed from denial to anger. Without additional information that a full investigation could have provided, the managers confronted the supervisor and demanded an explanation. This time, the supervisor said nothing. Irate, the managers fired him on the spot, without additional explanation. Firings like this jeopardize investigations and companies in several ways. First, if fraud has not been committed, the company may be subjected to litigation and sued for wrongful dismissal, slander, or libel. Second, harsh treatment jeopardizes further cooperation by the perpetrator. In this case, the basis for the termination was the several falsified credit memorandums (totaling between $300 and $400) located by the managers.

The audit that followed revealed over 100 falsified credit memos and losses totaling more than $5,000. The managers were surprised at the extent of the fraud. Their accusing the supervisor of fraud well before they could clearly demonstrate his guilt made the corporation vulnerable to litigation and potential liability.

Stage 3. Bargaining and Rationalization

After the supervisor was summarily terminated, the general manager worried that both he and the warehouse manager had acted too quickly; perhaps they should have given him one more chance. They soon realized their actions opened the company to liability. Although rehiring the supervisor was contrary to company policy, the general manager still felt he could "save" this "valued" employee.

Through these rationalizations, the general manager was trying to come to terms with the fact that a trusted friend and employee committed a fraud against the firm. He was "bargaining"—that is, trying to change the facts in some way that gave an acceptable explanation, although none existed.

Stage 4. Depression
After bargaining came depression; both the general manager and the warehouse manager grew less irritated and became much more withdrawn. Feelings of depression enveloped both individuals as they realized the scope of the situation. Their depression was reinforced by comments and reactions from other warehouse employees, as details of the fraud emerged. Interestingly enough, during this period neither manager discussed his feelings with the other. Rather, they kept their feelings to themselves, apparently because they felt that the employee had suffered enough and that the case should be closed.

Stage 5. Acceptance
The investigation conducted by corporate security and internal audit revealed the following facts:

- The supervisor had a substance abuse problem involving cocaine and alcohol. As a result of his confrontation with management, he was considering rehabilitation.
- The supervisor convinced himself that he was simply borrowing the money. He rationalized that he had every intention of repaying the money borrowed, but he was also caught up in the machinations of the fraud and expressed surprise that in less than one year he defrauded the company of over $5,000.
- The supervisor informed security personnel that he had spent almost his entire life savings on cocaine and had lost his family in the process. Losing his job was the last straw.
- In discussions with local management, investigators learned that several managers and employees had noticed a change in the supervisor's behavior over the previous several months. The changes, which no one acted on, included frequent mood swings; frequent tardiness and absenteeism; and a preoccupation with impressing other employees by taking them out to lunch, during which the supervisor chattered relentlessly.

Once these facts were known, both managers accepted the fraud as a reality and felt that they were back in control of the situation. Their desire at that point was to resolve the situation and get back to normal.

This fraud is typical of the reactions of innocent bystanders in a fraud. Interviewers who recognize and understand these reactions, who tailor their questions and interview approaches to the reaction stages their interviewees are in, and who can nudge interviewees to the acceptance stage will have much more successful interviews.

Planning an Interview

When you conduct interviews, follow a plan or outline to make sure that you meet your objectives. Proper planning allows you to get the most from the interview and to minimize the time spent. Such planning involves ascertaining in advance as many facts as possible about the offense and the interviewee, and establishing a location and time for the interview that are conducive to success.

To obtain facts about the offense and the interviewee, review relevant documents to gather as much other information as possible about the following factors:

The offense
- Legal nature of the offense
- Date, time, and place of occurrence

- Manner in which the crime appears to have been committed
- Possible motives
- All available evidence

The interviewee

- Personal background information—age, education, marital status, etc.
- Attitude toward investigation
- Any physical or mental conditions, such as alcohol or drug use

It is usually best (except with hostile interviewees) to conduct interviews at the interviewee's office or workplace, so that interviewees can access necessary papers, books, and other evidence. In addition, such locations are generally more convenient for interviewees. The interview room should be one where distractions from colleagues and telephones are nonexistent or minimal.

With friendly or neutral interviewees, set up an appointment and allow sufficient (even excess) time for the interview. When you set up the appointment, identify information that the interviewee will need. Wherever possible, interview only one person at a time.

The Interviewer's Demeanor

Take special pains to be efficient, courteous, polite, and careful with the language you use during interviews. Here are some suggestions:

- Sit fairly close to the interviewee with no desk or furniture between you. Don't walk around the room; stay seated.
- Do not talk down to the person. (Don't assume the person is less intelligent than you.)
- Be sensitive to the personal concerns of the witness, especially with regard to such matters as sex, race, religion, and ethnic background.
- Be businesslike. Conduct the interview in a professional manner. Be friendly but not social. Remember that you seek the truth; you are not trying to get a confession or a conviction.
- Avoid being authoritarian; do not dominate the interview.
- Be sympathetic and respectful. (If appropriate, tell the witness that anyone under similar conditions or circumstances might do the same thing.)
- Give careful thought to your language. Don't use technical jargon.
- Thank the witness for taking the time and trouble to cooperate.
- Keep pencil and paper out of sight during the interview.
- End every cooperative interview by expressing your sincere appreciation.

The Language of Interviews

Language is very important in interviews. Successful interviewers adhere to specific guidelines:

- Use short questions, confined to one topic, which can be clearly and easily understood.
- Ask questions that require narrative answers; whenever possible, avoid eliciting yes and no answers.
- Avoid questions that suggest part of the answer (called leading questions).
- Require witnesses to give the factual basis for any conclusions they state.
- Prevent witnesses from aimlessly wandering. Require direct responses.
- Don't let witnesses lead you away from the topic. Don't let them confuse the issue or leave basic questions unanswered.

- At any given point, concentrate more on the answer you are hearing than on the next question you plan to ask.
- Clearly understand each answer before you continue.
- Maintain full control of the interview.
- Point out some, but not all, of the circumstantial evidence.

Question Typology

Interviewers ask five types of questions: introductory, informational, assessment, closing, and admission-seeking. In routine interviews, where your objective is to gather information from neutral or friendly witnesses, only three of the five types are normally asked: introductory, informational, and closing questions. If you have reasonable cause to believe the respondent is not being truthful, then ask assessment questions. Finally, if you decide with reasonable cause that the respondent is responsible for misdeeds, admission-seeking questions can be posed.

Introductory Questions Interviewers use introductory questions for two purposes: to start the interview, and to get the respondent to verbally agree to cooperate. This is done in a step-by-step procedure in which you briefly state the purpose for the contact, then pose a question designed to get the respondent to agree to talk further.

Informational Questions Once the proper format for the interview is set, interviewers turn to the fact-gathering portion. Three types of questions are asked: open, closed, and leading. (We discuss these in more detail later in the chapter.) Each question type is used in a logical sequence in order to maximize the development of information. If you have reason to believe that the respondent is being untruthful, then pose assessment questions. Otherwise, bring the interview to a logical close.

Closing Questions In routine interviews, certain questions are asked at closing in order to reconfirm the facts, obtain previously undiscovered information, seek new evidence, and maintain goodwill. These three questions should always be asked in closing: (1) Do you know anyone else I should talk to? (2) Is there anything I have forgotten to ask that you believe would be relevant? And (3) if I need to talk to you again, would that be all right?

Assessment Questions If interviewers have reason to believe the respondent is being deceptive, certain types of hypothetical, nonaccusatory questions are posed. By observing the verbal and nonverbal responses of the respondent to these questions, you can assess the respondent's credibility with some degree of accuracy. Your assessment will form the basis of your decision about whether to pose admission-seeking questions to obtain a legal admission of wrongdoing.

Admission-Seeking Questions Admission-seeking interviews are reserved for individuals whose culpability is reasonably certain. Admission-seeking questions are posed in an exact order designed to (1) clear an innocent person or (2) encourage a culpable person to confess. These questions must not violate the rights and privileges of the person being interviewed.

Elements of Conversation

Since interviews are essentially structured conversations, it is helpful to understand the basic elements of effective communication. Whenever two or more human beings converse, several types of communication occur—either one at a time or in combination.

Expression A common function of conversation is self-expression in which one or more of the conversationalists express ideas, feelings, attitudes, or moods. The illusion of an audience is central to personal expression. The urge for spontaneous expression can be a vital asset in interviewing, and it should be encouraged in respondents. It can be directed by interviewers toward information-gathering objectives. A common error made by novice interviewers is yielding to the temptation to impress respondents with their knowledge of the subject of the interview. In doing so, interviewers risk making respondents feel threatened, resulting in respondents giving guarded responses rather than expressing their feelings frankly. Experienced interviewers have the discipline to control their own responses.

Persuasion. Persuasion and expression differ in that persuasion endeavors to convince the other person. There are times when persuasion can be effective in interviews; it is mostly used to convince respondents of the legitimacy of the interview.

Therapy. Making people feel good about themselves is often a function of effective communication. In our conversations with friends, we frequently express ideas and feelings to relieve emotional tension. This release, called *catharsis,* is encouraged in psychiatric interviews. There are many times when the information sought in an interview is closely related to the respondent's inner conflicts and tensions. For example, people embezzling money typically feel guilty. Skillful interviewers know the therapeutic implication of releasing such feelings in their attempts to develop information.

Ritual. Some aspects of conversation are ritualistic; that is, they are cultural expressions that have no significance other than to provide security in interpersonal relations. Examples include "Good morning!" and "How are you today?" It behooves you to learn to detect ritualistic answers by respondents, and to avoid giving them yourself. Be aware of the danger of engaging in ritualistic conversation; you don't want to confuse the results with valid information.

Information Exchange. Information exchange is the central purpose of interviews. The word "exchange" reminds us that the flow of information in interviews goes both ways. Interviewers are often so focused on the information they wish to obtain that they fail to properly exchange information with respondents. Although you should measure the details carefully, don't be "cagey." This tactic rarely works. Two basic problems occur in the exchange of information. One, the information sought by interviewers is not of equal importance to respondents. And second, communication barriers often exist between people of diverse backgrounds. These barriers are also common between strangers.

Inhibitors of Communication

To be an effective interviewer, you must understand that certain matters inhibit communication and others facilitate it. It is your task to minimize inhibitors and maximize facilitators. An *inhibitor* is any sociopsychological barrier that impedes the flow of relevant information by making respondents unable or unwilling to provide information. Carefully examine the eight inhibitors to communication listed below. The first four make respondents unwilling to cooperate; the last four make them unable to give information, even though they may be willing to do so.

Competing Demands for Time Respondents may hesitate to begin an interview because of other demands on their time. They are not necessarily placing a negative value on being interviewed, but are instead weighing the value of being interviewed against doing something else. Successful interviewers convince respondents that the interview is a good use of their time.

Threatened Egos Respondents in some cases withhold information because of a perceived threat to their self-esteem. There are three broad responses to ego threats: repression, disapproval, and loss of status.

- *Repression.* The strongest response to a threatened ego is repression. Respondents not only refuse to admit information, but they also refuse to admit the information inwardly. They are being honest when they answer that they don't know; they have truly "forgotten" (repressed) it. Embezzlers, for example, repress their memory of the act because it does not conform to their moral code.
- *Disapproval.* A less intense but more common response to threatened egos is found when respondents possess information but hesitate to admit it because they anticipate disapproval from the interviewer. If respondents are made to feel that the interviewer will not condemn them, they may welcome the opportunity to divulge information. A generally accepting and sympathetic attitude toward respondents goes a long way toward eliciting candid responses.
- *Loss of Status.* Sometimes respondents fear losing status if the information provided becomes public. This can sometimes be overcome by assuring them that the information will be handled confidentially.

Etiquette The etiquette barrier operates when an answer to a question contains information that the respondent perceives as inappropriate. Answering candidly would be considered in poor taste or evidence of a lack of proper etiquette. For example, there are certain things that men do not discuss comfortably in front of women and vice versa, that students do not tell teachers, and that doctors do not tell patients. The desire to avoid embarrassing, shocking, or threatening answers is distinct from the fear of exposing oneself. Often, the negative effects of the etiquette barrier can be forestalled by selecting the appropriate interviewer and setting for the interview.

Trauma Trauma denotes an acutely unpleasant feeling associated with crisis experiences. The unpleasant feeling is often brought to the surface when the respondent is reporting the experience. Trauma is common when talking to victims, and can usually be overcome by sensitive handling of the issue.

Forgetting A frequent inhibitor to communication is the respondent's inability to recall certain types of information. This is not a problem if the objectives of the interview deal only with current attitudes, beliefs, or expectations. The natural fading of memory over time makes it easier for the ego-defense system to reconstruct our own image of the past by omission, addition, or distortion.

The memory problem is a much more frequent obstacle than interviewers generally expect. Even the most simple and obvious facts cannot always be elicited. Three factors contribute to our recollection of an event.

First, the vividness of our recall relates to the event's original emotional impact, its meaningfulness at the time, and the degree to which our ego is involved. A second factor is the amount of time that has elapsed since the event. Third is the nature of the interview situation, including the interviewer's techniques and tactics. Knowledge of these factors will help you anticipate where problems may arise. And certain techniques (discussed later) will help you overcome many memory problems.

Chronological Confusion Chronological confusion is commonly encountered in interviews that seek case history information. This term refers to the respondent's tendency to confuse the order of events. This occurs in two ways: First, two or more events are correctly recalled, but the respondent is unsure of the sequence. Or, only one event is recalled, and it is incorrectly assumed to have been true at an earlier point.

Inferential Confusion This term denotes confusion and inaccuracies that result from errors of inference. These errors fall into two categories: induction and deduction. In *induction,* the respondent is asked to convert concrete experiences into a higher level of generalization. In *deduction,* the respondent is asked to give concrete examples of certain categories of experience.

Unconscious Behavior Often, interview objectives call for information about a person's unconscious behavior. There are three types of unconscious behavior: *custom* or *habit; circular reaction* (the immediate, unwitting response of one person to the subliminal, nonverbal clues of another, which arises under special circumstances); and *acute emotional crisis* (where the behavior does not follow a habitual pattern and where it does not result from a reaction to others).

Facilitators of Communication

Facilitators of communication are those sociopsychological forces that make conversations, including interviews, easier to accomplish. Facilitators require a basic understanding of what motivates people.

Fulfilling Expectations An important force in social interaction is our tendency to communicate, verbally or nonverbally, our expectations to the other person. The other person then tends to respond, consciously or unconsciously, to our expectations. This is one manifestation of the human tendency to conform to the group and to the anticipations of higher-status persons. It is in this conformity to group norms that security is sought.

In the interview setting, interviewers routinely communicate expectations to respondents. Strive to transmit both your general expectation of cooperation, as well as a more specific expectation that the respondent will answer the questions truthfully. Clearly distinguish between asking for information and expecting it. The former is mainly verbal communication; the latter is accomplished through nonverbal behavior.

Recognition We all need the recognition and the esteem of others. Social interaction often depends on an exchange of social goods. People "perform" in exchange for recognition and other social rewards. The need for recognition can be fulfilled by attention from people outside a person's social circle. Skillful and insightful interviewers take advantage of every opportunity to give respondents sincere recognition.

Altruistic Appeals Some people need to identify with a "higher" value or cause beyond their immediate self-interest. This sometimes takes the form of identifying with the objectives of the larger group. Altruistic deeds usually increase self-esteem whether or not the deeds are made public. This distinguishes altruism from publicity. Altruism is of major importance in motivating many respondents. Interviewers who understand their respondent's value system can use strategy and techniques that appeal to altruism.

Sympathetic Understanding We all need the sympathetic response of others. We like to share our joys, fears, successes, and failures. Our need for understanding differs from our need for recognition, which requires success and increased status. Interviewers who reflect a sympathetic attitude and who know how to direct that attitude toward the objectives of their interview find their percentages of success much higher than those who lack such abilities.

New Experience Some people welcome new experiences. Although variety is not everybody's spice of life, escape from dreary routine is sought by almost everyone. Sometimes respondents are motivated by curiosity regarding the interviewer. Experienced interviewers consider this when deciding what to say about themselves. Do not assume that just because an interview is a new experience it will satisfy the respondent's needs. Aspects of the respondent's perception of the new experience can also be ego-threatening. Respondents may be anxious about the impression they leave with interviewers. This apprehensiveness can often be detected at the beginning of the interview. Once these fears are dispelled, respondents frequently find interviews a new and interesting experience.

Catharsis *Catharsis* is the process by which we obtain release from unpleasant emotional tensions by talking about the source of these tensions. We often feel better after we talk about something that upsets us. Although we are all familiar with our own experiences with catharsis, we don't always perceive this need in others. After respondents confess, they may indicate that they feel much better about themselves. The need for sympathetic understanding and the need for catharsis are related, but they are not the same thing. Interviewers who do not have time to listen to what they consider inconsequential egocentric talk often find respondents unwilling to share important information.

Need for Meaning Another trait common to all of us is our need for meaning. Every society has a set of assumptions, values, explanations, and myths that serves to create order in the society. Our need for meaning is related to cognitive dissonance, the psychological tension we feel when we are aware of inconsistent facts, assumptions, and interpretations. This tension is painful, and reducing it is rewarding. In cases where the interview topic deals directly with information that disturbs a person's need for meaning, respondents are often strongly motivated to talk it through, if they are convinced of the interviewer's interest.

Extrinsic Rewards This term refers to rewards that motivate the respondent (other than those gained directly from being involved in the interview). Extrinsic rewards are helpful insofar as respondents see the interview as a means to an end. Various extrinsic rewards can come into play in interview situations, including money, job advancement, and retention of privileges. Remember that what is extrinsic to you as interviewer may not be extrinsic to respondents. Sensitive interviewers recognize what extrinsic rewards, if any, respondents receive from being interviewed.

Introductory Questions

One of the most difficult aspects of interviews is getting started. Indeed, the introduction is often the hardest part. In many instances, interviewers and respondents have not met before. Interviewers have a tall order: Meet the person, state a reason for the interview, establish necessary rapport, and get the information. The introduction is accomplished through questions as opposed to statements. Questions allow you to assess the respondent's feedback. This is an important aspect of the introduction. If the respondent is reluctant to be interviewed, that fact will come out through the introductory questions. They are designed to meet the objectives below.

Provide the Introduction Obviously, you must introduce yourself as the interview commences. You should generally indicate your name and company; avoid titles. This is not always the case, but the more informal the interview, generally the more relaxed the respondent.

Establish Rapport Webster's defines *rapport* as a "relation marked by harmony, conformity, accord, or affinity." In other words, establish some common ground before you begin your questioning. This is usually accomplished by spending a few minutes in "small talk." This aspect, however, should not be overdone. Most people are aware that the interviewer is not there to chit-chat.

Establish the Interview Theme State the purpose of your interview in some way prior to the commencement of serious questioning. Otherwise, the respondent may be confused, threatened, or overly cautious. Stating the purpose of the interview is known as "establishing the interview theme."

Observe Reactions You need to become skilled in interpreting the respondent's reactions to questions. Social scientists say that more than half the communication between individuals is nonverbal. You must, therefore, observe systematically (though in an offhand, unobtrusive manner) the various responses respondents give during interviews.

There are systematic ways to observe reactions. First pose nonsensitive questions as you establish rapport. During this phase, find some common ground so that you can "connect" with the respondent. As you establish rapport through normal conversation, observe the respondent's reactions. This is your baseline for observing later behavior, when you ask more sensitive questions. If the respondent's verbal and nonverbal behavior is inconsistent from one type of question to another, you can then attempt to determine why.

Develop the Interview Theme The interview theme may relate only indirectly to the actual purpose of the interview. The goal of the theme is to get the respondent to "buy in" to assisting in the interview. Generally, the most effective interview theme is that help is being sought. Nearly all of us get satisfaction from helping others.

In most interviews, it is best to treat respondents in such a manner that they feel important about helping. During this phase of the interview, respondents must not feel threatened in any way. An effective approach is the "Columbo-style" (although perhaps not so crumpled), in which at least two thoughts go through the mind of Columbo's subjects: (1) He is no threat to me; and (2) he really needs my help. In the following examples, assume you are introducing yourself.

WRONG	***RIGHT***
Interviewer: "I am ______ ______, a Certified Fraud Examiner with the store's fraud examination unit. I am investigating a case of suspected fraud, and you may know something about it. How long have you worked here at the company?"	Interviewer: "I'm ______ ______. I work here at the company. Have we met before?" Respondent: "I don't think so." Interviewer: "I am working on an assignment and I need your help. Do you have a few minutes I can spend with you now?"

Methodology

Respondents must perceive that they have something in common with you as interviewer, and should be made to feel good about the situation. This is best accomplished when respondents perceive you as open and friendly.

Make Physical Contact One way to promote respondents' perception of your being open and friendly is to shake hands at the beginning of the interview. Making physical contact helps break down psychological barriers to communication. (*Caution:* Do not invade the respondent's personal space; this makes people uncomfortable.)

Use body language to create the impression of trust during the interview: Gesture openly with your arms, clasp your hands together, and lean forward to indicate interest. You can also establish rapport verbally by using soft words, agreeing with the respondent, and avoiding negative terms.

Establish the Purpose of the Interview The purpose of your interview must be established. Obviously, when you make official contact with respondents, some reason must be given. The reason or purpose of your interview should be general and not specific. The specific purpose will be stated later. The general purpose for the interview should be one that is logical for respondents to accept and easy for you to explain. Normally, the more general, the better.

Example:

Interviewer:

"I'm working on a matter and I need your help."

OR

"I'm reviewing procedures here at the company."

OR

"I'm developing information on our purchasing procedures."

Don't Interview More Than One Person at a Time One basic rule—question only one person at a time. The testimony of one respondent will invariably influence the testimony of another. There are few hard and fast rules in interviewing, but this is one of them.

Conduct the Interview in Private Another basic rule—conduct interviews under conditions of privacy. Interviews are best conducted out of the sight and sound of friends, relatives, or fellow employees. People are reluctant to furnish information within the hearing of others.

Ask Nonsensitive Questions Sensitive questions should be scrupulously avoided until well into the interview. And then ask such questions *only* after careful deliberation and planning. During the introductory phase, avoid emotionally charged words of all types. Such words often put people on the defensive, and they are then reluctant to answer and even less likely to cooperate.

Nonsensitive Words

Instead of	Use
Investigation	*Inquiry*
Audit	*Review*
Interview	*Ask a few questions*
Embezzle/steal/theft	*Shortage or paperwork problems*

Get a Commitment for Assistance Failure to get a commitment from the respondent to assist you is a common mistake made even by experienced interviewers. This is a critical step and sets the tone of the entire interview. A commitment of assistance requires positive action on the part of the respondent. Remaining silent or simply nodding the head is generally not sufficient.

Ask for the commitment before the interview commences, and encourage respondents to voice that "yes" aloud. If you encounter silence the first time, repeat the question in a slightly different way until respondents verbalize commitment.

Example:

Interviewer:
"I'm _____ _____ with the company. I'm reviewing our sales returns and allowances. Do you have a few minutes?"

Respondent:
"Yes."

Interviewer:
"I'm gathering some information on certain company procedures. Maybe you can help me?"

Respondent:
(No response.)

Interviewer:
"Could I get you to help me, if you can?"

Respondent:
"Yes. What's this about?"

Establish a Transitional Statement At this point, you have a commitment for assistance and must now describe in more detail the purpose of the interview. This is done with a transitional statement that provides a legitimate basis for your inquiry, and explains to respondents how they fit into the inquiry. You can usually accomplish this using a broad, rather than a narrow, description. Note that employees in the same company will frequently assume that your request for assistance is legitimate. After describing the basic nature of the inquiry with the transitional statement, seek a second commitment for assistance.

Example:

Interviewer:
"I'm gathering some information about the sales return function and how it's supposed to work. It would be very helpful if I could start by asking you to basically tell me about your job. Okay?"

When interviewing complete strangers, you may have to give particulars about how the respondent's assistance is needed. This can be accomplished by one or more of the methods illustrated below.

Example:

Interviewer:
"It's pretty routine, really. As I say, I work for _______________ and I've been asked to gather information about some of their procedures. I thought it might be helpful to talk to you. Okay?"

OR

"It's pretty routine. I've been asked by the company to gather information on some of their procedures. I thought you might be able to help by answering a few questions. Okay?"

OR
"It's pretty routine, really. I've been asked by your company to gather some information, and they suggested I could contact you. Okay?"

Seek Continuous Agreement Throughout the process—from the introduction to the close—attempt to phrase questions that can be answered "yes." People find it easier to reply in the affirmative than the negative:

Example:
Interviewer:
"Okay?"
"Can you help me?"
"That's okay, isn't it?"

Do Not Invade Body Space During the introductory part of the interview, you should generally remain at a distance of four to six feet. Do not invade the respondent's personal zone (closer than about three feet), as it will make many respondents uncomfortable.

Set up the interview in a way where the respondent is free and clear—where you can see that person's movement from head to toe. You don't want to interview someone who is sitting behind his desk.

Informational Questions

Informational questions are nonconfrontational, nonthreatening, and are asked for information-gathering purposes. The great majority of questions fall into this category. Applications include:

- Interviews to gain an understanding of accounting control systems
- Interviews concerning documents
- Gathering information regarding business operations or systems
- Preemployment interviews

Informational questions seek to elicit unbiased factual information. Good interviewers are alert to inconsistency in facts or behavior. Informational questions—as well as others—fall into several general categories: open, closed, leading, double-negative, complex, and attitude.

Open Questions Open questions are worded in a way that makes it difficult to answer "yes" or "no." Typical open questions call for a monologue response, and can be answered in several different ways. During the informational phase of the interview, you should endeavor to ask primarily open questions. This stimulates conversation. Informational questions are open-ended questions and force more lengthy responses. Here is an open-ended question:

> *Do me a favor and just sort of explain what the purpose of a three parter is—how it gets filled out—these kinds of things.*

Here are a few other examples:

Example:
Interviewer:
"Please tell me about your job."
"Please tell me about the operation of your department."

"What do you think about this problem?"	"Please describe the procedures to me."

Closed Questions Closed questions require a precise answer—usually "yes" or "no." Closed questions also deal with specifics, such as amounts, dates, and times. As far as possible, avoid closed questions in the informational part of the interview. They are used extensively in closing questions, described later. Examples include:

Interviewer: "Do you work here?"	"What day of the week did it happen?"

Leading Questions Leading questions contain the answer as a part of the question. Most commonly, they are used to confirm already known facts. Although leading questions are usually discouraged in court proceedings, they can be effective in interviews. Here is a leading question:

> *All right, so you started here in November of '88—after working for Panasonic—to the best of your recollection?*

Double-Negative Questions Questions or statements that contain double negatives are confusing and often suggest an answer opposite to the correct one. Do not use them. Here is an example:

> Interviewer:
> "Didn't you suspect that something wasn't right?"

Complex Questions Complex questions and statements are not easily understood, cover more than one subject or topic, require more than one answer, and/or require a complicated answer. Simply put, avoid them—here is an example:

> Interviewer:
> "What are your duties here, and how long have you been employed?"

Attitude Questions Your attitude is conveyed not only by the structure of your questions and statements, but also by the manner in which you ask them. When you wish to establish a friendly mood, employ questions such as these:

Interviewer: "How are you doing this morning?"	"Do you like sports?"

It is always a good idea, however, to ask a question to which you know beforehand that the answer will be "yes."

Question Sequence

As a general rule, questioning should proceed from the general to the specific; that is, seek general information before you seek details. A variation is to "reach backward" with questions by beginning with known information and working toward unknown areas. An efficient way to do this is to recount the known information and then frame the next question as a logical continuation of the facts previously related. Figures and numbers are critical in accounting and fraud-related matters; unfortunately, witnesses aren't always able to recall specific amounts. You can jog the respondent's memory by comparing unknown items with items of known quantity:

Interviewer:
"Was the amount of money involved more than last year's figure?"

Controlled-Answer Techniques *Controlled-answer techniques* or statements are used to stimulate a desired answer or impression. These techniques direct the interview toward a specific point. For example, it may be possible to get a person to admit knowledge of a matter by phrasing the question thus: *"I understand you were present when the internal controls were developed, so would you please describe how they were constructed?"* This phrasing provides a stronger incentive for the respondent to admit knowledge than does *"Were you present when the internal controls were developed?"*

To stimulate the person to agree to talk or to provide information, you can use an example such as, *"Because you're not involved in this matter, I'm sure you wouldn't mind discussing it with me."* This provides a stronger incentive to cooperate than *"Do you have any objections to telling me what you know?"* Avoid negative constructions, such as, *"I don't guess you would mind answering a few questions."*

Free Narratives The *free narrative* is an orderly, continuous account of an event or incident, given with or without prompting. It is used to quickly summarize what is known about a matter. Be sure to explicitly designate the occurrence that you wish to discuss. Sometimes respondents must be controlled to prevent unnecessary digression. Otherwise, use a minimum of interruptions, and do not stop the narrative without good reason. Respondents will sometimes provide valuable clues when talking about things that are only partially related to the matter under inquiry.

Informational Question Techniques

The following suggestions improve the quality of interviews during the information-gathering phase:

- Begin by asking questions that are not likely to cause respondents to become defensive or hostile.
- Ask questions in a manner that develops the facts in the order of their occurrence, or in some other systematic order.
- Ask only one question at a time, and frame the question so that only one answer is required.

- Ask straightforward and frank questions; generally avoid shrewd approaches.
- Give respondents ample time to answer; do not rush.
- Try to help respondents remember, but do not suggest answers; be careful not to imply any particular answer by facial expressions, gestures, methods of asking questions, or types of questions asked.
- Repeat or rephrase questions, if necessary, to get the desired facts.
- Be sure you understand the answers, and if they are not perfectly clear, have respondents interpret them at that time instead of saving this for later.
- Give respondents an opportunity to qualify their answers.
- Separate facts from inferences.
- Have respondents give comparisons by percentages, fractions, estimates of time and distance, and other such comparisons to ascertain accuracy.
- Get all of the facts; almost every respondent can give you information beyond what was initially provided.
- After respondents give a narrative account, ask questions about the items discussed.
- Upon concluding the direct questioning, summarize the facts and have respondents verify that these conclusions are correct.

Note-Taking

As stated previously, note-taking is problematic during interviews. That said, interviewers will frequently need to take some notes. If this need arises, start each interview on a separate sheet of paper. This procedure is especially helpful should documents from a particular interview be subpoenaed. Do not try to write down all the information you are given during an interview, only the pertinent facts. Taking too many notes makes the interview process cumbersome and can inhibit respondents. If a quote is particularly relevant, try to write it down verbatim. Enclose all direct quotations in quotation marks. Do not slow down the interview process for note-taking. Instead, jot down key words or phrases, then go back over the details at the end of the interview. In general, it is better to err on the side of taking too few notes rather than too many.

If a record of an interview is necessary, taping the interview is a desirable alternative to extensive notes. While permission to tape an interview must usually be received from the interviewee, the tape recorder does not normally distract, once the interview begins.

Maintain Eye Contact Maintain eye contact with respondents in a normal way during note-taking. Just as eye contact personalizes other human communication, it also creates a more comfortable environment and facilitates the flow of information during interviews.

Opinions Avoid making notes regarding your overall opinions or impressions of a witness. Such notes can cause problems with your credibility if they are later produced in court. Be careful not to show excitement when note-taking. During interviews of targets and adverse witnesses, take notes in a manner that does not indicate the significance of the information; that is, never allow note-taking to "telegraph" your emotions.

Writing Down Questions Whenever possible, do not write down a list of interview questions. Let the interview flow freely. Inadvertently allowing respondents to read a written list of questions gives them an opportunity to fabricate answers. Writing down key points you want to discuss is appropriate, however.

Documenting Results Document the results of the interview as soon as possible after its conclusion—preferably immediately afterward. If this procedure is followed, you will not have to take copious notes during the interview. Law enforcement officials are generally required to maintain notes. In the private sector, the notes can usually be destroyed once a memorandum has been prepared summarizing the interview. Check with your lawyer when in doubt.

Observing Respondent Reactions

Interviewers must be knowledgeable about behavior during interviews. Most nonverbal clues fall within one of four categories: proxemics, chronemics, kinetics, or paralinguistics.

Proxemics

Proxemic communication is the use of interpersonal space to convey meaning. The relationship between interviewer and respondent is both a cause and an effect of proxemic behavior. If the distance between interviewer and respondent is greater, they both tend to watch each other's eyes for clues to meaning.

It is therefore important that the conversation occur at an acceptable distance. Correct conversational distances vary from one culture to another. In the Middle East, the distance is quite short; in Latin America, equals of the same sex carry on a conversation at a much closer distance than in North America. Often, as the subject matter of the interview changes, interviewers can note the changes in the proxemic behavior of respondents. If respondents are free to back away, they might do so when the topic becomes unpleasant or sensitive.

Chronemics

Chronemic communication refers to the use of time in interpersonal relationships to convey meaning, attitudes, and desires. For example, respondents who are late in keeping appointments may convey a lack of interest in the interview or may wish to avoid it.

The most important chronemic technique used by interviewers is in their timing of questions. Effective interviewers control the length of pauses and the rate of their speech. This is called *pacing*. Interviewers can also control the length of time after respondents finish a sentence before they pose another question. This is called the *silent probe*.

Pacing is one of the principal nonverbal ways to set an appropriate mood. Tense interviewers often communicate anxiety by a rapid-fire rate of speech, which in turn can increase anxiety in respondents. To establish the more thoughtful, deliberative mood that stimulates free association, interviewers strive to set a relaxed, deliberate pace.

Kinetics

Kinetic communication has to do with how body movements convey meaning. Even though posture, hands, and feet all communicate meaning, interviewers tend to focus attention on the face and are more accurate in their judgments of others if they can see facial movements and expressions. When you concentrate on facial expressions, your primary interest is eye contact. Eye contact primarily communicates the desire to make or avoid communication. People who feel shame normally drop their eyes to avoid returning glances. This not only avoids seeing the disapproval, but also conceals personal shame and confusion.

Paralinguistics

Paralinguistic communication involves the use of volume, pitch, and voice quality to convey meaning. One basic difference between written and verbal communication is that oral speech gives the full range of nonverbal cues. For example, a "no" answer may not really mean no; it depends on how the "no" is said.

Theme Development

All questions should be nonaccusatory during the information-seeking phase. Nothing closes up the lines of communication in interviews like accusatory questions. Therefore, be sure to formulate your questions in a way that does not elicit strong emotional reactions. *Move from nonsensitive to sensitive.* If respondents start to become uncomfortable with the questioning, go on to a different area and return to the sensitive question later, but from a different vantage point.

Some people do not volunteer information; they must be asked. You must not be reluctant to ask sensitive questions after you have established the proper basis. If you pose the question with confidence and show that you expect an answer, respondents are much more likely to furnish the requested information. If you are apologetic or lack confidence in the question, respondents are much less likely to answer.

Methodology

Once the introduction has been completed, you need a transition into the body of the interview. This is usually accomplished by asking respondents an easy question about themselves or their duties—for example:

Can you tell me what it is that you do as far as quality control?

Begin with Background Questions

Assuming that respondents do not have a problem answering the transitional question, you should then ask a series of easy, open questions designed to get them to talk about themselves.

Example:

Interviewer:

"What is your exact title?"

"What do your responsibilities involve?"

"How long have you been assigned here?"

"What do you like best about your job?"

"What do you like least about your job?"

"What would you eventually like to do for the company?"

Observe Verbal and Nonverbal Behavior

During the period when respondents talk about themselves, discreetly observe their verbal and nonverbal behavior. This will be discussed later in the chapter.

Ask Nonleading (Open) Questions

Open questioning techniques are used almost exclusively in the informational phase of interviews. The questions should seek information in a nonaccusatory way. Remember, the most effective questions are constructed as a subtle command.

Example:

Interviewer:

"Please tell me about ______________."

"Please tell me about your current job procedures."

"Please tell me what paperwork you are responsible for."

"Please explain the chain of command in your department."

"Please tell me what procedures are in effect to prevent errors in the paperwork."

"Please explain what you understand to be the system of checks and balances (or internal controls) in your department."

"Please explain where you see areas that need to be improved in the system of checks and balances in your department."

Once respondents answer open questions, you can go back and review the facts in greater detail. If the answers are inconsistent, try to clarify them. But do not challenge the honesty or integrity of respondents at this point.

Approach Sensitive Questions Carefully
Words such as "routine questions" play down the significance of the inquiry. It is important for information-gathering purposes that you do not react excessively to respondents' statements. In the following example, the interviewer is talking to a potential witness, and has decided to bring up the sensitive topic of a possible defalcation within the company. Several initial approaches could be used.

> ***Example:***
> Interviewer:
> "Part of my job is to prevent and uncover waste, fraud, and abuse. You understand that, don't you?"
> OR
> "Please tell me where you think the company is wasting assets or money."
> OR
> "Where do you think the company is vulnerable to someone here abusing his position?"

Dealing with Resistance

There is always the possibility that respondents will refuse a request for an interview. When respondent and interviewer have no connection, studies show that as many as 65% of the respondents will refuse an interview if contacted first by telephone. In contrast, one study concluded that only a third of respondents are reluctant to be interviewed when contacted in person.[3] The more unpleasant the topic, the more likely respondents are to refuse.

Inexperienced interviewers sometimes perceive resistance when there is none. As a result, interviewers frequently become defensive. You must overcome such feelings to complete the interview. Here are some examples of resistance you will encounter and how to try to overcome it.

"I'm Too Busy" When you contact a respondent without a previous appointment, the respondent may be too busy at the moment to cooperate. "I'm too busy" is also used to disguise the real source of the person's resistance, which may be lethargy, ego threat, or dislike of talking to strangers. Such objections can be overcome if you stress the following:

- The interview will be short.
- You are already there.
- The project is important.
- The interview will not be difficult.
- You need help.

"I Don't Know Anything About It" You will sometimes get this response immediately after stating the purpose of the interview. This resistance is typically softened by accepting the statement, and then returning with a question. For example, if the respondent says, "I don't know anything," a typical response would be:

Example: Interviewer: "I see. What do your duties involve, then?" OR	"Well, that was one of the things I wanted to find out. Do you know about internal controls, then?"

"I Don't Remember" This is not always an expression of resistance. Instead, it can also express modesty, tentativeness, or caution. One of the best ways to respond here is to simply remain silent while the person deliberates. He or she is saying, in effect, "Give me a moment to think." If this is not successful, you can then counter by posing a narrower question.

Example: Interviewer: "I understand you may not remember the entire transaction. Do you remember if it was over $10,000?"	OR "It's okay if you don't remember the details. Do you remember how it made you react at the time?"

"What Do You Mean by That?" When respondents ask this question, they may be signaling mild resistance. That is, they are attempting to shift the attention from themselves to you. They may also be stalling for time while they deliberate. Alternatively, they really may not understand your question. The best approach here is to treat the question as a simple request for clarification. Do not become defensive; to do so generally escalates the resistance.

Difficult People

Interviewers invariably encounter a few difficult people. Here are five commonsense steps to take with such individuals.

Don't React Sometimes respondents give interviewers a "hard time" for no apparent reason. In reality, there can be a multitude of reasons why people refuse to cooperate. There are three natural reactions for interviewers who are verbally assailed by respondents: strike back, give in, or terminate the interview. *Don't do them.* These tactics are not satisfactory; they do not lead to productive interviews. Instead, you should consciously ensure that you do not react to respondents' anger with hostility.

Disarm the Person A common mistake is to try to reason with unreceptive people. Don't! Try instead to disarm them. Your best tactic is surprise. Stonewalling respondents *expect* you to apply pressure; attacking respondents *expect* you to resist. Disarming them surprises them—so simply listen, acknowledge the point, and agree wherever you can.

Change Tactics In some situations, changing tactics is the only viable option to reduce hostility. This means recasting what respondents say in a form that directs attention back to the problem and to both your interests. This normally means that you ask respondents what they would do to solve the problem.

Make It Easy to Say "Yes" In negotiating with difficult people, interviewers usually make a statement and attempt to get respondents to agree with it. A better choice is to agree with one of *their* statements and go from there. It is also better to break statements into smaller ones that are harder to disagree with. This helps the difficult person save face.

Make it Hard to Say "No" You can make it difficult to say "no" by asking reality-based (what-if) questions. These questions get respondents to think of the consequences of not agreeing—for example:

> ***Example:***
> Interviewer:
> "What do you think will happen if we don't agree?"
> "What do you think I will have to do from here?"
> "What will you do?"

Volatile Interviews

Volatile interviews have the potential to elicit strong emotional reactions in respondents. Volatile interviews typically involve close friends and relatives of suspects, co-conspirators, and similar individuals.

The personalities of those involved in volatile interviews vary. Some individuals resent *all* authority figures; fraud examiners and law enforcement officers are authority figures.

Physical Symptoms

In volatile interviews, respondents typically react first—they don't think first. And they are frequently openly hostile to interviewers. People with high emotions often have dry mouths, so they tend to lick their lips and swallow more frequently than normal. Throat clearing is another audible sign of emotion. Restlessness shows in fidgeting, shifting in the chair, and foot-tapping. Persons under emotional stress frequently perspire more heavily.

Under stress, our complexion sometimes changes. We look red or flushed, or appear paler than normal. During stress, our heart beats more frequently; keen observers can actually see the carotid artery pulsate. (The carotid artery is the large artery on each side of the neck.) If in normal situations we maintain eye contact, we are probably under stress when we avoid eye contact. Note, however, that these symptoms are not present in all emotional situations.

Other Considerations

It is best to use two interviewers in potentially volatile situations—there is strength in numbers. Additionally, two interviewers serve as corroborating witnesses in the event the interview takes a turn for the worse. Although you will still need to obtain information regarding who, what, why, when, where, and how, the order of the questioning varies from other types of interviews.

Use surprise in potentially volatile interviews. In many instances, volatile respondents are unaware that they are going to be questioned, and will therefore be off guard. If you don't use surprise, you run the risk of the respondent not showing up, bringing a witness, or being present with co-workers or even counsel. In these interviews, ask questions out of sequence. This keeps volatile respondents from knowing exactly the nature of the inquiry, and where it is leading. Although you will endeavor to obtain information regarding who, what, why, when, where, and how, ask your questions out of order. This technique is especially important in situations where respondents are attempting to protect themselves.

Hypothetical questions are less threatening, and are therefore ideally suited for potentially volatile interviews. For example, suppose you are interviewing a suspect's boyfriend about his knowledge of her activities. Asking *"Did she do it?"* is a direct question. Instead, pose it as a hypothetical: *"Is there any reason why she would have done it?"*

Overcoming Objections

Volatile witnesses voice numerous objections to being interviewed. Here are some of the most common objections (along with suggested responses):

Example:

Respondent:
"I don't want to be involved."
Interviewer:
Point out that you would not be there, asking questions, if the respondent were not involved. Tell them that you are saving them trouble by discussing the matter "informally." (Do *not* say "off the record"—this can cause legal problems with the information.)
Respondent:
"Why should I talk to you?"
Interviewer:
Say that you are trying to clear up a problem, and that the respondent's assistance is important.

Respondent:
"You can't prove that!"
Interviewer:
Tell the person that you are not trying to prove or disprove; you are simply gathering information.
Respondent:
"You can't make me talk!"
Interviewer:
Tell the person that you are not trying to make them do anything; you are trying to resolve a problem, and would deeply appreciate help.

Assessment Questions

Assessment questions seek to establish the credibility of the respondent. They are used only when interviewers decide previous statements by respondents are inconsistent because of possible deception.

Once respondents answer all relevant questions about the event, and you have reason to believe they are being deceptive, establish a theme to justify additional questions. This theme can ordinarily be put forth by saying, *"I have a few additional questions."* Do not indicate in any way that these questions are for a purpose other than seeking information.

Norming or Calibrating

Norming or calibrating is the process of observing behavior before critical questions are asked, as opposed to doing so during the questioning. Norming should be a routine part of all interviews. People with truthful attitudes answer questions one way; those with untruthful attitudes generally answer them differently. Assessment questions ask for agreement on matters that are against the principles of most honest people. In other words, dishonest people are likely to agree with many of the statements, while honest people won't.

Assessment questions are designed primarily to get verbal or nonverbal reactions from respondents. Interviewers then carefully assess their reactions. Suggestions for observing the verbal and physical behavior of respondents include the following:

- Use your senses of touch, sight, and hearing to establish a norm.
- Do not stare or call attention to the person's behavior.
- Be aware of the respondent's entire body.

- Observe the timing and consistency of behavior.
- Note clusters of behaviors.

On the basis of respondents' reactions to the assessment questions, interviewers then consider all the verbal and nonverbal responses together (not in isolation) to decide whether to proceed to the admission-seeking phase of the interview. Don't rely too heavily on the results of the assessment questioning.

The Physiology of Deception

It is said that everyone lies and that we do so for one of two reasons: to receive rewards or to avoid punishment. In most people, lying produces stress. Our body attempts to relieve this stress (even in practiced liars) through verbal and nonverbal reactions.

Conclusions concerning behavior must be tempered by a number of factors. The physical environment in which the interview is conducted can affect behavior. If respondents are comfortable, fewer behavior quirks may be exhibited. The more intelligent the respondent, the more reliable the verbal and nonverbal clues. If the respondent is biased toward the interviewer, or vice versa, this will affect behavior. Stress-produced behaviors range from subtle to obvious.

Persons who are mentally unstable or who are under the influence of drugs will usually be unsuitable to interview. Because professional pathological liars are often familiar with interview techniques, they are less likely to furnish observable behavioral clues. Behavior cues of juveniles are generally unreliable. Carefully note racial, ethnic, and economic factors. Some cultures, for example, discourage looking directly at someone. Cultures use specific body languages that can be (and often are) misinterpreted by people from other cultures.

Verbal Clues

Verbal clues are those relating to wordings, expressions, and responses to specific questions. They are also numerous; here are a few examples.

Changes in Speech Patterns During deception, people often speed up or slow down their speech, or speak louder. There may be a change in the voice pitch; as we become tense, our vocal chords constrict. People also tend to cough or clear their throats during deception.

Repetition of the Question Liars frequently repeat questions to gain more time to think of answers. Deceptive individuals will say, *"What was that again?"* or use similar language.

Comments Regarding Interview Deceptive people often complain about the physical environment of the interview room, such as *"It's cold in here."* They also sometimes ask how much longer the interview will take.

Selective Memory Deceptive people often have a fine memory for insignificant events, but when it comes to the important facts, they "just can't seem to remember."

Making Excuses Dishonest people frequently make excuses about things that look bad for them, such as *"I'm always nervous; don't pay any attention to that."* Or they might say, *"Everybody does it."*

Oaths On frequent occasions, dishonest people will add what they believe to be credibility to their lies by use of emphasis. That is, they use such expressions as *"I swear to God,"* or *"Honestly,"* or *"Frankly,"* or *"To tell the truth."*

Character Testimony Liars often request that interviewers *"Check with my wife,"* or *"Talk to my minister."* This is done to add credibility to the false statement.

Answering with a Question Rather than deny the allegations outright, liars frequently answer with questions like *"Why would I do something like that?"* As a variation, deceptive people sometimes question the interview procedure by asking, *"Why are you picking on me?"*

Overuse of Respect Some deceptive people go out of their way to be respectful and friendly. When accused of wrongdoing, it is unnatural for a person to react in a friendly and respectful manner.

Increasingly Weaker Denials When honest people are accused of something they haven't done, they often become angry or forceful in their denial. The more they are accused, the more forceful their denial. Dishonest people, on the other hand, tend to "deny weakly." Upon repeated accusations, dishonest people's denials become weaker, to the point where they finally become silent.

Specific Denials Dishonest people are more likely to be very specific in their denials. An honest person offers a simple and resounding *"no,"* whereas dishonest people "qualify" the denial: *"No, I did not steal $15,000 from the Company on June 27."* Other qualified denial phrases include, *"To the best of my memory,"* and *"As far as I recall,"* or similar language.

Fewer Emotionally Charged Words Liars often avoid emotionally provocative terms such as "steal," "lie," and "crime." Instead, they prefer "soft" words such as "borrow," and "it" (referring to the deed in question).

Refusal to Implicate Other Suspects Both honest respondents and liars have a natural reluctance to name others involved in misdeeds. However, liars frequently continue to refuse to implicate possible suspects, no matter how much pressure is applied by interviewers. Why? Because doing so narrows the circle of suspicion.

Tolerance for Shady Conduct Dishonest people typically have tolerant attitudes toward miscreant conduct. For example, if interviewers in a theft case ask, *"What should happen to this person when he is caught?"* honest people will usually say, *"They should be fired/prosecuted."* Dishonest people, on the other hand, are much more likely to reply, *"How should I know?"* or, *"Maybe he is a good employee who got into problems. Perhaps he should be given a second chance."*

Reluctance to Terminate Interview Dishonest people are generally more reluctant to terminate interviews. They want to convince interviewers that they are not responsible, so that the investigation will not continue. Honest people generally have no such reluctance.

Feigned Unconcern Dishonest people often try to appear casual and unconcerned and frequently adopt an unnatural slouching posture. Additionally, they may react to questions with nervous or false laughter or feeble attempts at humor. Honest people typically are very concerned about being suspected of wrongdoing, and treat the interviewer's questions seriously.

Nonverbal Clues

Nonverbal clues to deception include various body movements and postures accompanying the verbal reply. Here are a few:

Full Body Motions When asked sensitive or emotional questions, dishonest people typically change posture completely—as if moving away from the interviewer. Honest people frequently lean forward toward the interviewer when questions are serious.

Anatomical Physical Responses Anatomical physical responses are our body's involuntary reactions to fright, such as increased heart rate, shallow or labored breathing, or excessive perspiration. These reactions are typical of dishonest persons accused of wrongdoing.

Illustrators "Illustrators" are motions made primarily with hands to demonstrate points when talking. During nonthreatening questions, illustrators are done at one rate. During threatening questions, illustrators may increase or decrease.

Hands Over the Mouth Frequently, dishonest people cover their mouths with their hand or fingers during deception. This reaction goes back to childhood, when many children cover their mouths when telling a lie. It is done subconsciously to "conceal" the statement.

Manipulators "Manipulators" are motions such as picking lint from clothing, playing with objects such as pencils, or holding one's hands while talking. Manipulators are displacement activities to reduce nervousness.

Fleeing Positions During the interview, dishonest people often posture themselves in a "fleeing position." That is, the head and trunk may face the interviewer, but the feet and lower portion of the body point toward the door. This is an unconscious effort to flee.

Crossing the Arms Crossing one's arms over the middle zones of the body is a classic defensive reaction to difficult or uncomfortable questions. A variation is crossing the feet under the chair and locking them. These crossing motions occur mostly when being deceptive.

Reaction to Evidence Although they try to appear outwardly unconcerned, guilty people have a keen interest in implicating evidence. Therefore, dishonest people often look at documents presented by interviewers, attempt to be casual about observing them, and then shove them away, as if wanting nothing to do with the evidence.

Lip Movements Genuine smiles usually involve the whole mouth; false ones are confined to the upper half. In deception, people tend to smirk rather than to smile. Most actions that interrupt the flow of speech are stress-related. Examples include:

- Closing the mouth tightly
- Pursing lips
- Covering the mouth with the hand
- Lip and tongue biting
- Licking the lips
- Chewing on objects

Methodology of Assessment Questions

If, based on all factors, you doubt the honesty of respondents, you can ask the following assessment questions. Note that these questions build from least sensitive to most sensitive. The initial questions seek agreement. Obviously, not all questions are asked in all situations.

In the following example, an interviewer is investigating missing funds. During a routine interview of one employee, the respondent makes several factually incorrect statements. The examiner then decides to ask a series of assessment questions and observe the answers. Here is how the interviewer starts the questioning:

Assessment Question 1:

Interviewer:

"The company is particularly concerned about fraud and abuse. There are some new laws in effect that will cost the company millions if abuses go on and we don't try to find them. Do you know which law I'm talking about?"

Explanation:

Most individuals do not know about the laws concerning corporate sentencing guidelines, and will therefore answer "no." The purpose of this question is to get the respondent to understand the serious nature of fraud and abuse.

Assessment Question 2:

Interviewer:

"Congress recently passed a law that allows for the levy of fines against companies that don't try to clean their own houses. Besides, when people take things from the company, it can cost a lot of money, so you can understand why the company's concerned, can't you?"

Explanation:

The majority of persons will say "yes" to this question. In the event of a "no" answer, you should explain the issue fully and, thereafter, attempt to get the respondent's agreement. If that agreement is not forthcoming, you should assess why not.

Assessment Question 3:

Interviewer:

"Of course, they are not talking about a loyal employee who gets in a bind. They're talking more about someone who is dishonest. But a lot of times, it's average people who get involved in taking something from the company. Do you know the kind of person we're talking about?"

Explanation:

Most people read the newspapers and are at least generally familiar with the problem of fraud and abuse. Agreement by the respondent is expected to this question.

Assessment Question 4:

Interviewer:

"Most of these people aren't criminals at all. A lot of times, they're just trying to save their jobs or just trying to get by because the company is so cheap that it won't pay people what they're worth. Do you know what I mean?"

Explanation:

Although both honest and dishonest people will probably answer "yes" to this question, honest people are less likely to accept the premise that these people are not wrongdoers. Many honest people will reply, *"Yes, I understand, but that doesn't justify stealing."*

Assessment Question 5:

Interviewer:

"Why do you think someone around here might be justified in taking company property?"

Explanation:

Because fraud perpetrators frequently justify their acts, dishonest people are more likely than honest ones to attempt a justification such as, *"Everyone does it,"* or *"The company should treat people better if they don't want them to steal."* Honest people, on the other hand, are much more likely to say, *"There is no justification for stealing from the company. It is dishonest."*

Assessment Question 6:

Interviewer:

"How do you think we should deal with someone who got in a bind and did something wrong in the eyes of the company?"

Explanation:

Similar to other questions in this series, honest people want to "throw the book" at the miscreant. Culpable individuals typically say, *"How should I know? It's not up to me,"* or, *"If they were a good employee, maybe we should give them another chance."*

Assessment Question 7:

Interviewer:

"Do you think someone in your department might have taken something from the company because he thought he was justified?"

Explanation:

Most people—honest and dishonest—answer "no" to this question. However, the culpable person will more likely say "yes" without elaborating. Honest people, if answering "yes," usually provide details.

Assessment Question 8:

Interviewer:

"Have you ever felt yourself—even though you didn't go through with it—justified in taking advantage of your position?"

Explanation:

Again, most people, both honest and dishonest, will answer "no." However, dishonest people are more likely to acknowledge having at least "thought" of doing it.

Assessment Question 9:

Interviewer:

"Who in your department do you feel would think they were justified in doing something against the company?"

Explanation:

Dishonest people usually don't answer this question, saying instead that, *"I guess anyone could have a justification if they wanted to."* Honest people may name names—albeit reluctantly.

Assessment Question 10:

Interviewer:

"Do you believe that most people will tell their manager if they believed a colleague was doing something wrong, like committing fraud against the company?"

Explanation:

Honest people have a sense of integrity and are much more likely to report misdeeds. Dishonest people are more likely to say "no." When pressed for an explanation, they typically say, *"No, nothing would be done about it, and they wouldn't believe me anyhow."*

Assessment Question 11:

Interviewer:

"Is there any reason why someone who works with you would say they thought you might feel justified in doing something wrong?"

Explanation:

This question is designed to place the thought in the mind of a wrongdoer that someone has named him as a suspect. Honest people typically say "no." Dishonest people are more likely to try to explain by saying something like, *"I know there are people around here who don't like me."*

Assessment Question 12:

Interviewer:

"What would concern you most if you did something wrong and it was found out?"

Explanation:

Dishonest people are likely to say something like, *"I wouldn't want to go to jail."* Honest people often reject the notion by saying, *"I'm not concerned at all, because I haven't done anything."* If an honest person does explain, it is usually along the lines of disappointing friends or family; dishonest people often mention punitive measures.

Closing Questions

Closing the interview on a positive note is a must in informational interviews. Closings serve several purposes. First, it is not unusual for interviewers to misunderstand or misinterpret statements of respondents. Therefore, interviewers should go over key facts to make certain they are accurate. The closing questions phase also seeks to obtain facts previously unknown. It provides respondents further opportunity to say whatever they want about the matter at hand. When you wind an interview down, be sure to do so positively so that you can call the person back and so that they will not feel that you represent a threat when you want to talk to them the second time.

If appropriate, ask if there are other documents or witnesses that would be helpful to the case. Do not promise confidentiality; instead, say, *"I'll keep your name as quiet as possible."*

People being interviewed often do not volunteer additional information regarding other witnesses or evidence. The theme, therefore, is to provide respondents opportunities to furnish further relevant facts or opinions. At the conclusion, attempt to determine which facts provided by the respondent are the most relevant. Do not go over all the information a second time.

Closing Question 1:

Interviewer:

"I want to make sure I have my information straight. Let me take a minute and summarize what we've discussed."

Tip:

Go over each of the key facts in summary form. The questions should be closed, so that the witness can respond either "yes" or "no."

Closing Question 2:

Interviewer:

"You have known her eight years, correct?"

OR

"You knew she had some financial problems, is that right?"

OR

"You suspect—but don't know for sure—that she still paid a lot of past due bills recently. Is that correct?"

Tip:

On absolutely vital facts provided by the respondent, add *"Are you sure?"*

Closing Question 3:

Interviewer:

"Are you sure?"

Tip:

To obtain additional facts, ask respondents if there is something else they would like to say. This gives the correct impression that you are interested in all relevant information, regardless of which side it favors. Try to actively involve respondents in helping solve the case—*"If you were trying to resolve this issue, what would you do?"* This technique is sometimes called "playing detective." Another excellent closing question is, *"Is there anything that I haven't asked you that you think would be worth[while] me asking you, that might be necessary in trying to figure this out?"*

Tip:

Ask respondents if they have been treated fairly. It is especially helpful to ask this when respondents have not been cooperative, or at the conclusion of an admission-seeking interview. Ask the question as if it were perfunctory. Ask if the respondent has anything else to say. This gives the respondent one final time to make a statement. Also ask if you can call with any additional questions. It leaves the door open to additional cooperation.

Tip:
Leave the respondent a business card or a telephone number. Invite the respondent to call about anything relevant. In some cases, try to obtain a commitment that the respondent will not discuss the matter. This step is not recommended with adverse or hostile respondents—it gives them ideas. Here is an example of the proper approach.

Closing Question 4:
Interviewer:
"In situations like this one, people's reputations can suffer because of rumor and innuendo. We don't want that to happen and neither do you. Therefore, I'd like your cooperation. Can I count on you not to discuss this until all the facts are out?"

Tip:
Shake hands with respondents, and thank them for their time and information.

Admission-Seeking Questions

Interviewers should ask accusatory or *admission-seeking questions* only when a reasonable probability exists that the respondent has committed the act in question. An assessment of culpability can be based on verbal and nonverbal responses to interview questions, as well as documents, physical evidence, and other interviews and evidence.

A transitional theme is necessary when you proceed from assessment to admission-seeking questions. The purpose of this theme is to suggest to miscreants that they have been caught. In ideal circumstances, you would leave the room for a few minutes, to "check on something." If you have incriminating documents, place copies of them in a folder and bring them back to the room. If no documents exist, you might even fill the file folder with blank paper. When you return to the room, place the file folder on the desk, and ask,

Example:
Interviewer:
"Is there something that you would like to tell me about __________?"

OR

"Is there any reason why someone would say that you ____________?"

Hand the documents to the respondent and ask for "comments." Do not introduce the evidence or explain it. In many cases, the miscreant will admit to incriminating conduct on the spot. If not, proceed.

Purpose of Questions

Admission-seeking questions have at least two purposes. The first purpose is to distinguish innocent persons from guilty ones. Culpable individuals frequently confess during the admission-seeking phase of interviews, while innocent people do not do so unless threats or coercion are used. In some instances, the only way to differentiate the culpable from the innocent is to seek an admission of guilt.

The second purpose is to obtain a valid confession. Confessions, under the law, must be voluntarily obtained. The importance of a valid and binding confession to wrongdoing cannot be overstated. Finally, the confessor should be asked to sign a written statement acknowledging the facts. Although oral confessions are legally as binding as written ones, written statements have greater credibility. They also discourage miscreants from later recanting.

Preparation

Schedule interviews when you can control the situation. Normally do not conduct them on the suspect's "turf"; they are also best conducted by surprise.

Interview Room The location should establish a sense of privacy. The door should be closed but not locked, and there should be no physical barriers preventing the target from leaving. This avoids allegations of "custodial interrogation"—that you held someone against their will.

Keep distractions to a minimum. Ideally, there should be no photographs, windows, or other objects to distract attention. Place chairs about six feet apart, and do not permit the accused to sit behind a desk. As stated, this prevents establishing a psychological barrier that allows the accused to "hide behind." Notes taken during the interview should be done in a way that does not reveal their significance.

Presence of Outsiders Do not suggest to the accused that they should have counsel present. Of course, this right cannot be denied. If counsel is present, you should have an understanding that he or she is an observer only; attorneys should not ask questions or object. Other than the accused and two examiners, no other observers are usually permitted in admission-seeking interviews. If the accused is a union member, a union representative may have the right to attend. However, this can present legal problems because it "broadcasts" the allegation to a third party. It is very difficult to obtain a confession with witnesses present. Examiners should therefore consider whether the case can be proven without a confession. If so, they may choose to omit the admission-seeking interview altogether.

Miranda Warnings Private investigators are not required to give Miranda warnings. Police are required to use them only if an arrest is imminent following the interview. Confessions are generally admissible in court if (1) they are obtained voluntarily and (2) interviewers have a reasonable belief that the confession is true. Always check with counsel.

Theme Development

People rarely confess voluntarily. However, they tend to confess when they perceive that the benefits of confession outweigh the penalties. Good interviewers, through the application of sophisticated techniques, can often convince respondents that a confession is in their best interest.

People generally will not confess if they believe that there is doubt in the mind of the accuser as to their guilt. Thus, you must convey absolute confidence in the admission-seeking accusation—even if not fully convinced. Make the accusation as a statement of fact. Accusatory questions do not ask, *"Did you do it?"* They ask, *"Why did you do it?"* Here is an example of an accusatory question:

> *Is this the first time that you have taken from the company? Is this the first time you have created an overdraft?*

Innocent people generally do not accept this question's premise. People confessing need adequate time to come to terms with their guilt; obtaining admissions and confessions takes patience. Therefore, admission-seeking interviews should be done only when there is sufficient privacy and time is not a factor. Do not express disgust, outrage, or moral condemnation about the confessor's actions. To do so goes against the basic strategy in obtaining confessions, which can be summed up as *maximize sympathy and minimize the perception of moral wrongdoing*.

Offer a morally acceptable reason for the confessor's behavior. Do not convey to accused that they are "bad people." Guilty people almost never confess under such conditions. Be firm, but also project compassion, understanding, and sympathy. Endeavor to keep the confessor from voicing a denial. Once the accused denies the act, overcoming that position will be very difficult.

It is generally considered legal to accuse innocent people of misdeeds they did not commit *as long as* the following holds:

- The accuser has reasonable suspicion or predication to believe the accused has committed an offense.
- The accusation is made under conditions of privacy.
- The accuser does not take any action likely to make an innocent person confess.
- The accusation is conducted under reasonable conditions.

But ALWAYS check with counsel.

Steps in the Admission-Seeking Interview

Effective admission-seeking interviews proceed in an orderly fashion. What follows is generally accepted as most likely to succeed in obtaining confessions. That said, the order always depends on the circumstances.

Accuse Directly The accusation should not be a question, but a statement. Avoid emotionally charged words such as "steal," "fraud," and "crime" in your accusations. Phrase the accusation so that the accused is psychologically "trapped," with no way out.

Direct Accusations

WRONG	***RIGHT***
"We have reason to believe that you . . ." OR "We think (suspect) you may have . . ."	"Our investigation has clearly established that you: • made a false entry (*avoid* "fraud") • took company assets without permission (*avoid using* "theft," "embezzlement," *or* "stealing") • took money from a vendor (*avoid* "bribe" *or* "kickback") • have not told the complete truth (*avoid* "lie" *or* "fraud") OR "We have been conducting an investigation into __________, and you are clearly the only person we have not been able to eliminate as being responsible."

Observe Reaction When accused of wrongdoing, some miscreants react with silence. If the accused does deny culpability, these denials are often weak. They may almost mumble their denial. It is common for culpable individuals to avoid outright denials. Rather, they give reasons why they could not have committed the act in question. Innocent people will sometimes react with genuine shock at being accused. It is not at all unusual for an innocent person, wrongfully accused, to react with anger. As opposed to guilty people, innocent people strongly deny carrying out the act or acts in question.

Repeat Accusation If the accused does not strenuously object to the accusation, repeat it with the same degree of conviction and strength.

Interrupt Denials Both truthful and untruthful people will normally object to the accusation and attempt denial. It is very important in instances where you are convinced of the individual's guilt that the denial be interrupted. Innocent people are unlikely to allow you to succeed in stopping their denial.

It is important to emphasize that both the innocent and culpable will make outright denials if forced to do so. Accordingly, interviewers should not solicit a denial at this stage of the admission-seeking interview.

Interrupting Denials

WRONG	***RIGHT***
"Did you do this?" OR "Are you the responsible person?"	"Why did you do this?"

Delays Delaying tactics are effective ways to stop or interrupt denials. Do not argue with the accused, but rather attempt to delay the outright denial.

Example:

Interviewer:

"I hear what you are saying, but let me finish first. Then you can talk."

Innocent people will usually not "hold on" or let you continue to develop this theme.

Interruptions Occasionally, you may have to interrupt the accused's attempted denials repeatedly. Because this stage is crucial, be prepared to increase the tone of your interruptions to the point where you say, *"If you keep interrupting, I am going to have to terminate this conversation."* Guilty individuals find this threatening, because they want to know the extent of incriminating evidence in your possession, and your terminating the interview blocks this.

Reasoning If the above techniques are unsuccessful, you may attempt to reason with the accused, and employ some of the tactics normally used for refuting alibis (see below). In this situation, you present the accused with some of the evidence that implicates them. Do not disclose *all* the facts, but rather only small portions here and there.

Establish Rationalization Once the accusation has been made, repeated, and the denials stopped, it is time to establish a morally acceptable rationalization that allows suspects to square their misdeeds with their conscience. This theme need not be related to the underlying causes of the misconduct. It is common and acceptable for suspects to explain away the moral consequences of the action by seizing on any plausible explanation other than being a "bad person."

If the accused do not seem to relate to one theme, continue on others until one seems to fit. Then develop that theme fully. Note that the theme explains away the moral—but not the legal—consequences of the misdeed. Interviewers are cautioned *not* to make any statements that would lead suspects to believe they will be excused from legal liability by cooperating. Interviewers must strike a balance between being in control of the interview and appearing compassionate and understanding. Again, no matter the conduct the accused has supposedly committed, never express shock, outrage, or condemnation.

Unfair Treatment Probably the most common rationalization for criminal activity in general (and fraud in particular) is in fraudsters' attempts to achieve equity. Studies show that counterproductive employee behavior—including stealing—is motivated primarily by job dissatisfaction. Employees and others feel that "striking back" is important to their self-esteem. Sensitive interviewers capitalize on these feelings by suggesting to suspects that they are victims.

Example:
Interviewer:
"I feel like I know what makes you tick. And I know it isn't like you to do something like this without a reason. You've worked hard here to get a good reputation. I don't think the company has paid you what you're really worth. And that's the way you feel too, isn't it?"

OR
"I've seen situations like this before. And I think the company brought this on themselves. If you had been fairly treated, this wouldn't have happened, don't you agree?"

Inadequate Recognition Some employees feel that their efforts have gone completely without notice. As with similar themes, interviewers strive to be empathetic.

Example:
Interviewer:
"I've found out a few things about you. It looks to me that you've given a lot more to this company than they recognize. Isn't that right?"

Financial Problems Internal criminals, especially executives and upper management, frequently engage in fraud to conceal their true financial condition—either personal or business.

Aberration of Conduct Many miscreants believe their conduct constitutes an aberration in their lives, and that it does not represent their true character. You can establish this theme using the following statements:

Example:
Interviewer:
"I know this is totally out of character for you. I know that this would never have happened if something wasn't going on in your life. Isn't that right?"
OR
"You've worked hard all your life to get a good reputation. I don't believe you would normally do something like this; it just doesn't fit. You must have felt forced into it. You felt forced, didn't you?"

Family Problems Some people commit fraud because of family problems—financial woes caused by divorce, an unfaithful spouse, or demanding children. Men especially—who may be socially conditioned to tie their masculinity to earning power—sometimes hold the notion that wealth garners respect. For their part, women often commit white-collar crime in response to the needs of their husbands and children. Skillful interviewers convert this motive to their advantage using one of the following approaches:

Example:
Interviewer:
"I know you've had some family problems. I know your recent divorce has been difficult for you. And I know how it is when these problems occur. You would have never done this if it hadn't been for family problems, isn't that right?"
OR
"Someone in your position and with your ethics just doesn't do things like this without a reason. And I think that reason has to do with trying to make the best possible life for your family. I know it would be difficult for me to admit to my family that we're not as well off as we were last year. And that's why you did this, isn't it?"

Accuser's Actions Don't disclose the accuser's identity if it is not already known. But in cases where the accuser's identity is known to the suspects, it is sometimes helpful to blame the accuser for the problem. The accuser can be a colleague, manager, auditor, fraud examiner, or any similar person, or the problem can be blamed on the company.

Example:
Interviewer:
"You know what these auditors are like. They are hired to turn over every stone. I wonder how they would look if we put *them* under a microscope. Compared to other things that are going on, what you've done isn't that bad. Right?"
OR
"I really blame a large part of this on the company. If some of the things that went on around this company were known, it would make what you've done seem pretty small in comparison, wouldn't it?"

Stress, Drugs, Alcohol Employees sometimes turn to drugs or alcohol to reduce stress. In some instances, the stress itself leads to aberrant behavior. The following rationalizations can work in these situations:

> ***Example:***
> Interviewer:
> "I know what you've done isn't really you. Inside, you've been in a lot of turmoil. A lot of people drink too much when they have problems. I have been through periods like that myself. And when things build up inside, it sometimes makes all of us do something we shouldn't. That's what happened here, isn't it?"
>
> OR
>
> "You're one of the most respected men in this company. I know you have been under tremendous pressure to succeed. Too much pressure, really. There is only so much any of us can take. That's behind what has happened here, isn't it?"

Revenge Similar to other themes, revenge can also be effectively developed as a motive. In this technique, you attempt to blame the offense on suspects' feelings that they must "get back" at someone or something.

> ***Example:***
> Interviewer:
> "What has happened is out of character for you. I think you were trying to get back at your supervisor for the time he passed you over for a raise. I would probably feel the same. That's what happened, isn't it?"
>
> OR
>
> "Everyone around here knows that the board has not supported you in your efforts to turn this company around. I would understand if you said to yourself, 'I'll show them.' Isn't that what happened?"

Depersonalizing the Victim In cases involving employee theft, an effective technique is to depersonalize the victim. Suspects are better able to cope with the moral dilemma of their actions if the victim is a faceless corporation or agency.

> ***Example:***
> Interviewer:
> "It isn't like you took something from a friend or neighbor. I can see how you could say, 'Well, this would be okay to do as long as it was against the company, and not my co-workers.' Isn't that right?"
>
> OR
>
> "It's not like what you've done has really hurt one person. Maybe you thought of it this way: 'At most, I've cost each shareholder a few cents.' Isn't that the way it was?"

Minor Moral Infraction In many cases, interviewers can reduce the accused's perception of the moral seriousness of the matter. To state again for emphasis, this is *not* to be confused with the legal seriousness of the act. Successful fraud examiners and interviewers avoid making statements that can be construed as relieving the accused of their legal responsibility. For example, do not state: *"It is not a big deal, legally. It's just a technical violation."* Instead, play down the moral side. One effective way is through comparisons, such as those illustrated here:

Example:
Interviewer:
"This problem we have doesn't mean you're 'Jack the Ripper.' When you compare what you've done to things other people do, this situation seems pretty insignificant, doesn't it?"
OR
"Everything is relative. What you've done doesn't even come close to some of the other things that have happened. You're not Ivan Boesky, right?"
OR
"I could see myself in your place. I probably would have done the same thing."

Altruism The moral seriousness of the matter can in many cases be deflected by claiming the action was for the benefit of others. This is especially true if accused view themselves as caring people.

Example:
Interviewer:
"I know you didn't do this for yourself. I have looked into this matter carefully, and I think you did this to help someone, didn't you?"
OR
"You have a big responsibility in this company. A lot of people depend on you for their jobs. I just know you did this because you thought you were doing the right thing for the company, didn't you?"

Genuine Need In a very small number of cases, fraud is predicated by genuine need. For example, the accused may be paying for the medical care of sick parents or a child. Or some other financial disaster has befallen the miscreant. In these situations, the following statements can be effective:

Example:
Interviewer:
"I don't know many people who've had so many bad things happen all at once. I can see where you thought this was pretty much a matter of life or death, right?"
OR
"You're like everyone else: you have to put food on the table. But in your position, it is very difficult to ask for help. You genuinely needed to do this to survive, didn't you?"

Refute Alibis

Even if suspects are presented with an appropriate rationalization, they often continue to deny culpability. When interviewers succeed in stopping the denials, the accused will then normally turn to various reasons why they could not have committed the act in question. The purpose here is to convince the accused of the weight of the evidence against them. Miscreants usually have a keen interest in material that implicates them. Alibis can be generally refuted using one of the methods listed below.

Display Physical Evidence Guilty people frequently overestimate the amount of physical evidence in the interviewer's possession. You want to reinforce this notion in the way you lay out the evidence. Therefore, display the physical evidence—usually documents in fraud matters—one piece at a time, in reverse order of importance. In this way, suspects do not immediately comprehend the full extent of the evidence. When they no longer deny culpability, stop displaying evidence.

Each time a document or piece of evidence is laid out, you should note its significance. During this phase, the accused are still trying to come to grips with being caught. Interviewers therefore expect that suspects will attempt to explain their way out of the situation. Like denials, it's best to stop the alibis and other falsehoods before they are fully articulated. Once alibis are shown to be false, you can return to the theme being developed.

Discuss Witnesses Discussing the testimony of witnesses is another way to refute alibis. The objective here is to give enough information about what other people will say without providing too much information. Ideally, your statement creates the impression in suspects' minds that many people are in a position to contradict their story.

Interviewers are again cautioned about furnishing too much information so that suspects can identify witnesses. This places witnesses in a difficult position, and suspects may contact witnesses in an effort to influence testimony. Suspects sometimes take reprisals against potential witnesses, although this is rare.

Example:

Respondent:

"I couldn't possibly have done this. It would require the approval of a supervisor."

Interviewer:

"In normal situations it would. The problem is that your statement doesn't hold up. There are several people who will tell a completely different story. I can understand how you would want me to believe that. But you're only worsening the situation by making these statements. If you will help me on this, you'll also be helping yourself. Understand?"

Discuss Deceptions The final technique is to discuss the accused's deceptions. The idea here is to appeal to their logic, not to scold or degrade. This technique is sometimes your only option if physical evidence is lacking. As with other interview situations, avoid the word "lying."

Present Alternatives After suspects' alibis have been refuted, they normally become quiet and withdrawn. Some people in this situation may cry. If so, comfort them. Do not discourage them from showing emotion. At this stage, suspects are deliberating about confessing. Interviewers at this point should present an alternative question to the accused. This question forces them to make one of two choices. One alternative allows the accused a morally acceptable reason for the misdeed; the other paints the accused in a negative light. Regardless of which answer suspects choose, they are acknowledging guilt.

Example:

Interviewer:

"Did you plan this deliberately, or did it just happen?"

OR

"Did you just want extra money, or did you do this because you had financial problems?"

OR "Did you just get greedy, or did you do this because of the way the company has treated you?"	

Benchmark Admission Either way suspects answer the alternative question—either yes or no—they have made a culpable statement, or *benchmark admission.* Once the benchmark admission is made, miscreants have made a subconscious decision to confess. The preceding questions are structured so that the negative alternative is presented first, followed by the positive one. In this way, suspects only have to nod or say "yes" for the benchmark admission to be made. They commonly answer in the negative.

Example: Respondent: "I didn't do it deliberately." OR "I didn't do it just because I wanted extra money."	OR "No, I'm not just greedy."

In the cases where suspects answer the alternative question in the negative, you should press further for a positive admission.

Example: Interviewer: "Then it just happened on the spur of the moment?" OR "Then you did it to take care of your financial problems?"	OR "Then you did it because of the way you've been treated here?"

Should the accused still not respond to the alternative question with the benchmark admission, repeat the questions, or variations thereof, until the benchmark admission is made. It is important that you get a response that is tantamount to a commitment to confess. Because only a commitment is sought at this point, the questions for the benchmark admission are constructed as leading questions. These questions can be answered "yes" or "no"; they do not require explanation. Explanations will come later.

Reinforce Rationalization Once the benchmark admission is made, it is time to reinforce the confessor's decision. Then you can make the transition to the verbal confession, where the details of the offense are obtained. Reinforcing the rationalization developed earlier helps confessors feel comfortable, believing that you do not look down on them.

Verbal Confession The transition to the verbal confession is made when suspects furnish the first detailed information about the offense. Thereafter, it is your job to probe gently for additional details—preferably including those that would be known only to the miscreant. As with any interview, there are three general approaches to obtaining the details: chronologically, by transaction, or by event. The approach you take is governed by the circumstances of the case.

During the admission-seeking interview, it is best to first confirm the general details of the offense. For example, you will want the accused's estimates of the amounts involved, other parties to the offense, and the location of physical evidence. After these basic facts are confirmed, you can return to the specifics, in chronological order. It is imperative that you obtain an early admission that the accused knew that the conduct in question was wrong. This confirms the essential element of intent.

Because of the psychology underlying confessions, most confessors lie about one or more aspects of the offense, even as they confirm their overall guilt. When this happens during the verbal confession, make a mental note of the discrepancy and proceed as if you have accepted the falsehood as truthful. That is, save such discrepancies until the accused provides all other relevant facts. If the discrepancies are material to the offense, then you should either resolve them at the end of the verbal confession or wait and correct them in the written confession. If not material, such information can be omitted from the written confession.

The following items of information should be obtained during the verbal confession:

The Accused Knew the Conduct Was Wrong As stated, intent is required in all matters involving fraud. Not only must confessors have committed the act, they must have *intended* to commit it. This information can be developed as follows:

Example:

Interviewer:

"Now that you've decided to help yourself, I can help you too. I need to ask you some questions to get this cleared up. As I understand it, you did this, and you knew it was wrong, but you didn't really mean to hurt the company, is that right?"

Facts Known Only to Confessor Once intent is confirmed, questioning turns to those facts known only to the confessors. These facts include—at a minimum—their estimates of the number of instances of wrongful conduct as well as the total amount of money involved. The questions should not be phrased so that they can answer "yes" or "no."

Estimate of Number of Instances/Amounts In fraud matters especially, it is common for suspects to underestimate the amount of funds involved, as well as the number of instances. This is probably because of our natural tendency to block out unpleasant matters. Take their figures with a grain of salt. If their response is "*I don't know,*" start high with the amounts and gradually come down.

Example:

Interviewer:

"How many times do you think this happened?"

Respondent:

"I don't have any idea."

Interviewer:
"Was it as many as 100 times?"
Respondent:
"No way!"
Interviewer:
"How about 75 times?"
Respondent:
"That's still too high. Probably not more than two or three times."
Interviewer:
"Are you pretty sure?" (If respondents' estimates are too low, gently get them to acknowledge a higher figure. But do not challenge the accused by calling them liars.)
Respondent:
"Maybe three times, but certainly not more than that."

Motive for the Fraud

Motive is an important element in establishing the crime. The motive may be the same as the theme you developed earlier—or it may not. The most common response is *"I don't know."* You should probe for additional information, but if it is not forthcoming, then attribute the motive to the theme you developed earlier. The motive should be established along these lines:

Example:
Interviewer:
"We have discussed what led you to do this. But I need to hear it in your words. Why do you think you did this?"

When the Fraud Commenced Interviewers need to find the approximate date and time that the fraud started. This information is usually developed by questions similar to the following:

Example:
Interviewer:
"I am sure you remember the first time this happened."
Respondent:
"Yes."
Interviewer:
"Tell me about it."
Respondent:
"Around the middle of January of last year."
Interviewer:
"I admire you for having the courage to talk about this. You're doing the right thing. Tell me in detail about the first time."

When/If Fraud Was Terminated When the crime is fraud, especially internal fraud, the offenses are usually continuous. That is, miscreants seldom stop before they are discovered. If appropriate, interviewers should seek the date the offense terminated. The question is typically phrased as follows:

> ***Example:***
> Interviewer:
> "When was the last time you did this?"

Others Involved

Most frauds are solo ventures—committed without accomplices. Rather than ask if anyone else was "involved," phrase the question something like this:

> ***Example:***
> Interviewer:
> "Who else knew about this besides you?"

By asking who else "knew," you are in effect not only asking for the names of possible conspirators, but also about others who knew what was going on but failed to report it. This question asks for specifics—not *"did someone else know?"* but rather *"who else knew?"*

Physical Evidence

Physical evidence—regardless of how limited it may be—should be obtained from perpetrators/confessors. In many instances, illicit income from fraud is deposited directly in their bank accounts. Interviewers typically want to ask confessors to surrender their banking records voluntarily for review. Ask for either (1) a separate written authorization or (2) language to be added to the confession noting the voluntary surrender of banking information. The first evidence is preferable.

If other relevant records can be obtained only with the confessor's consent, seek permission to review them during the oral confession. In some instances, it may be advisable to delay this step until you obtain the written confession. The request for physical evidence from confessors can be set up like this:

> ***Example:***
> Interviewer:
> "As a part of wrapping up the details, I will be needing your banking records (or other physical evidence). You understand that, don't you?"
> Respondent:
> "No, I don't."
> Interviewer:
> "Well, I just need to document the facts and clear up any remaining questions. You have decided to tell the complete story, including your side of it. I just want to make sure the facts are accurate and fair to you. We want to make sure you're not blamed for something someone else did. And I want to report that you cooperated fully and wanted to do the right thing, okay?" (Avoid the use of the word "evidence" or references to higher tribunals, for example, "courts" or "prosecutors.")
> Respondent:
> "Okay."
> Interviewer:
> "Where do you keep your bank accounts?"

(If the interviewer knows of at least one bank where the confessor does business, the question should be phrased: "Where do you do business besides First National Bank?")
Respondent:
"Just First National."
Interviewer:
"I'll need to get your okay to get the records from the bank if we need them. Where do you keep the original records?" (Do not ask their permission to look at the records; simply tell them the records are needed. Let them object if they have a problem with this request.)

Disposition of Proceeds If it has not come out earlier, find out what happened to any illicit income derived from the misdeeds. Typically, the money has long since been used for frivolous or ostentatious purposes. It is important, however, that confessors see their actions in a more positive light; you should therefore avoid comments or questions relating to "high living."

Example:
Interviewer:
"What happened to the money?" (Let the accused explain; do not suggest an answer unless they do not respond.)

Location of Assets In appropriate situations, you will want to find out if there are residual assets that confessors can use to reduce losses. Rather than ask them *"Is there anything left?"* the question should be phrased as *"What's left?"*

Example:
Interviewer:
"What do you have left from all of this?"
Respondent:
"Not much. I used most of the money to cover my bills and financial obligations. A little money and a car that is paid for is all I have."
Interviewer:
"Well, whatever it is, this whole thing will look a lot better if you volunteered to return what you could, don't you agree?"

Specifics of Each Offense

Once the major hurdles are overcome, interviewers then return to the specifics of each offense. Generally, you start with the first instance and work through chronologically in a logical fashion. Because these questions are information-seeking, they should be openly phrased so that the answer is independent of the question. It is best to seek the independent recollections of confessors first before you display physical evidence. If they cannot independently recall, use the documents to refresh their memory. It is generally best to resolve all issues on each instance before proceeding to the next. To determine the specifics of the offense, you can usually ask some of these questions:

Example:
Interviewer:
"Who has knowledge of this transaction?"
"What does this document mean?"
"When did this transaction occur?"
"Where did the proceeds of the transaction go?"
"Why was the transaction done?"
"How was the transaction covered up?"

Never promise immunity from prosecution. Confessors cannot be given immunity from prosecution by interviewers. There is a simple reason for this: Such promises can be interpreted as a way to unfairly extract statements that perpetrators would not have otherwise given.

Signed Statements

Verbal confessions should be reduced to short and concise written statements. Rarely should they exceed two or three handwritten pages. Interviewers prepare the statements (often in advance of the admission-seeking interview) and present them to the confessors for their signature. If a prepared confession needs to be changed, the changes can be added in ink, with everyone present initialing the changes. Such endorsed changes often lend credibility that the signed statements are legitimate and were voluntarily given.

The following points should be covered in every signed statement:

Voluntariness of Confessions Getting written admissions is difficult. Law that governs confessions requires that they be completely voluntary. This should be set forth specifically in the statement.

Intent There is no such thing as an accidental fraud or crime. Both require, as key elements of proof, that fraudsters knew the conduct was wrong and intended to commit the act. This is best accomplished using precise language. The statement should clearly and explicitly describe the act—for example, *"I wrongfully took assets from the company that weren't mine"* versus *"I borrowed money from the company without telling anyone."*

As a general rule, emotionally charged words, such as "lie" and "steal," should be avoided, because confessors often balk at signing statements that use these words. Here are some suggested wordings:

Instead of	Use
Lie	*I knew the statement/action was untrue.*
Steal	*Wrongfully took the property of ______ for my own benefit.*
Embezzle	*Wrongfully took ______'s property, which had been entrusted to me, and used it for my own benefit.*
Fraud	*I knowingly told ______ an untrue statement and he/she/they relied on it.*

Approximate Dates of Offense Unless the exact dates of the offense are known, the words "approximately" or "about" must precede any stated dates. If confessors are unsure about the dates, include language to that effect.

Approximate Amounts of Losses Include the approximate losses, making sure they are labeled as such. It is satisfactory to state a range (*"probably not less than $____ or more than $____"*).

Approximate Number of Instances Ranges are also satisfactory for the number of instances. This number is important because it helps establish intent by showing a pattern of activity.

Willingness to Cooperate When confessors perceive that the statement's language portrays them in a more favorable light, they have an easier time signing the statement. Confessors also convert this natural tendency to be seen favorably into cooperation and a willingness to make amends.

> ***Example:***
> "I am willing to cooperate in helping undo what I have done. I promise that I will try to repay whatever damages I caused by my actions."

Excuse Clause Mention the confessor's moral excuse in the statement. This helps the accused believe they are being portrayed in the most favorable light. Make sure that the excuse clause wording does not diminish legal responsibility.

> ***Example:***
> ***WRONG:***
> "I didn't mean to do this." (implies lack of intent)
>
> ***RIGHT:***
> "I wouldn't have done this if it had not been for pressing financial problems. I didn't mean to hurt anyone."

Confessor* Must *Read Statement Confessors must acknowledge that they read the statement and they should then initial every page in the statement. It may be advisable to insert intentional errors in the statement so that confessors will notice them as they read it. The errors are then crossed out, the correct information inserted, and the confessor asked to initial the changes. Whether this step is advisable depends on the likelihood that the confessor will attempt to retract the statement or claim it was not read.

Truthfulness of Statement The written statement should state specifically that it is true. This gives it added weight in ensuing litigation. However, the language should also allow for mistakes—for example:

> ***Example:***
> "This statement is true and complete to the best of my current recollection."

Key Points in Signed Statements

There is no legal requirement that statements must be in the handwriting or wording of declarants. Because examiners usually know how to draft valid statements, letting confessors draft the statement is generally not a good idea. A statement's wording should be precise. Declarants should read and sign the statement without undue delay. Do not ask confessors to sign the statement; instead, direct them—*"Please sign here."* Although there is no legal requirement, it is a good idea to have two people witness the signing of a statement.

There should not be more than one written statement for each offense. If facts are inadvertently omitted, they can later be added to the original statement as an addendum. For legal purposes, prepare separate statements for unrelated offenses. This rule applies because the target may be tried more than once (once for each offense). Preserve all notes taken during admission-seeking interviews, especially those concerning confessions. Access to pertinent notes aids in cross-examinations regarding the validity of signed statements. Stenographic notes, if any, should also be preserved. Once a confession is obtained, substantiate it through additional investigation, if necessary. A sample signed statement is included in Appendix A at the end of this chapter.

The Fraud Report

Interrogation of suspect(s) is usually the final stage of investigation (although circumstances may dictate an alternative sequencing of investigation methods). Once the investigation is completed, a fraud report is prepared. This report includes all findings, conclusions, recommendations and corrective actions taken. The report indicates all pertinent facts uncovered relative to the who, what, where, when, how, and why of the fraud. It also includes recommendations for control improvements that will minimize the exposure to similar occurrences in the future. It should not contain recommendations for disciplinary or legal action against anyone suspected of fraudulent or illegal activity, even when the investigation provides tenable evidence of probable culpability and/or complicity.

Particular care should be exercised to ensure that the general tone of the fraud report is neither accusatory nor conclusive as to guilt. Even when a confession of culpability or complicity is obtained during a fraud investigation, such confessions may not be considered valid or consequential evidence of guilt of fraud until a court of law decides. This is true even when management has already taken disciplinary action on the basis of the confession. Reports that refer to a confession obtained in the course of the investigation should state merely that admission of the alleged or suspected events was obtained—not that guilt was acknowledged. Attention to language is crucial here to ensure that subjective, inflammatory, libelous, or other prejudicial connotations are absent. To be objective, factual, unbiased, and free from distortion, reports should refer to "alleged" irregularities, activity, conduct, and so forth. Accordingly, the activities investigated and reported should be described as "purported" or "alleged" to have occurred. When findings support the allegations, couch reports in language such as the following:

- The investigation disclosed the existence of reasonably credible evidence to support the allegation.
- The investigation concludes with a rebuttal presumption that the allegations or suspicions are tenable.
- The investigation concludes with plausible evidence in support of the allegation.

Appendix B at the end of this chapter details an investigation of an employee fraud and an appropriate fraud report. This completed report covers the investigation of "Ivan Ben Steelin," a real estate purchasing representative who worked for "Resort and Properties Inc." Ivan accepted kickbacks from a company we'll call "Red Hot Real Estate" and he also inflated real estate prices as part of the scheme.

The fraud investigation documented by the report involved all four types of investigation procedures. The investigation was predicated on an anonymous tip received in a letter addressed to the company president. The investigation began with a review of the suspect's personnel records. It included one procedure to investigate the theft (surveillance of the suspects at a local restaurant) and several procedures to investigate the concealment (including computer searches of company databases; calculations of total purchase transactions by each real estate buyer; and determinations of the number of real estate agencies used, average price per acre paid, and the number of purchase transactions made with each vendor). The report documents the public records searches and net worth conversion. Searches were made of voter registration and marriage records, the secretary of state's records, as well as the real estate and contracting office records at the county level. Query procedures involved neutral interviews with the company's personnel manager, a home builder, and a company secretary, as well as a friendly interview with another real estate buyer and a hostile interview with the real estate agent who was suspected of making illegal payments to Ivan Ben Steelin. The interrogation of Ivan Ben Steelin (in order to gain access to his bank records) led to a signed confession. The investigation concluded with a signed confession statement and calculation of real estate overpayments (losses) by the company.

The report exemplifies the types of procedures and documentation that fraud investigations often include. We encourage you to read it carefully.

Summary

Interviewing is the most common investigation technique. Here, we have only touched the surface of this complex topic. If you are serious about pursuing fraud investigation as a career, become an excellent interviewer. Read several books on the subject, and take advantage of the excellent training that is available. Many frauds are solved, and many confessions and restitutions are obtained because of good interviewing skills. Fraud investigations often fail because of mistakes made during interviews. Counseling courses are another excellent way to develop listening and observation skills.

In this chapter, we have discussed interviewing etiquette, interview techniques, types of interviews, types of questions to ask and how to ask them, and ways to elicit confessions. When conducting admission-seeking interviews, the purpose is to get a confession or to exonerate (if innocent). In these types of interviews, almost always there is an invisible wall between the interviewer and the interviewee: the interviewee does not want to confess; the interviewer seeks a confession. Good interviewers find ways to break down this invisible wall. They use techniques such as those discussed in this chapter to (1) minimize the crime in the mind of the interviewee and (2) maximize the sympathy for the interviewee.

Wherever possible, fraud investigations should conclude with a signed confession of guilt from the perpetrator or perpetrators, and with an accurate calculation of the extent of the theft and losses. The confession and the loss calculation, as well as the fraud investigation techniques used, must be carefully documented so that civil, criminal, and other actions can be supported.

Questions and Cases

Discussion Questions

1. What are the three types of honesty testing?
2. What is an interview?
3. What are the five reactions to interviewees?
4. What are the five general types of questions that an interviewer can ask?
5. What are some of the different elements of communication?

6. What is an inhibitor of communication?
7. What are facilitators of communication?
8. What are informational questions?
9. What is meant by the "question sequence"?
10. What is a volatile interview?
11. What is the purpose of assessment questions?
12. What is norming or calibrating?

True/False

1. Paper-and-pencil honesty tests are most frequently used to determine whether someone has committed a crime.
2. Failure to pass a polygraph test means certain guilt.
3. Interviews during the rationalization stage are often not objective and can be harmful to the potential prosecution efforts.
4. The general tone of a fraud report should be neither accusatory nor conclusive as to guilt, even if the suspect has confessed his/her involvement in the crime.
5. An interviewer should always be sympathetic and respectful during an interview.
6. Confrontational interviews should always be conducted even if there is no evidence that can be obtained from the suspect.
7. Telling a significant lie and getting away with it during an interview is usually very difficult if the interviewer is well trained.
8. If a suspect continually repeats questions, it could be a verbal cue that he/she is lying.
9. The fraud report should include recommendations for disciplinary action.
10. The interview should always take place at the interviewee's place of work.

Multiple Choice

1. Which of the following is *not* a method of honesty testing?
   a. Graphology
   b. Voice stress analysis
   c. Body language test
   d. Pencil-and-paper test
2. Interviews should *not* be conducted with:
   a. Suspects
   b. Co-workers
   c. Clients
   d. Interviews can be conducted with all of the above.
3. Persons in the rationalization stage of reaction to a fraud:
   a. Make great interviewees because they want to punish the suspect
   b. Want to give the suspect one more chance
   c. Believe without a doubt that the suspect is guilty
   d. Have no sympathy for the suspect

4. Planning for interviews should *not* involve:
   a. Judging the guilt of the suspect based on available documents
   b. Establishing a location and time for the interview
   c. Ascertaining in advance as many facts as possible about the offense
   d. Understanding the attitude of the interviewee
5. Confrontational interviews should usually be conducted when:
   a. Police decide that the suspect is guilty.
   b. The examiner is starting the investigation.
   c. All other investigative procedures have been completed.
   d. The investigation is taking too long.
6. Which of the following is *not* an inquiry technique that should be used by interviewers?
   a. Use short questions, confined to one topic.
   b. Maintain full control of the interview.
   c. Point out some, but not all, of the circumstantial evidence.
   d. All of the above are good language techniques in an interview.
7. Which of the following honesty testing techniques deals with the study of handwriting for the purpose of character analysis?
   a. Polygraph
   b. Graphology
   c. Pencil-and-paper test
   d. Voice stress
   e. None of the above
8. Which of the following traits do polygraphs *not* measure when testing for stress?
   a. Pulse rate
   b. Blood pressure
   c. Galvanic skin response
   d. Respiration
   e. All of the above
9. Interviewing is:
   a. The systematic questioning of individuals who have knowledge of events, people, and evidence involved in a case under investigation
   b. The process of answering questions from an interviewer for the purpose of finding a job
   c. By far the most common technique used in investigating and resolving fraud
   d. a and c
   e. None of the above
10. Which of the following is the typical sequence of reactions to a crisis?
    a. Anger, denial, rationalization, depression, acceptance
    b. Rationalization, denial, anger, depression, acceptance
    c. Denial, anger, rationalization, depression, acceptance
    d. Depression, denial, anger, rationalization, acceptance
    e. None of the above

11. Which of the following reactions frequently involves appearing temporarily stunned, insisting there is some mistake, or not comprehending what has been said?
    a. Anger
    b. Denial
    c. Rationalization
    d. Depression
    e. Acceptance

Short Cases

Case 1. Jim-Bob has been a faithful employee of Daddy's Denture, Inc. (DD's) for four years. He has held various positions where he handles receipts, credit memos, and other accounting records. Along with recently added responsibility, Jim-Bob has discovered more opportunity to commit fraud.

Over the past three months, Jim-Bob figured out that he can create fictitious vendors and write checks from DD's to these fictitious vendors and deposit the checks in a new bank account he opened under a false name. Jim-Bob put this plan into action and has so far stolen $7,000 from DD's.

One day, Jim-Bob had to call in sick. A co-worker, Judd, assumed Jim-Bob's responsibilities for the day. As he reconciled cashed checks, Judd noticed Jim-Bob endorsed many of them himself. Judd doesn't believe what he sees. In fact, he leaves the reconciling for Jim-Bob to finish when he returns to work.

When Jim-Bob returns to work, everything seems normal at first. However, it eventually dawns on Judd that he caught Jim-Bob in the act of stealing. Judd becomes angry and confronts Jim-Bob. When Judd mentions the endorsements, Jim-Bob is dumbfounded and denies being dishonest. After Judd leaves, Jim-Bob gets angry, thinking, "What right did he have to take over my duties?" and "I'll be fired for sure!!"

Back in his office, Judd continues to think about Jim-Bob's dishonesty. He decides that Jim-Bob is just human, and that he let himself slip this once. Judd decides he should let the issue pass and just hope that Jim-Bob realizes his gig is up. Judd believes Jim-Bob is a basically good guy and will probably reconcile his misdoings and return to honest ways. Later that night, Judd feels sad knowing that his good friend, Jim-Bob, has done such a bad thing.

Meanwhile, Jim-Bob decides he shouldn't be angry with Judd. He is, after all, only doing what he's been told to do by his superiors. Jim-Bob feels horrible about what he has done, not to mention the fact that he got caught. He decides to fess up and let his boss know what he has been doing before he gets into any more trouble.

Name the five reactions to crises and briefly describe how both Jim-Bob and Judd proceed through each phase.

Case 2. Daffy Duck, the purchasing manager for ACME Corporation, is under suspicion for committing fraud. His superiors believe he is accepting kickbacks and bribes from various vendors. As the company's fraud expert, you are investigating this possible fraud and are preparing to interview Daffy. You suspect that Daffy will be defensive and possibly hostile when interviewed.

1. What investigation procedures should be completed before your admission-seeking interview with Daffy?
2. If you find evidence that proves Daffy is committing fraud at ACME, what might his initial reaction be when he is confronted? What other emotions and/or reactions might you expect from Daffy? How do you know this?

Case 3. An accountant for a small business is suspected of writing checks to "dummy" vendors and collecting the money himself. After a thorough investigation of the company, you determine that the company does not require authorization for vendor payments. In an interview with the suspect, you ask him if any controls are in place that could prevent someone from writing fraudulent checks. He quickly responds in the affirmative.

What type of questions could you ask next?

Case 4. Mike Trujillo has been involved in a serious relationship with his high school sweetheart, Bonny, for five years; they have even discussed marriage. One day, Bonny told Mike that she was seeing another man. "Mike, I love you, but I'm not in love with you." She then played a ridiculous song written by Sarah McLachlan that talked about how she would always remember him. Obviously, this was very difficult for Mike.

Over the course of the next few months, Mike had a bumpy ride emotionally. Initially, he simply couldn't believe it. He frequently caught himself thinking about Bonny as if they were still together. After a few days, Mike became bitter. He cut up all her pictures except for one. He hung that one on a dartboard and threw darts at it for hours. As his bitterness subsided, he looked for reasons why the breakup was actually beneficial. He told himself it was a blessing, that he wouldn't have to support Bonny's rich tastes anymore, that things were turning out for the best. However, during the next six months, Mike just couldn't get excited about dating other girls. He made himself go on dates, but he never really liked any of the girls he dated. He felt empty and didn't know how to fill the void in his heart. But after a few months, Mike did bounce back and started to take an interest in other girls. Within four months he found Amy, the girl of his dreams, and they got married about a year later.

1. What reactions do most people have to crises and how did Mike display these reactions?
2. How does Mike's experience relate to fraud examination?

Case 5. You manage a division that recently discovered a suspected fraud involving accounts receivable. For the past week, you and the internal auditors have been collecting documents, gathering information, and quietly interviewing personnel. It is now time to interview the suspect, who is your accounts receivable manager. She has access both to cash receipts and the accounts receivable ledger and has allegedly stolen $4,000 over the last year by writing off small accounts as uncollectable.

Pair up with another student in your class. One of you take the part of the interviewer and one that of the suspect. Develop a brief outline on how you will conduct your interview. Remember that your task as interviewer is to remain in control of the interview, but at the same time be sympathetic and understanding. If deemed appropriate, prepare a short, written confession statement like the example given in the chapter. Swap roles after the first interview and apply what you learned in it in a second interview.

Extensive Cases

Case 6. You are an internal auditor at BBB Company. An employee of BBB has phoned in an anonymous tip that a fellow worker, Jane X., might be embezzling money. Jane has been a trusted employee of the company for 13 years; she quickly moved through the ranks of the company because of her exemplary record and she is now Vice President in Charge of Treasury. Your internal audit team has done thorough audits of her department for years and has found its control environment to be exceptional. In addition, she is a good friend of the CEO and CFO. They have tremendous confidence in her abilities and honesty, and she is being groomed to succeed the current CFO when he retires.

The person making the anonymous tip claims to have noticed large fluctuations in certain financial statement accounts. Accompanying these fluctuations are unexplainable debits and credits that were all entered by Jane. The person also alleges that Jane's behavior has been erratic. She is usually kind and patient, but recently she has flown off the handle for no explainable reason. She insists on balancing certain accounts by herself because she claims that they are too critical to trust with anyone else. Finally, the informant feels like Jane's lifestyle as a single mother is well above what her salary would support.

Investigating allegations against such a trusted person in the company will cause considerable disruption. If you investigate, you will have to proceed very carefully, especially since you have only the word of one employee who could have ulterior motives.

1. Describe the steps you would take to investigate this suspected embezzlement.
2. As a first step in your investigation, would you interview Jane about the problem? Why or why not?
3. How would you conduct Jane's admission-seeking interview in order to be most effective?

Case 7. You have been talking with your best friend, John, for the past couple of weeks about a crisis in his company. He has just learned that his boss has been embezzling money for the past six months. The day he learns about the alleged fraud, he calls to tell you the news. In the telephone conversation, John tells you how much he respects his boss and that his boss is his mentor. You note that his voice seems distant and he doesn't respond well to your questions. Later that week, you meet John for lunch. His demeanor is completely changed since you last spoke with him. After a few drinks, John can't stop bad-mouthing his boss. John also makes a few insulting comments about you. You decide to leave him alone for a few days until he feels better.

A week later you again meet John for lunch. The subject of the fraud comes up, and John's attitude is again considerably changed. Instead of being angry, he compares his boss's life to his own. You think it a bit odd when John says, "I completely understand why he did it. His family life was suffering, his job was in jeopardy, and his mom just died. Given the same circumstances, I might have done the same thing." You finish lunch and go your separate ways. Later that week, John calls you again. This time, he tells you that he could have prevented the fraud. He feels embarrassed that it happened right before his eyes.

A week later you ask John if there are any new developments in the investigation. He tells you that he is helping with the investigation by providing all the facts he knows and his observations over the last few months. Now all John wants is to move on.

Identify John's reactions to the fraud, and explain each stage in detail.

Case 8. It is early Monday morning, and Brian is preparing to conduct his first interview as a fraud examiner. He is to meet with Sue, a laborer in the factory his firm is investigating. She is neither a suspect nor thought to be connected with the fraud. Her name simply came up in another investigator's interviews as someone who might be able to provide additional insight. They have arranged to meet at Brian's office, so he is simply awaiting her arrival.

"Hello," he hears someone say through his partially open door. "I'm Sue."

"Come in," he replies, remaining seated behind his large, oak desk. She enters and takes the empty seat across the desk from Brian. "Let me get right to the point," are his next words. "Are you aware of any reasonably credible or plausible evidence that the allegations of embezzlement at your place of employment are tenable?"

After a brief pause and a look of concern on Sue's face, Brian asks, "Do you know what embezzlement means?"

"Yes," replies Sue.

"Okay, then, do you know anyone who has embezzled from your employer?"

"No."

Sue becomes nervous as she sees Brian begin to take notes on a pad. He continues, "Specifically, have you seen Ralph perpetrating fraud?"

"No."

"Are you sure? You know that this is a big deal," he says as he stands and begins to pace around the room. "I can't imagine why anyone would steal from his own company, but he deserves to be caught if he has. It's wrong and bad, and only a horrible person would do something like this."

"I'm sure."

"Have you embezzled?"

"No," Sue states again.

"Well, then, I don't see any reason to continue. Goodbye."

Sue stands, excuses herself, and leaves the room.

What are some of the things Brian did wrong during this interview?

Internet Assignments

1. Go to the site http://www.fbi.gov/publications/leb/1996/oct964.txt and read the article about statement analysis, which discusses interviewing and how to know whether a person is lying or not. This article examines the case of Susan Smith, who killed her two sons by strapping them into the car and pushing the car into the river. The article uses the mother's statements to discuss four components of statement analysis that can help investigators know when a person is lying.

   Outline the four components of statement analysis and give a short definition of each.
2. Using the following Internet sites, identify the major characteristics or elements of fraud. What characteristics or elements are the most recognizable or most distinctive?

   http://www.pkf.co.uk/main/news_views/news_01_03_01o.html
   http://www.bus.lsu.edu/accounting/faculty/lcrumbley/fraudster.html
   http://www.bus.lsu.edu/accounting/faculty/lcrumbley/fraud1.htm
   http://www.mc2consulting.com/fraurisk.htm
3. Go to the site http://www.cieh.org.uk/events/pace.htm and read the advertisement for a course that teaches proper interview techniques.

   What do the criteria for analyzing how evidence was obtained teach about the importance of proper interview techniques?
4. Many Internet sites contain honesty tests for screening applicants or existing employees. Most of these charge a fee for their services, but they do provide an easy, quick way to test employees. At the web site queendom.com, you can access many free tests. In the relationship tab are several honesty tests. Go to this web site and look for honesty tests, or enter the following link http://www.queendom.com/tests/minitests/fx/honesty.html. Although this test is mainly for relationships, it is free and gives you an idea of what kind of questions are asked and what information can be derived from the answers.

   Take the test and obtain the results. Analyze the questions and try to determine why they are being asked. Do you think this is an accurate test? Why or why not?

Debate

1. The Employee Polygraph Protection Act passed by Congress made it difficult to use polygraphs in fraud investigations. Currently, 11 conditions must be met in order for polygraph tests to be used. Assume you are members of Congress debating the use of polygraphs. Discuss both sides of the issue and make *your* recommendation. Would you make it easier or harder to obtain permission to use a polygraph?
2. You and another fraud examiner are debating whether it is ethical to "lie" during an admission-seeking interview (such as claiming to have compelling evidence of guilt when you don't) to get a confession. You believe it is okay to lie. Your co-worker believes it is unethical to be deceptive. Who is correct?

End Notes

1. We would like to thank the Association of Certified Fraud Examiners and Chairman Joseph Wells, in particular, for allowing us to use their interview material in this book. Much of this chapter was taken from their self-study course on interviewing, *Beyond the Numbers: Professional Interview Techniques* (Austin, Texas), 1998.
2. See, for example, the works of Elizabeth Kübler Ross, such as *On Death and Dying,* which stresses that we are all operating at a psychological-steady state, and that crises knock us off that equilibrium (http://www.elisabethkublerross.com/).
3. *Beyond the Numbers: Professional Interview Techniques,* op. cit., page 38.

Sample Signed Statement

December 14, 20XX
Edison, New Jersey

I, Dominique Santana, furnish the following free and voluntary statement to Scott Barefoot of Major Electronics, Inc. No threats or promises of any kind have been used to induce this statement.

I am a cashier at Major Electronics, Inc. Part of my duties include processing and posting cash payments, sales, returns, and allowances, as well as handling cash. Commencing in early 2001 and continuing through the current time, I have taken about $7,000 in cash from the company, knowing the cash was not mine.

I took the company's money by creating fictitious merchandise returns, forging the signature of my manager, and posting the fictitious return to the computer. I then took out the resulting cash from the register. Later, I split the money with my boyfriend, Jerry Garza, who works here in the store. He knew what I was doing and helped me several times by signing a three-part return slip as if the merchandise had been returned when it had not. Most of the time, this scheme involved my own account. I bought televisions and other merchandise using my employee discount. I then sold them to outsiders for cash. Afterward, I prepared a document showing the television was returned when it was not.

Other than my boyfriend, Jerry, no one in the store knew what I was doing. I am aware my conduct is illegal, and violates the policies of Major Electronics, Inc. I participated in this scheme because I have had severe financial problems and my mother has been ill. I am truly sorry for my conduct, and promise to repay all losses. Some of the company's cash was deposited in my personal account, number 436-9241-7881 at the First National Bank, Edison, New Jersey. I hereby grant Scott Barefoot or representatives from Major Electronics permission to examine the account and to obtain copies of statements, checks, and deposits from First National Bank for the period January 1, 1992, to the present.

I have read this statement consisting of this page. I now sign my name below because this statement is true and correct to the best of my knowledge.

______________________________ ______________________________
Signature: Witness:

______________________________ ______________________________
Date Date

An Example Fraud Report

To demonstrate how frauds can be investigated and the type of report to prepare to document investigative procedures, we present a completed fraud report of the investigation of "Ivan Ben Steelin," a real estate purchasing representative who worked for "Silver Summit Real Estate." Ivan accepted kickbacks from a company we'll call "Red Hot Real Estate" and inflated real estate prices.

The fraud investigation documented in the report involves all four types of investigative procedures. The investigation is predicated on an anonymous tip received in a letter addressed to the company president. The investigation begins with a review of the suspect's personnel records. It includes one theft investigative procedure—surveillance of the suspects at a local restaurant. Several concealment-based investigative procedures are used, including computer searches of company databases, calculations of total purchase transactions by each real estate buyer, and determinations of the number of real estate agencies used, the average price paid per acre, and the number of purchase transactions made with each vendor. The report documents public records searches and net worth conversion investigative procedures. Searches were made of voter registration and marriage records, the secretary of state's records, and real estate and contracting office records at the county level. Query investigation procedures involved neutral interviews with the company's personnel manager, a home builder, and a company secretary, as well as a friendly interview with another real estate buyer and a hostile interview with the real estate agent who was suspected of making illegal payments to Ivan Ben Steelin. An interrogation of Ivan Ben Steelin in order to gain access to his bank records leads to a signed confession. The investigation concludes with the obtaining of a signed confession statement and the calculation of real estate overpayments (losses) by the company.

Although not perfect, the report does provide an excellent example of the investigative procedures and documentation that should be pursued in fraud investigations. We encourage you to read it carefully.

INVESTIGATIVE REPORT
ON IVAN BEN STEELIN

Silver Summit Real Estate

Internal Audit (or Corporate Security)
Special Cases File
030369

Silver Summit Real Estate
Internal Audit Special Cases File
(IASCF) 030369

Regarding
Ivan Ben Steelin

FILE INDEX

Silver Summit Real Estate

To: IASCF 030369
From: Scott R. Bulloch
Date: January 2, 2002
Re: Ivan Ben Steelin
Subject: Unsigned letter regarding Ivan Ben Steelin

On December 28, 2001, Vic Tumms, president and CEO of Silver Summit Real Estate, received an unsigned letter. The letter, dated December 27, 2001, referred to Ivan Ben Steelin. The letter, presented on page 2, is self-explanatory.

On December 30, 2001, the letter and its contents were discussed in a meeting at which Scott R. Bulloch (Silver Summit Real Estate's internal auditor), Vic Tumms, and Sue U. Buttz (Silver Summit Real Estate's legal counsel) were present.

Predicated on the contents of the letter, an investigation was commissioned by Sue U. Buttz, and was set to commence on January 1, 2002.

The original letter was initialed by Scott R. Bulloch and is maintained as evidence in IASCF 030369.

Silver Summit Real Estate

December 27, 2001

Mr. Vic Tumms
President
Silver Summit Real Estate
5511 Vero Beach Road
Denver, Colorado 84057

Dear Mr. Tumms:

I believe you should investigate the relationship between Ivan Ben Steelin, the real estate acquisition manager, and Red Hot Real Estate. I believe we paid significantly more than fair market value for the 200 acres we purchased in the river bottom, as well as for several other properties.

Sincerely,

A Concerned Associate

1-1-2001

2

Silver Summit Real Estate

To: IASCF 030369
From: Scott R. Bulloch
Date: January 3, 2002
Re: Ivan Ben Steelin
Subject: Interview with Rebecca Monson

Synopsis
Rebecca Monson, personnel manager of Silver Summit Real Estate, advised on January 2, 2002, that Ivan Ben Steelin had been employed at Silver Summit Real Estate since January 7, 1994. Steelin's salary in 2001 was $45,000, and his supervisor was RaNae Workman, vice president of external affairs.

Details
Rebecca Monson, personnel manager of Silver Summit Real Estate, was interviewed at her office, 5511 Vero Beach Road, Denver, Colorado, telephone (999) 555-3463, on January 2, 2002. Rebecca was advised of the identity of the interviewers, Scott R. Bulloch and Sue U. Buttz, and provided the following information. Rebecca was advised that the nature of the inquiry was an "internal investigation of misconduct," as per the company's code of conduct.

The personnel records reflect that Ivan Ben Steelin, white male, date of birth August 5, 1964, social security 999-06-2828, residing at 1156 North Ocean Boulevard, Denver, Colorado, telephone (999) 225-1161, had been employed at Silver Summit Real Estate since January 7, 1994. According to the records, Steelin was married and had four children.

Steelin's initial salary was $38,000 per year, and he was an investment analyst in the external affairs department. Steelin was enlisted in the management training program on his hire date. His supervisor after he became an investment analyst was Mickey Sheraton, vice president of external affairs.

On January 1, 1996, Steelin was promoted to a purchasing representative position, still in the external affairs department. Steelin's salary was $45,000 per year, as reflected by the 2001 salary file.

RaNae Workman became vice president of external affairs in August of 1997 and was Ivan's immediate supervisor.

According to the records, prior to his employment with Silver Summit Real Estate, Ivan Ben Steelin was employed by Rockwell Laboratories in St. Louis, Missouri. His reason for leaving Rockwell Laboratories, as stated on the personnel information card, was that he wanted to be closer to his family in Colorado.

No background investigation was conducted by the company prior to hiring Steelin at Silver Summit Real Estate.

First National, Second National, Third National, and Fourth National Banks called in February 1997 to confirm Steelin's employment with Silver Summit Real Estate. The personnel department enters the nature of the inquiry in the personnel database each time an outside party asks about employees. No other parties have requested information about Steelin since February 1997.

The original personnel information card and a copy of outside party inquiries (consisting of two pages), were obtained from Rebecca Monson and initialed and dated by Scott R. Bulloch. They are maintained in IASCF 030369. Copies were left with Rebecca Monson.

Rebecca Monson was advised to keep the interview and its issues confidential.

4

Personnel Information Card

Hire date: January 7, 1994
Name: Steelin, Ivan Ben

Social Security Number: 999-06-2828
Birth date: August 5, 1964

Address at time of hire:
1156 North Ocean Boulevard
Denver, CO 80234

Emergency Contact:
James Clintock
1145 North 8000 West
Denver, CO 80231

Relation: Father-in-law
(999) 555-7974

Previous Employers

Rockwell Laboratories
66 Market Street
St. Louis, MO 63101

Position: Sales agent
Supervisor: Jeff Cole, Sales Manager
Dates: 1988-1993

Reason for leaving: Would like to be closer to family in Colorado.

Ethics University
Denver, CO 80223

Position: Mail courier
Supervisor: Joseph Starks, Mail Manager
Dates: 1985-1988

Reason for leaving: Graduated from Ethics University and accepted a position in St. Louis.

Reason for leaving:

Other pertinent information

Ivan Ben Steelin — 1-7-1994
Signature — Date

Administrative Use Only
Background Check: No
Other: None

sb
1-2-2002

Outside Party Inquiries
Print date: January 3, 2002
Employee: Ivan Ben Steelin
File: 528062828

Date	*Party*	*Contact*	*Purpose*
2/2/97	First National Bank	Loan department	Confirm employment
2/4/97	Second National Bank	None given	Confirm employment
2/12/97	Third National Bank	Loan department	Confirm employment
2/16/97	Fourth National Bank	Credit department	Confirm employment

sb
1-2-2002

6

Silver Summit Real Estate

To: IASCF 030369
From: Scott R. Bulloch
Date: January 4, 2002
Re: Ivan Ben Steelin
Subject: Search of voter registration and marriage license records

Voter Registration

Voter registration records were examined on January 4, 2002, to confirm the information about Ivan Ben Steelin maintained by Silver Summit Real Estate's personnel department. The registration records substantiated that Steelin's address was 1156 North Ocean Boulevard, Denver, Colorado, 80234. Social security number, phone number, and date of birth were the same as maintained by the personnel department at Silver Summit Real Estate.

Marriage License

The marriage license of Mr. Steelin was inspected on January 4, 2002, at the Moore County Clerk's office. Ivan Ben Steelin was married to Clara Clintock on July 1, 1985. The records indicated that no previous marriages existed for either Mr. or Mrs. Steelin. The marriage license of Steelin revealed that his wife's parents, James and Jennifer Clintock, live at 1145 North 8000 West, Denver, Colorado, 80231—the address of Ivan Steelin at the time he was hired by Silver Summit Real Estate.

Silver Summit Real Estate

To: IASCF 030369
From: Scott R. Bulloch
Date: January 5, 2002
Re: Ivan Ben Steelin
Subject: Search of records at the Colorado secretary of state's office

The office of the secretary of state was visited on January 5, 2002, to survey:

- Business license records
- The UCC Records

Business License Records
It could not be determined whether Steelin had ever sought a business license in the state of Colorado. A computer search on Prentice Hall's national database did not provide information that would substantiate that Steelin had held a business license in any other state in the United States.

Uniform Commercial Code Records
The UCC records for Ivan Ben Steelin, 999-06-2828, 1156 North Ocean Boulevard, Denver, Colorado, reported the following information:

- Steelin made an acquisition of a boat at Ron's Boats, 25000 North State Street, Denver, Colorado, on November 12, 1998. The record reflected that a loan was not secured against the acquisition, though the cost of the boat was $23,000.
- On May 1, 1998, a purchase was made at Lund Furniture, 1400 West 1200 North, Denver, Colorado. The record reflects that the purchase, secured on store credit, cost a total of $9,425, with the acquisition items being the collateral for the credit. The purchase items consisted of:
  One (1) 44-inch Mitsubishi television set.
  One (1) Samsung home entertainment center.
  One (1) Broyhill bedroom set.
- On July 1, 1999, two automobiles were leased from Quickie Auto Imports, 1400 South State Street, Denver, Colorado, 80233.
  Auto 1: Audi 100, four-wheel-drive, VIN AUDI1234567891014.
  Auto 2: Subaru Legacy wagon, VIN SUBA1234567892024.
  The bargain purchase price, pending the end of the lease, was $45,000 less the cumulative lease payments of $1,150 per month.

8

- Cellular Three Telephone, 2200 Martin Parkway, Denver, Colorado, sold merchandise to Ivan Steelin on July 13, 1999. The record does not reflect that the acquisition was collateralized, though the cost was $2,000.
- Roger Tones Motors, 1275 South University Avenue, Denver, Colorado, sold one automobile to Ivan Ben Steelin on December 19, 2000. The automobile was partially paid for through a dealer loan, with the automobile being the collateral. The auto was a 2000 Volkswagen Passat Turbo touring sedan, VIN VW987654321123459. The purchase price was $26,497, and the amount of the loan was $10,000.
- On June 28, 2001, Bullard Jewelers Company, 1100 North University Avenue, sold merchandise on credit to Ivan Ben Steelin. The collateral to the purchase was the acquired merchandise, with the credit being extended by US Jewelers Credit Corporation of Denver, Colorado. The total cost of the acquisition was $8,200, with $4,000 being the credit amount. The description of the items identified:

  One (1) ring with 1.24 carat diamonds.

  Two (2) earrings, each with a 1.5 carat diamond.

Silver Summit Real Estate

To: IASCF 030369
From: Scott R. Bulloch
Date: January 7, 2002
Re: Ivan Ben Steelin
Subject: Search of real estate records

On January 7, 2002, the Moore County Land Office and the Moore County Tax Assessor's Office were visited to determine Ivan Ben Steelin's real estate holdings and their respective values.

County Land Office
The property records of Moore County, Colorado, indicate that Ivan Ben Steelin's real estate holdings consist of:

- 1.1 acres of improved property located at 1156 North Ocean Boulevard, Denver, Colorado, 80234.

As cited by the County Land Office records, Steelin acquired the property on April 4, 1997, from Red Hot Real Estate. The records maintain that the property, consisting of 1.1 acres of land and one single-family dwelling, is indebted to Fourth National Bank. The amount of the indebtedness was not available from these records.

County Tax Assessor's Office
The Moore County Tax Assessor's office records show a total tax base on the improved property, 1156 North Ocean Boulevard, Denver, Colorado, held by Ivan Ben Steelin, to be $275,000. The legal description of the property is as follows:

- 1.1 acres of property, with sewer and water.
- 4,100-square-foot single-family dwelling, built from building permit 19883000, issued on May 1, 1997.

The status of the tax payments, as reflected in the records, is that Steelin is current for his annual assessment.

10

Silver Summit Real Estate

To: IASCF 030369
From: Scott R. Bulloch
Date: January 8, 2002
Re: Ivan Ben Steelin
Subject: Search of records at the Moore County Contracting Office

On January 8, 2002, building permit 19883000 was examined at the Moore County Contracting Office.

The permit revealed the following information:

- The permit was issued to Ivan Ben Steelin on May 1, 1997.
- The designated licensed contractor on the building permit was Well's Custom Homes.
- The permit was for a single-family dwelling to be constructed at 1156 North Ocean Boulevard, Denver, Colorado, 80234.

The records accompanying the permit revealed that the dwelling passed code requirements and was available to be occupied on October 28, 1997.

Silver Summit Real Estate

To: IASCF 030369
From: Scott R. Bulloch
Date: January 8, 2002
Re: Ivan Ben Steelin
Subject: Interview with Jack Wells, owner of Wells Custom Homes

Synopsis
Jack Wells, owner of Wells Custom Homes, telephone (999) 222-1212, was interviewed over the phone on January 8, 2002. Wells revealed that the charge for building Ivan Ben Steelin's home at 1156 North Ocean Boulevard, Denver, Colorado, was $240,000.

Details
Jack Wells, owner of Wells Custom Homes, was interviewed over the phone on January 8, 2002. Wells was advised of the identity of the caller, Scott R. Bulloch, but not of the nature of the inquiry or of Scott R. Bulloch's position.

Wells stated that custom home construction is charged to clients on a square-foot basis. He stated that the average charge is $60 to $75 per square foot.

Wells remembered building a home for Ivan Ben Steelin. He stated that Steelin's home had been one of the first built by Wells Custom Homes. He revealed that the charge to Ivan Ben Steelin was $240,000.

Wells stated that payment had been received through a construction loan at Fourth National Bank, and that full payment had been received upon the house's passing the code requirements.

12

Silver Summit Real Estate

To: IASCF 030369
From: Scott R. Bulloch
Date: January 9, 2002
Re: Ivan Ben Steelin
Subject: Net worth analysis of Ivan Ben Steelin

Synopsis

On January 9, 2002, Scott R. Bulloch and Sue U. Buttz performed a net worth analysis of Ivan Ben Steelin. The analysis revealed, conservatively, that Mr. Steelin may have had estimated income from unknown sources of $17,000, $22,000, $34,000, and $23,000 in the years 1998, 1999, 2000, and 2001, respectively.

Details

On January 9, 2002, Scott R. Bulloch and Sue U. Buttz performed a net worth analysis of Ivan Ben Steelin. Conservative estimates and interpolations were made with regard to Mr. Steelin's assets and liabilities. The estimates and interpolations were derived from information acquired through public records, interviews, and personnel records maintained by Silver Summit Real Estate.

The net worth analysis indicated that Mr. Steelin may have had unknown sources of income in the amounts of $17,000, $22,000, $34,000, and $23,000, in the years, 1998, 1999, 2000, and 2001, respectively.

Attached is the worksheet that details the process of determining the above-stated figures. The worksheet consists of one page; it was initialed by Scott R. Bulloch and is maintained in IASCF 030369.

Net Worth Analysis

	1998	1999	2000	2001
Assets:				
Home	$275,000	$275,000	$275,000	$275,000
Cars	5,000	45,000	70,000	70,000
Boats	23,000	23,000	23,000	23,000
Furniture and other	10,000	20,000	20,000	28,000
Total assets	$313,000	$363,000	$388,000	$396,000
Liabilities:				
Home	$240,000	$240,000	$240,000	$240,000
Cars	0	45,000	55,000	55,000
Boats	0	0	0	0
Furniture and other	10,000	10,000*	10,000	14,000
Total liabilities	$250,000	$295,000	$305,000	$309,000
Net worth	$ 63,000	$ 68,000	$ 83,000	$ 87,000
Net worth increase	$ 10,000*	$ 5,000	$ 15,000	$ 4,000
Living expenses:				
Mortgage	$ 24,000	$ 24,000	$ 24,000	$ 24,000
Food, etc.	15,000	15,000	15,000	15,000
Cars	0	12,000	15,000	15,000
Total living expenses	$ 39,000	$ 51,000	$ 54,000	$ 54,000
Income	$ 49,000	$ 56,000	$ 69,000	$ 58,000
Known sources of income (net of taxes)	32,000	34,000	35,000	35,000
Funds from unknown sources	$ 17,000	$ 22,000	$ 34,000	$ 23,000

*Determined from 1997 figures, which are not provided.

sb
1-9-2002

14

Silver Summit Real Estate

To: IASCF 030369
From: Scott R. Bulloch
Date: January 11, 2002
Re: Ivan Ben Steelin
Subject: Average prices per acre paid by Silver Summit Real Estate

Synopsis

The records of the external affairs department were analyzed to track the average prices that each of the purchasing representatives has negotiated per acre of real estate purchased. Ivan Ben Steelin's average price is 23 to 42 percent higher than the average prices of the other three purchasing representatives.

Details

Four real estate purchasing representatives are employed by Silver Summit Real Estate. Each of the representatives is assigned purchasing tasks by the vice president of external affairs. The purchasing representative then initiates contacts and proceeds to fulfill their respective purchasing assignments.

The assignments are distributed equally among the four representatives. The records show that each representative executed the same number of real estate transactions as his or her counterpart representatives in the years 1998, 1999, 2000, and 2001.

A real estate purchasing project, for example (project 033189), to acquire 55 acres at 2000 North 8000 West, Boulder, Colorado, in 1989, revealed the following information:

- The 55-acre lot was owned by three different parties.
- Each of the three properties was listed by three different agencies, Red Hot Real Estate, Johnson Real Estate, and Monarch Real Estate, respectively.
- Steelin negotiated with Red Hot Real Estate, Peter Principle with Johnson Real Estate, and B.J. Integrity with Monarch Real Estate.
- Peter Principle's purchase of 21 acres cost $12,000, B.J. Integrity's purchase of 20.5 acres cost $10,500, and Steelin's purchase of 13.5 acres cost $10,000.

Data were gathered from purchase agreements, according to the purchasing representative, to determine the average price per acre of the real estate purchased. The data compilations revealed that Steelin's purchases were 23 to 42 percent higher than the purchases of the other purchasing representatives.

Attached (one page) are the data compilations extracted from the records of the external affairs department, as they pertain to the average prices per acre of real estate purchased. Scott R. Bulloch initialed and dated the document, and it is maintained in IASCF 030369.

Average Prices Paid per Acre of Real Estate Purchased by Silver Summit Real Estate

Purchasing Representative	1998	1999	2000	2001
Abraham Honest	515	535	543	576
B.J. Integrity	507	532	571	561
Peter Principle	555	567	581	592
Ivan Ben Steelin	678	775	898	988

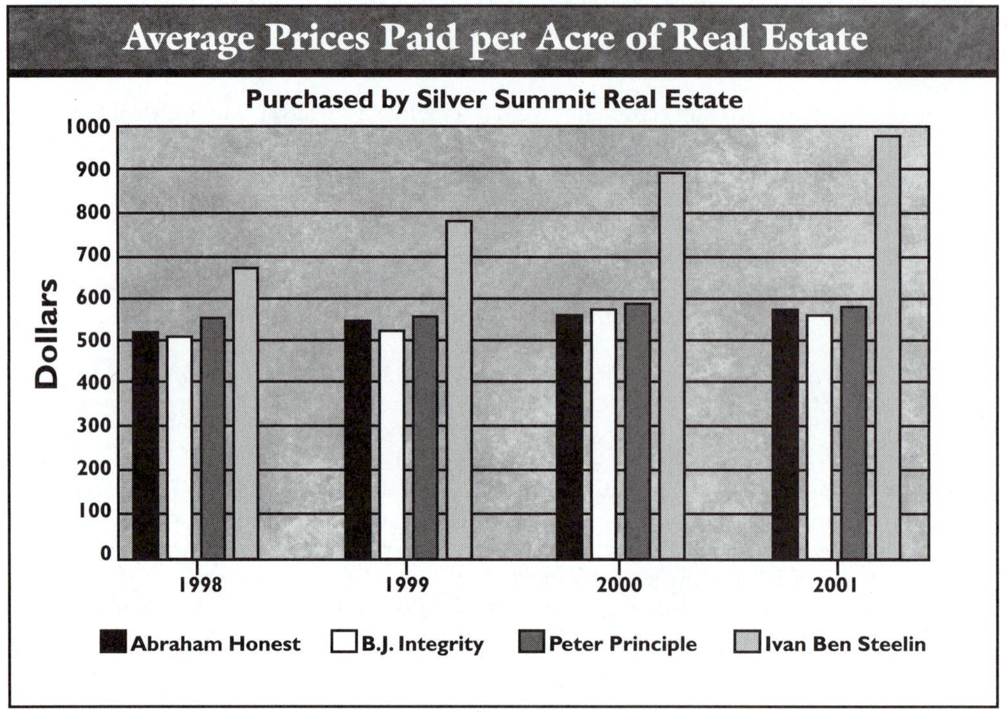

sb
1-11-2002

Silver Summit Real Estate

To: IASCF 030369
From: Scott R. Bulloch
Date: January 13, 2002
Re: Ivan Ben Steelin
Subject: Computer queries on Steelin's transactions with real estate agencies

Synopsis

Silver Summit Real Estate conducts real estate transactions through approved agencies that have listed the desired acquisition properties. Steelin has executed over 50 percent of his purchase transactions since January 1, 1998, through Red Hot Real Estate.

Details

Computer queries on the external affairs database were executed on January 13, 2002, to determine the extent of Steelin's relations with Red Hot Real Estate.

First, the number of total transactions per purchasing representative was queried. It was revealed that each purchasing representative has performed 165 purchasing arrangements since January 1, 1998.

Eleven real estate agencies have been utilized since January 1, 1998. The agencies, all located in Moore County, Colorado, are employed based on their listing of properties, which Silver Summer Real Estate seeks to acquire. If a property is not listed, the purchasing representatives are instructed, as per external affairs department policy, to rotate their dealings among the eleven agencies. The policy states "that by rotating among the approved agencies, equity is cultivated, which will encourage the agencies to offer competitive prices."

Since January 1, 1998, each of the four purchasing representatives has dealt with all the approved agencies. Steelin put 86 transactions through Red Hot Real Estate during the period in question, January 1, 1998, through December 31, 2001. Fifty-two percent of Steelin's transactions were made through Red Hot Real Estate.

The query regarding the distribution of purchasing transactions (one page) and charts extracted (two pages) were printed, initialed, and dated by Scott R. Bulloch. The three pages are maintained in IASCF 030369.

External Affairs Database
Distribution of Purchasing Transactions

January 13, 2002
User: Scott R. Bulloch
Dates searched: January 1, 1998, to December 31, 2001

Real Estate Agency	*Abraham Honest*	*B.J. Integrity*	*Peter Principle*	*Ivan Ben Steelin*
Red Hot	17	10	17	86
Johnson	16	11	12	8
Monarch	19	18	13	9
Rich	10	15	17	7
Martin	7	15	18	8
Labrum	21	19	11	7
Peterson	16	10	20	7
Century 46	22	20	14	9
Littleton	15	13	16	6
Selberg	10	15	16	6
Baker	12	19	9	8
Total	165	165	165	165

sb
1-13-2002

18

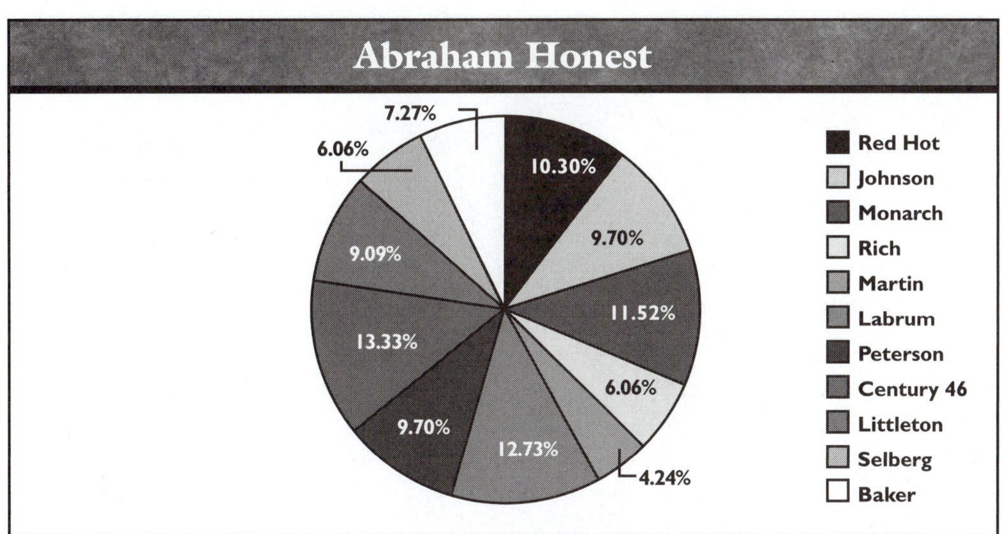
Abraham Honest
10.30%
9.70%
11.52%
6.06%
4.24%
12.73%
9.70%
13.33%
9.09%
6.06%
7.27%
Red Hot
Johnson
Monarch
Rich
Martin
Labrum
Peterson
Century 46
Littleton
Selberg
Baker

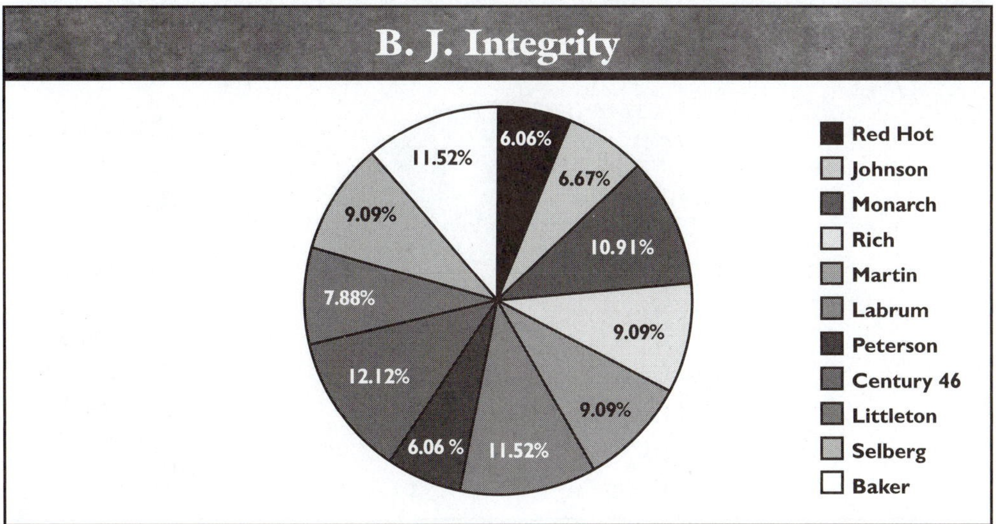
B. J. Integrity
6.06%
6.67%
10.91%
9.09%
9.09%
11.52%
6.06 %
12.12%
7.88%
9.09%
11.52%
Red Hot
Johnson
Monarch
Rich
Martin
Labrum
Peterson
Century 46
Littleton
Selberg
Baker

sb
1-13-2002

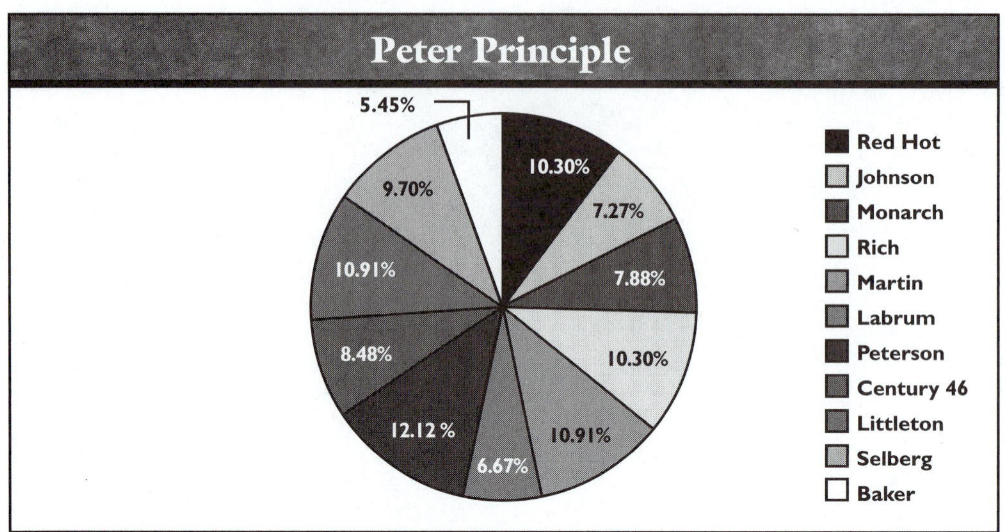

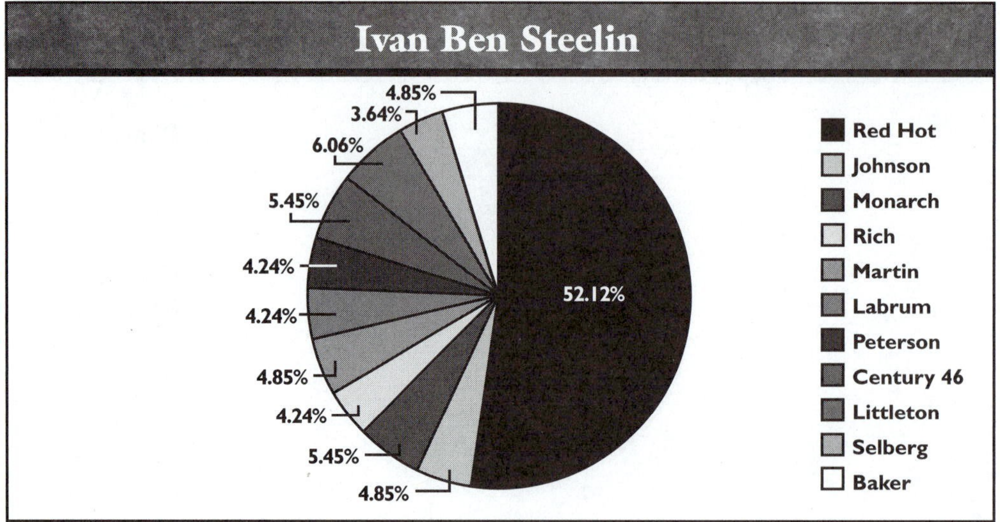

sb
1-13-2002

20

Silver Summit Real Estate

To: IASCF 030369
From: Scott R. Bulloch
Date: January 20, 2002
Re: Ivan Ben Steelin
Subject: Interview with Peter Principle

Synopsis
Peter Principle, a purchasing representative at Silver Summit Real Estate, stated that he believes that Ivan Ben Steelin conducts his Red Hot Real Estate transactions through Richey Rich, a broker at Red Hot Real Estate.

Details
Peter Principle, a purchasing representative at Silver Summit Real Estate, was interviewed in his office, 5511 Vero Beach Road, Denver, Colorado, telephone (999) 555-3463, on January 20, 2002. After being advised of the interviewer, Scott R. Bulloch, and the nature of the inquiry as an investigation of misconduct, Mr. Principle provided the following information regarding Ivan Ben Steelin:

Mr. Principle stated that Red Hot Real Estate is a very aggressive agency. In particular, Mr. Principle believed that one broker, Richey Rich, was the most aggressive broker that he had dealt with.

Mr. Principle stated that Richey Rich used to call him (Principle) to solicit deals. Principle became a purchasing representative in January of 1994. Mr. Principle cited that Rich became a bother at first, but after Mr. Principle worked for six months as a purchasing representative, Mr. Rich quit calling him (Principle).

Mr. Principle believes that Ivan Ben Steelin works very closely with Richey Rich. He stated that he overheard a conversation between Rich and Steelin, in Steelin's office, in which Steelin conveyed that he'd "send business his [Rich's] way."

Mr. Principle does not know of another broker at Red Hot Real Estate whom Ivan Ben Steelin has dealt with.

21

Silver Summit Real Estate

To: IASCF 030369
From: Scott R. Bulloch
Date: January 22, 2002
Re: Ivan Ben Steelin
Subject: Interview with Michelle Wang

Synopsis
Michelle Wang, a secretary at Silver Summit Real Estate in the external affairs department, advised that Ivan Ben Steelin had an appointment scheduled for 3:30 PM with Richey Rich on January 22, 2002, at the Burnt Oven Pizza Restaurant.

Details
Michelle Wang, a secretary at Silver Summit Real Estate in the external affairs department, was interviewed at her office, 5511 Vero Beach Road, Denver, Colorado, telephone (999)-555-3463, on the morning of January 22, 2002. Ms. Wang was informed of the nature of the inquiry and of the identity of the interviewer, Scott R. Bulloch. Ms. Wang provided the following information:

Ms. Wang is responsible for answering all incoming calls at the external affairs department. If the desired party is out or unavailable, Ms. Wang records a message on carbon-copied message slips.

Ms. Wang stated that she answered several calls a week from Richey Rich for Ivan Ben Steelin. On January 21, 2002, Ms. Wang documented a message telling Mr. Steelin to meet Richey Rich at the Burnt Oven Pizza Restaurant at 3:30 PM on January 22, 2002.

The duplicate copy of the message (one page) was obtained from Ms. Wang, was initialed and dated by Scott R. Bulloch, and is maintained in IASCF 030369.

External Affairs Department

To: Ivan
From: Richey Rich
Of: Red Hot Real Estate

Date: 1/21/2002
Time: 10:15 AM

_X_ Called

_____ Call Back at ____________________

_____ Stopped by

Message: Meet me at 3:30 PM on January 22—Burnt Oven Pizza Restaurant.

sb
1-22-2002

23

Silver Summit Real Estate

To: IASCF 030369
From: Scott R. Bulloch
Date: January 22, 2002
Re: Ivan Ben Steelin
Subject: Surveillance at Burnt Oven Pizza Restaurant

Synopsis

Ivan Ben Steelin had pizza and drinks with Richey Rich at the Burnt Oven Pizza Restaurant, 2750 East 1800 South, Denver, Colorado, on January 22, 2002. Steelin and Rich met from 3:30 PM to 4:45 PM. Steelin picked up the ticket of $14.50 and tipped the waiter a balance of a $20 bill. Rich gave Steelin a piece of paper before they left.

Details

During an interview, Michelle Wang, a secretary at Silver Summit Real Estate, advised of an appointment between Ivan Ben Steelin and Richey Rich. Ms. Wang provided a duplicate of a phone message slip regarding the appointment scheduled for 3:30 PM on January 22, 2002, at the Burnt Oven Pizza Restaurant.

According to the information provided, physical surveillance was established at the Burnt Oven Pizza Restaurant at 3:15 PM on January 22, and was terminated at 4:53 PM on the same date.

During the surveillance, Steelin and a white male, later identified as Richey Rich, had pizza and drinks. Steelin and Rich were observed writing in leather-like ring binders as they carried on a discussion.

After they consumed their provisions, Steelin put a $20 bill on the collection plate. As Steelin and Rich stood to leave, Rich was observed giving a piece of paper to Steelin, which Steelin placed in his left outside coat pocket.

The attached surveillance log furnished additional details. The surveillance log (one page) was initialed and dated by Scott R. Bulloch and is maintained in IASCF 030369.

January 22, 2002
Surveillance at the Burnt Oven Pizza Restaurant
Surveillance conducted by Scott R. Bulloch

3:15 PM	Established surveillance at the Burnt Oven Pizza Restaurant.
3:25 PM	Ivan Ben Steelin arrives at the restaurant.
3:33 PM	White male arrives and sits with Steelin.
3:40 PM	Steelin and white male place orders with waiter.
3:45 PM	Steelin and white male remove zipper ring binders from their briefcases, open them, and are observed writing in them as discussion takes place.
3:48 PM	Waiter refills glasses with clear fluid.
4:05 PM	Two pizzas are delivered to the table of Steelin and white male, and glasses are refilled with clear fluid.
4:30 PM	Waiter takes plates and tableware from table of Steelin and white male, refills glasses, and leaves a collection plate.
4:40 PM	Steelin and white male replace their zipper binders in their respective briefcases.
4:42 PM	Steelin places a form of currency on the collection plate.
4:45 PM	Steelin and white male stand up, white male hands Steelin a paper, and Steelin places the paper in his left outside coat pocket.
4:45 PM	Steelin and white male shake hands and leave the restaurant.
4:49 PM	Waiter, identified as Martin Lucky, states that the currency was a $20 bill and that the charge for the meal was $14.50. Lucky intends to keep the change as a tip. He advises that the white male is Richey Rich and that Rich is a frequent customer of the restaurant.
4:53 PM	Surveillance terminated.

sb
1-22-2002

Silver Summit Real Estate

To: IASCF 030369
From: Scott R. Bulloch
Date: January 28, 2002
Re: Ivan Ben Steelin
Subject: Interview with Richey Rich

Synopsis
Richey Rich, a real estate broker with Red Hot Real Estate, advised that he has conducted a few transactions with Ivan Ben Steelin. Rich denied having had any inappropriate relations with Ivan Ben Steelin. Rich denied having ever had meals with Ivan Ben Steelin at the Burnt Oven Pizza Restaurant.

Details
Richey Rich, a real estate broker with Red Hot Real Estate, was interviewed at his office, 3000 South Canyon Road, Denver, Colorado, on January 28, 2002. After being advised of the identity of the interviewer (Scott R. Bulloch) and the nature of the inquiry as an investigation of misconduct, Rich provided the following information:

"Red Hot Real Estate has done business with Silver Summit Real Estate for more than five years. Rich had conducted real estate transactions through all four of the purchasing representatives at Silver Summit Real Estate: Steelin, Honest, Integrity, and Principle."

Rich stated that he has conducted only a few transactions through Ivan Ben Steelin, because Steelin is "too demanding."

Richey Rich advised that not at any time have he and Steelin met for lunch at the Burnt Oven Pizza Restaurant, nor at any other restaurant.

Rich flatly denied furnishing bribes, kickbacks, or any other form of gratuities to Ivan Ben Steelin, or to any other purchasing representative at Silver Summit Real Estate. Rich stated that he suspects that other, unnamed agencies are furnishing gratuities to the purchasing representatives of Silver Summit Real Estate.

Silver Summit Real Estate

To: IASCF 030369
From: Scott R. Bulloch
Date: January 28, 2002
Re: Ivan Ben Steelin
Subject: Interview with Ivan Ben Steelin

Ivan Ben Steelin was interviewed at his office, 5511 Vero Beach Road, Denver, Colorado, telephone (999)-425-3463, on January 28, 2002. Steelin was advised that the interviewers were Scott R. Bulloch and Sue U. Buttz, and that an investigation was under way concerning an improper broker relationship.

Steelin was informed that the intent of the inquiry was to obtain a voluntary consent to examine his bank account records. Steelin stated that such a consent agreement was not necessary, and that he wished to meet in private at that time to discuss his predicament.

Ivan Ben Steelin was advised of his rights in regard to self-incrimination, and he executed an advice-of-rights form, a copy of which is attached. Steelin agreed to a videotaping of the interview that followed.

Steelin stated that family pressure to succeed and to measure up to his in-laws' expectations had led to his accepting payments from Richey Rich of Red Hot Real Estate. Steelin provided the attached free and voluntarily signed statement (two pages) regarding his association with Richey Rich, following the interview.

Silver Summit Real Estate

ADVICE OF RIGHTS*

Place: Silver Summit Real Estate, 5511 Vero Beach Road, Denver, Colorado
Date: January 28, 2002
Time: 11:30 AM

Before we ask you any questions, you must understand your rights.

You have the right to remain silent.

Anything you say can be used against you in court.

You have the right to talk to a lawyer for advice before we ask you any questions and to have a lawyer with you during questioning.

If you cannot afford a lawyer, one will be appointed for you before any questioning, if you wish.

If you decide to answer questions now without a lawyer present, you will still have the right to stop answering at any time. You also have the right to stop answering at any time until you talk to a lawyer.

WAIVER OF RIGHTS

I have read this statement of my rights and I understand what my rights are. I am willing to make a statement and answer questions. I do not want a lawyer at this time. I understand and know what I am doing. No promises or threats have been made to me and no pressure or coercion of any kind has been used against me.

Signed: *Ivan Ben Steelin* 1-28-2002

Witness: *Scott R. Bulloch*

Witness: *Sue U. Buttz*

Time: 11:30 AM

*Private citizens are not required to give Miranda warnings. However, many prosecutors prefer that they be given.

28

Silver Summit Real Estate

Denver, Colorado
January 28, 2002

I, Ivan Ben Steelin, furnish the following free and voluntary statement to Scott R. Bulloch and Sue U. Buttz, who have identified themselves to me as internal auditor and legal counsel, respectively, for Silver Summit Real Estate. No threats or promises of any kind have been used to induce this statement.

I have been advised that an internal inquiry has been and is being conducted to determine whether or not I have accepted any unlawful gratuities and violated the Silver Summit Real Estate code of conduct in my position as a purchasing representative for Silver Summit Real Estate. I have also been advised that I am the sole target of this internal inquiry; that the allegations could constitute a criminal act; and that I have a right to an attorney, should I choose.

I have been employed at Silver Summit Real Estate since January 7, 1994, and since January 1, 1996, have been a purchasing representative in the external affairs department, in Denver, Colorado.

I freely admit that I have accepted gratuities and other considerations from Richey Rich, real estate broker at Red Hot Real Estate, Denver, Colorado. The total amount of monies I have received is approximately $115,000 since January 1997. I have also received property, valued at approximately $35,000, from Richey Rich, on which property my personal residence was constructed.

Rich paid me the monies and provided the properties to ensure that I would continue to purchase real estate from Red Hot Real Estate. I was aware at the time I began taking money from Rich that such conduct was illegal and violated the Silver Summit Real Estate code of conduct. I committed these acts because of the financial pressure I felt to live up to others' expectations. I am sorry for my conduct, and I would like to begin to make reparations.

No one else at Silver Summit Real Estate was involved, nor did anyone else have knowledge of my activities.

29

I have read the above statement, consisting of this typewritten page and one other typewritten page. I have initialed the other page and now sign my name because this statement is true and correct to the best of my knowledge and belief.

Ivan Ben Steelin 1-28-2002

Ivan Ben Steelin

Scott R. Bulloch

Scott R. Bulloch January 28, 2002

Sue U. Buttz

Sue U. Buttz January 28, 2002

30

Silver Summit Real Estate

To: IASCF 030369
From: Scott R. Bulloch
Date: February 13, 2002
Re: Ivan Ben Steelin
Subject: Estimated overpayment to Red Hot Real Estate

Synopsis
Computations indicate that the estimated loss to Silver Summit Real Estate for the years 1997 through 2001 due to overpayment to Red Hot Real Estate is approximately $436,568.

Details
On February 13, 2002, estimates were prepared concerning possible overpayment to Red Hot Real Estate as a result of activities conducted between Ivan Ben Steelin and Richey Rich.

Data on four of the eleven agencies that Silver Summit Real Estate conducts transactions with were extracted from the external affairs database. The data were extrapolated to determine the average prices paid per acre of real estate purchased through each of the four agencies.

The average cost computation was then applied to the acreage purchased from Red Hot Real Estate to determine an approximate overpayment to that agency over the last five years.

The total of the losses, as reflected on the attached one-page worksheet, is approximately $436,568 for the years 1997 through 2001.

Average Cost per Acre

	1997	1998	1999	2000	2001
Johnson	$505.00	$525.00	$545.00	$565.00	$576.00
Labrum	508.00	520.00	541.00	560.00	573.00
Century 46	503.00	530.00	548.00	568.00	581.00
Monarch	510.00	524.00	545.00	567.00	575.00
Average cost	$506.50	$524.75	$544.75	$565.00	$576.25

Ivan Ben Steelin's Transactions with Red Hot Real Estate

Cost paid to Red Hot	$130,500.00	$176,280.00	$240,250.00	$332,260.00	$414,960.00
Acreage received	200	260	310	370	420
Average cost	$652.50	$678.00	$775.00	$898.00	$988.00
Expected cost for acreage	$101,200.00	$136,435.00	$168,872.50	$209,050.00	$242,025.00
Estimated overpayment	$29,200.00	$39,845.00	$71,377.50	$123,210.00	$172,935.00

Total loss = approximately $436,568

PART FIVE

MANAGEMENT FRAUD

Financial Statement Fraud

After studying this chapter, you should be able to:

1. Understand the role that financial statements play in U.S. businesses.
2. Understand the nature of financial statement fraud.
3. See how financial statement frauds occur and how they are concealed.
4. Understand how financial statement fraud is detected.
5. Identify financial statement fraud exposures.
6. Understand how information on company management and directors, the nature of organization, its operating characteristics, relationship with businesses, and financial results helps in assessing whether financial statement fraud is occurring.

You may not have heard of Cendant Corporation, but you are probably familiar with some of its subsidiaries—Days Inn, Ramada Inn, Avis Car Rental, and real-estate brokerage Century 21. Cendant Corporation was formed in 1997 when CUC International Inc. merged with HFS Inc. The intention was to create one of the world's largest hotel, car rental, reservation, and real-estate companies. But Cendant's hopes for success quickly faded when HFS Inc. learned that CUC International had inflated its income and earnings in order to appear highly profitable and successful. What started as a small fraud in 1983 quickly mushroomed into a large one. From 1995 to 1997, CUC International inflated its pre-tax operating income by more than $500 million. Many executives of CUC International were fired and prosecuted.

In 1999, Cendant Corporation agreed to pay $2.8 billion to settle a shareholder lawsuit. The attorneys for the plaintiffs earned $262 million in fees. On April 16, 1998, when the fraud was announced to the public, Cendant's stock dropped 46%; the company's paper value shrank by $14.4 billion in one day. Cendant survived and remains a diversified global provider of business consumer services. However, the fraud cost them precious time in a highly competitive business environment, negative public exposure in an industry where reputations count heavily, and, of course, more than $2.8 billion in hard-earned cash. Today the company has approximately 60,000 employees and operates in over 100 countries.[1]

The Growing Problem of Financial Statement Fraud

America's capital markets are the envy of the world. The efficiency, liquidity, and resiliency of our markets stand second to none. We cannot overstate the important role that financial statements play in keeping U.S. markets efficient. Financial statements are—normally—meaningful disclosures of where a company has been, where it is currently, and where it is going. Most statements present a fair representation of the financial position of the organization issuing them, and are prepared using GAAP (generally accepted accounting principles), which guide how transactions are to be accounted for. Although GAAP does allow some flexibility, standards of objectivity, integrity, and judgment are supposed to prevail.

Unfortunately, financial statements sometimes misrepresent an organization's position and results. The misstatement of financial statements happens because accounting records are manipulated, falsified, or altered. Misleading statements cause serious problems in the markets and in the economy. They result in large losses for investors, a break in the trust in our system, and litigation and embarrassment for individuals and organizations associated with the fraud.

The Nature of Financial Statement Fraud

Financial statement fraud, like other frauds, involves intentional deceit and attempted concealment. Financial statement fraud may be concealed through falsified documentation, including forgery, and through collusion by management, employees, or third parties. Unfortunately, like other fraud, financial statement fraud is rarely visible. Rather, symptoms of fraud—red flags—are observed. Because symptoms can be caused by legitimate factors, the presence of symptoms does not always mean that fraud exists. Documents are sometimes legitimately lost, the general ledger can be out of balance because of an unintentional (and real) accounting error, and unexpected analytical relationships can be the result of unrecognized changes in underlying economic factors. Caution must be used even when fraud tips come in, because the person may be mistaken or may be intentionally making false allegations.

Fraud symptoms cannot easily be ranked in order of importance, nor can they be combined into effective predictive models. Their significance varies widely. Some factors will be present when no fraud exists, and only a small number of symptoms may present themselves when fraud is occurring. Many times, the fraud is difficult to prove. Without a confession, obviously forged documents, or a number of repeated, similar thefts (so a pattern of fraud can be inferred), convicting someone of fraud is difficult. Because of the difficulty of detecting and proving fraud, always exercise extreme care when you conduct fraud examinations, quantify fraud, or perform other investigation activities.

Statistics on Financial Statement Fraud

How much financial statement fraud occurs is difficult to know. One way to measure it is to look at some of the Securities and Exchange Commission (SEC) enforcement releases (accounting and auditing enforcement releases—AAERs). AAERs are issued when financial statement fraud occurs at companies with publicly traded stock.

Several studies have examined AAERs. One of the first and most comprehensive was the Report of the National Commission on Fraudulent Financial Reporting (Treadway Commission). This report studied fraud during a 10-year period ending in 1987 and found that although financial statement frauds occur infrequently, they are extremely costly.[2]

In 1999, the Committee of Sponsoring Organizations (COSO) released a study of financial statement frauds that occurred between 1987 and 1997.[3] COSO found that approximately 300 financial statement frauds required AAERs during the period. A random sample of 204 of the COSO frauds revealed the following:

1. The average financial statement fraud period extended 23.7 months, and the frequency of fraudulent acts was fairly steady during the period.
2. These frauds were most commonly perpetrated by improper revenue recognition, overstating assets, and understating expenses. Revenue frauds were most commonly perpetrated (1) by recording fictitious revenues and (2) by record-

ing revenues prematurely. In inventory frauds, overstating actual assets was most common; recording fictitious assets or assets not owned was second; and capitalizing items that should be expensed was third. Other common financial statement frauds included misappropriation of assets (large enough to render the financial statements misleading) and inappropriate disclosure.

3. Accounts receivable, inventory, property, plant, and equipment, loans/notes receivable, cash, investments, patents, and natural resources were the assets most often misstated.
4. The mean cumulative misstatement was $25 million; the median cumulative misstatement was $4.1 million. (The mean was disproportionally increased by several very large frauds.) The mean largest single-year or quarterly misstatement of net income was $9.9 million.
5. In 72% of the cases, the CEO was the perpetrator. The next most frequent perpetrators (in descending order of frequency) were the CFO, controller, COO (chief operating officer), vice presidents, board of director members, lower-level personnel, and others. In 29% of the cases, the external auditor was named in an AAER. In these cases, the auditor was charged with either violating Rule 10(b)5 of the 1934 Securities Exchange Act or with aiding and abetting others in a violation of Rule 10(b)5.[4]
6. In 55% of the cases, the last audit report prior to the fraud was an unqualified audit opinion. In 24% of the frauds the last audit opinion noted going concern, litigation, or other uncertainties. In 17% of the cases, the opinion had modifications or qualifications due to a change in accounting principle or a change in auditors, and in 4% of the cases there were other qualifications, such as a scope limitation.[5]
7. Of companies involved in fraudulent financial statements reporting, the mean total assets were $532 million; the mean revenues were $232 million; and the mean shareholders' equity was $86 million. Medians were much lower, with $16 million in assets, $13 million in revenues, and $5 million in shareholders' equity.
8. Industries with the most frauds: computer hardware/software with 12%; other manufacturers with 12%; financial service providers with 11%; health care and health products with 9%; and retailers/wholesalers and other service providers with 7% each. Other industries with 3% or more were mining/oil and gas, telecommunications, insurance, and real estate.
9. Of the fraudulent companies, 78% were listed on the NASDAQ or other over-the-counter markets, 15% of the companies' stocks were traded on the New York Stock Exchange, and 7% were traded on the American Stock Exchange.
10. Severe consequences were usually associated with companies who committed financial statement fraud: (1) 36% eventually filed for Chapter 11 bankruptcy, were described as "defunct" in the AAERs, or were taken over by a state or federal regulator after the fraud was discovered. (2) 15% sold a large portion of their assets, merged with another company, or had a new controlling shareholder. (3) 21% had their stock delisted from the national stock exchange where the stock had traded. (4) 24% were sued and/or settled with shareholders or bondholders, often as part of the class action lawsuits filed subsequent to the disclosure of the fraud.
11. Most companies either had no audit committee or the audit committee met less than twice a year. Although 75% of the companies had an audit committee composed of outside directors, the committees generally met only annually.

12. Boards of directors were dominated by insiders and "grey" directors (outsiders with special ties to the company or with significant ownership and little experience serving as directors of other companies). Approximately 60% of the directors were insiders or grey directors. Collectively, the directors and officers owned nearly one-third of the company's stock. Nearly 40% of the boards had no directors who served as outside or grey directors on another company's board.
13. Family relationships between directors and/or officers were common, as were individuals who had significant power. In nearly 40% of the companies, the proxy provided evidence of family relationships between the directors and/or officers. The founder was on the board, or the original CEO/president was still in place in nearly one-half of the companies. In more than 20% of the companies, officers held incompatible job functions (for example, were both CEO and CFO).
14. Some companies were experiencing net losses or were just holding break-even positions in periods prior to the fraud. Financial strain or distress thus constituted the pressure factor for the fraud. The lowest quartile of companies were in a net loss position, and the median company had net income of only $175,000 in the year preceding the first year of the fraud period. Some companies were experiencing downward trends in net income preceding the first period; others were experiencing upward trends in net income. Thus, the frauds may have been designed to reverse downward spirals or to preserve upward trends.
15. All sizes of audit firms were associated with companies committing financial statement fraud. In the sample, 56% of the companies were audited by what was then a Big 8 or Big 6 auditor during the period of the fraud, and 44% were audited by auditors outside the Big 8/Big 6.
16. Financial statement fraud occasionally implicated the external auditor. Auditors were named in 56 of the 195 fraud cases (29) where AAERs named individuals for either alleged involvement in the fraud (30 of 56 cases) or for negligent auditing (26 of 56 cases). Most of the auditors named in AAERs (46 of 56) were not Big 8 or Big 6 auditors.
17. Some companies changed auditors during the fraud. Just over 25% of the companies changed auditors during the time frame between the last "clean" financial statement and the last fraud financial statement. A majority of the auditor changes occurred during the fraud period (so that two different auditors were used during the fraud).
18. Consequences associated with the fraud were severe for the individuals involved. Individual senior executives were subject to class action suits and SEC actions that resulted in severe personal financial penalties. A significant number of individuals were terminated or forced to resign. However, relatively few individuals admitted guilt or eventually served prison sentences.

These findings are consistent with a study conducted in the United Kingdom by the Auditing Practices Board (APB) of England.[6] APB also found two key aspects of financial statement frauds: (1) The majority are committed by company management, and (2) financial statement frauds involve no actual theft and are unlikely to be detected by statutory auditors.[7] Of the fraud cases reviewed by APB, 14 affected the company accounts financially. In all 14 cases, senior management played a key role, and 65% misstated financial data to boost share prices or disguise losses.[8]

An Example of Financial Statement Fraud

Although companies who report fraudulent financial statements remain a relatively small percentage of companies, the damage caused by even one set of fraudulent financial statements can be staggering. Consider, for example, the Phar-Mor fraud. Phar-Mor's COO, Michael "Mickey" Monus, was sentenced to 19 years and 7 months in prison. The fraud caused more than $1 billion in losses and the bankruptcy of the 28th largest private U.S. company. Phar-Mor's former auditors, a Big 5 firm, face claims of more than $1 billion (which it settled for significantly less).

The Phar-Mor fraud is a good example of how financial statement frauds typically occur. The first Phar-Mor store opened by Monus in 1982 sold a variety of household products and prescription drugs at prices substantially lower than at other discount stores. The low prices were possible because of "power buying," Monus's strategy of loading up on products whenever suppliers offered rock-bottom prices. At the time he started Phar-Mor, Monus was also president of Tamco, a family-held distributing company recently acquired by the Pittsburgh-based Giant Eagle grocery store chain. In 1984, David Shapira, president of Giant Eagle, funded the expansion of Phar-Mor with $4 million. Shapira then became CEO of Phar-Mor, and Monus was named president and COO. By 1985, Phar-Mor had 15 stores, and by 1992 (only a decade after the first store opened), 310 stores were operating in 32 states, posting sales of more than $3 billion.

Competitors marveled at how Phar-Mor could sell products so cheaply and still make a profit. It appeared to be well on its way to becoming the next Wal-Mart. In fact, Sam Walton once stated that the only company he feared was Phar-Mor. After five years, however, Phar-Mor began to lose money. Unwilling to allow these shortfalls to damage Phar-Mor's appearance of success, Monus and his team began to engage in creative accounting, and Phar-Mor never reported losses. Federal fraud examiners later discerned that Phar-Mor overstated pretax income for fiscal 1989 by $350,000 and that 1987 was the last year that Phar-Mor actually made a profit.

Relying on Phar-Mor's financial statements, investors and analysts alike viewed Phar-Mor as a sure way to cash in on the retailing craze. Among the big investors were Westinghouse Credit Corporation, Sears Roebuck & Co., mall developer Edward J. de Bartolo, and the prestigious Lazard Frères & Co. Prosecutors stated that banks and investors poured $1.14 billion into the company, because the financial statements looked so good.

To hide Phar-Mor's cash flow problems, attract investors, and make the company look profitable, Monus and his subordinate, Patrick Finn, altered inventory accounts to understate the cost of goods sold and overstate income. They also embezzled cash. The company's internal investigations estimated the embezzlement to be in excess of $10 million. Most of the stolen funds were used to support Monus's now-defunct World Basketball League.

Monus and Finn's embezzlement involved account manipulation, overstatement of inventory, and accounting rules manipulation of Phar-Mor's income statement. In 1985 and 1986, well before the large fraud began, Monus directed Finn to understate certain expenses that came in over budget and to overstate those expenses that came in under budget to make operations look efficient. Although the net effect of the first manipulations evened out, the accounting information was not accurate. Finn later stated that this seemingly harmless request by Monus was an important precursor to the later extensive fraud.

Finn also increased Phar-Mor's actual gross profit margin of 14.2% to around 16.5% by inflating inventory accounts. The company hired an independent firm to count inventory in its stores. After the third-party inventory counters submitted a report that detailed amounts and retail value for a store's inventory, Phar-Mor's accountants prepared a "compilation packet," which calculated the amount of inventory at cost. Journal entries were then prepared. Using the compilation numbers, accountants credited Inventory to properly report the sales activity, but rather than record a debit to Cost of Goods Sold, they debited so-called "bucket" accounts. To avoid auditor scrutiny they emptied the bucket accounts at the end of each fiscal year by allocating the balance to individual stores as Inventory. Because the related Cost of Goods Sold was understated, it appeared as if Phar-Mor was selling merchandise at higher margins. Because the cost of sales was understated, net income was overstated.

Phar-Mor regularly pressured vendors for large, up-front payments, called "exclusivity payments," in exchange for not selling competitors' products in their stores. Some vendors paid up to $25 million for these rights. Monus used this money to cover losses and to pay suppliers. Instead of deferring revenue from exclusivity payments over the life of the vendor's contracts—consistent with GAAP—Monus and Finn recognized all the revenue up-front. As a result, Phar-Mor was able to report impressive results in the short run.

Motivations Behind Financial Statement Fraud

The motivations behind fraudulent financial statements vary. Sometimes, perpetrators want to support a high stock price or a bond or stock offering. Sometimes they want to increase the company's stock price. Other times, top executives own large amounts of company stock, and a decrease in the stock price would significantly decrease their personal net worth.

Managers sometimes overstate financial results to meet the Street's expectations. Pressure to perform is high, and when faced with the choice between failure and cheating, some people choose cheating. In the Phar-Mor case, Monus wanted his company to grow quickly, so he lowered prices on 300 "price-sensitive" items. Prices were cut so much that items sold below cost—each sale resulted in a loss. The strategy may have helped Phar-Mor win new customers and open dozens of new stores each year, but it also resulted in huge losses for the company. Rather than admitting that the company was facing losses, Monus hid the drain and made Phar-Mor appear more profitable. The motivations for financial statement fraud differ, but the results are always the same—adverse consequences for the company, its principals, and its investors.

A Framework for Detecting Financial Statement Fraud

Identifying fraud exposures or opportunities for fraud is one of the most difficult steps in detecting financial statement fraud. To correctly identify exposures, you must clearly understand the operations and the nature of the organization you are examining as well as the industry and its competitors. You must understand the organization's management and what motivates them. You must also understand how the company is organized and be aware of the company's relationships with other parties and the influence that each party has on your client and its officers.

Financial statement frauds are rarely detected by analyzing financial statements alone. Rather, these frauds are detected by comparing financial statement numbers with real-world numbers. The context in which management is operating and by which they are being motivated must be understood. Changes in reported assets, liabilities, revenues, and expenses from period to period are examined. Company performance is compared to industry norms. In the ZZZZ Best fraud (see Chapter 7), for example, each period's financial statements looked correct.[9] Only when period-to-period changes in assets and revenues were examined and assets and revenues reported in the financial statements compared with actual projects was it determined that the statements were misstated.

The exposure rectangle shown on the next page is useful in identifying management fraud.

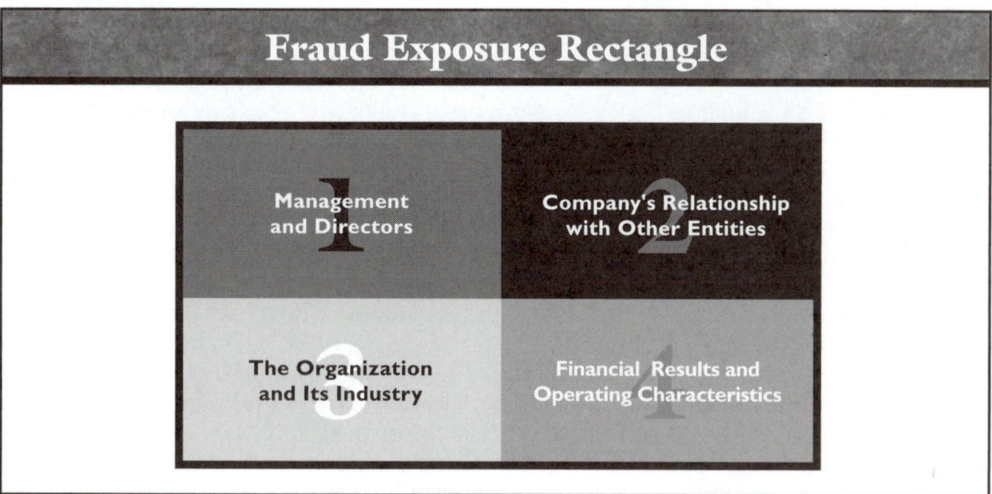

Although auditors traditionally focus almost entirely on the financial statements and results of operations in their endeavors to detect financial fraud, all four "corners" present fraud exposures that must be examined.

Management and the Board of Directors

As shown by the statistics presented earlier, top management is almost always involved in financial statement fraud. Unlike embezzlement and misappropriation, financial statement fraud requires the involvement of individuals high up in an organization, and most often *on behalf* of the organization as opposed to *against* the organization. Because of this, management and the directors must be investigated to determine their exposure to, and motivation for, committing fraud. Gaining an understanding of management and what motivates them is crucial. In particular, three aspects of management should be investigated:

1. Their backgrounds
2. Their motivations
3. Their influence in organizational decision making

With respect to backgrounds, as a fraud investigator, you need to understand what organizations and situations management and directors have been associated with in the past. Here is one example why. Remember the Lincoln Savings and Loan fraud? (See Chapter 2.) Before perpetrating the Lincoln Savings and Loan fraud, Charles Keating was sanctioned by the SEC for his involvement in a fraud in Cincinnati, Ohio. He had, in fact, signed a consent decree that he would never again manage another financial institution.

Here is another example—Comparator Systems, the Los Angeles-based fingerprint company accused of securities fraud in 1996.[10] CEO Robert Reed Rogers grew up in Chicago, majored in chemistry in college, and became a college lecturer in business and economics. He worked short stints at the consulting firm of McKinsey & Co. and at Litton Industries. In information sent to investors, he boasted of numerous accomplishments, describing himself as founder and president of various companies that developed products or processes. Missing from his biographical sketches was the fact that, in the mid-70s, he was president of Newport International Metals. Newport was involved in the speculative rage of the period—

precious metals. The company claimed to have "exclusive rights" to a certain mining process for producing jewelry. After obtaining $50,000 in securities from investors John and Herta Minar of New York to serve as collateral to secure start-up funds, Newport projected first-year revenue of $1.2 million. In 1976, Newport was cited by the State of California for unlawful sale of securities and was ordered to stop. The Minars sued and won judgment for $50,000. In 1977, a bench warrant was issued for Rogers's arrest for failure to appear in court in connection with a lawsuit filed by investors in Westcliffe International, of which Rogers was president. In 1977, as general partner of Intermedico Community Health Care, Rogers and three others borrowed $25,000 from Torrance, California, lawyer William MacCabe. Three years later, MacCabe won a court judgment for $31,000 against the group. Investors and others associated with Comparator Systems would, no doubt, have been extremely interested in such a tainted "resume."

You therefore need to know what motivates directors and management. Is their personal worth tied up in the organization? Are they under pressure to deliver unrealistic results? Is their compensation primarily performance-based? Must debt covenants or other financial measures be met? Are managers' jobs at risk? These questions—and others of similar ilk—must be asked and answered in order to properly understand management's motivations. Many financial statement frauds are perpetrated because management is under pressure to report positive or high income to support stock prices, or to show positive earnings for a public stock or debt offering, or to report profits to meet regulatory or loan restrictions.

Management's ability to influence organizational decisions is also important to understand because perpetrating fraud is much easier when only a few individuals have primary decision-making power. In organizations with democratic leadership, fraud is much harder to perpetrate. Most people who commit management fraud are first-time offenders, and their "first time" is tough on them. Things get even more difficult when the fraud requires two people to simultaneously be dishonest or three people to simultaneously be dishonest. When decision making is spread among several individuals, or when the board of directors takes an active role in the organization, fraud becomes very difficult to perpetrate. Because of this, most financial statement frauds do not occur in large, historically profitable organizations. Rather, they occur in smaller organizations where one or two individuals have almost total control over decision making, and where the board of directors and the audit committee are inactive. An active board of directors or an audit committee that is involved in major decisions does much to deter management fraud.

Here are some key questions that fraud examiners ask about management and the directors:

Understanding Management and Director Backgrounds

1. Have key executives or board members been associated with other organizations in the past, and what was the nature of those relationships?
2. Are key members of management promoted from within the organization or recruited from outside?
3. Do key members of management have past regulatory or legal problems, either personally or with prior organizations?
4. Have there been significant changes in the makeup of management or the board of directors?
5. Has there been a high turnover of management and/or board members?
6. Do any managers or board members have criminal backgrounds?
7. Are there other issues regarding the backgrounds of management and the board of directors?

Understanding What Motivates Management and the Board of Directors

1. Is key executives' personal worth tied up in the organization?
2. Is management under pressure to meet earnings or other financial expectations, or does management commit to achieving what appear to be unduly aggressive forecasts?

continues

3. Is management's compensation primarily performance-based (bonuses, stock options, etc.)?
4. Must management meet significant debt covenants or other financial restrictions?
5. Is the job security of key members of management at serious risk?
6. Is the organization's reported performance decreasing?
7. Is management excessively interested in maintaining or increasing the entity's stock price?
8. Does management have an incentive to use inappropriate means to minimize reported earnings for tax reasons?
9. Are there any other significant issues regarding motivations of management and board members?

Understanding the Scope of Influence of Management and the Board of Directors

1. Who among management or the board of directors has the most influence?
2. Do one or two people have dominant influence in the organization?
3. Is the management style autocratic or democratic?
4. Is management centralized or decentralized?
5. Does management effectively communicate and support the entity's values and ethics, or do they communicate inappropriate values or ethics?
6. Does management fail to correct known reportable conditions in internal control on a timely basis?
7. Does management set unduly aggressive financial targets and expenditures for operating personnel?
8. Does management have too much involvement in, or influence over, the selection of accounting principles or the determination of significant estimates?
9. Are there other significant issues regarding the influence of management and/or the board of directors?

Relationships with Others

Financial statement fraud is often perpetrated with the help of other real or fictitious organizations. Lincoln Savings and Loan, for example, structured sham transactions with "straw buyers" to make its negative performance appear profitable. A real estate limited partnership, the DuVall Limited Real Estate Partnerships, structured fraudulent transactions with bankers to hide mortgages on their holdings. Relationships with related parties are problematic because they often allow for other than arms-length transactions. The management of ESM Government Securities, for example, hid a $400 million financial statement fraud by creating a large receivable from a nonconsolidated entity.

Although relationships with all parties should be examined to determine if they present opportunities for management fraud, relationships with financial institutions, related organizations and individuals, external auditors, lawyers, investors, and regulators should be carefully scrutinized. Relationships with financial institutions and bondholders are important because they indicate the extent to which the company is leveraged. Here are typical questions to ask about debt relationships:

- How leveraged is the company, with which financial institutions, and is it in line with the industry?
- What assets has the organization pledged as collateral?
- What debt or other restrictive covenants must be met?
- Do the banking relationships appear normal, or are there strange relationships with financial institutions, such as using institutions in unusual geographical locations?
- Are there relationships between the officers of the financial institutions and your client organization?

In the DuVall Limited Real Estate Partnerships referred to earlier, a Wisconsin company took out unauthorized loans from a bank located in another state, where it had no business operations. The partnership was used because the client company's CEO had a relationship with the bank president, who later falsified an audit confirmation. The loans were discovered when auditors performed a lien search on properties owned. The bank president denied the existence of the loans, so liabilities were significantly understated on the balance sheet.

Related organizations and individuals (related parties) should be examined because structuring improper and unrealistic transactions with related organizations and individuals is an easy way to perpetrate financial statement fraud. These symptoms are identified by examining large and/or unusual transactions, especially those that occur at strategic times (such as at the end of an accounting period) to make the financial statements look better. Here are transactions events that should be carefully examined:

- Large transactions that result in revenues and/or income for the organization
- Sales and/or purchases of assets between related entities
- Transactions that result in goodwill or other tangible assets being recognized in the financial statements
- Loans and other financing transactions between related entities
- Transactions that appear to be unusual or questionable for the organization, especially unrealistically large ones

A company's relationship with its auditors is important to analyze for several reasons. If there has been a recent change in auditors, there is probably a good reason for the change. Auditing firms do not easily give up clients, and the termination of an auditor-auditee relationship is often caused by (1) failure of the client to pay, (2) an auditor-auditee disagreement, (3) the auditor's suspicion of fraud or other problems, or (4) the auditee's view that the auditor's fees are too high. Although high fees don't usually signal fraud, the other three reasons can. The fact that an auditor was dismissed or resigned, together with the difficulties that first-year auditors will encounter in discovering financial statement fraud, is cause for concern.

Relationships with lawyers pose an even greater risk. Auditors are supposed to be independent and are obliged to resign if they suspect inaccurate or inappropriate financial results. However, lawyers act as advocates for their clients, and therefore tend to follow and support their clients until it is extremely obvious that fraud has occurred. In addition, lawyers are often privy to information about a client's legal difficulties, regulatory problems, and other significant occurrences. Like auditors, lawyers rarely give up a profitable client unless something is very wrong. Thus a change in legal firms can be cause for concern. And, unlike changing auditors, where publicly held companies have to file a 10-K, changing lawyers entails no such reporting requirement.

Relationships with investors are important because financial statement fraud is often motivated by wanting to promote a debt or equity offering to investors. In addition, a knowledge of the number and types of investors (public vs. private company, major exchange vs. small exchange, etc.) often indicates the level of pressure and public scrutiny management faces in its performance. If an organization is publicly held, investor groups and investment analysts are following the company very closely and can often provide information that something is wrong. For example, "short" investors are always looking for bad news that makes a stock go down. If they suspect something awry, they may contact management, the media, or even the auditors to vent their concerns. Investor groups focus on information very different from that used by auditors, and sometimes fraud symptoms are more obvious to them.

Finally, understanding the client's relationship with regulators is important. If your client company is publicly held, you need to know whether the SEC has ever issued an enforcement release against them. You also need to know whether annual, quarterly, and other reports are filed on a timely basis. If the client is in a regulated industry, such as banking, you need to know what their relationship is with appropriate regulatory bodies. Are there significant issues raised by those bodies? Does the organization owe back taxes to the federal or state government or to other taxing districts? Because of the recourses and sanctions available to taxing authorities, organizations don't fall behind on their payments unless something is very wrong or they are having serious cash flow problems. These are typical questions to ask about a company's relationships:

Relationships with Financial Institutions

1. With what financial institution does the organization maintain significant relationships?
2. How leveraged is the organization through its bank or other loans?
3. Do loan or debt covenants or restrictions pose significant problems for the organization?
4. Do banking relationships appear normal, or are there unusual attributes about the relationships (strange geographical locations, too many banks, etc.)?
5. Do members of management or the board have personal or other close relationships with officers of the company's major banks?
6. Have there been significant changes in the financial institutions the company uses? If so, why?
7. Are there significant bank accounts or subsidiary or branch operations in tax havens for which there appears to be no clear business justification?
8. Have critical assets of the company been pledged as collateral on risky loans?
9. Are there other questionable financial institution relationships?

Relationships with Related Parties

1. Are there significant transactions with related parties not in the ordinary course of business or with related parties that have not been audited or that were audited by another firm?
2. Are there large and/or unusual transactions at or near the end of a period that significantly improve the company's reported financial performance?
3. Are there significant receivables and/or payables between related parties?
4. Is a significant amount of the organization's revenues and/or income derived from related-party transactions?
5. Is a significant part of the company's income or revenues derived from one or two large transactions?
6. Are there any other questionable related-party relationships?

Relationships with Auditors

1. Have there been frequent disputes with current or preceding auditors on accounting, auditing, or reporting matters?
2. Has management placed unreasonable demands on its auditors, including unreasonable time constraints?
3. Has the company placed formal or informal restrictions on auditors that inappropriately limit their access to people or information or limit their ability to communicate effectively with the board of directors or the audit committee?
4. Is management behavior toward auditors domineering? Has management attempted to influence the scope of the auditor's work?
5. Has there been a change in auditors, and if so, for what reason?
6. Are there other questionable auditor relationships?

Relationships with Lawyers

1. Has there been significant litigation involving the company in matters that could severely and adversely affect its performance?
2. Has there been an attempt to hide litigation from auditors or others?
3. Has there been a change in outside counsel, and if so, for what reason?
4. Are there other questionable lawyer relationships?

Relationships with Investors

1. Is the organization in the process of issuing an initial or secondary public debt or equity offering?
2. Are there investor-related lawsuits?
3. Are there problematic or questionable relationships with investment bankers, stock analysts, or others?
4. Has there been significant "short selling" of the company's stock, and if so, for what reasons?
5. Are there questionable investor relationships?

continues

Relationships with Regulatory Bodies

1. Does management disregard regulatory authorities?
2. Have there been claims against the entity or its senior management that allege fraud or violations of securities laws?
3. Have 8-Ks been filed with the SEC, and if so, for what reasons?[11]
4. Are there any new accounting, statutory, or regulatory requirements that could impair the financial stability or profitability of the entity?
5. Are there significant tax disputes with the IRS or other taxing authorities?
6. Is the company current on paying its payroll taxes and other payroll-related expenses, and is the company current on paying other liabilities?
7. Are there other questionable relationships with regulatory bodies?

Organization and Industry

Perpetrators sometimes mask financial statement fraud by creating an organizational structure in which hiding fraud is easy. For example, Enron used complicated and even off-book organizational structures to mask problems such as large liabilities. Several Enron transactions, such as the famous Chewco and LMJ1 transactions, were hidden in off-balance-sheet partnerships. Another example is Lincoln Savings and Loan, a subsidiary of American National, which had over 50 other subsidiaries and related companies. Lincoln Savings and Loan also had several subsidiaries, some with no apparent business purpose. A significant part of the fraud involved the structuring of supposedly "profitable" transactions near the end of each quarter by selling land to "straw buyers."[12] To entice buyers to participate, perpetrators often made the down payment themselves by having Lincoln Savings and Loan simultaneously loan the straw buyers the same amount of money (or more) that they needed for the down payments. The simultaneous transactions were not easily identifiable because Lincoln Savings and Loan sold the land themselves but had another entity make the loan. The complexity functioned as "smoke" to hide illicit transactions. The same was true of ESM. In that case, organizations were established solely to make it look like receivables were due them when, in fact, they were not audited and could not have been paid even a small portion of what they were owed.

Organizational attributes that typically suggest potential frauds include unduly complex organizational structures, lack of an internal audit department, a board of directors with few outsiders, control of related parties by a small group of individuals, offshore affiliates with no apparent business purpose, or new subsidiaries with no apparent business purpose. Investigators must understand exactly who owns the organization. Sometimes silent or hidden owners use organizations in questionable activities.

The COSO-sponsored study of the attributes of firms that commit financial statement fraud concluded the following:

> *The relatively small size of fraud companies suggests that the inability or even unwillingness to implement cost-effective internal controls may be a factor affecting the likelihood of financial statement fraud (e.g., override of controls is easier). Smaller companies may be unable or unwilling to employ senior executives with sufficient financial reporting knowledge and experience.*
>
> *The concentration of fraud among companies with under $50 million in revenues and with generally weak audit committees highlights the importance*

> *of rigorous audit committee practices even for smaller organizations. In particular, the number of audit committee meetings per year and the financial expertise of the audit committee members may deserve closer attention. Investors should be aware of the possible complications arising from family relationships and from individuals (founders, CEO/board chairs, etc.) who hold significant power or incompatible job functions.*[13]

The industry of your client organization must also be carefully examined. Some industries are riskier than others. In addition, the organization's performance relative to that of similar organizations in the industry should be examined. These are typical questions you should ask about organizational structure and industry attributes:

1. Does the company have an overly complex organizational structure; that is, does it have legal entities, managerial lines of authority, or contractual arrangements without apparent business purpose?
2. Is there a legitimate business purpose for each separate entity of the business?
3. Is the board of directors comprised primarily of officers of the company or other related individuals?
4. Is the board of directors passive, or active and independent?
5. Is the audit committee comprised primarily of insiders or outsiders?
6. Is the audit committee passive, or active and independent?
7. Is the internal audit department independent and active?
8. Does the organization have offshore activities without an apparent business purpose?
9. Is the organization a new entity without a proven history?
10. Have there been significant recent changes in the nature of the organization?
11. Is there adequate monitoring of controls?
12. Is there an effective accounting and information technology staff?
13. Does the organization face stiff competition or market saturation for its products, accompanied by declining margins?
14. Is the client's industry declining—that is, is it experiencing increasing business failures and significant decreases in customer demand?
15. Is the industry subject to rapidly changing technology or rapid product obsolescence?
16. Is the company's performance similar or contrary to other firms in the industry?
17. Are there other significant issues about the organization and the industry?

Financial Results and Operating Characteristics

Much can be learned about exposure to financial statement fraud by closely examining management and the board of directors, relationships with others, and the nature of the organization, and looking at those three elements is always a good idea. In examining financial statements to assess a company's exposure to fraud, effective investigators take a nontraditional approach to financial statements. As we noted earlier, fraud symptoms often exhibit themselves through changes in the financial statements. Footnotes are another key item to examine; in fact, understanding what they are *really* saying is very important. Many times, footnotes strongly hint that fraud is occurring, but auditors and others miss it.

When investigators use a company's financial statements and its operating characteristics to determine whether fraud is occurring, they compare the statement balances with those of similar organizations in the industry, and they also check to see whether the real-world numbers match the statement numbers. That is, the $2 million inventory on a statement has to be located somewhere, and it will require space to store it, forklifts and other equipment to move it, and people to manage it. Investigators therefore ask, are the statement numbers realistic, given the inventory that is on hand?

In order to use financial statements in this manner, you must understand the nature of the client's business, the types of accounts that should be included in the statements, the types of fraud that the organization is particularly vulnerable to, and the symptoms these frauds generate. For example, the activities of a manufacturing company typically divide into sales and collections, acquisition and payment, financing, payroll, and inventory and warehousing. To identify fraud, you would break an organization down into activities like these and then identify the functions performed in each activity, the inherent risk in each function, the abuses and frauds that can occur, and the symptoms these frauds generate. You can then use detection techniques to determine whether fraud is occurring in these activities. Here are critical questions to ask about financial statement relationships and operating results:

1. Are the changes in financial statement account balances unrealistic?
2. Are the account balances themselves realistic given the nature, age, and size of the company?
3. Do actual physical assets exist in the amounts and values reported in the statements?
4. Have there been significant changes in the nature of the organization's revenues or expenses?
5. Do one or a few large transactions account for a significant portion of an account balance or amount?
6. Are there significant end-of-period transactions that positively impact results, especially ones that are unusual or complex or that pose "substance over form" questions?
7. Do financial results appear consistent on a quarter-by-quarter or month-by-month basis, or are there unrealistic amounts in a subperiod?
8. Is the organization reporting earnings and earnings growth, yet having trouble generating cash flow?
9. Is the organization continually having to obtain additional capital to stay competitive?
10. Are reported assets, liabilities, revenues, or expenses based on estimates that involve unusually subjective judgments or uncertainties or that are subject to potential significant change in the near term in a manner that may have a financially disruptive effect on the entity—such as ultimate collectibility of receivables, timing of revenue recognition, realizability of financial instruments based on the highly subjective valuation of collateral or difficult-to-assess repayment sources, or significant deferral of costs?
11. Is profitability growing at an unusually rapid pace, especially compared with other companies in the industry?
12. Is the organization particularly vulnerable to changes in the interest rates?
13. Are sales or profitability incentive programs unrealistically aggressive?
14. Does the organization face imminent bankruptcy or foreclosure? Is it threatened by a hostile takeover?
15. Are adverse consequences probable on pending transactions, such as a business combination or contract award, if poor financial results are reported?
16. Is there a poor or deteriorating financial position in which management has personally guaranteed significant debts of the entity?
17. Does the firm continuously operate in "crisis" mode or without a careful budgeting and planning process?

18. Does the organization have difficulty collecting receivables? Does it have other cash flow problems?
19. Does the organization's success depend on one or two key products or services? Can these products or services quickly become obsolete? Do its competitors adapt better to market swings?
20. Do statement footnotes contain information about difficult-to-understand issues?
21. Are there adequate disclosures in the footnotes?
22. Are there questionable or suspicious aspects in the financial results or operating characteristics?

Summary

In this chapter, we covered the first steps in detecting financial statement fraud. Four areas must be examined: (1) management and directors, (2) relationships with others, (3) the organization and its industry, and (4) financial results and operating characteristics. Perpetrators choose fraud schemes as much for their "ease to commit and conceal" than for any other factor. Most fraud symptoms, especially those that show up in the financial results and the organization's operating characteristics, are scheme-specific. In the next two chapters, we will discuss understatement of liability frauds, overstatement of asset frauds, and inadequate disclosure frauds. For each type of scheme, we will discuss which symptoms indicate that fraud may be occurring, ways to search for fraud symptoms, and ways to determine whether observed symptoms are occurring because of fraud or because of some other reason.

New Terms

Accounting and Auditing Enforcement Release (AAER): Public document released by the SEC when a company commits financial statement fraud or other inappropriate activities.

Committee of Sponsoring Organizations (COSO): Organization made up of representatives from major accounting firms that focus on internal controls and financial statement fraud.

Financial statement fraud: Intentional misstatement of financial statements by omitting critical facts or disclosures, misstating amounts, or misapplying GAAP.

Financial statements: Financial reports that summarize the profitability and cash flows of an entity for a specific period and the financial position of the entity as of a specific date.

Securities and Exchange Commission (SEC): Government body responsible for regulating stock trading and the financial statements and reports of public companies.

10-K: Annual report filed by publicly traded companies to the SEC.

10-Q: Quarterly report filed by publicly traded companies to the SEC.

Treadway Commission: National Commission on Fraudulent Financial Reporting that made recommendations on financial statement fraud and other matters in 1987.

Questions and Cases

Discussion Questions

1. Why are financial statements important to the effective operation of capital markets?
2. What is financial statement fraud?
3. Who usually commits financial statement fraud?
4. Why are CEOs often perpetrators of financial statement fraud?

5. Compare and contrast financial statement fraud with embezzlement and misappropriation, especially with respect to who tends to perpetrate each type of fraud. Also contrast these frauds with respect to who benefits from them.
6. What are common ways to conceal financial statement frauds?
7. Why does an active audit committee help to deter financial statement fraud?
8. What motivates perpetrators to commit financial statement fraud?
9. What four areas must be examined to detect financial statement fraud?
10. How are financial statement fraud schemes identified?
11. For the following fraud symptoms, identify where the risk is greatest: management and directors, relationships with others, organization and industry, or financial results and operating characteristics.
    a. The personal worth of directors is tied up in the organization.
    b. The company has a complex organizational structure.
    c. The audit committee rarely holds meetings.
    d. The company recently switched to a new law firm.
    e. Although sales appear to be increasing, the cost of goods sold and inventory levels remain constant.
    f. The company is about to go through a debt offering.
    g. A background check indicates that the new controller has been fired from five previous jobs.
12. Why must management and the board of directors be investigated when fraud examiners search for financial statement fraud?
13. Why are relationships with others examined when investigators search for financial statement fraud?
14. When looking for financial statement fraud, why is it important to analyze the company's relationship with its auditors?
15. Why must the organization's structure be examined when investigators search for financial statement fraud?

True/False

1. Unlike other types of fraud, financial statement fraud is usually not concealed and is therefore relatively easy to spot.
2. Fraud symptoms can be caused by fraud or by legitimate factors.
3. Without a confession, forged documents, or repeated fraudulent acts that establish a pattern of dishonesty, convicting someone of fraud is difficult.
4. According to the 1999 COSO study of fraudulent financial reporting, overstating liabilities is the most common way to perpetrate financial statement fraud.
5. Most companies that commit financial statement fraud have no audit committee or have an audit committee that meets less than twice a year.
6. In identifying management fraud, it is useful to think of the fraud exposure rectangle, which includes (1) management and directors, (2) organizations and industry, and (3) relationships with others.
7. Financial statement fraud is committed by entry-level accountants against an organization.
8. In searches for financial statement fraud, three aspects of directors and management that should be investigated are (1) their backgrounds, (2) their motivations, and (3) their influence on organizational decision making.

9. A company's relationship with other organizations and individuals is of no interest to a fraud examiner.
10. Recording fictitious revenues is a common way to perpetrate financial statement fraud.
11. Most often, the corporation's controller or CFO is the perpetrator of financial statement fraud because of their knowledge of accounting and unlimited access to accounts.
12. Financial statement fraud, like other types of fraud, is most often committed against an organization instead of on behalf of the organization.
13. People who commit management fraud tend to be repeat offenders.
14. Most financial statement frauds occur in large, historically profitable organizations.

Multiple Choice

1. Financial statement fraud tends to be committed by:
   a. Executives
   b. Managers
   c. Stockholders
   d. Outsiders
   e. a and b
2. Which company officer is most likely to perpetrate financial statement fraud?
   a. Chief financial officer (CFO)
   b. Controller
   c. Chief operating officer (COO)
   d. Chief executive officer (CEO)
3. When searching for financial statement fraud, auditors should look for fraud symptoms by:
   a. Examining financial statements
   b. Evaluating changes in financial statements
   c. Examining company relationships with other parties
   d. Examining the company's operating characteristics
   e. All of the above
   f. None of the above because auditors are not responsible for finding financial statement fraud.
4. The three aspects of management that fraud examiners need to be aware of include all of the following *except*:
   a. Their backgrounds
   b. Their motivations
   c. Their religious convictions
   d. Their influence in making decisions for the organization
5. Which of the following is least likely to be considered a financial statement fraud symptom?
   a. Grey directors
   b. Family relationships between directors or officers
   c. Large increases in accounts receivable with no increase in sales
   d. Size of the firm

6. Many fraud symptoms are circumstantial; that is, they can also be caused by factors other than fraud. This makes convicting someone of fraud difficult. Which of the following types of evidence is most helpful in proving that someone committed fraud?
   a. Missing documentation
   b. An out-of-balance general ledger
   c. Analytical relationships that don't make sense
   d. A repeated pattern of similar fraudulent acts
7. In the PharMor fraud, the perpetrator used several methods to manipulate the financial statements. These included all of the following *except:*
   a. Funneling losses into unaudited subsidiaries
   b. Overstating inventory
   c. Recognizing revenue that should have been deferred
   d. Manipulating accounts
8. Most financial statement frauds occur in smaller organizations with simple management structures, rather than in large, historically profitable organizations. This is because:
   a. People in small organizations are less honest.
   b. Smaller organizations do not have investors.
   c. Management fraud is more difficult to commit when there are formal organizational structures.
   d. People in large organizations are more honest.
9. Management fraud is usually committed on behalf of the organization rather than against it. Which of the following is *not* a motivation of fraud on behalf of an organization?
   a. The CEO needs a new car.
   b. The industry is highly competitive.
   c. Pressure is high to meet expected earnings.
   d. Debt restructuring can't be met.
10. All of the following are symptoms of financial statement fraud *except*:
   a. Unusually rapid growth of profitability
   b. Threat of a hostile takeover
   c. Dependence on one or two products
   d. Large amounts of available cash

Short Cases

Case 1. Rural Electra is a new electronics company that produces circuit boards for personal computers and has located in a small southern town. The three founders, who previously worked for another electronics company, appointed themselves chairman/CEO, president/COO, and controller/treasurer. They are also members of the board of directors in Rural Electra. Two of the three founders together owned approximately 10.7% of the company's common stock. The board of directors has seven members, and they meet about four times a year, for which they receive an annual retainer of $4,500 plus a fee of $800 for each meeting attended. Their new company is well received by the townspeople, who are excited about its prospects and what it may mean for the local economy. The city showed its enthusiasm by providing Rural Electra with an empty building, and the local bank came up with an attractive credit arrangement. In turn, the company asked the bank's president to serve on its board of directors. Two years later, the three founders began to commit financial statement fraud, which went on for about three years. The fraud involved overstating inventory, understating the cost of goods sold, overstating the gross margin, and overstating net income.

Identify the fraud symptoms present in this case.

Case 2. As you can see from the chart below, Microsoft would have to report huge losses if its employees were paid only in cash rather than in cash and stock options as they are now. However, it is able to show a profit because current GAAP allow companies to carry stock options "off the books." This in effect understates costs and overstates earnings because these are unfunded liabilities. However, Microsoft's 2001 press releases imply that it took a tax deduction for "stock option wages" of between \$2.5 and \$4 billion. None of the "stock option wages" were charged against earnings.

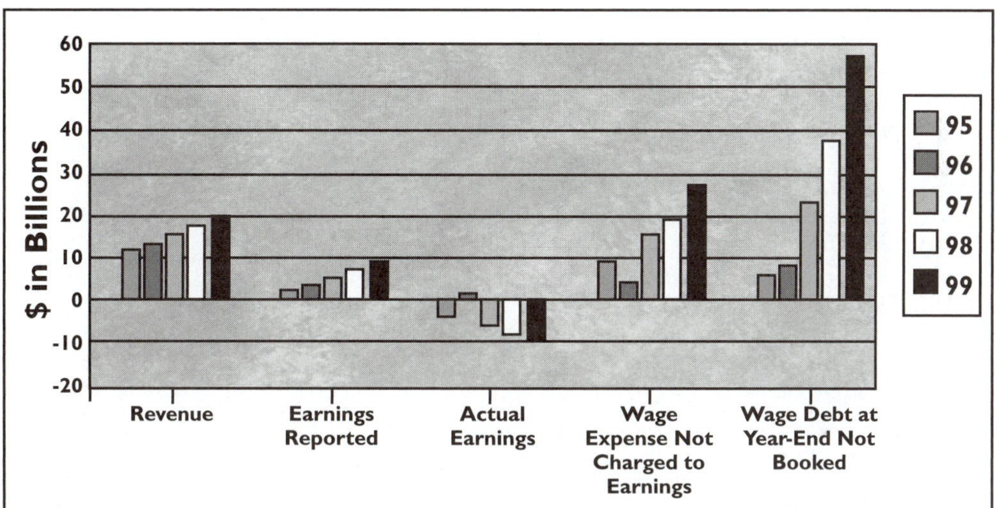

How do you think the investing public would react if they realized that Microsoft actually lost \$10 billion in 1999, rather than earning \$7.8 billion as reported? Is this financial statement fraud?

Case 3. ABC Company manufactures and sells software packages to small businesses. The company has enjoyed great success since it began business in 1998. Last year, ABC doubled its revenues, and its management is now looking closely at going public. Its goal is to make an initial public offering (IPO) next September. Senior management is attempting to increase sales by offering its sales reps generous commissions.

ABC's CEO, CFO, and COO have been in business together for 20 years. Two of them were high school "buddies." They and their wives are still very close socially.

In completing your background check on the company, you find that ABC has a positive relationship with private investors, who are excited about the proposed IPO next September. One investor did inform you, however, that ABC changed auditors last year because of a dispute over a "strict" revenue recognition rule.

ABC's board of directors and audit committee meet twice a year to discuss how the business is doing. The board recently decided to meet four times over the next year because of the upcoming IPO. The board speaks highly of management and compensates them generously with stock options for the "good work."

What red flags indicate that financial statement fraud may be occurring?

Extensive Case

Case 4. You have been hired to investigate financial statement fraud for the Chipmunk Company. You are given the following the financial statements.

THE CHIPMUNK COMPANY
Balance Sheet
December 31, 2003 and 2002

	2003	2002
ASSETS		
Current assets		
Cash	$ 1,320,096	$ 1,089,978
Accounts receivable: net	1,646,046	1,285,593
Inventories	15,524,349	12,356,400
Prepaid expenses	17,720	15,826
Deposits	7,916	5,484
Total current assets	$16,516,127	$14,753,281
Property, plant, and equipment		
At cost, less accumulated depreciation	596,517	612,480
TOTAL ASSETS	$17,112,644	$15,365,761
LIABILITIES		
Current liabilities		
Notes payable—Bank	$ 5,100,000	$ 4,250,000
Accounts payable	1,750,831	1,403,247
Accrued liabilities	257,800	217,003
Federal income taxes payable	35,284	45,990
Current portion of long-term debt	5,642	5,642
Total current liabilities	$ 7,149,557	$ 5,921,882
Long-term liabilities		
Long-term debt	409,824	415,466
TOTAL LIABILITIES	$ 7,559,381	$ 6,337,348
STOCKHOLDERS' EQUITY		
Common stock	$ 10,000	$ 10,000
Additional paid-in capital	2,500,000	2,500,000
Retained earnings	7,043,263	6,518,413
Total stockholder's equity	$ 9,553,263	$ 9,028,413
TOTAL LIABILITIES AND STOCKHOLDERS' EQUITY	$17,112,644	$15,365,761

THE CHIPMUNK COMPANY
Statement of Income and Retained Earnings
For the years ended December 31, 2003 and 2002

	2003	2002
Sales	$26,456,647	$22,889,060
Sales returns and allowances	37,557	27,740
Net sale	$26,419,090	$22,861,320
Cost of sales	19,133,299	16,530,114
Gross profit	$ 7,285,791	$ 6,331,206
EXPENSES		
Accounting	$ 48,253	$ 46,750
Advertising	28,624	27,947
Depreciation	46,415	46,578
Bad debts	148,252	162,344
Business publications	1,231	872
Cleaning services	15,817	12,809
Fuel	64,161	53,566
Garbage collection	4,870	4,674
Insurance	16,415	16,303
Interest	427,362	364,312
Legal	69,752	29,914
Licensing and certification fees	33,580	27,142
Linen service	3,044	1,939
Medical benefits	4,178	4,624
Miscellaneous	47,739	16,631
Office supplies	26,390	23,289
Payroll benefits	569,110	461,214
Pension expense	40,770	37,263
Postage and courier	8,623	20,962
Property taxes	3,978	27,947
Rent	158,526	120,000
Repairs and maintenance	51,316	26,439
Salaries and wages	4,310,281	3,970,092
Security	96,980	100,098
Telephone	5,707	7,092
Travel and entertainment	21,633	16,303
Utilities	63,329	41,919
Total expenses	$ 6,316,336	$ 5,669,023
Net income before income tax	$ 969,455	$ 662,183
Income tax expense	344,605	239,406
NET INCOME	$ 624,850	$ 422,777
Retained earnings at beginning of year	6,518,413	6,195,636
Less: Dividends	100,000	100,000
Retained earnings at end of year	$ 7,043,263	$ 6,518,413

As part of your analysis, you are required to:

1. Calculate the 2003 and 2002 liquidity and equity ratios identified below. Also calculate the change and percentage change for the ratios and complete the table below. (Formulas are given to shorten the time spent on the assignment.)
2. Analyze the Chipmunk Company's ratios for both years and compare the figures with the given industry ratios. Based on the ratios identified, where do you think fraud may have occurred?

Ratio Analysis 12/31/03					
LIQUIDITY RATIOS:	**12/31/03**	**12/31/02**	**Change**	**Percent Change**	**Industry Average**
Current ratio (current assets ÷ current liabilities)					1.21
Quick ratio (current assets − inventory ÷ curr. liab)					0.35
Sales ÷ Receivable (net sales ÷ net ending receivables)					23.42
Number of days sales in A/R (net ending receivables ÷ net sales ÷ 365)					15.58
Inventory turnover (cost of sales ÷ average inventory)					1.29
EQUITY POSITION RATIOS:					
Owner's equity ÷ total assets (total stockholder equity ÷ total assets)					0.28
Long-term assets ÷ total owners' equity (net long-term assets ÷ total stockholder equity)					0.54
Current liabilities ÷ owners' equity (current liabilities ÷ total stockholder equity)					1.29
Total liabilities ÷ owners' equity (total liabilities ÷ total stockholder equity)					2.58

Internet Assignments

1. The Internet is a great place to find information about financial statement fraud. Using your favorite search engine, try various word combinations to see what you can find about financial statement fraud. What did you find that interested you? Now go to the following web address: http://www.electronicaccountant.com/html/atoday/090301nw-3.htm. This web site features an article from the *Electronic Accountant* about fraud in financial statement audits. What are some key points made in the article? What did you learn after reading this article?
2. As we discussed in this chapter, upper management motivations can indicate possible financial statement fraud. Another symptom of financial statement fraud is related-party transactions. Go to the web site http://www.cnn.com/2002/LAW/02/03/enron/index.html and read the article on Enron. Briefly explain how this article illustrates that management motivation and related-party transactions can be symptoms of fraud.

Debate

1. Some business analysts believe that the accounting profession industry has fallen out of touch with the realities of business. They believe that accounting standards were developed for a manufacturing environment and do not fit modern needs. As a result, they contend that financial statements are now a game in which companies try to match the earnings forecasts set by financial analysts.

   Are these statements true, or do you think that they are too cynical? To assist you in this debate, you may want to study the research paper, "Measuring Intellectual Investment: The Boundaries of Financial Reporting and How to Expand Them," by Baruch Lev and Paul Zarnum of New York University. (See http://www1.oecd.org/dsti/sti/industry/indcomp/prod/paper11.pdf.)
2. One of the most controversial topics recently affecting the accounting profession is earnings management. Today, companies routinely try to manage their earnings to match analysts' projections. Although the accounting literature doesn't give accounting professionals a clear definition of earnings management, many analysts have been critical of companies for doing this, saying that managed financial statements are by their very nature fraudulent.

   Analyze the pros and cons of earnings management and debate whether earnings management is financial statement fraud.

End Notes

1. Daniel Wise, "Cendant Lawyers Get Record $262 Million in Securities Fraud Case," *New York Law Journal* (Aug. 22, 2000).
2. National Commission on Fraudulent Financial Reporting (NCFFR). 1987 *Report of the National Commission on Fraudulent Financial Reporting*. New York: AICPA.
3. COSO. *Fraudulent Financial Reporting 1987–1997, An Analysis of U.S. Public Companies.* 1999. Research Commissioned by the Committee of Sponsoring Organizations of the Treadway Commission.

4. Rule 10(b)5 is the section of the federal Securities Exchange Act of 1934 that has been the principal focus of CPA liability litigation. The rule states: It shall be unlawful for any person directly or indirectly, by the use of any means or instrumentality of interstate commerce, or of the mails or of any facility of any national securities exchange, (a) to employ any device, scheme, or artifice to defraud, (b) to make any untrue statement of a material fact or omit to state a material fact necessary in order to make the statements made, in the light of the circumstances under which they were made, not misleading, or (c) to engage in any act, practice, or course of business which operates or would operate as a fraud or deceit upon any person in connection with the purchase or sale of any security.

5. Modifications or qualifications are one of the types of auditor's opinion. It means that a strict clean or unqualified opinion was not given, but that the auditor felt it necessary to explain something to readers or to "modify" his or her report from the standard opinion. A scope limitation means that an auditor was not able to conduct all the tests and procedures he or she deemed necessary in the circumstances. In other words, he or she couldn't perform the "full scope" of the audit. There are two kinds of scope limitations: (1) those caused by a client and (2) those caused by conditions beyond the control of either the client or the auditor.

6. M. S. Beasley, J. V. Carcello, and D. R. Hermanson, *Fraudulent Financial Reporting: 1987–1997: An Analysis of U.S. Public Companies,* Committee of Sponsoring Organizations (COSO), 1999.

7. These are auditors required by law. In some countries (like Japan), they actually work inside companies. In other countries, they are hired from the outside.

8. *Fraudulent Financial Reporting: 1987–1997: An Analysis of U.S. Public Companies,* op. cit.

9. "Lessons to Be Learned—ZZZZ Best, Regina, and Lincoln Savings," W. Steve Albrecht, James D. Stice, and Leslie M. Brown, Jr., *The CPA Journal,* April 1991, pp. 52–53.

10. http://www.sec.gov/litigation/litreleases/lr15855.txt

11. Form 8-K is the SEC report filed at the end of any month in which significant events have occurred that are of interest to public investors. Such events include the acquisition or sale of a subsidiary, a change in officers or directors, an addition of a new product line, or a change in auditors.

12. A straw buyer helps someone commit fraud by pretending to buy the property at an inflated price. A straw buyer is an "unreal" buyer that is being represented as buying something, when in reality he or she is only helping the perpetrator commit fraud. In Lincoln's case, straw buyers (friends of Keating) were told that if they would "park" the properties on their financial statements for a time, Keating would assume all the risk and even take the properties back.

13. *Fraudulent Financial Reporting: 1987-1997: An Analysis of U.S. Public Companies,* op. cit., p. 80.

CHAPTER ELEVEN

Revenue and Inventory Frauds

After studying this chapter, you should be able to:

1. Understand revenue fraud.
2. Identify revenue fraud schemes.
3. Use financial statements to proactively search for revenue fraud.
4. Understand inventory and cost of goods sold fraud.
5. Identify symptoms of inventory fraud.
6. Use financial statements to proactively search for inventory fraud.

In April 1997, Bre-X Minerals, a Canadian company, was considered one of the most valuable companies in Canada. Hailed as the mining find of the century, Bre-X had just discovered the largest gold deposit ever reported. The gold mine, located on a remote island in the East Kalimantan Province of Indonesia, supposedly had so much gold that the price of gold on the open market plummeted because investors anticipated a huge spike in supplies. Within a few months, thousands of Canadians—big investors, pension and mutual funds, and many small investors, including hardware store owners and factory workers—got caught up in Bre-X fever. The company's stock price shot up from pennies to more than $250 per share before a 10-for-1 stock split was announced. Thousands of investors believed they were about to become millionaires.

The story began to seriously unravel, however, when Michael de Guzman, Bre-X's chief geologist and one of only a handful of company insiders entrusted with the mine's core samples, committed suicide by jumping out of a helicopter. Involved parties frantically scrambled for cover:

> *The search for a jungle El Dorado is over; the search for culprits in an astounding gold mine fraud has begun. Investigators opened investigations into how Bre-X Minerals, a tiny exploration company from Alberta, Canada, managed to convince countless experts and investors that a tract of land in Borneo contained the biggest gold find of the century.*
>
> *After two years as a stock market superstar, Bre-X was suddenly a pariah after an independent consulting company reported that the Busang site was worthless. It said thousands of seemingly promising crushed rock core samples collected by Bre-X had been doctored with gold from elsewhere in a scam "without precedent in the history of mining."*
>
> *Partners in the Indonesian project promptly jumped ship. The Indonesian government, which held a 10% stake, vowed to punish whoever was responsible. New Orleans-based Freeport-McMoRan Copper & Gold—the first to cast doubts on Busang's value—said it was withdrawing from its planned partnership with Bre-X.*

The company that reported the fraud, Strathcona Mineral Services, did not attempt to fix blame for the tampering, but offered to assist in subsequent investigations. Industry analysts said that senior Bre-X personnel were involved, but there was no consensus whether the culprits were executives, geologists in the field, or both.

Mining analysts say only a small amount of gold—perhaps a few pounds—would have been enough to doctor the Bre-X samples to make it appear that the Busang mine was a world-class gold deposit.

Bre-X's president, David Walsh, who launched the Busang project from his Calgary basement while bankrupt in 1993, expressed shock at the evidence of tampering and said his company would conduct its own investigation.

Walsh, 51, sold off some of his Bre-X shares last year, along with other senior company officials, who together reaped more than $56 million in profits. They have been targeted by at least eight class-action lawsuits in Canada and the United States, alleging that Bre-X executives misled shareholders about Busang's potential while selling off some of their own shares.

Revenue Fraud

By far, the most common accounts manipulated when financial statement fraud is perpetrated are revenues and/or accounts receivable. A study by the Committee of Sponsoring Organizations (COSO) found that over half of all financial statement frauds involve revenues and/or accounts receivable.[1] The COSO study also found that the most common way to manipulate revenue accounts is by recording fictitious revenues and the second most common is by recording revenues prematurely. Other studies have found similar results.[2] In fact, because of the frequency of revenue frauds, the AICPA published "Audit Issues in Revenue Recognition" on its web site (http://www.aicpa.org) in January 1999. This publication contains guidance to help auditors identify and respond to warning signals of improper revenue reporting. It focuses on issues related to the sale of goods and services in the ordinary course of business and also discusses management's responsibility to report revenues accurately and the applicable accounting standards. Several other AICPA activities also address earnings management and financial statement fraud practices that threaten the integrity of the financial reporting process.[3]

Revenue frauds are common for two reasons. First, there are acceptable alternatives for recognizing revenue, and each approach can be interpreted and applied in situation-specific ways. Just as organizations differ, the types of revenues they generate also differ, and each revenue type requires specific recognition and reporting methods. A company that collects cash before delivering goods or performing services, such as a franchiser, for example, recognizes revenue differently than a company that collects cash after the delivery of goods or the performance of a service, such as a manufacturing firm. A company that has long-term, construction-type contracts uses different revenue recognition criteria than one whose revenue is based on small, discrete work tasks. In many cases, identifying the most significant events that should control the timing of revenue recognition is difficult.

Consider, for example, a corporation that explores, refines, and distributes oil that we'll call Teapot Oil. When should that company recognize revenue from its oil—when it discovers oil deposits in the ground (for which there is a ready market and an easily assessed price), when it refines the crude oil or condensate into products such as jet and diesel fuel, when it distributes its products to its service stations for resale, or when it sells the products at the gas pump?

Similarly, consider a company, SRO Health, that performs human clinical trials on new drugs developed by pharmaceutical companies to determine whether the drugs should be approved by the Food and Drug Administration for sale and distribution to the public. A contract with a pharmaceutical company, Meds Inc., states that the drug will be tested on 100 patients over a period of six months, and each patient will be observed and tested weekly. SRO Health is to be paid $100 per patient visit for a total of $2,600 (26 visits) per patient and a total contract amount of $260,000 ($2,600 per patient × 100 patients). Meds Inc. does not want to be billed every time a patient is tested, so it directs SRO Health to submit bills only when "billing milestones" are reached (at 25, 50, 75, and 100 patient visits). When should SRO Health's revenues be recognized—when patient visits take place, when bills are submitted to Meds Inc., when all visits have occurred, or at some other time?

These difficult issues require significant judgment. In these and many other situations, both conservative and liberal criteria for revenue recognition can be used. Even financial reporting experts don't always agree when an organization has sufficient performance to recognize revenue and what the major revenue-recognition criteria should be. The accounting industry debates these and other complex revenue-recognition issues continually, and they form the heart of numerous fraud lawsuits. The differences in revenue-recognition and performance criteria across organizations make it very difficult to develop absolute rules that can be applied in every case. And because significant judgment must be exercised to determine when and how much revenue to recognize, the inherent subjectivity provides opportunities for financial statement manipulation by managers who want to "cook the books."

There is another reason why revenue frauds are so common: It is easy to manipulate net income using revenue reporting and receivable accounts. In the video "Cooking the Books," produced by the Association of Certified Fraud Examiners, Barry Minkow, mastermind of the ZZZZ Best fraud, states, "Receivables are a wonderful thing. You create a receivable and you have revenue." When you have revenue, you have income. Need to increase reported net income? Just add a little revenue and a few more receivables. In addition, revenue and receivables can be easily manipulated in other ways.

Recently, a number of power trading companies have admitted that they entered into buy and sell transactions with each other in order to give the impression that their revenues were higher than they really were. Another example is an organization that creates additional revenues by simply holding its books open for a time after the end of the accounting period in order to include in the current period revenues that should be recognized in the next period. This revenue fraud is often called "early recognition of revenues" or "abusing the cut-off." In long-term construction contracts, early recognition is especially easy because the revenues recognized depend on the project's percentage of completion, and that is often an estimate. Or, a company creates fictitious documentation that makes sales appear higher than they actually were for the period. Alternatively, contracts on which the revenue recognition is based are altered or forged. In the most egregious cases, companies use topside journal entries to create revenues and receivables without underlying documentation.

Revenue Fraud Schemes

As you will see, various schemes are used to misstate financial statements. One of the best ways to understand how financial statement frauds are perpetrated using revenue is to first identify the various types of transactions that bring in revenue. Diagrams of the various transactions between an organization and its customers are really helpful here to analyze accounts involved in each transaction, and to determine how misstatements can occur. As a fraud examiner, you might diagram a company's revenue-related transactions as follows:

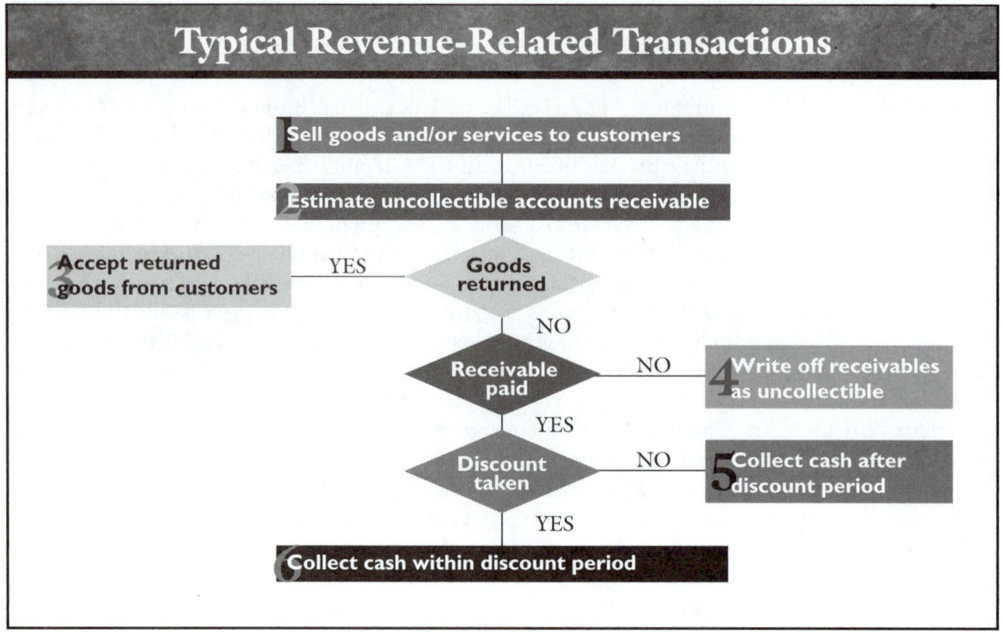

Once you have diagrammed the company's revenue transactions, a good way to determine possible avenues for financial statement fraud is to correlate the accounts involved in each transaction with typical manipulation. The following table uses numbers from the preceding diagram to identify likely transactions.

Transaction	Accounts Involved	Possible Schemes
1. Sell goods and/or services to customers	Accounts receivable, revenues (e.g., sales revenue)	1. Record fictitious sales (related parties, sham sales, sales with conditions, consignment sales, etc.) 2. Recognize revenues too early (improper cut-off, percentage of completion, etc.) 3. Overstate real sales (alter contracts, inflate amounts, etc.)
2. Estimate uncollectible accounts receivable	Bad debt expense, allowance for doubtful accounts	4. Understate allowance for doubtful accounts, thus overstating receivables
3. Accept returned goods from customers	Sales returns, accounts receivable	5. Don't record returned goods from customers 6. Record returned goods after the end of the period
4. Write off receivables as uncollectible	Allowance for doubtful accounts, accounts receivable	7. Don't write off uncollectible receivables 8. Write off uncollectible receivables in a later period.

continues

Transaction	Accounts Involved	Possible Schemes
5. Collect cash after discount period	Cash, accounts receivable	9. Record bank transfers as cash received from customers 10. Manipulate cash received from related parties
6. Collect cash within discount period	Cash, sales discounts, accounts receivable	11. Don't record discounts given to customers

As you have no doubt noticed, all 11 schemes result in overstated revenues and overstated net income. Of course, companies can also commit fraud by understating revenues and net income. However, such frauds are extremely rare and usually occur only when a company wants to pay lower income taxes.

Once you have identified the various schemes that are possible, you can then list scheme-specific symptoms of fraud, proceed with proactive auditing and/or investigation, and follow up on observed symptoms to determine whether fraud exists.

Revenue-Related Fraud Symptoms

As you now know by this point in your course, unlike murder or bank robbery, fraud is rarely observed directly. Instead, employees, customers, auditors, and fraud examiners observe only symptoms, or red flags. To detect fraud, you must be able to identify something as a symptom. As noted earlier, we divide fraud symptoms (for all types of fraud) into six categories: analytical symptoms, accounting or documentary symptoms, extravagant lifestyle,* breakdown in accounting controls, behavioral and verbal flags, and tips and complaints. With revenue frauds, the most common symptoms in the five relevant categories are as follows:

Analytical Symptoms

1. Reported revenue or sales account balances appear too high.
2. Reported sales discounts account balances appear too low.
3. Reported sales returns account balances appear too low.
4. Reported bad debt expense account balances appear too low.
5. Reported accounts receivable account balances appear too high or are increasing too fast.
6. Reported allowance for doubtful accounts account balances appear too low.
7. Too little cash is collected from reported revenues.

Accounting or Documentary Symptoms

1. Revenue-related transactions are not recorded in a complete or timely manner or are improperly recorded as to amount, accounting period, classification, or entity policy.
2. Balances are unsupported, or transactions are unauthorized.
3. Last-minute revenue adjustments significantly improve financial results.
4. Documents in the revenue cycle are missing.

continues

* *Note*: Although fraud in smaller companies and other types of misappropriation are often driven by lifestyle, this symptom is often not relevant in financial statement fraud in large organizations.

5. Original documents are unavailable; only photocopies are used to support transactions.
6. Significant items on bank and other reconciliations are not explained.
7. Revenue-related ledgers (sales, cash receipts, etc.) do not balance.
8. Unusual discrepancies exist between revenue-related records and corroborating evidence (such as accounts receivable confirmation replies).

Control Symptoms

1. Management overrides significant internal control activities related to the revenue cycle.
2. New, unusual, or large customers do not appear to have gone through the customer-approval process.

Behavioral or Verbal Symptoms

1. Responses from management or employees about revenue or analytical procedures are inconsistent, vague, or implausible.
2. Auditors are denied access to facilities, employees, records, customers, vendors, or others from whom revenue-related audit evidence might be sought.
3. Undue time pressures are imposed by management to resolve complex revenue-related issues.
4. Unusual delays occur in providing requested information.
5. Responses to auditors' queries are untrue.
6. Behavior of management when asked about revenue-related transactions or accounts is suspicious.

Lifestyle Symptoms

Managers and other company officers live lavish lifestyles.

Tips and Complaints

There is an uptick in tips or complaints about revenue-related fraud.

Obviously, this list is not exhaustive, but it is indicative of the symptoms that you may observe when examining revenues.

Actively Looking for Symptoms

As a fraud examiner, to detect financial statement fraud you must recognize fraud symptoms when you observe them. In certain famous revenue frauds, symptoms should have been readily recognized by auditors and others but were not, hard as it is to believe in retrospect. In fact, in many cases symptoms are often observed and even inquired about, but the alternative explanations that management provides are accepted. As an auditor or examiner, you can find fraud symptoms in two ways: You can wait until you stumble on symptoms—that is, trust chance, *or* you can proactively search for symptoms. For years, auditors and accountants relied primarily on chance to discover symptoms. Because of developments in technology and lessons learned from research, we now have tools available that allow us to actively search for fraud symptoms. How you search for symptoms depends on the types of symptoms you are looking for.

Searching for Analytical Symptoms

As we noted in earlier chapters, analytical symptoms are anomalies like accounts that are too high or too low, increase too fast or not fast enough, and other abnormal relationships. But, you must ask, too high, too low, or unusual relative to what? To determine whether analytical symptoms exist, you need a point of reference, an expectation, or some reasonable balance or relationship to compare to recorded amounts. This is where your knowledge of financial statement accounting kicks in. You can then compare the company's financial statements, focusing on suspicious changes by:

1. Analyzing the balances and relationships within the statements.
   - Look for unusual changes in revenue-related account *balances* from period to period (looking at trends), and
   - Look for changes in revenue-related *relationships* from period to period.
2. Comparing the statement amounts and relationships with other data.
   - Compare the company's financial results and trends with those of similar firms in the same industry, and
   - Compare financial statement amounts with the assets they are supposed to represent.

Changes in Period-to-Period Amounts

Recorded amounts from one period can be compared to recorded amounts in another period in three ways. The first and least effective method is to focus on changes in the actual financial statement *numbers* themselves. It is often difficult, however, to assess the magnitude or significance of changes in account balances looking only at raw data, especially when the numbers are large.

The second (much easier) method uses horizontal analysis (described in Chapter 5). Recall that in horizontal analysis we examine percentage changes in account balances from period to period. Here is how percentage change is calculated:

$$\frac{\text{Period 2 account balance} - \text{Period 1 account balance}}{\text{Period 1 account balance}}$$

Thus, if an organization has an accounts receivable balance of $100,000 in period 1 and $130,000 in period 2, horizontal analysis reveals a percentage change of 30%, calculated as follows:

$$\frac{\$130{,}000 - \$100{,}000}{\$100{,}000} = 30\%$$

The third way to examine period-to-period changes is to study the statement of cash flows. Why do we perform horizontal analysis only on the income statement and balance sheet, but not on the statement of cash flows? Because horizontal analysis converts income statements and balance sheets to "change statements," and the statement of cash flows is already a change statement. Every number on the statement of cash flows represents the change in account balances from one period to the next, and the changes in accounts receivable, inventory, accounts payable, and other accounts appear on the statement itself. Studying the statement of cash flows, then, is like looking at the differences in raw numbers on the balance sheet and income statement from one period to the next, except that the calculations have been made for you. When searching for fraud, examining the statement of cash flows is as effective as comparing actual changes in account balances. It is probably easier than recalculating the differences between two successive financial statements, but it is usually much less effective than using horizontal analysis.

Changes in Revenue Relationships

Examining changes in period-to-period revenue relationships is an especially effective way to discover analytical symptoms; this can be done in two primary ways. (1) Focus on period-to-period changes in various ratios, or (2) use vertical analysis. The following are the most common ratios used to discover revenue-related analytical fraud symptoms.

Gross Profit Margin. The gross profit margin measures the markup as a percentage of sales.

$$\textbf{Gross profit margin} = \frac{\textbf{Gross profit}}{\textbf{Net sales}} = \frac{\textbf{Net sales} - \textbf{Cost of goods sold}}{\textbf{Net sales}}$$

If someone is perpetrating revenue-related fraud by overstating sales (revenues), understating sales discounts or sales returns, overstating sales by recording fictitious sales, or recognizing next period's sales this period, this ratio will increase. (The ratio will also increase if management understates the cost of goods sold by overstating inventory, understating purchases, or by using other means.) When a company's gross profit percentage increases dramatically, something inappropriate may be going on, and that something could be fraud.

Sales Return Percentage. This ratio gives the percentage of sales being returned by customers.

$$\textbf{Sales return percentage} = \frac{\textbf{Sales return}}{\textbf{Total sales}}$$

A high number means too many goods are being returned. A low number may signal fraud. One of the main methods perpetrators used in the MiniScribe fraud (see Chapter 5) was to understate sales returns.[4] In fact, the fraud became so egregious that at one time bricks were boxed and shipped as software, with revenues recognized at the time of shipment. When the bricks were returned by customers, they were stored in a separate location and not recorded as sales returns, allowing revenues and income to be overstated.

Sales Discount Percentage. Similar to the sales return percentage, this ratio measures the percentage of sales discounts taken by customers.

$$\textbf{Sales discount percentage} = \frac{\textbf{Sales discounts}}{\textbf{Gross sales}}$$

A sudden decrease in this ratio can mean that customers are simply taking longer to pay (and not taking the discounts), or it can mean that the discounts are not being recorded in the accounting records and fraud is occurring.

Accounts Receivable Turnover. Accounts Receivable Turnover is one of the most widely used ratios to analyze revenues.

$$\textbf{Accounts receivable turnover} = \frac{\textbf{Net sales}}{\textbf{Accounts receivables}}$$

This ratio is used to examine the efficiency with which receivables are collected, but it is also an excellent tool for identifying fraud symptoms. One of the easiest ways to perpetrate revenue frauds is to record fictitious receivables and revenues. Unless the ratio equals 1, adding the same amount to the numerator (net sales) and denominator (accounts receivable) changes the ratio. If the ratio exceeds 1, recording fictitious sales decreases the ratio. If the ratio is less than 1, recording fictitious sales increases the ratio. Only in rare cases will recording significant fictitious revenues and receivables *not* affect this ratio. Sudden changes in this ratio are flags that fraud may be occurring.

Number of Days in Receivables. This ratio provides the same information as the Accounts Receivable Turnover ratio. The advantage of this ratio is that it measures how fast or slowly receivables are being collected in number of days, which is easy to understand.

$$\textbf{Number of days in receivables} = \frac{\textbf{Accounts receivable turnover}}{\textbf{365}}$$

Adding fictitious receivables generally increases the number of days it takes to collect receivables for an obvious reason—the fictitious receivables will not be collected.

Allowance for Uncollectible Accounts as a Percentage of Receivables. This ratio gives the percentage of receivables that are expected to be uncollectible.

$$\textbf{Percent of uncollectible accounts} = \frac{\textbf{Allowance for uncollectible accounts}}{\textbf{Total accounts receivable}}$$

Receivables (and hence net income) are commonly overstated by not recording bad accounts receivable as uncollectible. In one famous fraud, this percentage shrank from 4% to less than 0.5% before the fraud was discovered.

Asset Turnover. This ratio measures sales revenue generated with each dollar of company-owned assets.

$$\textbf{Asset turnover} = \frac{\textbf{Total sales}}{\textbf{Average total assets}}$$

When a company records fictitious revenues, this ratio increases. And, as with other ratios, unusually large increases in this ratio can indicate fraud. Note, however, that this ratio is not as sensitive to receivable and revenue frauds as the preceding ratios.

Working Capital Turnover. This ratio indicates how much working capital is used to generate sales for the period.

$$\textbf{Working capital turnover} = \frac{\textbf{Sales}}{\textbf{Average working capital}} = \frac{\textbf{Sales}}{\textbf{Current assets} - \textbf{Current liabilities}}$$

Significant increases in this ratio can signal that revenue fraud is occurring. As with asset turnover, this ratio is not as sensitive as the previous ratios in highlighting revenue frauds.

Operating Performance Margin. This ratio measures a company's profit margin.

$$\textbf{Operating performance margin} = \frac{\textbf{Net income}}{\textbf{Total sales}}$$

Often, when revenue frauds occur, fictitious revenues are added without additional expenses. Such entries increase revenues and net income; the result is a dramatic increase in this ratio.

Earnings Per Share. This very commonly used ratio measures the profitability of an organization.

$$\textbf{Earnings per share} = \frac{\textbf{Net income}}{\textbf{Shares of stock outstanding}}$$

A dramatic increase in this ratio may be signaling fraud but is not necessarily indicative of revenue fraud. This is one of the least sensitive ratios for detecting revenue fraud.

When you use ratios to look for fraud symptoms, remember that the size or direction of the ratio is usually not important; rather, *changes* (and the speed of changes) in the ratios are flags for possible fraud.

With Outside Data Analysis

The second way auditors use financial statements to look for symptoms of fraud is to convert the statements to common-size statements (percentages) and perform vertical analysis (see Chapter 5). Just as horizontal analysis is effective in identifying changes in account balances, vertical analysis is effective in identifying changes in statement relationships that should be investigated. With ratios, you generally focus on only one or two relationships at a time. Vertical analysis enables you to view the number relationships on the balance sheet or income statement simultaneously.

The trick with using horizontal analysis, vertical analysis, and other tools to search for analytical fraud symptoms is knowing when a change is significant. This is where your experience with a company, its history, these analytical tools, and other firms in the same industry are helpful. Generally, the more dramatic the change in an indicator, the higher the likelihood that something unusual (possibly fraud) is occurring. However, you should *never* conclude on the basis of analytical evidence alone that management is perpetrating fraud. At best, analytical tools merely identify potential problem areas or "circumstantial evidence" that need further analysis and investigation.

Comparing Companies' Financial Statements

One of the best ways to detect financial statement fraud is to compare the performance of the company you are examining with the performance of other, similar companies in the industry. Performance that runs counter to the performance of other firms in the same industry can signal fraud, among other problems. For example, in the Equity Funding fraud (see Chapter 2), financial statements showed a highly profitable and growing insurance company at a time when the insurance industry was struggling.[5] Economic and industrywide factors tend to affect similar firms in similar ways. Comparisons with other firms can be made by horizontal or vertical analysis, ratio analysis, or by comparing statements of cash flow or the statement numbers themselves. Common-sizing statements is especially helpful when making inter-firm comparisons and can quickly draw attention to, and thus encourage the investigation of, variations in performance. Working with percentages is much easier than comparing raw data.

Comparing Statement Amounts with Actual Assets

Comparing financial statement numbers with tangible assets, although an excellent way to detect fraud, is not as useful for detecting revenue frauds as it is for detecting cash, inventory, and physical-asset frauds. Generally, nonmonetary assets cannot be examined via revenue numbers. The notable exception, of course, is a company that earns revenue constructing assets such as buildings, bridges, and highways and then recognizes the revenue on the percentage-of-completion method. In those cases, constructed assets can be examined to determine whether the revenue recognized is reasonable, given the degree of completion.

Search for Control Weaknesses

The importance of identifying control weaknesses as possible fraud symptoms has been discussed in detail in earlier chapters. However, two control-related points warrant mentioning here with respect to revenue frauds. First, accountants are accustomed to accepting a limited number of control exceptions when assessing the adequacy of an internal control system. This approach is used because accountants view control breakdowns or weaknesses as something that needs to be fixed "in the future." As a fraud examiner, you must remember that frauds are typically motivated by the fraud triangle that we have discussed—pressure/opportunity/rationalization.

When an organization unduly experiences pressures in the business environment and management rationalizes that the pressures are only short-term and will correct themselves in the future, all that is needed to commit financial statement fraud is a perceived opportunity. Usually, opportunity presents itself as a control weakness, a control breakdown, or an overriding of key controls. For that reason, fraud examiners look at control breakdowns not only as something that must be fixed in the future, but also as something that must be examined to see whether it has been abused in the past. In fact, frauds are very frequently detected by investigating control weaknesses.

Another key factor in financial statement frauds is that the control environment (rather than specific control activities or procedures) is often very weak. You will find that, in many financial statement frauds, the audit committee and/or board of directors is weak or inactive, the internal audit department is weak or inactive, and usually only one or two executives have controlling power in the organization.

Searching for Behavior and Lifestyle Flags

Lifestyle symptoms are less helpful in detecting financial statement frauds than they are in detecting employee fraud because most financial statement frauds do not benefit perpetrators directly. Rather, these frauds make the organization look like it is performing better than it really is. To be sure, the perpetrators can benefit handsomely, but it is indirectly—through a higher stock price, not defaulting on a restrictive agreement, and so on. The same is not true of behavioral and verbal symptoms, however. In fact, one detection tool frequently underused by fraud examiners and auditors is verbal inquiries and personal observations. Management typically has difficulty committing fraud without guilt and without others knowing about the fraud. Savvy fraud examiners and auditors routinely ask such questions as:

- Is there anything suspicious I should be aware of in this company?
- Why do you think revenues (or returns, discounts, bad debts, allowances, etc.) have increased (decreased) so dramatically?
- Are there certain people whom you think I should pay particular attention to?
- What part of this organization (or which individuals) keeps you awake worrying at night?

In many frauds, some of the perpetrators are looking for a way out of the fraud, or for someone to talk to. They would like to "spill the beans," but they do not because no one asks them. Certainly, auditors and fraud examiners should strive to communicate better with audit clients and their personnel, and not rely so much on the financial statements themselves. Extensive conversations with a manager in the midst of financial statement fraud often reveals inconsistencies that help you understand that everything is not the way it is being presented. Lying consistently takes work and an excellent memory, and alert auditors and fraud examiners often detect inconsistencies. Certainly you will not catch all the lies. You are not trained as a truth analyst. However, the likelihood of your catching a lie is much greater when you make it a point to get to know your clients through casual conversations, as well as business ones.

Finally, with respect to behavior, remember that committing fraud, especially for first-time offenders, creates high levels of stress. Perpetrators must find a way to cope with that stress, and it usually shows up in their behavior. Although auditors and fraud examiners may not be familiar enough with management to recognize behavior changes, others in the organization are. In these situations, asking questions of lots of people often reveals that something is not right.

Searching for Tips and Complaints

One way to search for tips and complaints about revenue fraud, and any fraud for that matter, is to institute an ombudsman, hotline, or toll-free telephone number that people can call anonymously. Certainly, instituting hotlines is not the purview of auditors and fraud examiners; however, you can strongly encourage your clients to do so. In many frauds, some individuals have knowledge that fraud is occurring but are afraid to come forward because of the reasons that we identified in Chapter 3.

- They don't know who to tell or how to come forward.
- They don't want to wrongly accuse someone.
- They are afraid of "whistle-blower" repercussions.
- They only have suspicions rather than actual knowledge.

Hotlines are effective in obtaining information from these types of individuals. If a company has a hotline, auditors and fraud examiners should always review the records and transcripts to see what kind of information is coming in. Tips or complaints about top management or other key personnel or about fraud in financial statements should be pursued vigorously.

Following Up on Symptoms

As a fraud investigator, the presence of fraud symptoms gives you predication—that is, "reason to believe that fraud may be occurring." When predication exists, and if conditions warrant, an investigation should take place. The specific investigative procedures that you will use, and the order in which you will use them, depends on what type of fraud you suspect and the ease of collecting evidence. (See Chapters 7, 8, and 9.)

Inventory and Cost of Goods Sold Frauds

After revenue frauds, the next most common financial statement fraud is the manipulation of inventory and/or cost of goods sold (COGS) accounts. Many high-profile financial statement frauds involve overstating inventory. Phar-Mor, for example, significantly overstated the value of its inventory, and then moved inventory back and forth between stores, so that it could be counted multiple times.

Inventory frauds historically have been such a persistent problem that a few years ago the *Wall Street Journal* ran a front-page article titled "Inventory Chicanery Tempts More Firms, Fools More Auditors."[6] To understand why inventory and/or cost of goods sold frauds are so common, you need to understand the income statement. The format for a typical income statement is as follows:

Income Statement	Overstated Inventory
Gross revenues (sales)	No effect
− Sales returns	No effect
− Sales discounts	No effect
Net revenues (sales)	No effect
− Cost of goods sold	Understated
Gross margin	Overstated
− Expenses	No effect
Net income	Overstated

From this format, you can see that if inventory is overstated, cost of goods sold is understated, and net income is overstated by an equal amount (less the tax effect). To better understand the effect of cost of goods sold on inventory, consider how this account balance is calculated.

Cost of Goods Sold	Overstated Ending Inventory	Understated Purchases
Beginning Inventory	No effect	No effect
+ Purchases of inventory	No effect	Understated
− Returns of inventory to vendor	No effect	No effect
− Purchase discounts on inventory purchases	No effect	No effect
Goods available for sale	No effect	Understated
− Ending Inventory	Overstated	No effect
Cost of goods sold	Understated	Understated

This calculation shows how cost of goods sold can be understated—by understating purchases or by overstating inventory. (It can also be understated by overstating purchase returns or purchase discounts.) Of these alternatives, overstating the end-of-period inventory tends to be the "fraud of choice" because it not only increases net income, it also increases recorded assets and makes the balance sheet look better.

Identifying Inventory/Cost of Goods Sold Frauds

As with revenue frauds, an easy way to identify financial statement frauds is to diagram the various types of inventory transactions that occur in an organization. For many companies, that diagram might appear as follows:

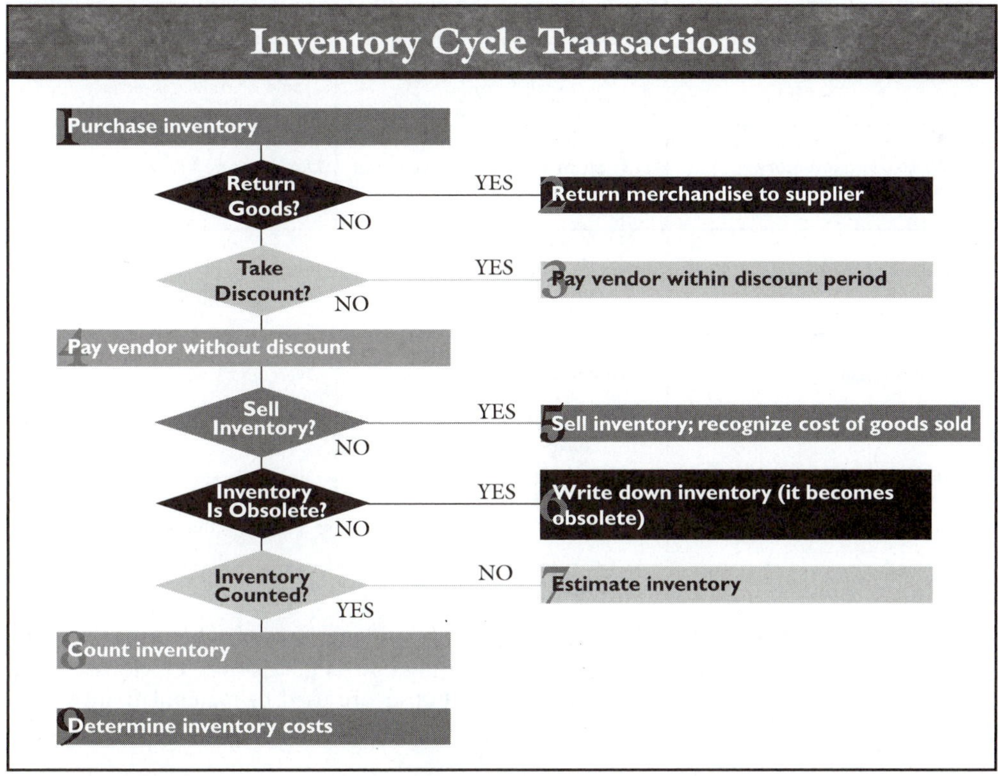

As you can see from this diagram, nine different transactions and counts are involved in accounting for inventories and the cost of goods sold. The following table shows the accounts involved in each transaction and common fraud schemes. You can use this table to determine vulnerabilities in situations you are investigating or analyzing. The effect on cost of goods sold and potential fraud schemes are the same under the perpetual and periodic inventory systems.

Transaction	Accounts Involved	Fraud Schemes
1. Purchase inventory	Inventory, accounts payable	• Underrecord purchases • Record purchases too late (cut-off problem) • Not record purchases
2. Return merchandise to supplier	Accounts payable, inventory	• Overstate returns • Record returns in an earlier period (cut-off problem)
3. Pay vendor within discount period	Accounts payable, inventory, cash	• Overstate discounts • Don't reduce inventory cost
4. Pay vendor without discount	Account payable, cash	• Don't reduce inventory cost • Record purchase and payment in a later period
5. Sell inventory; recognize cost of goods sold	Cost of goods sold, inventory	• Record at too low an amount • Don't record cost of goods sold or reduce inventory
6. Write down inventory (it becomes obsolete)	Loss on write-down of inventory, inventory	Don't write off or write down obsolete inventory
7. Estimate inventory	Inventory shrinkage, inventory	Overestimate inventory (use incorrect ratio, etc.)
8. Count inventory	Inventory shrinkage, inventory	Overcount inventory (double counting, etc.)
9. Determine inventory costs	Inventory, cost of goods sold	• Use incorrect costs • Make incorrect extensions • Record fictitious inventory

As you can see, by focusing on transactions and inventory counts, we have identified 17 schemes for overstating inventory and/or understating cost of goods sold. Obviously, some of these schemes are more common than others, but all are used to manipulate inventory and cost of goods sold on financial statements. And, as with revenue frauds, these schemes all have the effect of increasing net income. (Obviously, although rare, it is also possible to commit inventory fraud by understating inventory and net income if, for example, a company wanted to pay less taxes.)

Inventory overstatement frauds present a more difficult challenge to perpetrators than do revenue frauds. With revenue frauds, reported revenues are overstated in the current period, and accounts receivable are overstated on the balance sheet. Thus, a compounding effect does not occur in the subsequent period. With inventory frauds, however, the "overstated ending inventory" of one period becomes the "overstated beginning inventory" of the next period and causes net income to be understated in the second period. Thus, if management wants to continue the fraud and overstate net income in the ensuing periods (and most frauds are multiple-period frauds), it must not only offset the overstated beginning inventory, it must then increase net income over and above the offsetting manipulation. The results are ever larger misstatements of inventory, which rapidly becomes easy to detect. Fortunately, most financial statement frauds are perpetrated out of desperation, and perpetrators are focused on how they can overstate income in the current period, with no thought to the accounting problems facing them in subsequent periods.

Identifying Inventory/Cost of Goods Sold Fraud Symptoms

Once again, the six categories of fraud symptoms also apply to inventory and cost of goods sold frauds. The most common symptoms with these frauds are listed below.

Analytical Symptoms

- Reported Inventory balances appear too high or are increasing too fast.
- Reported Cost of Goods Sold balances appear too low or are decreasing too fast.
- Reported "Purchase Returns" appear too high or are increasing too rapidly.
- Reported "Purchase Discounts" appear too high or are increasing too rapidly.
- Reported "Purchases" appear too low for inventory levels.

Accounting or Documentary Symptoms

- Inventory and/or cost of goods sold transactions are not recorded in a complete or timely manner or are improperly recorded as to amount, accounting period, classification, or entity.
- Inventory/cost of goods sold–related transactions are unsupported or unauthorized.
- End-of-period inventory and/or cost of goods sold adjustments significantly affect the entity's financial results.
- Inventory and/or cost of goods sold documents are missing.
- Original documents to support inventory and/or cost of goods sold transactions are unavailable; only photocopies are presented.
- Cost of goods sold–related accounting records (purchases, sales, cash payments, etc.) do not balance.
- Unusual discrepancies exist between the entity's inventory and/or cost of goods sold records and corroborating evidence (such as inventory counts).
- Inventory counts and inventory records differ systematically.
- Receiving reports and inventory actually received differ.
- Purchase orders, purchase invoices, receiving records, and inventory records differ.
- Purchases from suppliers are not approved on vendor lists.
- Inventory is missing.
- Purchase orders or invoice numbers are duplicated.
- Vendors are not listed in Dun & Bradstreet or telephone directories.

continues

Control Symptoms
• Management overrides significant internal control activities related to purchases, inventory, and/or cost of goods sold. • New or unusual vendors do not go through the regular vendor-approval process. • Weaknesses in the inventory counting process exist.
Behavioral or Verbal Symptoms
• Management or employees give inconsistent, vague, or implausible responses to inventory, purchase, or cost of goods sold–related inquiries or analytical procedures. • Auditors/investigators are denied access to facilities, employees, records, customers, vendors, or others from whom evidence might be sought. • Undue time pressures are imposed by management to resolve contentious or complex inventory and/or cost of goods sold–related issues. • Unusual delays occur in providing requested inventory and/or cost of goods sold–related information. • Management responses to inventory and/or cost of goods sold or other queries made by auditors are untrue or questionable. • The behavior or responses of management are suspicious when they are asked about inventory and/or cost of goods sold–related transactions, vendors, or accounts.
Lifestyle Symptoms
• As with revenue frauds, lifestyle symptoms are often not particularly relevant to inventory frauds involving large organizations. In smaller companies, however, where officers can benefit personally from higher stock prices or from obtaining bank loans, they can be relevant.
Tips and Complaints
• Tips or complaints suggest that inventory, purchase, and/or cost of goods sold fraud (any of the schemes discussed earlier) might be occurring.

Obviously these lists are not exhaustive. Rather, they represent common symptoms of inventory and/or cost of goods sold–related fraud.

Searching for Inventory Control Symptoms

Because inventory frauds, like revenue frauds, are so easy to perpetrate, a good control environment and control procedures are crucial. Recall that the COSO study found that most companies that commit financial statement fraud are relatively small, have "inactive" audit committees, have boards of directors dominated by insiders and "grey" directors with significant equity ownership and little experience serving as directors of other companies, and have family relationships among directors and/or officers.[7] The relatively small size of these companies suggests that the inability or even unwillingness to implement cost-effective controls is a factor that increases the likelihood of inventory fraud. (In these environments overriding of controls is easier.)

As a result, controls over inventory must be examined closely. Keep in mind that the lack of a key control provides the opportunity that completes the fraud triangle. With respect to inventory, purchases, and cost of goods sold, as a fraud examiner you are primarily concerned with controls over the purchasing process (purchase requisitions, purchase orders, etc.); receiving (receiving reports, physical control, etc.); recording of liabilities (vendor's invoice, debit memos, etc.); cash disbursements (checks, etc.); storage, processing, and shipping of inventory; transferring the cost of inventory sold; accurately tracking inventory costs (especially in manufacturing firms); and physically observing inventory. In each case, make sure that recorded inventory represents goods actually received or manufactured, existing acquisition transactions are recorded, transaction amounts are accurate, and that transactions are properly classified, are recorded in the proper periods, and are included in the proper financial statement accounts. Where inventory controls are weak or easily overridden, a missing control or an observance of an override represents a fraud symptom, not merely a control weakness. As such, it should be pursued with the same vigilance as any other fraud symptom.

Searching for Behavior and Lifestyle Flags

As with other financial statement frauds, lifestyle symptoms are not effective in helping you find inventory fraud because these frauds don't benefit perpetrators directly. However, searching for behavioral and verbal symptoms can be fruitful. Often, recorded inventory amounts are subject to management's intent. For example, if managers believe they can sell existing inventory, they will not write inventory amounts off as obsolete. Usually, the best evidence of intent comes from inquiries to management. Their responses should be corroborated, but this is not always possible. With inventory, it is very important that auditors and fraud examiners ask detailed questions about the nature, age, salability, and other characteristics of inventory as well as inventory levels (increases or decreases), significant changes in vendors, and so on. The best way to determine whether management is lying is to identify inconsistencies between what you observe (for example, analytical and documentary symptoms) and what management tells you.

Searching for Tips and Complaints

Tips and complaints are useful in detecting inventory frauds. In most cases, inventory must be brought into a firm, handled within the firm, and shipped out when sold. All this movement means that many people must be involved in managing the physical flow of inventory. Usually, these employees do not understand the nature of audits or forensic examinations, nor the frauds that can occur. To underscore the value of asking questions and responding to tips, consider the case of an outside auditor who audited the inventory of a sprinkler pipe manufacturer. Some of the inventory looked old and unsalable. However, the CFO and CEO told the auditor that the inventory was fine and would be sold in the normal course of business. Curious, he brought a sack lunch the next day and ate with the warehouse workers. After "chatting them up," he asked them about how the various types of pipe were used. They were forthright—most of the pipe on hand would never be sold because it was "useless." With his firm's backing, he insisted that the client write down the pipe inventory by several million dollars. The moral of this story? Talk to the people who actually handle the inventory.

In addition to talking to the people who handle the inventory, it is often helpful to communicate directly with vendors and to determine their relationships with the company. Of course, you must in no way intrude in the company's business and put its relationships with its vendors at risk (unless you like lawsuits!), but vendors can often give you valuable information about inventory costs, amounts of purchases, and other factors. Similarly, talking with large customers and assessing inventory quality and product returns often provides crucial evidence—they will know whether bricks are shipped as software and whether inventory is overvalued.

The important point to remember here is that you must actively seek out tips. As we stated earlier, there are often individuals who suspect that something is awry, but are afraid to come forward or are simply not asked. And be sure you review hotline records to see whether any calls have come in about suspicious inventory.

Looking for Inventory and/or Cost of Goods Sold–Related Fraud Symptoms

As with other frauds, for inventory and/or cost of goods sold financial statement frauds to be detected, symptoms must be observed and recognized. Take the MiniScribe Corporation financial statement fraud, for example.[8] MiniScribe's management, assisted by financial officers and other employees, overstated inventory and materially inflated reported net income. Because the Inventory account was used (and inventory errors offset in subsequent periods, which required the misstatement of larger and larger amounts), the fraud grew rapidly. The inventory overstatement was $4.5 million in the first year, $22 million in the second year, and $31.8 million in the third year (two quarters only)! To understand the scope and variety of presenting symptoms, let's look at how management perpetrated the MiniScribe fraud. In the first year, senior managers broke into the auditors' files to obtain inventory lists that designated which items had been test-counted. With this information, the officers inflated the values of items that had *not* been test-counted. With the second year came the need to misstate inventory by a much larger amount, so management used three different approaches:

1. Created fictitious "inventory in transit" amounts.
2. Recorded a transfer of $9 million in nonexistent inventory from MiniScribe's U.S. books to their Far East subsidiaries' books.
3. Received raw materials into inventory just prior to the end of the fiscal year without recording the corresponding Accounts Payable liability.

In the third year, management resorted to more flagrant ways to manipulate inventory. As an example of their desperation, they labeled boxes of bricks as disk drives, shipped them to two MiniScribe distributors, and recorded the shipments as consigned inventory. Perhaps they felt cocky and reckless when they named the computer program they created to generate fictitious inventory numbers "Cook Book"! They also accumulated scrap that had been written off the company's books, repackaged it, and recorded it as inventory. Employees also prepared false inventory tickets to increase recorded inventory.

In the first year, the fraud was no doubt difficult to detect. When management is willing to break into auditors' files and forge computer records, a fraud has little chance of being caught. People's behavior or responses to auditors' inquiries might change here and there, and someone might provide a tip, but not many other symptoms would present themselves in the early stages. Also, the fraud in that first year was only $4.5 million, so the analytical symptoms were not significant yet.

In the second year, as the fraud grew to $22 million and took on different forms, symptoms began to proliferate—the huge increase in the inventory balance, to name one. Obviously, there were questions that didn't get asked. For example, why did inventory increase so fast, yet the relationships between inventory, sales, and cost of sales stayed the same? What about the large year-end "in-transit" inventory amounts? Together with the $9 million transfer of inventory from the books of the U.S. parent company to the Asian subsidiary's books, these two transactions alone should have raised concerns. Certainly, inventory that is listed as an asset without recording the corresponding purchases raises an accounting flag. With these suspicious year-end transactions, inquiries into management procedures should have increased, providing auditors and fraud examiners with opportunities to observe inconsistencies in behavior and other responses. In the second year, some overriding of key controls and maybe even a tip or two had to appear as knowledge about the fraud inevitably spread.

In the third year, when boxes of bricks were being shipped, consigned inventory increased, and the "Cook Book" computer program was written, employees had to be "stumbling over" symptoms. Returns of "merchandise" (the bricks), increasing customer complaints, expanding circles of employees involved (and thereby higher probabilities of tips and complaints), false inventory tickets, the reclassification of obsolete inventory as good inventory—all these symptoms were present and probably flagrant at this stage of the "game."

Searching for Inventory/Cost of Goods Sold Analytical Symptoms

As with all other types of fraud, inventory and cost of goods sold fraud symptoms can be found in one of two ways:

- Happen on to them by chance.
- Proactively search for them.

How you search for symptoms depends on what symptoms you are looking for. Remember that analytical symptoms show accounts as being too high or too low or exhibiting unusual characteristics. Also remember that you need a point of reference—an expectation or some basis against which to compare recorded amounts. As with revenue fraud symptoms, the most practical way to look for analytical symptoms in inventory fraud is to focus on financial statements. The following table applies the methods we previously discussed to inventory:

Analysis of Period-to-Period Changes	Comparison of Statement Amounts
Inventory account balances 1. Focus on changes in statement numbers. 2. Study statement of cash flow. 3. Use horizontal analysis.	*With industry competitors* 1. Compare statement results with similiar companies. 2. Compare company's trends with those of similiar companies.
Inventory relationships 1. Examine changes in relevant ratios. 2. Use vertical analysis.	*With real-world numbers* 1. Compare statement amounts with the assets they are supposed to represent.

Changes in Period-to-Period Inventory Balances. Recall from our previous discussion that there are three ways to focus on changes in period-to-period balances. The first, and usually least effective, method is to focus on the changes in the statement *numbers.* Because the numbers for inventory and cost of goods sold are often large, it is often difficult to assess the magnitude of changes or to distinguish significant from insignificant changes. The second method is to study the statement of cash flow to identify changes in account balances from one period to the next. The advantage of focusing on the statement of cash flows is that the "change" numbers have already been calculated.

Horizontal analysis is the easiest way to examine period-to-period changes in account balances. As you will recall, horizontal analysis allows you to examine percentage changes from period to period. Although performing horizontal analysis on all balance sheet and income statement accounts works best when you don't know what type of fraud you are looking for, inventory/cost of goods sold frauds are often discovered via unusual changes in inventory on the balance sheet and cost of goods sold on the income statement. Generally, fraud may be present if inventory increases are too high to be realistic, period-to-period inventory balances increase monotonically, or cost of goods sold increases don't mirror the increases in either sales or inventory. However, any change that appears to be unusual or unrealistic can be an analytical fraud symptom.

Period-to-Period Changes in Relationships. As with revenue frauds, the two primary methods for inventory fraud focus on changes in relationships from period to period: (1) Examine ratio changes from one period to the next, and (2) convert financial statements to common-size statements and use vertical analysis. The most helpful ratios used to examine inventory and cost of goods sold relationships are as follows:

Gross Profit Margin (Gross profit ÷ Sales). When a company overstates its inventory balance, cost of goods sold is usually understated. The result is an increase in the gross profit margin. Thus, a significant increase in the gross profit margin can be signaling either a revenue or an inventory fraud.

Inventory Turnover (Cost of goods sold ÷ Average Inventory). This ratio helps determine whether inventory is overstated or cost of goods sold is understated. Generally, overstating inventory has the effect of decreasing this ratio because the denominator is increased. Similarly, understating cost of goods sold also decreases this ratio.

Number of Days' Sales in Inventory (Days in a Period ÷ Inventory turnover). This ratio measures the average time it takes to sell inventory. Thus, if cost of goods sold is $500, average inventory is $200, and there are 365 days in a year, the inventory turnover ratio is 2.5 ($500 ÷ $200), and the number of days' sales in inventory is 146 (365 ÷ 2.5). This means that the company "turns" or sells its inventory, on average, every 146 days. When a company overstates inventory, inventory turnover numbers decrease, and the number of days' sales in inventory increases. For example, if the company overstates inventory by $100 or reports $300 in inventory, the inventory turnover is 1.67 ($500 ÷ $300), and the number of days' sales in inventory is about 219 days (365 ÷ 1.67).

Four other ratios are also helpful in detecting inventory and/or cost of goods sold–related frauds. Although not as sensitive as the three ratios discussed above, asset turnover, working capital turnover, operating performance ratio, and earnings per share can sometimes be useful in identifying inventory frauds. Asset turnover is most helpful in detecting fraud when inventory comprises a large percentage of the total assets of an organization. When inventory is overstated, the denominator of this ratio increases, causing working capital turnover to decrease. Again, this ratio is most helpful when inventory comprises a major portion of current assets. The operating performance ratio measures the profit margin of a company. When inventory is overstated and/or cost of goods sold is understated, net income is artificially increased, causing this ratio to increase. Finally, earnings per share, the most commonly used ratio, measures the profitability of an organization. When net income is overstated, earnings per share increase. When earnings increase dramatically, the cause should be investigated, because you may find overstated inventory and/or understated cost of goods sold.

Remember that a large or small ratio does not mean much. Rather, the *change* in the ratios from period to period is what is of interest.

Fraud examiners also explore financial statement relationships by converting the statements to common-size statements and performing vertical analysis. If inventory as a percentage of total assets or as a percentage of sales keeps increasing, or if cost of goods sold as a percentage of net sales keeps decreasing, there could be fraud. Take the financial statement fraud at Crazy Eddie, Inc.[9] At one point, Crazy Eddie, Inc. was the hot name in consumer electronics. What began in 1970 as a single store selling TVs, stereos, and other electronic products mushroomed into an empire with so many stores that *The New Yorker* magazine once ran a cartoon in which all roads led to Crazy Eddie. The piercing slogan "C-r-r-r-azy Eddie! His prices are ins-a-a-a-ne!" blurted incessantly on radio and TV stations and brought customers in droves. At one point, Crazy Eddie stock traded for as much as $43.25 per share.

In the end, however, the company was under court-protected bankruptcy because of its much-publicized inventory problems. As much as $65 million in inventory was suddenly and inexplicably missing. When new management took over the company in a desperate rescue attempt, the $65 million inventory write-off more than erased *all* previous earnings. Apparently, during inventory counts, company officers drafted phony inventory count sheets and improperly included merchandise, which made reported ending inventory and net income higher. The artificially high profits and stock price allowed its founder, Eddie Antar, to rake in $68.4 million from stock sales.

These inventory increases substantially increased the inventory balances from period to period, increased the gross profit margin, decreased the inventory turnover ratio, increased the number of days' sales in inventory, and were quite obvious in the percentage changes using vertical and horizontal analysis. Indeed, Crazy Eddie, Inc. was awash in analytical symptoms.

Comparing Companies' Financial Statements. Maintaining large amounts of inventory is expensive, especially if inventory is large, bulky, heavy, or requires special handling. Because handling, warehousing, and financing inventory are extremely expensive today, most companies take extreme steps to keep the inventory they have on hand at minimum levels. Dell Computer, for example, keeps very little, if any, inventory. It purchases inventory to make computers ordered by its customers "just in time." Today's investors view high inventory levels as flags for management ineptitude and lack of efficiency in operations. Therefore, when the reported inventory balance increases, it behooves you to ask why. Increasing inventory levels are especially questionable when competing companies are not increasing their inventories. Economic and industrywide factors tend to affect similar firms in similar ways. Financial results that are inconsistent with those of other similar firms quite often signal problems. To make comparisons, use horizontal or vertical analysis, ratio analysis, changes reported in the statement of cash flows, or changes in the financial statement numbers themselves.

As you compare inventory balances and trends with other similar companies, also consider the type of inventory. Increasing inventory balances in industries that are rapidly changing (such as the computer or software industries), that have high amounts of spoilage or obsolescence (such as groceries), or that normally don't have high inventory balances should raise questions. When inventory balances are increasing, either by themselves or in relation to other numbers, always ask yourself what it is about this company that makes it different from other similar firms. If a ready answer is not forthcoming, you may have a fraud on your hands.

Comparing Statement Amounts with Actual Assets. Comparing recorded amounts in the financial statements with the assets they are supposed to represent is an excellent way to detect inventory frauds. In the Laribee case, the inventory represented by the financial statement amounts "would have required three times the capacity of the buildings" the company had to store it.[10] In another case, cited in Chapter 5, auditors were suspicious of the inventory numbers reported on a company's financial statements. Their observation of inventory revealed no serious shortages but didn't square with the statement numbers. Why would the company's inventory increase fivefold in one year? Suspecting that something was awry, the auditors looked at the physical attributes of the actual inventory. Their investigation revealed that the sheet metal inventory was grossly overstated. Management falsified the inventory by preparing fictitious records. Company management also prepared inventory tags and delivered them to the auditors. The auditors verified the inventory shown on the tags and deposited them in a box in the conference room they used during the audit. At night, a manager then added spurious tags to the box. The manager also substituted new inventory reconciliation lists to conform with the total of the valid and spurious tags.

The fraud was discovered when the auditors performed volume tests on the inventory. First, they converted the purported $30 million of sheet metal stock into cubic feet and determined the volume of the warehouse that was supposed to contain the inventory. At best, it could contain one-half the reported amount—it was far too small to house the total. Next, they examined the inventory tags and found that some rolls of sheet metal were supposed to weigh 50,000 pounds. However, none of the forklifts that were supposed to move the inventory could lift over 3,000 pounds. Finally, the auditors verified the reported inventory purchases and found purchase records supporting an inventory of about 30 million pounds. Yet, the reported amount was 60 million pounds. Faced with this evidence, management admitted that it grossly overstated the value of the inventory to show increased profits. Management had forecast increased earnings, and without the overstatement, earnings would have fallen far short of target.

Summary

Revenue and inventory frauds are closely related, because revenues are generated by selling inventory. Inventory, by its nature, has physical characteristics that should be compared to ascertain whether the numbers reported on the financial statements match. This ensures that the reported inventory levels are realistic.

New Terms

Accounts receivable turnover: Sales divided by average accounts receivable; a measure of the efficiency with which receivables are being collected.

Allowance for doubtful accounts: A contra-asset (receivable) account representing the amount of receivables that are estimated to be uncollectible.

Allowance for uncollectible assets as a percentage of receivables: Allowance for doubtful accounts divided by accounts receivable; a measure of the percentage of receivables estimated to be uncollectible.

Asset turnover: Total sales divided by average total assets; a measure of the amount of sales revenue generated with each dollar of assets.

Bad debt expense: An expense representing receivables and/or revenues that are presumed not to be collectible.

Common-size financial statements: Financial statements that have been converted to percentages.

Cost of goods sold: The cost of goods sold to customers; calculated by subtracting ending inventory from the sum of beginning inventory plus purchases.

Earnings per share: Net income divided by the number of shares of stock outstanding; a measure of profitability.

Gross profit margin: Gross profit margin divided by net sales; a measure of markup.

Number of days in receivables: 365 (number of days in a year) divided by accounts receivable turnover; a measure of how long it takes to collect receivables.

Operating performance ratio: Net income divided by total sales; a measure of the percentage of revenues that become profits.

Revenue recognition: Determining that revenues have been earned and are collectible and thus should be reported on the income statement.

Sales return percentage (ratio): Sales returns divided by total sales; a measure of the percentage of sales being returned by customers.

Sales returns (sales returns and allowances): Sold merchandise that is returned by customers and/or damaged, or other sold merchandise for which credit is given.

Working capital turnover ratio: Sales divided by average working capital; a measure of the amount of working capital used to generate revenues.

Questions and Cases

Discussion Questions

1. What are some common revenue fraud schemes?
2. How can you proactively search for revenue frauds?
3. Why is it important to follow up on revenue fraud symptoms?
4. What are some of the most common inventory fraud schemes?
5. What are some of the ways to proactively search for inventory frauds?

6. What are common-size financial statements?
7. Why do you think revenue frauds are so common and inventory frauds are next in number?
8. What is the effect on net income of not recording sales returns?
9. What is the effect on net income of overstating ending inventory?

True/False

1. Understated revenues and understated net income are among the most common types of financial statement fraud.
2. Two of the reasons revenue fraud is so prevalent are because revenue recognition can be highly subjective and because revenue is so easily manipulated.
3. Performing a horizontal analysis of the statement of cash flow is an excellent way to proactively search for revenue fraud.
4. The most common accounts manipulated when perpetrating financial statement fraud are revenues and/or accounts receivable.
5. An increase in gross margin and an increase in number of days' sales in inventory could be an indication of inflated inventory fraud.
6. A "sales discount" amount that appears too low could be a fraud symptom.
7. Comparing financial results and trends of a company with those of similar firms is an ineffective way to look for fraud symptoms.
8. Focusing on changes in financial statements from period to period can help identify analytical fraud symptoms.
9. Controls over inventory should be closely examined when searching for fraud symptoms.
10. The gross profit margin is calculated by dividing gross profit by cost of goods sold.

Multiple Choice

1. The most common accounts manipulated when perpetrating financial statement fraud are:
   a. Expenses
   b. Inventory
   c. Revenue
   d. Accounts Payable
2. Why would a company want to understate net income?
   a. To increase profits
   b. To increase stock price
   c. To gain consumer confidence
   d. To pay less taxes
3. Reported Revenue and Sales account balances that appear too high are examples of:
   a. Analytical symptoms
   b. Documentary symptoms
   c. Lifestyle symptoms
   d. Verbal symptoms

4. Horizontal analysis is a method that:
   a. Examines financial statement numbers from period to period
   b. Examines percent changes in account balances from period to period
   c. Examines transactions from period to period
   d. None of the above
5. Adding fictitious receivables will usually result in a(n):
   a. Sales return percentage that remains constant
   b. Increased sales discount percentage
   c. Increase in accounts receivable turnover
   d. Increase in the number of days in receivables
6. Comparing recorded amounts in financial statements with actual assets is effective in detecting:
   a. Cash and inventory fraud
   b. Accounts payable fraud
   c. Revenue frauds
   d. Accounts receivable fraud
7. Lifestyle symptoms are most effective with:
   a. Revenue frauds
   b. Inventory fraud
   c. Employee frauds
   d. Accounts payable fraud
8. Which of the following is *not* an inventory-related documentary symptom?
   a. Duplicate purchase orders
   b. Missing inventory during inventory counts
   c. Unsupported inventory sales transactions
   d. All of the above are inventory-related documentary symptoms.
9. When looking for inventory fraud, an important question to ask is:
   a. What is the nature of inventory?
   b. What is the age of inventory?
   c. What is the salability of inventory?
   d. All are important questions.
10. Which of the following ratios would *not* generally be used to look for inventory and cost of goods sold–related frauds?
   a. Accounts payable turnover
   b. Gross profit margin
   c. Inventory turnover
   d. Number of days' sales in inventory

Short Cases

Case 1. During the audit of a major client, you notice that revenues increased dramatically from the third to the fourth quarter and especially over the previous periods of last year. You've received tips alleging that the company is overstating its revenues. What steps would you take to examine the legitimacy of management's assertions regarding its reported revenue?

Case 2. Thomas is the CEO of a business that just went public. He is feeling intense pressure for the business to succeed because all of his relatives have invested heavily in his company. Since going public, sales have been flat, and Thomas is worried about not meeting analysts' and even relatives' expectations. Which financial statement accounts might Thomas attempt to manipulate in order to meet analysts' projected earnings?

Case 3. The following information is provided for Technoworld, a company that provides Internet technology assistance to clients:

	2001	**2002**	**2003**	**2004**
Cash	$1,000	$1,200	$1,400	$1,500
Accounts receivable	250	375	600	900
Inventory	600	700	825	975
Property, plant and equipment (net)	1,500	1,700	1,800	1,950
Notes receivable	500	500	500	500
Total assets	$3,850	$4,475	$5,125	$5,825
Accounts payable	$700	$900	$1,000	$1,100
Other current liabilities	200	300	350	425
Notes payable	1,200	1,400	1,500	1,750
Total liabilities	$2,100	$2,600	$2,850	$3,275
Stock outstanding	$1,000	$1,000	$1,000	$1,000
Retained earnings	750	875	1,275	1,550
Total shareholders' equity	$1,750	$1,875	$2,275	$2,550
Total liabilities and shareholders' equity	$3,850	$4,475	$5,125	$5,825

Perform a horizontal analysis of this balance sheet and identify accounts that may be questionable. Take into account technology industry trends when you perform the analysis.

Cases 4 and 5. For Cases 4 and 5, use the following information:

Five-Year Financial Data for Company AAA

	Year 1	Year 2	Year 3	Year 4	Year 5
Sales	$100,000	$105,000	$110,250	$137,812	$206,718
COGS	75,000	78,750	82,687	66,150	59,535
Margin	25,000	26,250	27,562	71,662	147,183

Case 4. Perform horizontal analysis of the data to find red flags for possible overstatement of sales.

Case 5. Perform vertical analysis of the data to search for red flags for possible understatement of the cost of goods sold (COGS).

Extensive Cases

Case 6. Fraud investigators found that 70% of the nearly $160 million in sales booked by an Asian subsidiary of a European company between September 1999 and June 2000 were fictitious. In an effort to earn rich bonuses tied to sales targets, the Asian subsidiary's managers used sophisticated schemes to fool auditors, including funneling bank loans through third parties to make it look as though customers had paid, when in fact they hadn't.

In a lawsuit filed by the company's auditors, it was alleged that former executives "deliberately" provided "false or incomplete information" to the auditors and conspired to obstruct the firm's audits. To fool the auditors, the subsidiary used two schemes. The first involved factoring unpaid receivables to banks to obtain cash up front. Side letters that were concealed from the auditors gave the banks the right to take the money back if they couldn't collect from the company's customers. Hence, the factoring agreements amounted to little more than loans.

The second, more creative, scheme was used after the auditors questioned why the company wasn't collecting more of its overdue bills from customers. The subsidiary told many customers to transfer their contracts to third parties. The third parties then took out bank loans, for which the company provided collateral, and then "paid" the overdue bills to the company using the borrowed money. The company was, in effect, paying itself. When the contracts were later canceled, the company paid "penalties" to the customers and the third parties to compensate them "for the inconvenience of dealing with the auditors."

The investigators also found that the bulk of the company's sales came from contracts signed at the end of quarters, so managers could meet ambitious quarterly sales targets and receive multimillion-dollar bonuses. For example, 90% of the revenue recorded by the subsidiary in the second quarter of 2000 was booked in several deals signed in the final nine days of the quarter. But the company was forced to subsequently cancel 70% of those contracts because the customers—most of them tiny start-ups—didn't have the means to pay.

List revenue fraud symptoms and schemes used in this case. Briefly discuss how actively searching and understanding revenue fraud symptoms could have led to discovery of the fraud.

Case 7. Toolsito is a medium-sized company that buys copper rod and plastic materials to produce insulated copper wiring. Toolsito operates out of a single building of about 500,000 square feet that includes office space (3%), production area (57%), shipping and receiving (15%), and finished goods and raw materials inventory warehousing (25%). You have gathered the following data about the company's inventories and performance, and now you are ready to conduct an analysis on these numbers to discover possible fraud symptoms.

	2002	**2001**
Finished goods inventory (Approx. 300 million ft.–2002)	$1,654,500	$1,175,500
Copper rod inventory (Approx. 5.9 million lbs.–2002)	$2,625,000	$1,650,000
Plastics inventory (Approx. 1.1 million lbs.–2002)	$ 224,500	$ 182,000
Accounts payable (for inv. purchases)	$ 450,000	$ 425,000
Days purchases in A/P	43.6 days	44.2 days
Days sales in receivables	56.3 days	48.4 days
Market price of insulated wire (per foot)	$0.008	$0.009
Market price of copper rod (per lb.)	$0.480	$0.480
Market price of plastics (per lb.)	$0.120	$0.190

How would you go about looking for red flags? Determine if you think possible fraud symptoms are present in 2002.

Internet Assignments

1. Horizontal and vertical analyses are effective ways to search for analytical fraud symptoms. Search the Internet for the annual report of a company of your choice. Perform both a horizontal and vertical analysis for the assets portion of the balance sheet. You may find it helpful to use Excel or similar spreadsheet software.
2. Go to IBM's web site (http://www.ibm.com) and download IBM's most recent financial statements. In the notes to the financial statements, read the significant accounting policies concerning revenue and inventory. Do the policies seem legitimate? What concerns might you have? Then, go to the financial statements and do a year-to-year comparison of the three accounts. Were the changes as expected? Is anything unusual? Does IBM explain any unusual fluctuations in the notes?

Debate

Jorge Mendoza is considering investing in IBM. He is captivated by IBM's annual average growth rate of 27% per year since 1994. IBM has made a remarkable transition from a struggling company to a leading company in the personal computer market. Mendoza asks for your advice: Do you think the growth is genuine? He suspects there might have been some fraudulent or unethical actions taken by IBM to increase its income.

After a brief look at the recent history and performance of IBM, you decide to look more closely at the financial statements. As you review the financial statements, you begin to have some concerns about the true nature of IBM's growth. Certain accounting procedures cause you to have doubt as to whether the growth came from IBM's core business operations or from carefully planned accounting adjustments that seem to be unethical. As you proceed in your investigations, you pay particular attention to the following areas:

Pensions

IBM changed its pension plan to a cash balance plan. The returns of this plan exceeded the amount recognized as an expense. Accounting rules require the company to add the excess returns to earnings, but the gains cannot be spent on anything other than pension benefits. IBM increased its earnings per share by making the above adjustment.

Stock Repurchases

Since 1995, IBM has spent millions on stock repurchases. A stock repurchase can be beneficial to a company by increasing earnings per share, because there are fewer shareholders across which to spread the earnings.

You conclude that IBM's financial statements are in accordance with GAAP, and you are confident that all accounting rules were followed. However, you have to explain to Mendoza whether the behavior was ethical. What would you tell him?

End Notes

1. M. S. Beasley, J. V. Carcello, and D. R. Hermanson, 1999, *Fraudulent Financial Reporting: 1987–1997: An Analysis of U.S. Public Companies,* Committee of Sponsoring Organizations (COSO).

2. See, for example, National Commission on Fraudulent Financial Reporting (NCFFR), 1987, Report of the National Commission on Fraudulent Financial Reporting, New York: AICPA.
3. For example, see the AICPA's self-study course on fraud: W. Steve Albrecht, *Fraudulent Financial Transactions,* American Institute of Certified Public Accountants, Self-Study Course on Fraud, 2000.
4. See http://www.sec.gov/litigation/admin/34-39589.txt, Auditing and Accounting Enforcement Release No. 1007, January 28, 1998.
5. http://www.nwfusion.com/newsletters/sec/2002/01190226.html
6. "Inventory Chicanery Tempts More Firms, Fools More Auditors," *Wall Street Journal* (Dec. 14, 1992), p. 1.
7. Beasley, et. al. op. cit.
8. http://www.sec.gov/litigation/admin/34-39589.txt, op. cit.
9. Joseph T. Wells, *Frankensteins of Fraud,* Obsidian Publishing Company, Inc., Austin, Texas, 2000, pp. 215–261.
10. http://college.hmco.com/accounting/resources/students/readings/25-read.html

CHAPTER TWELVE

Liability, Asset, and Inadequate Disclosure Frauds

After studying this chapter, you should be able to:

1. Identify fraud schemes that understate liabilities.
2. Understand the understatement of liabilities.
3. Identify fraud schemes that overstate assets.
4. Understand the overstatement of assets.
5. Identify fraud schemes that inadequately disclose financial statement information.
6. Understand inadequate disclosure fraud.

Sunbeam Corporation began developing home appliances in 1910. Over the years, Sunbeam made some of the nation's best home appliances, such as the electric iron and pop-up toaster.

In July 1996, "Chainsaw Al" Dunlap became Sunbeam's new CEO and chairman of the board. Dunlap promised a rapid turnaround in Sunbeam's performance. Six months later, the new CEO could not show the magical results he had so widely touted. Desperate, Chainsaw Al turned to the fraudster's "laundry list" to improve Sunbeam's performance.

Dunlap initially created "cookie jar" reserves, which increased Sunbeam's 1996 reported losses, but which then enabled Dunlap to inflate income in 1997, thus giving the picture of a rapid turnaround. In 1997, Chainsaw Al caused the company to recognize revenues for sales that did not meet applicable accounting rules. As a result, at least $60 million of Sunbeam's record-setting $189 million reported 1997 earnings came from accounting fraud.

In early 1998, Dunlap took even more desperate measures to conceal the company's mounting financial problems. He again recognized revenue for sales that did not meet applicable accounting rules. He also caused Sunbeam to accelerate sales revenue from a later period and deleted corporate records to conceal pending returns of merchandise.[1]

On February 6, 2001, Sunbeam Corporation filed voluntary petitions with the United States Bankruptcy Court for the Southern District of New York, under Chapter 11 of Title 11 of the United States Code. Al Dunlap agreed to pay $15 million to settle a shareholder lawsuit accusing him and other Sunbeam executives of inflating stock share prices. A civil trial for the suit is still going on. The class action lawsuit accused Sunbeam and its officers of misleading investors about the appliance maker's sales and earnings in 1997 and 1998. The suit also alleged that the executives used inflated stock prices to complete mergers with Coleman, Signature Brands USA Inc., and First Alert Inc. The company restated financial results for the six quarters before Dunlap was fired.

The revenue and inventory frauds discussed in Chapter 11 are the most common financial statement frauds. However, three other financial statement frauds occur frequently: (1) understating liabilities, (2) overstating assets, and (3) inadequate disclosure.

Liability Fraud

We begin with an example of understating liabilities. A number of years ago, one of the Big 5 CPA firms was sued for failing to detect a financial statement fraud in its GAAS (generally accepted auditing standards) audits. The company that misstated its financial statements, DuVall Limited Real Estate Partnerships, organized a series of real estate limited partnerships under Wisconsin's Uniform Limited Partnership Act. The largest partnership—and the one with the most fraud—had more than 5,000 limited partners and two general partners. The partnerships were formed to acquire, own, and operate commercial real estate, which consisted of new and existing convenience-store properties. Using a triple net basis,[2] DuVall leased the properties to franchisers of national and regional retail chains under long-term leases. The lessees were primarily restaurants (fast-food, family style, and casual theme, such as Wendy's, Hardees, Peso's Country Kitchen, Applebee's, Popeye's, Arby's, and Village Inns), but also included Blockbuster Video stores and child-care centers. Money supplied by limited partners was used to purchase, construct, and fully pay for the properties. None of the properties had mortgages.

The two general partners also had significant real estate investments of their own and needed money to support their cash-strapped, personal investments. They saw DuVall equity as a great source of cash. Accordingly, they approached a Kansas bank (where they didn't think the loans would be discovered) and borrowed millions of dollars against DuVall equity assets, thus incurring significant amounts of debt for the partnership.

Fortunately, auditors were concerned that the "triple net" nature of the leases meant that DuVall had significant risk, because a lessee's failure to pay local property taxes or utilities could encumber the properties with liens. As a result, to determine whether lessees were current on their obligations, the auditors performed lien searches on all properties. What they found surprised them considerably. Their searches revealed liens against Arizona and Texas properties by a Kansas bank. Because the partnership operated no businesses in Kansas, the liens garnered significant scrutiny. The auditors first approached management and asked about the liens. They were told that the liens were recorded as part of a lending arrangement with the bank that was never completed and should have been released. To corroborate management's explanations, the auditors sent a confirmation letter to the Kansas bank:

> *In connection with the audit of the DuVall partnership for the year ending December 31, 1995, our auditors became aware of several mortgage liens held by your bank on properties located in Arizona and Texas. These liens were recorded as part of a lending arrangement with your bank which was not completed. Because the liens have not been released, our auditors would like confirmation from you on the enclosed form as to the balance of loans or other liabilities outstanding to your bank from the DuVall partnership at December 31, 1995. If such balance was zero at that date, please so state.*
>
> *Your prompt response will be appreciated. Please fax a copy of your response to the attention of [named auditor] at [telephone number] and also return the enclosed form in the envelope provided. Thank you for your attention to this matter.*

In response, the auditors received both a fax and an original letter dated April 12, 1996, from the bank's executive vice president:

> *In response to [name of signer] letter of January 24, 1996, regarding your audit of DuVall Limited Real Estate Partnerships, please be advised as follows: (1) DuVall Limited Real Estate Partnerships has no debt or obligation outstanding to the bank, and (2) the bank's attorneys are in the process of releasing the collateral liens, since it is the bank's understanding that the borrower does not intend to utilize its existing line of credit arrangements.*

Like the auditors in this case, at this point you might have been satisfied that DuVall had no unrecorded liabilities and that the line of credit had never been used. Unfortunately, you would have assumed wrong. Read the letters again. Although the auditor's letter specifies December 31, 1995, as the date for which they wanted to know whether liabilities existed, note that the bank's response does not specify a date, only the letter itself was dated April 12. In reality, significant liabilities existed on December 31, 1995, and continued until April 11, 1996, at which time they were removed. On April 12, there were no *recorded* liabilities, but on April 13, 1996, the liabilities were again recorded. In other words, the no-liability situation existed for only one day—April 12. DuVall's general partners coerced the bank's president and executive vice president into removing the liabilities for April 12 and responding thus to the auditors—they were acting in collusion with the general partners. This was not the only financial statement fraud perpetrated by the general partners, but it was the largest. The unrecorded liabilities, which could never be paid off, resulted in significant adverse consequences for DuVall.

Frauds that entail understating liabilities are difficult for auditors to detect. In fact, all financial statement frauds fall on a continuum of "easy to detect/should be detected" to "difficult to detect/cannot be detected" by auditors performing a GAAS audit. The following are some of the factors that make frauds difficult to detect:

- Collusion with outsiders
- Forgery, which GAAS auditors are not trained to detect
- Complex audit trails or frauds that are mainly revealed on internal reports that are not reviewed in financial statement audits
- Lying by management and other key people
- Frauds that mimic normal transactions (in other words, are not unusual)
- Silence by individuals "in the know"
- Off-book frauds (no records on the company's books are fraudulent)
- Misleading documentation
- Small frauds relative to financial statement balances

Identifying Liability Frauds

As with revenue and inventory frauds, the first step in uncovering liability frauds is to identify transactions that involve liabilities and that can be understated. To do this, you must understand what type of organization you are dealing with, because different types of companies have different liabilities and perpetrate different liability frauds. The following table lists the six transactions that can create liabilities for retail or wholesale companies. When you analyze the accounts involved in these transactions, you will note at least 19 different ways (some are similar) to understate liabilities in financial statements.

Liability Fraud		
Transaction	**Accounts Involved**	**Fraud Schemes**
1. Purchase inventory	Inventory, Accounts payable	1. Record payables in subsequent period 2. Don't record purchases 3. Overstate purchase returns and purchase discounts 4. Record payments made in later periods as paid in earlier periods 5. Fraudulent recording of payments (e.g., kiting)
2. Incur payroll and other accrued liabilities	Payroll tax expense, Salary expense, Various expenses, Salaries payable, Payroll taxes payable, Various accrued liabilities	6. Don't record accrued liabilities 7. Record accruals in later period
3. Sell products purchased	Accounts receivable, Sales revenue, Unearned revenue	8. Record unearned revenues as earned revenues
4. Service products sold, repay deposits, or repurchase something in the future (future commitments)	Warranty (service) expense, Warranty or service liability	9. Don't record warranty (service) liabilities 10. Underrecord liabilities 11. Record deposits as revenues 12. Don't record repurchase agreements and commitments
5. Borrow money	Cash, Notes payable, Mortgages payable, etc.	13. Borrow from related parties at less than arms-length transactions 14. Don't record liabilities 15. Borrow against equities in assets 16. Write off liabilities as forgiven 17. Claim liabilities as personal debt rather than as debt of the entity
6. Incur contingent liabilities	Loss from contingencies, Losses payable	18. Don't record contingent liabilities that are probable 19. Record contingent liabilities at too low an amount

Understating Accounts Payable

The first fraud scheme involves various cut-off problems related to purchasing inventory. Although minor cut-off problems occur in many companies, large statement misstatements can result from these frauds. In one case, auditors discovered a $28 million liability for inventory purchased before year-end that was not recorded as a liability because management altered purchasing records, bank statements, and correspondence to make it look like the inventory was paid for before year-end.

Understating accounts payable is the flip side of the transactions we considered in Chapter 11. When accounts payables are understated, purchases and inventory are often understated as well, or the ledgers do not balance. In the case of ZZZZ Best, Barry Minkow and his colleagues used interbank transfers or kites to make it appear as though liabilities had been paid (as cash received). Perpetrators understate accounts payable by doing the following: (1) not recording purchases or recording them after year-end, (2) overstating purchase returns or purchase discounts, *and* (3) making it appear as though liabilities are paid off or forgiven (like ZZZZ Best did or by predating a payment made in a subsequent period so it looked like it was paid during the current period). Such understatements are a common way to misstate financial statements. Note that, if a purchase is not recorded but the inventory is counted and included in a period's ending inventory, the net income overstatement equals the understatement (less tax effects).

Understating Accrued Liabilities

Several accrued liabilities that need to be recorded at the end of accounting periods often add up to millions of dollars. These include salaries payable, payroll taxes payable, rent payable, utilities payable, and interest payable. When these liabilities are not recorded or are understated, net income is overstated because the other (debit) side of an accrual entry is to an expense account. Although these frauds tend to be small, they are easy to perpetrate. For example, one company understated payroll taxes payable by $2.1 million and accrued salaries by $1 million.

Recognizing Unearned Revenue as Earned Revenue

The third liability that can be understated is unearned revenues. Sometimes cash is received prior to the performance of a service or the shipment of goods. Or a company requires tenants or others to make deposits that can be recorded as revenue. When someone pays in advance of the performance of a service or the sale of a product, the journal entry should recognize the cash received and a liability for the future service or product. Later, when the service is performed or the product shipped, the liability is eliminated and the revenue is recognized. A company that collects cash in advance and wants to understate liabilities merely records revenues at the time cash is received, rather than later when the service is performed. Recognizing revenues instead of recording a liability has a positive effect on the financial statements because it understates liabilities and overstates revenues and net income; this of course makes the company look better. Similarly, a company that collects deposits (which may have to be returned in the future) and recognizes them as revenues is overstating revenues and understating liabilities.

Underrecording Future Obligations

This fraud, underrecording warranty or service obligations, is also easy to perpetrate and, like the others, also results in overstated net income and understated liabilities. For example, every time an automobile manufacturer sells a car, it provides a warranty, such as 3-year, 36,000-mile bumper-to-bumper coverage. According to the matching rule, the expense (and liability) that will be incurred to service these warranties must be recorded in the same period in which the cars are sold. To understate this liability, companies simply do not record the liability or record amounts that are too low. Consider a health spa chain, or any other company for that matter, that offers a money-back guarantee if you aren't satisfied after 30 days. If revenue is collected when customers enroll as members, and an adequate expense is not recorded for the estimated number of customers who will demand their money back, liabilities can be significantly understated.

In the Lincoln Savings and Loan case (see Chapter 5), revenue was recognized on land sale transactions, even though promises were made to buyers that Lincoln would buy the property back in two years at a higher price. According to Statement of Financial Accounting Standards No. 66, "Accounting for Sales of Real Estate," revenue should not have been recognized on these kinds of transactions. Similarly, in the ESM case, significant repurchase commitments were recorded, but were offset by fictitious receivables from an affiliated company that was not audited. In reality, the affiliated company had no assets, and the reported receivable was just a ruse to hide the fact that liabilities exceeded assets by approximately $400 million. A footnote from the ESM financial statement explains these liabilities as follows:

> *The Company entered into repurchase (liability) and resale (receivable) agreements with customers whereby specific securities are sold or purchased for short durations of time. These agreements cover securities, the rights to which are usually acquired through similar purchase/resale agreements. The Company has agreements with an affiliated company for securities purchased under agreements to resell (receivables. meaning the company will get cash when it resells the securities) amounting to approximately $1,308,199,000 and securities sold under agreement to repurchase (liabilities) amounting to approximately $944,356,000 at December 31, 1983.*

The financial statement that accompanied this footnote reported that the total amounts of repurchase and resell agreements were equal on the balance sheet. (This anomaly needed an explanation all by itself. How many financial statements show total receivables as exactly equal to total liabilities for three consecutive years, as occurred in this case?) Thus, comparing the balance sheet numbers with this footnote showed a net receivable from an affiliate of $353,843,000 ($1,308,199,000 − $944,356,000) and a net liability to third parties of the very same amount. This net obligation to repurchase securities was camouflaged by a fictitious receivable from a related-party entity.

Whether the future obligation is to service or provide warranty on a product, to repay a deposit, or to repurchase securities, the result is the same—understated liabilities. Cash must be spent or returned, service must be performed, or a product must be delivered at a future date.

Underrecording Debt

The DuVall Limited Real Estate Partnerships fraud demonstrates one way to understate debt—unauthorized borrowing against company equity. Other ways to underrecord liabilities include:

- Not reporting or underrecording debt (notes, mortgages, etc.) to related parties
- Borrowing but not disclosing debt incurred on existing lines of credit
- Not recording loans incurred
- Claiming that existing debt has been forgiven by creditors
- Claiming that debt on the company's books is personal debt of the owners or principals, rather than debt of the business

Because of inadequate internal controls, Marsh & McLennan allegedly allowed $1.2 billion in one year and $2.1 billion in the next year in undisclosed corporate liabilities to accumulate in the form of repurchase agreements. Marsh's books and records apparently did not accurately reflect the value, nature, terms, and profitability of its investments. Internal controls relating to investment activities were inadequate to ensure that investments were executed according to management's authorization, and that these investments were recorded to permit preparation of accurate financial statements. Total liabilities and total assets were apparently understated, and income before taxes and earnings per share were overstated. Futher, disclosures in the financial statements allegedly did not reflect that Marsh held a substantial position in intermediate and long-term marketable securities.[3]

Not Recording Contingent Liabilities

Statement of Financial Accounting Standards No. 5, "Accounting for Contingencies," requires contingent liabilities to be recorded as liabilities on the balance sheet if the likelihood of loss or payment is "probable." If the likelihood of loss is a reasonable possibility, the contingent liability should be disclosed in the statement footnotes. If the probability of payment is "remote," the liability does not have to be mentioned in the financial statements. Contingent liabilities are misstated by underestimating the probability of occurrence and then not recording and/or not disclosing the contingent liabilities in the statements. Consider the case of Pfizer, a pharmaceutical company.[4] In a civil case, plaintiffs alleged that Pfizer failed to disclose material information concerning the Shiley heart valve. This material information included the results of at least one product liability suit that Pfizer lost. Four years earlier, Pfizer reportedly knew that the Shiley heart valve was problematic, and it took the valve off the market. However, by that time, approximately 60,000 valves had been implanted. As of the date of the complaint, 389 fractures of the valve had been reported, and the FDA attributed 248 deaths to failed Shiley valves. Moreover, Pfizer maintained that surgery to replace the implanted valves would be riskier than leaving them in. Pfizer did not record a contingent liability for this potential liability.

Symptoms of Liability Fraud

In our discussion on detecting liability frauds, we consider only accounting/documentary and analytical symptoms. As was the case with inventory and revenue frauds, we don't cover control symptoms in detail because they are adequately covered in other texts and standards. Neither do we cover lifestyle symptoms, except to note that when principals use company assets to benefit themselves personally, their lifestyles typically exhibit red flags. Behavior and tips for liability frauds are no different than for other financial statement frauds and so will not be discussed further in this chapter. Remember, however, that inconsistent, vague, or implausible responses or behavior by or from management or employees constitute fraud symptoms.

Analytical Symptoms

In accounts payable understatements, one analytical symptom is balances that appear too low. Other symptoms include purchase or cost of goods sold numbers that appear too low, or purchase returns or purchase discounts that appear too high. In unearned revenues, symptoms are reported payroll, payroll tax, rent, interest, utility, or other accrued liabilities that appear too low. To determine whether these balances are "too low," you must compare recorded amounts to balances in past periods, relationships with other accounts, and to equivalent balances in similar companies. Analytical symptoms for premature recognition of unearned revenues involve unearned liability account balances that appear too low and revenue accounts that appear too high. Significant judgment is needed, in most cases, to determine whether revenues are being recognized before they are earned; this often means examining terms of contracts, sales agreements, and other revenue-related documentation. Analytical symptoms for the under- and nonrecording of service warranties or other future commitments include balances in warranty, repurchases, or deposits that appear too low. In many cases, investigators compare them with other accounts—for example, they compare warranties with sales—to make the determination.

Analytical symptoms for unrecorded notes and mortgages payable involve unreasonable relationships between interest expense and recorded liabilities; significant decreases in recorded debt; significant purchases of assets with no recorded debt; and recorded amounts of notes payable, mortgages payable, lease liabilities, pension liabilities, and other debts that appear to be too low. Finally, analytical symptoms are not especially helpful in discovering contingent liabilities that should be recorded because it is difficult to determine whether a contingent liability should be recorded and, if so, for how much. Frequently, the past amounts needed for the comparisons do not exist, and identifying an expectation against which the amount of a contingent liability should be recorded is difficult.

Accounting or Documentary Symptoms

Symptoms of fraud show up in documentation as vendor statements received with no liability recorded; large purchases recorded at the beginning of a period; large payments made in subsequent periods, backdated to the current period; receiving reports with no recorded liability; and errors in cut-off tests. The following are documentary symptoms for liability frauds:

- Photocopied purchase records where originals should exist
- Unusual discrepancies between the entity's records and confirmation replies
- Transactions not recorded in a complete or timely manner or improperly recorded as to amount
- Accounting period, classification, or entity policy; unsupported or unauthorized balances or transactions
- Last-minute adjustments by the entity that significantly affect financial results
- Missing documents; significant unexplained items on reconciliations
- Denied access to records, facilities, certain employees, customers, vendors, or others from whom audit evidence might be sought

Specific accounts can show symptoms of fraudulent documentation. With payroll, for example, the red flags will be employees with no withholdings, lack of payments to governmental entities, no accruals at year-end, payroll tax rates that are too low, fewer employees paid than are listed on the payroll records, and capitalization of employee wages as start-up or other deferred costs when they should be expensed. If interest is understated, you may find notes payable with no interest expense, bank confirmations of notes that are not recorded by the company, and interest expense deducted on tax returns but not recorded on the financial statements. Other symptoms include inconsistencies between revenue recognition criteria and the timing specified in contracts and sales agreements, the method and timing with which revenues are recognized, large reclassification entries near the end of a period that increase revenues and lower liabilities, differences between confirmation balances and revenue recognized by the company, no shipping documentation for recorded revenues, revenues recognized before customers are billed, and inconsistencies in the timing or method of recording unrecorded liabilities.

Symptoms for frauds perpetrated by under- or nonrecording of service or other future obligations take the form of differences between amounts expensed as warranty or service costs and amounts that should be expensed, based on sales contracts or sales agreements; improper treatment of deposits; differences between confirmations of repurchase agreements, deposits, or other confirmed amounts and balances reported on the financial statements; and differences between what contracts say should be recorded as liabilities and what the company is doing. When liabilities are underrecorded or not recorded, you will find bank confirmations of liabilities that are not recorded by the company, unrecorded liens, differences between contract amounts and recorded loans, interest expense with no recorded debt, liabilities written off without payment, significant purchases of assets without a comparable decrease in cash or increase in liabilities, and significant repayment of debt immediately prior to year-end, with new borrowing immediately after year-end.

Documentary symptoms are the best way to find underrecorded contingent liabilities. These symptoms include identification of lawsuits by attorneys; payments to attorneys without acknowledged litigation; litigation mentioned in corporate minutes; correspondence with governmental agencies, such as the Environmental Protection Agency, or the Securities and Exchange Commission; significant payments to plaintiffs and others; filing of an 8-K with the SEC;[5] withdrawal or issuance of less-than-clean audit opinion by previous auditors; and correspondence from previous auditors, banks, regulators, and others.

Searching for Symptoms of Liability Fraud

In the DuVall Limited Real Estate Partnerships fraud discussed earlier in this chapter, auditors found liens on properties that were supposed to be lien-free. The liens were discovered only because auditors were concerned that, under the triple-net lease arrangement, some lessees might put partnership properties at risk by not paying property taxes, utilities, and other expenses. As often happens, the fraud was discovered by accident. Proactive searching is much more effective.

As you will recall, proactive searching for analytical symptoms means looking for accounts that appear too high or too low or that are unusual in some other way—that is, we look for unusual changes and then we make comparisons. The table shown here for liability fraud is parallel to the table in Chapter 11 for inventory and revenue fraud.

Analysis of Period-to-Period Changes	Comparison of Statement Amounts
Liability account balances 1. Focus on changes in statement numbers. 2. Study statement of cash flow. 3. Use horizontal analysis.	*With industry competitors* 1. Compare statement results with similiar companies. 2. Compare company's trends with those of similiar companies.
Liability relationships 1. Examine changes in relevant ratios. 2. Use vertical analysis.	*With real-world numbers* 1. Compare statement amounts with the real-world assets they are supposed to represent.

Changes in Recorded Balances

As you look for balances that are too low, take care to scrutinize all reported liabilities and to search for liabilities that have not been recorded. As noted in the table above, you can focus on period-to-period changes in liability account balances by looking for changes in the actual numbers, by studying the statement of cash flows (which shows actual change numbers but may not list every liability account separately), or by using horizontal analysis, which is our preferred method. As you use these methods, you should compare balances over several years and pay special attention to liabilities that have been eliminated, significant changes in the write-down of long-term liabilities, accruals and service liabilities that have not been recorded or are recorded at significantly lower balances than in previous periods, and contingent liabilities that have been disclosed in the footnotes but that need to be recorded as liabilities in the financial statements. Using horizontal analysis, you can quickly examine percentage changes in the liability accounts and determine whether they are unusual. For example, an expert retained as a witness in the ESM fraud case (Chapter 2) performed a horizontal analysis on ESM's balance sheets and income statements. What he found was liability (and other) account balances that changed by 400%, 1,700%, 250%, and so forth, which are extremely large changes, especially in accounts with large balances. He concluded that someone manipulated the financial statements—the changes were simply too large to be believable. As it turned out, management was indeed manipulating the financial statements and plugging in numbers to make them balance.

When you search for changes in account balances, remember that every liability account is a candidate for fraud. Therefore, as you go over the results of your horizontal analysis, examine each liability, consider the most common liability frauds (discussed in the first part of this chapter), and then check to see if the changes suggest any of those frauds. For example, if long-term notes payable changes from $2.1 million to $1.1 million and back to $2.1 million in three consecutive years, you might be concerned about year 2 and would focus on whether liabilities were paid off with the intent of immediately restoring them after year-end. Similarly, if service or warranty liabilities decreased from $3.2 million to $2.2 million, and then to $1.7 million at the same time total sales increased, you should be very concerned that warranty liabilities were significantly understated. Analytical symptoms only make sense when you follow a careful and orderly process:

1. Ask what kind of fraud could be occurring.
2. Identify what symptoms those frauds would generate.
3. Determine whether those symptoms exist.
4. Follow up to determine if the symptom signals fraud, or an abnormality caused by something else.

Changes in Relationships

Using period-to-period changes in relationships to identify analytical symptoms is a good way to detect liability frauds. Key ratios are listed in the following table:

Liability Fraud	Ratios to Examine
Underrecording accounts payable	1. Acid-test ratio (Quick assets ÷ Current liabilities) 2. Current ratio (Current assets ÷ Current liabilities) 3. Accounts payable ÷ Purchases 4. Accounts payable ÷ Cost of goods sold 5. Accounts payable ÷ Total liabilities 6. Accounts payable ÷ Inventory Each ratio should be examined over time in order to observe changes. These ratios focus on the reasonableness of the accounts payable balance relative to different account balances. Increases in the first two ratios and decreases in the last four ratios indicate fraud.
Underrecording accrued liabilities, including salaries, payroll taxes, interest, rent, etc.	7. Various accruals ÷ Number of days to accrue compared with same ratio in previous years 8. Various accruals ÷ Related expenses The amount to be accrued depends on the length of time between the accounting year-end and the last point at which expenses were recorded. Lack of accruals or significant decreases in these ratios from previous years on a per-day basis is cause for concern. With certain accruals, you can examine the relationship between various expenses (payroll tax expense ÷ salary expense, for example) to see whether sufficient payroll taxes have been recorded.
Underrecording of unearned revenues (a liability)	9. Unearned revenue ÷ Revenue Finding good ratios to uncover unrecorded, unearned revenues is difficult. To determine whether revenues have been recognized as earned when they are, in fact, unearned, you need to examine actual contracts and sales agreements to ascertain what services need to be performed or what products provided.
Underrecording of service (warranty) liabilities and other liabilities to perform something in the future (repurchase securities, repay deposits, etc.)	10. Warranty expense ÷ Sales The amount of warranty or service expense and liability relates directly to sales volume. Ratios that reveal that deposit, repurchase agreements, or other similar liabilities are understated are more difficult to find.

continues

Liability Fraud	Ratios to Examine
Underrecording of miscellaneous liabilities (notes, mortgages, leases, pensions, etc.)	11. Interest expense ÷ Notes payable 12. Long-term debt ÷ Stockholders' equity 13. Various types of debt ÷ Total assets 14. Total liabilities ÷ Total assets 15. Pension expense ÷ Salary expense 16. Lease expense ÷ Total fixed assets Choose from these ratios by focusing on individual liabilities on the balance sheet. Always ask, what should this liability balance relate to, and has that relationship changed over time. If so, why?
Contingent liabilities not recorded	No ratios apply. You must look for documentary symptoms to find unrecorded or undisclosed contingent liabilities.

The second way to focus on financial statement relationships is to prepare common-size financial statements and perform vertical analysis. Using this approach, you compute each liability as a percent of total assets (or total liabilities and stockholders' equity) and then focus on the change in these percentages. In conducting this analysis, remember that large financial statement balances generally do not change very much, while small liability balances may change significantly and be normal. Ask yourself why every major change is occurring, and whether you think it is unusual, given other changes in the financial statements. For example, purchasing significant amounts of fixed assets and not incurring additional long-term debt may be unusual, especially if the company does not have a large cash balance. Similarly, liabilities decreasing but interest expense increasing, or vice versa, would be rare.

Comparisons with Industry Competitors

Generally, comparing a company's liability balances with those of other companies is not as useful as comparing revenues, accounts receivable, inventory, and other balances. Companies use three sources to finance their operations:

- Earnings
- Borrowing
- Owner (stockholder) investments

The amount of operations financed by each source is a matter of management philosophy—it is not an industry norm. For example, in the computer industry, Hewlett Packard has historically very little debt and finances its operations mostly from owner investments and earnings; Texas Instruments, on the other hand, has traditionally financed its business mostly through borrowing. The relationships between interest expense and debt, the amount of warranty expense as a percentage of sales, and other similar relationships can be compared across firms, however. You should be very concerned if a company's warranty expense is only 1% of sales, when other companies in the same industry record warranty expense of 3% of sales.

Comparisons with Real-World Assets

Because liabilities typically don't represent specific assets, comparing liability balances with actual asset amounts is difficult. The notable exception, of course, is mortgage liabilities, which are loans secured with collateral—specific assets. You can therefore examine these assets. Eliminating a mortgage payable or finding no mortgages on new buildings (when company practice is to mortgage all buildings) are symptoms that should be investigated.

Searching the Documentation

Documentation can be very helpful in detecting liability frauds. The specific symptoms you search for will vary according to the liability that is understated. The following table summarizes the most common symptoms by liability account. In most cases, computer searches can be designed, using either commercial packages, such as ACL, or tailored queries, to look for these symptoms.

Liability Account	Fraud Symptoms
Accounts Payable	1. Payments made in subsequent period for liabilities that existed at the balance sheet date and were not recorded 2. More inventory counted than identified through purchasing and inventory records 3. Receiving reports near period-end, without corresponding purchase invoices 4. Amounts listed on vendor statements not recorded as purchases 5. Confirmation differences not easily reconciled with purchase records 6. Discrepancies in cut-off tests
Accrued Liabilities	7. 1099s with no withholdings, where withholdings should exist 8. Employees with no withholdings 9. Vendor statements (utilities, etc.) with no recorded liability 10. Loans with no interest 11. Leased buildings with no rent or lease expense
Unearned Revenues	12. Reclassification entries near period-end that increase earned revenues and decrease unearned revenues 13. Differences between customer confirmations and company records about earned revenue
Service (Warranty) Liabilities, Deposits, Repurchase Agreements—Obligations to Perform Services, Deliver Products, or Return Money in the Future	14. Inconsistencies in customer agreements or contracts and recording of expenses 15. Differences in customer confirmations regarding client obligations (repurchase agreements, etc.) 16. Warranty payments that exceed warranty liabilities 17. Deposits recognized as revenues
Liabilities to Pay Money (Notes Payable, Mortgage Payable, Pension Liabilities, Lease Liabilities, etc.)	18. Liens on properties that are supposed to be paid for 19. Loans approved by board of directors but not listed as liabilities 20. Loans listed on bank confirmations but not recorded by company 21. Lack of pension accrual 22. Lease payments with no lease liability 23. Conservative assumptions used to calculate pension liability 24. Unusually large credits on bank statements

continues

Liability Account	Fraud Symptoms
Contingent Liabilities	25. Discussion of contingent liabilities in board minutes 26. Contingencies discussed in footnotes 27. Significant payments to lawyers 28. Lawsuits brought to your attention for the first time in attorney letters 29. Letters from regulators (OSHA, EPA, SEC, etc.)

Because so many types of liabilities exist and they can be understated in such different ways, following up on observed symptoms is crucial. Companies in trouble have a strong motivation to understate liabilities. Sometimes the understatements are small, sometimes they are large ($350 million in the ESM case).

Because understated liabilities may involve only one or two omitted transactions, unusual revelations, such as surprise liens, surprise loan contracts, written-off debt, and surprise debt on bank confirmations, must be carefully scrutinized. In many cases, management will offer alternative explanations—the lien or contract is a mistake, it is personal debt, or it is a line of credit never activated. You must verify these explanations, and find corroborating evidence to support their explanations to the extent deemed necessary under the circumstances.

Asset Fraud

In Chapter 10, we described the revenue fraud discovered at Cendant Corporation, which was created from the merger of CUC International Inc. and HFS Inc. In 1998, Cendant issued a 200-page 8-K in response to the SEC's investigation into the credibility of CUC's financial statements. The 8-K explained the extent to which CUC misrepresented its financial statements prior to the merger, using a variety of fraud schemes, including improper revenue recognition and capitalization of costs.

A membership-based consumer services company, CUC marketed its services to credit-card holders and reported increasing profits each year. CUC committed financial statement fraud various ways. Among other things, they deferred costs that should have been expensed into future periods by recording them as deferred charges (assets).

The deferral of expenses related to the recognition of marketing expenses incurred in selling customer memberships. For example, CUC sold a service called "Shoppers Advantage," in which customers bought memberships that allowed them to call an 800 number or use an online service to compare prices on certain brand-name products. Customers then had the option of buying the product from CUC at the "lowest price available" or buying it elsewhere.

CUC stated that its revenue and expense recognition policies followed the matching principle. In retrospect, that was not the case. In multiple instances, CUC recognized all the revenue from sales of membership contracts at the time of sale, but deferred the marketing expenses incurred in making the sale to future periods. Thus, membership contract revenue would be fully booked in January, but marketing expenses for the contracts were amortized and expensed over a 12-month period. In another scheme, near the end of each fiscal year, CUC's management imposed moratoriums on recognizing expenses (they recognized them after year-end), further inflating net income. The deferral of expenses appears to have been intentional and pervasive.

Cendant's improper capitalizing of costs is one way perpetrators overstate assets on balance sheets. We will explore other ways in which perpetrators fraudulently overstate assets to make their financial statements look better. As we examine asset fraud, we will follow the same format used for liability fraud—that is, we will first examine types of asset fraud, then discuss symptoms, and finally show you how to search for symptoms of asset fraud. There are many ways to overstate assets, so instead of using transactions to identify accounts, we first provide examples of asset frauds that have been perpetrated. In many cases, the determination of asset overstatement depends on whether the accounting principles followed are appropriate and on management's improper manipulation of assets.

Identifying Asset Fraud

Most organizations show different types of assets on their balance sheets. In the Cendant case, management overstated assets by improperly deferring costs. As was the case with liabilities, different assets are overstated in different ways. The following exhibit identifies five types of assets that are commonly overstated:

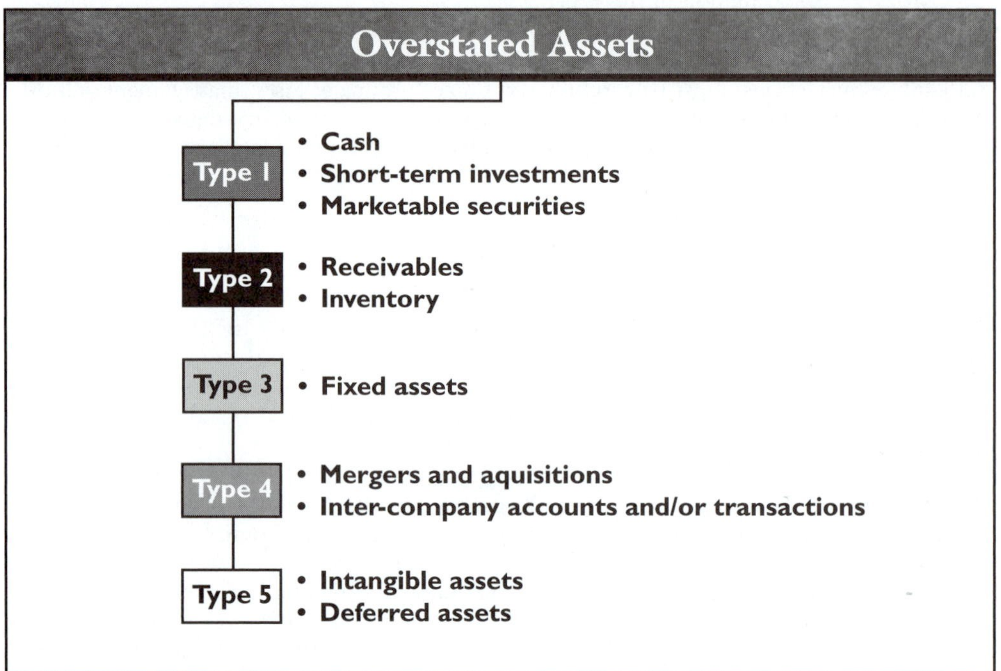

Overstated Assets
Type 1
• Cash
• Short-term investments
• Marketable securities
Type 2
• Receivables
• Inventory
Type 3
• Fixed assets
Type 4
• Mergers and aquisitions
• Inter-company accounts and/or transactions
Type 5
• Intangible assets
• Deferred assets

Improper Capitalizing or Expensing

Even though most financial statement frauds occur in smaller, less established companies, CPAs must also be alert to the fraud symptoms when they audit large, well-established companies. Remember that any company can encounter problems with profitability, and financial statement fraud is a quick fix during trying times. To make their financial statements look better, start-up companies often overstate assets by capitalizing as intangible assets such things as start-up or pre-operation costs, advertising costs, research and development, marketing costs, and certain salaries, and other initial costs. Management often argues that they are in the start-up or development phase and therefore these costs must be capitalized as deferred charges and written off against future profitable operations. In some cases, the deferred charges are justified; in other cases, they are clearly fraudulent. The question of whether these costs should be capitalized is one of whether the costs being incurred will truly generate future revenues and whether the future revenues will be sufficient to cover the costs. Consider the following cases where litigation or SEC action took place.[6]

Computer Science Corporation (CSC) developed and sold computer services known as proprietary systems, one of which was called "Computicket." An interested investor, Marx, availed himself of CSC's financial data, which explained how CSC capitalized development expenses. Per their stated policy, CSC initially capitalized development expenses instead of treating them as charges against current income. When a system (such as Computicket) became fully operational (defined as generating revenue in excess of expenses), CSC then amortized the capitalized expenses over a specified period of time, presumably over the revenue-generating time period. At one point, CSC claimed approximately $6.8 million in capitalized costs for Computicket. In a registration statement filed with the SEC, CSC stated that it expected to amortize these capitalized expenses later.

From its inception, Computicket did not meet internal projections for market capture; it also experienced problems getting equipment installed, and ran monthly deficits of $500,000. In addition, the system lost a major contract. Moreover, CSC attempted, without success, to sell Computicket proprietary packages to various prospects for differing amounts. In October and November, CSC discussed abandoning the system. The inference was clear: The prospects for Computicket's commercial success continued to diminish over time.

Marx sued CSC for violations of SEC Rule 10b-5. The court in Marx v. Computer Sciences Corporation, 507 F.2d. 485, *stated that the failure to disclose facts indicating that Computicket was in serious financial trouble was an omission "to state a material fact necessary, in order to make the statements not misleading."*

In another case, Savin, an office equipment manufacturer, was charged with materially overstating its assets and net worth and materially understating its losses.[7] It did so by improperly classifying certain costs incurred in the research and development of a new line of photocopiers as "start-up" costs. As a result, Savin improperly capitalized more than $42 million as an asset.

In most cases, fraudulent capitalization of deferred charges does not occur all at once. Rather, it starts by capitalizing borderline (or questionable) deferred charges and progresses to management routinely capitalizing costs that are not even remotely appropriate. Many times, capitalizing deferred charges, like other financial statement frauds, becomes the proverbial slippery slope: It is hard to stop once it starts, especially if the organization is experiencing profit pressures, and justifying it becomes easier and easier.

Capitalizing costs that should be expensed increases net income by the same amount of the capitalized costs. Why? Because expenses that should be deducted from revenues are not deducted until future periods when they are amortized. In many cases, these illicit capitalizations are not written off for many years.

Inflating Assets in Mergers, Acquisitions, and Restructurings

There have been several financial statement frauds where companies involved in mergers or acquisitions overstated their assets by either (1) using market values instead of book values, (2) having the wrong entity act as purchaser, or (3) improperly allocating book values to assets (assigning higher book values to assets that will be amortized or depreciated over longer periods or not depreciated at all, and lower values to assets that will be amortized or depreciated over shorter periods). In fact, Warren Buffet, the legendary chairman of Berkshire Hathaway, included the following comments in a March 1999 letter to his shareholders:

> *Many managements purposefully work at manipulating numbers and deceiving investors when it comes to mergers and big restructurings. . . . During mergers, major auditing firms sometimes point out the possibilities for a little accounting magic (or a lot).*

Consider the case of Malibu Capital Corporation.

> *For at least three and a half years, Lehman, Lucchesi & Walker (LLW) performed audits for Malibu Capital Corporation. Malibu subsequently merged with Colstar Petroleum Corporation. Prior to the combination with Colstar, Malibu had no business purpose other than to merge with or acquire one or a small number of private companies. LLW gave Malibu an unqualified opinion on their financial statements, which identified Colstar as the "acquired corporation." The combination was treated as a "purchase" of Colstar by Malibu, and Colstar's primary asset was adjusted up from $11,055 to $1,342,600.*
>
> *Under GAAP, the combination should have been treated as a "reverse purchase" with Colstar as the "acquiring corporation" (and therefore no adjustment to Colstar's assets). As a result of the improper accounting treatment, Malibu overstated its assets 102 times.*[8]

In this case, the "asset"—Colstar—was written up by having the wrong entity—Malibu—act as the purchaser. In other cases, companies overstate assets in mergers by using market values instead of book values.

Malibu's case shows that whenever assets are revaluated or two companies merge there is an opportunity to use inappropriate values. This is especially true when the merging companies are related parties, when companies are struggling, or when they have a strong incentive to report profits.

Fraud is also perpetrated by manipulating inter-company accounts and/or transactions. Consider the AFCO fraud in the late 1970s, which involved manipulating inter-company transactions to make the company appear more profitable than it really was.

> *AFCO started as a medical-dental equipment leasing business. One owner was a former insurance salesman, and the other was two years out of law school. The company was mildly successful during its first two years. Several new branches were formed, including a land development company. The land development company purchased 1,000 acres of undeveloped property in Sardine Canyon in northern Utah and began to develop an "old English" family resort called Sherwood Hills. The resort included summer and winter sports, making it a year-round enterprise. Although it was reasonably popular in the summer, the heavy winter snows and poor accessibility made it an unappealing winter resort. To raise money for additional development and marketing efforts, limited partnerships were sold, mostly to physicians and dentists.*
>
> *Other AFCO projects included a shopping center, apartment complexes, a medical center, and a 700-acre site in West Jordan, Utah. This development, known as Glenmoor Village, was touted as Utah's biggest real estate development. It was to include 1,400 homes in a totally planned community, an 18-hole golf course, and equestrian facilities.*

As with Sherwood Hills, the development of Glenmoor Village was extremely expensive. Maintenance of a positive cash flow depended on lot sales, but sales were slow because the area lacked essential services, such as roads and utilities. AFCO borrowed heavily to make these investments, but only 400 of the 1,400 lots were sold. Residents complained that promised improvements were never made.

Because of severe cash shortages and an inability to obtain additional bank financing, AFCO turned to middle-class homeowners for funding. The company's salesmen contacted friends, acquaintances, and referrals and offered them "a chance to get in on the ground floor." Using elaborate flip charts and relying on the reputation of other investors, salespeople persuaded homeowners to allow the company to borrow on the equity in their homes. If homeowners allowed the second mortgage, AFCO promised to service the second mortgage and pay the homeowner an additional 10% on the money used. Second mortgage rates were approximately 20% at that time, so AFCO was, in effect, offering a 30% return. AFCO was very accommodating: If a homeowner didn't want the return in cash, it leased a BMW or a Mercedes for the homeowner and serviced the lease!

Although the investment sounded legitimate, the promised returns were based on inflated financial statements and empty promises. The investment was a Ponzi scheme. Early investors were paid the 10% returns from subsequent investments, but the second-mortgage payments were never made. The Assistant U.S. Attorney called the president of AFCO "one of the most ruthless swindlers seen in these parts in years." He sweet-talked about 650 people, many of them business people, into investing some $70 million in his schemes. He later declared bankruptcy, foreclosing forever on his investors' chances of getting their money back.

To get people to invest in AFCO, the owners used fraudulent financial statements to make the company look better than it really was. Carefully examine the two sets of financial statement numbers—the company's fraudulent ones and the correctly restated numbers:

AFCO
Balance Sheet, Statement of Income, and Retained Earnings

	Original Numbers	**Restated Numbers**
Assets		
Current assets:		
Cash	$ 1,299	$ 1,299
Current portion of contract receivable	276,084	0
Interest receivable	124,197	0
Total current assets	401,580	1,299
Contract receivable long-term portion	$ 8,373,916	0
Investment property:		
Real estate Jackson Village (at market)	$10,832,480	
Real estate Mountainland Hills	1,800,000	?
	$12,623,480	?
Total assets	$21,398,480	$1,299+?

Liabilities and stockholders' equity		
Current liabilities:		
Accounts payable to related parties	$ 27,000	$ 27,000
Accrued interest	176,965	176,965
Current portion of long-term debt	902,944	902,944
Total current liabilities	$ 1,106,909	$ 1,106,909
Long-term debt less current portion	$12,781,668	$12,781,688
Deferred income taxes	$ 3,041,729	$ 3,041,729
Contingencies		
Stockholders' equity:		
Common stock, par value $1.00, authorized 50,000 shares; issued and outstanding, 1,000 shares	$ 1,000	$ 1,000
Appraisal increase	1,663,606	0
Retained earnings	2,804,044	?
Total stockholders' equity	$ 4,468,650	?
Total liabilities and stockholders' equity	$21,398,976	?
Gain on sales of Mountain Hills	$ 4,887,000	0
Interest income	324,197	0
Total income	$ 5,211,197	
Interest expense	$ 627,796	$ 627,796
General and administrative expenses	27,190	27,190
	$ 654,986	$ 654,986
Income before income taxes	$ 4,556,211	$ (654,986)
Provision for federal and state income taxes	2,258,855	0
Net income	$ 2,297,356	$ (654,986)

In this case, the auditors issued an adverse opinion because assets had been stated at fair market value instead of at cost and because a large portion of AFCO's assets consisted of a receivable and interest due from the sale of property to a related party. Because of the related-party sale, auditors could not determine whether the transaction was arm's length.

In AFCO's case, the adverse opinion signaled that something was wrong. As it turned out, the sale of land to the related party, the income from this sale, the receivable arising from that transaction, and the interest on the receivable all involved a phantom transaction. When the phantom sale and its impacts were subtracted from AFCO's balance sheet, all that remained was $1,299 in cash and some real estate whose cost statement readers could not evaluate because it was recorded at market value. The real total assets of $1,299 were nowhere near the $21 million claimed by the company.

Overstating Fixed Assets

Fixed assets (property, plant, and equipment) can be overstated in many ways. The most common ways leave worthless or expired assets on the books (not writing them off), underreport depreciation expense, overstate residual values, record fixed assets at inflated values (sometimes through sham or related-party purchases), or simply fabricate fixed assets for the financial statements. One company recorded assets on its balance sheet at their "estimated fair market value" when, in fact, the assets had been fully depreciated in prior years. In the AFCO case, company management recorded a large asset they called "refunds forthcoming" for workers' compensation reimbursements, for which they had no assurance that reimbursement would be forthcoming. In another case, a health provider collected large overpayments from customers and classified them as assets, even though they were legally obligated to return them.

Asset overstatements can be significant. In 1999, the *Wall Street Journal* reported that the "Baby Bells" (Bell Atlantic Corp., SBC Communications, Inc., Nynex Telephone Company, Southern Bell Telephone, and Bell South) could not locate $5 billion in telecommunications and other equipment that they carried on their balance sheets as assets.[9] Whether these companies committed fraud is a question that would have to be investigated, but the *Wall Street Journal* noted that a Federal Communications Commission (FCC) audit of these companies could not locate one-tenth of the equipment and recommended that the assets be written off.

Consider yet another aspect of the Lincoln Savings and Loan scandal:

> *One of the major frauds perpetrated by Lincoln Savings and Loan involved purchasing property at inflated amounts and then reselling it at even higher amounts to "straw buyers." This "land flipping" resulted in overstated assets on the balance sheet and unrealistically high profits when the land was "sold." Such transactions were routine at Lincoln, and they frequently happened at the end of quarters so that reported quarterly income would be positive. One was the "Continental Ranch" transaction. In this transaction, Lincoln purchased land at arguably inflated prices and recorded the asset on its financial statements. Then, on September 30, 1986, desperate for profits, Lincoln sold 1,300 acres of the ranch to RA Homes (a straw buyer) for $25 million, including $5 million in cash and a $20 million note receivable. What was not easily detectable by auditors and others was that a related-party entity loaned RA Homes $3 million on September 25, 1986, and another $2 million on November 12, 1986. In essence, Lincoln "paid the down payment to itself." This transaction, like so many others in the company, had the intermediate effect of allowing inflated land values to be reported on the balance sheet, and the end effect of reporting high profits on the transaction and overstated accounts receivable.*

Finally, fixed assets can be overstated by underrecording depreciation expense. To do this, companies use asset lives that are too long; allocate too much cost in a basket purchase of land and building to land that is not depreciated; use salvage values that are too high; or fail to make the accrual entries for depreciation.

Overstating Cash and Marketable Securities

There are several famous cases where marketable securities were materially overstated, but it is difficult to overstate cash because cash balances can be easily confirmed with banks and other financial institutions. What does happen with cash is employees or vendors steal cash in magnitudes significant enough to result in misstated financial statements (without management's knowledge). Consider these three cases: a small thrift institution where a vice president embezzled several million dollars over a period of 16 years; a small, five-branch bank where a proof operator embezzled $7 million over eight years; and General Motors, where one car dealer embezzled $436 million. These large cash thefts resulted in financial statement fraud of a different type than we have been discussing in this book—financial statement misstatement without management's knowledge.

It is much easier to perpetrate asset fraud by overstating marketable securities, especially when the securities in question are not widely traded. What many people don't realize is that the term "publicly traded" means much more than "companies whose securities are traded on the New York Stock Exchange, the American Stock Exchange, and NASDAQ." Many smaller, over-the-counter stocks are traded only rarely and are not actively listed by even over-the-counter stock exchanges, but whose stock prices are circulated among brokers via "pink sheets." These pink sheets are distributed daily to brokers and listing dealers who might be willing to buy and sell through other methods. Assigning market values to many of these securities is often problematic (and placing market values on securities that are not publicly traded is even more difficult), and once in a while, management commits fraud by materially overstating their values. One well-known fraud (Lincoln Savings and Loan) involved sham transactions between the company and related parties, and materially overvalued securities were listed as current assets on the balance sheet. Another case involved a minority investment in another company that was carried at several million dollars when, in fact, the company had negative stockholders' equity and losses of several million dollars in each of the preceding five years. The securities should have been written off because the investment was basically worthless.

Overstating Accounts Receivable or Inventory

In Chapter 11, we discussed how accounts receivable are inflated by recording fictitious revenues and how inventory is overstated and cost of goods sold understated. Accounts receivable and inventory are also overstated in order to overstate assets and cover thefts of cash. That is what happened in the ESM fraud where management stole $350 million and covered the theft by creating a fictitious receivable from a related entity. In the Phar-Mor fraud, inventory was overstated to offset cash that Monus took out of the business to support his World Basketball League.

Summary of Asset Fraud

It behooves us to summarize the various asset fraud schemes we have discussed thus far. Although not exhaustive, the following table lists the most common schemes:

Asset Overstated	Accounts Involved	Fraud Schemes
By improper capitalizing costs as assets that should be expensed	Various deferred charge and intangible assets accounts	1. Inappropriately capitalizing assets as: • start-up costs • marketing costs • salaries • R&D costs • other such expenditures
• Through mergers, acquisitions, and restructuring • Through manipulating inter-company accounts and/or transactions	Any asset account	2. Using market values rather than book values to record assets 3. Having wrong entity be "purchaser" 4. Allocating costs among assets in inappropriate ways 5. Recording fictitious assets or inflating the value of assets in inter-company accounts or transactions
By overstating fixed assets	• Land, Buildings • Equipment • Leasehold Improvements • etc.	6. Sham purchases and sales of assets using "straw buyers" 7. Overstating asset costs with related parties 8. Not recording depreciation 9. Collusion with outside parties to overstate assets (e.g., allocating inventory costs to fixed assets)

continues

Asset Overstated	Accounts Involved	Fraud Schemes
By overstating cash marketable securities	• Cash • Marketable Securities • Other Short-Term Assets	10. Misstating marketable securities using related parties
By overstating accounts receivable and/or inventory to hide thefts of cash by management	• Accounts Receivable • Inventory	11. Covering thefts of cash or other assets by overstating receivables or inventory

Symptoms of Asset Fraud

Symptoms that indicate assets are overstated closely parallel those that indicate understated liabilities. Thus, often just one or two large fictitious accounting entries, rather than a series of smaller entries, result in asset overstatement. In some ways, however, asset overstatements are easier to detect than other financial statement frauds because the overstated assets are always included on the balance sheet, whereas understated liabilities do not show up on the financial statements. Fraud investigators search for symptoms by examining the actual assets that make up the reported amounts, to make sure they really exist and to verify that they are listed in appropriate amounts.

In the following paragraphs, we discuss asset fraud using the five types of asset overstatement shown in the chart on page 400. Because asset overstatements differ dramatically, we will focus on relevant symptoms and searching for those symptoms together. Once again, we don't focus on control, lifestyle, behavioral, and tips/complaint symptoms here because, for the most part, they are not unique to asset frauds. Rather, we focus on analytical and documentary symptoms and discuss other symptoms where appropriate. Note that this does not mean that these other symptoms are not important. In many cases, they are the most reliable or most easily observed symptoms.

Inappropriately Capitalizing Costs

In identifying symptoms, the first thing you must ask is whether the deferred charges of interest exist on the balance sheet. In many companies, they do not. When they do exist, you should "assume guilt, then try to prove innocence." That is, consider them candidates for fraud and then convince yourself that their capitalization is appropriate; don't assume they are appropriate and try to determine whether they are fraudulent. Such skepticism is justified because of the "intangible" nature of these assets and the ease with which they can be abused. Questions you should ask include:

1. Do the deferred charges have future benefits that are specifically identifiable?
2. Is it likely that future revenues and profits will be sufficient for writing off the costs, and if so, when?
3. Are the deferred charges types that are acceptable under GAAP (in most cases, for example, R&D costs are not) and are capitalized by other, similar companies?
4. Are there strong incentives for management to manage earnings or "find profits" in this company?

Analytical Symptoms. In most cases, analytical symptoms show up in the size of the deferred charges on the balance sheet relative to prior periods and to other similar companies. You should be concerned, for example, if deferred charges make up a major portion of a company's total assets. Other analytical symptoms to look for include the size of various deferred charges (say, advertising expense) compared to the amount of advertising or other expenses on the income statement. You would probably be less concerned with a company that capitalizes only a small part of its advertising costs than you would with a company that capitalizes all of its advertising costs.

The four ways to search for analytical symptoms parallel those shown for liability fraud (see page 396):

1. Analyze changes and trends in asset account balances.
2. Analyze changes and trends in statement asset relationships.
3. Compare statement balance amounts with actual assets.
4. Compare statements with those of similar companies.

As you consider which analyses to conduct to determine whether costs have been improperly capitalized, note that actual assets can be associated with only a few deferred charges. One notable exception is, of course, when companies acquire other entities or enter new ventures, in which case you might expect additional capitalization of deferred charges. You can therefore look for significant events where it would make sense to capitalize certain kinds of expenditures. If you are looking at trends in account balances, you might be concerned if deferred charges increase substantially without triggering events. In addition, you would normally expect more capitalization in the early years of a business; thus, increasing balances in the deferred charge accounts of a mature company could be symptomatic of asset fraud. If anything, you would expect that amortizing such costs would cause deferred charge balances to decrease.

Although changes in account balances may provide limited information, examining changes in deferred charge ratios from period to period can be particularly rewarding. You also need to compare statement amounts and capitalization policies with those of similar companies. Here are some of the most appropriate ratios to focus on:

- Total deferred charges ÷ Total assets
- Total deferred charges ÷ Total intangible assets
- Deferred charge write-offs (amortization) ÷ Deferred charge balance

Examining these and other ratios over time helps you quickly determine whether deferred charges are increasing as a percentage of total assets or total intangible assets, and what percentage of deferred charges are being written off or amortized each year.

One of the best ways to find symptoms of inappropriate cost capitalization is to make comparisons with similar companies. If your client is the only firm that capitalizes certain expenditures as deferred charges, skepticism is in order. Ask yourself, What is unique about my client that makes capitalizing more appropriate for them than for these other companies? If you cannot arrive at a clear, defensible answer, your client may be overstating assets to inflate reported income.

Accounting or Documentary Symptoms. As with other frauds, documentary symptoms are of two types: (1) general symptoms that relate to most financial statement frauds, and (2) documentary symptoms that relate to improper capitalization of costs. General symptoms are presented here:

- Asset transactions not recorded in a complete or timely manner or improperly recorded as to amount, accounting period, classification, or entity policy
- Unsupported or unauthorized asset balances or transactions
- Last-minute asset adjustments that significantly improve financial results
- Missing documents related to assets
- No original documents to support asset transactions

- Asset ledgers do not balance
- Unusual discrepancies between records and corroborating evidence or management explanations

Documentary symptoms include invoices from related parties that misstate the nature of expenses; year-end reclassifications or journal entries that reduce expenses and increase deferred charges; and differences between costs on invoices and recorded costs.

In many cases, examining management motivations to see where strong incentives exist to overstate assets can be more important than searching for documentary and analytical symptoms. Perhaps there are strong management incentives to show profits; perhaps the organization is new or is in an industry where capitalization is not appropriate; perhaps recent financial results and operating characteristics motivate misstatement.

Mergers, Acquisitions, Restructurings, and Inter-Company Manipulations

Understanding the context of a merger or an inter-company transaction can be more important in determining whether fraud exists than identifying specific symptoms. If you are concerned about a merger causing overstatement of assets, ask yourself if the accounts used by the merged companies are appropriate; if how the merger was recorded is appropriate, given the nature of the companies involved; if after-merger book values are higher or lower than pre-merger amounts and, if so, why; what motivated the merger; and whether the appropriate company was the purchaser or the entity purchased. Again, understanding management and its motivations, the nature of the companies involved, whether the merged companies were related parties, and what financial results or operating characteristics motivated the merger is very important.

Analytical Symptoms. Analytical symptoms are usually not helpful in determining asset overstatements in mergers and restructurings. Analytical symptoms help you compare trends and changes, but the merger is a new, reformatted entity with no history. As a result, you cannot look for changes in statement account balances or relationships. However, it can be helpful to compare various asset ratios for the individual companies pre-merger and the post-merger company. By looking at such asset ratios, you can quickly get an idea of how company structure has changed. There is cause for concern if, for example, total intangible assets as a percentage of total assets increase from a pre-merger average of 10% to a post-merger average of 40%, especially if the transaction was handled as a business combination (pooling) rather than as a purchase.

Comparing post-merger recorded assets with actual assets is often helpful. If reported asset values increase substantially, for example, you need to verify that balance sheet asset amounts do not exceed their fair market values. However, finding similar companies with which to compare statement balances can be difficult.

Accounting or Documentary Symptoms. When you audit mergers, one of your first steps should be to make sure that the accounting methods used are appropriate and consistent with GAAP. After that, you can examine the specific transactions to make sure that the types of transactions and the amounts make sense. Inconsistencies between appraised and recorded amounts for assets is a strong documentary symptom. Similarly, if post-merger assets have longer amortization or depreciation periods than pre-merger assets, a closer examination is in order. In the Malibu Capital Corporation case cited earlier in this chapter, post-merger asset values were significantly inflated over the pre-merger assets. Upon further analysis, investigators determined that the lesser-known company did not exist—it was fabricated to make the financial statements look better "through a merger."

Fixed Assets

Fixed assets are overstated on financial statements in one of three ways:

1. Inflated amounts are recorded in non-arm's-length purchase transactions.
2. Assets are not written down to appropriate book, market, or residual values because insufficient depreciation is recorded, they are obsolete, or their values are otherwise impaired.
3. Nonexistent assets are recorded in statement accounts.

In the famous Penn Central fraud, railroad cars that had been abandoned in old mine shafts for years were still carried on the balance sheet at significant book values. These "assets" could not have been recovered even had the company wanted to, because many of the tracks to the mineshafts had been long since removed, and the railroad ties sold to landscaping companies. Similarly, in another case, an oil company reported significant fixed asset amounts for a refinery that was no longer in use and oil reserves.

Analytical Symptoms. Horizontal analysis, analysis of the statement of cash flow, and period-to-period comparisons of account balances can all be used to track changes in fixed asset account balances. Unrealistically large changes in land, property, equipment, or other fixed asset account balances may indicate that fraud is occurring. Fixed asset relationships can also be examined by computing ratios such as the following:

1. Total fixed assets ÷ Total assets
2. Individual fixed asset account balances ÷ Total fixed assets
3. Total fixed assets ÷ Long-term debt
4. Depreciation expense for various categories of assets ÷ Assets being depreciated
5. Accumulated depreciation ÷ Depreciable assets (per asset category)

Ratios 1 and 2 provide evidence about the reasonableness of fixed asset balances relative to other asset balances. Ratio 3 measures solvency. If fixed assets increase significantly but long-term debt does not, fraud may exist, especially if cash, marketable securities, or other assets were not used to purchase the fixed assets. Ratios 4 and 5 indicate whether fixed assets are being adequately depreciated.

Vertical analysis over several periods shows percentage changes in statement balances and relationships over time. You might be concerned if, for example, fixed assets increase from 50% of total assets to 70% at a time when company revenues are not increasing much.

Because fixed assets are tangible, you can compare statement balances with actual assets to verify that the recorded amounts do indeed represent actual assets and in approximately the appropriate amounts. Although determining how complicated or company-specific assets should be valued can be difficult, you can attack the problem using other analyses. If you are concerned about a retail company like Sears or Wal-Mart, you can compute total assets on a per-store basis and see how that changes over time. You would not expect to find dramatic per-store changes, unless the companies started building larger superstores (for example). You can also ask questions: Does it make sense that this type of company would have these types of assets, would have assets in these locations, or could have increased assets so much without significant changes in the company structure?

Finally, comparing total fixed assets or fixed assets as a percentage of total assets with similar companies is always helpful in determining whether recorded asset totals are reasonable. Suppose you are comparing two automobile manufacturing companies. If one has $50 of fixed assets for every $1 of sales and the other has $100 of fixed assets for every $1 of sales, you should ask, Why? Perhaps company 1 is that much more efficient, company 2 has just spent millions renovating its manufacturing facilities and thus has newer and less depreciated fixed assets, *or* company 2 is overstating its assets and committing fraud—all are alternatives to consider. Another analytical test that is often helpful is to determine the percentage of a class of asset costs that is depreciated each year (a measure of depreciable life). If one company depreciates its assets over 10 years and a similar company uses 20-year asset lives, further analysis is in order.

Accounting or Documentary Symptoms. Overstating fixed assets by recording inflated amounts is typical of fraudulent related-party transactions. Therefore, determining whether large purchases of fixed assets are arm's-length transactions or are purchases between related parties is important. If the vendor or provider of the assets is a related party, you need to determine why the company bought the assets from that entity and whether the amounts recorded are reasonable. Here are some key questions to ask:

- Were there appraisals of purchased fixed assets?
- Were the purchase transactions recorded near year-end?
- Did the transaction(s) involve exchanges of assets or a purchase of assets?
- Are the assets purchased assets that this company would normally purchase, or are they tangential to the business?
- Are there inconsistencies in the documentation?
- Are the assets recorded on your client's books at the same or lower amounts as on the seller's books?

Cash and Marketable Securities

As stated earlier, management has difficulty overstating cash by a significant enough amount to materially impact the financial statements. There are two reasons for this: First, corroborating recorded amounts of cash is easy—all one has to do is confirm bank and financial institution balances. To conceal cash frauds on bank confirmations requires the collusive efforts of outsiders, which occurs only rarely. Second, the amount of cash that a company has is usually small relative to its receivables, inventory, and fixed assets. (What can happen, though, is that enough cash is *embezzled* from a company to materially and adversely affect its financial statements.)

Analytical Symptoms. For both cash and marketable securities, it helps to perform all four analyses. Recorded amounts of individual categories of cash and marketable securities can be examined over time to determine whether the changes are unrealistic. Usually, if marketable securities increase, cash decreases by a similar amount, because securities are typically purchased with cash (unless debt was used or some other asset was traded for the securities). Various relationships can also be examined over time, using overhead analysis and/or the following ratios:

- Current ratio: Current assets ÷ Current liabilities
- Quick ratio: Current assets (inventory & prepaids) ÷ Current liabilities
- Current assets ÷ Total assets
- Marketable securities ÷ Total current assets
- Cash ÷ Total current assets

These ratios help you understand whether the relationship between cash or marketable securities is reasonable in relation to total current assets or total assets.

Because cash balances can be confirmed, recorded amounts of cash can be confirmed by other sources. Banks provide independent verifications that recorded amounts are appropriate. With securities, you can confirm market values and amounts with brokers or by checking the financial pages of newspapers. Comparing cash and security balances with those of similar companies is usually not helpful. Even similar companies often have significantly different amounts of cash and securities because they use different business strategies and incur different spending patterns. To determine whether recorded amounts of cash and securities are reasonable, ask questions such as, Does it makes sense for the company to have this amount of cash or securities? Reasons given for large balances should be plausible because, in many cases, having large amounts of cash on hand does not make sense.

Accounting or Documentary Symptoms. The best symptoms for discovering cash and/or marketable security frauds are usually the differences between recorded amounts and amounts confirmed by banks, brokers, and other independent parties. You should be concerned (1) if it makes sense for the company to have physical possession of security certificates and they do not; (2) if they should have bank statements and/or bank reconciliations and they do not; or (3) if they have bank statements that cannot be reconciled. You should also be concerned if the company uses off-shore banks, banks in other locations, or the banks have characteristics that do not make business sense.

Receivables and Inventory

Almost always, when accounts receivable are overstated, revenues are overstated. Similarly, when inventory is overstated, the cost of goods sold is understated. Once in a while, however, inventory and/or accounts receivable (or other assets) are overstated to conceal large thefts of cash or other assets. As stated earlier, much of the PharMor inventory overstatement was used to conceal Monus's large thefts of cash. Similarly, the ESM perpetrators overstated accounts receivable by about $350 million to hide the fact that the three principals embezzled $350 million.

Inadequate Disclosure

The final financial statement fraud we discuss is disclosure fraud. In inadequate disclosures, fraudulent or misleading statements or press releases are issued without line-item effects. That is, somewhere in its annual report or through press releases or other media, management makes statements that are wrong but which do not impact the statement numbers. Disclosure fraud can also be perpetrated by *omission*—statements that should have been but were not made by management (that is, they mislead because of what they *don't* say).

Because inadequate disclosure does not impact the financial statements, analytical symptoms do not exist. However, there may or may not be documentary symptoms, depending on the type of misstatement.

Disclosure frauds are a different "animal" than liability and asset fraud. Misleading disclosures can be made about anything; therefore, symptoms vary from fraud to fraud. As a result, generalizing symptoms is difficult.

One thing you should remember is that fraud vulnerability are particularly relevant to disclosure frauds. Management rarely makes willful misstatements if there are no significant pressures or opportunities to do so. Therefore, when you observe management, organizational structure, relationships with other parties, and operating characteristic vulnerability, keep your level of skepticism higher than normal, not only about statement numbers, but also about management disclosures and representations made in annual reports and in other information distributed by the company.

Types of Disclosure Fraud

Disclosure frauds misrepresent:

1. The nature of the company or its products, through news reports, interviews, annual reports, and elsewhere
2. The company's performance in management discussions and in annual reports, 10-Ks, 10-Qs, and other reports
3. Unusual business dealings in footnotes to the financial statements

Misrepresenting the Company or Its Products

All too often, the business press mouths misrepresentations that a company puts out about itself or about its products. Here are two examples:

They called it the "dog-and-pony" show. A "prospect" would be brought to *Comparator Systems* (see Chapter 10), a tiny Los Angeles-based company that, in June 1996, was accused of securities fraud by the SEC.[10] On a table would be a small machine, a fingerprint identification device that Comparator said could help the world stop imposters and make investors who bought its penny-priced shares rich. Imagine a technology that would one day let businesses and governments quickly and affordably verify that people are who they claim to be. Robert Reed Rogers, Comparator's chairman and CEO, was particularly adept at telepathically "beaming" confidence. The company's small band of employees, who might not have been paid in months, wore their most respectable outfits. Comparator executives demonstrated the technology, sometimes using a machine that the SEC says was stolen from Scottish inventors. These demonstrations were part and parcel of one of the largest stock market scandals of the 1990s. The SEC charges that Comparator told a convincing tall tale about a phony product, and turned the tale into big money through stock sales.

Comparator is the story of how a company snagged investors from Middle America and the hallowed halls of Harvard to rising business districts in Malaysia. It is also the story of how a company with allegedly worthless assets, a product it did not own, a 29-person payroll it had not met for 11 of 13 years, and a stock market value of $40 million became worth $1 billion in three days of frenzied trading on the NASDAQ. For three days in May 1996, not only was the stock of this virtually unknown company the most active ever on NASDAQ, sky rocketing from 6 cents a share to $2 a share, it also accounted for one-fourth of NASDAQ trading volume. In the end, chastened investors found out the hard way: Comparator was an imposter—ironically, the same kind of imposter its "technology" was supposed to detect.

In 1997, *Bre-X Minerals* (see Chapter 11) found itself at the center of a storm of controversy. Bre-X claimed a discovery of as much as 71 million ounces of gold, worth $21 billion, in Indonesian Borneo. The hype surrounding Bre-X transformed the tiny Calgary, Alberta–based firm over three years into a company with a market value of $4.5 billion. The stock's run-up also made instant millionaires of its executives. The gold "discovery" was faked by adding outside gold to samples taken from the Busang site in Borneo. Industry experts say that it was almost impossible to perpetrate the scam without management knowing about it, given the extent of the fraud. Bre-X's stock was traded in Toronto and Montreal and on NASDAQ, and the stock's price plummeted 80% in one day when the fraud was discovered. After the discovery, Bre-X announced that the company was pulling out of the Busang project.

Comparator and Bre-X are companies that misrepresented themselves and/or their products. Comparator never had a state-of-the-art fingerprinting machine. And Bre-X never had a fabulous mine in Borneo. Yet, these companies cost investors hundreds of millions of dollars and together had an aggregate market value of nearly $6 billion. Unfortunately, these companies are not alone. Many companies claim to be something they are not. Perpetrators of disclosure fraud are "imposters." They are no different than a person who enters a bank, claims to be a certain bank customer, and withdraws money from that customer's account using fictitious or stolen identification.

Misrepresentations in Financial Reports

In recent years, a company's annual report has become as much a public relations document as it is a report of financial condition and operations. Most annual reports include various statements by management, including management's "discussion and analysis," historical performance charts, announcements of new products and strategic directions, and plans and goals for the future. Sometimes, management's statements contain false disclosures and outright lies. Other times, management fails to make disclosures that are necessary to help investors and creditors understand what is really going on. Consider the E.F. Hutton case:

> *In the early 1980s, E.F. Hutton Group developed a cash management system for moving customer funds received by Hutton branch offices through bank accounts maintained at regional offices and ultimately to Hutton's corporate bank accounts in New York City and Los Angeles. The system required branch offices to calculate daily net activity in their branch accounts, and then to remove from the accounts all funds in excess of the required compensating balances. On certain days, the branches overdrafted their bank accounts to offset excess collected on other days. If, on the day after a branch overdrafted its bank account, insufficient funds were collected from customers to cover the overdraft, or if there was a delay in the check clearing process, the branch deposited a "reimbursement check" in the bank account to make up the difference. Branch reimbursement checks were drawn on zero balance checking accounts that were funded at the end of each day.*
>
> *Certain members of senior management encouraged greater use of the drawdown procedures, which increased Hutton's interest income and reduced their interest expense. Net interest income figured significantly in Hutton's financial statements. Hutton failed to disclose in its management discussion and analysis that the increased use of the overdrafting practices was a material cause of the significant increase in net interest income. The complaint also alleged that Hutton failed to disclose in its management discussion and analysis that the reduced use of bank overdrafting practices the next year was a material cause of the significant decrease in Hutton's net interest income that year.*[11]

In Hutton's case, the company materially changed the nature of its operations, making as much money from using bank floats and kiting as from selling securities. The management discussion and analysis section of the annual report should have described these events. As you can see, fraudulent financial reporting can occur as much from failure to disclose—omission—as from disclosing misleading information.

Misleading Statement Footnotes

Another way to perpetrate disclosure fraud is through misleading footnotes or by omitting key or required disclosures. A company's footnotes *must* provide all necessary relevant disclosures, to help investors and creditors understand the financial statements so they can make sound investment and credit decisions. Sometimes, disclosures that should be made in the footnotes are missing, and other times the footnotes are misleading. Many of these misleading disclosures affect financial statement balances, but some do not. In this section, we focus on those that do not impact the financial statement numbers.

Probably the most frequent type of footnote disclosure fraud is failure to disclose related-party transactions. Auditors and others are required by both GAAP and GAAS to look closely at related-party transactions, and often management believes it can avoid such scrutiny if it does not reveal the existence of related parties. Disclosure frauds also fail to disclose:

- Contingent liabilities that are reasonably possible or probable and that would create a loss for the company
- Contractual obligations, including restrictions on specific assets and/or liabilities
- Information regarding loans to creditors
- Significant events

Alternatively disclosure frauds inadequately or incorrectly state:

- Contingent gains that are probably not going to occur
- Significant accounting policies
- Information about market value declines of assets, including marketable securities
- Information about pension or other long-term liabilities

Of course, to be fraud, the lack of disclosure or misleading disclosures has to be intentional. Consider the Centennial Savings and Loan fraud.[12]

> *Centennial Savings and Loan began in the mid-1970s with about $18 million in assets. The company eventually increased those assets to a supposed $408 million before the fraud was discovered. In 1985, examiners began to uncover discrepancies in the company's financial statements. In January 1986, the FBI began an investigation of Centennial and found numerous illegal activities. Centennial conspired with executives of other savings and loans to create loans for former Centennial officials. These loans violated federal regulations that prevent thrifts from making more than $100,000 in unsecured loans to affiliated persons. Executives of Centennial received and paid kickbacks to help these loans go through. In addition, the company was involved in suspicious joint ventures that were highly speculative. They also engaged in real estate deals that significantly overstated asset values. None of this information was ever disclosed in the statement footnotes.*

Centennial's financial statement fraud involved not disclosing related-party transactions, among other things. In other fraud cases, disclosures about asset impairment, contingent liabilities, and significant events are either missing or misleading. Sometimes, as was the case with the ESM footnote disclosure discussed earlier, information about fraud that is occurring is actually provided in the footnotes, but is concealed in such a way that most readers will not detect it.

Identifying Disclosure Fraud

Identifying disclosure fraud is harder than other frauds. In fact, without a tip or complaint, it is difficult to know that disclosure fraud is even occurring. Misleading disclosures are easier to detect than missing disclosures. Also, the symptoms differ, depending on which type of disclosure fraud is occurring. In overall misrepresentations of a company or its products, for example, symptoms will relate to the nature of the company, its assets and organization, its management, and its operating characteristics.

Symptoms of Disclosure Fraud

Taking a broad view, symptoms you look for to find frauds like those of Comparator and Bre-X resemble the symptoms we find in investment scams and Ponzi schemes.

Company Misrepresentations

To help you discover whether companies like AFCO, Comparator, or Bre-X are misrepresenting themselves or their product, you need to understand their financial situation, financial goals and objectives, and risk tolerance. Other flags are companies that have unrealistically large growth in assets, revenues, or profits and companies that have a short history, involve unknown management, or have other characteristics that make their performance or other representations look suspicious. In addition, the following questions are useful in helping you identify whether a company and its products are legitimate:

- Does the company's performance make sense when compared with the performance of similar companies?
- Is the company cash-poor? Is it desperate for investors to put money into it immediately?
- Does the company's success depend on a special tax loophole or tax avoidance scheme?
- Is there anything that cannot be fully disclosed because it is one of the company's "unique" reasons for success?
- Is the business new in town?
- What is the background of the principals? Where do they come from, and what were their operations in previous locations?
- Have any of the principals been involved in bankruptcy or scandals?
- Are the appraisal figures and financial claims provided by company's representatives true?
- Does the company's success depend on kickbacks, complicated marketing schemes, special concessions to those who have money, or unwritten deals that cannot be talked about because of domestic or foreign laws?
- Are the company's financial reports audited? If so, for how many years? What type of audit opinion did they receive?
- Does the company's success depend on someone's "unique" expertise (such as an uncanny ability to predict commodity prices or unusually good salesmanship) for financial success?
- What would happen if one person's special skills were removed from the company?
- Is the company making guaranteed promises? Can the promises be verified?
- Does the company's success depend on high financial leverage?
- Would investors be liable if the company's debts were not paid?
- Are the principals living "high on the hog," even though the business is relatively new?
- Is the company's stock listed on a national exchange? If so, which one, and what has been its history on that exchange?
- What is the nature of the company and its board of directors? Does the company have an audit committee and/or internal auditors?
- Is the company's success based on a recent announcement of a major success or discovery? If so, have independent sources confirmed the truthfulness of the announcements?

In the Comparator fraud, for example, the company compiled bad debts in approximately 27 cases, owing $478,554 in principal and accrued interest from final court judgments, according to the company's final 10-K report to the SEC. Another eight cases, worth $300,000, were in dispute. The company's bad debts included rent owed for three different Los Angeles area offices. The company used stock to pay veterinarian, dental, and legal bills. Rogers distributed shares of stock like water. Rogers was past president of several companies that had previous brushes with the law. In one, his company claimed to have "exclusive rights" to certain mining processes for producing jewelry. In another, a bench warrant was issued for his arrest for failure to appear in court in connection with a lawsuit filed by investors. As the general partner of a health care company, Rogers and his partners were sued and had judgments against them. Comparator was also late with, and did not make, some filings to the SEC. In fact, dealers stopped trading Comparator, and the company was dropped from newspaper stock listings and from the public's eyes for a while. One investor called the company's balance sheet "puff" and "inflated," because it included worthless patents and other assets.

In another disclosure fraud, a professor received a call from a colleague at another university, who asked him about a company his university was investing in. The colleague was suspicious, because the company claimed that his university would double its endowments in a year or less. The company had a wealthy investor who would match any amount the university invested. The more the colleague described the company, the more it sounded like a classic Ponzi scheme. After listening for about 30 minutes, the professor mused, "I don't know whether this company is fraudulent. But, I've always believed if something crawled like a snake, looked like a snake, and acted like a snake, it probably is a snake." He told his colleague that the company had all the characteristics of an investment scam. His colleague proceeded to investigate the company and discovered the now famous "New Era" fraud.[13]

Misleading Financial Reports and Statement Footnotes

Several fraud investigation techniques can be used to identify inadequate disclosures. First, look for inconsistencies between disclosures and information in the financial statements and other information you are aware of. Second, make inquiries of management and other personnel concerning related-party transactions, contingent liabilities, and contractual obligations. Make these inquiries at several levels of management and do them separately and judiciously. Inquiries should also be made about different accounting policies that management is aware of. Even though some of these inquiries may be routine or involve basic questions, differences in responses may tip you off that management is engaging in fraudulent activities.

Another way to identify inadequate disclosures, especially those concerning related parties, is to review the company's files and records with the SEC and other regulatory agencies. Check for names of officers and directors who occupy management or directorship positions in other companies. It is also possible, given the number and variety of databases available today, to search for common ownership and directorship interests. If you suspect something awry, use databases such as Lexis/Nexis to perform background searches on key individuals. Other good places to look for inadequate disclosures are the board of director minutes, correspondence and invoices from attorneys, confirmations with banks and others, contracts, loan agreements, loan guarantees, leases, correspondence from taxing and regulatory authorities, pension plan documents, sales agreements, and any type of legal document.

In many disclosure frauds, financial statement auditors actually "get their hands on the fraud" but don't recognize it for what it is. To identify disclosure fraud and other financial statement frauds, auditors and others must realize that such things as inconsistencies between financial statements and other information often represent fraud symptoms and not merely mistakes. If something doesn't look right, is not consistent with GAAP, or has other characteristics that make you uncomfortable, do not let management explain away the problem. Detecting fraud requires you to look beyond transactions, documents, and other information and to ask what possible explanations exist for its occurrence or for it being reported or represented in the way it is. These days, acquiring answers to questions you have about business relationships, management backgrounds, and other information from publicly available sources is not difficult. If something looks suspicious or questionable, research the issue or gather independent evidence, rather than merely accepting management representations. If management can commit financial statement fraud, they can certainly lie to you.

Summary

Looking for fraud is not unlike hiking in a forest. Perpetrators stand camouflaged and motionless as they try to conceal themselves and their fraud. Many people walk right by deer or elk in the forest; they don't see the animal unless they look for movement, changes in color or shadows, or changes in shapes, or the animal is pointed out to them. Likewise, to discover fraud, we look for analytical symptoms (movements), accounting or documentary symptoms (changes in color), behavioral and lifestyle symptoms (changes in shapes), control symptoms (changes in shadows), and tips and complaints (the evidence that is pointed out).

We have completed three chapters on financial statement fraud and have looked at specific types of financial statement misstatements. GAAP requires that companies prepare their financial statements using accrual-based accounting. Because of accrual-based accounting, reconciling the difference between the cash a company is generating and its reported net income is sometimes difficult. Indeed, that is one of the major purposes of the statement of cash flows. Timing and other elements create differences between a company's cash flows and its accrual-based net income. Over the life of a firm, however, these timing and other differences should even out so that the cash generated is approximately equal to the net income that is reported.

One of the best overall fraud indicators we have found is to track the differences and trend between cash flows (only cash can pay debts and keep a company liquid) and reported net income. We track this difference using the following ratio:

$$\frac{\textbf{Net Income} - \textbf{Cash Flow from Operations}}{\textbf{Total Assets}}$$

The numerator is the difference between reported net income (from the income statement) and cash flow from operations (from the statement of cash flows.) The denominator is total assets (from the balance sheet) and is used to standardize the numerator. Over time, this ratio should hover around zero, with some positive years and some negative years. Progressive deterioration in this ratio (measured by increasingly longer positive numbers) can often spell trouble and hint that financial statement fraud is occurring, with reported net income increasing and cash flows decreasing.

As an example, consider the case of Aviation Sales, a company whose management was alleged to have committed financial statement fraud during 1995–1998. Its cash flows and net income (in millions) during this period were:

Year	Net Income	Cash Flow from Operations	Total Assets
1995	$186.0	$ 14	$ 42
1996	22.3	(8)	89
1997	35.0	(49)	145
1998 (3 months)	(32)		

The ratios, calculated for 1995–1997, are:

1995

$$\frac{\$186 - \$14}{\$42} = .109$$

1996

$$\frac{\$22.3 + \$8}{\$89} = .50$$

1997

$$\frac{\$35 + \$48.9}{\$145} = .58$$

As you can see, this ratio progressively decreased from .109 to .50 to .58, indicating that there is an increasingly larger difference between cash flows from operations and net income. While this ratio doesn't provide information about the kind of fraud that may be occurring, it is an excellent warning sign to show (1) that financial statement fraud may be occurring and that net income is being manipulated, or (2) that even if fraud isn't occurring, the company is having serious cash flow problems. Either way, the news isn't good.

New Terms

Accrued liability: Liabilities arising from end-of-period adjustments, not from specific transactions.

Acquisition: The purchase of something, such as the purchase of one company by another company.

Capitalization: Recording expenditures as assets rather than as expenses. (For example, start-up costs that are "capitalized" are recorded as assets and amortized.)

Contingent liability: A possible liability. If the likelihood of payment is "probable," the contingent liability must be reported as a liability on the financial statements; if likelihood of payment is reasonably possible, it must be disclosed in the footnotes to the financial statements; if likelihood of payment is remote, no mention of the possible liability needs to be made.

Deferred asset: Expenditure that has been capitalized to be expensed in the future.

Fixed assets: Property, plant, and equipment assets of an organization.

Footnotes: Information that accompanies a company's financial statements and that provides interpretive guidance to the financial statements or includes related information that must be disclosed.

Disclosure fraud: The issuance of fraudulent or misleading statements or press releases without financial statement line-item effect or the lack of appropriate disclosures that should have been, but were not, made by management.

Intangible asset: An asset that has no tangible existence (for example, goodwill).

Lease: Obligation to make periodic payments over a specified period for use or "rent" of an asset; does not involve ownership of the asset.

Marketable securities: Stocks, bonds, and other non-cash assets; sometimes called short-term investments.

Merger: Combining of two organizations into one business entity.

Mortgage: Long-term loan secured by property, such as a home mortgage.

Asset fraud: Financial statement fraud in which assets are recorded at higher amounts than they should be.

Pension: Postretirement cash benefits paid to former employees.

Repurchase agreements: Agreement to buy back something previously sold.

Restructuring: Reevaluation of a company's assets because of impairment of value or for other reasons. Restructured companies usually have lower amounts of assets and look quite different than before the restructuring.

Liability frauds: Financial statement fraud in which liabilities (amounts owed to others) are understated.

Unearned revenues: Amounts that have been received from customers but for which performance of a service or sale of a product has not yet been made.

Warranty liabilities: Obligation to perform service and repair items sold within a specific period of time and/or use after sale.

Questions and Cases

Discussion Questions

1. Why are liability frauds difficult to discover?
2. What are the four analytical analyses used to search for financial statement fraud symptoms? Give an example of each method and show how you would use it to search for liability fraud symptoms.
3. What is meant by "cut-off problems" as they relate to accounts payable?
4. Why might liabilities be understated if proper adjusting entries are not made at the end of an accounting period?
5. What is the difference between unearned revenue and earned revenue?
6. If a "contingent liability" is only a "possible liability," why might not disclosing contingent liabilities constitute financial statement fraud?
7. Why can improper capitalization of amounts spent result in financial statement fraud and overstatement of assets?
8. Is cash an asset that is frequently overstated when committing financial statement fraud? Why or why not?
9. In what ways can financial statement fraud result from a merger?
10. If all statement amounts are presented appropriately, can financial statement fraud still be occurring?

True/False

1. Fraud auditors are usually concerned with liabilities being overstated as well as understated.
2. Confirmations with vendors are an effective way to discover unrecorded liabilities.
3. Accrued liabilities are an important account to look at when searching for fraud because it is easier to understate liabilities in these accounts.
4. Symptoms of unrecorded contingent liabilities can be found by performing analytical procedures on certain financial statement ratios.
5. Some misleading footnotes have no effect on the financial statement balances.
6. Liability fraud is generally more difficult to find than asset fraud.
7. When searching for unrecorded liabilities, investigating vendors with zero balances is just as important as investigating vendors with large balances.
8. The assets most often improperly capitalized are fixed assets.
9. Financial statement fraud involving footnote disclosures can be frauds of omission or frauds of commission.
10. A company that claims to be something it is not in a 10-K report is committing a kind of financial statement fraud.

Multiple Choice

1. Which of the following are primary types of transactions that can create liabilities for a company?
    a. Purchasing inventory
    b. Borrowing money
    c. Selling purchased goods
    d. Leasing assets
    e. All of the above

2. When accounts payable–related liabilities are understated, purchases and inventory are often __________, or the financial statements don't balance.
   a. Overstated
   b. Understated
   c. Correctly stated
   d. It is impossible to tell.
3. Recognizing something as a revenue instead of as a liability has a positive effect on the reported financial statements because:
   a. It understates liabilities.
   b. It overstates revenues.
   c. It overstates net income.
   d. It overstates assets.
   e. All of the above.
   f. a, b, and c are correct.
4. The most common fraud involving car companies and the warranties they offer is:
   a. Overstating accrued liabilities
   b. Recognizing unearned revenue
   c. Not recording or underrecording future obligations
   d. Not recording or underrecording various types of debt
5. FAS 5 requires contingent liabilities to be recorded as liabilities on the balance sheet if the likelihood of loss or payment is:
   a. Remote
   b. Reasonably possible
   c. Probable
   d. Not determinable
6. Analytical symptoms of accounts payable fraud show up as reported Accounts Payable balances that appear:
   a. Too low
   b. Too high
   c. Too perfect
   d. Unchanged
7. Searching for analytical symptoms of financial statement fraud means looking for accounts that appear:
   a. Too low
   b. Too high
   c. Unusual
   d. Any of the above
8. When focusing on changes, you should consider period-to-period changes in:
   a. Recorded balances
   b. Relationships between balances
   c. Balances of other dissimilar companies
   d. Both a and b
   e. All of the above

9. Overstating cash is difficult because:
   a. Cash balances can be easily confirmed with banks and other financial institutions.
   b. Cash is hard to steal.
   c. Cash is normally not a fraudulent account.
   d. Cash is usually a small asset.
10. Inadequate disclosure frauds involve:
   a. Statements in the footnotes that are wrong but do not impact the financial statement
   b. Disclosures that should have been made in the footnotes, but were not
   c. Both a and b
   d. Neither a or b

Short Cases

Case 1. John is president and manager of a small computer sales and support chain, Electronics, Inc. His stores are located throughout the state of California and are competitive with all of the major computer providers in the state. Electronics is known for its quick support and friendly service. The company often offers deals that include free service or low-priced service for products purchased. Electronics' competitors offer the same deals to their customers, but because of Electronics' small size, the chain is better able to provide the quick service that customers demand. John has raised funding through issuing stock. He hasn't used external loans much in the past. Electronics operates about 50 stores in California, and is in the process of securing new-store locations in other states. John's main business strategy is the quick customer service that Electronics provides. He believes his company can charge higher prices because people are willing to pay the initial higher price on computer components for the added customer service on the back end. In recent years, however, the competition has become more successful in providing quick services and low-maintenance products.

Managers in all stores report directly to John. They do not communicate regularly with other store managers on inventory issues or the availability of customer service reps. Electronics provides financial statements on a yearly basis so investors can follow the company's success. With the growing success of competitors, John has found it more difficult to show revenue growth. During the past year, Electronics recorded significant revenues from sales that will require warranty service over the next few years. However, the company reported that warranty expenses stayed the same. In addition, reported inventory levels remained approximately the same as in previous years. No additional financing or loans were recorded on the financial statements, even though assets continued to grow. Revenue was the only financial statement amount that changed dramatically.

What are possible fraud symptoms in this case? What symptoms look like fraud but could be explained by industry trends?

Case 2. Enron, the large energy trading company, recently imploded because of massive alleged fraud. Their "new-economy" approach to accounting allowed them to record liabilities in related-party partnerships that were not consolidated or combined with Enron's financial statements. Company executives maintain that they did not know about these massive off-balance-sheet liabilities, which are estimated to run into billions of dollars.

As a fraud investigator, how would you go about verifying the existence of these liabilities and partnerships?

Case 3. Qwest is the dominant local telephone company in 14 states and the owner of an international fiber-optic network. In 2002, the company was investigated by the SEC for not including certain expense items related to its merger with U S WEST, among other issues.

Why would the SEC be concerned if Qwest does not include certain expense items in merger documentation?

Case 4. Until its involvement as Enron's auditor, Arthur Andersen was one of the most respected CPA firms in the world. Arthur Andersen, like other large CPA firms, operates as a limited liability corporation (LLC). At the time that its involvement as Enron's auditor was making headlines, it wasn't clear whether the LLC form of organization could protect the personal assets of Andersen's partners from creditors' lawsuits.

Assume that there are 2,000 Andersen partners, and that creditor claims in the Enron case total $50 billion. Further assume that Arthur Andersen is a corporation. How would you expect creditor litigation to be reported in the financial statements? Would failure to report the litigation constitute financial statement fraud?

Case 5. In its 2001 annual report, investors of Adelphia Communications were startled to find a footnote to the financial statements that reported that the company had guaranteed as much as $2.7 billion in loans to a private entity owned by CEO John Rigas and his family.[14] As a result of the footnote, Adelphia lost more than 50% of its market value in a little more than a week.

Why do you think the market value of Adelphia fell so dramatically with this footnote disclosure?

Case 6. The officers of an oil refiner, trader, and hedger based in New York City were arrested by the FBI for committing massive financial statement fraud. The executives perpetrated the fraud using many schemes, one of which was to hide a $30 million accounts payable and show it as a payable arising in the following year. To conceal the fraud, they altered purchasing records, using white-out, and provided only photocopies of the records to auditors. The Big 5 firm that audited this company was later sued for audit negligence in not finding this fraud.

In your opinion, were the auditors negligent for accepting photocopies of purchasing records and thus not detecting this accounts payable understatement?

Extensive Case

Case 7. The following are the comparative balance sheets and statements of income for XYZ Company for the years 2001–2003.

CONSOLIDATED BALANCE SHEETS — XYZ Company

	2003	2002	2001
Assets			
Current assets			
Cash and cash equivalents	$ 1,542	$ 851	$ 317
Receivables	5,602	4,115	3,329
Inventories	1,524	1,112	900
Deferred income taxes	851	302	456
Total current assets	$ 9,519	$ 6,380	$ 5,002
Land	22,547	15,239	12,045
Buildings	10,982	8,475	7,698
Machinery	6,233	5,008	3,511
Accumulated depreciation	(396)	(305)	(235)
Total assets	$48,885	$34,797	$28,021

Liabilities and Stockholders' Equity			
Current liabilities			
Accounts payable	$ 5,603	$ 4,112	$ 4,758
Taxes payable	786	543	235
Total current liabilities	$ 6,389	$ 4,655	$ 4,993
Long-term debt	16,987	16,115	19,546
Deferred income taxes	845	562	354
Stockholders' Equity			
Common stock	22,220	12,764	2,907
Retained earnings	2,444	701	221
Total liabilities and stockholders' equity	$48,885	$34,797	$28,021

CONSOLIDATED STATEMENTS OF INCOME — XYZ Company

	2003	**2002**	**2001**
Revenues	$26,534	$22,473	$18,739
Cost of goods sold	18,201	18,161	15,406
Gross margin	$ 8,333	$ 4,312	$ 3,333
Operating expenses	5,428	3,512	2,965
Operating income before taxes	$ 2,905	$ 800	$ 368
Income taxes	1,162	320	147
Net income	$ 1,743	$ 480	$ 221

Calculate all ratios needed to determine whether XYZ is possibly underreporting accounts payable. If you observe symptoms, explain why you think fraud might exist.

Internet Assignment

Go online and enter the following page: http://www.kpmg.bb/interactive/articles/Best_of_IRM_Insights_Part_1.PDF

The first two pages of this report contain a summary of the 2000 KPMG Caribbean Fraud Survey. Review these pages and answer the following questions.

1. What facts in this report directly relate to the financial statement frauds discussed in this chapter?
2. What are some interesting facts about fraud in the Caribbean that are surprisingly consistent with the information about fraud in the United States provided in this book?

Debate

The following excerpt is taken from an article that appeared in a local newspaper:[15]

"Off-Balance-Sheet Land Is Where Death Spirals Lurk"

What occurred at the Enron Corporation, at considerable distance from the assets and liabilities on its balance sheet, may of course prove an anomaly. The company, now in bankruptcy but once the world's dominant energy trader, was an aggressive user of partnerships separated from the parent but

> *for which the parent's shareholders remained on the hook. Perhaps worse, it also committed the ultimate sin of omission—it failed to disclose the extent of its contingent liabilities related to those partnerships. Under U.S. federal securities laws, those details should probably have been listed in at least the footnotes to the company's financial statements.*
>
> *In itself, off-balance-sheet financing is no vice. Companies can use it in perfectly legitimate ways that carry little risk to shareholders. The trouble is, while more companies are relying on off-balance-sheet methods to finance their operations, investors are usually unaware until it is too late that a company with a clean balance sheet may be loaded with debt.*
>
> *Critics contend that one intent of these structures is to try to move debt off the radar screen so that companies appear less financially leveraged than they actually are. As a result, if investors take the financial statements at face value and not delve very deeply into these off-balance-sheet arrangements, the financial statements can be misunderstood.*

Is it ethical to keep the types of liabilities discussed in this article off the balance sheet, or is this a type of financial statement fraud?

End Notes

1. http://www.securitiessleuth.com/roguesgallery/chainsaw_al_5_17_01.htm
2. A triple-net lease means that the lessee is responsible for paying property taxes, maintenance, insurance, and utilities. Most of the leases were for periods of 14 years or more.
3. Securities & Exchange Commission. *In the Matter of Marsh & McLennan Companies, Inc.,* Exchange Act Ref. No. 24023, Accounting and Auditing Enforcement Release No. 124.
4. See *Fraud Examination for Managers and Auditors,* Jack C. Robertson, Viesca Books, Austin, Texas, 1997, p. 139. Thanks to Prof. Robertson for allowing us to use this and a few other examples from his book.
5. Form 8-K is the report filed at the end of any month in which significant events have occurred that are of interest to public investors. Such events include the acquisition or sale of a subsidiary, a change in officers or directors, an addition of a new product line, or a change in auditors.
6. *Fraud Examination for Managers and Auditors,* op. cit., pp. 137–138.
7. *Fraud Examination for Managers and Auditors,* op. cit., p. 136.
8. *Fraud Examination for Managers and Auditors,* op. cit., p. 132.
9. "Audit Showing Baby Bells Can't Locate $5 Billion in Gear Could Spur Rate Cuts," *Wall Street Journal,* March 17, 1999. Also see http://www.newnetworks.com/fccaudit.html.
10. http://www.sec.gov/litigation/litreleases/lr15855.txt
11. Seiler v. E. F. Hutton & Co., Inc., 102 F.R.D. 880 (D.N.J. 1984), and Glick v. E. F. Hutton & Co., Inc., 106 F.R.D. 446 (E.D. Pa. 1985).

12. Stephen Pizzo, Mary Fricker, and Paul Muolo, *Inside Job: The Looting of America's Savings and Loans.* See http://www.fictionwise.com/ebooks/eBook2072.htm.
13. http://www.christianitytoday.com/ct/7tc/7tc86a.html
14. http://www.buffalonews.com/editorial/20020519/1033589.asp
15. http://old.smh.com.au/news/0112/29/text/biztech3.html

PART SIX

OTHER TYPES OF FRAUD

Fraud Against Organizations

After studying this chapter, you should be able to understand:

1. The various ways in which corrupt employees, vendors, and customers steal assets.
2. How cash is stolen through larceny, skimming, and fraudulent disbursements.
3. The nature of thefts of inventory and other assets.
4. The nature of bribery.

David Miller first sold insurance in Wheeling, West Virginia, but was fired after ten months for stealing $200. After an assortment of odd jobs, Miller moved to Ohio and worked as an accountant for a local baker, where he was caught embezzling funds. He paid back the $1,000 he stole, and he was also dismissed, but his crime was not reported to authorities.

Miller then returned to Wheeling and went to work for Wheeling Bronze, Inc., a bronze-casting maker. In December 1971, the president of Wheeling Bronze discovered a $30,000 cash shortfall and several missing returned checks. An extensive search uncovered a number of canceled checks with forged signatures. Miller was questioned, and he confessed to the scheme. Faced with the choice of paying back the stolen amount or going to jail, Miller talked his parents into taking out a mortgage on their home to pay back the stolen money. No charges were filed.

Several months later, in Pennsylvania, Miller went to work for Robinson Pipe Cleaning. Miller embezzled funds yet again and was caught, and he again avoided prosecution by repaying the $20,000. In 1974, Crest Industries hired Miller as an accountant. Considered an ideal employee, Miller was dedicated, worked long hours, and did outstanding work; he was quickly promoted to office manager. Soon after, he purchased a new home, a new car, and a new wardrobe. In 1976, Miller's world unraveled once more when Crest's auditors discovered that $31,000 was missing. A tearful confession ensued as he promised to repay all the stolen money. Miller confessed that he wrote checks to himself and then recorded payments to vendors on the copies of the checks. To cover his tracks, he altered the company's monthly bank statements. He used the money he stole to finance his lifestyle and to repay Wheeling Bronze and Robinson Pipe Cleaning.

Miller claimed that he had never before embezzled funds. He showed such sincere remorse that Crest hired a lawyer for him! After giving Crest a lien on his house, he was quietly dismissed. The president of Crest did not want the publicity to harm Miller's wife and three children, so Crest never pressed charges.

Miller next took a job as an accountant in Steubenville, Ohio, with Rustcraft Broadcasting Company, a chain of radio and TV stations. Associated Communications acquired Rustcraft in 1979, and Miller moved to Pittsburgh, where he became Associated's new controller. Miller immediately began dipping into Associated's accounts. Over a six-year period, he embez-

zled approximately $1.36 million, $445,000 of that in 1984 when he was promoted to CFO. Miller used various methods to embezzle the money. In one approach, he circumvented the need for two signatures on every check by asking another executive who was going on vacation to sign several checks "just in case" the company needed additional cash while he was gone. Miller used these checks to siphon off funds to his personal accounts. Miller maintained a very comfortable lifestyle that included a new house, several expensive cars, vacation property, and a very expensive wardrobe.

Miller's life came crashing down around him in December 1984, while he was on vacation. A bank officer called to inquire about a check written to Mr. Miller. An investigation ensued, and Miller confessed to embezzling funds. As part of the 1985 out-of-court settlement with Miller, Associated Communications received most of Miller's personal property. After leaving Associated, Miller was hired by a former colleague. Miller underwent therapy and believes he has resolved his compulsion to embezzle.

When interviewed about his past activities, Miller said that he felt his problem with theft was an illness, just like alcoholism or compulsive gambling. The illness was driven by his need to be admired and liked by others. He thought that by spending money others would like him. Miller stated that once he got started, he couldn't stop.[1]

In Part 5 of this book, we discussed financial statement frauds. In this chapter, we look at how employees, customers, and vendors perpetuate fraud against organizations. This fraud is sometimes called occupational fraud, and we focus on two aspects of it: misappropriation and corruption. In Chapter 14, we discuss frauds associated with bankruptcies. Note that we do not cover every type of fraud in this book. For example, we don't cover investment scams (where perpetrators trick individuals into investing their money in fake investments). As you think about the various types of fraud, always remember that fraud perpetrators are creative, and they come up with new schemes every day. We introduce you to the most common types of fraud here to whet your appetite for further study.

Fraud Statistics

In this chapter, we draw heavily from Joe Wells's book, *Occupational Fraud and Abuse,* as well as his other works. This book contains by far the best taxonomy of the various types of fraud.[2]

In 1993, under Wells's direction, the Association of Certified Fraud Examiners (ACFE) embarked on a major research project that examined over 2,600 different frauds reported by over 2,000 certified fraud examiners. The study provides many useful findings about fraud, one of which is the classification of occupational fraud and abuse into three main categories: asset misappropriation, corruption, and fraudulent financial statements. Within these main categories, 44 separate fraud schemes are identified and classified.

Some key statistics about occupational fraud revealed in the ACFE's study are stated here:

- Of frauds against organizations, 58% are perpetrated by employees, 30% by management, and 12% by owners.
- Median loss to organizations by type of perpetrator: $60,000 by employees, $250,000 by managers, and $1,000,000 by owners.
- Median loss by sex of perpetrator: $185,000 by males, $48,000 by females.

- Median fraud losses increase with the age of perpetrators:
  - Less than 25 years old $ 12,000
  - 26–30 years old 50,000
  - 31–35 years old 54,000
  - 36–40 years old 100,000
  - 41–50 years old 196,000
  - 51–60 years old 280,000
  - Over 60 years old 346,000
- Median fraud losses differ by marital status:
- Married (72% of all perpetrators) $150,000
  - Divorced (8% of all perpetrators) 80,000
  - Single (11% of all perpetrators) 54,000
  - Separated (9% of all perpetrators) 50,000
- Median fraud losses vary by level of education:
  - High school (42% of all perpetrators) $ 50,000
  - College (45% of all perpetrators) 200,000
  - Postgraduate (13% of all perpetrators) 275,000
- Median fraud losses vary by size of the victim organization:
  - 1–100 employees $120,000
  - 101–1,000 employees 100,000
  - 1,001–10,000 employees 80,000
  - Over 10,000 employees 126,000

Asset Misappropriations

Dishonest employees, vendors, and customers have three opportunities to steal assets: They can (1) steal *receipts* of cash and other assets as they come into the organization, (2) steal cash and other assets that are *on hand*, or (3) commit *disbursement fraud* (the organization pays for something it shouldn't pay for or pays too much for purchases). With each type of fraud, perpetrators can act alone or in collusion with others. The following diagram outlines possible ways to misappropriate funds:

The fraud taxonomy developed by Wells is more complicated and detailed than the one we show above. He divides asset misappropriations into two major categories: (1) thefts of cash and (2) thefts of inventory and other assets. Thefts of cash he further subdivides as follows: (1) larceny (intentionally taking an organization's cash without its consent and against its will), (2) skimming (removing cash prior to its entry into the accounting system), and (3) fraudulent disbursements. Thefts of inventory and other assets he also divides into two groups: (1) larceny and (2) misuse. We will discuss the misappropriation of assets using Wells's classification scheme.

Theft of Cash Through Larceny

In larceny, cash is stolen by employees or others after it has been recorded in the company's accounting system. As a result, larceny is easier to detect than skimming and is far less common. The ACFE found that cash larceny accounts for only 2.95% of all frauds, and that the median loss is only $22,000 per incident, third lowest among all types of fraud.[3]

Cash larcenies take place in situations in which perpetrators have access to cash. Commonly, perpetrators take cash or currency on hand (in cash registers or cash boxes) or from bank deposits. Cash larcenies are most successful when they involve relatively small amounts over extended periods of time. With such thefts, businesses often write the small missing amounts off as "shorts" or "miscounts," rather than as thefts. For example, in one bank, annual cash shortages by tellers exceed $3 million per year. Some of this teller shortage is no doubt truly miscounting, and certainly customers are more likely to inform their teller when they are given too little cash than when they are given too much cash. However, a significant portion of the shortage is also caused by larceny.

Theft of Cash Through Skimming

An example of skimming is the fraud perpetrated by Marvin Culpepper. Culpepper was the business manager at Muffler's Incorporated. Among his duties were to collect cash from customers and open all incoming mail. He also made the daily bank deposits. At Muffler's Incorporated, customers paid for their automobile repairs by check, cash, or credit card. Over a period of six years, Culpepper skimmed approximately half the cash receipts, over $600,000. He concealed his thefts by simply not recording the work as being done. He did not skim money from the check or credit-card receipts because that would have been much harder to conceal.

Culpepper's theft illustrates the most basic skimming scheme—taking money from the sale of goods or services but not recording the sale. Another example is the ice cream store cashier who sells two-scoop ice cream cones to customers and either doesn't enter the sales into the cash register or enters the sales as single-scoop sales.

More complicated skimming schemes occur when employees (1) understate sales and collections by recording false or larger-than-reality sales discounts; (2) misappropriate customer payments and write off the receivable as "uncollectible"; (3) embezzle a first customer's payment and then credit that customer's account when a second customer pays (a delayed recognition of payment, called *lapping*); or (4) collude with customers so they either pay later than required or less than required. As an example of this latter scheme, consider the $2.2 million fraud perpetrated on a Fortune 500 company: An employee who collected receivables gave a high-volume customer extra time to pay receivables without reporting them as delinquent. As a result of this fraud, the dishonest customer earned interest on cash that should have been used to pay the accounts payable; the interest exceeded $2 million. The money was then split with the accounts receivable manager, who worked for the victim company. The victim company lost (1) the interest they should have been earning on the receivables, and (2) the interest they had to pay out on loans to cover the shortfall. This fraud encompassed both skimming and corruption.

Theft of Cash Through Fraudulent Disbursements

The ACFE research project found that fraudulent disbursements comprise by far the highest percentage of asset misappropriations. In fact, based on the sample studied, fraudulent disbursements represent 67% of all cases, more than double the total of skimming (38.9% of all misappropriations) and larceny (4.1% of all cases).

The ACFE divides fraudulent disbursements into six major types: (1) check tampering, (2) register-disbursement schemes, (3) billing schemes, (4) expense schemes, (5) payroll schemes, and (6) others. In terms of frequency and amount of losses, billing schemes are the largest, as shown below:

Type of Disbursements Fraud	Percent of Total Cases	Percent of Total Losses
Billing schemes	33.3%	51.6%
Check tampering	24.5%	13.2%
Payroll schemes	16.5%	10.7%
Expense schemes	14.9%	4.0%
Other fraudulent disbursements	8.1%	.1%
Register-disbursement schemes	2.7%	20.4%

Check Tampering. Check tampering is a disbursement scheme in which employees either (1) prepare fraudulent checks for their own use, or (2) intercept checks intended for a third party and convert the checks to cash for their own use. Check tampering is unusual among the disbursement frauds in that perpetrators physically prepare the fraudulent checks. In most disbursement schemes, culprits generate payments to themselves by submitting false documents to the victim company, such as invoices or timecards. The false documents represent a claim for payment and cause the victim company to issue a check, which the perpetrator then converts. These frauds are basically trickery: Perpetrators fool companies into handing over their money. Check-tampering schemes are fundamentally different. With check tampering, perpetrators take physical control of checks and make them payable to themselves by either forging the maker (signing the check), forging endorsements, or altering payees.

Register-Disbursement Schemes. Register-disbursement schemes are the least costly of the disbursement schemes, averaging only $22,500 per incident. Two basic schemes take place at the register: false refunds and false voids. With false refunds, perpetrators process transactions as if a customer were returning merchandise, even though there is no actual return. Perpetrators then take money from the cash register in the amount of the false return. The register tape shows that a merchandise return has been made, so the disbursement appears legitimate. The concealment problem for perpetrators is that, with false refunds, a debit is made to the inventory system that shows merchandise has been returned. Since no inventory was returned, the recorded inventory amount is overstated and an inventory count can reveal the missing inventory. A similar but more difficult fraud to detect is refund overstatement. In these cases, merchandise is actually returned, but the value of the return is overstated. For example, suppose a customer returns merchandise costing $10. The dishonest employee records the return as $15, gives the customer $10, and pockets $5.

Fictitious voids resemble refund schemes in that they generate disbursements from the cash register. When a sale is voided on a register, a copy of the customer's receipt is attached to a void slip, along with the signature or initials of a manager that indicates that the transaction has been approved. To process a false void, cashiers keep the customer's receipt at the time of sale and then ring in a voided sale after the customer leaves. Whatever money the customer paid for the item is removed from the register as though it was returned to the customer. The copy of the customer's receipt attached to the voided slip verifies the authenticity of the transaction. Unfortunately for perpetrators, voided sales create the same kind of concealment problems that false returns do—that is, missing inventory.

Billing Schemes. Both check tampering and register-disbursement schemes require perpetrators to physically take cash or checks from their employers. With billing schemes, perpetrators avoid the risk of taking company cash or merchandise. In billing schemes, perpetrators submit or alter invoices that cause their employer to issue checks. Although the support for the checks is fraudulent, the disbursement itself appears valid. Billing schemes are common and expensive. The median loss of billing schemes in the ACFE study is $250,000, by far the highest of all asset misappropriations. Because most businesses' disbursements are made in the purchasing cycle, larger thefts can be hidden using false billing schemes. Employees who concoct billing schemes are just going where the money is.

The three most common billing schemes are (1) setting up dummy companies (shell companies) to submit invoices to the victim organization, (2) altering or double-paying nonaccomplice vendor's statements, and (3) making personal purchases with company funds. Dummy or shell companies are fictitious entities created for the sole purpose of committing fraud. Many times, they are nothing more than a fabricated name and a post office box that the perpetrator uses to collect disbursements from false billings. However, since the checks received are made out in the name of the shell company, perpetrators normally set up a bank account in the new company's name, listing themselves as the authorized signer.

Some perpetrators generate fraudulent disbursements by using invoices of nonaccomplice vendors. For example, they may double-pay an invoice, and request the recipient to return one of the checks—the perpetrator then pockets the returned check. Alternatively, fraudsters intentionally pay the wrong vendor and then ask them to return the payment. Or, they intentionally overpay a legitimate vendor and ask for a return in the amount of the overpayment.

Finally, perpetrators make personal purchases with company funds. The purchases can be for themselves or for their businesses, their families, or others.

Expense Schemes. Expense and payroll schemes are similar to billing schemes. In these frauds, perpetrators produce false documentation that causes the victim company to unknowingly make a fraudulent disbursement. In payroll schemes, false documentation uses items like timecards, sales orders, and expense reports. Expense schemes overbill the company for car travel and other related business expenses, such as business lunches, hotel bills, and air travel.

The four common expense disbursement schemes (1) mischaracterize expenses, (2) overstate expenses, (3) submit fictitious expenses, and (4) submit the same expenses multiple times. In the first type, a personal expense is mischaracterized to make it look like a business expense. For example, personal travel is claimed as a business trip, a personal lunch as a business lunch, or a personal magazine subscription as a company subscription. Overstating expenses usually involves doctoring a receipt or other supporting documentation to reflect a higher cost than what was actually paid. Fraudsters may use eradicating fluid, ball point pens, or some other method to change the price on the receipt. If the company does not require original documents as support, perpetrators generally attach a copy of the receipt to their expense report. In some cases (like taxi receipts), they complete the receipt themselves, writing in an amount higher than they actually spent.

In expense schemes, perpetrators create bogus support documents, such as false receipts. The proliferation of graphics programs for personal computers has made it easy to create realistic-looking counterfeit receipts. Alternatively, perpetrators sometimes obtain blank receipts from vendors or printers, and then fill them out and submit them. The least common expense scheme is the submission of multiple reimbursements for the same expense.

Payroll Schemes. Payroll schemes account for only a very small percentage of all frauds—1.9% of the total losses in the ACFE study. Payroll schemes fall into four major categories: (1) ghost employees, (2) falsified hours and salary, (3) commission schemes, and (4) false worker compensation claims. Of all payroll fraud schemes, ghost-employee schemes generate the largest losses. According to the ACFE, their average loss is $275,000 per occurrence. In ghost-employee schemes, fraudsters put someone on the payroll (or keep a former employee on the payroll) who doesn't actually work for the victim company. By falsifying personnel or payroll records, fraudsters cause paychecks to be generated to the ghost employee. These paychecks are then cashed by the perpetrators or their accomplices.

For ghost-employee schemes to succeed, four things have to happen: (1) the ghost must be added to the payroll, (2) timekeeping and wage rate information must be collected, (3) a paycheck must be issued to the ghost (unless direct deposits are used), and (4) the check must be delivered to the perpetrator or an accomplice. By far the most common method of misappropriating funds from payroll is the overpayment of wages: this accounts for 55.4% of all payroll frauds. For hourly employees, the size of a paycheck is based on two essential factors: the number of hours worked and the rate of pay. Therefore, for hourly employees to fraudulently increase the size of their paychecks, they must either falsify the number of hours worked or falsify the wage rate. Because salaried employees don't receive compensation based on their time at work, in most cases these perpetrators generate fraudulent wages by increasing their rate of pay.

Commissions are a form of compensation calculated as a percentage of transaction amounts that a salesperson or other employee generates. This form of compensation is not based on hours worked or a set yearly salary. Rather, commissioned employees' wages are based on the amount of sales they generate and the percentage of those sales they are paid. Thus, perpetrators on commission fraudulently increase their pay by (1) falsifying the amounts of their sales, or (2) increasing their rate of commission. Commission-based payroll frauds commonly falsify the amount of sales. This is done (1) by creating fictitious sales, (2) by falsifying the value of sales by altering prices on the sales documents, or (3) by overstating sales by claiming sales made by another employee or in another period.

Some commission plans are structured in ways that almost encourage fraud. Take, for example, a graduated commission plan, such as one that pays 5% if sales are less than $100,000, 7% if sales fall between $100,000 and $200,000, and 10% if they exceed $200,000. Working under this system, sales agents have a very strong incentive to generate revenues exceeding $200,000 so they can earn a 10% commission on all sales. Thus, if their total sales fall just short of $200,000, they may be tempted to create "additional revenues" that help them qualify for the higher commission rate.

Workers' compensation is not a payroll account, but rather an insurance expense. It is an employee benefit that entitles employees injured on the job to compensation while they heal. By far the most common way to commit workers' compensation fraud is to fake an injury and collect payments from the victim company's insurance carrier. In some cases, fraudsters collude with doctors, who process bogus claims for unnecessary medical treatments and then split the payments for the fictitious treatments with the "injured" employees.

The primary victim of a workers' compensation scheme is not the employer, but rather the insurance carrier. The insurance carrier pays for the fraudulent medical bills and the unnecessary absences of the perpetrator. Nevertheless, employers are also victims of these crimes because bogus claims often result in higher premiums for the company in the future.

Theft of Inventory and Other Assets

Fraudsters misappropriate company assets other than cash in one of two ways. They misuse (or "borrow") the asset or they steal it. Simple misuse is obviously the less egregious of the two types of fraud. Assets that are misused but not "technically" stolen include company vehicles, company supplies, computers, and other office equipment. These assets are also used by perpetrators to conduct personal work on company time. In many instances, the side businesses are of the same nature as the employer's business, so the fraudster is essentially competing with the employer and using the employer's equipment to do it.

Although the misuse of company property is a problem, the theft of company property is a much greater problem. Losses from inventory theft run into the millions of dollars. The means employed to steal company property range from simple larceny—walking off with company property—to more complicated schemes that involve falsifying company documents and records. Larceny usually involves taking inventory or other assets from the company premises, without attempting to conceal it in the books and records or "justify" its absence. Most noncash larceny schemes are not very complicated. They are typically committed by employees (such as warehouse personnel, inventory clerks, and shipping clerks) who have access to inventory and other assets.

Another common noncash asset theft is the use of asset requisitions and other forms that allow assets to be moved from one location in a company to another location. Often, perpetrators use internal documents to gain access to merchandise that they otherwise might not be able to handle without raising suspicion. Transfer documents allow them to move assets from one location to another and ultimately take the merchandise for themselves. The most basic scheme occurs when fraudsters requisition materials to complete a work-related project and then steal the materials. In more extreme cases, perpetrators completely fabricate a project that necessitates the use of the assets that they want to steal.

A third noncash asset theft uses a company's purchasing and receiving functions. In purchasing-scheme frauds, perpetrators use company funds to purchase items for their personal use. In noncash asset frauds, assets are intentionally purchased by the company and then misappropriated by perpetrators. In these schemes, victim companies lose three ways. The company is deprived not only of the cash it paid for the merchandise, but also of the merchandise itself. And, because the organization doesn't have as much inventory on hand as it thinks it has, stock-outs and unhappy customers often result.

Corruption

The schemes we have discussed thus far in this chapter are asset misappropriation frauds. Perpetrators also commit fraud against organizations through corruption. Corruption and embezzlement are the oldest white-collar crimes. "Paying off" officials, both public and private, for preferential treatment is rooted in our crudest business systems.

Corruption breaks down into four types: (1) bribery, (2) conflicts of interest, (3) extortion, and (4) illegal gratuities. By far the largest of these is bribery, which accounts for 89.2% of all corruption losses, compared to 9% for conflicts of interest, 1.6% for extortion, and 0.2% for illegal gratuities. Although bribery is not as common as some types of fraud, the median loss from bribery is by far the highest of any of the schemes discussed in this chapter—over $500,000 per incident.

Bribery

Bribery involves offering, giving, receiving, or soliciting anything of value in order to influence an official act. The term "official act" means that traditional bribery involves payments made to influence the decisions of government agents or employees. Examples of famous briberies abound. Consider the Teapot Dome scandal that rocked the nation in the early 1920s, and involved key members of President Warren Harding's staff mishandling the leasing of naval oil reserve lands. The paper trail of corruption led directly to the White House Cabinet and nearly implicated President Harding.

A lot of corruption involves commercial bribery, in which something of value is offered to influence a business decision (rather than an official act of government). In commercial bribery, payment is received by corrupt employees without the employer's consent. That is, they accept under-the-table payments in return for influence over a business transaction.

Bribery generally falls into two broad categories: kickbacks and bid-rigging schemes. Kickbacks are undisclosed payments made by vendors to employees of the purchasing companies. The purpose is to enlist the corrupt employee in an overbilling scheme. Sometimes vendors pay kickbacks simply to get extra business from the victim company. Unfortunately, once vendors pay kickbacks, the control of purchasing transactions transfers from the buyer to the vendor. When corrupt vendors are in control of purchasing transactions, goods are sold at higher prices, and their quality can deteriorate substantially.

In Chapter 3, we described the kickback scheme in which Mark-X Corporation bought approximately $11 million of unneeded guard uniforms at higher prices and lower quality. In common kickback schemes vendors submit fraudulent or inflated invoices to the victim company, and corrupt employees of that company make sure that payment is made on the false invoice. For their assistance, these employees receive a kickback from the vendor; it can be cash, reduced prices for goods purchased, the hiring of a relative, the promise of subsequent employment, or numerous other forms. Kickback schemes almost always attack the purchasing function of the victim company.

Bid-rigging schemes occur when corrupt employees help vendors falsely win a contract through "competitive" bidding. This process, in which suppliers or contractors vie for contracts in what can be cutthroat environments, is tailor-made for bribery. Any advantage a vendor gains over competitors in this arena is extremely valuable. The benefit of "inside influence" can ensure that a vendor wins a sought-after contract. Many vendors are willing to pay for this influence. How the bidding is rigged depends largely on the level of influence of the corrupt employee. The more power a person has over the bidding process, the more likely they can influence the selection process. Therefore, employees who participate in bid-rigging schemes (like those in kickback schemes) often have a good measure of influence over the bidding process, or access to influence. Potential targets for bribes include buyers, contracting officials, engineers and technical representatives, quality or product assurance representatives, subcontractor liaison employees—in short, anyone with authority over the awarding of contracts.

Conflicts of Interest

A conflict of interest occurs when an employee, manager, or executive has an undisclosed economic or personal interest in a transaction that adversely affects the company. As with other corruption schemes, conflicts of interest involve corrupt employees exerting influence to the detriment of their company. Conflicts usually involve self-dealing by these employees. In some cases, their act benefits a friend or relative, even though they receive no financial benefit themselves.

To be classified as a conflict of interest scheme, the employee's interest in a transaction must be undisclosed. The essential element in conflict cases is that perpetrators take advantage of their employers: The victim company is unaware that its employee has divided loyalties. If an employer *knows* of the employee's interest in a business deal or negotiation, there can be no conflict of interest, no matter how favorable the arrangement is for the employee.

Conflict schemes fall into one of two categories: purchase schemes and sales schemes. In purchase schemes, corrupt employees (or a friend or relative of the employee) have some kind of undisclosed ownership or employment interest in the vendor that submits the invoice. The bill must originate from a real company in which the perpetrator has an economic or personal interest, and the perpetrator's interest in the company must be undisclosed to the victim company.

In common sales schemes, corrupt employees with a hidden interest have the victim company sell its goods or services below fair market value, which results in a lower profit margin or even a loss on the sale for the company. As an example, a few years ago a large U.S. paper-and-pulp company uncovered a major sales fraud. To get wood for making paper, the company owns its own forests and purchases lumber from others. One of the vendors providing lumber to the company turned out to be a group of its own employees who cut timber on the company's own forest reserves and then sold the timber back to the company. In this case, the company lost twice—it paid for lumber it already owned, and had less of its own lumber to process.

Economic Extortion and Illegal Gratuities

Compared to bribery and conflicts of interests, extortion and illegal gratuities occur relatively infrequently and are usually quite small. Economic extortion is basically the flip side of bribery. Instead of a vendor *offering* payments for influence, corrupt employees *demand* payments from vendors for deciding in the vendors' favor. Thus, situations that are ripe for bribery are also ripe for extortion. Illegal gratuities is really a subcategory of bribery; here corrupt employees are rewarded for making favorable decisions. Illegal gratuities are made after deals are approved.

Summary

The following graphic summarizes the taxonomy used to describe misappropriation and corruption schemes in this chapter. This classification scheme was developed by Joe Wells,

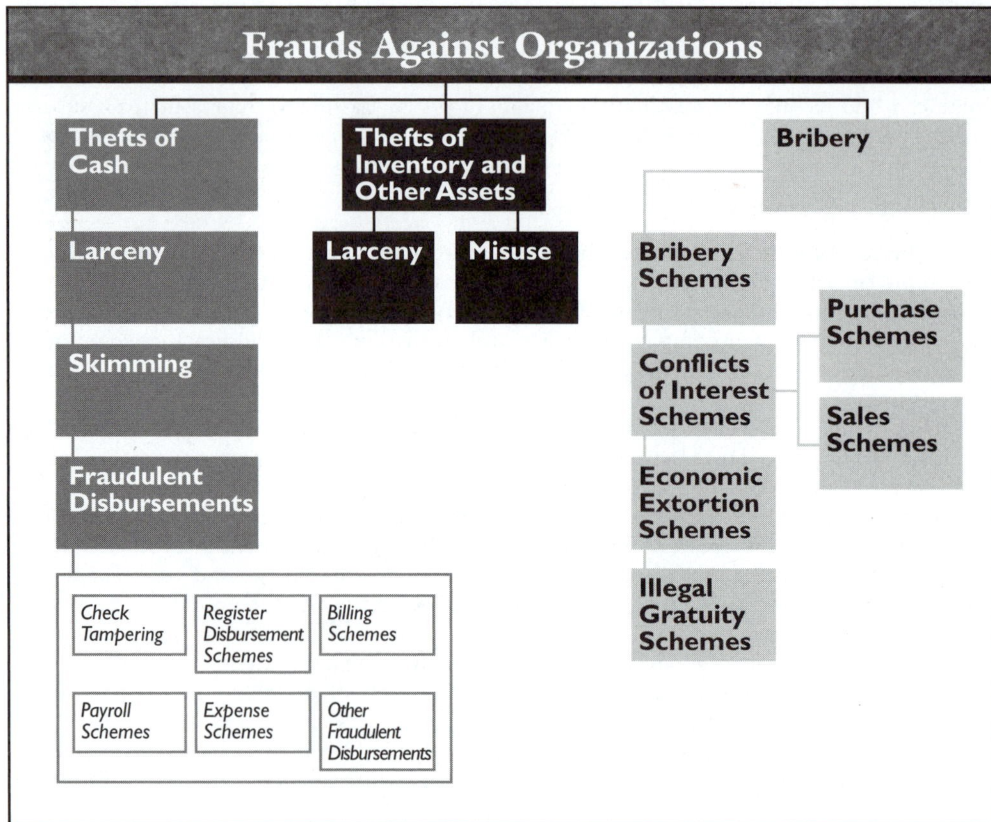

Chairman and CEO of the Association of Certified Fraud Examiners. Although it isn't the only fraud taxonomy available, it is exceptionally complete and is based on an empirical study of over 2,600 frauds.

Organizations that understand the types of frauds that they are particularly vulnerable to can "customize" this taxonomy for their individual situation and thereby pinpoint where their risks are greatest. They can then take proactive steps to reduce and/or eliminate the risks and begin to audit for frauds that may be occurring.

New Terms

Asset misappropriations: Theft that is committed by stealing receipts, stealing assets on hand, or by committing some type of disbursement fraud.

Bid-rigging scheme: Collusive fraud wherein an employee helps a vendor illegally obtain a contract that was supposed to involve competitive bidding.

Billing scheme: Submission of a false or altered invoice that causes an employer to willingly issue a check.

Bribery: The offering, giving, receiving, or soliciting anything of value to influence an official act.

Check tampering: Scheme in which dishonest employees (1) prepare fraudulent checks for their own benefit, or (2) intercept checks intended for a third party and convert the checks for their own benefit.

Corruption: Dishonesty that involves the following schemes: (1) bribery, (2) conflicts of interest, (3) economic extortion, and (4) illegal gratuities.

Disbursement fraud: Having an organization pay for something it shouldn't pay for or pay too much for something it purchases.

Dummy or shell company: Fictitious entity created for the sole purpose of committing fraud; usually involves an employee making fraudulent payments to the dummy company.

Economic extortion scheme: Involves an employee demanding payment from a vendor in order to make or influence a decision in that vendor's favor.

Expense scheme: Scheme in which perpetrators produce false documents to claim false expenses.

Illegal gratuities: Similar to bribery, except that there is no intent to influence a particular business decision, but rather to reward someone for making a favorable decision.

Investment scam: Scheme in which perpetrators deceive individuals into putting their money into a fake investment.

Lapping: Fraud that involves stealing one customer's payment and then crediting that customer's account when a subsequent customer pays.

Larceny: Intentionally taking an employer's cash or other assets without the consent and against the will of the employer, after it has been recorded in the company's accounting system.

Payroll fraud scheme: Using the payroll function to commit fraud, such as creating ghost employees or overpaying wages.

Register disbursement scheme: Scheme that involves false refunds or false voids.

Skimming: Removal of cash from a victim organization prior to its entry in an accounting system.

Questions and Cases

Discussion Questions

1. What three types of occupational fraud schemes do corrupt employees, vendors, and customers use to steal an organization's assets?
2. What is theft of cash through larceny?
3. What is theft of cash through skimming?
4. How does the ACFE categorize fraudulent disbursements?
5. What is check tampering?
6. What is a register-disbursement scheme?
7. What is a billing scheme?
8. What are expense fraud schemes?
9. What are payroll disbursement fraud schemes?
10. What is meant by the term "corruption"?
11. What is meant by the term "bribery"?
12. When does a conflict of interest occur? Give an example.

True/False

1. At the present time, approximately 25,000 members make up the Association of Certified Fraud Examiners.
2. Employee frauds constitute a greater percentage of all frauds and have greater median losses than management and owner frauds combined.
3. Statistics show that fraud losses are directly proportional to age and inversely proportional to education.
4. Larceny, skimming, and misuse are all subdivisions of theft of cash.
5. Skimming schemes are far less common than larceny schemes.
6. Billing schemes have by far the highest median losses per incident of all frauds.
7. Kickback schemes always involve the purchasing function of the victim company.
8. Bribery is one of the four types of corruption.
9. Commercial bribery is different from traditional bribery, in that the offer made in commercial bribery is to influence an official act of government, and traditional briberies never involve government officials.
10. Failure to account for missing inventory that was supposed to have been returned is a problem found in voided sales frauds.
11. Asset misappropriations are divided into two categories: theft of cash and theft of inventory.
12. In larceny, employees steal cash before the cash is recorded in the company's accounting system.
13. Understating sales and stealing cash is an example of skimming.
14. The two basic register-disbursement schemes are false refunds and false voids.
15. Ghost-employee schemes usually generate the largest losses among the payroll disbursement fraud schemes.
16. Corruption is divided into four types of schemes: (1) bribery, (2) conflict of interest, (3) extortion, and (4) illegal services.

17. Kickbacks are undisclosed payments made to vendors by employees of purchasing companies.
18. Compared to bribery and conflicts of interest, economic extortion fraud schemes occur relatively infrequently.
19. Illegal gratuities are made before deals are approved but after payment has been accepted.

Multiple Choice

1. Most frauds against organizations are perpetrated by:
   a. Employees
   b. Owners
   c. Vendors
   d. A collusion of two of the above
2. What are three types of asset misappropriation?
   a. Stealing receipts, purchasing fraud, and disbursement fraud
   b. Stealing receipts, purchasing fraud, and stealing assets on hand
   c. Stealing receipts, disbursement fraud, and stealing assets on hand
   d. Stealing receipts, disbursement fraud, and purchasing fraud
3. Which of the following types of fraud is committed least often?
   a. Skimming schemes
   b. Larceny
   c. Check schemes
   d. Payroll
4. Which of the following is *not* a common billing scheme?
   a. Setting up dummy companies to submit invoices to the victim organization
   b. Changing the quantity or price on an invoice to favor a customer
   c. Altering or double-paying nonaccomplice vendor's statements
   d. Making personal purchases with company funds
5. The most affected party in workers' compensation frauds is which of the following?
   a. Employer
   b. Employer's insurance carrier
   c. Other employees
   d. Government
6. Which of the following is a major difference between larceny and skimming?
   a. Larceny is committed before the cash is entered into the accounting system, whereas skimming is committed after the cash is entered into the system.
   b. Larceny is committed after the cash is entered into the accounting system, whereas skimming is committed before the cash is entered into the system.
   c. Larceny involves fraudulent disbursements of cash, whereas skimming involves fraudulent receipts of cash.
   d. Larceny involves fraudulent receipts of cash, whereas skimming involves fraudulent disbursements of cash.

7. Which of the following disbursement fraud schemes occurs *least frequently*?
   a. Expense tampering
   b. Payroll schemes
   c. Register-disbursement schemes
   d. Billing schemes
8. Which of the following results in the highest loss *per case*?
   a. Expense tampering
   b. Payroll schemes
   c. Register-disbursement schemes
   d. Billing schemes
9. Which of the following is *not* considered a misappropriation of assets?
   a. Payroll disbursement schemes
   b. Kickbacks
   c. Expense schemes
   d. Skimming
10. Which of the following is *not* true of billing schemes?
    a. Perpetrators take physical possession of their employer's cash.
    b. Perpetrators often set up "dummy" companies.
    c. It is one of the most commonly committed disbursement schemes.
    d. It usually involves dealing with the victim organization's purchasing department.

Short Cases

Case 1. Regina has finally landed her dream job at Abercroanie & Fetch. After just a couple of days on the job, we find out why. Often, when customers return merchandise, Regina rings up on her cash register that they return items of higher value than the original pricetag. She then pockets the extra cash and gives the customer the amount due. Regina finds this method very effective because people really are returning something, so inventories and the register totals are not out of balance at the end of the day.

1. What type of fraud is Regina committing?
2. How could her employer detect this kind of fraud?

Case 2. In a Las Vegas casino, an employee discovered a weakness in the accounting system. The accounts payable clerk realized that he could change the names of vendors in the computer to his name. He then created false invoices and issued a check for the false invoice. He next changed the name on the check to his. After the check was printed, he changed the name in the system back to the appropriate vendor. The check register showed only the vendor's name. The employee had authorization to sign checks under $1,000. By writing small checks, he defrauded the company of $10,000. This fraud was caught by accident. An employee in another department was looking through the vendor list on her computer during the period when the fraudster had his name on the invoice, but a few entries later, the invoice showed the vendor's name. Puzzled, she showed the discrepancy to her supervisor, and soon after, the perpetrator was caught.

1. What kind of fraud is being committed?
2. What percent of frauds are of this type?
3. How could this fraud have been prevented?

Case 3. As the assistant to the controller of a small, privately owned company, you create weekly reports of the company's inventories. For the past several months, you have excluded from your report a room full of damaged and obsolete inventory. Although these assets have little or no market value, one of the owners recently found an interested buyer who wants to purchase the goods for scrap material at a deep discount. Even with this discount, the sales price of these items will be approximately $50,000.

The company has been experiencing severe financial difficulties. Today, in fact, the owners filed for bankruptcy. The controller asks you to create one last inventory report, reminding you to ignore the damaged/obsolete inventory as usual. When you ask him about the potential buyer, he says that the owner found the buyer only by a stroke of luck, and that the goods really are worthless, so you should record them as such.

1. What should you do?
2. What issues are involved?

Case 4. Ed Neilson is the purchasing agent for Style, an online women's high-fashion store. He joined the company after graduating from college five years ago, and has now a close relationship with one of the vendors—Sarah Love. Sarah has a small line of exclusive French fashions and accessories. Ed and Sarah became engaged four months ago. Sarah's fashions have historically sold very well in the Style chain, but with the recent decline in the retail industry, high-fashion, high-cost-item sales have decreased substantially. Ed believes this is a short-term trend and thus decides to help his fiancée by guaranteeing $50,000 monthly purchases for Sarah's line.

Is Ed involved in a fraud? If so, what kind of scheme is it, and how might he go about perpetrating it?

Extensive Case

Case 5. In 1987, Bill Eaves worked in the purchasing department of Marion County. In 1990, Eaves became the county's human resources administrator. Five years later, Eaves was promoted to County Administrative Officer (the county's top executive), and he hired James Hart from Billings County to replace him as the county's human resources administrator. In 1999, Eaves retired as County Administrative Officer, but he continued to manage the county as a contract employee while the county searched for his successor. James Hart was eventually selected to replace Eaves.

Following his retirement, Eaves believed county landfills could turn a profit if operated privately, so he asked Bell Waste Systems Company if he could buy them out of their contract to operate some of the county's landfills. Bell Company turned down Eaves's offer, but hired him as a consultant to help it develop and pitch a proposal to take over the operation of all the county's landfills. Eaves asked Hart for help, and Hart promised to help Bell Company win county business in exchange for thousands of dollars in cash or in-kind payments from Eaves. Eaves accepted this exchange.

Eaves signed a consulting agreement with Bell Company, which ultimately paid him $4.6 million. Under the agreement, Bell Company promised to pay Eaves $1 million if the county allowed Bell to operate the county landfill system and $50,000 per month if the garbage dumped at county landfills exceeded 850,000 tons a year. The county then issued municipal bonds to finance landfill closure and postclosure of maintenance.

Hart headed the County Board of Supervisors and approved a contract with Bell to operate all the county's landfills worth more than $20 million a year. Bell started work on the contract. Hart, his friends, and other county officials were given free lodging, meals, fishing, and golf in Cabo San Lucas, the costs of which were covered by Eaves. In addition, Hart signed a promissory note for $90,000 he received from Eaves.

Hernandez Trucking started paying kickbacks to Robert Max, Vice President of Bell Company, equaling about $2 per truckload of dirt delivered to county landfills to cover garbage. Max received approximately $256,000, which he shared with Eaves and Hart.

In January 2001, Eaves, Hart, and Max found themselves under FBI investigation because of a tip from a county official. They were among numerous people to testify in front of a special grand jury convened to investigate a failed trash project and political corruption in the county.

Identify the type of fraud being committed here and explain your reasons.

Internet Assignments

1. Visit the Association of Certified Fraud Examiners web site and read a short introduction on Joe Wells: http://www.cfenet.com//about/josephtwells.asp
    1. What was Mr. Wells's background before he became chairman of the Association of Certified Fraud Examiners? What major aspects of his background would be crucial to his success as a CFE?
    2. What books has Mr. Wells written?
    3. What organizations and/or groups is Mr. Wells currently a member of?
2. Visit the following Internet address: http://www.securitymanagement.com/library/000714.html

    Once you have logged onto the site, read the article "A Fistful of Dollars," by Joe Wells.
    1. According to the article, who is most likely to steal from a company?
    2. According to Mr. Wells, what three areas should a company focus on in order to successfully deter fraud? Which areas of focus do you think would be most effective in deterring fraud?
    3. What is the fourth suggestion to deter and detect fraud in organizations? Do you think this is a cost-beneficial way to deal with occupational fraud?

Debate

Look at the various fraud statistics on pages 430–431 in this chapter. Determine the characteristics of the person most likely to perpetrate a large fraud. Debate why people with certain characteristics are more likely to be fraud perpetrators.

End Notes

1. Bryan Burrough, "David L. Miller Stole from His Employer and Isn't in Prison," *Wall Street Journal* (Sept. 19, 1986):1.
2. Material from *Occupational Fraud and Abuse*, published by Obsidian Publishing Company, Inc., in 1997 (800 West Avenue, Austin, Texas 78701), is used with permission. After working for the FBI, Joe Wells started Wells & Associates, a group of consulting criminologists that concentrates on white-collar crime prevention, detection, and education. That venture led to the formation of the Association of Certified Fraud Examiners, a professional organization of fraud professionals that now has approximately 25,000 members. Since its inception, Joe Wells has been the Chairman of the Board of Directors and CEO.
3. Ibid., p. 131.

Bankruptcy and Divorce Fraud

After studying this chapter, you should be able to understand:

1. Why fraud is so prevalent in bankruptcy and divorce cases.
2. The nature of bankruptcy and the bankruptcy codes.
3. Civil and criminal bankruptcy fraud statutes.
4. Key participants in the bankruptcy process.
5. Different bankruptcy and divorce fraud schemes.
6. How fraudsters conceal and transfer assets and income in bankruptcies and divorces.

Robert Brennan, a former penny-stock tycoon, was convicted in April 2001 of bankruptcy fraud. He was sentenced to jail for 9 years and 2 months on federal convictions. Jurors found Brennan guilty of hiding $4.5 million in assets from the federal government before he filed for bankruptcy in 1995. The legal proceedings spanned six weeks, including 19 days of testimony and arguments that revealed the high-stakes action at the Mirage hotel-casino in Las Vegas and the complexities of international finance.

Brennan was well known in Las Vegas because of his ties to the now-imploded El Rancho hotel-casino on the Strip. At one point, a Brennan company, International Thoroughbred Breeders, talked of redeveloping the dilapidated property into a new casino resort, but the plans never materialized.

The case alleged that Brennan continued to live a lavish lifestyle, despite being millions of dollars in debt. There was testimony from or references to a soap-opera star that Brennan dated, a Catholic cardinal that Brennan knew, international arms trading, and former football coach Bill Parcells, who posted assets for Brennan's bond.

Brennan, 57, was convicted on seven of thirteen counts. The jury was convinced he hid money offshore, and that he cashed in casino chips without reporting them just three weeks after he filed for bankruptcy protection. He was found guilty of spending $100,000 on private flights around the world, but innocent of illegally spending $60,000 on a yacht cruise. Brennan was acquitted on charges that cash was delivered to him in a handoff in a London hotel.

Brennan filed for bankruptcy protection just before he was due to pay millions to compensate First Jersey investors whom Manhattan U.S. District Judge Richard Owen determined that Brennan cheated. This judgment, won by the Securities and Exchange Commission, was for more than $78 million. The ruling led to a series of other legal setbacks for Brennan, who is now barred from the securities industry after regulators found he continued to use high-pressure "boiler room" tactics to sell stocks.

Brennan's bankruptcy fraud represents an ever-growing problem in the United States. Entering false financial information on bankruptcy petitions and schedules is responsible for many of the cases. Fraud in divorce cases is also growing at an alarming rate. Although statistics aren't available, many divorces with significant assets include allegations of fraud. Why is fraud so common in bankruptcies and divorces? Because, in both situations, assets are taken away from one party and given to other parties. To keep their assets from being taken, individuals and organizations often attempt to illegally hide or transfer assets so that they won't be counted in the proceedings. Transfers of assets to offshore bank accounts, relatives, friends, and other hiding places are all too common in both bankruptcy and divorce proceedings.

Although you may know something about divorce, you are probably less familiar with the workings of bankruptcy.[1] Thus, our focus in this chapter is primarily on bankruptcy. Note, however, that motivations for fraud and the schemes for perpetrating it are similar in both situations.

Bankruptcy and divorce fraud can involve criminal or civil proceedings.[2] Criminal divorce and bankruptcy frauds are often investigated by the FBI or other law enforcement agencies. Civil bankruptcy and divorce frauds are investigated by trustees, examiners, creditors, and creditors' committees appointed by Bankruptcy and Divorce Courts.

CPAs and other fraud examiners often play important roles in investigating bankruptcy and divorce frauds. For example, they can:

- Serve as examiners or trustees in bankruptcy cases.
- Serve on creditors' committees or represent creditors' committees by investigating the debtor's financial affairs and preparing investigation reports in bankruptcy cases.
- Assist the U.S. Department of Justice, the Office of the U.S. Trustee, Panel Trustees, and others by preparing detailed reports of investigation findings in bankruptcy cases.
- Assist in recovering assets for creditors in both divorce and bankruptcy cases.
- Serve as private investigators to find hidden assets or examine the lifestyle of the participants in a divorce or bankruptcy.

Bankruptcy and divorce frauds can be categorized as follows:

- *Fraud causes the bankruptcy or divorce.* When fraudulent activity results in too few assets remaining to pay creditors and investors, an entity generally files bankruptcy. Similarly, when marriage partners discover that their marital partner has committed fraud, they may seek divorce to salvage their reputation or because they no longer trust the partner.
- *The bankruptcy or divorce is used to perpetrate the fraud.* During bankruptcy and divorce, courts often grant an automatic "stay"; during this period creditors or marital partners are prohibited from taking action against the debtor or marriage partner. Some debtors and spouses use the stay to perpetrate fraud. For example, they fraudulently transfer assets to other organizations or individuals to prevent them from "being on the table" during negotiation.
- *The bankruptcy or divorce is used to conceal the fraud.* These frauds generally result in the books and records of the debtor/marital partner being destroyed, inaccurate, or hard to locate.

When fraud examiners investigate a "bankruptcy or divorce resulting from fraud," they focus on the fraudulent activity occurring *before* the bankruptcy filing or divorce. Such fraud may be any of the fraud types that we have discussed throughout this book.

In this chapter, we focus on the situations in which bankruptcies and divorces are used to perpetrate fraud or to conceal fraud. Because bankruptcy is more difficult to understand, we first provide an overview of the Bankruptcy Code and the various types of bankruptcy, and then examine the civil and criminal statutes for bankruptcy and divorce fraud. In the third section of this chapter, we discuss the activities of key participants in the bankruptcy and divorce process, and finally, we discuss two common bankruptcy/divorce frauds—bustouts and the concealment of assets or income and fraudulent transfers of assets.

The Bankruptcy Code

When people or organizations are unable to pay their debts and have more liabilities than assets, they can file for bankruptcy. To do this, they file a bankruptcy petition with the courts; this initiates a legal process under the jurisdiction of the U.S. District Court that automatically refers the petition to the Bankruptcy Court. Bankruptcies have several purposes; they give debtors relief from creditors and foreclosure actions and protect creditors from unfair collection efforts by other creditors. A bankruptcy filing follows one of two paths: (1) It allows the debtor to work out an orderly plan to settle debts, *or* (2) it liquidates assets and distributes the proceeds to creditors in a manner that treats creditors with equal status. The filing creates a separate entity, an "estate," that consists of the debtor's property or income that will be used to settle the debts and over which the Bankruptcy Court has control.

Title 11 of the U.S. Code is referred to as the Bankruptcy Code; this is the federal statute that governs the bankruptcy process. The Code provides for several types of bankruptcy. Chapters 1, 3, and 5 in the Code contain general provisions that apply to all bankruptcies, and Chapters 7, 11, and 13 apply to specific types of bankruptcy.

Chapters 7 and 11 are used by corporations or individuals. A Chapter 7 bankruptcy is a complete liquidation or "shutting down of the business." In this situation, all assets are liquidated and used to pay creditors, usually for some percentage of debts owed. In contrast, in a Chapter 11 bankruptcy, the creditors are directed to give the bankrupt entity time to reorganize its operational and financial affairs and settle its debts, so that it can eventually operate in a reorganized fashion. Chapter 13 bankruptcies are reorganizations (similar to Chapter 11) that can be used by individuals who meet certain tests (regular income and debts of $1 million or less). Debtors make regular payments to creditors over a specified number of years under Chapter 13. If reorganization doesn't work in Chapters 11 or 13 bankruptcies, judges often order a complete adjudication, or Chapter 7 bankruptcy.

In Chapter 11 cases, if the bankruptcy court confirms a plan for reorganization (or liquidation) in corporate cases or a discharge in individual cases, it becomes legally binding on the debtor and creditors. Only obligations provided for in the reorganized plan remain (settled in the amount, time, and manner provided for in the plan). If assets are liquidated, the proceeds are distributed to creditors in the order of priority specified in the Bankruptcy Code. For example, secured creditors are usually paid before unsecured creditors.

Civil and Criminal Bankruptcy Fraud Statutes

Criminal bankruptcy fraud cases are generally prosecuted by the U.S. Attorney's office in U.S. District Court, and the government must prove its case beyond a reasonable doubt. Convictions can result in jail sentences or other criminal penalties.

Here are some relevant sections of the Bankruptcy Code as it relates to criminal fraud:

Concealment of Assets, False Oaths and Claims, and Bribery (18 USC 152).[3] This section makes it a crime for a person to "knowingly and fraudulently" do any of the following:

- Conceal property of a debtor's estate from creditors or from the bankruptcy trustee, custodian, or other officer of the court charged with custody of the property.
- Make a false oath or account in a bankruptcy case.

- Make a false declaration, certification, verification, or statement under penalty of perjury, such as intentionally omitting property, debt, or income from an Official Form required in a bankruptcy case. The court may infer fraudulent intent from the existence of an unexplained false statement if the debtor cannot prove that the false statement was an unintentional, honest mistake.
- Present a false proof of claim against the debtor's estate. A proof of claim is a document filed with the bankruptcy court by a creditor stating the nature and amount of the claim against the debtor. The debt settlement plan takes into account "allowed" claims—that is, claims that the bankruptcy court accepts as valid claims. A creditor would be the likely perpetrator of this crime.
- Receive a "material amount of property" from a debtor after the filing of a bankruptcy petition, with the "intent to defeat the provisions" of the Bankruptcy Code.
- "Give, offer, receive, or attempt to obtain money or property, remuneration, compensation, reward, advantage or promise thereof for acting or forbearing to act" in a bankruptcy case.
- In a personal capacity or as an agent or officer of a person or corporation, transfer or conceal his or the other person's or corporation's property, in contemplation of a bankruptcy case involving himself or the other person or corporation, or with the "intent to defeat the provisions" of the Bankruptcy Code.
- In contemplation of a bankruptcy filing, or after such a filing, "conceal, destroy, mutilate, falsify, or make a false entry in any recorded information (including books, documents, records, and papers)" relating to the debtor's "property or financial affairs."
- After a bankruptcy filing, "withhold any recorded information (including books, documents, records, and papers)" relating to the debtor's "property or financial affairs" from a custodian, trustee, or other officer of the court.

Obviously, this statute targets fraudulent acts by people or organizations filing bankruptcy. Note that although criminal statutes for divorce aren't as specific as those for bankruptcy, the same types of offenses can be criminally prosecuted in divorce cases.

Embezzlement Against the Debtor's Estate (18 USC 153). This section applies to bankruptcy trustees, custodians, attorneys, or other court officers, and to anyone engaged by a court officer to perform a service for a debtor's estate. The statute makes it a crime for such persons to "knowingly and fraudulently appropriate to [their] own use, embezzle, spend, or transfer" any property, or to hide or destroy any document, belonging to the debtor's estate. This section of the Code focuses on those who are appointed to assist in the orderly transfer of assets in a bankruptcy. As an example of a prosecution under this section of the Code, a court-appointed trustee was convicted of stealing $15 million from a debtor's assets before the remaining assets were distributed to creditors. Similarly, many divorce lawyers hired to assist in divorce cases of the wealthy have been prosecuted for misappropriating assets of the divorced couple.

Adverse Interest and Conduct of Officers (18 USC 154). This section prohibits a custodian, trustee, marshal, or other court officer from knowingly:

- Purchasing, directly or indirectly, any property of the debtor's estate of which the person is an officer in a bankruptcy case.
- Refusing to permit a reasonable opportunity for the inspection by parties in interest of the documents and accounts relating to the affairs of the estate in the person's charge when directed by the court to do so.

- Refusing to permit a reasonable opportunity for the inspection by the U.S. Trustee of the documents and accounts relating to the affairs of the estate in the person's charge.

This section of the Code targets conflicts of interest by those appointed or hired to equitably dissolve assets in bankruptcy cases. For example, this section makes it an offense for court-appointed individuals to purchase property of a debtor for fear that an unreasonably low price will be paid.

Bankruptcy Fraud. This section makes it a crime to do any of the following to execute or conceal a fraud scheme:

- File a bankruptcy petition.
- File a document in a bankruptcy proceeding.
- Make a false or fraudulent representation, claim, or promise with respect to a bankruptcy proceeding, either before or after the bankruptcy petition is filed.

The bankruptcy fraud section is the "catchall" section that prohibits every other type of fraud associated with bankruptcies.

Civil Bankruptcy Statutes

As you learned earlier in this course, criminal laws endeavor to "right a wrong" or send someone to jail or have them pay fines, and civil laws endeavor to find monetary remedies in order to recover stolen funds.

Bankruptcy cases often involve civil proceedings conducted in the U.S. Bankruptcy Court. Plaintiffs may seek remedies when they are damaged by inappropriate conduct, for example, in a fraudulent transfer matter. The plaintiff (who is usually a trustee) need only demonstrate a preponderance of evidence (or sometimes clear and convincing evidence) that the defendant (normally the debtor or a related party) is liable for civil remedies. The specific remedies that are sought depend on the charges involved. The following are some of the most pertinent sections of the Bankruptcy Code that provide civil remedies for bankruptcy fraud.

Offenses Leading to Revocation of Debt Discharge in Chapter 11 and Chapter 13 Cases. Section 1144 of the Bankruptcy Code provides for the revocation of a Chapter 11 reorganization plan and for the revocation of debt forgiveness or discharge in a Chapter 11 bankruptcy if the plan's approval was obtained through fraudulent means.[4] Similarly, Code Section 1328(e) provides for the revocation of debt forgiveness or discharge in a Chapter 13 case if the discharge was obtained through fraud actions. Sections 1144 and 1328(e) are not specific as to what constitutes fraud, but they include intentional deceit and criminal action. As an example of the type of fraud targeted by this section, if a debtor lies about (usually by understating) the amount of his or her assets in order to get the debts forgiven, the forgiveness or discharge of the debts may be revoked.

Fraudulent Transfers. Section 548 of the Bankruptcy Code defines a fraudulent transfer as a transfer made, or obligation incurred, *within one year before the bankruptcy petition's filing date* that was:

1. Made with the actual intent to hinder, delay, or defraud creditors, for example, by giving debtor property to relatives with the intent of placing it beyond the reach of creditors, or

2. Made for less than reasonably equivalent value if
   - The debtor is insolvent or becomes insolvent as a result of the transfer, or
   - The debtor's capital remaining after the transfer is unreasonably small (for instance, the debtor is constantly behind in paying bills after the transfer), or
   - The debtor intends to incur debts or believed that debts would be incurred that could not be repaid at maturity.

This statute is a workhorse in the Bankruptcy Code because hiding assets or trading or selling them at amounts below market value to relatives or friends is a very common fraud.

Participants in the Bankruptcy Process

As a fraud investigator, you need to understand the roles of these key participants in the bankruptcy process: Bankruptcy Court, U.S. Trustee, court-appointed trustee or panel trustee, examiner, debtor, creditors, and adjusters (operations or field agents).

Bankruptcy Court. Bankruptcy petitions are filed with the U.S. Bankruptcy Clerk's Office. All bankruptcy petitions are subject to U.S. District Court jurisdiction, but are automatically referred to the U.S. Bankruptcy Court for supervision. Bankruptcy judges hear cases involving debtors' and creditors' rights, approve reorganization plans, award professional fees, and conduct hearings and trials to resolve disputes. Divorce Courts play a similar role in divorce hearings.

U.S. Trustee. The Office of the U.S. Trustee is an agency in the Department of Justice that is responsible for such functions as:

- Administering bankruptcy cases
- Appointing trustees, examiners, and Chapter 11 committees
- Overseeing and monitoring trustees
- Reviewing employees and fee applications
- Appearing in court on matters of interest to the debtor's estate and creditors

A U.S. Trustee or Assistant Trustee heads each of the 21 regions in the United States. Each regional office of the U.S. Trustee may have the following staff:

- *Staff attorneys,* who review fee applications, motions to appoint trustees and examiners, motions to convert or dismiss a case, and other pleadings. They also represent the U.S. Trustee as a party in interest.
- *Bankruptcy analysts,* who review operating reports and other financial information and oversee the debtor's case to assure compliance with the Bankruptcy Code and to protect the estate's assets.
- *Special investigative units (SIUs).* Some regions have SIUs that investigate criminal complaints in bankruptcy cases.

Court-Appointed or Panel Trustee. Court-appointed or panel trustees are individuals or firms, such as accountants or lawyers, who identify and collect a debtor's assets and then allocate those assets to creditors in an orderly manner. The duties of a court-appointed or panel trustee in Chapter 7 cases, as set forth in 11 USC 704, are as follows:

1. Collect and liquidate the property of the debtor's estate and close the estate as quickly as is compatible with the best interests of parties in interest.
2. Account for all property received.

3. Ensure that the debtor files the statement of intention to retain or surrender property as specified in 11 USC 521 (2)(B).
4. Investigate the financial affairs of the debtor.
5. If necessary, examine proofs of claims and object to improper claims.
6. If appropriate, oppose the discharge of the debtor.
7. Furnish information about the estate and its administration when requested by a party in interest, unless the court orders otherwise.
8. If the business of the debtor is authorized to be operated, file with the court, the U.S. Trustee, and any applicable tax-collecting governmental unit, periodic reports and summaries of the operation of the business, including a statement of receipts and disbursements and such other information as the U.S. Trustee or the court requires.
9. Make a final report and file a final account of the administration of the estate with the court and with the U.S. Trustee.

In Chapter 11 cases, the court-appointed or panel trustee's duties, as set forth in 11 USC 1106, are as follows:

1. Perform the duties of the trustee specified in items 2, 5, 7, 8, and 9 in the preceding list.
2. If the debtor has not done so, file the list, schedule, and statement required under 11 USC 521 (1).
3. Except to the extent that the court orders otherwise, investigate the acts, conduct, assets, liabilities, and financial condition of the debtor, the operation of the debtor's business and the desirability of the continuance of that business, and any other matter relevant to the case or to the formulation of a plan.
4. As soon as practical:
   - File a statement of any investigation conducted under item 3, above, including any fact ascertained pertaining to fraud, dishonesty, incompetence, misconduct, mismanagement, or irregularity in the management of the affairs of the debtor, or to a cause of action available to the estate.
   - Transmit a copy or a summary of any such statement to any creditors' committee or equity security holders' committee, to any indenture trustee, and to such other entity as the court designates.
5. As soon as practical, file a reorganization plan under 11 USC 1121, file a report of why the trustee will not file a plan, or recommend conversion of the case to a case under Chapters 7, 12, or 13 or dismissal of the case.
6. For any year for which the debtor has not filed a tax return required by law, furnish, without personal liability, such information as may be required by the governmental unit with which such tax return was to be filed, in light of the condition of the debtor's books and records and the availability of such information.
7. After confirmation of a plan, file such reports as are necessary or as the court orders.

Bankruptcy trustees often hear allegations of fraud by the debtor or its principals. In Chapter 11 cases, alleged fraud is generally the reason the court appoints a trustee. The trustee's authority to investigate fraud involves investigating the affairs of the debtor in Chapter 7 bankruptcies and (1) investigating the acts, conduct, assets, liabilities, and financial condition of the debtor, the operation of the debtor's business and the desirability of the continuance of such business, and (2) filing a statement of investigation conducted in the case of a Chapter 11 bankruptcy. If the trustee conducts an investigation and decides that sufficient evidence of bankruptcy fraud exists, a report on the results of the investigation should be filed with the U.S. Attorney.

The trustee has significant powers to gather information in an investigation. A trustee, in effect, assumes the role of the debtor with all the rights thereto. Thus, the trustee can obtain information from the debtor's attorneys and accountants. The trustee can even break the attorney-client privilege because the trustee becomes the client. The trustee can also obtain access to the debtor's records that are in the hands of the criminal authorities.

Examiners. Examiners (usually some type of fraud examiner or investigator) are appointed by bankruptcy judges in Chapter 11 proceedings to investigate allegations of fraud or misconduct by the debtor or its principals. The examiner investigates and reports the results of the investigation to the court and other interested parties as soon as possible. Examiners can subpoena records and depose witnesses. Generally, they cannot operate businesses, make business decisions, or propose reorganization plans. However, the court may expand an examiner's role to perform some functions of the trustees or debtors-in-possession.[5]

Debtors. A debtor is the "person" or "entity" who is the subject of a Chapter 11 filing. A debtor in an involuntary or "forced" bankruptcy proceeding is called an "alleged debtor."

The debtor's primary goal in a bankruptcy proceeding is to settle its obligations as favorably to its interest as possible. Individual debtors often commit bankruptcy fraud by concealing assets or making false statements on office forms. Organizations who commit bankruptcy fraud often inflate debt and underreport assets.

Creditors. A creditor is defined as one who holds a valid claim against a debtor. The Bankruptcy Code allows committees to represent classes of creditors. In Chapter 11 cases, creditors' committees have the power to investigate the acts, conduct, and financial condition of a debtor and any other matters relevant to the case.

Adjusters. Adjusters are also known as operations or field agents. Adjusters assist the trustee by performing such duties as securing business facilities and assets, locating assets of the debtor's estate, locating business records, opening new bank accounts, investigating asset thefts, and arranging asset sales.

Participants in Divorce Cases

Divorce laws and statutes are much simpler than bankruptcy laws. Divorce actions are usually initiated by disgruntled spouses who believe they have been "wronged" or "injured" in some way.[6] The parties involved include the husband and wife, attorneys for both sides, and a Divorce Court. When allegations of fraud arise (such as hiding or illegally transferring assets), attorneys for the party alleging fraud frequently hire investigators to locate the hidden assets. Investigative techniques include surveillance, public records searches, and subpoenas of private records. Evidence discovered by hired investigators is presented to the Divorce Court by attorneys to obtain favorable divorce settlements. Most divorce fraud cases are civil cases, but when evidence of *egregious* fraudulent acts by one marital partner exist, law enforcement officials may be called in to investigate, and criminal charges can be filed.

Fraud Investigator's Relationship to Participants in Bankruptcy Proceedings

Code Section 327(a) allows trustees to employ, with the court's approval, attorneys, accountants, or other professionals to represent or assist the trustee. Also, Code Section 1103 allows a creditors' committee to employ, with the court's approval, attorneys, accountants, or their agents to perform services for the committee. Although the Code does not specifically authorize it, Bankruptcy Courts typically allow examiners to employ CFEs and even CPAs and other professionals. Fraud examiners and accountants may be used to conduct fraud investigations and to provide consulting and other financial services.

Before professionals can be compensated from estate funds, they must be employed under Code Section 327. The court must approve the employment of those professionals. Code Section 330 sets forth the conditions regarding compensation of professionals and lists specific requirements relating to retention.

A creditor may engage a CFE, CPA, or other professional independently from the court to investigate allegations of bankruptcy fraud. In such cases, the creditor usually compensates the investigator directly without court approval. Under certain conditions, the creditor may apply to the court to have the costs of the investigation paid by the state if they result in criminal prosecution.

The retention of a fraud examiner or investigator in a bankruptcy proceeding must be approved by the bankruptcy judge. This approval is required whenever the investigator is paid by the debtor's estate, whether the investigator is engaged by the debtor, trustee, debtor-in-possession, creditors' committee, or stockholders. However, in the rare cases in which an investigator provides services to, and is directly paid by, an individual creditor or stockholder, these requirements do not apply.

When a fraud investigator is retained, an affidavit of a proposed investigator is prepared. (See the sample affidavit in Appendix A at the end of the chapter.) The affidavit is addressed to the court and is submitted by the attorney for the person or entity who engaged the investigator (such as the trustee, examiner, or creditors' committee) as part of the application for retention. The affidavit is a legal document that is sworn under oath (under penalties of perjury) and that must be notarized. The exact content and extent of detail required in an affidavit vary by jurisdiction.

A description of the proposed services is particularly important. U.S. Trustees require the services of professionals to be categorized and have developed broad categories of service. One such category is litigation consulting, which includes fraud examination or forensic accounting. Fraud investigation services come under this category. Another category is asset analysis and recovery, which is relevant to an engagement to search for possible fraudulent transfers.

The description of services should be reasonably detailed, but the extent of detail required depends on the preferences of the bankruptcy judge. In considering the request for compensation, the judge will compare actual services rendered to proposed services in the application and order for retention. Judges often disallow compensation for services that were not authorized.

Once the services of the fraud investigator are approved, an application for retention is prepared by the attorney for the person engaging the investigator; it is based primarily on information in the affidavit and discussions with the investigator. (See sample application in Appendix B at the end of the chapter.)

Once the application for retention is approved, the judge issues an order authorizing the services. Investigators should always secure a signed order before they begin work.

The Planned Bankruptcy Fraud

The two most common bankruptcy frauds are the planned bankruptcy (the "bustout") and the illegal concealment of assets during, or in contemplation of, a bankruptcy. This latter scheme is also common in divorce cases.

Bustouts can take several forms, but all involve intentionally obtaining loans or purchasing inventory on a credit basis and concealing, or absconding with, the proceeds from the loan or sale of the inventory or with the inventory itself before the creditors are paid. Insolvency is declared and bankruptcy is filed, but the creditors find that no assets are left with which to pay the creditors. If the scam works, the perpetrators retain the proceeds from the loan and sales or take the inventory, but they escape liability for the debt. Government statistics estimate that losses to creditors from bustouts amount to $1 billion a year.

Perpetrators involved in bustouts either set up new companies or use established companies. In the first scheme, perpetrators set up a new company and operate it legitimately for a while in order to establish credibility (a reputation for honesty) and a credit rating with banks (that provide loans) or suppliers (who sell goods on credit). The new company may take a name similar to a well-known, reputable company in order to trick unwary lenders and suppliers into thinking they are dealing with the well-known company or with its subsidiary or affiliate. The scam company may also submit intentionally misstated financial statements to suppliers or creditors to inflate its financial position and profitability.

In the second bustout scheme, perpetrators quietly buy an established company with a good reputation and credit rating and take over its management. Credit-rating agencies are usually not aware of the ownership/management change. The perpetrators then rely on the established credit rating to get credit from suppliers and loans from banks.

In both schemes, perpetrators buy large amounts of inventory on credit from numerous suppliers. They may also obtain bank loans. At first, the perpetrators pay suppliers promptly; this builds up their credit rating and encourages suppliers to extend more credit. To pay suppliers, the perpetrators borrow from banks or sell the goods at deep discounts through co-conspirators in other markets. (The merchandise is usually of a type that can be sold quickly at cost.) The perpetrators buy more inventory on credit and eventually stop paying the suppliers. They stockpile the inventory and either conceal it for later sale in another location or secretly liquidate it at bargain prices. If the perpetrators obtain bank loans, they siphon off some or all of the proceeds into accounts of hidden "shell" corporations.

The perpetrators then either claim insolvency and file for bankruptcy or simply close up shop and abscond with the money. The company appears to be insolvent because their bargain or liquidation prices reduced profits and cash flow, and the siphoning off of the sales proceeds reduced assets and cash. Of course, the liabilities to lenders and suppliers remain. If the perpetrators flee without filing for bankruptcy, the unpaid lenders and suppliers may file an involuntary bankruptcy petition against the company. In either case, however, the lenders and suppliers find that there are few or no assets left in the company for paying creditors.

In bustouts, perpetrators intend from the beginning to make the company insolvent and to either file bankruptcy or skip town. Note that if the perpetrators do not file a bankruptcy petition, they cannot be charged with bankruptcy fraud. Almost all bustout schemes involve concealing assets—either sales or loan proceeds, or inventory.

Bustouts can be hard to detect. If a company claims insolvency and files for bankruptcy, creditors can't always detect that the insolvency is the result of actions deliberately taken to perpetrate a fraud. The following are flags that indicate the bankruptcy is a bustout:

1. A company's only listed address and phone number are a post office box and an answering service. (Investigators should be aware that post office boxes can appear as street addresses.)
2. A new company is owned and managed by people from another state, or the company is vague about its ownership or type of business.
3. A sudden change is made in management, especially if the change is made without public notice.
4. Credit references either cannot be verified or seem too eager to provide favorable references. (These may be phony or collusive references.)
5. The size of orders placed on credit and the credit balances with suppliers suddenly and dramatically increase.

6. The inventory suddenly disappears, without explanation.
7. "Customers" have a history of buying goods at unreasonable discounts.

Fraudulent Concealment of Assets or Income in Bankruptcies or Divorces

Although bustouts are unique to bankruptcy, fraudulent concealment of assets or income is a common fraud in both bankruptcy and divorce. In this section, we discuss what constitutes the debtor's or divorce partner's estate (that is, what assets and income might be concealed), methods of concealment, and investigation procedures.

The Debtor's or Divorce Partner's Estate

When a company or individual (including someone who owns an unincorporated business) files for bankruptcy under Chapters 7, 11, or 13 of the Bankruptcy Code, or an individual files or is involved in a divorce, an estate is created. This estate consists of the property (or income, in some cases) of the debtor or divorce partner that will be used to settle debts and over which the Bankruptcy or Divorce Court has control. In a Chapter 7 bankruptcy, the estate assets are liquidated and the proceeds are used to settle debts. In Chapters 11 or 13 bankruptcies, some of the estate's assets may be liquidated or turned over to creditors to settle debt, but most estate assets are normally not liquidated or turned over to creditors because Chapters 11 and 13 bankruptcies allow the individual or organization to retain assets and to settle debts from future income. In a divorce case, the estate or assets of the married couple are usually divided between the two spouses after the couple's debts are paid.

Generally, the debtor's estate or divorce partner's assets consist of all property as of the date the bankruptcy or divorce petition was filed and the postpetition proceeds or earnings from such property. For example, an estate could include a building owned as of the petition date and the rent earned from the building during the postpetition period. Or, an estate could include postpetition collections of accounts receivable that existed as of the petition date.

Bankruptcy Statutes Concerning Concealment of Assets

Title 18, Section 152, of the U.S. Code makes it a crime to knowingly and fraudulently conceal property of a debtor's estate or to falsify any documents, records, or statements during, or in contemplation of, a bankruptcy. As previously discussed, the Bankruptcy Code provides for revocation of debt forgiveness or discharge obtained through fraud, including (the authors believe) concealment of assets or intentional misstatement of records or statements filed in the case. Even if the debtor is not convicted of criminal or civil fraud, concealed assets or income that are located can be brought back into the estate to be used to settle debts.

Concealing Assets or Income

As previously noted, concealment of assets or income is a common bankruptcy and divorce fraud. The following are some ways in which assets or income are concealed:

1. Cash received in payment of receivables is diverted to another entity, usually a related party.
2. Inventory is shipped to an off-site location or sold to a related party, fence, or other co-conspirator at a steeply discounted price.

3. Assets or income is shifted to another entity controlled by the debtor or a divorced party. The transfer may be accomplished by changing the title to assets, by depositing amounts into accounts of other individuals or companies, or by paying bogus or padded fees and expenses.
4. Sales are not reported in the debtor company's books; instead the sales proceeds are diverted.
5. Payments are made to fictitious individuals or vendors and the amounts diverted to the debtor or to a divorced party. Also, payments to conspiring vendors or individuals are padded, or purchase discounts are not recorded, and overpayment is diverted to the debtor or a spouse.
6. Income from controlled organizations is intentionally understated by overstating expenses. Also, the debtor company can pay excessive compensation to owners.
7. The debtor's personal expenses are paid by the company and mischaracterized as business expenses.
8. The debtor's or divorced partner's books and records or other financial information are damaged or hidden.
9. Interests in partnerships, corporations, lawsuit proceeds, and so on, are not disclosed.

Indicators of Concealment

Some indicators of possible asset or income concealment include the following:

1. Transfers of property or large payments to related parties or individuals, such as insiders, shareholders, or relatives
2. Frequent and unusual transfers between bank accounts, particularly between business and personal accounts
3. Transactions frequently made in cash but normally made on account (sales, purchases, etc.)
4. Unusually large payments to particular vendors that are not explainable
5. Unusual or rapid reductions in assets
6. Increases in operating losses that are not explained by economic factors facing the company or individual
7. Inconsistencies between financial statements or tax returns and the Official Forms filed for the bankruptcy or the records filed in divorce cases
8. Travel to off-shore tax havens or locations that allow secret bank accounts
9. Missing, inaccurate, or damaged records

Fraudulent Transfers

Section 548 of the Bankruptcy Code defines a fraudulent transfer as a transfer made, or obligation incurred, within one year before the bankruptcy petition's filing date that was

1. Made with the intent to hinder, delay, or defraud creditors, for example, by giving debtor property to relatives with the intent of placing it beyond the reach of creditors, *or*
2. Made for less than the reasonably equivalent value if:
   - The debtor was insolvent or became insolvent as a result of the transfer (insolvency for this purpose is defined beginning in paragraph 906.5), *or*
   - The debtor's capital remaining after the transfer was unreasonably small (for instance, the debtor was constantly behind in paying bills after the transfer), *or*
   - The debtor intended to, or believed it would, incur debts it would be unable to repay when they matured.

Part 1 of this definition constitutes actual fraud, for which fraudulent intent must be shown. Part 2 constitutes constructive fraud, for which intent to defraud need not be shown, as long as one of the conditions in part 2 is met. The one-year cutoff date applies to either type of fraudulent transfer. However, in bankruptcy cases, longer cutoff periods can be designated if state statutes apply.

Note that a fraudulent transfer may be made with or without actual intent to defraud creditors. The statutes discussed in Section 901 apply when *actual intent* to defraud creditors is proved. Also, the Bankruptcy Court can void (cancel) the transfer and bring the property back into the estate for use to settle debts.

The Bankruptcy Code also contains provisions that apply when a transfer meets the Code's definition of constructive fraud, even if the transfer cannot be shown to involve actual intent to defraud creditors. The Bankruptcy Court can void constructively fraudulent transfers and bring the assets back into the estate for use to settle debts.

Civil Liability for False Accusations

An important issue for fraud investigators in bankruptcy and divorce cases is the risk of civil liability for false accusations. Debtors and divorced partners often have little to lose by challenging investigators on every word in their report. In this situation, investigators may find themselves on the defensive. Investigators should take great care to ensure that all report findings and conclusions are properly supported with evidence. Unsupported conclusions can expose investigators to charges of false accusations, which can result in costly civil litigation.

Summary

Fraud is common in divorces and bankruptcies because, in both situations, assets are being taken away from one party and given to the other party. To keep assets from being taken, involved parties often attempt to fraudulently hide or transfer assets so they can't be discovered. Both bankruptcy and divorce fraud can be criminal and civil matters.

Bankruptcies go through a legal process under the jurisdiction of a U.S. District Court that automatically refers the case to a Bankruptcy Court. Title 11 of the U.S. Code is the federal statute that governs the bankruptcy process. A Chapter 7 bankruptcy is a complete liquidation of all assets, whereas a Chapter 11 bankruptcy provides the bankrupt entity some time to reorganize its operational and financial affairs, settle its debts and continue to operate in a reorganized fashion.

Divorce laws are much simpler than bankruptcy laws. Divorce actions are initiated by disgruntled spouses who believe they have been "wronged" or "injured" in some way. Most divorce cases are handled civilly, and fraud examiners may be hired by the attorneys for one party or the other to locate hidden assets or to discover or validate suspected inappropriate activity by a spouse.

Some bankruptcies and divorces are planned in advance in order to perpetrate fraud. A bustout, for example, is a planned bankruptcy whereby the perpetrators intentionally obtain loans or purchase inventory on a credit basis and then conceal or abscond with the proceeds from the loan or sale of inventory before creditors are paid.

Because bankruptcy statutes are detailed and complicated, fraud examiners should make sure that their terms of employment are both approved by the appropriate officials and consistent with legal requirements. Divorce-related assignments, on the other hand, are typically contractual arrangements where the terms can vary from case to case.

New Terms

Bankruptcy: A legal process that either allows a debtor to work out an orderly plan to settle debts or to liquidate a debtor's assets and distribute them to creditors.

Bankruptcy Code: Title 11 of the U.S. Code—the federal statute that governs the bankruptcy process.

Bankruptcy Court: The federal court that supervises all bankruptcy proceedings.

Bustout: A planned bankruptcy.

Chapter 7 bankruptcy: Complete liquidation or "shutting down of a business" and distribution of any proceeds to creditors.

Chapter 11 bankruptcy: Bankruptcy that allows the bankrupt entity time to reorganize its operational and financial affairs, settle its debts, and continue to operate in a reorganized fashion.

Creditor: A person or entity owed money by a debtor.

Debtor: A person or entity declaring bankruptcy.

Divorce: The legal separation of two married partners resulting in the dissolution of their marriage.

Trustee: Individual or firm who collects a debtor's assets and distributes them to creditors.

Questions and Cases

Discussion Questions

1. What are the purposes of bankruptcy?
2. Are bankruptcy and divorce fraud civil or criminal matters?
3. What is the difference between Chapter 11 and Chapter 7 bankruptcies?
4. How are bankruptcy petitions filed?
5. What is a fraud examiner's role in bankruptcy fraud cases?
6. What are the two most common bankruptcy fraud schemes?
7. What are some common means of concealing assets or income?
8. Why do fraud investigators need to be careful of civil liability for false accusations?

True/False

1. Civil bankruptcy cases are usually investigated by the FBI and other law enforcement agencies.
2. A person acting as an officer in a bankruptcy case is prohibited from purchasing any property of the debtor's estate.
3. Fraudulent transfers can occur up to two years before the debtor files for bankruptcy.
4. Bustout schemes involve the concealment of assets, sales proceeds, and inventory.
5. Debtors in bankruptcy cases can sue investigators over false accusations.
6. Chapter 11 bankruptcies represent the complete liquidation or shutting down of a business.

7. A "debtor" is the person or entity who is subject to a bankruptcy filing.
8. Most divorce-related fraud cases are civil rather than criminal.
9. The retention of a fraud investigator in a bankruptcy case must always be approved by the bankrupt's judge.
10. A "planned bankruptcy" is called a bustout.

Multiple Choice

1. Which of the following describes a Chapter 13 bankruptcy?
   a. All assets are liquidated and used to pay creditors.
   b. Reorganizations can be used by individuals with debts less than a million dollars.
   c. The entity is given time to reorganize its financial affairs, settle debts, and continue operations.
   d. Debtors receive all their payments up front from liquidated assets.
2. Which of the following is *not* a section of the Bankruptcy Code relating to fraud?
   a. Concealment, false oaths, and bribery
   b. Embezzlement against the debtor's estate
   c. Illegal liquidation of assets and processes to settle debts
   d. Adverse interest and conduct of officers
3. Bankruptcy courts do *not* have which of the following responsibilities?
   a. Appoint trustees, examiners, and committees
   b. Supervise bankruptcy petitions
   c. Approve reorganization plans
   d. Conduct hearings and trials to resolve disputes
4. Which of the following is *not* a characteristic of an affidavit of a proposed investigator?
   a. Content and the detail required do not vary by jurisdiction.
   b. Document is prepared when a fraud investigator is retained.
   c. Legal document is sworn under oath and must be notarized.
   d. Document is addressed to the court and is submitted by an attorney for the person who engaged the investigator.
5. Which of the following is the least likely symptom of a possible "bustout"?
   a. Company's only listed address is a post office box.
   b. Size of credit orders has dramatically increased.
   c. Public notice of change in management is posted.
   d. Inventory suddenly decreases.
6. Which of the following is the major reason for so much divorce fraud?
   a. Assets are being taken away from one divorce partner and are given to another.
   b. Divorce proceedings usually take a long time.
   c. States make divorces very difficult.
   d. Children usually get most assets in divorce cases.

7. Which of the following investigative methods is used more often in divorce cases than in bankruptcy cases?
   a. Surveillance
   b. Public records searches
   c. Subpoena of private records
   d. Interviews
8. The retention of a fraud investigator in a bankruptcy proceeding must be approved by the bankruptcy judge *unless*:
   a. The debtor's estate pays the investigator.
   b. The trustee pays the investigator.
   c. The creditors' committee pays the investigator.
   d. An individual creditor or shareholder pays the investigator.
9. Which of the following is *not* an indicator of a possible bustout?
   a. An address that is a post office box
   b. New ownership of a company
   c. Slow buildup of inventory
   d. Dramatic increase in the size of credit orders
10. Which of the following may indicate possible concealment of assets in a divorce?
    a. Assets transferred to an off-site location
    b. Changing the title to assets
    c. Payments made to fictitious individuals
    d. All of the above

Short Cases

Case 1. Brothers Willy and Buck Forsythe specialize in shady business deals and swindle people with depressing regularity. Willy and Buck have embarked on a new "venture." A small hardware store in town, Pop's, has a good reputation for honesty and friendly service. Willy and Buck decide to use the money they have accumulated from other schemes to buy Pop's. They make the owner an offer he can't refuse, and they are soon in the hardware business.

As Pop's new managers, Willy and Buck make some key changes. They order bigger shipments from suppliers and pay them off promptly, using money they acquired through loans. They sell off a lot of these shipments at cost to their unruly friend Billy the Kid. Because payments remain prompt, suppliers are willing to extend more and more credit to Pop's new owners. Also, business appears to be good, so the bank lends more money.

Things are going just as planned for our crooked friends. The moment they have a good stash of cash from bank loans, they sell off huge amounts of inventory that they purchased on credit to Billy and file for bankruptcy. The suppliers and the bank are stunned, especially when they find that Willy and Buck have no money to pay them back or inventory to liquidate.

What kind of scheme are Willy and Buck involved in, and how could the bank and the suppliers have detected it sooner?

Case 2. A small credit union has asked you to investigate an alleged fraud in a bankruptcy case they are involved in. They are worried that the debtor is destroying evidence vital to their case, so they direct you to start immediately. They have not yet received permission from the judge on the case to put you under contract, but they assure you that if you find fraud, there will be no problem securing the judge's permission.

What should your response be?

Case 3. As a fraud auditor, you are examining the assets of Lorrell Corporation, which recently filed Chapter 11 bankruptcy. The company manufactures and sells circuit boards for computerized toys. You have access to its financial statements and warehouses. The company is a closely held corporation. There have been suggestions that the company is fraudulently concealing assets.

Give three red flags that you would look for that might indicate fraudulent concealment of assets.

Case 4. Trek, Inc., has experienced two bad financial years and now has significantly more liabilities than it does assets. It does not believe it can pay off its debts, and sees no alternative to declaring bankruptcy. If Trek files for bankruptcy, what are its bankruptcy options and which one do you believe would be best for Trek? The answer, of course, depends on whether or not Trek can work itself out of its problems (Chapter 11) or if it should terminate business.

Case 5. In the fall of 2001, Enron, the eighth largest corporation in the United States, unexpectedly declared bankruptcy, and investors lost approximately $60 billion. From your reading about this famous case, does Enron's bankruptcy involve fraud? If so, what type? (Many articles have been written about this case. See for example: http://news.bbc.co.uk/hi/english/business/newsid_1780000/1780075.stm and http://www.charm.net/~marc/chronicle/enron_apr02.shtml. If you want to perform your own search and read more about this case, just key in your web search engine such key words as "Enron Bankruptcy" or "Enron Fraud," and you will find hundreds of articles.)

Case 6. John Dewey, husband of Mary Dewey, is the CEO of a large public relations firm. Mary recently filed for divorce, alleging mental cruelty, and is asking for half of John's and the couple's assets. In the six months prior to being served for divorce, John took business trips to the Cayman Islands, Switzerland, Hong Kong, and Barbados. This was the first time John had ever done business in these locations. When John's and the couple's assets are identified during the divorce proceedings, Mary is shocked to learn that John's and his company's net worth total only $50,000, and that she is entitled to only $25,000. Prior to the divorce, John had been giving her $200,000 per year to cover their personal expenses.

What type of fraud is most likely in this case?

Extensive Cases

Case 7. BBB Company has been a successful manufacturer of quality electronics products for the past 20 years. It is a publicly traded company with 1 million shares outstanding. However, BBB has fallen on hard times. Profit margins in the electronics manufacturing industry have been squeezed due to competition in Japan. For most of BBB's history, research and development costs were a substantial portion of expenses. However, in the last three years, there have been no R&D expenses. This no doubt caused the decline in quality about which customers have expressed concern.

Suppliers have also been complaining. BBB has been buying more and more inventory on credit and has pressured suppliers to loosen credit terms. However, the company shows a decreasing inventory over the last three years even though sales declined. Recently, the company CFO talked the local bank into increasing BBB's credit limit, and the company very quickly used its entire line of credit. The CFO convinced the bank's management that the current downturn in sales was temporary and that BBB's new product line would be very lucrative.

With all its financial pressures, the company recently decided to file for bankruptcy. It cannot cover the interest payments on loans, nor can it meet its growing accounts payable balance. As creditors begin to seek monetary recovery through assets, they discover that there is very little inventory, and expenses are extraordinarily high for the current year. Also, some cash has disappeared, and there is no paper trail.

1. Is there evidence here that the company has been planning to declare bankruptcy?
2. If this bankruptcy was planned and assets have disappeared, will BBB Company still be allowed to declare bankruptcy?

Case 8. Abbott Insurance Company (AIC) is based in Florida. Because the company is experiencing financial problems, the state's regulatory board directed the company to either find an infusion of capital or declare bankruptcy. The officers found a group of investors who purchased 90% of the company for $4 million. Unfortunately, once in control, the new owners offered single-premium annuities with higher-than-market interest rates. They used the money from the annuities to fund mortgages for their friends. Most of the mortgages were bad, and the company declared bankruptcy. Subsequent investigation revealed that the new owners stole nearly $200 million from AIC's coffers.

What investigation techniques most likely disclosed the fraudulent acts of the new owners?

Internet Assignment

1. Visit the FBI's economic crimes unit web site at http://www.fbi.gov/hg/cid/fc/ec/about/about_bf.htm and answer the following questions:
   1. What effect does the increase of bankruptcy frauds have on the economy?
   2. What type of fraud comprises approximately 70% of bankruptcy fraud?
   3. What are the two most popular ways to perpetrate multiple bankruptcy filing frauds?
2. The Internet contains many resources for learning about bankruptcy and bankruptcy fraud. Many firms and professionals that participate in bankruptcy and fraud investigations maintain web sites. One such web site is maintained by William G. Hays & Associates, Inc. Go to their web site, located at http://www.wghaysinc.com/ and find the link to "Bankruptcy and Receiver Services." List 10 ways in which the company or its president have been involved with the U.S. Department of Justice in bankruptcy proceedings.

End Notes

1. For more technical material on bankruptcy fraud, see *Fraud Investigations,* by W. Steve Albrecht, D. R. Carmichael, M. M. Stanton, D. K Wilson, M. L. Reed, and C. W. Shipp, Practitioners Publishing Company, Ft. Worth, Texas, March 1999. Chapter 9 is on bankruptcy.
2. The differences between civil and criminal proceedings are covered in detail in Chapter 16.
3. This is a reference to Title 18, Section 152, of the U.S. Code. To look up such references, enter the title number and code number (such as 18 USC 152) into any web search engine, and that section of the code will be displayed.
4. Chapter 11 allows the person declaring bankruptcy to have time to work out a reorganization plan. If there are found to be lies, hidden assets, or other problems that led to this ruling, the Chapter 11 bankruptcy or the debt forgiveness can be "revoked," meaning that there is no debt forgiveness or Chapter 11 bankruptcy. Rather, the person declaring bankruptcy is ordered to pay the debts and/or declare complete bankruptcy.

5. A debtor-in-possession is a Chapter 11 or Chapter 12 debtor that operates its own business and remains in possession of its assets and property. For purposes of the Code, a debtor-in-possession has substantially all the rights and powers of a trustee. The bankruptcy judge may order that the debtor-in-possession be replaced by a trustee appointed by the U.S. Trustee. For a complete list bankruptcy terms and their definitions, see http://www.abiworld.org/media/terms.html.

6. Many states have now instituted "no fault" divorce statutes. No-fault divorce laws have eliminated the need to prove one party is at fault for causing the breakdown of a marriage. No-fault divorce is divorce granted on the basis of a showing by either spouse that a marriage is "irretrievably broken." As a practical matter, a couple agreeing to a divorce can now negotiate a property settlement and other details. The court will usually approve such an agreement in a short, simple hearing. The financial settlements regarding the divorce are now based on need, ability to pay, contribution to the family economy, and special circumstances, rather than on fault, as was common under the previous law. However, in more difficult cases, parties in a divorce hire lawyers to contest divorce arrangements. A lawyer's job is to represent a client's best interests by serving as an advocate and negotiator and by knowing the procedures to follow and the papers to file. Often, two people who are in the process of dissolving a marriage are unable to negotiate calmly and rationally. Sometimes they do not even agree that a divorce is the best solution. There are many web sites and firms that specialize in finding hidden assets in divorce cases. See, for example: http://www.nolo.com/lawcenter/ency/article.cfm/objectID/96F03E94-0FA6-4973-89D685E63A6AAA7A/catID/101C121B-3FFB-42F9-B60C2CC50B6921C6.

Affidavit of Proposed Investigator

UNITED STATES BANKRUPTCY COURT
WESTERN DISTRICT OF TEXAS

In the Matter of ARCHIBALD, WALL & CO. Debtor.	No. X5-30870-BKC-RAM AFFIDAVIT FOR RETENTION AS INVESTIGATOR FOR THE EXAMINER

STATE OF TEXAS)
) SS:
COUNTY OF SAGE)

MARY JONES, being duly sworn, deposes and says:

1. THAT I am a Certified Fraud Examiner (CFE) or Certified Public Accountant (CPA), licensed under the laws of the State of Texas and a member of the firm of Jones, Sally, and Doo, LLP with offices at 950 N. Beacon Street, Monroe, Texas 77034.

2. THAT neither deponent nor any member of deponent's firm is related to or has any business association with the debtor, the examiner, or the official Creditors' Committee except that our firm may have been retained in other matters in which some of the aforementioned persons may have been parties.

3. THAT deponent's firm maintains offices in Monroe, Texas. Total personnel numbers approximately 45 of whom nine are partners. Applicant has been known for many years for its expertise in accounting practice as related to the field of bankruptcy and fraud investigation, and has frequently been requested to serve in such matters by the legal, financial, and business community.

4. THAT deponent has surveyed the books and records of the debtor and is familiar with the matter and is familiar with the work to be done. That work is contemplated to be the following:

   a. Review of incorporation documents and other documents of the Debtor related to the formation and operation of the Debtor and consideration of whether they indicate that two separate entities were one entity.

b. Investigation of the circumstances of the Debtor's obtaining of bank loans, including review of bank loan applications and related documents and financial statements submitted in obtaining the loans, and interviews of bank officials about the loan applications.
c. Tracing of the disposition of loan proceeds and transfers of certain assets.
d. Investigation of the Debtor's accounts receivable collection effort, including analysis of accounts receivable history, write-offs, setoffs, and collections, and review of the collectibility of account balances.
e. Interviews of current or former principals of the Debtor with respect to the foregoing matters.
f. Provision of litigation consulting services and expert witness testimony if necessary and requested by examiner.
g. Performance of other services as requested by the examiner consistent with professional standards to aid the examiner in its investigation of the Debtor.

5. THAT in addition to the foregoing, the firms of JONES, SALLY, & DOO, LLP may be required to attend before the Bankruptcy Court with respect to the acts and conduct of the Debtor.

6. THAT the cost of the foregoing services is based on the following current hourly rates:

Partner	$250 per hour
Senior	$100 per hour
Paraprofessional	$ 30 per hour

7. ACTUAL and necessary out-of-pocket expenses will be incurred in connection with the rendition of these services. These will be billed separately in addition to the above.

WHEREFORE, your deponent respectfully requests that an Order be entered authorizing the retention of JONES, SALLY & DOO, LLP to perform the above mentioned services.

____

MARY JONES

Sworn to before me this
10th day of May 2003

____

NOTARY PUBLIC

Application for Retention of Investigator

Phillip Gallagher, Esq.
GALLAGHER, JOHNSON & SMITH
P.O. Box 75609
Sage, Texas 76031

ATTORNEYS FOR GEORGE SMITH, EXAMINER

IN THE UNITED STATES BANKRUPTCY COURT
FOR THE WESTERN DISTRICT OF TEXAS

IN RE:	§	
	§	
ARCHIBALD, WALL & CO., PA	§	CASE NO. X5-30870-BKC-RAM
	§	
DEBTOR.	§	

APPLICATION FOR AUTHORITY TO
EMPLOY INVESTIGATOR FOR THE EXAMINER

TO THE HONORABLE Linda Alright, U.S. BANKRUPTCY JUDGE:

COMES NOW, George Smith, the Court-appointed Examiner herein ("Examiner"), by and through his counsel, and files this his Application for Authority to Employ Investigator for the Examiner ("Application"), and in support thereof would respectfully show this Court as follows:

1. On March 15, 2003, Archibald, Wall & Co., PA ("Debtor") filed its voluntary petition under Chapter 11 of the Bankruptcy Code ("Code"), 11 U.S.C. §§ 101, *et seq.*, thereby commencing the above-captioned bankruptcy case. Thereafter, on May 5, 2003, George Smith was appointed the Examiner of the Debtor's estate and continues to act in that capacity.

2. Your Examiner requests authority to employ the firm of Jones, Sally, & Doo, LLP (the "Firm").

3. Your Examiner has selected the Firm for the reason that it has had considerable experience in matters of this nature and he believes that the Firm is well qualified to provide him with investigation services in his capacity as Examiner.

4. The professional services, which the Firm is anticipated to render, include: (a) to provide the Examiner with litigation consulting and forensic accounting services in connection with allegations of bank fraud and bankruptcy fraud by current or former principals of the Debtor; (b) to provide financial analysis in connection with the write-offs and collectibility

of accounts receivable balances of the Debtor estate; (c) to investigate the disposition and transfers of certain loan proceeds and assets for possible fraudulent transfers; (d) to provide evidence for determining whether there is cause for the appointment of a trustee; and (e) to perform all other investigation services for your Examiner which may be, or become, necessary herein.

5. As evidenced by the Affidavit of Proposed Investigator attached hereto as Exhibit A and incorporated herein by reference, to the best of your Examiner's knowledge, the Firm has no relationship that would raise a possible disqualification or conflict of interest. Consequently, the employment of the Firm is in compliance with § 327 of the Code.

6. Your Examiner believes that the employment of the Firm would be in the best interest of this estate by providing your Examiner with the necessary and beneficial services set forth in paragraph four (4) above.

WHEREFORE, PREMISES CONSIDERED, your Examiner respectfully requests that this Court enter an Order authorizing him to employ Jones, Sally, & Doo, LLP as Investigator of the Examiner in this bankruptcy proceeding; and for such other and further relief to which he may be justly entitled.

Respectfully submitted,
GALLAGHER, JOHNSON & SMITH
By:______________________________
Phillip Gallagher, Esq.

Fraud in E-Commerce[1]

After studying this chapter, you should be able to:

1. Understand e-commerce fraud risk.
2. Take measures to prevent fraud in e-commerce.
3. Detect e-business fraud.

The United Kingdom, one of the most powerful nations in the world, is facing a new danger. At the beginning of 2000, the U.K. local authorities called for more resources to combat escalating fraud. The cost of detecting fraud in local governments in the U.K. now exceeds more than £100 million annually.

The United Kingdom is planning to put all government services online by 2008. This creates a major problem for local authorities and police. Not only must local police and authorities implement the new technology, but they must also have the training and expertise to do so in place. Local authorities and police need more funding to combat fraud. Bruce Strugnell, a computer auditor for Portsmouth City Council, stated, "An explosion is taking place in computer fraud. We have to find innovative ways of funding. The people perpetrating the crimes are better equipped with technology than we are. The technology has become cheaper and more widely available, but the ability to upgrade our technology is a problem. Having more government services online makes it easier to maintain false identities."[2]

Many U.K. police argue that resources are insufficient to meet government's escalating needs for combatting computer fraud. They also argue that security issues are not addressed in their planning process. With the lack of funds, lack of training, and lack of planning, computer fraud poses an ever more serious threat in the United Kingdom and elsewhere.

Theft involves stealing assets, such as cash, inventory, or even valuable information. Thefts can occur manually or electronically. Concealment involves the steps taken by the perpetrator to hide the fraud from others. Concealment can involve altering financial records, miscounting cash or other assets, mis-programming a computer, or destroying evidence. Conversion involves benefiting from the stolen goods and usually involves selling the stolen assets or converting them into cash and then spending the cash.

In recent years, the technology revolution has provided perpetrators with new ways to commit and conceal fraud, and also to convert the ill-gotten gains. Consider Internet and electronic business (e-business) transactions. Essentially, e-business uses information technology and electronic communication networks to exchange business information and to conduct paperless transactions. Compared to other inventions, the Internet is truly revolutionary. It took radio more than 35 years and television 15 years to reach 60 million people. In contrast, the Internet reached over 90 million people in just three years. Internet traffic doubles every 100 days.[3] In 1999, an estimated 200–275 million people used the Internet, and the year 2005 may see 800 million to 1 billion users. When Jack Welch (former CEO of General Electric) was asked where the Internet ranks in priority in his company, he responded that "it's numbers 1, 2, 3 and 4."[4] In the year 2000, approximately 600,000 companies engaged in e-business transactions, up from just 100,000 in 1997. Business-to-business electronic transactions are forecasted to grow from $43 billion in 1998 to $1.3 trillion in 2003.[5]

In this chapter, we discuss unique aspects of e-business fraud, risks specific to e-business, and how to prevent electronic fraud. We will discuss e-business fraud detection briefly, but do not discuss fraud investigation because the methods used to investigate e-business fraud are the same as for other frauds. Remember that e-businesses conduct regular transactions (for example, purchasing and selling products and services)—only their medium of exchange is different. Once you understand the risks inherent in this new area of fraud, you will know where to target your detection efforts.

Fraud Risks in E-Commerce

Although fraud can occur in any environment, several aspects of e-business environments present unique risks. These characteristics of the "new economy," which is basically Internet-driven, create pressures and opportunities specific to e-commerce fraud. (Just like other frauds, these new frauds are perpetrated when pressures, opportunities, and rationalizations come together.) E-commerce elements that create increased or unique risks include the following:

Pressures

- Dramatic growth, which has created tremendous cash flow needs.
- Merger or acquisition activity, which creates pressures to "improve the reported financial results."
- Borrowing or issuing stock, additional pressures to "cook the books."
- New products, which require intensive and expensive marketing and for which an existing market does not yet exist.
- Unproven or flawed business models, with tremendous cash flow pressures.

Opportunities

- New and innovative technologies for which security developments often lag transaction developments.
- Complex information systems that make installing controls difficult.
- The transfer of large amounts of information, a factor that poses theft and identity risks such as illegal monitoring and unauthorized access.
- Removal of personal contact, which allows for easier impersonation or falsified identity.
- Lack of "brick-and-mortar" and other physical facilities that facilitate falsifying web sites and business transactions.
- Inability to distinguish large and/or established companies from new and/or smaller companies, making it easy to deceive customers by falsifying identity and/or business descriptions.
- Electronic transfer of funds, allowing large frauds to be committed more easily.
- Compromised privacy, which results in easier theft by using stolen or falsified information.

Increased Propensity to Rationalize

- The perceived distance that decreases the personal contact between customer and supplier.
- Transactions between anonymous or unknown buyers and sellers—you can't see who you are hurting.
- New economy thinking contends that traditional methods of accounting no longer apply.

Preventing Fraud in E-Commerce

Preventing fraud in every business setting involves reducing or eliminating the elements that motivate fraud: pressure, opportunity, and rationalization. In e-business settings, reducing pressures and eliminating rationalizations has thus far proved difficult. The lack of personal contact makes it hard to know what pressures exist or what rationalizations perpetrators are using. Therefore, the best businesses can hope for is to avoid conducting transactions with firms that are experiencing high pressures or have dishonest managers. Generally, the best way to prevent fraud in e-business settings is to focus on reducing opportunities, usually through the implementation of appropriate internal controls.

In traditional businesses, internal controls involve five different elements: (1) the control environment, (2) risk assessment, (3) control activities or procedures, (4) information and communication, and (5) monitoring. In e-businesses, the first three elements are far more relevant and important in preventing fraud than the last two. Therefore, we limit our discussion to control environment, risk assessment, and control activities.

The Control Environment

The essence of effectively controlled organizations lies in the attitude of their management. If top management believes that control is important, others in an organization will respond by conscientiously observing established controls. On the other hand, if it is clear to employees that management is only giving lip service to the idea of controls, rather than meaningful support, the organization's control objectives will almost certainly not be achieved, and fraud is a more likely occurrence. Because controls are so important, firms endeavoring to prevent e-business fraud must do everything possible to establish and observe good controls. Another key strategy is understanding the controls in place in the companies with whom the organization conducts its electronic business.

As noted in earlier chapters, the following are the most important components of the control environment:

Integrity and Ethical Values. An organization's culture of integrity and ethics is the product of what its standards are and how they are communicated and reinforced in the firm. This includes management's actions to remove or reduce incentives and temptations that might prompt personnel to engage in fraud. It also includes the communication of organizational values and behavioral standards to personnel through policy statements and codes of conduct and by example. A good question to ask about companies that engage in electronic business is whether they have a formal code of conduct and whether it is available to be examined.

Board of Directors and Audit Committee Participation. An effective board of directors is independent of management, and its members carefully scrutinize management's activities. The board delegates responsibility for internal control to management, but they undertake regular, independent assessments of management-established internal controls. In addition, the presence of an active and objective board often discourages management from overriding existing controls. A study of financial statement frauds during the period 1987 to 1997 revealed that a weak or ineffective board was one of the most common elements in firms that issued fraudulent financial statements.[6]

Management's Philosophy and Operating Style. Management provides clear signals to employees about the importance of internal controls. For example, does management take significant risks, or are they risk-averse? Are profit plans and budget data set as "best possible" plans or "most likely" targets? Can management be described as "fat and bureaucratic," "lean and mean," dominated by one or a few individuals, or is it just right? Understanding these and similar aspects of management's philosophy and operating styles provides a sense of management's attitude about internal controls and fraud.

Human Resources Policies and Practices. The most important aspect of internal control is personnel. If employees are competent and trustworthy, other controls can be absent and reliable transactions will still result. Honest, efficient people are able to perform at a high level, even when there are few other controls to support them. However, dishonest people can reduce to shambles a system with numerous controls in place.

Risk Assessment

Risk assessment identifies the risks of doing business with e-business partners. A key part of the assessment focuses on the control environment of those organizations. Another part identifies key risks in the electronic exchange of information and money, so that control procedures tailored to the special challenges that these exchanges present can be installed—procedures that counter the risk of data theft, sniffing, unauthorized access to passwords, falsified identity, spoofing, customer impersonation, false web sites, and e-mail or web site hijacking.

Data Theft. The theft of money is often the first thing that comes to mind when we think of fraud. In the electronic environment, however, the theft of data is an even larger concern. For example, stolen personal information about customers can be sold or misused, and individuals can be blackmailed. The theft of electronic data is thus a concern for both businesses and consumers. Information technology (IT) managers and assurance providers therefore need to be aware of the critical points in e-business infrastructures at which data can be stolen.

Sniffing. Sniffing is the viewing of information that passes along a network communication channel. Specialized hardware sniffers can be attached to a network to monitor or record all traffic passing through the network. Sniffing software is readily available and can be used legitimately to monitor message and data flow within a company's e-business infrastructure. However, unauthorized parties can also use sniffing techniques to capture passwords and other sensitive information. Sniffing is effective only when the data are transferred in plaintext form, or if perpetrators have a key that enables decryption of encoded messages.

Unauthorized Access to Passwords. In today's interconnected world of e-business, password protection is often the only barrier to unauthorized access. Knowledge of passwords makes electronic fraud very easy to commit.

Falsified Identity. Falsified identity is a major source of risk in e-business. For an electronic transaction to take place, each party to the transaction needs to be confident that the claimed identity of the other party is authentic. These threats are less of a concern in traditional electronic data interchange (EDI) settings because traditional EDI uses relatively limited access points, dedicated lines, and established value-added network providers as intermediaries. But authenticity is a significant concern for transactions conducted through electronic channels in e-business.

Spoofing. Spoofing changes the information in e-mail headers or IP addresses. Perpetrators hide their identities by simply changing the information in the header, thus allowing unauthorized access. Imposters that pose as computer support technicians or network managers can easily convince employees to divulge passwords or other confidential information.

Customer Impersonation. Like traditional businesses that accept checks or credit cards, e-businesses must also verify customer identity. When customers have falsified their identities, businesses lose money on fraudulent requests for products or services.

False Web Sites. As noted in Chapter 14, one of the most common frauds in traditional business is the "bustout"—the planned bankruptcy. In its simplest form, perpetrators set up a business, buy inventory on credit, sell it for low prices, and then run off with the money before the bills are paid. Bustouts are especially problematic in e-business. Instead of renting a "brick-and-mortar" store, the perpetrators merely establish (at significantly less cost) a false web site. The false web site may grab confidential information or conduct fraudulent transactions. False web sites look like the site of a real bank or an online broker or retailer and collect identification and credit-card numbers from unsuspecting customers. Alternatively, perpetrators use false web sites to conduct business transactions that they never intend to pay for.

Hijacking. E-mail messages and web visits can be hijacked because subtle differences in Internet host names often go unnoticed by Internet users. For example, "computer.com" and "computer.org" are two completely different host names that can be easily confused. If the two names are owned by different entities, one site could mimic the other and trick users into thinking they are dealing with the original web site or e-mail address.

Obviously, our listing of the electronic environment fraud risks is not complete. Perpetrators are extremely ingenious. All the traditional frauds are still possible. In addition, creative fraudsters will continue to develop new schemes. Just about the time we in the industry have one scheme figured out and know how to prevent or detect it, perpetrators develop new ones.

Preventing Fraud Through Control Activities

As you learned earlier in this textbook, control activities are the policies and procedures that ensure that necessary actions are taken to address risks and frauds. As you also learned, control activities generally fall into the following five types:

1. Adequate separation of duties
2. Proper authorization of transactions and activities
3. Adequate documents and records
4. Physical control over assets and records
5. Independent checks on performance

Although all of these activities can be used to prevent fraud in many forms in traditional organizations and transactions, they are not as effective in e-businesses.

Adequate Separation of Duties

In e-business, this control is useful for making sure that individuals who authorize transactions are different from those who actually execute them. Probably the most common frauds in purchasing and sales transactions are kickbacks and bribery. Kickbacks occur where one individual becomes too close to suppliers or customers. Adequate segregation of duties prevents bribery because employees don't have complete control of transactions.

Proper Authorization of Transactions and Activities

Proper authorization is another key control in e-business. The most common authorization controls are passwords, firewalls, digital signatures and certificates, and biometrics. Every transaction must be properly authorized.

Passwords. Passwords are a vital part of the security of any electronic system, but they are also an Achilles' heel. Why? Because they involve people. Compromising passwords allows unauthorized transactions to be made. To prevent fraud, organizations should have clearly communicated policies regarding selecting, changing, and disclosing passwords. In an electronic environment, no other control can better prevent fraud than the wise use of passwords.

Digital Signatures and Certificates. Just as signatures on paper documents serve as authorization or verification, digital signatures reassure users that transactions are valid. Digital signatures and certificates thus prevent falsified identity and impersonation and as such are increasingly important.

Biometrics. One of the most promising areas of technology and systems security is biometrics—the use of unique features of the human body to create secure access controls. Because each of us possesses unique biological characteristics (for example, iris and retina patterns, fingerprints, voice tones, facial structures, and writing styles), scientists are developing specialized security devices that have the potential to be highly accurate in authenticating identity. Access and permission to execute a transaction is granted or denied, based on how similar the subsequent reading is to the reference template.

Adequate Documents and Records

Documents and records (sales invoices, purchase orders, subsidiary records, sales journals, employee time cards, and even checks) are the physical objects by which transactions are entered and summarized.

In e-business, most documents are electronic. This lack of hard-copy documentation, the very essence of e-business, creates new opportunities for fraud. Documents and records typically are detective controls, not preventive controls. They are the audit trail and enable auditors and fraud examiners to investigate suspected wrongdoing. Although most computer systems create records of transactions that can be accessed or reconstructed, smart perpetrators figure out how to remove evidence of transactions from servers and computers.

Because many of the traditional document controls aren't available in e-commerce, controls must be put in place. The primary electronic transaction and document control is encryption, which protects confidential and sensitive information (such as checks or purchase or sales transactions) from being "sniffed" or stolen.[7] Public-key encryption allows information to be sent in encrypted format over unsecured networks like the Internet, and is widely used to protect data and ensure privacy. In public-key arrangements, communicating parties have two keys, one that is made public and another that is held private. These keys are inversely related: If one key is used to "lock" a message, the other must be used to "unlock" it. Thus, a message locked by a public key can be read only by the party holding the private key. Similarly, a message that can be unlocked by a particular public key can have originated only from the party holding the corresponding private key. Public-key encryption is thus used for privacy (by locking a message with the intended recipient's public key) and for authenticity (by locking a message with the originator's private key).

Physical Control Over Assets and Records

When records—be they electronic or paper—are not adequately protected, they can be stolen, damaged, or lost. Highly computerized companies need to go to special lengths to protect computer equipment, programs, and data files.

Three categories of controls protect IT equipment, programs, and data files from fraud. As with other types of assets, physical controls are used to protect computer facilities. Examples are locks on doors to the computer room and terminals and adequate and safe storage space for software and data files. In addition to software-based security, the software and hardware that comprise the IT infrastructure must be physically secure. Remember that authorized personnel that can access computers and servers can also execute unauthorized transactions or steal sensitive information. Sometimes physical infrastructure is so sensitive and critical to e-business operations that the system is placed in an isolated location with only high-level security access.

Independent Checks on Performance

As with traditional business, a key component in e-business controls is the careful and continuous review of the other four components—the independent checks and internal verification. The need for independent checks arises because internal controls change over time. Personnel forget or fail to follow procedures, or become careless—*unless* someone observes and evaluates their performance. The likelihood of fraudulent transactions goes up when controls break down.

Independent checks are particularly important in preventing fraud in e-business. Organizations should always conduct checks on their e-business partners. These checks can range from simple Dun & Bradstreet reviews to full-fledged investigations of the firm and its officers. A quick search of Lexis-Nexis and other financial databases or the Internet often reveals problems the organization should be aware of before they conduct electronic business.

Electronic fraud, especially that perpetrated by smaller companies, is often committed by individuals high in the organization, and quite often on behalf of the organization as opposed to against the organization. Because management is often involved, management and the directors or business partners must be investigated to determine their exposure to, and motivation for, committing fraud. To prevent fraud, gaining an understanding of the management or the organization's business partners and what motivates them is important. In particular, three items—(1) backgrounds, (2) motivations, and (3) decision-making influence—must be examined. What organizations and situations have management and directors been associated with in the past? What really drives and motivates the organization's leaders? Is their personal worth tied up in the organization? Are they under pressure to deliver unrealistic results? Is their compensation primarily performance-based? Are there debt covenants or other financial pressures that must be met? Management's ability to influence decisions is important to understand because perpetrating fraud when only one or two individuals have primary decision-making power is much easier.

Detecting E-Business Fraud

In Chapter 6, we introduced proactive fraud detection, in which the types of fraud that can occur are identified and then technology and other activities are used to look for fraud symptoms. That is, fraud examiners (1) endeavor to understand the business or operations of the organization, (2) identify what frauds can occur in the operation, (3) determine the symptoms that the most likely frauds would generate, (4) use databases and information systems to search for those symptoms, and (5) follow up on the symptoms to determine if they are being caused by actual fraud or by other factors.

This method of fraud detection works very well in detecting e-business fraud. Instead of using this approach on a one-time basis, once the types of frauds that can be committed and their symptoms have been identified (steps 2 and 3), e-business fraud detection works best when the queries (step 4) are automated, so that they examine every business transaction and business relationship.

Planting automated queries in electronic purchasing records that examine changes in the percentage of goods purchased from different vendors by individual buyer, price changes, the number of returns (indicating lower quality), and comparisons of these factors with other vendors is easy. These variables can even be analyzed on a combined basis; for example, the system will look for increased purchases from the vendor whose prices are increasing the fastest. Computer systems can be programmed to provide information when changes equal or exceed a certain amount. For example, price changes of a certain percentage within a certain period might be queried.

The advantage of e-business transactions is that information about the transactions is captured in databases that can be analyzed in numerous ways. This data makes fraud detection much easier than ever before. The most difficult aspect of detecting e-business fraud is correctly specifying the types of frauds that can occur and the symptoms they will generate. Also, symptoms are only circumstantial evidence at best. There may be perfectly legitimate explanations for factors that appear to be symptoms. However, just as e-business transactions make fraud easier to commit, they also make it much easier to detect.

Summary

Electronic fraud is a significant problem that is increasing both in frequency of occurrence and in amount. Because personal contact is limited in e-business settings and because defrauding people is easier when perpetrators can't see the personal hurt they are causing, fraud risks are higher than in other settings. Because of the ease of perpetrating electronic fraud, organizations must have proactive fraud prevention and detection efforts in place. Fraud prevention, of course, is the most cost-effective element in a proactive strategy. Organizations and individuals that install proactive prevention measures find that they pay big dividends. Passwords, firewalls, digital signatures and certificates, and biometrics are prevention measures designed specifically to protect electronic transactions.

The bad news is, electronic fraud cannot be totally eliminated. The good news is, the very nature of e-commerce provides the perfect audit trail.

New Terms

Biometrics: Using unique features of the human body (for example, retinal scans) to create secure access controls.

Data theft: Theft of data or personal information through such means as sniffing, spoofing, and customer impersonation.

Digital signatures and certificates: A signature sent over the Internet.

E-business: The use of information technology and electronic communication networks to exchange business information and conduct transactions in electronic, paperless form.

Falsified identity (customer impersonation): Pretending to be someone you're not—a major problem in e-business transactions.

Passwords: Secret codes or names that allow users to access networks and other computer systems.

Sniffing: Illegal or unauthorized viewing of information as it passes along a network communication channel.

Spoofing: Changing the information in an e-mail header or an IP address to hide identities.

Web-visit hijacking: Mimicking another, similarly named web site in order to trick or confuse e-mail and e-business users into sending information to a business other than the intended one.

Questions[8]

Discussion Questions

1. In what ways do e-business transactions pose heightened fraud risks?
2. What are some common ways e-business fraud is perpetrated?

3. How can the authenticity of a party to an e-business transaction be verified?
4. What is sniffing?
5. Why is spoofing a significant risk in e-business?
6. What is a password?
7. Why does biometrics offer significant promise as a way to authenticate e-business transactions?
8. Is the deductive, five-step detection approach relevant to e-business fraud detection?
9. Why can it be dangerous to provide credit-card information over the Internet?
10. Can e-business fraud risks ever be completely eliminated?

True/False

1. Fraud risks are higher when the entity with whom you are transacting business can't be seen.
2. Data theft is a bigger problem in e-business transactions than money theft.
3. Sniffing changes e-mail headers or IP addresses.
4. Falsified identity and customer impersonation are the same thing.
5. In many e-business sales, password protection is the only barrier to unauthorized access.
6. Customer impersonation is similar to a "bustout" fraud.
7. Segregation of duties is an important control in preventing e-business fraud.
8. Digital signatures use human features to create secure access controls.
9. Biometrics is a form of authorization control.
10. It is often easier to analyze e-business transaction data than data from other types of transactions because information is captured in databases that can be manipulated.

Multiple Choice

1. Which of the following is *not* a fraud risk unique to e-business transactions?
   a. Innovative technologies where security lags process development
   b. Selling new products
   c. Complex information systems
   d. Removal of personal contact
2. E-business transactions make it easier to commit which of the following types of frauds?
   a. Kickbacks
   b. Customer impersonation
   c. Setting up dummy companies
   d. Stealing petty cash
3. Which of the following is *not* an element of a company's control environment?
   a. Audit committee participation
   b. Management's philosophy
   c. Hiring policies
   d. Independent checks

4. Which of the following is *not* an internal control activity or procedure?
   a. Physical safeguards
   b. Segregation of duties
   c. Internal auditors
   d. Documents and records
5. Which of the following fraud risks involves changing IP addresses?
   a. Spoofing
   b. Sniffing
   c. False web sites
   d. Customer impersonation
6. Which of the following fraud risks involves viewing information as it passes along network channels?
   a. Sniffing
   b. Spoofing
   c. False web sites
   d. Web hijacking
7. Using a subtly different Internet host name to mimic another business is known as:
   a. Spoofing
   b. Sniffing
   c. Web-visit hijacking
   d. Falsified identity
8. Passwords and biometrics are both:
   a. Authorization controls
   b. Independent check controls
   c. Physical controls
   d. Document controls
9. Which of the following human features is generally *not* used in biometrics?
   a. Fingerprints
   b. Voice tones
   c. Retina patterns
   d. Weight
10. Which of the following types of controls is *not* used to protect IT processing equipment?
   a. Physical controls
   b. Authorization controls
   c. Independent checks or reference
   d. Document and records

End Notes

1. Much of this chapter was extracted from material written by the authors, "Preventing and Detecting Fraud in Electronic Commerce Systems," *The E-Business Handbook,* pp. 315–338, St. Lucie Press, Boca Raton, FL, 2002.

2. http://www.vnunet.com/News/106245

3. This discussion was taken from *E-Business: Principles and Strategies for Accountants,* Steven M. Glover, Stephen W. Liddle, and Douglas F. Prawitt, Prentice-Hall, 2001.

4. Naanette Brynes and Paul C. Judge, "Internet Anxiety," *Business Week,* June 28, 1999.

5. *E-Business: Principles and Strategies for Accountants,* op. cit., p. 1.

6. M. S. Beasley, J. V. Carcello, and D. R. Hermanson, 1999, *Fraudulent Financial Reporting: 1987–1997: An Analysis of U.S. Public Companies,* Committee of Sponsoring Organizations (COSO).

7. Encryption is the conversion of data into a form, called a ciphertext, that cannot be easily understood by unauthorized people. Decryption is the process of converting encrypted data back into its original form, so it can be understood.

8. *Note*: Because this chapter discusses an emerging type of fraud, where new developments occur almost daily, the end-of-chapter materials are limited to discussion questions, true/false questions, and multiple choice questions.

PART SEVEN

RESOLUTION OF FRAUD

CHAPTER SIXTEEN

Legal Follow-Up[1]

After studying this chapter, you should be able to understand:

1. The court system.
2. The civil litigation process.
3. The criminal litigation process.
4. The nature of an expert witness.

FBI and IRS Raid Offices of Slatkin[2]

Federal regulators pounced on EarthLink co-founder Reed E. Slatkin, raiding his offices and persuading a federal judge to freeze his bank and brokerage accounts to prevent him from hiding investors' money or destroying documents.

The actions turned what had been a civil matter—with investors accusing Slatkin of running a 16-year Ponzi scheme—into a criminal investigation.

At 8 A.M., agents from the FBI and Internal Revenue Service began hauling boxes of documents from the converted garage of Slatkin's former home in the Santa Barbara suburb of Goleta, which since the early 1990s has housed his stock-trading and money management businesses. Regulators also took documents from the Santa Fe, New Mexico, office of Slatkin's bookkeeper.

At the same time, the Securities and Exchange Commission asked a U.S. district judge for the Central District of California to freeze Slatkin's assets, claiming that he had been operating a fraudulent investment scheme since 1986. The request was granted.

Slatkin's attorney, Brian Sun, said his client was "fully cooperating" with the investigations. Slatkin, through his attorneys, provided computer passwords and a computer hard drive to investigators at the scene, Sun said.

The SEC charged that Slatkin provided investigators with investor account statements and year-end summaries showing that he invested in a wide variety of large- and small-company stocks. The SEC stated that its investigation of Slatkin's bank and brokerage records showed Slatkin used part of a $10 million deposit made by one investor to make payments to other investors.

When a fraud occurs, investigators and/or victim organizations and individuals must decide what actions to take against the perpetrators. These actions range from doing nothing to merely transferring or punishing the perpetrator to termination and pursuing various legal remedies. Obviously, such actions should not be pursued until the investigation is complete and the identity of the perpetrator is known, along with a sense of the schemes used, the amounts taken, and other important facts in the case. In this chapter, we discuss various legal remedies that are available. We will begin by discussing the state and federal court system in the United States. We then discuss civil and criminal fraud trials and the various elements of trials that fraud examiners should be familiar with.

The Court System

To understand the types of legal answers that are available in the United States, you first need some knowledge of how our federal and state courts operate. The U.S. justice system combines separate interlocking courts. State and local courts throughout the United States handle nearly every type of case. Only the U.S. Constitution, the state's constitution, and the state's laws govern state courts.

The state and local courts generally handle fraud cases. Federal courts handle only those cases over which the U.S. Constitution or federal laws give them authority. The federal courts will therefore hear fraud cases that involve federal laws and/or include several states.

State Courts

Although the organization of state courts differs from state to state, the following diagram shows how they are typically organized.

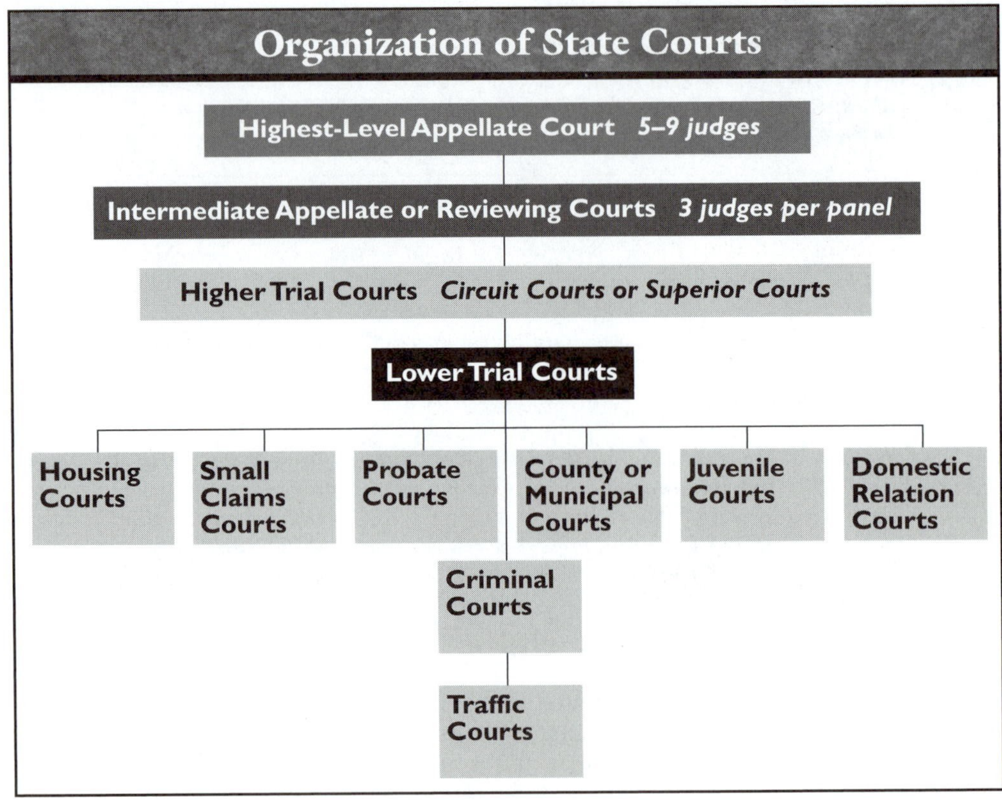

The lower trial courts try misdemeanors (small crimes) and preliminaries (pretrial issues) for felony and civil cases that are below a determined dollar amount, usually below $10,000. Several types of lower trial courts exist, including housing courts that hear housing and landlord/tenant issues, small claims courts where individuals can inexpensively bring small actions against others, probate courts where the assets of deceased persons are distributed, and so forth. These actions are judged initially in lower trial courts.

Initial actions are also heard in the higher trial courts, which try felony and civil cases that are above a determined dollar amount, usually above $10,000. The distinguishing factors between the lower and higher trial litigation are the amounts and seriousness of the crimes.

Plaintiffs or defendants who are not satisfied with the outcomes of lower or higher trial courts can appeal court decisions to appellate courts. Usually, the first level of review is conducted by the appellate or reviewing courts. If these courts can satisfy plaintiffs and defendants, there are no further appeals.

The last level of appeals at the state level is the highest-level appellate courts.[3] These courts review decisions made by the lower appellate courts, and their decisions are final.

Federal Courts

The following diagram shows how our federal courts are organized. The federal courts enforce federal laws and statutes. The bankruptcy courts adjudicate bankruptcy proceedings and the tax courts hear tax cases. Although bankruptcy fraud cases are normally tried in bankruptcy courts and tax fraud cases in tax courts, fraud cases that involve federal laws or statutes (such as mail fraud, Racketeering Influence Corrupt Organization [RICO], banking, and securities regulations) are tried in U.S. district courts. These courts try criminal and civil cases under federal laws.

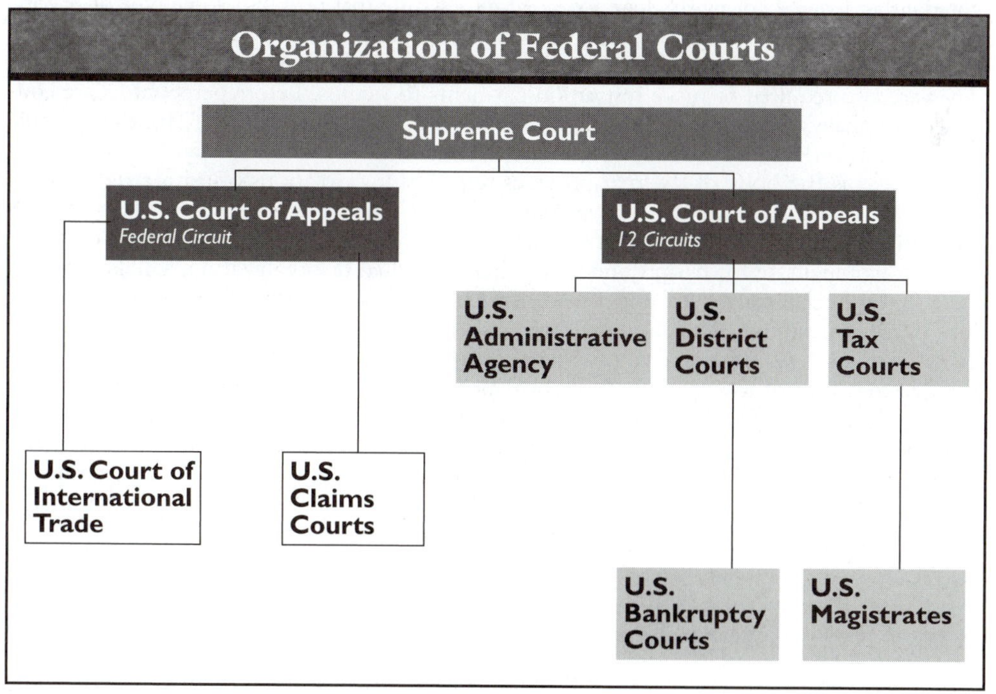

If defendants or plaintiffs are not satisfied with judgments rendered in district court, they can appeal the findings in one of 12 circuit courts of appeal. The final court of appeal is the U.S. Supreme Court, which reviews decisions made by appellate courts.

As an example of how appellate courts work, consider the following: In 1994, a jury in Anchorage, Alaska, ordered Exxon Corporation to pay $5 billion to thousands of commercial fisherman and property owners for damages done in 1989 when the tanker *Exxon Valdez* spilled 11 million gallons of oil in Alaska's Prince William Sound. Plaintiffs alleged that the black "goo" that spread across 1,500 miles of shoreline reduced property value and damaged fishing and hunting grounds. When Exxon appealed the findings, the three-judge panel of the 9th U.S. Circuit Court of Appeals said that some damages were justified, but that $5 billion was excessive. The appeals court ordered the lower court to determine a smaller amount of damages.[4]

Civil and Criminal Fraud Trials

Individuals who commit fraud can be prosecuted criminally and/or civilly. Once sufficient evidence is obtained through a fraud investigation, the defrauded company must decide whether to pursue the case criminally, civilly, or both, or to take no action at all. Many times, defrauded companies do not pursue cases in criminal or civil court because they want to avoid additional expenses and negative publicity. Rather, they merely fire the perpetrator and file a claim with their bonding company. (Sometimes the bonding company pursues legal actions against the perpetrators.) When defrauded companies pursue civil remedies in court, cases are frequently settled before they go to trial. Even in criminal cases, plea bargains are often pursued in order to avoid lengthy and costly trials.

As we discussed in Chapter 1, criminal law is that branch of law that deals with offenses of a public nature. Criminal laws deal with offenses against society as a whole. They are prosecuted either federally or by the state for violating a statute that prohibits some type of activity. All states and the federal government have statutes that prohibit a wide variety of practices. When perpetrators are convicted criminally, they usually serve jail sentences and/or pay fines. They are also required to make restitution payments to victims. Before perpetrators are convicted criminally, they must be proven guilty "beyond a reasonable doubt." Juries must rule unanimously on guilt for the perpetrator to be convicted.

Civil law is the body of law that provides remedies for violations of private rights. Civil law deals with rights and duties between individuals. Civil claims begin when one party files a complaint against another in order to gain financial restitution. The purpose of a civil lawsuit is to compensate for harm done to another individual or organization. Unlike criminal cases, juries in civil cases need not consist of 12 jurors, but may have as few as 6 jurors. The jury's verdict need not be unanimous. Civil cases are often heard by judges instead of juries. To be successful, plaintiffs in civil cases must only prove their case by the "preponderance of the evidence." In other words, only slightly more evidence must support the plaintiff than supports the defendant. In both civil and criminal proceedings, the parties may call expert witnesses to help jurors and judges understand technical matters. Fraud examiners and accountants are often used as experts in fraud cases to compute and testify to the amount of damages, the nature of the fraud, and whether the parties were negligent in their actions and thus committed fraud.

The Civil Litigation Process

During civil litigation, cases proceed through common stages. In every civil case, there are four basic stages:

- Investigation and pleadings
- Discovery
- Motion practice and negotiation
- Trial and appeal

Most fraud cases follow these four stages, although in some cases the stages overlap. For example, investigation can occur during motion practice.

Investigation and Pleadings

The civil litigation process usually begins when a client in a case of suspected fraud approaches an attorney. Before the attorney is notified, the investigator should have gathered important evidence about the facts of the case, such as how the fraud occurred, the amount of the fraud, the accused perpetrator, and so forth.

For litigation to begin, it is necessary for the plaintiff to file an "initial pleading" or "complaint." The complaint explains the alleged violation of the law and the monetary expenses or damages sought in the case. The court's response to the claim is called a motion or answer. The motion is an objection to the plaintiff's complaint that points out defects of the case and asks for a specific remedy. The remedy may include dismissal of all or part of the original complaint. The answer is the response to the complaint that denies or admits various allegations. Sometimes, defendants in civil cases file counterclaims, such as sex, race, or age discrimination or invasion of privacy rights. For example, a defendant may claim that he lost his job because of sex discrimination in order to divert the jury's attention away from the fraud.

Discovery

Discovery is the legal process by which each party's attorneys try to find all information about the other side's case before the trial begins. Because discovery is time-consuming and expensive, this stage can be the most difficult part of litigation. To obtain information about the other side's case, attorneys file motions for the production of documents, file interrogatories, file requests for admissions, obtain subpoenas, and take depositions of both parties and nonparties to the litigation.[5]

Production Requests. A production request is a means of securing documents in the other party's possession that are relevant to the issues of the case. These documents can be bank statements, property titles, stock holdings, accounting records, and other important information. Attorneys may request documents to establish that the opposing party has no documents or to avoid presenting at trial documents that have not been reviewed. The production request should be specific, contain the facts of the case, and be defensible in court, should that become necessary. Fraud investigators provide significant assistance in preparing production requests because of their knowledge of the case. Fraud investigators also assist in evaluating whether documents produced by the opposing side satisfy requests. Document requests are typically made at the beginning of discovery. This allows attorneys time to review all relevant documents before they elicit the testimony of witnesses or consultants. After both parties receive responses (and if the responses contain no objections), the counsel of both parties arrange to exchange documents at a time and place convenient for all parties.

Interrogatories. An interrogatory is a series of written questions that specifically identify information needed from the opposing party. Fraud investigators often provide important interrogatory service by suggesting relevant questions to ask the other side. Fraud investigators also draft responses to questions received and ensure that answers are consistent with the presentation to be made at trial. Normally, responses to interrogatories must be made within 30 days. If answers are not given in a timely fashion, the court may issue an order demanding that all questions be answered and may charge the noncomplying party with fees and costs incurred by the other party in obtaining the order. Interrogatories ask questions about personnel, documents, and the nature of the organization, although other questions can also be asked. Often, responses to interrogatories include statements such as "the request is unduly burdensome" or "the infraction is unavailable."

Requests for Admission. A request for admission asks the opposing party to admit designated facts relevant to litigation. These facts may relate to the authenticity of documents or to precise facts about certain issues. For example, a request for admission may ask the opposing party to admit that the company was incorporated in a particular state during a specific period. Request for admissions must be answered within a certain time period. If answers are not given in a timely fashion, the court may issue an order demanding that all questions be answered and may charge the noncomplying party with fees and costs incurred by the other party.

Subpoenas. A subpoena is a written order in the name of the court that requires a witness to submit to a deposition, give testimony at trial, or report to an administrative body. A *subpoena duces tecum* requires the recipient to produce documents pertinent to the case. The court clerk or an attorney as an officer of the court may issue subpoenas. Subpoenas are often the only method of ensuring production of information or documents from witnesses who are not parties to a lawsuit. For example, a subpoena can be used to require a brokerage house to produce records pertaining to the opposing party's account. Subpoenas are sometimes necessary to obtain documents to compare documents produced by the opposing party. If the witness believes that the defendant has altered a bank statement sent as part of a document request, a copy of the defendant's bank statement might be subpoenaed from the bank, and documents supporting the transactions may be vouched to the statement to establish the completeness of information.

Depositions. A deposition is testimony taken before trial begins. Judges usually are not present at depositions. The conditions are less formal than in a courtroom, but the rules and regulations of court apply. The opposing side's attorney takes fact and expert witness depositions.

A deposition is a powerful tool in the hands of skilled attorneys. They shrewdly note how witnesses react to questioning. If witnesses are not prepared to be deposed, the attorneys may be able to obtain admissions or errors not possible at trial. Attorneys may also get witnesses to commit to a particular position at deposition that prevents them from suddenly "recalling" a favorable matter at trial.

The individual being deposed is under oath, and a court reporter records the questions and answers and later transcribes the notes. The witness is given an opportunity to approve the written transcript and make any necessary corrections. Deposition transcripts are read to the court at trial for a variety of reasons. One of these is to impeach or question the accuracy of the trial testimony of the witness. For example, if the witness gives seemingly contradictory evidence at deposition and trial, the transcript may be read to convince the jury to give less weight to the witness's testimony. In some cases, depositions are videotaped and the tape is shown at trial.

Fraud investigators assist the client's attorney by preparing questions to ask opposing witnesses during depositions. Fraud investigators sometimes attend the depositions of other witnesses. Although only attorneys ask questions during depositions, fraud investigators can communicate with the attorney during breaks or by using written notes. Attending the depositions of opposing experts can be especially helpful for fraud investigators. These depositions may reveal information and opinions that are not accurately reflected in the expert's written report or work papers. A fraud investigator's technical knowledge of the areas of testimony can help ensure that the deposition reveals all of the opposing expert's opinions as well as the methodologies and supporting information used to reach those opinions. In many ways, being deposed is much more difficult than testifying in court. Expert witnesses, for example, are questioned by the other side's attorneys but not by their own, except to clarify answers given to the other attorneys. Effective witnesses realize that it is best to be a good "defensive" witness in depositions and a good "offensive" witness in court.

Motion Practice and Negotiation

At various stages during discovery, the opposing parties may seek rulings from the trial judge on a variety of questions. For example, a defendant may file a motion for summary judgment before a case even goes to trial. In a motion for summary judgment, counsel requests the court to rule that all or a part of the claim should be dismissed because there is no genuine issue of a material fact. At times during discovery, the witness may be requested to execute an affidavit on a relevant fact in support of a motion. (An affidavit is a written declaration given under oath.)

Settlement Negotiations. Either party may negotiate a settlement at any time during the litigation. If a settlement is reached, the case is resolved. However, settlement discussions and negotiations cannot be introduced at trial. Fraud investigators can be useful during settlement negotiations because they can help resolve differences between the two parties. Most large civil cases are ultimately settled and do not go to trial.

Trial and Appeal

If the case is not closed by motion practice or settlement, it then goes to trial. Before the trial begins, attorneys for both sides meet with the judge and agree to certain ground rules regarding the scope of the litigation, what documents will be admitted, and how long the trial will last. In most jurisdictions, litigating parties have the right to demand a jury trial, and in most cases, a jury trial will be held. Often when one side prefers a jury, the other side wants a judge or vice versa. If either party wants a jury, a jury trial is usually held.

A fraud investigator's testimony is intended to help the jury understand the technical issues involved. In addition to providing trial testimony, fraud investigators also develop questions that will be asked of the opposing side's expert or fact witnesses during cross-examination by the client's attorney.

In jury trials, the judge determines issues of the law. At the conclusion of the trial, the judge "charges the jury." This means that the judge instructs the jury on the law to be applied in reaching its verdict. After the jury returns a verdict, a limited period ensues during which the parties can file motions to have the verdict set aside in whole or in part or to have the judge grant a new trial. If these motions are overruled, a judgment is entered, and both parties have a specified time to appeal.

Appeals typically relate to matters of law and not to facts of the case. They are requests to a higher court to overturn the verdict or order a retrial due to some legal defect during the trial. For example, an appeal may be based on the contention that some inappropriate evidence was admitted during the trial, or that the trial judge wrongfully instructed the jury on one or more legal issues.

The Criminal Litigation Process

Litigation in criminal cases differs significantly from that in civil cases because the criminal justice system provides more protections for the rights of defendants. These protections arise primarily from three amendments to the U.S. Constitution—the Fourth Amendment, the

Fifth Amendment, and the Sixth Amendment. Each stage of criminal litigation is also governed by rules established by the jurisdiction in which the case is tried. The Federal Rules of Evidence and Federal Rules of Criminal Procedures apply to testimony in federal courts. Many state courts follow the federal rules with little modification. The typical stages through which criminal cases progress are discussed in the following paragraphs.

Filing Criminal Charges

After investigators believe they have enough evidence to prosecute a defendant, the defrauded party determines whether to pursue criminal charges. If the decision is made to pursue criminal charges, the victim contacts the district attorney for the county in which the fraud was perpetrated. The district attorney coordinates with the local police, so that an arrest warrant or summons is prepared. If the case involves a federal crime, notice is also sent to the U.S. Attorney's Office.

Arresting and Charging the Defendant

Representatives of the government do not have unlimited power to search or arrest citizens. Instead, they must comply with the requirements of the U.S. Constitution, including the Fourth and Fifth Amendments.

The Fourth Amendment. The Fourth Amendment protects defendants against unreasonable searches and seizures by the government. It requires that probable cause exist before a defendant is arrested or searched. Probable cause is the level of evidence required for a reasonable person to believe that a crime has been committed and that the accused committed it. The level of evidence necessary to show probable cause is less than certainty, but more than speculation or suspicion. Evidence seized without meeting this requirement can be excluded from trial. Searches at the place of business by employers or investigators hired by employers are generally not subject to this amendment, unless they were carried out in a prejudicial or careless manner. In fraud trials, documents seized by the employer are frequently turned over to the government. The government can use these documents as evidence, even though a search warrant was not issued to obtain the evidence. However, if the defendant's attorney can show that fraud investigators were really an agent of the district attorney when they gathered the information, and therefore were subject to the rules against unreasonable searches and seizures, the government may not be able to use some of the evidence gathered.

The Fifth Amendment. The Fifth Amendment provides defendants the following protections:

- Requires an indictment of a grand jury before a defendant is held for a capital crime (one where the death penalty, or other certain punishments are possible).
- Precludes a person from being tried twice for the same crime.
- Gives defendants the right to refuse to incriminate themselves—often referred to as "pleading the fifth."
- Requires the state to apply due process of law.
- Forbids the state from taking a private party's property without just compensation.

As we stated earlier, agents of the government must have probable cause before they can arrest people. There are three ways one can be arrested for a crime:

1. Arrest without a warrant by a private citizen or police officer who observes a crime being committed.
2. Arrest after a warrant has been issued (to obtain a warrant, a preliminary showing of probable cause must have been made).

3. Arrest after an indictment by the grand jury. (The purpose of the grand jury is to determine whether probable cause exists; grand jury indictments are generally used in fraud cases.)

Preliminary Hearings

If the accused is arrested based on a warrant, either a preliminary hearing or a grand jury proceeding follows, depending on whether the defendant's attorney or prosecutor reaches a judge first. The purpose of a preliminary hearing is to determine whether there is "probable cause" to charge the defendant with a crime—not to establish their guilt or innocence. Although preliminary hearings are held before judges, hearsay and illegally obtained evidence can be heard. The defendant is represented by an attorney who can cross-examine the prosecution's witnesses. The defendant attempts to demonstrate that the prosecution does not have enough evidence to show probable cause. If there is not enough evidence to show probable cause, charges are dismissed and the defendant is released. However, this does not preclude the government from instituting a later prosecution for the same offense, once it has gathered better evidence.

Grand Jury

Because a preliminary hearing is an opportunity for the defendant to obtain discovery of the prosecution's case without disclosing their own evidence, the prosecution generally prefers to obtain a grand jury indictment. Once the defendant is indicted by a grand jury, probable cause is satisfied and a preliminary hearing is not held. The defense, however, can file a motion to obtain most, if not all, of the factual information they could have obtained during a preliminary hearing.

A grand jury is a body of 16–23 people, selected from the community, who are sworn as jurors and who deliberate in secret. Grand jurors listen to evidence presented by witnesses and prosecutors. Grand juries also have the right to subpoena witnesses and documents and can issue contempt orders, fines, or jail terms to enforce the subpoena. Grand juries can consider any evidence, even that which would not be admissible at trial. Defendants do not have to be notified that a grand jury is considering evidence against them. Nor are they allowed to review the evidence, confront their accusers, or present evidence in their defense. Defendants who appear before a grand jury cannot be accompanied by their attorneys. However, defendants can periodically leave the grand jury room to discuss their cases with counsel. Defendants appearing before grand juries retain the right against self-incrimination. At least 12 grand jurors must agree for an indictment to be issued. An indictment is not a conviction. At trial, the defendant will have the Sixth Amendment protections denied during the grand jury process.

Sixth Amendment protections relate only to trials and provide a defendant with the right to:

- Receive a speedy and public trial.
- Be heard by an impartial jury.
- Have a trial held in the state and district in which the crime was committed.
- Be informed of the accusation.
- Confront witnesses against him or her.
- Compel witnesses to attend the trial.
- Be represented by legal counsel.

Arraignment

Generally, in a fraud trial, the grand jury will hear evidence of wrongdoing before the defendant is in custody. Once defendants are indicted, they will receive a summons to attend an arraignment that includes the time and place to appear. Alternatively, they may be arrested and brought to arraignment. At arraignment, the charges against the defendant are read. The defendant may plead guilty, not guilty, or *nolo contendere* (the defendant does not contest the charges but does not admit guilt). If the defendant pleads "not guilty," a trial will be held and bail will be set. If the defendant pleads "guilty" or "*nolo contendere,*" sentencing follows.

Discovery

Pretrial discovery in criminal trials differs significantly from that in civil trials. Depositions are allowed only in exceptional circumstances (such as the illness or anticipated death of a witness). According to Rule 16 of the Federal Rules of Criminal Procedure, upon request defendants may obtain the following:[6]

1. Copies of all relevant statements made by the defendant that are in the government's possession.
2. A copy of the defendant's prior criminal record.
3. All documents, items, test results, written reports of expert witnesses, or other evidence the government intends to introduce at trial or that are necessary to the defense.
4. Copies of all prior statements made by witnesses relevant to the information about which they have testified.

If defendants request the prosecution to produce any or all of the items listed in item 3 they must also provide the same items to the prosecution. However, defendants are not required to disclose information that is self-incriminatory—only information expected to be introduced as evidence at trial.

Pretrial Motions

Before a criminal trial, defendants can file motions with the court. This process resembles that in civil trials. These two motions are frequently made to request:

- That the charges be dismissed as a matter of law, and
- That certain evidence be suppressed because it was illegally obtained

Trial and Appeal

In state courts, civil fraud trials are sometimes held before criminal trials because prosecutors may choose not to investigate until the defrauded company finds evidence of fraud. In these cases, the defrauded party's attorney notifies the district attorney of the investigation. The district attorney may wait to indict the defendant until enough evidence has been obtained in the defrauded party's investigation to show probable cause, and might use that evidence in the criminal trial. However, in federal courts, criminal trials are generally held first. Having a civil trial first can benefit the prosecution because the defendant may make admissions during the civil trial that can be used in the criminal trial. Also, in civil trials, the defrauded party may have greater access to the documents of the defendant during discovery. If defendants do not present requested documents during a civil trial, they can be held in contempt of court and fined.

Burden of Proof. Defendants in criminal trials are considered innocent until proven guilty. Although an unanimous jury decision is not required in civil cases, in most jurisdictions a jury's decision in a criminal trial must be unanimous. The burden of proof necessary to find a defendant guilty in a criminal trial is also significantly greater than the level needed to prove civil liability. Civil actions require that the "preponderance of the evidence" (usually interpreted to mean more than 50%) support one side of the action. In a criminal case, the guilt of the accused must be established "beyond a reasonable doubt."

Appeal. After the jury returns the verdict, the defendant may file motions to have the verdict set aside. If that is unsuccessful, the defendant may appeal the verdict. An appeal is a request to a higher court to overturn the verdict or order a retrial due to some legal defect in the trial proceedings.

Being an Expert Witness

Because fraud examiners and accountants are often retained as expert witnesses in both civil and criminal cases, we conclude this chapter by discussing the role that expert witnesses play in trials and guidelines that will help you become an effective expert witness. Most witnesses in a fraud trial are fact or character witnesses. The exception is the expert witness who can offer opinions about the fraud based on experience, education, or training. In the process of qualifying an expert witness to testify, known as *voir dire,* the judge rules on whether an expert witness is qualified to provide evidence on a matter before the court. Once qualified, expert witnesses can testify about the nature of the fraud, the damages suffered in the fraud, the negligence of the victim in allowing the fraud to happen, standards (such as accounting standards) that were violated, and other aspects related to the fraud.

Expert witnesses study the facts of the case during the discovery stage of the trial. To prepare, they read fact witness depositions, study relevant documents and other materials related to the case, and make sure they understand all the authoritative literature related to the issues of the case. Often, experts are required or asked to prepare a report that sets out their opinions.

After the fact discovery period ends, experts are deposed by attorneys on the opposing side.[7] The deposition is probably the most stressful part of the case because, except for a few clarifying questions at the end, the opposition's attorneys ask the questions. Those attorneys have several goals during the deposition of the expert: (1) to understand the expert's opinions on the case, (2) to understand the expert's credentials and experience, (3) to identify evidence that can either impeach the expert or be used against his or her testimony during the trial, and (4) to assess how difficult an opponent the expert will be.

During the deposition, good experts take a defensive posture—answering only the questions that are asked in the most abbreviated way possible. Good experts never volunteer anything beyond what is asked, and they always listen carefully to the questions to make sure they hear exactly what is being asked. Before answering, experts pause to give the attorneys for their side an opportunity to object to the question on the basis of relevance, foundation, or some other reasonable basis of objection. At times, experts are instructed by their attorneys not to answer specific questions. Ethical expert witnesses never forget that their opinions are only as good as their reputation and integrity. They therefore never sell their opinions to the highest bidder, but rather give their honest opinions at all times.

Following the deposition, experts work with the attorneys representing their side to prepare for trial. During this period, the experts decide how to best present their opinions to the judge or jury. Graphics and other visuals are often helpful in conveying, in simple terms, complex fraud issues.

During the trial, expert witnesses first encounter direct examination by the attorneys representing their side of the case. At the beginning of direct examination, the attorney asking the questions covers the qualifications of the expert, so that the judge or jury hearing the case can establish in their minds how well qualified the expert is. Once the expert's qualifications are established, attorneys then ask the expert questions that, when answered honestly, will support the case they are trying to make. Following direct examination, the expert is cross-examined by opposing attorneys.

Articles that coach individuals on how to be effective expert witnesses abound in the literature.[8] Just remember, there is no substitute for good preparation. No matter how extensive an expert's personal qualifications, their credibility is weakened if they are unprepared or not familiar with the facts of the case. Most experts agree that, once prepared, the following do's and don'ts should be followed when testifying as an expert.

Do's and Don'ts at Deposition or Trial

1. Listen carefully and concentrate on each question.
2. Think about the question and digest it before attempting to respond; don't give snap answers.
3. Don't try to guess or bluff your way through an answer. If you do not know the answer to a question or do not understand the question, say so.
4. Restrict your answer to the question asked; don't editorialize your answer or volunteer information.
5. Don't respond to statements or observations, only to questions.
6. Answer questions convincingly; don't repeatedly attempt to hedge your answers or be overcautious.
7. Don't memorize answers to questions you expect to be asked; phrase your response in your own words.
8. Answer questions honestly; don't attempt to figure out what the best answer to each question might be.
9. Speak out the answer to each question. Body language, such as hand signals or nods, cannot be recorded by the stenographer.
10. Before answering a hypothetical question, be cautious, make sure you understand the assumptions, and then spell them out as part of your answer.
11. Try to "read messages" intended by objections to questions by lawyers with whom you are working. Their objection may be designed to caution you about some risk or problem with the question.
12. Don't hesitate to take the time necessary to review exhibits put before you before responding to any questions based on them.
13. Explain all assumptions on which your conclusions are based and be prepared for opposing counsel to attack them.

Additional Do's and Don'ts at Trial

1. Be mindful that your personal characteristics and professionalism may influence the jury as much as or even more than the substantive content of your testimony.
2. Be yourself; jurors are apt to sense when you are not being natural.
3. Do your best to appear authoritative, credible, businesslike, serious, assertive, polite, assured, self-confident, sincere, candid, forthright, fair, and spontaneous.
4. Don't appear pompous or aggressive.
5. Remember that you are independent; avoid bias or unnecessary advocacy of the client's position.
6. Focus on the lawyer asking the questions, but remember to look at and direct your answers to the jury as well. Don't overlook the reactions of the jurors to your answers; do try to be responsive to their nonverbal signals.
7. Correct any errors you make as soon as you can.
8. Tailor your answers to the jury's educational level and do your best to speak in plain English; don't use technical terms that laypeople will not understand.
9. Don't bore the jury; try to speak with clarity and feeling and avoid long, overly detailed answers.
10. Don't hesitate to raise your voice; pause or use some other natural gesture to emphasize an important point.
11. Speak just loud enough and just fast enough to be comfortably understood by the jury.
12. Don't bring notes, work papers, or other material to the witness stand unless counsel for your side approves.
13. Don't try to play lawyer while on the stand. Your job is to answer the questions honestly and responsively; counsel for your side will take care of the legal matters.
14. Don't look to counsel for your side or the judge or anyone else to bail you out if a question stumps you or you otherwise get yourself into a hole.

continues

Do's and Don'ts in Cross-Examination

1. Don't lose your temper or become angry or antagonistic; recognize that it is opposing counsel's job to attempt to discredit you.
2. Don't be concerned if opposing counsel scores points. This is entirely to be expected when your side relinquishes the offensive to the other side; all you can do is try to keep the damage to a minimum.
3. Don't quibble unduly or become argumentative with opposing counsel.
4. Don't respond evasively or ambiguously to questions, no matter how difficult they may be.
5. Be extra careful if opposing counsel takes on a friendly air. Their intent may be solely to catch you off guard.
6. Don't become hostile if opposing counsel tries to bully you. Jurors respect you for not becoming unduly perturbed and sympathize with you if you get "beat up."
7. Resist responding with simple "yes" or "no" answers that may be misleading without some qualification or explanation. Either provide the qualification or explanation directly by responding "yes, but" or "no, but" or request the opportunity to do so.
8. Do your best to recognize signals, such as careless answers, that you may be getting tired or losing your competitive edge. If this happens, it is advisable to indicate the need for a break.
9. Don't allow opposing counsel to entice you into coming up with answers to questions addressing matters outside of your area of expertise.
10. Maintain the position you took in your direct testimony.
11. Don't allow opposing counsel to con you into an advocacy role; unduly taking your client's side can cause you to lose your independence in the eyes of the jury.

New Terms

Affidavit: Written statement or declaration given under oath.

Appellate court: Review court to which participants in lower court cases can have their cases reviewed or retried if they are unhappy with the outcome.

Arraignment: Court hearing where charges against the defendant are read. At the arraignment, the defendants may plead guilty, not guilty, or *nolo contendere*.

Bankruptcy courts: Federal courts that hear only bankruptcy cases.

Civil law: Body of law that provides remedies for violation of private rights—deals with rights and duties between individuals.

Complaint: Request filed by a plaintiff to request civil proceedings against someone—usually to seek damages.

Criminal law: Branch of law that deals with offenses of a public nature or against society.

Deposition: Sworn testimony taken before a trial begins. At depositions, the opposing side's attorneys ask questions of witnesses.

Discovery: Legal process by which each party's attorneys try to find all information about the other side's case before a trial begins.

Expert witness: Trial witness who can offer opinions about a matter, based on unique experience, education, or training.

Federal courts: Courts established by the federal government to enforce federal laws and statutes.

Fifth Amendment to the U.S. Constitution: Provides defendants certain protections, including (1) an indictment by a grand jury before being held for a capital crime, and (2) not being tried twice for the same crime.

Fourth Amendment to the U.S. Constitution: Protects defendants against unreasonable searches and seizures by the government.

Grand jury: Body of 4–23 individuals who deliberate in secret to decide whether there is sufficient evidence to charge someone in a preliminary hearing.

Higher trial courts: State courts that try felony (larger crimes) and civil cases above a predetermined amount.

Initial pleading: Complaint filed by a plaintiff to request legal proceedings against someone.

Interrogatory: A series of written questions that specifically identify information needed from the opposing party.

Lower trial courts: State courts that try misdemeanors (small crimes) and pretrial issues.

Motion: Response to a complaint or pleading by the defendant. Sometimes "motion" refers to any request made to the judge for a ruling in a case by either party.

Motion for dismissal: Request to the judge to dismiss a claim because there is no genuine issue of a material fact.

Nolo contendere: Plea by a defendant that does not contest the charges but does not admit guilt.

Preliminary hearing: Pretrial hearing to determine whether there is "probable cause" to charge the defendant with a crime.

Remedy: Judgments asked for in civil cases (what it would take to right a private wrong).

Request for admission: Request that the opposing party admit designated facts relevant to litigation.

Settlement: Negotiated pretrial agreement between the parties to resolve a legal dispute.

Sixth Amendment to the U.S. Constitution: Provides trial-related protections to defendants, such as the right to a speedy trial and the right to be heard by an impartial jury.

Subpoenas: Written orders in the name of the court, requiring a witness to submit to a deposition, give testimony at trial, or report to an administrative body.

Tax courts: Federal courts that hear only tax cases.

Voir dire: Legal process of qualifying an expert witness.

Warrant: Order issued by a judge to arrest someone.

Questions and Cases

Discussion Questions

1. How are state courts organized?
2. How are federal courts organized?
3. How do civil and criminal fraud trials differ?
4. What steps are involved in the civil litigation process?
5. What is an interrogatory?
6. What is a deposition?
7. Why are depositions a powerful tool in obtaining information?
8. What steps are involved in the criminal litigation process?
9. What is discovery?
10. How are fraud examiners used as expert witnesses?
11. What are some of the do's and don'ts of being an expert witness?
12. What aspects of a fraud can an expert witness testify about?
13. During deposition, what posture should an expert witness display?

True/False

1. Most fraud cases are tried in federal courts.
2. Civil cases must consist of a jury of at least six jurors.
3. The prosecution usually prefers to present evidence at a grand jury because the accused does not have the right to hear the evidence.
4. If, during a preliminary hearing, there is not sufficient evidence to show probable cause, the defendant can still be prosecuted at a later time when more evidence is available.
5. The burden of proof necessary to prove a defendant is guilty in a criminal trial is significantly greater than in a civil trial.
6. To be successful, plaintiffs in civil cases must prove their case beyond a reasonable doubt.
7. Investigation is the legal process by which each party's attorneys try to find all information about the other side's case before the trial begins.
8. An interrogatory is a series of written questions that specifically identify information needed from the opposing party.
9. A request for confession asks the opposing party to admit designated facts relevant to litigation.
10. The parties in a civil case may negotiate a settlement during any stage of litigation.
11. Federal courts only hear cases that involve federal law, more than one state, or a federal statute.
12. Defendants can choose to have their case tried in either a state lower court or a state higher court.
13. An individual committing fraud can be prosecuted either criminally or civilly, but not both.
14. A deposition is a testimony taken before the trial begins in a situation that is less formal than a courtroom, but in which the court rules and regulations still apply.

Multiple Choice

1. To be convicted in a criminal case, the standard of evidence is:
   a. Beyond a shadow of a doubt
   b. Beyond a reasonable doubt
   c. Preponderance of the evidence
   d. All of the above
2. Most court cases are decided in state courts, except when:
   a. Federal laws are in question.
   b. The case involves several states.
   c. The amount exceeds $100,000.
   d. Both a and b are correct.

3. Which of the following rights is *not* provided by the Fifth Amendment?
   a. Double jeopardy (being tried twice for the same crime)
   b. States forbidden from seizing private property without just compensation
   c. Right to refuse to incriminate oneself
   d. Reading of Miranda rights upon arrest
4. During a trial or deposition, expert witnesses should:
   a. Respond aggressively
   b. Bring notes and work papers to cite
   c. Answer questions convincingly, without hedging their answers
   d. Memorize well-crafted responses to say what they think sounds effective
5. During cross-examination, expert witnesses should:
   a. Address areas outside of their areas of expertise
   b. Appreciate opposing counsel when they act very friendly
   c. Respond evasively and ambiguously to tough questions
   d. Maintain the same positions taken during direct testimony
6. When deposing an expert witness, the opposing attorneys try to achieve all of the following goals *except*:
   a. Understanding the expert's opinion
   b. Understanding the expert's credentials
   c. Seeking admission of guilt
   d. Obtaining an assessment of how difficult the expert will be in the case
7. Having a civil trial before a criminal trial has the following benefits:
   a. Defendant may make admissions during civil trial that can be used in criminal trial.
   b. Greater access to documents of the defendant.
   c. Defendant is not guaranteed the right to an attorney.
   d. Both a and b are correct.
8. Which of the following is *not* one of the common stages of a criminal case?
   a. Filing a criminal charge
   b. Filing a complaint
   c. Discovery
   d. Trial and appeal
9. In a civil trial, settlements may be negotiated:
   a. At any time during the litigation
   b. After arraignment
   c. No settlement may be reached once negotiation begins
   d. Only after judge orders negotiation between parties
10. Which of the following actions can fraud victims pursue after sufficient evidence is obtained?
    a. Prosecute in a criminal court
    b. Pursue civil litigation
    c. Take no action at all
    d. All of the above

Short Cases

Case 1. Mr. Bill is the sole proprietor of a small play-dough production company. Over the last few months, he has noticed revenues dropping and he wonders what is going on. After giving it much thought, he realizes that his accountant is cooking the books and stealing money from him—at least that is what seems to be the case. Mr. Bill is pretty upset and immediately runs down to the local courthouse and files a complaint against his accountant. Too anxious to wait for the workings of the legal process, Mr. Bill goes to his accountant's personal residence and searches for evidence of fraud. To his delight, he finds papers that document his accountant's illegal activities.

Mr. Bill hurries to the office, where he confronts his accountant and shows him what he found at his house, informing him that a complaint has been filed. His accountant, Mr. Pringles, calmly laughs and walks away, apparently not affected at all by what Mr. Bill has told him.

Why is Mr. Pringles not worried about Mr. Bill's discovery?

Case 2. In April of 1994, a Wall Street bond trader turned on the television and saw a news report accusing him of committing a large securities scam. This trader learned that his employer had accused him of creating $300 million of phony profits and, as a result, getting bogus bonuses of $8 million. He claimed he was innocent, and it took him three years to prove his innocence. In the months that followed the accusations, he was investigated by the Securities and Exchange Commission, the National Association of Securities Dealers, and the Justice Department. In 1997, this bond trader was cleared of all major charges brought against him.[9]

1. What type of legal action would you as his employer seek against this bond trader? Why?
2. What type of court would your case more likely be assigned to? Why?

Case 3. In June of 2000, the SEC brought civil charges against seven top executives of Cendant Corporation. The commission alleged that these officials had, among other things, inflated income by more than $100 million through improper use of company reserves. These proceedings were a result of a long-standing investigation by the SEC of financial fraud that started back in the 1980s.

In your opinion, how far along is this case? Why?

Case 4. Briefly research a recent well-publicized fraud and become familiar with the major facts in the case. Identify ways that a fraud investigator could add value in (1) the investigation, (2) legal follow-up, and (3) designing and implementing controls to prevent similar problems in the future.

Case 5. When O. J. Simpson was tried for the murder of his wife, Nicole Simpson, he was ruled "not guilty" in the criminal court hearings. However, when Nicole Simpson's family sued Mr. Simpson civilly, he was ordered to compensate Nicole's family several millions of dollars. How could that be?

Case 6. You manage a large department store. It has recently come to light that a receiving clerk has been stealing merchandise. About $5,000 has been stolen. The clerk has stopped stealing, and the internal control weaknesses that allowed the fraud have been fixed. No action has been taken to punish the perpetrator, who still works at his same job. The clerk happens to be the nephew of another manager, who, although he understands that his nephew's behavior was unacceptable, would like to keep the theft "under wraps."

What action, if any, should be taken against the receiving clerk in this situation? What consequences might result from that action?

Case 7. Answer the following questions:

1. After being named as a defendant in a corporate fraud case, the XYZ accounting firm was found guilty of negligence and fined $25 billion. As a partner in the firm, what would you recommend as the next course of action, and how would you go about pursuing that action?
2. As part of your preparations for a large financial statement fraud case, you issue a production request to see the other party's bank statements. When the statements are provided to you, some of them are only photocopies. The opposing party claims that the originals were accidentally destroyed. What can you do in this situation?

Case 8. You have been retained by the Mitchell Company shareholders as an expert witness in a case of alleged fraud by top management against the corporation. Supposedly, working in collusion, top management defrauded the company of $5 million over two years. The allegations suggest that the fraud was concealed by overstating expense accounts and manipulating balance sheet accounts.

Following the initial discovery of this alleged fraud, Mitchell's shareholders brought a civil lawsuit against top management. The case is now in the discovery phase.

What will your role likely be as an expert witness? At what point in the process will you be most involved? How can you assist the prosecution?

Case 9. Bobby Jones, an accountant for ABC Corporation, is suspected of committing fraud. Information already gathered about the fraud points a finger at Bobby Jones as the most likely perpetrator. In his scheme, Bobby supposedly stole more than $5 million over the past three years. Due to the magnitude of the fraud, and to set an example in the company, ABC decides to prosecute Bobby both civilly and criminally.

Describe what will happen to Bobby Jones and ABC during each stage of the civil litigation.

Extensive Cases

Case 10. *Supreme Court Declines to Hear Cendant Stock Fraud Case*

Recently, the Supreme Court declined to hear a securities fraud case pitting disgruntled investors against former Cendant Corporation executives. The justices, acting without comment, turned away an appeal by former Cendant Chairman Walter Forbes and Vice Chairman Christopher McLeod of a ruling on how to establish whether a fraud is made "in connection with" a securities offering.

The executives argued that the June 2000 ruling by the Third Circuit U.S. Court of Appeals is so broad that it could unleash a flood of securities fraud lawsuits. The ruling stems from a lawsuit in which a New Jersey district court dismissed securities fraud claims against Cendant and former top executives. Investors appealed that ruling to the federal appeals court, and the appellate court sent the case back to the district court for further review, prompting the former executives to appeal to the Supreme Court.

The case revolves around allegedly misleading statements about Cendant's financial health in conjunction with a proposed 1998 merger with American Bankers Insurance Group, Inc., which promised American Bankers' shareholders $67 per share in cash or Cendant stock.

Disgruntled investors said they relied on Cendant's upbeat assessment of its finances, and "lost enormous sums of money" when American Bankers Insurance stock fell from nearly $65 to $35.50 when the merger was terminated. A New Jersey district court rejected the claims, saying connections between any misrepresentations by Cendant and the investors' purchases of American Bankers Insurance Group shares were too tenuous to be deemed to be "in connections with 'those purchases.' "

1. Why were the securities fraud claims against Cendant ultimately dismissed?
2. What appeals process was followed by the prosecuting investors? Is this process concurrent with what you learned in the chapter?
3. Do you think the Supreme Court's decision was valid? Do you think they should have at least heard the case? Why or why not?

Case 11. Daren has been retained as an expert witness in a recent fraud case by the defendant. He will provide information concerning the defendant's activities, explaining why the defendant's activities are in accordance with GAAP and normal business practice. Throughout the litigation process, Daren has been completely honest with the attorneys through his deposition and other correspondence. Daren believes that the activities of the defendant are in accordance with GAAP. The case continues and is brought to trial. A few days before Daren is called to testify in the trial, he discovers new documents and information, which possibly represent fraudulent behavior by the defendant.

What ethical issues does Daren face in the light of this new information? What concerns should Daren have? What are some possible actions Daren can take?

Debate

Sam's Electronics Universe has discovered and investigated a kickback fraud perpetrated by its purchasing agent. The fraud lasted eight months and cost the company $2 million in excess inventory purchases. The perpetrator received kickbacks of $780,000. Your boss wants to seek restitution for what the company has lost, but is worried about the ramifications of a trial and how it might hurt Sam's image in the market. She is trying to decide if she should pursue restitution through a civil trial or turn the case over to the district attorney to prosecute the perpetrator criminally. Pair up with a class member and choose sides. Discuss the pros and cons of each approach.

End Notes

1. We appreciate the Association of Certified Fraud Examiners and its chairman, Joseph T. Wells, for allowing us to reference extensively the association's self-study course "Recovering the Proceeds of Fraud," and its video "The Fraud Trial."
2. Liz Pulliam Weston: "Money Talk, FBI and IRS Raid Offices of Slatkin," *Los Angeles Times,* May 12, 2001. See http://www.slatkinfraud.com/media.shtml.
3. Most states refer to their highest-level appellate court as the state supreme court.
4. *USA Today,* Nov. 8, 2001, p. 6A.
5. Nonparties are other witnesses, both fact and experts, who have information or will render an opinion about the case.
6. The Federal Rules of Criminal Procedure can be found at: http://www.courtrules.org/frc.htm.
7. While depositions are common in court cases, they are usually not taken in arbitration hearings. For example, the New York Stock Exchange settles most lawsuits brought against registered companies (brokers, etc.) through arbitration. In these arbitration

hearings, most of the elements discussed in this chapter apply (fact discovery, interrogatories, etc.), except that there are no depositions prior to the arbitration. Arbitrations are usually decided by a panel of three impartial members.

8. The *Journal of Accountancy,* a publication of the AICPA, has published several articles on this topic. Some good Internet references are: http://www.courtrules.org/frc.htm and http://www.e3power.com/Search/Courses/ProfessionalDevelopment/ExpertWitness.htm.

9. You can read about the case at: http://www.smeal.psu.edu/faculty/huddart/Courses/BA521/Jett/JettWSJ98.shtm.

Financial Statement Fraud Standards

This textbook contains three chapters on financial statement fraud. Because of the high costs associated with financial statement fraud, regulators have paid much attention over the years to this problem. Such scrutiny has resulted in both auditing standards as well as influential reports issued by organizations and parties interested in the fair presentation of financial statements. In this appendix, we review the professional standards and reports related to financial statement fraud in order to provide you with the necessary background to understand issues related to fraudulent financial statements. Standards and reports are presented chronologically.

Auditors' Responsibility to Detect Financial Statement Fraud: A Brief History

During the early part of this century, there was universal agreement, even among auditors, that the detection of fraud was one of the primary purposes for conducting an audit of financial statements. Indeed, as noted in a best-selling auditing textbook by Carmichael and Willingham (1971), detecting fraud is deeply rooted in the historical role of auditors, dating back to the early sixteenth century. As late as the 1930s, most auditors emphasized that one of the primary purposes of an audit was detection of fraud. Mautz and Sharaf (1961) stated, "Until recently there was substantial acceptance of the idea that an independent audit had as one of its principal purposes the detection and prevention of fraud and other irregularities."[1] An early edition of Montgomery (the first auditing text) listed three objectives of the audit:

1. The detection of fraud,
2. The detection of technical errors, and
3. The detection of errors in principle.

By the late 1930s, a visible change occurred in the auditing profession's willingness to accept responsibility for fraud detection as a purpose for auditing financial statements. This revolutionary change culminated in the issuance of Statement on Auditing Procedure (SAP) No. 1, *Extensions of Auditing Procedure*. SAP No. 1 contained the following statement:

> *The ordinary examination incident to the issuance of financial statements, accompanied by a report and opinion of an independent certified public accountant, is not designed to discover all defalcations, because that is not its primary objective, although discovery of defalcation frequently results. . . . To exhaust the possibility of all cases of dishonesty or fraud, the independent auditor would have to examine in detail all transactions. This would entail a prohibitive cost to the great majority of business enterprises—a cost which would pass all bounds of reasonable expectation of benefit or safeguard therefrom, and place an undue burden on industry.*

Since SAP No. 1 was issued, the profession has struggled to refine and articulate its position on detecting fraud and to establish standards capable of convincing users that auditors should have only a limited role in detecting fraud. During the late 1950s, SAP No. 1, as well as the profession, endured vigorous attacks, and pressure mounted for the AICPA to reconsider its official position as stated in SAP No. 1. The AICPA responded in 1960 by issuing a new standard, SAP No. 30, *Responsibilities and Functions of the Independent Auditor in the Examination of Financial Statements.* Many accounting professionals viewed SAP No. 30 as unresponsive to user concerns because it added no new responsibility to detect fraud. Specifically, SAP No. 30 stated an auditor's responsibility to detect irregularities as follows:

> *The ordinary examination incident to the expression of an opinion on financial statements is not primarily or specifically designed, and cannot be relied upon, to disclose defalcations and other similar irregularities, although their discovery may result. Similarly, although the discovery of deliberate misrepresentations by management is usually more closely associated with the objective of the ordinary examination, such examination cannot be relied upon to assure its discovery.*

Although the standard did stress that an auditor was obliged to "be aware of the possibility that fraud may exist," it also clarified that an auditor held no responsibility beyond the minimum duty to design tests that would detect fraud.

Although the courts appeared to hold auditors responsible for failure to detect fraud, it took the Equity Funding case and its associated scrutiny of the profession to determine that SAP No. 30 was inadequate.

The Committee on Auditor's Responsibility (Cohen Commission), comprised largely of non-AICPA members, reached a different conclusion, however. The Cohen Commission issued a report in 1978 that highlighted the widening gap between auditor performance and financial statement user expectations. The Cohen report primarily targeted the development of conclusions and recommendations regarding appropriate responsibilities of independent auditors, including the auditor's responsibility for the detection of fraudulent financial reporting. According to the Cohen Commission, the auditor:

> *. . . has a duty to search for fraud, and should be expected to detect those frauds that the examination would normally uncover.*

The commission went on to say that

> *. . . users of financial statements should have a right to assume that audited financial information is not unreliable because of fraud. . . . An audit should be designed to provide reasonable assurance that the financial statements are not affected by material fraud.*

SAS No. 16, *The Independent Auditor's Responsibility for the Detection of Errors or Irregularities,* was issued in 1977, admitting some obligation to search for fraud in the normal course of a GAAS audit. According to SAS No. 16:

> *The independent auditor's objective in making an examination of financial statements in accordance with (GAAS) is to form an opinion on whether the financial statements present fairly financial position, results of operations, and the changes in financial position in conformity with (GAAP). . . . Consequently, under (GAAS), the independent auditor has the responsibility, within the inherent limitations of the auditing process . . . to plan his examination to search for (material) errors and irregularities.*

Although SAS No. 16 required auditors to "search for" fraud, it did not require them to "detect" fraud. Even after SAS No. 16 was issued, auditors remained unwilling to accept or acknowledge a substantial responsibility for detecting fraud. SAS No. 16 contained similar "defensive and qualifying" language that was included in SAP No. 1 and SAP No. 30: phrases such as "inherent limitations of the auditing process" and "unless the auditor's examination reveals evidentiary matter to the contrary, his reliance on the truthfulness of certain representations and the genuineness of records and documents obtained during the examination was reasonable" allowed auditors to justify the unwillingness to detect fraud.

Report of the National Commission on Fraudulent Financial Reporting

In October 1987, the National Commission on Fraudulent Financial Reporting (Treadway Commission) issued a landmark report in response to concerns about fraudulent financial reporting. This report helped refocus the business community on the problem of fraudulent financial reporting. Considered an update to the Cohen report, the Treadway study of incidents of financial statement fraud also focused on a broader range of parties playing a vital role in the financial reporting process. The report included 49 extensive recommendations embracing the roles of top management and boards of directors of public companies, independent public accountants and the public accounting profession, the SEC and other regulatory and law enforcement bodies, and the academic community. The Treadway Commission identified numerous causal factors that can lead to financial statement fraud.

Although the Treadway report is not covered in detail in this book, it is strongly recommended that you become familiar with its contents. The report highlights many of the problems that lead to financial statement fraud and provides a basis for activity by organizations such as the AICPA and others. Since the issuance of the Treadway report, there have been many efforts to build upon the commission's findings—that is, to minimize incidents of fraudulent financial reporting. These efforts have primarily focused on the roles that auditors, managers, boards of directors, and audit committees play in the financial statement process.

Efforts Related to the Role of Auditors—SAS No. 53

Soon after the issuance of the Treadway report, the AICPA's Auditing Standards Board (ASB) issued Statement on Auditing Standards No. 53, *The Auditor's Responsibility to Detect and Report Errors and Irregularities.* The ASB issued SAS No. 53 to strengthen the auditor's responsibility related to the detection of instances of material fraudulent financial reporting. SAS No. 53 modified the auditor's responsibility to require the auditor to "design the audit to provide reasonable assurance of detecting errors and irregularities." SAS No. 53 was designed to narrow the expectation gap between the assurances auditors provide and what financial statement users expect regarding the detection of fraudulent financial reporting. SAS No. 53 required the auditor to provide reasonable assurance that material irregularities would be detected, which extended the auditor's responsibility beyond what was required by SAS No. 16.

Public Oversight Board's 1993 Special Report

Subsequent to the issuance of SAS No. 53, the Public Oversight Board of the AICPA SEC Practice Section (the POB) issued a Special Report entitled *In the Public Interest: Issues Confronting the Accounting Profession.* The report was issued primarily in response to continuing signs of failing public confidence in public accountants and auditors, particularly the widespread belief that auditors have a responsibility for detecting management fraud, which many viewed auditors as not meeting. Based on the POB's belief that the integrity and reliability of audited financial statements are critical to the U.S. economy, the Special Report contained specific recommendations for improving and strengthening the accounting profession's performance by enhancing its capacity and willingness to detect fraud and improve the financial reporting process. It also called for improved guidance beyond that in SAS No. 53 to assist auditors in assessing the likelihood of fraud, a strengthening of the process to ensure auditor independence and professionalism, and changes in the corporate governance process. The POB was especially interested in enhancing the auditing profession's potential for detecting management fraud.

AICPA Board of Director's 1993 Report

Also in 1993, the AICPA's Board of Directors issued its report, *Meeting the Financial Reporting Needs of the Future: A Public Commitment for the Public Accounting Profession.* In that report, the AICPA Board of Directors expressed its determination to keep the U.S. financial reporting system the best in the world, supporting the recommendations and initiatives of others to assist auditors in the detection of material misstatements in financial statements resulting from fraud, and encouraged every participant in the financial reporting process—management, their advisors, regulators, and independent auditors—to share in this responsibility.

AICPA SEC Practice Section Initiatives

Soon after the issuance of the POB's Special Report and the AICPA's Board of Directors' report, the AICPA undertook efforts related to improving the integrity of the financial reporting process, particularly through improved detection of fraudulent financial reporting. The AICPA's SEC Practice Section formed a Professional Issues Task Force that has published guidance about emerging or unresolved practice issues that surface through litigation analysis, peer review, or internal inspection. The SEC Practice Section also amended membership requirements to require that concurring partners provide assurance that those consulting on accounting and auditing matters are aware of all relevant facts and circumstances related to the consultation issue and to the auditee, to ensure that the conclusion reached is an appropriate one. The AICPA SEC Practice Section also created the Detection and Prevention of Fraud Task Force. That task force issued a document in 1994 entitled *Client Acceptance and Continuance Procedures for Audit Clients.*[2] That document emphasized that understanding the components of engagement risk is critical to deciding whether to accept new clients, continue old ones, and in any event to manage the "audit risk" that accompanies those decisions.

Panel on Audit Effectiveness

At the request of the chairman of the SEC, the Public Oversight Board appointed a panel of eight members, charging it to thoroughly examine the current audit model. The panel made recommendations that it believed would result in more effective audits that improve the reliability of financial statements, enhance their credibility, contribute to investors' confidence in the profession, and improve the efficiency of the capital markets. One of the panel's recommendations was that because "audit firms may have reduced the scope of their audits and level of testing and because the auditing profession may not have kept pace with a rapidly changing environment, the profession needs to address vigorously the issue of fraudulent financial reporting, including fraud in the form of illegitimate earnings management." They recommended that the auditing standards should create a "forensic-type" fieldwork phase on all audits. They suggested that this work should be based on the possibility of dishonesty and collusion, overriding of controls, and falsification of documents. Auditors would be required during this phase, in some cases on a surprise basis, to perform substantive tests directed at the possibility of fraud. The panel's recommendations also call for auditors to examine non-standard entries, and to analyze certain opening financial statement balances to assess, with the benefit of hindsight, how certain accounting estimates and judgments or other matters were resolved. The intent of the panel's recommendations was twofold: to enhance the likelihood that auditors will be able to detect material fraud, and to establish implicitly a deterrent to fraud by positing a greater threat to its successful concealment.[3]

SAS No. 82

In 1997, the AICPA responded to various calls for improved auditing guidance related to the detection of material misstatements due to fraudulent financial reporting by issuing SAS No. 82, *Consideration of Fraud in a Financial Statement Audit*. SAS 82 was written to help reduce the "expectation gap" that exists between financial statement auditors and users of financial statements. SAS 82 will only be successful in narrowing the expectation gap if, as a result of applying the standard, (1) auditors detect more fraud sooner (that is, the standard bolsters the actual fraud detection performance of auditors), or (2) the standard is successful in convincing financial statement users that auditors should not be held responsible for detecting all financial statement fraud. Although many people are optimistic about the standard accomplishing the first of these possibilities, few believe that the second result will ever happen.

Although we refer often to, and liberally excerpt from, SAS 82 in this textbook, we would encourage you to read the entire standard. In studying SAS 82, consider what SAS 82 is and what it is not. Also, the key provisions of SAS 82 and how it differs from previous fraud-related auditing standards are important.

What SAS 82 Is

At the time this book was published, SAS 82 was the existing GAAS fraud standard. However, an exposure draft for another fraud standard that would revise SAS 82 had been issued.

SAS 82 is an auditing standard that clarifies the fraud detection responsibilities of certified public accountants (CPAs) and provides guidance to those who perform financial statement audits. Like all other standards, SAS 82 offers instructions on how the ten generally accepted auditing standards (GAAS) should be interpreted and followed. SAS 82 primarily provides guidance on how financial statement auditors should consider the possibility of fraud when:

- Exercising due professional care (general auditing standard No. 3)
- Planning an audit (fieldwork standard No. 1)
- Evaluating internal controls (fieldwork standard No. 2), and
- Gathering sufficient, competent evidentiary matter to support the audit opinion (fieldwork standard No. 3)

SAS 82 relates only to audits of financial statement performed in accordance with GAAS, and represents the American Institute of Certified Public Accountant's most recent attempt to deal with the difficult issue of fraud.

SAS 82 is much more comprehensive than the preceding fraud-related auditing standards. Although it does not change the overall responsibilities of GAAS auditors to provide "reasonable assurance that material misstatement of the financial statement does not exist," it more explicitly identifies what auditors must do to try to discover such fraud. The following are key provisions of the standard that are intended to remove the "fuzziness" that existed with previous standards, and that should help auditors better detect material financial statement misstatement caused by fraud.

1. SAS 82 is the first-ever auditing standard that solely addresses fraud. Previous standards addressed "errors" and irregularities" together.
2. SAS 82 is the first GAAS auditing standard to use the term *fraud*. Previous standards have used the more nebulous term *irregularity* when referring to fraud.
3. SAS 82 makes it clear that the auditor's responsibilities with respect to fraud extend throughout the entire audit and do not end when the planning phase is finished. Previous standards were not clear regarding post-planning responsibilities.
4. SAS 82 requires GAAS auditors to document how they assessed the risk of fraud in their audits. Previous fraud standards did not require specific documentation. There was a general feeling among SAS 82 task force members that requiring documentation would, in many cases, drive behavior that is consistent with the standard.
5. SAS 82 requires GAAS auditors to document how they responded to the risks of fraud they discovered when conducting their audits. Previous standards hardly mentioned how risks of fraud should be documented, evaluated, or addressed.
6. SAS 82 emphasizes the need for "professional skepticism" in dealing with clients.
7. SAS 82 provides specific guidance to auditors about the kind of risks they must consider (more than 30 different examples of risk factors are presented), and how observed risk factors should be considered and addressed.
8. SAS 82 requires GAAS auditors to ask management specifically about the risks of fraud, what they perceive to be the company's greatest fraud exposures, and whether they have knowledge of fraud that has been perpetrated on or within the company.

Proposed Statement on Auditing Standards: Considerations of Fraud in a Financial Statement Audit[4]

The proposed statement on auditing standards (SAS) establishes standards and provides guidance to auditors in fulfilling their responsibility as it relates to fraud in an audit of financial statements conducted in accordance with generally accepted auditing standards (GAAS). The proposed statement does not change the auditor's responsibility to plan and perform the audit to obtain reasonable assurance about whether the financial statements are free of material misstatement, whether caused by error or fraud. However, the proposed statement does establish standards and provide guidance to auditors in fulfilling that responsibility, as it relates to fraud. The following is an overview of the content of the proposed statement:

Description and characteristics of fraud. This section of the proposed statement describes fraud and its characteristics, including the aspects of fraud particularly relevant to an audit of financial statements.

Discussion among engagement personnel regarding the risks of material misstatement due to fraud. This section requires, as part of planning the audit, that there be a discussion among the audit team members to consider the susceptibility of the entity to material misstatement due to fraud and to reinforce the importance of adopting an appropriate mindset of professional skepticism.

Obtaining the information needed to identify the risks of material misstatement due to fraud. This section requires the auditor to gather the information necessary to identify the risks of material misstatement due to fraud, by the following:

1. Making inquiries of management and others within the entity.
2. Considering the results of the analytical procedures performed in planning the audit. (The proposed statement also requires that the auditor perform analytical procedures relating to revenue.)
3. Considering fraud risk factors.
4. Considering certain other information.

Identifying risks that may result in a material misstatement due to fraud. This section requires the auditor to use the information gathered above to identify risks that may result in a material misstatement due to fraud.

Assessing the identified risks after taking into account an evaluation of the entity's programs and controls. This section requires the auditor to evaluate the entity's programs and controls that address the identified risks of material misstatement due to fraud, and to assess the risks taking into account this evaluation.

Responding to the results of the assessment. This section requires the auditor to respond to the results of the risk assessment. This response may include the following:

1. A response to identified risks that has an overall effect on how the audit is conducted; that is, a response involving more general considerations apart from the specific procedures otherwise planned.
2. A response to identified risk that involves the nature, timing, and extent of the auditing procedures to be performed.
3. A response involving the performance of certain procedures to further address the risk of material misstatement due to fraud involving management override of controls.

Evaluating audit test results. This section requires the auditor's assessment of the risk of material misstatement due to fraud to be ongoing throughout the audit and that the auditor evaluate at the completion of the audit whether the accumulated results of auditing procedures and other observations affect the assessment. It also requires the auditor to consider whether identified misstatements may be indicative of fraud and, if so, directs the auditor to evaluate their implications.

Communicating about fraud to management, the audit committee, and others. This section provides guidance regarding the auditor's communications about fraud to management, the audit committee, and others.

Documenting the auditor's consideration of fraud. This section describes related documentation requirements.

The Roles of Management, Boards of Directors, and Audit Committees

Although auditors play a vital role in the detection of instances of material fraudulent financial reporting, the Treadway Commission's 1987 report noted that the prevention and early detection of fraudulent financial reporting must start with the entity that prepares the financial statements. Every fraudulent financial statement for which the auditor has been held responsible was prepared by executives who intentionally misstated financial information to deceive not only shareholders, investors, and creditors, but the auditor as well. Thus, the

Treadway report contains several recommendations for public companies, particularly addressing responsibilities of top management, the board of directors, and audit committees. The Treadway report calls for all public companies to maintain internal controls that provide reasonable assurance that fraudulent financial reporting will be prevented or subjected to early detection. The Treadway Commission specifically calls for the development of additional, integrated guidance on internal controls.

COSO's 1992 Report

In 1992, COSO issued *Internal Control—Integrated Framework* in response to calls for better internal control systems to help senior executives better control the enterprises they run. In addition to noting that internal controls can help an entity achieve its performance and profitability targets and prevent the loss of resources, COSO's report also notes that internal control can significantly help an entity ensure reliable financial reporting. Specifically, the COSO report:

- Provides a high-level overview of the internal control framework directed to the chief executive and other senior officers, board members, legislators, and regulators.
- Defines internal control, describe its components, and provide criteria against which managements, boards of directors, and others can assess their internal control systems.
- Provides guidance to those entities that report publicly on internal control over the preparation of their published statements.
- Contains materials that might be useful in conducting an evaluation of internal controls.

Audit Committee Requirements of Major U.S. Stock Exchanges

Often, boards of directors of companies assign responsibility for oversight of the financial reporting process to an audit committee, comprised of a subgroup of the board. In the United States, all three major securities markets—the New York Stock Exchange (NYSE), American Stock Exchange (AMEX), and National Association of Securities Dealer's Automated Quotation System (NASDAQ)—have requirements addressing audit committee composition. The NYSE requires, and the AMEX recommends, that listed companies have audit committees made up entirely of outside directors.[5] NASDAQ requires only that a majority of the audit committee consist of outside directors for companies trading on the National Market System; however, companies trading as a NASDAQ Small-Cap Issue are not required to maintain a minimum number of outside directors on their audit committees. These audit committee requirements were generally in place by the time the Treadway report was issued. However, other regulatory actions were undertaken in the 1990s related to the corporate governance process. For example, the Federal Deposit Insurance Corporation implemented new audit committee composition requirements mandating the inclusion of independent directors who, for certain large depository institutions, must include individuals with banking experience.[6]

Public Oversight Board's Advisory Panel Report

In 1994, the POB issued a report entitled *Strengthening the Professionalism of the Independent Auditor.* This report encouraged boards of directors to play an active role in the financial reporting process and for the auditing profession to look to the board of directors—the shareholders' representative—as its client. The Advisory Panel urged the POB, the SEC, and others to encourage adoption of proposals such as increasing the representation of outsiders on the board and reducing board size to strengthen the independence of boards of directors and their accountability to shareholders. In addition to strengthening the role of the board of directors in the oversight of management, the Advisory Panel recommended that audit committees should expect auditors to be more forthcoming in communicating first with the audit committee and then with the full board to provide the auditor's perspective on the company's operations, as well as the company's financial reporting policies and practices.

Public Oversight Board's 1995 Report

The POB stated in their 1995 publication, *Directors, Management, and Auditors: Allies in Protecting Shareholder Interests,* that practices followed by well-governed corporations should foster an environment where the independent auditor, management, audit committee, and board of directors play interactive and timely roles in the financial reporting process.

After the Enron "debacle," there was significant controversy about the accounting profession and its regulation and oversight. Because of the criticism of the Public Oversight Board, it went out of business effective March 31, 2002.[7]

The Independence Standards Board

To strengthen the role of the auditor as an independent assurer of credible financial information and a major source of information for the audit committee and board, the accounting profession and the SEC agreed in 1997 to establish a new private sector body—the Independence Standards Board—to set independence rules and guidance for auditors of public companies. The Independence Standards Board did not make a significant difference in the profession.

A Different Form of Oversight

All of these efforts have helped focus attention on and reduce the number of incidences of fraudulent financial reporting. It is important that CPAs understand the high level of attention that has been paid to this problem. It is highly unlikely that the problem of fraudulent financial statements will ever go away completely. However, CPAs who follow the guidelines of SAS 82, who practice the principles set forth in this book when performing audits and providing consulting services to clients, and who work only with organizations that exhibit the kind of boards and audit committees recommended by Treadway, the stock exchanges, and others, will rarely find themselves associated with a fraudulent financial statement problem.

In addition to the reports and standards discussed here, you should also know that fraudulent financial reporting has been a subject of great academic research interest. Practitioners who have a keen interest in fraudulent financial reporting may want to read some of the relevant academic studies listed in the Bibliography.

In November 2001, Enron Corporation declared bankruptcy. Following this largest bankruptcy in history, allegations quickly focused on Enron's "financial statement manipulations" and the "failure of Enron's auditor to provide proper, objective oversight." The Enron debate led to calls for new and different oversight of the CPA profession with claims that the Independence Standards Board was ineffective. At the time this book went to press, several bills calling for different types of oversight had been introduced in Congress and other calls were being made for improved oversight.

End Notes

1. Marx, R. K., and H. A. Sharaf, "The Philosophy of Auditing," American Accounting Association, 1961.

2. http://www.aicpa.org/members/div/secps/lit/practice/943.htm

3. The Panel on Audit Effectiveness: Report and Recommendations, August 31, 2000, c/o The Public Oversight Board, One Station Place, Stamford, CT 06902. This report can be found at http://www.probauditpanel.org.

4. http://www.aicpa.org/members/div/auditstd/consideration_of_fraud.htm

5. http://www.sec.gov/rules/sro/ny9939o.htm

6. This information can be accessed at the Federal Deposit Insurance Corporation web site at http://www.fdic.gov/regulations/laws/rules/2000-8500.html. Section D: Audit Committees.

7. http://www.smartpros.com/x33441.xml

BIBLIOGRAPHY

Albrecht, W. Steve, M. B. Romney, D. J. Cherrington, I. R. Payne, and A. J. Roe, 1982, *How to Detect and Prevent Business Fraud,* Englewood Cliffs, NJ: Prentice-Hall.

Albrecht, W. Steve, and M. B. Romney, 1986, "Red-flagging Management Fraud: A Validation," *Advances in Accounting* 3: 323–333.

Albrecht, W. Steve, and J. J. Willingham, 1993, "An Evaluation of SAS No. 53: The Auditor's Responsibility to Detect and Report Errors and Irregularities," *The Expectation Gap Standards: Progress, Implementation Issues, Research Opportunities,* New York: AICPA.

Albrecht, W. Steve, G. W. Wernz, and T. L. Williams, 1995, *Fraud: Bringing Light to the Dark Side of Business,* New York, New York: Irwin Professional Publishing, pp. 56–59 and 118–119.

Albrecht, W. Steve, K. R. Howe, and M. B. Romney, 1982, *Detecting Fraud: The Internal Auditor's Perspective,* Maitland, FL: The Institute of Internal Auditors Research Foundation.

Ashton, R. E., and A. Wright, 1989, "Identifying Audit Adjustments with Attention-Directing Procedures," *The Accounting Review,* Vol. LXIV, No. 4 (October): 710–728.

Association of Certified Fraud Examiners, 1995, *Report to the Nation: Occupational Fraud and Abuse,* Austin, Texas.

Beasley, M. S., J. V. Carcello, and D. R. Hermanson, 1999, *Fraudulent Financial Reporting: 1987–1997: An Analysis of U.S. Public Companies,* Committee of Sponsoring Organizations (COSO).

Bell, T. B., and J. V. Carcello, 1998, "Assessing the Likelihood of Fraudulent Financial Reporting," Working paper, Montvale, NJ: KPMG.

Bonner, S. E., Z. V. Palmrose, and S. M. Young, 1998, "Fraud Type and Auditor Litigation: An Analysis of SEC Accounting and Auditing Enforcement Releases," *The Accounting Review* 73 (October): 503–532.

Cressy, D. R., 1953, *Other People's Money: The Social Psychology of Embezzlement,* New York: Free Press.

Deshmukh, A., K. E. Karim, and P. H. Siegel, 1998, "An Analysis of the Efficiency and Effectiveness of Auditing to Detect Management Fraud: A Signal Detection Theory Approach," *International Journal of Auditing:* 127–138.

DeZoort, F. T., and T. A. Lee, 1998, "The Impact of SAS No. 82 on Perceptions of External Auditor Responsibility for Fraud Detection," *International Journal of Auditing:* 167–182.

Eining, M. M., and P. B. Dorr, 1991, "The Impact of Expert System Usage on Experiential Learning in an Audit Setting," *Journal of Information Systems* (Spring): 1–16.

Eining, M. M., D. R. Jones, and J. K. Loebbecke, 1997, "Reliance on Decision Aids: An Examination of Management Fraud," *Auditing: A Journal of Practice and Theory* 16 (Fall): 1–19.

Elliott, R. K., and J. J. Willingham, Jr., 1980, *Management Fraud: Detection and Deterrence,* New York: Petrocelli Books, Inc.

Geis, G., 1982, *On White-Collar Crime,* Lexington, MA: Lexington Books.

Geis, G., and R. F. Meier, 1977, *White-Collar Crime: Offenses in Business, Politics, and the Professions,* Revised Edition, New York: The Free Press.

Green, B. P., and J. H. Choi, 1997, "Assessing the Risk of Management Fraud Through Neural Network Technology," *Auditing: A Journal of Practice and Theory* 16 (Spring): 14–28.

Guy, D. M., and J. M. Mancino, 1998, *Consideration of Fraud in a Financial Statement Audit: What Every CPA Should Know About SAS No. 82,* A 4-hour CPE course, New York, New York: AICPA, pp. 4-7.

Hackenbrack, K., 1993, "The Effects of Experience with Different Sized Clients on Auditor Evaluations of Fraudulent Financial Reporting Indicators," *Auditing: A Journal of Practice and Theory* 12 (Spring): pp. 99–110.

Hollinger, R. C., 1989, *Dishonesty in the Workplace: A Manager's Guide to Preventing Employee Theft,* Park Ridge, IL: London House Press.

Hylas, R. E., and R. H. Ashton, "Audit Detection of Financial Statement Errors," *The Accounting Review,* Vol. LVII, No. 4 (October): 751–765.

Loebbecke, J. K., and J. J. Willingham, Jr., 1988, "Review of SEC Accounting and Auditing Enforcement Releases," Working paper, University of Utah.

Loebbecke, J. K., M. M. Eining, and J. J. Willingham, Jr., 1989, "Auditors' Experience with Material Irregularities: Frequency, Nature, and Detect-Ability," *Auditing: A Journal of Practice and Theory* 9 (Fall): 1–28.

Merchant, K. A., 1987, *Fraudulent and Questionable Financial Reporting: A Corporate Perspective,* Morristown, NJ: Financial Executives Research Foundation.

Palmrose, Z. V., 1987, "Litigation and Independent Auditors: The Role of Business Failures and Management Fraud," *Auditing: A Journal of Practice and Theory* 6 (Spring): 90–103.

Pincus, K. V., 1989, "The Efficacy of a Red Flags Questionnaire for Assessing the Possibility of Fraud," *Accounting, Organizations, and Society* 14: 153–163.

Romney, M. B., W. Steve Albrecht, and D. J. Cherrington, March 1980, "Red-flagging the White-Collar Criminal," *Management Accounting,* pp. 51–57.

Summers, S. L., and J. T. Sweeney, 1998, "Fraudulently Misstated Financial Statements and Insider Trading: An Empirical Analysis," *The Accounting Review* 73 (January): 131–146.

Sutherland, E. H., 1949, *White-Collar Crime,* New York: Dryden Press.

Zimbelman, M. F., 1997, "The Effects of SAS No. 82 on Auditors' Attention to Fraud Risk Factors and Audit Planning," *Journal of Accounting Research* 35 (Supplement): 75–97.

GLOSSARY

A

Accounting and Auditing Enforcement Release (AAER) Public document released by the SEC when a company commits financial statement fraud or other inappropriate activities.

Accounting anomalies Inaccuracies in source documents, journal entries, ledgers, or financial statements.

Accounting cycle Procedures for analyzing, recording, classifying, summarizing, and reporting the transactions of a business.

Accounting system Policies and procedures for recording economic transactions in an organized manner.

Accounts receivable turnover ratio The rate at which a company collects its receivables; computed by dividing sales by average accounts receivable.

Accounts receivable turnover Sales divided by average accounts receivable; a measure of the efficiency with which receivables are being collected.

Accrued liability Liabilities arising from end-of-period adjustments, not from specific transactions.

Acquisition The purchase of something, such as the purchase of one company by another company.

Affidavit Written statement or declaration given under oath.

Allowance for doubtful accounts A contra-asset (receivable) account representing the amount of receivables that are estimated to be uncollectible.

Allowance for uncollectible assets as a percentage of receivables Allowance for doubtful accounts divided by accounts receivable; a measure of the percentage of receivables estimated to be uncollectible.

Analytical anomalies Relationships, procedures, or events that do not make sense.

Appellate Court Review court to which participants in lower court cases can have their cases reviewed or retried if they are unhappy with the outcome.

Arraignment Court hearing where charges against the defendant are read. At the arraignment, the defendants may plead guilty, not guilty, or nolo contendere.

Asset fraud Financial statement fraud in which assets are recorded at higher amounts than they should be.

Asset misappropriations Theft that is committed by stealing receipts, stealing assets on hand, or by committing some type of disbursement fraud.

Asset turnover Total sales divided by average total assets; a measure of the amount of sales revenue generated with each dollar of assets.

Association of Certified Fraud Examiners (ACFE) An international organization, based in Austin, Texas, dedicated to fighting fraud and white-collar crime.

Audit command language (ACL) Popular commercial data-mining software; helps investigators detect fraud.

Audit trail Documents and records that can be used to trace transactions.

Autocratic management Management conducted by a few key people who do not accept advice or participation from other employees.

B

Bad debt expense An expense representing receivables and/or revenues that are presumed not to be collectible.

Balance sheet Financial statement that reports a company's assets, liabilities, and owners' equity as of a particular date.

Bankruptcy A legal process that either allows a debtor to work out an orderly plan to settle debts or to liquidate a debtor's assets and distribute them to creditors.

Bankruptcy Code Title 11 of the U.S. Code—the federal statute that governs the bankruptcy process.

Bankruptcy Courts Federal courts that hear only bankruptcy cases.

Benford's law Mathematical algorithm that accurately predicts that, for many data sets, the first digit of each group of numbers in a random sample will begin with a 1 more than a 2, a 2 more than a 3, a 3 more than a 4, and so on; predicts the percentage of time each digit will appear in a sequence of numbers.

Bid-rigging scheme Collusive fraud wherein an employee helps a vendor illegally obtain a contract that was supposed to involve competitive bidding.

Billing scheme Submission of a false or altered invoice that causes an employer to willingly issue a check.

Biometrics Using unique features of the human body (for example, retinal scans) to create secure access controls.

Bribery The offering, giving, receiving, or soliciting anything of value to influence an official act.

Bustout A planned bankruptcy.

C

Capitalization Recording expenditures as assets rather than as expenses. (For example, start-up costs that are "capitalized" are recorded as assets and amortized.)

Chain of custody Maintaining detailed records about documents from the time they are received in the investigation process until the trial is completed. Helps to substantiate that documents have not been altered or manipulated since coming into the investigator's hands.

Chapter 11 bankruptcy Bankruptcy that allows the bankrupt entity time to reorganize its operational and financial affairs, settle its debts, and continue to operate in a reorganized fashion.

Chapter 7 bankruptcy Complete liquidation or "shutting down of a business" and distribution of any proceeds to creditors.

Check tampering Scheme in which dishonest employees (1) prepare fraudulent checks for their own benefit, or (2) intercept checks intended for a third party and convert the checks for their own benefit.

Civil law Body of law that provides remedies for violation of private rights—deals with rights and duties between individuals.

Collusion Fraud perpetrated by two or more employees or others, each of whose job responsibilities is necessary to complete the fraud.

Commercial data-mining software Commercial software packages that use query techniques to detect patterns and anomalies in data that may suggest fraud.

Committee of Sponsoring Organizations (COSO) Organization made up of representatives from major accounting firms that focus on internal controls and financial statement fraud.

Common-size financial statements Financial statements that have been converted to percentages.

Complaint Request filed by a plaintiff to request civil proceedings against someone—usually to seek damages.

Concealment investigative methods Investigating a fraud by focusing on the cover-up efforts, such as the manipulation of source documents.

Contingent liability A possible liability. If the likelihood of payment is "probable," the contingent liability must be reported as a liability on the financial statements; if likelihood of payment is reasonably possible, it must be disclosed in the footnotes to the financial statements; if likelihood of payment is remote, no mention of the possible liability needs to be made.

Control activities or procedures Specific error-checking routines performed by company personnel.

Control environment The actions, policies, and procedures that reflect the overall attitudes of top management, the directors, and the owners about control and its importance to the entity.

Corruption Dishonesty that involves the following schemes: (1) bribery, (2) conflicts of interest, (3) economic extortion, and (4) illegal gratuities.

Cost of goods sold The cost of goods sold to customers; calculated by subtracting ending inventory from the sum of beginning inventory plus purchases.

Covert operations Placing an agent in an undercover role in order to observe the suspect.

Creditor A person or entity owed money by a debtor.

Criminal law Branch of law that deals with offenses of a public nature or against society.

Current ratio Measure of the liquidity of a business; equal to current assets divided by current liabilities.

Customer fraud Customers not paying for goods purchased, getting something for nothing, or deceiving organizations into giving them something they should not have.

D

Data theft Theft of data or personal information through such means as sniffing, spoofing, and customer impersonation.

Database Set of interrelated, centrally controlled data files that are stored with as little redundancy as possible. A database consolidates many records previously stored in separate files into a common pool of data and serves a variety of users and data processing applications.

Debtor A person or entity declaring bankruptcy.

Debt-to-equity ratio The number of dollars of borrowed funds for every dollar invested by owners; computed as total liabilities divided by total equity.

Deductive fraud detection Determining the types of frauds that can occur and then using query techniques and other methods to determine if those frauds may actually exist.

Deferred asset Expenditure that has been capitalized to be expensed in the future.

Deposition Sworn testimony taken before a trial begins. At depositions, the opposing side's attorneys ask questions of witnesses.

Digital signatures and certificates A signature sent over the Internet.

Disbursement fraud Having an organization pay for something it shouldn't pay for or pay too much for something it purchases.

Disclosure fraud The issuance of fraudulent or misleading statements or press releases without financial statement line-item effect or the lack of appropriate disclosures that should have been, but were not, made by management.

Discovery sampling Sampling used in fraud detection that assumes a zero expected error rate. The methodology allows an auditor to determine confidence levels and make inferences from the sample to the population.

Discovery Legal process by which each party's attorneys try to find all information about the other side's case before a trial begins.

Divorce The legal separation of two married partners resulting in the dissolution of their marriage.

Document examiner Specialized investigator who applies forensic chemistry, microscopy, photography, and other scientific methods to determine whether documents or other evidence are genuine, forged, counterfeit, or fraudulent.

Documentary evidence Evidence gathered from paper, documents, computer records, and other written, printed, or electronic sources.

Documents and records Documentation of all transactions in order to create an audit trail.

Dummy or shell company Fictitious entity created for the sole purpose of committing fraud; usually involves an employee making fraudulent payments to the dummy company.

E

Earnings per share Net income divided by the number of shares of stock outstanding; a measure of profitability.

E-Business The use of information technology and electronic communication networks to exchange business information and conduct transactions in electronic, paperless form.

Economic extortion scheme Involves an employee demanding payment from a vendor in order to make or influence a decision in that vendor's favor.

Electronic surveillance Using video, e-mail, wiretapping, and so on to watch fraud suspects.

Elements of fraud The theft act, concealment, and conversion that are present in every fraud.

Embezzlement Theft or fraudulent appropriation of money through deception; often used interchangeably with the term fraud.

Employee Assistance Programs (EAPs) Programs that help employees deal with problems such as substance abuse, gambling, money management and debt, health, family, and other pressures.

Employee embezzlement Employees deceiving their employers by taking company assets.

Evidence square A categorization of fraud investigative procedures that includes testimonial evidence, documentary evidence, physical evidence, and personal observation.

Evidential matter The underlying data and all corroborating information available about a fraud.

Expense scheme Scheme in which perpetrators produce false documents to claim false expenses.

Expert witness Trial witness who can offer opinions about a matter, based on unique experience, education, or training.

F

Falsified identity (customer impersonation) Pretending to be someone you're not—a major problem in e-business transactions.

Federal Courts Courts established by the federal government to enforce federal laws and statutes.

Fifth Amendment to the U.S. Constitution Provides defendants certain protections, including (1) an indictment by a grand jury before being held for a capital crime, and (2) not being tried twice for the same crime.

Financial statement fraud Intentional misstatement of financial statements by omitting critical facts or disclosures, misstating amounts, or misapplying GAAP.

Financial statements Financial reports such as the balance sheet, income statement, and statement of cash flows that summarize the profitability and cash flows of an entity for a specific period and the financial position of the entity as of a specific date.

Fixed assets Property, plant, and equipment assets of an organization.

Fixed point surveillance Watching a fraud suspect from a fixed point, such as a restaurant, office, or other set location.

Footnotes Information that accompanies a company's financial statements and that provides interpretive guidance to the financial statements or includes related information that must be disclosed.

Fourth Amendment to the U.S. Constitution Protects defendants against unreasonable searches and seizures by the government.

Fraud "A generic term that embraces all the multifarious means which human ingenuity can devise, which are resorted to by one individual, to get an advantage over another by false representations. No definite and invariable rule can be laid down as a general proposition in defining fraud, as it includes surprise, trickery, cunning and unfair ways by which another is cheated. The only boundaries defining it are those which limit human knavery."

G

Gramm-Leach Bliley Act Passed in 1999, this law prohibits the use of false pretenses to access the personal information of others. It does allow banks and other financial institutions to share or sell customer information, unless customers proactively "opt out" and asks that their information not be shared.

Grand jury Body of 4 to 23 individuals who deliberate in secret to decide whether there is sufficient evidence to charge someone in a preliminary hearing.

Gross profit margin Gross profit margin divided by net sales; a measure of markup.

H

Higher trial courts State courts that try felony (larger crimes) and civil cases above a predetermined amount.

Horizontal analysis Tool that determines the percentage change in balance sheet and income statement numbers from one period to the next.

I

Illegal gratuities Similar to bribery, except that there is no intent to influence a particular business decision, but rather to reward someone for making a favorable decision.

Income statement Financial statement that reports the amount of net income earned by a company during a specified period.

Independent checks Procedures for verifying and monitoring other controls.

Inductive fraud detection Proactively searching for fraud by identifying anomalies or unusual or unexpected patterns and/or relationships, without determining in advance the kinds of fraud you are looking for.

Inherent risks A business's susceptibility to fraud, assuming that appropriate controls are not in place.

Initial pleading Complaint filed by a plaintiff to request legal proceedings against someone.

Intangible asset An asset that has no tangible existence (for example, goodwill).

Internal control structure Specific policies and procedures designed to provide management with reasonable assurance that the goals and objectives it believes important to the entity will be met.

Internal control weakness Weakness in the control environment, accounting system, or the control activities or procedures.

Interrogatory A series of written questions that specifically identify information needed from the opposing party.

Inventory turnover ratio Measure of the efficiency with which inventory is managed; computed by dividing cost of goods sold by average inventory for a period.

Investment scams The selling of fraudulent and worthless investments to unsuspecting investors.

Invigilation Imposing strict temporary controls on an activity so that, during the observation period, fraud is virtually impossible. Involves keeping detailed records before, during, and after the invigilation period and comparing suspicious activity during the three periods to obtain evidence about whether fraud is occurring.

J

Jurisdiction The limit or territory over which an organization has authority.

K

Kickback fraud Fraud perpetrated by an employee and the employee's vendor or customer. Usually involves the employee buying goods or services from the vendor at an overstated price or giving the customer a lower-than-normal price, and in return the vendor or customer pays the employee a "kickback."

Kiting Fraud that conceals cash shortages by (1) transferring funds from one bank to another and (2) recording the receipt on or before the balance sheet date and the disbursement after the balance sheet date.

L

Labeling Teaching and training.

Lapping Fraud that involves stealing one customer's payment and then crediting that customer's account when a subsequent customer pays.

Larceny Intentionally taking an employer's cash or other assets without the consent and against the will of the employer, after it has been recorded in the company's accounting system.

Lease Obligation to make periodic payments over a specified period for use or "rent" of an asset; does not involve ownership of the asset.

Liability frauds Financial statement fraud in which liabilities (amounts owed to others) are understated.

Lien Claim on property for the satisfaction of just debt.

Lower trial courts State courts that try misdemeanors (small crimes) and pretrial issues.

M

Management fraud Deception perpetrated by an organization's top management through the manipulation of financial statement amounts or disclosures.

Marketable securities Stocks, bonds, and other non-cash assets; sometimes called short-term investments.

Marking the evidence Placing unique identification tags or descriptions on documents when they are received, so that they can be identified during the investigation and trial process.

Merger Combining of two organizations into one business entity.

Miscellaneous fraud Deception that doesn't fall into any of the other five categories of fraud.

Mobile observation Another term for tailing.

Modeling Setting an example.

Mortgage Long-term loan secured by property, such as a home mortgage.

Motion Response to a complaint or pleading by the defendant. Sometimes "motion" refers to any request made to the judge for a ruling in a case by either party.

Motion for dismissal Request to the judge to dismiss a claim because there is no genuine issue of a material fact.

Moving surveillance Another term for tailing; involves following suspects wherever they go (within limits) and observing or recording their activities.

N

National Crime Information Center (NCIC) The major criminal database maintained by the FBI. This database contains information on stolen vehicles, securities, boats, missing persons, and other information helpful in fraud investigations.

Net income An overall measure of the performance of a company; equal to revenues minus expenses for the period.

Net worth method Analytical method that estimates a suspect's unexplained income. Liabilities are subtracted from assets to give net worth, then the previous year's net worth is subtracted to find the increase in net worth. Living expenses are then added to the change in net worth to determine a person's total income, and finally known income is subtracted from total income to determine the unknown income.

Nolo contendere Plea by a defendant that does not contest the charges but does not admit guilt.

Nonsampling risk Risk that a sample will be examined and the characteristics of the sample will be misinterpreted.

Number of days in receivables 365 (number of days in a year) divided by accounts receivable turnover; a measure of how long it takes to collect receivables.

O

Operating performance ratio Net income divided by total sales; a measure of the percentage of revenues that become profits.

Opting-out right Right of customers to give written notice to financial institutions that prohibits the institution from sharing or selling customer's personal information.

P

Participative management Management style that expects everyone in the organization to take ownership and responsibility for their conduct and responsibilities and that allows input into decisions.

Passwords Secret codes or names that allow users to access networks and other computer systems.

Payroll fraud scheme Using the payroll function to commit fraud, such as creating ghost employees or overpaying wages.

Pension Postretirement cash benefits paid to former employees.

Perceived opportunity A situation where people believe they have a favorable or promising combination of circumstances to commit fraud and not be detected.

Perceived pressure A situation where people perceive they have a need to commit fraud; a constraining influence on the will or mind, as a moral force.

Perpetrator A person who has committed a fraud.

Personal observation evidence Evidence that is sensed (seen, heard, felt, etc.) by investigators.

Physical evidence Evidence of a tangible nature—includes fingerprints, tire marks, weapons, stolen property, identification numbers or marks on stolen objects, and so on—that can be used in an investigation to provide information about a fraud or other crime.

Physical safeguards Vaults, fences, locks, and so on that protect assets from theft.

Population Collection of all units with similar characteristics from which samples are drawn.

Postal inspectors Inspectors or investigators hired by the U.S. Postal Service to handle major fraud cases that are perpetrated through the U.S. mail system.

Predication Circumstances that, taken as a whole, would lead a reasonable, prudent professional to believe that a fraud has occurred, is occurring, or will occur.

Preliminary hearing Pretrial hearing to determine whether there is "probable cause" to charge the defendant with a crime.

Profit margin Measure of the profit generated from each dollar of revenue; calculated by dividing net income by revenue. Also known as return on sales, profit margin percentage, profit margin ratio, operating performance ratio.

Psychopath A person with a personality disorder, especially one manifested in aggressively antisocial behavior.

Q

Quick (acid-test) ratio Measure of a firm's ability to meet current liabilities, computed by dividing net quick assets (all current assets, except inventories and prepaid expenses) by current liabilities.

R

Rationalization Self-satisfying but incorrect reasons for one's behavior.

Register disbursement scheme Scheme that involves false refunds or false voids.

Remedy Judgments asked for in civil cases (what it would take to right a private wrong).

Repurchase agreements Agreement to buy back something previously sold.

Request for admission Request that the opposing party admit designated facts relevant to litigation.

Restructuring Reevaluation of a company's assets because of impairment of value or for other reasons. Restructured companies usually have lower amounts of assets and look quite different than before the restructuring.

Return on equity Measure of the profit earned per dollar of investment; computed by dividing net income by equity.

Revenue recognition Determining that revenues have been earned and are collectible and thus should be reported on the income statement.

Revenue Increases in a company's resources from the sale of goods or services.

Risk assessment The identification, analysis, and management of risk, such as the risk associated with the possibility of fraud.

S

Sales return percentage (ratio) Sales returns divided by total sales; a measure of the percentage of sales being returned by customers.

Sales returns (sales returns and allowances) Sold merchandise that is returned by customers and/or damaged, or other sold merchandise for which credit is given.

Sample Portion of the population that is examined in order to draw inferences about the population.

Sampling risk Risk that a sample is not representative of the population.

Search warrant Order issued by a judge that gives the investigator consent to search a suspect's personal information, such as bank records, tax returns, or their premises.

Securities and Exchange Commission (SEC) Government body responsible for regulating stock trading and the financial statements and reports of public companies.

Segregation of duties Division of tasks into two parts, so one person does not have complete control of the task.

Settlement Negotiated pretrial agreement between the parties to resolve a legal dispute.

Sixth Amendment to the U.S. Constitution Provides trial-related protections to defendants, such as the right to a speedy trial and the right to be heard by an impartial jury.

Skimming Removal of cash from a victim organization prior to its entry in an accounting system.

Sniffing Illegal or unauthorized viewing of information as it passes along a network communication channel.

Spoofing Changing the information in an e-mail header or an IP address used to hide identities.

Statement of cash flows Financial statement that reports an entity's cash inflows (receipts) and outflows (payments) during an accounting period.

Static surveillance Another term for fixed-point surveillance.

Stationary surveillance Locating a scene to be observed, anticipating the actions that are most likely to occur at the scene, and keeping detailed notes on tape or film on all activities involving the suspect.

Statistical analysis The use of statistics and number patterns to discover relationships in certain data, such as Benford's law.

Statute A law or regulation; a law enacted by the legislative branch of a government.

Subpoena (subpoena duces tecum) Order issued by a court or a grand jury to produce documents or requiring a witness to submit to a deposition, give testimony at trial, or report to an administrative body.

Surveillance Investigation technique that relies on the senses, especially hearing and seeing.

System of authorizations A system of limits on who can and cannot perform certain functions.

T

Tailing Secretly following a fraud suspect in an attempt to gain additional information; another name for moving surveillance.

Tax courts Federal courts that hear only tax cases.

10-K Annual report filed by publicly traded companies to the SEC.

10-Q Quarterly report filed by publicly traded companies to the SEC.

Testimonial evidence Evidence based on querying techniques, such as interviewing, interrogation, and honesty testing.

Theft investigation methods Investigation methods that focus on the actual transfer of assets from the victim to the perpetrator; helps determine how the theft was committed and often includes methods such as surveillance and covert operations, invigilation, and the obtaining of physical evidence.

Trash investigation Searching through a person's trash for possible evidence in an investigation.

Treadway Commission National Commission on Fraudulent Financial Reporting that made recommendations on financial statement fraud and other matters in 1987.

Trustee Individual or firm who collects a debtor's assets and distributes them to creditors.

U

Unearned revenues Amounts that have been received from customers but for which performance of a service or sale of a product has not yet been made.

V

Vendor fraud An overcharge for purchased goods, the shipment of inferior goods, or the nonshipment of goods even though payment is made.

Vertical analysis Tool that converts financial statement numbers to percentages so that they are easy to understand and analyze.

Victim The person or organization deceived by the perpetrator.

Voir dire Legal process of qualifying an expert witness.

Vulnerability chart Tool that coordinates the various elements of a fraud investigation to help identify possible suspects.

W

Warrant Order issued by a judge to arrest someone.

Warranty liabilities Obligation to perform service and repair items sold within a specific period of time and/or use after sale.

Web-visit hijacking Mimicking another, similarly named web site in order to trick or confuse e-mail and e-business users into sending information to a business other than the intended one.

Working capital turnover ratio Sales divided by average working capital; a measure of the amount of working capital used to generate revenues.

INDEX

A

B

C

D

G

H

I

J

K

L